The World's Multinational Enterprises

The World's Multinational Enterprises

A Sourcebook of Tables Based on a Study of the
Largest U.S. and Non-U.S. Manufacturing Corporations

JAMES W. VAUPEL
JOAN P. CURHAN
Graduate School of Business Administration
Harvard University

Division of Research
Graduate School of Business Administration
Harvard University
Boston · 1973

Library of Congress Catalog Card No. 73-76600
ISBN 0-87584-107-4

Faculty research at the Harvard Business School is undertaken with the expectation of publication. In such publication the author responsible for the research project is also responsible for statements of fact, opinions, and conclusions expressed. Neither the Harvard Business School, its Faculty as a whole, nor the President and Fellows of Harvard College reach conclusions or make recommendations as results of Faculty Research.

Printed in the United States of America

Foreword

For the past half decade, research on the subject of multinational enterprises has been one of the leading growth industries among scholars. From the beginning, such scholarship has been inhibited by the paucity of elementary facts. A few official sources, notably the U.K. Board of Trade, the U.S. Department of Commerce, and the OECD, have provided systematic compilations of some of the current activities of multinational enterprises around the globe. But the current picture is still incomplete. Even less is known about the patterns by which such multinational activities have evolved over the past decades.

The tabulations in this volume cannot pretend fully to have remedied the underlying lack; but they do represent a major step forward. These tabulations are the by-product of an effort that began at the Harvard Business School in 1965. The first phase of that sustained effort, covering a five-year period, concentrated principally upon the evolution of U.S.-based multinational enterprises; that is, enterprises consisting of a U.S. parent and of producing subsidiaries located outside the United States. In that phase, the development of some 10,000 such subsidiaries of 187 U.S. parent companies was traced from 1900. Five hundred pages of data based on these materials were published in 1969 in a book by James W. Vaupel and Joan P. Curhan, *The Making of Multinational Enterprise* (Boston: Division of Research, Harvard Business School, 1969). The foreign direct investments of these 187 parent companies represented over 70% of all foreign direct investment in manufacturing by U.S. firms—over 80%, if Canada is not included in the "foreign" category.

This book draws modestly on the earlier study, reproducing certain selected figures in new formats. But the main advance represented by the present compilation is the extension of our reporting network. Some 15,000 foreign subsidiaries of parent companies based in countries other than the United States provide the core of the data in the present compilations. From a statistical point of view, these compilations cover territory and subject matter that is almost totally unexplored.

Those who intend to use the data for comparative purposes are warned to proceed with caution. As a result of our desire to capitalize on the experience gained in the first compilation, the coverage of subsidiaries of non-U.S. parents in this volume differs in some respects from the coverage of the subsidiaries of U.S. parents contained in the first volume. The details of those differences are presented in the Orientation. For comparative purposes, a special set of tables are presented, in which parallel coverage is provided. Nevertheless, it can be said of both the U.S. and the non-U.S. compilations that each has managed to cover the great bulk of foreign private direct investment generated out of their respective areas.

A large proportion of the data in this book was obtained from public records. The extensive resources of Baker Library at the Harvard Business School turned up annual reports to stockholders, business histories, business periodicals, and similar resources. These records were then verified and elaborated by interviews with most of the companies contained in the compilation. For that purpose, the Centre d'Etudes Industrielles in Geneva, and the London School of Business provided bases for European research efforts. Dr. John M. Stopford, Reader in Business Policy at the London Graduate School of Business Studies, supervised the British interviews and Dr. Lawrence G. Franko, Faculty Member at Centre d'Etudes Industrielles, was responsible for the interviews on the European continent. The extraordinary efforts of Urs Schneider in connection with the continental interviews deserve special mention.

Partly as a result of the efforts of our colleagues in Europe, the cooperation secured from European enterprises was excellent in general. In the end, the coverage of the non-U.S. data proved to be somewhat better than that of the earlier U.S. data; and this, despite the fact that even more sensitive figures were sought from the non-U.S. enterprises, such as figures on sales and assets. During the course of the interviews, commitments to preserve the confidentiality of some of the underlying materials were undertaken.

The collection of the Japanese data was under the general supervision of two colleagues associated in the Multinational Enterprise Project at the Harvard Business School: Michael M. Yoshino, of the University of California at Los Angeles, and Yoshihiro Tsurumi, Visiting Associate Professor at the Harvard Business School.

The tabulations presented here have been selected from the data bank with an eye to their general utility for researchers. In some cases, our obligations to cooperating companies have imposed limits on the data that could be published. We propose, however, to follow the precedent that was established with respect to our first volume, making the underlying data available to academic researchers under suitable conditions that guarantee the preservation of confidentiality.

The present compilation was completed in a relatively brief period of time; the entire operation took place within an 18-month period. This performance, of course, would have been impossible if it were not for the fact that the two principal authors, James W. Vaupel and Joan P. Curhan, were also responsible for producing the first volume. Vaupel is at Duke University while Curhan is an Associate in Research at the Harvard Business School. Vaupel's main contribution was in designing the necessary data storage and data processing systems, and developing the form and structure of this volume. Curhan's contribution consisted of devising the methods for collecting the basic data, then creating and managing the far-flung collection apparatus.

Another indispensable member was added to the team for the data-processing phase of the work. George Middleton performed the critical and exacting task of creating the master computer data bank and checking it for errors.

The Multinational Enterprise Project is supported primarily by a grant from the Ford Foundation to the Harvard Business School. A large group of research assistants, drawn together by Curhan from a dozen universities during the summer months and from a few universities in the Boston area during the rest of the year, were supported primarily by the College Work-Study Program (sponsored by the U.S. Department of Health, Education, and Welfare). To both of these sources of support, to the staff of Baker Library at the Harvard Business School, and to the 400 or so cooperating companies, we express our appreciation.

RAYMOND VERNON
Coordinator, Multinational Enterprise Project
Harvard Business School

Soldiers Field
Boston, Massachusetts
June 1973

Table of Contents

Orientation

ORIENTATION

1. Background

Since 1965, the Harvard Business School has been engaged in a detailed analysis of the problems and practices of so-called multinational enterprises — that is, large business firms that have extensive interests in subsidiaries and branches outside their home countries. In connection with this study, a unique file of statistical data was collected on the more than 28,000 "foreign" subsidiaries of the world's largest manufacturing enterprises. (A "foreign" subsidiary of an enterprise is any subsidiary located outside the national base of the parent enterprise.) This publication presents several hundred tabulations and cross-tabulations of the data in this file.

The data were collected in two stages. From 1965 through 1969, data were gathered on the foreign subsidiaries of the largest U.S.-based manufacturing enterprises. From 1971 through 1973, data were gathered on the foreign subsidiaries of the largest manufacturing enterprises based outside the United States. The data collected in the two stages of the study differ in three key respects.

First, the foreign subsidiaries of the U.S.-based enterprises were traced from 1900 until January 1, 1968, while the foreign subsidiaries of the enterprises based outside the United States were traced from 1900 until January 1, 1971.

Second, the data questionnaire used in the second stage of the study asked somewhat fewer questions and required less detailed responses than the data questionnaire used in the first stage of the study. Partially as a result of this, the rate of response in the second stage of the study was generally higher than in the first stage of the study, especially with regard to financial data.

Third, different rules were used in the two stages of the study to select the enterprises whose foreign subsidiaries were to be investigated. (The rules used are discussed in Section 2, below.)

Because the data gathered in the two stages of the study differ in these three important ways, throughout this publication statistics pertaining to the foreign subsidiaries of U.S.-based enterprises are presented separately from statistics pertaining to the foreign subsidiaries of enterprises based outside the United States. In addition, some statistics are presented that are based on roughly comparable data pertaining to the foreign subsidiaries of a special "world subset" of U.S.-based and non-U.S.-based enterprises.

2. The Enterprises Studied

This section describes the rules used to select the U.S.-based enterprises, the non-U.S.-based enterprises, and the "world subset" of U.S.-based and non-U.S.-based enterprises.

The U.S.-based enterprises were required to meet the following three criteria:

(1) the enterprise appeared on Fortune's list of the "500 Largest U.S. Industrial Corporations" for the year 1963 or 1964;

(2) by the end of 1963, the enterprise held or had held equity interests in manufacturing firms located in 6 or more countries outside the United States, such equity interest in each case amounting to 25% or more of the total equity; and

(3) the enterprise was not the subsidiary of another enterprise.

More than 190 enterprises met these three criteria, but mergers between some of these enterprises reduced this number to 187 enterprises by the terminal date of the study, January 1, 1968. (These 187 enterprises are listed in Section 11, below.)

In the second stage of the study, data were gathered on the foreign subsidiaries of all the enterprises that appeared on Fortune's list of the "200 Largest Non-U.S. Industrial Corporations" for the year 1970. In addition, data were collected on the foreign subsidiaries of 12 manufacturing enterprises that did not appear on the Fortune list but that had sales as large as the enterprises that did appear on the list. Finally, data were also gathered on the foreign subsidiaries of 6 major Japanese "trading companies" and on the foreign subsidiaries of 2 German enterprises and 6 Japanese zaibatsu that were broken up at the end of World War II. Altogether 226 enterprises were investigated. (The enterprises are listed in Section 12, below.) Of these enterprises, 209 had at one time or other at least one foreign subsidiary.

As a result of these selection criteria, the smallest of the U.S.-based enterprises studied had sales of about $100 million, while the smallest of the non-U.S.-based enterprises studied had sales of about $400 million. Moreover, the least "multinational" of the U.S.-based enterprises had an equity interest of at least 25% in manufacturing subsidiaries in at least 6 foreign countries, while some of the non-U.S.-based enterprises only had a small equity interest in subsidiaries, not necessarily manufacturing subsidiaries, in one or two foreign countries.

The "world subset" of U.S.-based and non-U.S.-based enterprises was selected to eliminate these differences. To qualify for this subset, an enterprise had to have had:

(1)   sales of at least $400 million in 1967, and

(2)   an equity interest of at least 25% in manufacturing subsidiaries in at least 6 foreign countries as of January 1, 1968.

A total of 261 enterprises met these additional criteria, of which 133 were based in the United States and 128 were based outside the United States.

3.   The Foreign Subsidiaries

Once an enterprise qualified for the study, data were gathered on all of its foreign subsidiaries, non-manufacturing as well as manufacturing. A firm was considered to be a subsidiary if a total of at least 5%

of the firm's equity was held by the enterprise or by
companies in which the enterprise held at least 25% of
the equity. As mentioned above, the foreign subsidiaries of the 187 U.S.-based enterprises were traced from
1900 until January 1, 1968, while the foreign subsidiaries of the 226 enterprises based outside the United
States were traced from 1900 until January 1, 1971.
Altogether, data were gathered on 11,742 firms that
were foreign subsidiaries of one or more of the
U.S.-based enterprises, and 16,576 firms that were
foreign subsidiaries of one or more of the enterprises
based outside the United States.

4. Coverage of the Sample

It would be helpful for some purposes to know how
large this sample of 28,318 foreign subsidiaries is
relative to the universe of all foreign subsidiaries.
Unfortunately, data on this universe are sparse and
only a few, rough comparisons can be given.

As explained in greater detail in an earlier
publication[1], we estimate that over the period from
1900 through 1967 the foreign manufacturing subsidiaries of the 187 U.S.-based enterprises constituted
roughly 40% of the total number of foreign manufacturing subsidiaries of all U.S. companies and more than
50% of the number outside of Canada. In terms of value
of investment, we estimate that the sample included
over 70% of U.S. foreign direct investment in manufacturing and over 80% of U.S. foreign direct investment
in manufacturing outside of Canada.

An estimate of sales in 1970 was obtained for more
than 60%, and an estimate of either sales or nominal
share capital in 1970 for more than 80% of the foreign
manufacturing subsidiaries of the non-U.S.-based enterprises. These data, when extrapolated, indicate that

----

[1]J. W. Vaupel and J. P. Curhan, The Making of Multina-
tional Enterprise: A Sourcebook of Tables Based on a
Study of 187 Major U.S. Manufacturing Corporations,
(Boston: Division of Research, Harvard Business
School, 1969), p. 3.

the aggregate value of sales in 1970 of these subsidiaries exceeded $80 billion.

5. The Data

Although the questionnaire used for the foreign subsidiaries of the enterprises based outside the United States differed somewhat from the questionnaire used for the foreign subsidiaries of the U.S.-based enterprises, the same basic information was sought in each case. The information included: the country in which the subsidiary was incorporated and the country in which the subsidiary's principal activity was performed; how and when the subsidiary became part of its parent multinational enterprise; the principal activity of the subsidiary -- manufacturing, sales, extraction, etc. -- in each year of its existence; the principal market of the subsidiary; if the subsidiary was a manufacturing firm, the product categories manufactured; the value of the sales and nominal share capital of the subsidiary; and the equity interest held in the subsidiary by its parent company or companies.

For the more than 28,000 subsidiaries in the study, most of the information was obtained from library sources, including government documents, annual reports to stockholders, business histories, business periodicals, and similar sources. This library research was augmented and verified through visits to the headquarters of most of the parent enterprises studied. More than 150 students worked at one time or other during summers or part-time during school years gathering and coding the data. Some 167 of the 187 U.S.-based parent enterprises generously provided information on their foreign subsidiaries as did 170 of the 209 parent enterprises based outside the United States. Commitments were made to cooperating enterprises to publish data only in aggregate form and not on a company-by-company basis. Although strenuous efforts were made to insure the completeness and the accuracy of the data, the data are incomplete and almost certainly contain some errors. The response rates for nearly all the variables used in this publication were above 50% and in most instances above 80%.

6. The Variables Used in This Publication

In the tabulations and cross-tabulations of this publication, subsidiaries are classified according to 29 different variables. These variables, which were computed from the master data bank, are listed below. (Detailed definitions of these variables are given in Section 9.) The phrase "parent system" refers to the ultimate parent company of a subsidiary and all the subsidiaries of this ultimate parent company and its subsidiaries. When used in reference to the foreign subsidiaries of the non-U.S.-based parent systems the "terminal date" is January 1, 1971; when used in reference to the foreign subsidiaries of the U.S.-based parent systems or the foreign subsidiaries of the "world subset" of U.S.-based and non-U.S.-based parent systems the "terminal date" is January 1, 1968. "Date of entry" refers to the date the subsidiary was formed or acquired by its parent system.

Variable 1: Subsidiary's Country.

Variable 2: Geographical Region of Subsidiary's Country.

Variable 3: GNP per Capita in 1970 of Subsidiary's Country.

Variable 4: GNP in 1970 of Subsidiary's Country.

Variable 5: Principal Industry of Subsidiary at Date of Entry.

Variable 6: Principal Industry of Subsidiary at Terminal Date.

Variable 7: Principal Industry-Group of Subsidiary at Date of Entry.

Variable 8: Principal Industry-Group of Subsidiary at Terminal Date.

Variable 9: Percentage of Subsidiary's Equity Owned by Parent System at Date of Entry.

Variable 10: Percentage of Subsidiary's Equity Owned by Parent System at Terminal Date.

Variable 11: Category of Subsidiary's Principal Outside Owner (if Any) at Date of Entry.

Variable 12: Category of Subsidiary's Principal Outside Owner (if Any) at Terminal Date.

Variable 13: Subsidiary's Method of Entry into Parent System.

Variable 14: Subsidiary's Method of Exit from Parent System.

Variable 15: Subsidiary's Principal Market at Terminal Date.

Variable 16: Subsidiary's Principal Customer at Terminal Date.

Variable 17: Subsidiary's Date of Entry into Parent System.

Variable 18: Value of Subsidiary's Sales in Year Prior to Terminal Date.

Variable 19: Subsidiary's Principal Activity at Date of Entry.

Variable 20: Subsidiary's Principal Activity at Terminal Date.

Variable 21: National Base of Subsidiary's Parent System.

Variable 22: Value of Sales of Subsidiary's Parent System in Year Prior to Terminal Date.

Variable 23: Principal Industry-Group of Subsidiary's Parent System at Terminal Date.

Variable 24: Number of Countries in Which Parent System Manufactured at Subsidiary's Date of Entry.

Variable 25: Number of Countries in Which Parent System Manufactured at Terminal Date.

Variable 26:   Percentage of Parent System's Employees Outside Parent System's National Base at Terminal Date.

Variable 27:   Number of Industries in Which Parent System Manufactured Within National Base at Terminal Date.

Variable 28:   Number of Industries in Which Parent System Manufactured Outside National Base at Terminal Date.

Variable 29:   Parent System's R&D Expenditures as a Percentage of Sales in Year Prior to Terminal Date.

7.   The Tables in this Publication

This publication contains two types of tables, which are labelled "Tabulations" and "Cross-Tabulations".

Each "Tabulation" breaks subsidiaries down according to one of the variables listed above. Data are presented separately for all subsidiaries, for manufacturing subsidiaries, and for sales subsidiaries. In each case, the percentage of subsidiaries that fall into each category of the variable is listed separately for the subsidiaries of non-U.S.-based parent systems, for the subsidiaries of U.S.-based parent systems, and for the subsidiaries of the "world subset" of U.S.-based and non-U.S.-based parent systems. In addition, for the subsidiaries of non-U.S.-based parent systems, a separate table lists the percentage of the total sales of the subsidiaries in 1970 accounted for by the subsidiaries that fall into each category of the variable. That breakdown is not presented for the subsidiaries of U.S.-based parent systems or for the subsidiaries of the special subset of U.S.-based and non-U.S.-based parent systems, as sales data were sparse for the subsidiaries of U.S.-based parent systems.

Each "Cross-Tabulation" breaks subsidiaries down according to two of the variables listed in Section 6 above. The Cross-Tabulations present data only on subsidiaries that are known to be manufacturing subsidiaries. For every pair of variables considered, data are presented in separate tables for the subsidiaries of non-U.S.-based parent systems and the subsidiaries of U.S.-based parent systems. In one case, data are presented in separate tables for the subsidiaries of parent systems based in the United Kingdom, Continental Europe (i.e., West Germany, France, Italy, Belgium, Luxemburg, the Netherlands, Sweden, and Switzerland), and Japan. The Cross-Tabulations in this publication array data on only a fraction of all possible pairs of the 29 variables listed in Section 6: efforts were made to limit the Cross-Tabulations to those of greatest general interest.

8. Uses of this Publication

The Tabulations and Cross-Tabulations of this publication were designed with three basic uses in mind.

First, the tables have been designed to aid recognition of salient patterns in the structure and development of multinational enterprises. In many cases, data on the foreign subsidiaries of parent systems based in different countries are presented separately to facilitate detection of international differences in these patterns.

Second, the tables have been designed to permit the testing of a wide range of hypotheses about multinational enterprises, either directly or with some additional calculations using the data presented.

Third, the tables have been designed to provide an overview of the master data bank. The Harvard Business School is taking measures to provide access to the data bank for academic researchers, with suitable safeguards to protect the confidentiality of the data.

9. Definitions of the Variables in this Publication

Variable 1: Subsidiary's Country. A subsidiary's country is defined as the country in which the subsidiary performed its principal activity. For more than 95% of the subsidiaries studied, this country was also the country in which the subsidiary was incorporated or legally registered. The category "Other Europe" includes, among other countries and areas, Cyprus, Gibraltar, and Malta; "Germany" refers to Germany before World War II and West Germany after World War II; "Other Mid East" consists of Bahrain, Iraq, Jordan, Kuwait, Lebanon, Muscat and Oman, Qatar, Saudi Arabia, Southern Yemen (Aden), Syria, the Trucial States, and Yemen; "Other (British) Africa" refers to African countries, not separately listed, that were British colonies--among other countries, Mauritius and the Sudan are included in this category; "Other (French) Africa" refers to African countries that were (or are) French colonies--among other countries, Reunion is included in this category; "China (Taiwan)" refers to China before 1949 and Taiwan after 1949.

Variable 2: Geographical Region of Subsidiary's Country. This variable groups subsidiaries' countries into five categories: North America, Latin America, Europe, Africa and the Middle East, and Other Asia and Oceania. "North America" consists of the United States and Canada; "Latin America" includes Bermuda; "Europe" includes Cyprus, Gibraltar, Malta, and Turkey; "Africa and Middle East" includes Afghanistan, Iran, Israel, and Pakistan.

Variable 3: GNP per Capita in 1970 of Subsidiary's Country. For this variable, countries are grouped into five categories according to the countries' GNP per capita in 1970. The GNP per capita figures used are those reported in the 1971 World Almanac, pages 617 and 618.

Variable 4: GNP in 1970 of Subsidiary's Country. For this variable, countries are grouped into five categories according to the countries' GNP in 1970. The GNP figures used are those reported in the 1971 World Almanac, pages 617 and 618.

Variable 5: Principal Industry of Subsidiary at Date of Entry. Fifty-four industry categories are used for this variable. The correspondence between these categories and Standard Industrial Classification (SIC) Codes[2] is as follows:

Industry	SIC Code
Ordnance	19
Meat Products	201
Dairy Products	202
Canned or Frozen Foods	203
Grain Mill Products	204
Bakery Products	205
Confectionery Products	207
Beverages	208
Other Food Products	206 and 209
Tobacco Products	21
Textiles	22
Apparel	23
Lumber and Wood	24
Furniture	25
Paper Products	26
Printed Matter	27
Industrial Chemicals	281
Plastic and Synthetics	282
Drugs	283
Soap and Cosmetics	284
Paints	285
Agricultural Chemicals	287
Other Chemicals	286 and 289
Refined Petroleum	291
Other Petroleum Products	295 and 299
Tires	301
Other Rubber Products	Other 30
Leather Products and Shoes	31
Glass Products	321 - 323
Stone, Clay, and Concrete	324 - 329
Iron and Steel Products	331, 332, and 339

----

[2]U.S. Technical Committee on Industrial Classification, Standard Industrial Classification Manual (Washington, D.C.: U.S. Government Printing Office, 1967).

Industry	SIC Code
Non-Ferrous Smelting	333 and 334
Non-Ferrous Products	335 and 336
Metal Cans	341
Structural Metal Products	344
Fabricated Wire Products	348
Other Fabricated Metal	Other 34
Engines and Turbines	351
Farm Machinery	352
Construction Machinery	353
Special Industry Machinery	355
General Industry Machinery	356
Office Machines and Computers	357
Other Non-Electrical Machinery	Other 35
Electric Transmission Equipment	361
Electrical Lighting and Wiring	364
Radios, T.V.'s and Appliances	363 and 365
Communications Equipment	366
Electronic Components	367
Other Electrical Equipment	362 and 369
Motor Vehicles and Equipment	371
Other Transportation Equipment	Other 37
Precision Goods	38
Miscellaneous Products	39

"Principal industry of subsidiary" pertains only to manufacturing subsidiaries. More than 80% of the subsidiaries studied manufactured products that fell entirely within a single industry category. For those subsidiaries that manufactured products in more than one industry category, the principal industry of the subsidiary was defined as the industry category that included the 3 digit SIC industry category that accounted for the largest share of the subsidiary's manufacturing output. As indicated in Section 6, "date of entry" refers to the date the subsidiary was formed or acquired by its parent enterprise. Thus, variable 5 is not defined for those subsidiaries that commenced manufacturing after their date of entry: such subsidiaries account for fewer than 10% of the manufacturing subsidiaries studied.

Variable 6: Principal Industry of Subsidiary at Terminal Date. See discussion of variable 5 for definition of "principal industry of subsidiary." As indicated in Section 6, the "terminal date" is January 1, 1971 when used in reference to the foreign subsidiaries of the non–U.S.–based parent systems and January 1, 1968 when used in reference to the foreign subsidiaries of the U.S.–based parent systems or the foreign subsidiaries of the "world subset" of U.S.–based and non–U.S.–based parent systems.

Variable 7: Principal Industry-Group of Subsidiary at Date of Entry and Variable 8: Principal Industry-Group of Subsidiary at Terminal Date. For these variables, the fifty-four industries defined above are grouped into twelve broader categories. A subsidiary is classified into the industry-group that includes the subsidiary's principal industry. The correspondence between industry-groups and SIC codes is as follows:

Industry	SIC Code
Food and Tobacco	20 and 21
Textiles and Apparel	22 and 23
Wood, Furniture and Paper	24, 25, and 26
Chemicals	28
Petroleum	29
Rubber and Tires	30
Primary Metals	33
Fabricated Metals and Non-Electrical Machinery	34 and 35, except 357
Electric and Electronic Products	36 and 357
Transportation Equipment	37
Precision Goods	38
Other	19, 27, 31, 32, and 39

Variable 9: Percentage of Subsidiary's Equity Owned by Parent System at Date of Entry and Variable 10: Percentage of Subsidiary's Equity Owned by Parent System at Terminal Date. The "percentage of subsidiary's equity owned by parent system" was calculated as the sum total of the equity interests directly owned by those members of the parent system in which the parent system held at least a 25% equity interest.

14

Variable 11: Category_of_Subsidiary's__Principal_
Outside__Owner__(if__Any)_at_Date_of_Entry and Variable
12:__Category_of_Subsidiary's_Principal__Outside__Owner_
(if__Any)__at__Terminal__Date. These variables pertain
only to subsidiaries for which the "percentage of
subsidiary's equity owned by parent system" amounted to
less than 95 percent. The outside owners of such
subsidiaries are classified under four headings:
"local private," "local state," "foreign private," and
"stock widely dispersed." A "local private" enterprise
is any enterprise located in the subsidiary's country
that is not known to be a subsidiary of a foreign
enterprise. A "local state" enterprise (or agency) is
an enterprise controlled by the government of the
subsidiary's country. A "foreign private" enterprise
is an enterprise whose national base is not the
subsidiary's country. The category "stock widely dispersed" was used in all cases for which no outside
owner held as much as 5% of the subsidiary's equity.
There is a somewhat greater chance that "local state"
outside owners were mis-coded as "local private" outside owners in the case of the foreign subsidiaries of
U.S.-based parent systems than in the case of non-U.S.-
based parent systems.

Variable 13: Subsidiary's Method of Entry into
Parent__System. This variable classifies a subsidiary
according to the method by which the subsidiary became
a subsidiary of its parent system. Methods of entry
are grouped into four categories: "newly formed,"
"reorganization," "acquired directly," and "acquired
through acquisition." The category "reorganization" is
used if the subsidiary was formed as a result of the
merger or break-up of existing subsidiaries. The
category "newly formed" is used if the subsidiary was
established by its parent system to perform a function
not previously performed by other subsidiaries of the
parent system. A subsidiary was "acquired directly" if
its parent system directly purchased at least 5% of its
equity. A subsidiary was "acquired through acquisition" if its parent system purchased at least 25% of
the equity of a firm that held at least 5% of the
equity of the subsidiary. The distinction between
"acquired directly" and "acquired through acquisition"
was not made for the subsidiaries of U.S.-based parent
systems; in the tables in this publication all such
subsidiaries that were acquired are classified as being
"acquired directly."

Variable 14: Subsidiary's Method of Exit from Parent Enterprise. This variable classifies subsidiaries into five categories: "sold," "confiscated or expropriated," "liquidated, function ended," "liquidated, function continued" (by other subsidiaries), and "did not exit." A subsidiary is considered to have been sold when the percentage of the subsidiary's equity held by its parent system fell below 5 percent.

Variable 15: Subsidiary's Principal Market at Terminal Date. The category "local country" is used if more than 50% of a subsidiary's business is with customers located in the subsidiary's country; otherwise the category "export markets" is used. Data for this variable and for variable 16 were so sparse for the foreign subsidairies of U.S.-based parent systems that Cross-Tabulations of these variables with other variables are sometimes presented only for the foreign subsidiaries of non-U.S.-based parent systems.

Variable 16: Subsidiary's Principal Customer at Terminal Date. The category "parent system" is used if more than 50% of the subsidiary's business is conducted with fellow members of its parent system; otherwise the category "outside customers" is used.

Variable 17: Subsidiary's Date of Entry into Parent System. "Subsidiary's date of entry into parent system" is the earliest date on which the subsidiary was in existence and on which at least 5% of the subsidiary's equity was collectively owned by those members of its parent system in which its parent system held at least a 25% equity interest.

Variable 18: Value of Subsidiary's Sales in Year Prior to Terminal Date. This variable classifies subsidiaries into five categories on the basis of the value of the subsidiaries' sales in the year prior to the terminal date of the study.

Variable 19: Subsidiary's Principal Activity at Date of Entry and Variable 20: Subsidiary's Principal Activity at Terminal Date. These variables classify subsidiaries into five categories on the basis of the nature of the subsidiaries' business activities. The category "some manufacturing" is used if a subsidiary did any manufacturing, assembling, or packaging. The category "inactive" is used if a subsidiary was legally in existence but did not perform any business activity, except, perhaps, the protection of a brand name. Otherwise, a subsidiary is classified by its primary activity——"sales or service," "extraction," or "other."

Variable 21: National Base of Subsidiary's Parent System. For the non-U.S.-based parent systems, the national base used is the country of the subsidiary's ultimate parent, as given on Fortune's list of the "200 Largest Non-U.S. Industrial Corporations" for the year 1970. Royal Dutch/Shell was assigned to the Netherlands, Unilever to the United Kingdom, and Agfa-Gevaert to West Germany. Parent systems with national bases in Argentina, Australia, Brazil, India, Mexico, the Netherlands Antilles, South Africa, and Zambia were grouped together in a category labelled "other."

Variable 22: Value of Sales of Subsidiary's Parent System in Year Prior to Terminal Date. Parent systems are classified into five categories on the basis of their consolidated, world-wide sales.

Variable 23: Principal Industry-Group of Subsidiary's Parent System at Terminal Date. This variable was computed on the basis of data provided on Fortune's list of the "500 Largest U.S. Industrial Corporations" for the year 1967 and Fortune's list of the "200 Largest Non-U.S. Industrial Corporations" for the year 1970. Annual reports and other published data were used for those parent systems not appearing on the Fortune lists.

Variable 24: Number of Countries in Which Parent System Manufactured at Subsidiary's Date of Entry and Variable 25: Number of Countries in Which Parent System Manufactured at Terminal Date. For these two variables, the "number of countries" includes the parent system's national base. A country is not counted unless the parent system is known to own at least 25% of the equity of a manufacturing subsidiary in the country.

Variable 26: Percentage of Parent System's Employees Outside Parent System's National Base at Terminal Date. For this variable and for variables 27 and 28, the national base of Royal Dutch/Shell and of Unilever was taken to include both the Netherlands and the United Kingdom and the national base of Agfa-Gevaert was taken to include both West Germany and Belgium. Data for variable 26 were not gathered for U.S.-based parent systems.

Variable 27: Number of Industries in Which Parent System Manufactured Within National Base at Terminal Date and Variable 28: Number of Industries in Which Parent System Manufactured Outside National Base at Terminal Date. "Number of industries" is measured by the number of 3 digit SIC (Standard Industrial Classification) categories in which the system manufactured products.

Variable 29: Parent System's R&D Expenditures as a Percentage of Sales in Year Prior to Terminal Date. For U.S.-based parent systems, the data for this variable were taken from Newsfront magazine, April 1969. For non-U.S.-based parent systems, the data were gathered from various sources, including company interviews.

10. Additional Notes on the Data and Tables

(1) Percentages in the tables were rounded as follows:

Figures greater than 99% but less than 100% were rounded to 99%.
Figures between 10% and 99% were rounded to the nearest percent. Thus 69.73% is given as 70%.
Figures between 0.1% and 10% were rounded to the nearest tenth of a percent. Thus, 3.84% is given as 3.8% and 0.37% is given as 0.4%.
Figures less than 0.1% but greater than 0% were rounded to 0.1%.
The figure 100% is used only to represent exactly 100% and the figure 0% is used only to represent exactly 0%.

(2) In a Cross-Tabulation, a figure of 0% for a category may mean that <u>by definition</u> no subsidiary can be classified into that category. For example, none of the foreign subsidiaries of U.S.-based parent systems can have the United States as their country.

(3) The tables in this publication were numbered as follows. For the Tabulations, the first number is the number of the variable being tabulated; the second number is 1 if the tabulation is of "number of subsidiaries" and 2 if the tabulation is of "sales of subsidiaries." For the Cross-Tabulations, the first number is the number of the variable listed across the top of the table and the second number is the number of the variable listed down the side of the table. The third number is 1 if the Cross-Tabulation pertains to the foreign subsidiaries of non-U.S.-based parent systems and 2 if it pertains to the foreign subsidiaries of U.S.-based parent systems.

(4) When indicated by the phrase "as of 1/1/71" or "as of 1/1/68," tables pertain to the stock of subsidiaries in existence as of 1/1/71 or 1/1/68. Otherwise, the tables pertain to all the subsidiaries studied.

(5) Subsidiaries that were known to be subsidiaries of more than one of the U.S.-based parent systems were assigned to the parent system whose name appeared first on the list of U.S.-based parent systems given in Section 11 below. Similarly, subsidiaries that were known to be subsidiaries of more than one of the non-U.S.-based parent systems were assigned to the parent system whose name appeared first on the list of non-U.S.-based parent systems given in Section 12 below.

11. List of U.S.-Based Enterprises

Abbott Laboratories
ABEX Corporation
Addressograph-Multigraph Corporation
Allied Chemical Corporation
Allis-Chalmers Manufacturing Company
Aluminum Company of America
American Can Company
American Cyanamid Company
American Home Products Corporation
American Machine & Foundry Company
American Metal Climax, Incorporated
American Smelting and Refining Company
American Standard
Archer-Daniels-Midland Company
Armco Steel Corporation
Armour & Company
Armstrong Cork Company
Atlas Chemical Industries, Incorporated

Beatrice Foods Company
Beech-Nut Life Savers, Incorporated
Bendix Corporation
Black & Decker Manufacturing Company
Borden Company
Borg-Warner Corporation
Bristol-Myers Company
Brunswick Corporation
Budd Company
Burlington Industries, Incorporated

Cabot Corporation
Campbell Soup Company
Carborundum Company
Carnation Company
Caterpillar Tractor Company
Celanese Corporation
Champion Spark Plug Company
Chemetron Corporation
Chesebrough-Pond's Incorporated
Chicago Pneumatic Tool Company
Chrysler Corporation
Cities Service Company
Clark Equipment Company

Clevite Corporation
Coca-Cola Company
Colgate-Palmolive Company
Combustion Engineering, Incorporated
Container Corporation of America
Continental Can Company, Incorporated
Continental Oil Company
Corn Products Company
Corning Glass Works
Crane Company
Crown Cork & Seal Company, Incorporated

Dana Corporation
Deere & Company
Del Monte Corporation
Dow Chemical Company
Dresser Industries, Incorporated
E.I. du Pont de Nemours & Company

ESB Incorporated
Eastman Kodak Company
Eaton, Yale & Towne, Incorporated
ELTRA Corporation
Emhart Corporation
Engelhard Minerals and Chemicals Corporation

FMC Corporation
Federal-Mogul Corporation
Federal Pacific Electric Company
Firestone Tire & Rubber Company
Ford Motor Company
Foremost-McKesson, Incorporated
Fruehauf Corporation

General American Transportation Corporation
General Dynamics Corporation
General Electric Company
General Foods Corporation
General Mills, Incorporated
General Motors Corporation
General Telephone & Electronics Corporation
General Tire and Rubber Company
Genesco Incorporated
Gillette Company

Glen Alden Corporation
B.F. Goodrich Company
The Goodyear Tire & Rubber Company
W.R. Grace & Company
Gulf Oil Corporation

H.J. Heinz Company
Hercules, Incorporated
Hobart Manufacturing Company
Honeywell, Incorporated
Hoover Company
Hygrade Food Products Corporation

Ingersoll-Rand Company
Interchemical Corporation
International Business Machines Corporation
International Harvester Company
International Packers Limited
International Paper Company
International Telephone & Telegraph Corporation

Johns-Manville Corporation
Johnson & Johnson
Joy Manufacturing Company

Kaiser Industries Corporation
Kellogg Company
Kendall Company
Kimberly-Clark Corporation
Koppers Company, Incorporated

Libby, McNeill & Libby
Eli Lilly & Company
Litton Industries, Incorporated
Lockheed Aircraft Corporation

P.R. Mallory & Company Incorporated
Maremont Corporation
Martin Marietta Corporation
Merck & Company, Incorporated
Miles Laboratories, Incorporated
Minnesota Mining and Manufacturing Company

Mobil Oil Corporation
Monsanto Company

National Biscuit Company
National Cash Register Company
National Dairy Products Corporation
National Distillers & Chemical Corporation
National Lead Company
Norton Company

Olin Mathieson Chemical Corporation
Otis Elevator Company
Owens-Corning Fiberglas Corporation
Owens-Illinois, Incorporated

Parke, Davis & Company
Pennsalt Chemicals Corporation
PepsiCo, Incorporated
Pet Incorporated
Chas. Pfizer & Company, Incorporated
Phelps Dodge Corporation
Philip Morris Incorporated
Phillips Petroleum Company
Pillsbury Company
Pittsburgh Plate Glass Company
H.K. Porter Company, Incorporated
Procter & Gamble Company
Purex Corporation, Limited

Quaker Oats Company

Radio Corporation of America
Ralston Purina Company
Raytheon Company
Revlon, Incorporated
Reynolds Metals Company
Rheem Manufacturing Company
Richardson-Merrell, Incorporated
H.H. Robertson Company
Rockwell Manufacturing Company
Rohm & Haas Company

SCM Corporation
St. Regis Paper Company
Schering Corporation
Scott Paper Company
Scovill Manufacturing Company
Simmons Company
Singer Company
Smith Kline & French Laboratories
Sperry Rand Corporation
A.E. Staley Manufacturing Company
Standard Brands, Incorporated
Standard Oil Company of California
Standard Oil Company (Indiana)
Standard Oil Company (New Jersey)
Stauffer Chemical Company
Sterling Drug, Incorporated
Studebaker-Worthington, Incorporated
Sunbeam Corporation
Swift & Company

TRW Incorporated
Texaco Incorporated
Texas Instruments Incorporated
Time Incorporated
The Timken Roller Bearing Company

Union Carbide Corporation
UNIROYAL, Incorporated
United Merchants & Manufacturers, Incorporated
United Shoe Machinery Corporation
Upjohn Company

Warner-Lambert Pharmaceutical Company
Westinghouse Air Brake Company
Westinghouse Electric Corporation
Weyerhaeuser Company
Wm. Wrigley, Jr. Company

12. List of Enterprises Based Outside the United States

Allgemeine Elektricitats-Gesellshaft AEG-Telefunken	Germany
Ste Nationale Industrielle Aerospatiale	France
Agfa-Gevaert A.G.	Germany-Belgium
L'Air Liquide	France
AKZO (N.V.)	Netherlands
Alcan Aluminium Limited	Canada
Allied Breweries Limited	United Kingdom
Swiss Aluminum Ltd. (Alusuisse)	Switzerland
Societe Anonyme des Acieries Reunies de Burbach — Eich — Dudelange (ARBED)	Luxemburg
Asahi Chemical Industry Co., Ltd.	Japan
Asano Honsha	Japan
Allmanna Svenska Elektriska Aktiebolagets (ASEA)	Sweden
Associated British Foods Ltd.	United Kingdom
Ataka & Co. Ltd.	Japan
A. Johnson & Co. H.A.B.	Sweden
Badische Anilin & Soda - Fabrik Aktiengesellschaft (BASF)	Germany
Bass Charrington Brewers Limited	United Kingdom
Farbenfabriken Bayer Aktiengesellschaft Leverkusen	Germany
Beecham Group Limited	United Kingdom
Broken Hill Proprietary Company, Limited	Australia
Bayerische Motoren Werke Aktiengesellschaft Munchen	Germany
Bosch (Robert) GMBH	Germany
Boussois Souchon Neuvesel	France
Bowater Corporation Ltd.	United Kingdom
Bridgestone Tire Company Ltd.	Japan
British-American-Tobacco Company Limited	United Kingdom
British Insulated Callender's Cables, Limited	United Kingdom
British Leyland Motor Corporation	United Kingdom
British Oxygen Company, Ltd.	United Kingdom
British Petroleum Company, Limited	United Kingdom
British Steel Corporation	United Kingdom

Brooke Bond Liebig Ltd.	United Kingdom
Brown, Boveri & Cie in Baden	Switzerland
Buderussche Eisenwerke	Germany
Burmah Oil Company, Limited	United Kingdom
Cadbury Schweppes Limited	United Kingdom
Canada Packers, Limited	Canada
Charbonnages de France	France
Ciba-Geigy Limited	Switzerland
Compagnie Francaise des Petroles	France
Compagnie Generale d'Electricite	France
Societe Anonyme Andre Citroen	France
J&P Coats Patons & Baldwins Ltd.	United Kingdom
Cockerill — Ougree — Providence et Esperance — Longdoz, S.A.	Belgium
Consolidated Gold Fields Limited	United Kingdom
Consolidated Tin Smelters Limited	United Kingdom
Continental Gummi-Werke Aktiengesellschaft	Germany
Courtaulds, Limited	United Kingdom
Colonial Sugar Refining Co., Ltd.	Australia
Daimler-Benz A.G.	Germany
DeBeers Consolidated Mines, Limited	South Africa
Degussa	Germany
Delta Metal Company Limited	United Kingdom
Distillers Company, Limited	United Kingdom
Distillers Corporation — Seagrams, Limited	Canada
Domtar Limited	Canada
DSM NV Nederlandse Staatsmijmen	Netherlands
Dunlop Company Limited	United Kingdom
Enterprise de Recherches et D'Activites Petrolieres (E.R.A.P.)	France
EMI Limited	United Kingdom
ENI	Italy
Telefonaktiebolaget LM Ericsson	Sweden
I.G. Farben AG	Germany
Feldmuhle Aktiengesellschaft	Germany
Fiat Societa per Azioni	Italy
Friedrich Flick K.G.	Germany
Fujitse Limited	Japan

Furukawa Electric Company, Ltd.	Japan
Gelsenberg Aktiengesellschaft	Germany
The General Electric Company, Limited	United Kingdom
Granges Aktiebolag	Sweden
Guest, Keen and Nettlefolds Limited	United Kingdom
Gutehoffnungshutte Aktienverein	Germany
Hawker Siddeley Group Limited	United Kingdom
Henkel GMBH	Germany
Hindustan Steel Limited	India
Hitachi Ltd.	Japan
Hitachi Shipbuilding & Engineering Co., Ltd.	Japan
Farbwerke Hoechst Aktiengesellschaft	Germany
Hoesch Aktiengesellschaft	Germany
F.Hoffmann - LaRoche & Co. Aktiengesellschaft	Switzerland
Honda Motor Company Ltd.	Japan
Koninklijke Nederlandsche Hoogovens en Staalfabrieken N.V.	Netherlands
Idemitsu Kosan Co. Ltd.	Japan
Imperial Chemical Industries Limited	United Kingdom
Imperial Tobacco Group Limited	United Kingdom
Indian Oil Blending Ltd.	India
The International Nickel Company of Canada, Limited	Canada
Istituto per la Ricostruzione Industriale	Italy
ISCOR	South Africa
Ishikawajima-Harima Heavy Industries Co. Ltd.	Japan
Isuzu Motors Ltd.	Japan
Italsider	Italy
C. Itoh & Co. Ltd.	Japan
Johnson, Matthey & Co. Limited	United Kingdom
Kanegafuchi Spinning Co. Ltd.	Japan
Kanematsu-Gosho Ltd.	Japan
Kawasaki Heavy Industries Ltd.	Japan
Kawasaki Steel Corp.	Japan
Kirin Brewery Company, Limited	Japan

Klockner — Humboldt — Deutz Aktiengesellschaft	Germany
Klockner—Werke AG	Germany
Kobe Steel Ltd.	Japan
Komatsu Manufacturing Co. Ltd.	Japan
Kooperativa Forbundet	Sweden
Fried. Krupp Huttenwerke AG.	Germany
Kubota Iron & Machinery Works Ltd.	Japan
Librairie Hachette Societe Anonyme	France
Lonrho Limited	United Kingdom
Joseph Lucas (Industries) Limited	United Kingdom
J. Lyons & Company Limited	United Kingdom
MacMillan, Bloedel & Powell River Co. Ltd.	Canada
Mannesman Aktiengesellschaft	Germany
Marubeni — Iida Co. Ltd.	Japan
Maruzen Oil Co. Ltd.	Japan
Massey—Ferguson Limited	Canada
Matsushita Electric Industrial Co. Ltd.	Japan
The Metal Box Company Limited	United Kingdom
Metallgesellschaft AG	Germany
Metallurgie Hoboken—Overpelt	Belgium
Compagnie General des Etablissements Michelin	France
Mitsubishi Honsha Ltd.	Japan
Mitsubishi Chemical Industries Ltd.	Japan
Mitsubishi Corporation	Japan
Mitsubishi Electric Corporation	Japan
Mitsubishi Heavy Industries, Ltd.	Japan
Mitsubishi Metal Mining Co. Ltd.	Japan
Mitsubishi Oil Co., Ltd.	Japan
Mitsubishi Rayon Company, Ltd.	Japan
Mitsui Honsha Ltd.	Japan
Mitsui & Company Ltd.	Japan
Mitsui Shipbuilding & Engineering Co., Ltd.	Japan
Montedison S.p.A.	Italy
Moore Corporation Limited	Canada

National Coal Board	United Kingdom
Nchanga Consolidated Copper Mines Ltd.	Zambia
Nestle Alimentana S.A.;	
Unilac Inc.	Switzerland
Nichimen Company	Japan
Nippon Electric Co. Ltd.	Japan
Nippon Kokan Kabushiki Kaisha	Japan
Nippon Mining Co. Ltd.	Japan
Nippon Steel Corporation	Japan
Nissan, Ltd.	Japan
Nissan Motor Co. Ltd.	Japan
Nisshin Steel Co. Ltd.	Japan
Nissho-Iwai Co. Ltd.	Japan
Noranda Mines Limited	Canada
Norddeutsche Affinerie	Germany
The Northern Electric Co.	Canada
Ing. C. Olivetti & C., S.p.A.	Italy
Compagnie Pechiney S.A.	France
Petroleos Mexicanos	Mexico
Petrofina S.A.	Belgium
Petroleo Brasileiro S.A./Petrobas	Brazil
Peugeot S.A.	France
N.V. Philips' Gloeilampenfabrieken	Netherlands
Pirelli S.p.A.	Italy
The Plessey Company Limited	United Kingdom
Ranks Hovis McDougall Limited	United Kingdom
Reckitt & Colman Limited	United Kingdom
Reed International Limited	United Kingdom
Regie Nationale de Usines (Renault)	France
Rheinstahl Aktiengesellschaft	Germany
Rhone Poulenc S.A.	France
The Rio Tinto-Zinc Corporation Limited	United Kingdom
Roan Consolidated Mines Limited	Zambia
Rolls Royce Ltd.	United Kingdom
N.V. Koninklijke Nederlandsche	
Petroleum Maatschappij	
(Royal Dutch/Shell)	Neth.-U.K.

Saab-Scania Aktiebolag	Sweden
Compagnie de Saint-Gobain-Pont-a-Mousson	France
Salzgitter AG	Germany
Sandoz AG	Switzerland
Sanyo Electric Co. Ltd.	Japan
Schlumberger Limited	Neth. Antilles
Schneider S.A.	France
Sharp Manufacturing Co.	Japan
Showa Denko K.K.	Japan
Siemens Aktiengesellschaft	Germany
SKF Aktiebolaget Svenska Kullagerfabriken	Sweden
Snia Viscosa	Italy
Snow Brand Milk Products, Ltd.	Japan
Societe Generale de Belgique	Belgium
Solvay & Cie S.A.	Belgium
Sony Corp.	Japan
Spillers Limited	United Kingdom
The Steel Company of Canada Limited	Canada
Gebruder Sulzer Aktiengesellschaft	Switzerland
Sumitomo Honsha Ltd.	Japan
Sumitomo Chemical Co. Ltd.	Japan
Sumitomo Electric Industries Ltd.	Japan
Sumitomo Metal Industries Ltd.	Japan
Sumitomo Shoji Kaisha Ltd.	Japan
Swedish Match Company Limited	Sweden
Taiyo Corporation	Japan
Takeda Chemical Industries Ltd.	Japan
Tate and Lyle Limited	United Kingdom
Teijin Ltd.	Japan
Compagnie Francaise Thomson Houston-Hotchkiss Brandt	France
Thorn Electrical Industries Limited	United Kingdom
ATH August Thyssen-Hutte Aktiengesellschaft	Germany
Toa Nenryo Kogyo Kabushiki Kaisha	Japan
Tokyo Shibaura Electric Co. Ltd.	Japan
Toray Industries	Japan
Toyobo Co., Ltd.	Japan
Toyo Kogyo Company Ltd.	Japan
Toyo Menka Kaisha, Ltd.	Japan
Toyota Motor Co. Ltd.	Japan
Tube Investments Limited	United Kingdom

Ube Cycon Limited	Japan
Ugine Kuhlmann	France
Unigate Limited	United Kingdom
Unilever Limited	U.K.-Neth.
The Union International Co. Ltd.	United Kingdom
Unitika Ltd.	Japan
Union Siderurgique du Nord et de l'Est de la France S.A. (Usinor)	France
Usines a Tubes de Lorraine-Escaut et Vallourec Reunies	France
Varta Aktiengesellschaft	Germany
Veba Aktiengesellschaft	Germany
Vereinigte Österreichische Eisen- und Stahlwerke AG	Germany
Vickers Limited	United Kingdom
VW Volkswagenwerk Aktiengesellschaft	Germany
Aktiebolaget Volvo	Sweden
Wendel-Sidelor Societe Anonyme	France
Whitbread and Company Limited	United Kingdom
Yacimientos Petroliferos Fiscales	Argentina
Yasuda Hozensha	Japan

NOTE Of the companies on the above list, the following had no known foreign subsidiaries: Asano Honsha, Hindustan Steel Limited, Indian Oil Blending Ltd., ISCOR, Italsider, Kirin Brewery Company, Limited, Mitsubishi Oil Co., Ltd., Mitsui Shipbuilding & Engineering Co., Ltd., National Coal Board, Nchanga Consolidated Copper Mines Ltd., Nissan, Ltd., Petroleos Mexicanos, Petroleo Brasileiro S.A./Petrobas, Roan Consolidated Mines Limited, Toa Nenryo Kogyo Kabushiki Kaisha, Ube Cycon Limited, and Yacimientos Petroliferos Fiscales.

Tabulations
and
Cross-Tabulations

TABULATION 1.1: PERCENTAGE BREAKDOWN OF NUMBER OF SUBSIDIARIES BY
SUBSIDIARY'S COUNTRY
FOR VARIOUS CATEGORIES OF SUBSIDIARIES

CATEGORY OF SUBSIDIARY	SUBSIDIARY'S COUNTRY						
	UNITED STATES	CANADA	MEXICO	CENTRAL AMERICA +CARIB.	VENE-ZUELA	COLOMBIA	PERU
NON-U.S.-BASED SYSTEMS (AS OF 1/1/71):							
ALL SUBSIDIARIES........	7.8	5.3	1.3	2.0	0.8	0.4	0.5
MANUFACTURING SUBS......	7.1	4.8	1.7	1.6	0.8	0.5	0.5
SALES SUBSIDIARIES......	8.4	4.2	1.5	1.9	1.1	0.6	0.8
U.S.-BASED SYSTEMS (AS OF 1/1/68):							
ALL SUBSIDIARIES........	0.	14.	4.9	5.1	3.6	2.1	1.3
MANUFACTURING SUBS......	0.	13.	6.8	3.3	3.2	2.7	1.2
SALES SUBSIDIARIES......	0.	9.7	2.3	4.8	2.1	1.4	1.5
WORLD SUBSET OF SYSTEMS (AS OF 1/1/68):							
NON-U.S.-BASED SYSTEMS:							
ALL SUBSIDIARIES........	7.4	6.9	1.4	2.6	0.9	0.5	0.6
MANUFACTURING SUBS.....	6.5	7.3	1.8	1.9	0.7	0.7	0.7
SALES SUBSIDIARIES......	6.3	4.5	1.3	2.3	1.0	0.6	0.7
U.S.BASED-SYSTEMS:							
ALL SUBSIDIARIES........	0.	14.	4.8	5.5	3.2	2.3	1.3
MANUFACTURING SUBS.....	0.	13.	6.6	3.5	3.6	2.9	1.2
SALES SUBSIDIARIES......	0.	11.	2.1	5.0	2.1	1.7	1.6

(TABLE CONTINUED ON NEXT PAGE)

TABULATION 1.1: PERCENTAGE BREAKDOWN OF NUMBER OF SUBSIDIARIES BY SUBSIDIARY'S COUNTRY FOR VARIOUS CATEGORIES OF SUBSIDIARIES (CONTINUED)

CATEGORY OF SUBSIDIARY	SUBSIDIARY'S COUNTRY						
	CHILE	ARGEN-TINA	BRAZIL	OTHER SOUTH AMERICA	GERMANY	FRANCE	ITALY
NON-U.S.-BASED SYSTEMS (AS OF 1/1/71):							
ALL SUBSIDIARIES.........	0.5	1.8	2.2	0.5	5.8	7.1	2.9
MANUFACTURING SUBS.......	0.5	2.1	3.3	0.4	5.7	7.8	3.6
SALES SUBSIDIARIES.......	0.7	1.6	1.5	0.6	6.6	5.3	2.6
U.S.-BASED SYSTEMS (AS OF 1/1/68):							
ALL SUBSIDIARIES.........	0.8	2.7	3.3	1.3	5.5	5.5	3.8
MANUFACTURING SUBS.......	1.0	3.2	4.2	1.0	5.8	5.6	4.4
SALES SUBSIDIARIES.......	0.7	1.7	1.9	1.4	6.1	5.1	3.1
WORLD SUBSET OF SYSTEMS (AS OF 1/1/68):							
NON-U.S.-BASED SYSTEMS:							
ALL SUBSIDIARIES........	0.5	2.2	2.1	0.5	5.4	6.6	2.8
MANUFACTURING SUBS......	0.5	2.8	3.2	0.3	5.8	5.6	3.5
SALES SUBSIDIARIES......	0.7	1.6	0.9	1.0	5.6	5.2	2.6
U.S.-BASED-SYSTEMS:							
ALL SUBSIDIARIES........	0.8	2.6	3.2	1.4	5.5	5.3	3.6
MANUFACTURING SUBS......	1.0	3.2	4.0	1.2	5.8	5.4	4.4
SALES SUBSIDIARIES......	0.8	1.3	1.7	1.4	5.8	5.0	2.9

(TABLE CONTINUED ON NEXT PAGE)

TABULATION 1.1: PERCENTAGE BREAKDOWN OF NUMBER OF SUBSIDIARIES BY SUBSIDIARY'S COUNTRY FOR VARIOUS CATEGORIES OF SUBSIDIARIES (CONTINUED)

CATEGORY OF SUBSIDIARY	SUBSIDIARY'S COUNTRY						
	BELGIUM AND LUX-EMBURG	THE NETHER-LANDS	UNITED KINGDOM	IRELAND	DENMARK	NORWAY	SWEDEN
NON-U.S.-BASED SYSTEMS (AS OF 1/1/71):							
ALL SUBSIDIARIES.........	3.7	2.6	6.5	1.7	1.0	0.9	1.3
MANUFACTURING SUBS.....	2.8	2.5	4.5	1.7	0.7	0.8	1.3
SALES SUBSIDIARIES.....	4.2	3.0	9.9	2.0	2.0	1.5	1.8
U.S.-BASED SYSTEMS (AS OF 1/1/68):							
ALL SUBSIDIARIES.........	2.7	2.4	9.8	0.7	1.1	0.8	1.4
MANUFACTURING SUBS.....	2.4	2.1	9.5	0.7	0.8	0.5	0.9
SALES SUBSIDIARIES.....	4.5	3.7	7.9	0.8	2.3	1.3	3.1
WORLD SUBSET OF SYSTEMS (AS OF 1/1/68):							
NON-U.S.-BASED SYSTEMS:							
ALL SUBSIDIARIES.........	3.1	2.2	7.4	1.3	1.1	1.0	1.6
MANUFACTURING SUBS.....	2.7	2.0	5.0	1.5	0.9	1.0	1.8
SALES SUBSIDIARIES.....	4.0	2.9	12.	1.3	2.0	1.5	2.0
U.S.-BASED-SYSTEMS:							
ALL SUBSIDIARIES.........	2.5	2.4	9.6	0.6	1.1	0.8	1.4
MANUFACTURING SUBS.....	2.5	2.2	8.8	0.6	0.8	0.5	0.9
SALES SUBSIDIARIES.....	4.0	2.9	8.4	0.8	2.4	1.2	3.1

(TABLE CONTINUED ON NEXT PAGE)

TABULATION 1.1: PERCENTAGE BREAKDOWN OF NUMBER OF SUBSIDIARIES BY SUBSIDIARY'S COUNTRY FOR VARIOUS CATEGORIES OF SUBSIDIARIES (CONTINUED)

SUBSIDIARY'S COUNTRY

CATEGORY OF SUBSIDIARY	FINLAND	SWITZ-ERLAND	AUSTRIA	PORTUGAL	SPAIN	GREECE	TURKEY
NON-U.S.-BASED SYSTEMS (AS OF 1/1/71):							
ALL SUBSIDIARIES.........	0.5	2.4	1.6	0.8	2.5	0.4	0.4
MANUFACTURING SUBS.......	0.4	1.0	1.6	1.0	3.4	0.5	0.6
SALES SUBSIDIARIES.......	0.9	2.8	2.2	1.1	1.8	0.6	0.4
U.S.-BASED SYSTEMS (AS OF 1/1/68):							
ALL SUBSIDIARIES.........	0.3	2.8	0.6	0.4	2.2	0.5	0.3
MANUFACTURING SUBS.......	0.1	0.8	0.5	0.5	2.9	0.5	0.4
SALES SUBSIDIARIES.......	1.0	5.3	1.7	0.7	1.9	0.7	0.4
WORLD SUBSET OF SYSTEMS (AS OF 1/1/68):							
NON-U.S.-BASED SYSTEMS:							
ALL SUBSIDIARIES.........	0.5	2.5	1.5	1.0	2.8	0.5	0.6
MANUFACTURING SUBS.......	0.4	1.0	1.0	0.9	3.8	0.5	0.8
SALES SUBSIDIARIES.......	1.0	3.0	2.0	1.7	2.0	0.6	0.5
U.S.-BASED-SYSTEMS:							
ALL SUBSIDIARIES.........	0.3	2.7	0.6	0.5	2.2	0.5	0.4
MANUFACTURING SUBS.......	0.1	0.8	0.4	0.5	3.1	3.5	0.4
SALES SUBSIDIARIES.......	1.0	5.4	1.7	0.8	1.6	0.5	0.4

(TABLE CONTINUED ON NEXT PAGE)

35

TABULATION 1.1: PERCENTAGE BREAKDOWN OF NUMBER OF SUBSIDIARIES BY
SUBSIDIARY'S COUNTRY
FOR VARIOUS CATEGORIES OF SUBSIDIARIES
(CONTINUED)

SUBSIDIARY'S COUNTRY

CATEGORY OF SUBSIDIARY	OTHER EUROPE +ISRAEL	PAKISTAN	IRAN	OTHER MID EAST+LIB-YA+EGYPT	UNION OF S. AFRICA	RHODESIA	ZAMBIA
NON-U.S.-BASED SYSTEMS (AS OF 1/1/71):							
ALL SUBSIDIARIES.........	0.7	0.6	0.5	0.6	6.1	1.2	0.8
MANUFACTURING SUBS......	0.7	0.7	0.4	0.5	6.6	1.0	0.7
SALES SUBSIDIARIES......	0.5	0.7	0.6	0.6	3.0	0.8	1.0
U.S.-BASED SYSTEMS (AS OF 1/1/68):							
ALL SUBSIDIARIES.........	0.5	0.3	0.5	1.2	2.2	0.4	0.5
MANUFACTURING SUBS......	0.4	0.4	0.4	0.7	2.9	0.3	0.2
SALES SUBSIDIARIES......	0.8	0.4	0.4	0.5	1.8	0.7	0.7
WORLD SUBSET OF SYSTEMS (AS OF 1/1/68):							
NON-U.S.-BASED SYSTEMS:							
ALL SUBSIDIARIES.........	1.0	0.7	0.5	0.8	4.0	1.1	0.4
MANUFACTURING SUBS......	0.9	0.8	0.4	0.6	5.1	1.1	0.3
SALES SUBSIDIARIES......	0.4	0.8	0.8	0.9	2.4	0.8	0.6
U.S.-BASED-SYSTEMS:							
ALL SUBSIDIARIES.........	0.5	0.3	0.5	1.5	2.0	0.3	0.6
MANUFACTURING SUBS......	0.3	0.4	0.5	0.9	2.7	0.3	0.2
SALES SUBSIDIARIES......	1.1	0.4	0.5	0.7	1.6	0.5	0.5

(TABLE CONTINUED ON NEXT PAGE)

TABULATION 1.1: PERCENTAGE BREAKDOWN OF NUMBER OF SUBSIDIARIES BY
SUBSIDIARY'S COUNTRY
FOR VARIOUS CATEGORIES OF SUBSIDIARIES
(CONTINUED)

SUBSIDIARY'S COUNTRY

CATEGORY OF SUBSIDIARY	TANZANIA	KENYA	NIGERIA	OTHER (BRITISH) AFRICA	MOROCCO, ALGERIA + TUNISIA	OTHER (FRENCH) AFRICA	OTHER AFRICA
NON-U.S.-BASED SYSTEMS (AS OF 1/1/71):							
ALL SUBSIDIARIES.........	0.5	1.0	1.1	1.4	1.4	1.6	1.1
MANUFACTURING SUBS.......	0.4	0.8	1.0	1.0	0.9	0.9	0.6
SALES SUBSIDIARIES.......	0.5	1.0	1.4	2.4	1.6	2.4	1.5
U.S.-BASED SYSTEMS (AS OF 1/1/68):							
ALL SUBSIDIARIES.........	0.1	0.2	0.3	0.3	0.5	0.5	0.4
MANUFACTURING SUBS.......	0.	0.2	0.3	0.1	0.4	0.2	0.1
SALES SUBSIDIARIES.......	0.1	0.3	0.2	0.6	1.1	0.7	0.4
WORLD SUBSET OF SYSTEMS (AS OF 1/1/68):							
NON-U.S.-BASED SYSTEMS:							
ALL SUBSIDIARIES.........	0.4	0.7	1.0	1.1	1.8	1.8	1.2
MANUFACTURING SUBS.......	0.3	0.7	1.0	0.9	1.2	1.0	0.7
SALES SUBSIDIARIES.......	0.6	0.7	1.2	2.0	2.0	2.7	1.9
U.S.-BASED-SYSTEMS:							
ALL SUBSIDIARIES.........	0.1	0.2	0.3	0.3	0.5	0.5	0.5
MANUFACTURING SUBS.......	0.	0.2	0.4	0.1	0.4	0.2	0.1
SALES SUBSIDIARIES.......	0.2	0.3	0.3	0.8	1.3	0.8	0.5

(TABLE CONTINUED ON NEXT PAGE)

TABULATION 1.1: PERCENTAGE BREAKDOWN OF NUMBER OF SUBSIDIARIES BY
SUBSIDIARY'S COUNTRY
FOR VARIOUS CATEGORIES OF SUBSIDIARIES
(CONTINUED)

CATEGORY OF SUBSIDIARY	SUBSIDIARY'S COUNTRY						
	AUSTRALIA	NEW ZEALAND	JAPAN	CHINA (TAIWAN)	HONG KONG	THE PHILIP- PINES	MALAYSIA
NON-U.S.-BASED SYSTEMS (AS OF 1/1/71):							
ALL SUBSIDIARIES.........	6.6	1.6	1.1	0.8	0.5	0.3	0.7
MANUFACTURING SUBS......	7.2	2.0	1.5	1.7	0.5	0.4	1.0
SALES SUBSIDIARIES......	3.6	1.2	1.1	0.1	1.1	0.2	0.3
U.S.-BASED SYSTEMS (AS OF 1/1/68):							
ALL SUBSIDIARIES.........	4.8	1.0	2.8	0.3	0.5	1.1	0.4
MANUFACTURING SUBS......	5.5	1.1	3.7	0.4	0.2	1.3	0.4
SALES SUBSIDIARIES......	4.2	1.1	3.0	0.5	1.4	1.1	0.7
WORLD SUBSET OF SYSTEMS (AS OF 1/1/68):							
NON-U.S.-BASED SYSTEMS:							
ALL SUBSIDIARIES........	7.1	1.7	1.3	0.2	0.5	0.3	0.7
MANUFACTURING SUBS.....	8.8	2.0	1.4	0.5	0.4	0.4	0.7
SALES SUBSIDIARIES.....	3.6	2.0	1.5	0.1	0.9	0.1	0.6
U.S.-BASED-SYSTEMS:							
ALL SUBSIDIARIES........	4.1	0.8	2.8	0.4	0.5	1.1	0.4
MANUFACTURING SUBS.....	5.1	0.8	3.9	0.4	0.1	1.5	0.4
SALES SUBSIDIARIES.....	4.0	1.1	2.6	0.6	1.5	1.3	0.7

(TABLE CONTINUED ON NEXT PAGE)

TABULATION 1.1: PERCENTAGE BREAKDOWN OF NUMBER OF SUBSIDIARIES BY
SUBSIDIARY'S COUNTRY
FOR VARIOUS CATEGORIES OF SUBSIDIARIES
(CONTINUED)

CATEGORY OF SUBSIDIARY	SUBSIDIARY'S COUNTRY						
	SINGA-PORE	INDO-NESIA	THAILAND	INDIA	OTHER ASIA + OCEANIA	TOTAL PERCENT	TOTAL NUMBER
NON-U.S.-BASED SYSTEMS (AS OF 1/1/71):							
ALL SUBSIDIARIES.........	0.6	0.5	0.7	1.6	1.0	100.	13774
MANUFACTURING SUBS.......	0.9	0.5	1.2	2.7	1.1	100.	5639
SALES SUBSIDIARIES.......	0.6	0.4	0.7	0.8	0.7	100.	3304
U.S.-BASED SYSTEMS (AS OF 1/1/68):							
ALL SUBSIDIARIES.........	0.2	0.3	0.3	1.0	0.5	100.	9776
MANUFACTURING SUBS.......	0.3	0.1	0.4	1.6	0.5	100.	4246
SALES SUBSIDIARIES.......	0.5	0.4	0.4	0.7	0.4	100.	1664
WORLD SUBSET OF SYSTEMS (AS OF 1/1/68):							
NON-U.S.-BASED SYSTEMS:							
ALL SUBSIDIARIES.......	0.6	0.2	0.4	2.1	0.9	100.	6143
MANUFACTURING SUBS.....	0.8	0.1	0.5	3.4	0.8	100.	2735
SALES SUBSIDIARIES.....	0.4	0.3	0.5	1.2	1.0	100.	1631
U.S.-BASED-SYSTEMS:							
ALL SUBSIDIARIES.......	0.2	0.4	0.3	1.0	0.5	100.	8144
MANUFACTURING SUBS.....	0.2	0.1	0.4	1.6	0.6	100.	3334
SALES SUBSIDIARIES.....	0.4	0.5	0.5	0.8	0.4	100.	1309

TABULATION 1.2: PERCENTAGE BREAKDOWN OF SALES OF SUBSIDIARIES IN 1970 BY
SUBSIDIARY'S COUNTRY
FOR ALL SUBSIDIARIES, MANUFACTURING SUBSIDIARIES AND SALES SUBSIDIARIES
OF NON-U.S.-BASED SYSTEMS

SUBSIDIARY'S COUNTRY

CATEGORY OF SUBSIDIARY	UNITED STATES	CANADA	MEXICO	CENTRAL AMERICA + CARIB.	VENE- ZUELA	COLOMBIA	PERU
ALL SUBSIDIARIES............	18.	5.8	0.7	1.6	0.8	0.2	0.2
MANUFACTURING SUBSIDIARIES...	18.	5.9	0.8	1.8	0.8	0.2	0.2
SALES SUBSIDIARIES..........	25.	3.2	1.0	0.7	0.8	0.2	0.3

TABLE CONTINUED ON NEXT PAGE

TABULATION 1.2: PERCENTAGE BREAKDOWN OF SALES OF SUBSIDIARIES IN 1970 BY
SUBSIDIARY'S COUNTRY
FOR ALL SUBSIDIARIES, MANUFACTURING SUBSIDIARIES AND SALES SUBSIDIARIES
OF NON-U.S.-BASED SYSTEMS
(CONTINUED)

SUBSIDIARY'S COUNTRY

CATEGORY OF SUBSIDIARY	CHILE	ARGEN-TINA	BRAZIL	OTHER SOUTH AMERICA	GERMANY	FRANCE	ITALY
ALL SUBSIDIARIES............	0.2	1.8	2.7	0.2	11.	8.3	3.4
MANUFACTURING SUBSIDIARIES...	0.1	2.1	3.7	0.1	13.	9.3	4.1
SALES SUBSIDIARIES..........	0.5	1.6	1.0	0.1	8.1	6.3	2.6

TABLE CONTINUED ON NEXT PAGE

TABULATION 1.2: PERCENTAGE BREAKDOWN OF SALES OF SUBSIDIARIES IN 1970 BY
SUBSIDIARY'S COUNTRY

FOP ALL SUBSIDIARIES, MANUFACTURING SUBSIDIARIES AND SALES SUBSIDIARIES
OF NON-U.S.-BASED SYSTEMS
(CONTINUED)

SUBSIDIARY'S COUNTRY

CATEGORY OF SUBSIDIARY	BELGIUM AND LUX-EMBURG	THE NETHER-LANDS	UNITED KINGDOM	IRELAND	DENMARK	NORWAY	SWEDEN
ALL SUBSIDIARIES..........	3.4	2.1	6.3	0.5	0.7	0.6	1.0
MANUFACTURING SUBSIDIARIES...	2.7	2.0	5.3	0.5	0.4	0.6	1.0
SALES SUBSIDIARIES..........	3.3	2.8	8.1	0.6	2.5	1.2	2.0

TABLE CONTINUED ON NEXT PAGE

TABULATION 1.2: PERCENTAGE BREAKDOWN OF SALES OF SUBSIDIARIES IN 1970 BY
SUBSIDIARY'S COUNTRY
FOR ALL SUBSIDIARIES, MANUFACTURING SUBSIDIARIES AND SALES SUBSIDIARIES
OF NON-U.S.-BASED SYSTEMS
(CONTINUED)

SUBSIDIARY'S COUNTRY

CATEGORY OF SUBSIDIARY	FINLAND	SWITZ-ERLAND	AUSTRIA	PORTUGAL	SPAIN	GREECE	TURKEY
ALL SUBSIDIARIES............	0.3	1.8	1.1	0.5	1.9	0.3	0.3
MANUFACTURING SUBSIDIARIES...	0.2	0.6	0.9	0.4	2.1	0.3	0.4
SALES SUBSIDIARIES...........	1.0	2.9	1.4	1.1	1.7	0.4	0.1

TABLE CONTINUED ON NEXT PAGE

TABULATION 1.2: PERCENTAGE BREAKDOWN OF SALES OF SUBSIDIARIES IN 1970 BY
SUBSIDIARY'S COUNTRY
FOR ALL SUBSIDIARIES, MANUFACTURING SUBSIDIARIES AND SALES SUBSIDIARIES
OF NON-U.S.-BASED SYSTEMS
(CONTINUED)

SUBSIDIARY'S COUNTRY

CATEGORY OF SUBSIDIARY	OTHER EUROPE +ISRAEL	PAKISTAN	IRAN	OTHER MID EAST+LIB- YA+EGYPT	UNION OF S. AFRICA	RHODESIA	ZAMBIA
ALL SUBSIDIARIES............	0.2	0.5	0.7	2.8	2.8	0.2	0.1
MANUFACTURING SUBSIDIARIES...	0.2	0.4	0.4	2.9	2.7	0.2	0.1
SALES SUBSIDIARIES...........	0.2	0.6	1.1	0.3	2.0	0.1	0.1

TABLE CONTINUED ON NEXT PAGE

TABULATION 1.2: PERCENTAGE BREAKDOWN OF SALES OF SUBSIDIARIES IN 1970 BY
SUBSIDIARY'S COUNTRY

FOR ALL SUBSIDIARIES, MANUFACTURING SUBSIDIARIES AND SALES SUBSIDIARIES
OF NON-U.S.-BASED SYSTEMS
(CONTINUED)

SUBSIDIARY'S COUNTRY

CATEGORY OF SUBSIDIARY	TANZANIA	KENYA	NIGERIA	OTHER (BRITISH) AFRICA	MOROCCO, ALGERIA + TUNISIA	OTHER (FRENCH) AFRICA	OTHER AFRICA
ALL SUBSIDIARIES............	0.1	0.5	0.4	0.4	0.9	1.3	0.5
MANUFACTURING SUBSIDIARIES...	0.1	0.3	0.3	0.3	0.5	0.7	0.1
SALES SUBSIDIARIES..........	0.3	1.1	0.5	0.6	0.7	1.3	0.7

TABLE CONTINUED ON NEXT PAGE

TABULATION 1.2: PERCENTAGE BREAKDOWN OF SALES OF SUBSIDIARIES IN 1970 BY
SUBSIDIARY'S COUNTRY
FOR ALL SUBSIDIARIES, MANUFACTURING SUBSIDIARIES AND SALES SUBSIDIARIES
OF NON-U.S.-BASED SYSTEMS
(CONTINUED)

SUBSIDIARY'S COUNTRY

CATEGORY OF SUBSIDIARY	AUSTRALIA	NEW ZEALAND	JAPAN	CHINA (TAIWAN)	HONG KONG	THE PHILIP-PINES	MALAYSIA
ALL SUBSIDIARIES............	6.1	0.5	1.6	0.5	0.2	0.3	0.4
MANUFACTURING SUBSIDIARIES...	5.6	0.5	2.1	0.7	0.1	0.5	0.5
SALES SUBSIDIARIES..........	3.8	0.7	1.4	0.2	0.5	0.1	0.3

TABLE CONTINUED ON NEXT PAGE

TABULATION 1.2: PERCENTAGE BREAKDOWN OF SALES OF SUBSIDIARIES IN 1970 BY
SUBSIDIARY'S COUNTRY
FOR ALL SUBSIDIARIES, MANUFACTURING SUBSIDIARIES AND SALES SUBSIDIARIES
OF NON-U.S.-BASED SYSTEMS
(CONTINUED)

SUBSIDIARY'S COUNTRY

CATEGORY OF SUBSIDIARY	SINGA-PORE	INDO-NESIA	THAILAND	INDIA	OTHER ASIA + OCEANIA	TOTAL PERCENT	TOTAL ($ MIL)
ALL SUBSIDIARIES..............	0.3	0.2	0.3	1.7	0.7	100.	132401
MANUFACTURING SUBSIDIARIES...	0.4	0.1	0.4	2.1	0.3	100.	82412
SALES SUBSIDIARIES...........	0.4	0.4	0.3	1.2	0.4	100.	23243

CROSS-TABULATION 1. 8.1: PERCENTAGE BREAKDOWN OF NUMBER (AS OF 1/1/71) OF
MANUFACTURING SUBSIDIARIES OF NON-U.S.-BASED PARENT SYSTEMS BY
SUBSIDIARY'S COUNTRY
FOR SUBSIDIARIES CLASSIFIED BY
PRINCIPAL INDUSTRY-GROUP OF SUBSIDIARY AS OF 1/1/71

SUBSIDIARY'S COUNTRY

PRINCIPAL INDUSTRY- GROUP OF SUBSIDIARY AS OF 1/1/71	UNITED STATES	CANADA	MEXICO	CENTRAL AMERICA + CARIB.	VENE- ZUELA	COLOMBIA	PERU
FOOD AND TOBACCO.............	6.4	5.5	0.9	3.1	0.6	0.1	0.6
TEXTILES AND APPAREL.........	1.8	3.2	1.1	2.5	1.4	1.1	0.7
WOOD, FURNITURE AND PAPER....	5.7	13.	0.5	1.4	0.	1.0	0.
CHEMICALS....................	7.6	3.7	2.7	1.1	1.0	0.8	0.7
PETROLEUM....................	6.3	3.6	0.	2.6	0.5	0.	0.
RUBBER AND TIRES.............	1.9	1.9	0.	1.9	0.9	0.	0.
PRIMARY METALS...............	5.6	7.0	0.5	1.9	0.5	0.2	0.2
FABR. METAL + NON-EL. MACH...	9.3	5.3	2.0	1.3	0.7	0.3	0.2
ELECTRIC AND ELECTRONIC......	9.0	2.2	2.9	1.1	0.8	0.5	0.6
TRANSPORTATION EQUIPMENT.....	2.4	7.7	2.0	1.2	1.2	1.2	2.8
PRECISION GOODS..............	31.	2.6	0.	0.	0.	0.	0.
OTHER........................	7.7	8.0	1.2	1.5	0.6	0.3	0.

TABLE CONTINUED ON NEXT PAGE

CROSS-TABULATION 1. 8.1: PERCENTAGE BREAKDOWN OF NUMBER (AS OF 1/1/71) OF MANUFACTURING SUBSIDIARIES OF NON-U.S.-BASED PARENT SYSTEMS BY SUBSIDIARY'S COUNTRY FOR SUBSIDIARIES CLASSIFIED BY PRINCIPAL INDUSTRY-GROUP OF SUBSIDIARY AS OF 1/1/71 (CONTINUED)

SUBSIDIARY'S COUNTRY

PRINCIPAL INDUSTRY-GROUP OF SUBSIDIARY AS OF 1/1/71	CHILE	ARGEN-TINA	BRAZIL	OTHER SOUTH AMERICA	GERMANY	FRANCE	ITALY
FOOD AND TOBACCO............	0.1	1.3	1.5	0.9	3.8	6.0	1.6
TEXTILES AND APPAREL........	0.7	1.8	4.3	0.7	5.4	3.2	1.4
WOOD, FURNITURE AND PAPER....	0.5	1.4	1.0	0.	4.8	5.2	2.9
CHEMICALS...................	1.0	2.8	3.9	0.5	6.3	9.6	4.2
PETROLEUM...................	0.	0.5	0.	1.0	8.3	6.3	4.2
RUBBER AND TIRES............	0.	2.8	0.9	0.	6.6	6.6	2.8
PRIMARY METALS..............	0.	2.9	2.7	0.5	5.1	7.0	1.9
FABR. METAL + NON-EL. MACH...	0.	2.0	4.3	0.2	7.1	8.4	4.5
ELECTRIC AND ELECTRONIC......	0.4	2.0	3.7	0.	4.7	6.0	5.1
TRANSPORTATION EQUIPMENT.....	1.6	3.3	5.7	0.	2.8	5.3	2.0
PRECISION GOODS.............	1.3	2.6	1.3	0.	5.1	17.	12.
OTHER......................	0.3	1.8	4.2	0.	8.6	7.1	3.9

TABLE CONTINUED ON NEXT PAGE

CROSS-TABULATION 1. 8.1: PERCENTAGE BREAKDOWN OF NUMBER (AS OF 1/1/71) OF
MANUFACTURING SUBSIDIARIES OF NON-U.S.-BASED PARENT SYSTEMS BY
SUBSIDIARY'S COUNTRY
FOR SUBSIDIARIES CLASSIFIED BY
PRINCIPAL INDUSTRY-GROUP OF SUBSIDIARY AS OF 1/1/71
(CONTINUED)

SUBSIDIARY'S COUNTRY

PRINCIPAL INDUSTRY-GROUP OF SUBSIDIARY AS OF 1/1/71	BELGIUM AND LUX-EMBURG	THE NETHER-LANDS	UNITED KINGDOM	IRELAND	DENMARK	NORWAY	SWEDEN
FOOD AND TOBACCO..............	2.5	1.9	2.0	5.7	1.0	0.4	1.3
TEXTILES AND APPAREL..........	1.1	0.7	1.8	0.4	0.	0.	0.7
WOOD, FURNITURE AND PAPER.....	3.3	3.8	6.7	3.3	1.0	2.9	1.9
CHEMICALS.....................	2.3	2.5	4.1	1.4	0.9	0.4	1.0
PETROLEUM.....................	3.6	2.6	5.7	1.6	1.6	0.5	2.1
RUBBER AND TIRES..............	3.8	3.8	3.8	1.9	0.	0.	0.9
PRIMARY METALS................	2.7	2.7	3.1	0.5	0.7	1.5	0.7
FABR. METAL + NON-EL. MACH....	2.6	2.5	6.4	1.0	0.2	1.0	1.2
ELECTRIC AND ELECTRONIC.......	3.0	1.5	6.0	1.4	1.4	1.8	2.4
TRANSPORTATION EQUIPMENT......	4.1	2.4	0.8	0.8	0.	0.4	0.4
PRECISION GOODS...............	0.	2.6	9.0	0.	1.3	1.3	0.
OTHER.........................	4.8	4.5	9.8	0.6	0.3	0.3	1.2

TABLE CONTINUED ON NEXT PAGE

CROSS-TABULATION 1.8.1: PERCENTAGE BREAKDOWN OF NUMBER (AS OF 1/1/71) OF MANUFACTURING SUBSIDIARIES OF NON-U.S.-BASED PARENT SYSTEMS BY SUBSIDIARY'S COUNTRY

FOR SUBSIDIARIES CLASSIFIED BY
PRINCIPAL INDUSTRY-GROUP OF SUBSIDIARY AS OF 1/1/71
(CONTINUED)

SUBSIDIARY'S COUNTRY

PRINCIPAL INDUSTRY-GROUP OF SUBSIDIARY AS OF 1/1/71	FINLAND	SWITZ-ERLAND	AUSTRIA	PORTUGAL	SPAIN	GREECE	TURKEY
FOOD AND TOBACCO..........	0.3	0.9	0.4	0.7	1.8	0.1	0.3
TEXTILES AND APPAREL......	0.	1.1	0.7	1.4	3.6	0.	0.4
WOOD, FURNITURE AND PAPER....	0.5	0.5	1.0	0.5	1.0	0.	0.
CHEMICALS.................	0.4	1.0	2.5	1.4	4.8	0.6	1.2
PETROLEUM.................	0.	2.1	2.1	0.5	1.6	0.	0.5
RUBBER AND TIRES..........	0.	0.9	0.9	0.9	7.5	1.9	0.9
PRIMARY METALS...........	1.0	0.5	1.7	1.2	2.2	0.2	0.2
FABR. METAL + NON-EL. MACH...	0.3	1.2	1.3	0.7	2.1	0.3	0.3
ELECTRIC AND ELECTRONIC......	0.6	1.1	2.4	0.5	3.6	1.3	0.6
TRANSPORTATION EQUIPMENT....	0.8	0.	0.4	2.0	5.7	0.	1.6
PRECISION GOODS...........	0.	1.3	1.3	0.	2.6	0.	0.
OTHER.....................	0.	0.6	2.1	0.6	4.8	0.3	0.

TABLE CONTINUED ON NEXT PAGE

CROSS-TABULATION 1. 8.1: PERCENTAGE BREAKDOWN OF NUMBER (AS OF 1/1/71) OF
MANUFACTURING SUBSIDIARIES OF NON-U.S.-BASED PARENT SYSTEMS BY
SUBSIDIARY'S COUNTRY
FOR SUBSIDIARIES CLASSIFIED BY
PRINCIPAL INDUSTRY-GROUP OF SUBSIDIARY AS OF 1/1/71
(CONTINUED)

SUBSIDIARY'S COUNTRY

PRINCIPAL INDUSTRY-GROUP OF SUBSIDIARY AS OF 1/1/71	OTHER EUROPE +ISRAEL	PAKISTAN	IRAN	OTHER MID EAST+LIB-YA+EGYPT	UNION OF S. AFRICA	RHODESIA	ZAMBIA
FOOD AND TOBACCO..........	0.9	0.4	0.	0.	12.	2.9	2.3
TEXTILES AND APPAREL.........	1.8	0.7	0.4	0.	5.4	0.4	0.
WOOD, FURNITURE AND PAPER.....	0.	0.	0.5	0.	8.6	1.0	0.5
CHEMICALS.................	0.6	1.2	0.3	0.5	4.9	0.7	0.6
PETROLEUM.................	0.	1.6	1.0	2.1	3.1	0.5	0.
RUBBER AND TIRES.............	0.	0.	0.	0.	12.	0.9	0.9
PRIMARY METALS.............	0.2	0.5	0.2	0.7	8.2	1.5	0.2
FABR. METAL + NON-EL. MACH...	0.8	0.7	0.5	0.5	5.3	0.3	0.3
ELECTRIC AND ELECTRONIC......	0.8	0.9	0.8	0.5	5.5	0.5	0.1
TRANSPORTATION EQUIPMENT.....	0.8	0.4	0.8	0.8	7.3	1.2	0.
PRECISION GOODS..............	0.	0.	0.	0.	5.1	0.	0.
OTHER.....................	1.2	0.3	0.6	0.	3.0	0.3	2.4

TABLE CONTINUED ON NEXT PAGE

52

CROSS-TABULATION 1. 8.1: PERCENTAGE BREAKDOWN OF NUMBER (AS OF 1/1/71) OF
MANUFACTURING SUBSIDIARIES OF NON-U.S.-BASED PARENT SYSTEMS BY
SUBSIDIARY'S COUNTRY
FOR SUBSIDIARIES CLASSIFIED BY
PRINCIPAL INDUSTRY-GROUP OF SUBSIDIARY AS OF 1/1/71
(CONTINUED)

SUBSIDIARY'S COUNTRY

PRINCIPAL INDUSTRY-GROUP OF SUBSIDIARY AS OF 1/1/71	TANZANIA	KENYA	NIGERIA	OTHER (BRITISH) AFRICA	MOROCCO, ALGERIA + TUNISIA	OTHER (FRENCH) AFRICA	OTHER AFRICA
FOOD AND TOBACCO.................	0.7	1.3	1.5	2.3	0.	0.6	0.7
TEXTILES AND APPAREL............	1.4	0.7	2.2	1.4	0.	0.4	3.2
WOOD, FURNITURE AND PAPER......	0.	0.5	1.9	2.4	1.0	0.5	0.5
CHEMICALS.......................	0.2	0.8	0.8	0.9	0.5	0.6	0.4
PETROLEUM.......................	0.5	0.5	0.5	1.6	4.2	6.8	1.6
RUBBER AND TIRES................	0.	0.9	1.9	0.9	0.	0.	0.
PRIMARY METALS..................	0.2	0.5	1.0	0.5	0.2	1.9	0.7
FABR. METAL + NON-EL. MACH....	0.3	0.8	0.5	0.7	1.0	0.2	0.5
ELECTRIC AND ELECTRONIC........	0.3	0.5	0.8	0.4	1.5	0.4	0.
TRANSPORTATION EQUIPMENT.......	1.2	0.4	0.8	0.8	0.4	1.6	0.8
PRECISION GOODS.................	0.	0.	0.	0.	0.	0.	0.
OTHER...........................	0.3	1.5	0.6	0.6	0.6	0.6	0.

TABLE CONTINUED ON NEXT PAGE

CROSS-TABULATION 1.8.1: PERCENTAGE BREAKDOWN OF NUMBER (AS OF 1/1/71) OF MANUFACTURING SUBSIDIARIES OF NON-U.S.-BASED PARENT SYSTEMS BY SUBSIDIARY'S COUNTRY FOR SUBSIDIARIES CLASSIFIED BY PRINCIPAL INDUSTRY-GROUP OF SUBSIDIARY AS OF 1/1/71 (CONTINUED)

SUBSIDIARY'S COUNTRY

PRINCIPAL INDUSTRY-GROUP OF SUBSIDIARY AS OF 1/1/71	AUSTRALIA	NEW ZEALAND	JAPAN	CHINA (TAIWAN)	HONG KONG	THE PHILIP-PINES	MALAYSIA
FOOD AND TOBACCO..........	13.	4.1	0.3	0.1	0.1	0.3	0.7
TEXTILES AND APPAREL......	7.2	0.4	0.7	14.	4.7	0.4	0.4
WOOD, FURNITURE AND PAPER..	15.	1.4	0.	0.	0.	0.	1.9
CHEMICALS.................	5.1	1.3	2.5	0.8	0.3	0.6	0.8
PETROLEUM.................	6.3	1.6	1.6	0.	0.	0.5	2.1
RUBBER AND TIRES..........	7.5	2.8	2.8	6.6	0.	0.	0.9
PRIMARY METALS...........	14.	3.4	1.0	0.	1.0	0.5	1.0
FABR. METAL + NON-EL. MACH...	4.8	1.5	2.3	1.7	0.3	0.2	1.5
ELECTRIC AND ELECTRONIC......	5.3	2.4	1.9	2.5	0.3	0.4	1.0
TRANSPORTATION EQUIPMENT.....	5.7	0.4	0.4	1.2	0.	1.6	2.4
PRECISION GOODS..............	1.3	0.	0.	0.	0.	0.	0.
OTHER........................	4.2	1.8	0.6	0.9	0.3	0.6	0.6

TABLE CONTINUED ON NEXT PAGE

CROSS-TABULATION 1. 8.1: PERCENTAGE BREAKDOWN OF NUMBER (AS OF 1/1/71) OF
MANUFACTURING SUBSIDIARIES OF NON-U.S.-BASED PARENT SYSTEMS BY
SUBSIDIARY'S COUNTRY
FOR SUBSIDIARIES CLASSIFIED BY
PRINCIPAL INDUSTRY-GROUP OF SUBSIDIARY AS OF 1/1/71
(CONTINUED)

SUBSIDIARY'S COUNTRY

PRINCIPAL INDUSTRY-GROUP OF SUBSIDIARY AS OF 1/1/71	SINGA-PORE	INDO-NESIA	THAILAND	INDIA	OTHER ASIA + OCEANIA	TOTAL PERCENT	TOTAL NUMBER
FOOD AND TOBACCO..............	1.0	0.6	0.4	1.0	0.7	100.	685
TEXTILES AND APPAREL.........	1.4	1.4	5.4	1.4	3.2	100.	279
WOOD, FURNITURE AND PAPER.....	1.0	0.	0.	0.5	0.	100.	210
CHEMICALS.....................	0.6	0.6	0.4	2.8	1.0	100.	1258
PETROLEUM.....................	2.6	0.	0.	1.6	2.1	100.	192
RUBBER AND TIRES..............	0.9	0.	1.9	2.8	1.9	100.	106
PRIMARY METALS................	0.5	0.5	1.9	3.9	0.5	100.	413
FABR. METAL + NON-EL. MACH....	1.2	0.2	1.3	5.0	1.2	100.	605
ELECTRIC AND ELECTRONIC.......	0.8	0.5	1.1	2.8	1.4	100.	787
TRANSPORTATION EQUIPMENT......	1.2	0.	4.1	4.9	1.6	100.	246
PRECISION GOODS...............	0.	0.	0.	2.6	0.	100.	78
OTHER.........................	1.5	0.3	0.6	1.2	0.6	100.	336

CROSS-TABULATION 1.8.2: PERCENTAGE BREAKDOWN OF NUMBER (AS OF 1/1/68) OF MANUFACTURING SUBSIDIARIES OF U.S.-BASED PARENT SYSTEMS BY SUBSIDIARY'S COUNTRY FOR SUBSIDIARIES CLASSIFIED BY PRINCIPAL INDUSTRY-GROUP OF SUBSIDIARY AS OF 1/1/68

SUBSIDIARY'S COUNTRY

PRINCIPAL INDUSTRY-GROUP OF SUBSIDIARY AS OF 1/1/68	CANADA	MEXICO	CENTRAL AMERICA + CARIB.	VENE-ZUELA	COLOMBIA	PERU
FOOD AND TOBACCO................	16.	5.9	6.1	4.5	3.9	2.8
TEXTILES AND APPAREL...........	17.	9.8	2.0	11.	5.9	2.0
WOOD, FURNITURE AND PAPER......	16.	3.0	6.0	7.0	2.5	2.0
CHEMICALS......................	10.	8.6	4.3	2.6	3.4	1.2
PETROLEUM......................	7.3	1.5	3.4	3.4	3.4	1.0
RUBBER AND TIRES...............	7.1	8.0	4.4	4.4	2.7	1.8
PRIMARY METALS.................	18.	6.3	0.9	1.8	1.8	0.
FABR. METAL + NON-EL. MACH.....	16.	6.2	1.3	1.7	1.7	0.4
ELECTRIC AND ELECTRONIC........	12.	8.1	1.9	1.7	1.7	0.6
TRANSPORTATION EQUIPMENT.......	14.	7.5	0.9	3.1	1.8	0.9
PRECISION GOODS................	9.5	4.1	1.4	0.	2.7	1.4
OTHER..........................	9.9	6.4	0.	3.9	2.1	1.3

TABLE CONTINUED ON NEXT PAGE

CROSS-TABULATION 1. 8.2: PERCENTAGE BREAKDOWN OF NUMBER (AS OF 1/1/68) OF MANUFACTURING SUBSIDIARIES OF U.S.-BASED PARENT SYSTEMS BY SUBSIDIARY'S COUNTRY FOR SUBSIDIARIES CLASSIFIED BY PRINCIPAL INDUSTRY-GROUP OF SUBSIDIARY AS OF 1/1/68 (CONTINUED)

SUBSIDIARY'S COUNTRY

PRINCIPAL INDUSTRY-GROUP OF SUBSIDIARY AS OF 1/1/68	CHILE	ARGEN-TINA	BRAZIL	OTHER SOUTH AMERICA	GERMANY	FRANCE	ITALY
FOOD AND TOBACCO	1.6	2.6	2.9	1.2	5.3	3.5	2.9
TEXTILES AND APPAREL	0.	1.0	2.0	2.9	2.9	5.9	3.9
WOOD, FURNITURE AND PAPER	0.	2.0	4.5	1.5	4.0	5.0	4.5
CHEMICALS	0.6	3.5	4.1	1.2	3.8	5.2	4.6
PETROLEUM	0.5	1.9	2.4	1.0	10.	3.4	6.8
RUBBER AND TIRES	0.	5.3	4.4	1.8	3.5	3.5	2.7
PRIMARY METALS	0.9	4.5	3.6	0.9	3.6	3.6	1.8
FABR. METAL + NON-EL. MACH.	0.4	2.6	4.0	0.8	8.5	6.4	5.7
ELECTRIC AND ELECTRONIC	1.1	2.5	6.4	0.3	6.7	7.2	5.6
TRANSPORTATION EQUIPMENT	0.4	8.0	7.1	0.4	5.3	6.6	4.0
PRECISION GOODS	1.4	4.1	6.8	0.	19.	12.	5.4
OTHER	2.6	4.3	5.2	1.7	6.0	6.4	6.4

TABLE CONTINUED ON NEXT PAGE

CROSS-TABULATION 1.8.2: PERCENTAGE BREAKDOWN OF NUMBER (AS OF 1/1/68) OF MANUFACTURING SUBSIDIARIES OF U.S.-BASED PARENT SYSTEMS BY SUBSIDIARY'S COUNTRY FOR SUBSIDIARIES CLASSIFIED BY PRINCIPAL INDUSTRY-GROUP OF SUBSIDIARY AS OF 1/1/68 (CONTINUED)

| | | | SUBSIDIARY'S COUNTRY | | | | |
PRINCIPAL INDUSTRY-GROUP OF SUBSIDIARY AS OF 1/1/68	BELGIUM AND LUX-EMBURG	THE NETHER-LANDS	UNITED KINGDOM	IRELAND	DENMARK	NORWAY	SWEDEN
FOOD AND TOBACCO............	1.8	2.4	9.2	1.8	1.2	0.2	0.6
TEXTILES AND APPAREL........	2.9	0.	11.	0.	0.	0.	1.0
WOOD, FURNITURE AND PAPER...	2.0	1.5	5.5	0.	0.5	0.	1.0
CHEMICALS...................	3.0	2.6	8.1	0.6	0.5	0.3	1.3
PETROLEUM...................	1.9	2.4	6.3	0.	2.9	1.5	2.4
RUBBER AND TIRES............	1.8	1.8	4.4	1.8	0.	0.9	1.8
PRIMARY METALS..............	1.8	4.5	15.	0.	0.	3.6	0.
FABR. METAL + NON-EL. MACH..	2.8	2.5	12.	0.4	0.4	0.	0.4
ELECTRIC AND ELECTRONIC.....	0.6	1.9	11.	0.3	0.3	0.6	1.1
TRANSPORTATION EQUIPMENT....	0.9	0.9	12.	1.3	1.3	0.	0.4
PRECISION GOODS.............	4.1	2.7	18.	0.	0.	0.	0.
OTHER.......................	3.0	1.3	8.6	1.7	0.4	1.3	0.4

TABLE CONTINUED ON NEXT PAGE

CROSS-TABULATION 1.8.2: PERCENTAGE BREAKDOWN OF NUMBER (AS OF 1/1/68) OF MANUFACTURING SUBSIDIARIES OF U.S.-BASED PARENT SYSTEMS BY SUBSIDIARY'S COUNTRY FOR SUBSIDIARIES CLASSIFIED BY PRINCIPAL INDUSTRY-GROUP OF SUBSIDIARY AS OF 1/1/68 (CONTINUED)

SUBSIDIARY'S COUNTRY

PRINCIPAL INDUSTRY-GROUP OF SUBSIDIARY AS OF 1/1/68	FINLAND	SWITZ-ERLAND	AUSTRIA	PORTUGAL	SPAIN	GREECE	TURKEY
FOOD AND TOBACCO.........	0.	0.6	0.4	0.6	3.3	0.2	0.2
TEXTILES AND APPAREL......	0.	3.9	0.	1.0	2.0	0.	0.
WOOD, FURNITURE AND PAPER.....	0.	0.	0.	0.5	4.5	0.5	0.
CHEMICALS........	0.2	0.4	0.3	0.6	3.4	0.7	0.3
PETROLEUM........	0.	0.	1.5	0.	2.9	0.5	0.5
RUBBER AND TIRES.....	0.	0.9	0.	2.7	2.7	0.	1.8
PRIMARY METALS......	0.	3.9	0.	0.	0.9	1.8	0.9
FABR. METAL + NON-EL. MACH...	0.	0.8	0.9	0.2	3.2	0.4	0.4
ELECTRIC AND ELECTRONIC.....	0.6	1.7	0.6	0.	1.1	0.3	1.1
TRANSPORTATION EQUIPMENT.....	0.4	0.	0.4	0.4	2.7	0.	0.9
PRECISION GOODS........	0.	0.	1.4	0.	0.	0.	0.
OTHER........	0.4	0.9	0.	0.4	1.7	0.4	0.

TABLE CONTINUED ON NEXT PAGE

CROSS-TABULATION 1.8.2: PERCENTAGE BREAKDOWN OF NUMBER (AS OF 1/1/68) OF
MANUFACTURING SUBSIDIARIES OF U.S.-BASED PARENT SYSTEMS BY
SUBSIDIARY'S COUNTRY
FOR SUBSIDIARIES CLASSIFIED BY
PRINCIPAL INDUSTRY-GROUP OF SUBSIDIARY AS OF 1/1/68
(CONTINUED)

SUBSIDIARY'S COUNTRY

PRINCIPAL INDUSTRY-GROUP OF SUBSIDIARY AS OF 1/1/68	OTHER EUROPE +ISRAEL	PAKISTAN	IRAN	OTHER MID EAST+LIB-YA+EGYPT	UNION OF S. AFRICA	RHODESIA	ZAMBIA
FOOD AND TOBACCO..........	0.2	0.4	0.2	0.6	2.2	0.	0.2
TEXTILES AND APPAREL......	0.	0.	0.	0.	1.0	0.	0.
WOOD, FURNITURE AND PAPER.	0.5	0.5	0.	0.	11.	1.5	1.0
CHEMICALS.................	0.3	0.9	0.5	0.5	3.0	0.2	0.2
PETROLEUM.................	0.	0.5	1.9	4.9	0.5	1.0	0.
RUBBER AND TIRES..........	0.	0.9	1.8	0.9	3.5	0.	0.
PRIMARY METALS............	0.	0.	0.	0.9	2.7	0.9	0.9
FABR. METAL + NON-EL. MACH....	0.2	0.	0.2	0.	3.8	0.	0.
ELECTRIC AND ELECTRONIC......	0.3	0.3	0.3	0.	1.1	0.6	0.
TRANSPORTATION EQUIPMENT.....	0.4	0.	0.	0.	4.0	0.	0.
PRECISION GOODS...........	0.	0.	0.	0.	0.	0.	0.
OTHER.....................	1.3	0.	0.4	0.4	3.4	1.3	0.

TABLE CONTINUED ON NEXT PAGE

CROSS-TABULATION 1.8.2: PERCENTAGE BREAKDOWN OF NUMBER (AS OF 1/1/68) OF
MANUFACTURING SUBSIDIARIES OF U.S.-BASED PARENT SYSTEMS BY
SUBSIDIARY'S COUNTRY
FOR SUBSIDIARIES CLASSIFIED BY
PRINCIPAL INDUSTRY-GROUP OF SUBSIDIARY AS OF 1/1/68
(CONTINUED)

SUBSIDIARY'S COUNTRY

PRINCIPAL INDUSTRY-GROUP OF SUBSIDIARY AS OF 1/1/68	TANZANIA	KENYA	NIGERIA	OTHER (BRITISH) AFRICA	MOROCCO, ALGERIA + TUNISIA	OTHER (FRENCH) AFRICA	OTHER AFRICA
FOOD AND TOBACCO..........	0.	0.2	0.4	0.	0.4	0.	0.
TEXTILES AND APPAREL......	0.	0.	0.	0.	0.	0.	0.
WOOD FURNITURE AND PAPER...	0.	0.	0.	0.	0.5	0.5	0.
CHEMICALS.................	0.	0.2	0.4	0.1	0.3	0.2	0.
PETROLEUM.................	0.	0.5	0.	0.	0.5	1.5	0.5
RUBBER AND TIRES..........	0.	1.8	0.	0.	1.8	0.	0.9
PRIMARY METALS............	0.	0.	0.	1.8	0.9	0.	0.
FABR. METAL + NON-EL. MACH...	0.	0.	0.	0.	0.4	0.4	0.
ELECTRIC AND ELECTRONIC......	0.	0.3	0.6	0.	0.3	0.3	0.
TRANSPORTATION EQUIPMENT...	0.	0.	0.	0.	0.4	0.	0.4
PRECISION GOODS...........	0.	0.	0.	1.4	0.	0.	0.
OTHER.....................	0.	0.4	1.3	0.	0.4	0.	0.

TABLE CONTINUED ON NEXT PAGE

CROSS-TABULATION 1.8.2: PERCENTAGE BREAKDOWN OF NUMBER (AS OF 1/1/68) OF
MANUFACTURING SUBSIDIARIES OF U.S.-BASED PARENT SYSTEMS BY
SUBSIDIARY'S COUNTRY
FOR SUBSIDIARIES CLASSIFIED BY
PRINCIPAL INDUSTRY-GROUP OF SUBSIDIARY AS OF 1/1/68
(CONTINUED)

SUBSIDIARY'S COUNTRY

PRINCIPAL INDUSTRY-GROUP OF SUBSIDIARY AS OF 1/1/68	AUSTRALIA	NEW ZEALAND	JAPAN	CHINA (TAIWAN)	HONG KONG	THE PHILIP-PINES	MALAYSIA
FOOD AND TOBACCO............	5.5	1.8	2.4	0.2	0.	2.4	0.8
TEXTILES AND APPAREL........	1.0	0.	8.8	0.	0.	0.	0.
WOOD, FURNITURE AND PAPER...	4.0	0.5	2.5	0.	0.	2.0	0.5
CHEMICALS...................	5.3	1.9	4.5	0.7	0.3	1.6	0.3
PETROLEUM...................	8.3	1.5	4.4	0.5	0.	1.0	0.5
RUBBER AND TIRES............	5.3	1.8	4.4	0.	0.	1.8	0.9
PRIMARY METALS..............	7.1	0.	2.7	0.	0.	0.	0.
FABR. METAL + NON-EL. MACH..	7.4	0.8	3.4	0.	0.	0.9	0.2
ELECTRIC AND ELECTRONIC.....	4.2	0.8	5.0	0.8	0.8	1.9	0.6
TRANSPORTATION EQUIPMENT....	6.2	0.9	1.8	0.	0.	0.9	0.
PRECISION GOODS.............	2.7	0.	0.	0.	0.	0.	0.
OTHER.......................	5.6	0.	3.9	0.	0.4	0.9	0.4

TABLE CONTINUED ON NEXT PAGE

CROSS-TABULATION 1.8.2: PERCENTAGE BREAKDOWN OF NUMBER (AS OF 1/1/68) OF MANUFACTURING SUBSIDIARIES OF U.S.-BASED PARENT SYSTEMS BY SUBSIDIARY'S COUNTRY FOR SUBSIDIARIES CLASSIFIED BY PRINCIPAL INDUSTRY-GROUP OF SUBSIDIARY AS OF 1/1/68 (CONTINUED)

SUBSIDIARY'S COUNTRY

PRINCIPAL INDUSTRY-GROUP OF SUBSIDIARY AS OF 1/1/68	SINGA-PORE	INDO-NESIA	THAILAND	INDIA	OTHER ASIA + OCEANIA	TOTAL PERCENT	TOTAL NUMBER
FOOD AND TOBACCO	0.2	0.	0.4	0.2	0.	100.	509
TEXTILES AND APPAREL	0.	0.	0.	1.0	1.0	100.	102
WOOD, FURNITURE AND PAPER	0.	0.	0.5	0.5	0.	100.	199
CHEMICALS	0.2	0.	0.4	2.2	0.5	100.	1093
PETROLEUM	0.	0.	0.	1.9	1.5	100.	206
RUBBER AND TIRES	0.	1.8	0.9	1.8	0.	100.	113
PRIMARY METALS	0.9	0.	1.8	2.7	0.	100.	112
FABR. METAL + NON-EL. MACH	0.2	0.	0.	1.7	0.4	100.	530
ELECTRIC AND ELECTRONIC	0.6	0.3	0.8	2.5	0.6	100.	359
TRANSPORTATION EQUIPMENT	0.4	0.	0.	2.2	0.	100.	226
PRECISION GOODS	0.	0.	0.	2.7	0.	100.	74
OTHER	0.9	0.	0.4	1.7	0.	100.	233

CROSS-TABULATION 1.17.1: PERCENTAGE BREAKDOWN OF NUMBER OF
MANUFACTURING SUBSIDIARIES OF NON-U.S.-BASED PARENT SYSTEMS BY
SUBSIDIARY'S COUNTRY
FOR SUBSIDIARIES CLASSIFIED BY
SUBSIDIARY'S DATE OF ENTRY INTO PARENT SYSTEM

SUBSIDIARY'S COUNTRY

SUBSIDIARY'S DATE OF ENTRY INTO PARENT SYSTEM	UNITED STATES	CANADA	MEXICO	CENTRAL AMERICA + CARIB.	VENE-ZUELA	COLOMBIA	PERU
PRE 1914	5.2	3.0	0.4	0.9	0.	0.	0.
1914 - 1919	11.	4.8	0.	0.	0.	0.	0.
1920 - 1929	12.	2.6	0.5	2.0	0.	0.5	0.3
1930 - 1939	6.5	3.0	0.4	0.9	0.	0.	0.
1940 - 1945	9.7	0.7	0.7	2.2	0.	0.	0.
1946 - 1952	4.2	4.5	1.7	0.8	0.3	0.	0.3
1953 - 1955	4.3	11.	3.2	1.6	1.6	1.1	0.5
1956 - 1959	5.4	18.	2.0	1.2	0.	0.4	0.8
1960 - 1961	9.2	5.6	1.4	2.3	1.1	0.8	0.6
1962 - 1964	9.1	4.1	1.2	1.3	1.2	0.9	0.9
1965 - 1967	7.6	5.3	2.1	1.8	0.4	0.8	0.8
1968 - 1970	7.8	5.3	1.6	1.0	0.8	0.2	0.2

TABLE CONTINUED ON NEXT PAGE

CROSS-TABULATION 1.17.1: PERCENTAGE BREAKDOWN OF NUMBER OF
MANUFACTURING SUBSIDIARIES OF NON-U.S.-BASED PARENT SYSTEMS BY
SUBSIDIARY'S COUNTRY
FOR SUBSIDIARIES CLASSIFIED BY
SUBSIDIARY'S DATE OF ENTRY INTO PARENT SYSTEM
(CONTINUED)

SUBSIDIARY'S COUNTRY

SUBSIDIARY'S DATE OF ENTRY INTO PARENT SYSTEM	CHILE	ARGEN-TINA	BRAZIL	OTHER SOUTH AMERICA	GERMANY	FRANCE	ITALY
PRE 1914	0.	2.6	0.4	0.9	13.	10.	5.6
1914 - 1919	0.	3.6	2.4	1.2	8.4	1.2	4.8
1920 - 1929	0.5	1.8	1.5	0.3	12.	4.3	7.4
1930 - 1938	1.3	3.5	3.0	1.3	6.5	4.3	1.3
1939 - 1945	0.7	0.7	2.2	1.5	3.7	3.0	0.7
1946 - 1952	0.3	3.1	4.2	0.	2.2	4.2	1.4
1953 - 1955	0.5	2.7	6.9	0.	3.7	7.4	1.6
1956 - 1958	0.8	4.4	8.8	0.4	3.2	6.8	1.2
1959 - 1961	0.	3.0	1.4	0.	3.8	5.3	4.4
1962 - 1964	1.0	1.5	1.2	0.6	3.4	5.5	3.4
1965 - 1967	0.2	1.3	3.7	0.2	6.3	6.6	3.1
1968 - 1970	0.7	1.4	3.2	0.3	5.9	12.	4.1

TABLE CONTINUED ON NEXT PAGE

CROSS-TABULATION 1.17.1: PERCENTAGE BREAKDOWN OF NUMBER OF
MANUFACTURING SUBSIDIARIES OF NON-U.S.-BASED PARENT SYSTEMS BY
SUBSIDIARY'S COUNTRY
FOR SUBSIDIARIES CLASSIFIED BY
SUBSIDIARY'S DATE OF ENTRY INTO PARENT SYSTEM
(CONTINUED)

SUBSIDIARY'S DATE OF ENTRY INTO PARENT SYSTEM	SUBSIDIARY'S COUNTRY						
	BELGIUM AND LUX-EMBURG	THE NETHER-LANDS	UNITED KINGDOM	IRELAND	DENMARK	NORWAY	SWEDEN
PRE 1914	1.3	1.3	10.	0.9	2.2	2.6	1.7
1914 – 1919	2.4	3.6	7.2	1.2	1.2	6.0	0.
1920 – 1929	3.8	1.8	5.9	1.0	0.8	2.0	1.0
1930 – 1938	2.2	6.1	6.9	2.6	2.6	3.5	1.3
1939 – 1945	0.7	3.0	5.2	0.	3.0	1.5	0.
1946 – 1952	2.8	0.3	5.6	0.8	0.6	0.6	1.1
1953 – 1955	2.1	1.6	8.5	0.5	0.5	0.5	1.6
1956 – 1958	2.4	1.2	5.2	0.8	0.4	0.8	0.8
1959 – 1961	2.4	0.9	4.1	2.9	0.8	0.5	2.1
1962 – 1964	2.4	2.7	4.4	1.6	0.7	0.1	1.6
1965 – 1967	2.8	2.7	7.2	2.1	0.8	0.5	1.0
1968 – 1970	2.9	3.1	4.2	1.6	0.5	0.5	1.0

TABLE CONTINUED ON NEXT PAGE

CROSS-TABULATION 1.17.1: PERCENTAGE BREAKDOWN OF NUMBER OF
MANUFACTURING SUBSIDIARIES OF NON-U.S.-BASED PARENT SYSTEMS BY
SUBSIDIARY'S COUNTRY
FOR SUBSIDIARIES CLASSIFIED BY
SUBSIDIARY'S DATE OF ENTRY INTO PARENT SYSTEM
(CONTINUED)

SUBSIDIARY'S COUNTRY

SUBSIDIARY'S DATE OF ENTRY INTO PARENT SYSTEM	FINLAND	SWITZ-ERLAND	AUSTRIA	PORTUGAL	SPAIN	GREECE	TURKEY
PRE 1914	0.0	1.7	6.1	0.4	5.6	0.	0.4
1914 - 1919	0.	2.4	6.0	1.2	7.2	0.	1.2
1920 - 1929	1.0	2.8	2.8	0.3	3.3	1.5	1.3
1930 - 1938	1.7	2.2	3.9	0.4	3.5	1.3	0.4
1939 - 1945	1.5	0.	1.5	0.	6.0	0.	0.
1946 - 1952	0.3	0.8	1.9	0.8	2.2	0.3	0.6
1953 - 1955	0.	1.6	0.5	1.1	3.7	1.1	2.1
1956 - 1958	0.	0.8	1.2	0.	3.6	0.	1.2
1959 - 1961	0.2	0.2	1.5	1.2	1.8	0.6	0.3
1962 - 1964	0.	0.6	0.9	1.2	4.0	0.3	0.9
1965 - 1967	0.2	0.8	1.4	0.7	3.5	0.3	0.7
1968 - 1970	0.4	1.1	1.8	1.2	3.3	0.6	0.2

TABLE CONTINUED ON NEXT PAGE

CROSS-TABULATION 1.17.1: PERCENTAGE BREAKDOWN OF NUMBER OF
MANUFACTURING SUBSIDIARIES OF NON-U.S.-BASED PARENT SYSTEMS BY
SUBSIDIARY'S COUNTRY
FOR SUBSIDIARIES CLASSIFIED BY
SUBSIDIARY'S DATE OF ENTRY INTO PARENT SYSTEM
(CONTINUED)

SUBSIDIARY'S COUNTRY

SUBSIDIARY'S DATE OF ENTRY INTO PARENT SYSTEM	OTHER EUROPE +ISRAEL	PAKISTAN	IRAN	OTHER MID EAST+LIB-YA+EGYPT	UNION OF S. AFRICA	RHODESIA	ZAMBIA
PRE 1914	13.	0.	0.	0.	1.7	0.4	0.
1914 - 1919	6.0	0.	0.	0.	1.2	0.	0.
1920 - 1929	8.4	0.	0.	0.3	1.5	0.8	0.3
1930 - 1938	3.5	0.	0.	1.3	1.7	0.4	0.4
1939 - 1945	3.0	0.	0.	1.5	5.2	1.5	0.
1946 - 1952	1.9	3.1	0.	0.	21.	1.1	0.
1953 - 1955	1.6	1.1	0.5	0.5	5.3	0.5	0.
1956 - 1958	0.	1.6	0.	0.8	4.8	2.0	0.
1959 - 1961	0.	1.1	0.3	0.3	5.0	3.2	0.2
1962 - 1964	0.4	1.0	0.1	1.0	6.5	0.7	3.0
1965 - 1967	0.7	0.5	0.6	0.3	4.6	0.7	1.2
1968 - 1970	0.5	0.2	0.6	0.2	7.1	0.5	0.2

TABLE CONTINUED ON NEXT PAGE

CROSS-TABULATION 1.17.1: PERCENTAGE BREAKDOWN OF NUMBER OF
MANUFACTURING SUBSIDIARIES OF NON-U.S.-BASED PARENT SYSTEMS BY
SUBSIDIARY'S COUNTRY
FOR SUBSIDIARIES CLASSIFIED BY
SUBSIDIARY'S DATE OF ENTRY INTO PARENT SYSTEM
(CONTINUED)

SUBSIDIARY'S COUNTRY

SUBSIDIARY'S DATE OF ENTRY INTO PARENT SYSTEM	TANZANIA	KENYA	NIGERIA	OTHER (BRITISH) AFRICA	MOROCCO, ALGERIA + TUNISIA	OTHER (FRENCH) AFRICA	OTHER AFRICA
PRE 1914	0.	0.	0.4	0.	0.4	0.	0.
1914 - 1919	0.	0.	2.4	0.	0.	0.	0.
1920 - 1929	0.	0.	0.3	0.5	0.3	0.8	0.8
1930 - 1938	0.4	0.	0.	0.9	0.	0.	1.3
1939 - 1945	0.	0.	0.7	0.	0.	0.	0.
1946 - 1952	0.3	0.6	0.3	1.1	1.7	0.3	0.6
1953 - 1955	0.	0.5	1.1	1.1	1.1	1.1	0.5
1956 - 1958	0.	0.4	0.	0.4	0.4	2.0	0.
1959 - 1961	0.	1.8	2.4	1.1	2.0	0.3	0.6
1962 - 1964	0.4	0.6	0.9	1.0	0.4	0.7	0.7
1965 - 1967	1.1	1.4	0.5	1.3	0.9	0.9	0.4
1968 - 1970	0.3	0.4	1.2	0.5	0.9	0.9	0.5

TABLE CONTINUED IN NEXT PAGE

CROSS-TABULATION 1.17.1: PERCENTAGE BREAKDOWN OF NUMBER OF MANUFACTURING SUBSIDIARIES OF NON-U.S.-BASED PARENT SYSTEMS BY SUBSIDIARY'S COUNTRY

FOR SUBSIDIARIES CLASSIFIED BY SUBSIDIARY'S DATE OF ENTRY INTO PARENT SYSTEM

(CONTINUED)

SUBSIDIARY'S DATE OF ENTRY INTO PARENT SYSTEM	SUBSIDIARY'S COUNTRY						
	AUSTRALIA	NEW ZEALAND	JAPAN	CHINA (TAIWAN)	HONG KONG	THE PHILIPPINES	MALAYSIA
PRE 1914	2.2	0.9	0.9	0.	0.	0.	0.
1914 - 1919	7.2	0.	1.2	0.	1.2	0.	0.
1920 - 1929	4.1	1.0	0.8	1.0	0.	0.3	0.3
1930 - 1938	7.8	1.3	0.4	1.7	0.	0.4	0.
1939 - 1945	8.2	0.	0.7	16.	0.	0.	0.7
1946 - 1952	13.	2.2	3.9	0.6	0.	0.	0.6
1953 - 1955	4.3	1.6	1.1	0.5	0.	0.5	0.
1956 - 1958	7.6	0.8	0.8	0.4	0.	0.	0.8
1959 - 1961	9.6	3.0	0.9	0.9	0.8	0.3	1.4
1962 - 1964	11.	1.0	0.9	1.3	1.2	0.4	0.6
1965 - 1967	7.5	2.1	1.1	1.9	0.3	0.3	1.1
1968 - 1970	6.3	2.0	1.5	2.5	0.5	0.5	1.1

TABLE CONTINUED ON NEXT PAGE

CROSS-TABULATION 1.17.1: PERCENTAGE BREAKDOWN OF NUMBER OF
MANUFACTURING SUBSIDIARIES OF NON-U.S.-BASED PARENT SYSTEMS BY
SUBSIDIARY'S COUNTRY
FOR SUBSIDIARIES CLASSIFIED BY
SUBSIDIARY'S DATE OF ENTRY INTO PARENT SYSTEM
(CONTINUED)

SUBSIDIARY'S COUNTRY

SUBSIDIARY'S DATE OF ENTRY INTO PARENT SYSTEM	SINGA- PORE	INDO- NESIA	THAILAND	INDIA	OTHER ASIA + OCEANIA	TOTAL PERCENT	TOTAL NUMBER
PRE 1914	0.	1.3	0.	0.4	0.4	100.	231
1914 - 1919	0.	0.	0.	0.	3.6	100.	83
1920 - 1929	0.	0.5	0.	2.3	0.8	100.	392
1930 - 1938	0.4	0.9	0.4	4.3	0.9	100.	231
1939 - 1945	0.	0.	0.	3.0	11.	100.	134
1946 - 1952	0.6	0.3	0.	1.4	0.3	100.	359
1953 - 1955	0.	0.	0.	4.3	1.1	100.	188
1956 - 1958	0.	0.	0.	3.6	0.8	100.	251
1959 - 1961	0.5	0.	1.1	4.9	1.2	100.	666
1962 - 1964	2.2	0.	1.9	4.7	0.7	100.	676
1965 - 1967	1.6	0.1	1.2	2.2	0.5	100.	1159
1968 - 1970	0.6	1.0	1.5	0.8	1.5	100.	2083

CROSS-TABULATION 1.17.2: PERCENTAGE BREAKDOWN OF NUMBER OF
MANUFACTURING SUBSIDIARIES OF U.S.-BASED PARENT SYSTEMS BY
SUBSIDIARY'S COUNTRY
FOR SUBSIDIARIES CLASSIFIED BY
SUBSIDIARY'S DATE OF ENTRY INTO PARENT SYSTEM

SUBSIDIARY'S COUNTRY

SUBSIDIARY'S DATE OF ENTRY INTO PARENT SYSTEM	CANADA	MEXICO	CENTRAL AMERICA + CARIB.	VENE-ZUELA	COLOMBIA	PERU
PRE 1914	27.	2.5	0.8	0.	0.	1.6
1914 - 1919	45.	1.4	2.8	0.	0.	0.
1920 - 1929	28.	2.3	1.0	1.0	0.	0.7
1930 - 1938	22.	6.0	4.8	0.	1.6	0.3
1939 - 1945	23.	8.7	4.1	5.2	5.2	4.1
1946 - 1952	22.	9.3	3.6	3.1	3.4	0.8
1953 - 1955	22.	7.8	2.1	4.6	3.5	1.8
1956 - 1958	14.	9.8	5.5	4.8	2.1	1.6
1959 - 1961	9.9	7.2	2.9	4.2	3.2	0.8
1962 - 1964	10.	5.2	3.6	2.5	2.5	1.0
1965 - 1967	11.	7.5	5.7	2.2	2.1	1.0

TABLE CONTINUED ON NEXT PAGE

CROSS-TABULATION 1.17.2: PERCENTAGE BREAKDOWN OF NUMBER OF MANUFACTURING SUBSIDIARIES OF U.S.-BASED PARENT SYSTEMS BY SUBSIDIARY'S COUNTRY FOR SUBSIDIARIES CLASSIFIED BY SUBSIDIARY'S DATE OF ENTRY INTO PARENT SYSTEM (CONTINUED)

SUBSIDIARY'S COUNTRY

SUBSIDIARY'S DATE OF ENTRY INTO PARENT SYSTEM	CHILE	ARGEN- TINA	BRAZIL	OTHER SOUTH AMERICA	GERMANY	FRANCE	ITALY
PRE 1914...........	0.8	1.6	0.	0.8	13.	9.8	5.7
1914 - 1919.......	1.4	4.2	7.0	0.	4.2	1.4	0.
1920 - 1929.......	1.7	2.7	3.0	0.7	8.0	8.4	2.0
1930 - 1938.......	0.3	5.7	2.2	0.3	5.7	6.3	1.6
1939 - 1945.......	2.3	7.6	9.3	1.7	0.6	2.3	0.6
1946 - 1952.......	0.8	2.3	7.0	1.3	3.4	3.1	3.4
1953 - 1955.......	0.4	3.9	6.7	1.1	5.7	4.6	2.8
1956 - 1958.......	0.	4.1	8.2	1.6	4.8	4.3	4.3
1959 - 1961.......	0.8	3.0	3.4	0.6	6.1	8.5	6.9
1962 - 1964.......	0.9	2.8	2.0	0.5	5.8	7.8	6.0
1965 - 1967.......	1.1	1.7	2.7	1.1	6.4	5.1	3.6

TABLE CONTINUED ON NEXT PAGE

CROSS-TABULATION 1.17.2: PERCENTAGE BREAKDOWN OF NUMBER OF
MANUFACTURING SUBSIDIARIES OF U.S.-BASED PARENT SYSTEMS BY
SUBSIDIARY'S COUNTRY
FOR SUBSIDIARIES CLASSIFIED BY
SUBSIDIARY'S DATE OF ENTRY INTO PARENT SYSTEM
(CONTINUED)

SUBSIDIARY'S COUNTRY

SUBSIDIARY'S DATE OF ENTRY INTO PARENT SYSTEM	BELGIUM AND LUX-EMBURG	THE NETHER-LANDS	UNITED KINGDOM	IRELAND	DENMARK	NORWAY	SWEDEN
PRE 1914........................	0.3	0.	20.	0.8	0.8	2.5	2.5
1914 - 1919.....................	1.4	1.4	7.0	0.	2.8	1.4	0.
1920 - 1929.....................	1.7	1.7	16.	0.	0.3	1.3	1.0
1930 - 1938.....................	2.2	1.9	17.	0.3	0.6	0.6	0.6
1939 - 1945.....................	0.	1.7	7.0	0.6	0.	0.	0.
1946 - 1952.....................	1.3	2.1	11.	1.3	0.	0.3	0.8
1953 - 1955.....................	1.4	1.4	7.4	1.1	0.4	0.	0.7
1956 - 1958.....................	1.4	2.5	8.7	0.2	0.7	0.2	0.5
1959 - 1961.....................	3.0	2.3	9.4	0.7	0.1	0.4	0.8
1962 - 1964.....................	2.6	1.9	8.6	1.0	1.3	0.4	1.3
1965 - 1967.....................	3.4	2.5	8.8	0.6	1.1	0.2	0.9

TABLE CONTINUED ON NEXT PAGE

CROSS-TABULATION 1.17.2: PERCENTAGE BREAKDOWN OF NUMBER OF
MANUFACTURING SUBSIDIARIES OF U.S.-BASED PARENT SYSTEMS BY
SUBSIDIARY'S COUNTRY
FOR SUBSIDIARIES CLASSIFIED BY
SUBSIDIARY'S DATE OF ENTRY INTO PARENT SYSTEM
(CONTINUED)

SUBSIDIARY'S COUNTRY

SUBSIDIARY'S DATE OF ENTRY INTO PARENT SYSTEM	FINLAND	SWITZ-ERLAND	AUSTRIA	PORTUGAL	SPAIN	GREECE	TURKEY
PRE 1914	0.	0.	1.6	0.	0.	0.	0.
1914 - 1919	0.	0.	0.	0.	1.4	0.	0.
1920 - 1929	0.	0.3	1.3	0.3	3.0	0.	0.3
1930 - 1938	0.	1.0	1.3	0.6	1.3	0.	0.
1939 - 1945	0.	0.	0.6	0.6	0.	0.	0.
1946 - 1952	0.	0.3	0.	0.3	1.6	0.3	0.5
1953 - 1955	0.4	0.	0.	0.4	2.5	0.	0.4
1956 - 1958	0.	0.2	0.	0.5	1.1	0.2	0.5
1959 - 1961	0.2	1.0	0.4	0.4	1.9	0.6	0.4
1962 - 1964	0.2	1.0	0.6	0.2	3.5	0.5	0.4
1965 - 1967	0.	0.4	0.2	1.0	6.0	1.5	0.3

TABLE CONTINUED ON NEXT PAGE

CROSS-TABULATION 1.17.2: PERCENTAGE BREAKDOWN OF NUMBER OF
MANUFACTURING SUBSIDIARIES OF U.S.-BASED PARENT SYSTEMS BY
SUBSIDIARY'S COUNTRY
FOR SUBSIDIARIES CLASSIFIED BY
SUBSIDIARY'S DATE OF ENTRY INTO PARENT SYSTEM
(CONTINUED)

SUBSIDIARY'S COUNTRY

SUBSIDIARY'S DATE OF ENTRY INTO PARENT SYSTEM	OTHER EUROPE +ISRAEL	PAKISTAN	IRAN	OTHER MID EAST+LIB-YA+EGYPT	UNION OF S. AFRICA	RHODESIA	ZAMBIA
PRE 1914...........	4.1	0.	0.	0.	0.8	0.	0.
1914 - 1919.......	0.	0.	0.	0.	1.4	0.	0.
1920 - 1929.......	1.3	0.	0.	0.7	1.7	0.	0.
1930 - 1938.......	0.6	0.	0.	0.3	4.1	0.	0.
1939 - 1945.......	1.2	0.	0.	0.6	2.9	0.	0.
1946 - 1952.......	1.0	0.3	0.	0.8	2.8	0.3	0.
1953 - 1955.......	0.	0.	0.4	0.4	3.5	0.	0.4
1956 - 1958.......	0.	0.7	0.	0.	2.5	0.5	0.
1959 - 1961.......	0.3	0.6	0.3	0.2	1.7	0.	0.1
1962 - 1964.......	0.4	0.5	0.6	0.3	4.5	0.7	0.2
1965 - 1967.......	0.4	0.2	0.7	1.0	1.5	0.2	0.3

TABLE CONTINUED ON NEXT PAGE

CROSS-TABULATION 1.17.2: PERCENTAGE BREAKDOWN OF NUMBER OF
MANUFACTURING SUBSIDIARIES OF U.S.-BASED PARENT SYSTEMS BY
SUBSIDIARY'S COUNTRY
FOR SUBSIDIARIES CLASSIFIED BY
SUBSIDIARY'S DATE OF ENTRY INTO PARENT SYSTEM
(CONTINUED)

SUBSIDIARY'S COUNTRY

SUBSIDIARY'S DATE OF ENTRY INTO PARENT SYSTEM	TANZANIA	KENYA	NIGERIA	OTHER (BRITISH) AFRICA	MOROCCO, ALGERIA + TUNISIA	OTHER (FRENCH) AFRICA	OTHER AFRICA
PRE 1914	0.	0.	0.	0.	0.	0.	0.
1914 - 1919	0.	0.	0.	0.	0.	0.	0.
1920 - 1929	0.	0.	0.	0.	0.	0.	0.
1930 - 1938	0.	0.	0.	0.	0.	0.	0.
1939 - 1945	0.	0.	0.	0.	0.	0.	0.
1946 - 1952	0.	0.3	0.	0.	0.5	0.	0.
1953 - 1955	0.	0.	0.	0.	0.	0.	0.
1956 - 1958	0.	0.5	0.2	0.	0.7	0.	0.2
1959 - 1961	0.	0.2	0.1	0.3	0.3	0.3	0.
1962 - 1964	0.	0.1	0.9	0.1	0.3	0.5	0.
1965 - 1967	0.	0.3	0.1	0.4	0.7	0.1	0.1

TABLE CONTINUED ON NEXT PAGE

CROSS-TABULATION 1.17.2: PERCENTAGE BREAKDOWN OF NUMBER OF
MANUFACTURING SUBSIDIARIES OF U.S.-BASED PARENT SYSTEMS BY
SUBSIDIARY'S COUNTRY
FOR SUBSIDIARIES CLASSIFIED BY
SUBSIDIARY'S DATE OF ENTRY INTO PARENT SYSTEM
(CONTINUED)

SUBSIDIARY'S COUNTRY

SUBSIDIARY'S DATE OF ENTRY INTO PARENT SYSTEM	AUSTRALIA	NEW ZEALAND	JAPAN	CHINA (TAIWAN)	HONG KONG	THE PHILIP- PINES	MALAYSIA
PRE 1914	1.6	0.	0.8	0.	0.	0.	0.
1914 - 1919	7.0	0.	1.4	1.4	0.	0.	0.
1920 - 1929	4.0	0.3	1.0	0.7	0.	1.7	0.
1930 - 1938	6.0	1.9	0.6	0.	0.	0.6	0.3
1939 - 1945	4.1	4.1	1.2	0.	0.	0.6	0.
1946 - 1952	3.6	1.0	3.4	0.	0.	1.3	0.
1953 - 1955	6.4	1.1	1.4	0.	0.4	2.5	0.4
1956 - 1958	5.5	0.9	1.6	0.2	0.2	1.6	0.2
1959 - 1961	8.4	0.4	3.0	0.2	0.2	0.9	0.7
1962 - 1964	3.3	0.9	5.3	0.6	0.4	1.5	0.4
1965 - 1967	5.4	0.7	4.2	0.8	0.3	0.7	0.6

TABLE CONTINUED ON NEXT PAGE

CROSS-TABULATION 1.17.2: PERCENTAGE BREAKDOWN OF NUMBER OF
MANUFACTURING SUBSIDIARIES OF U.S.-BASED PARENT SYSTEMS BY
SUBSIDIARY'S COUNTRY
FOR SUBSIDIARIES CLASSIFIED BY
SUBSIDIARY'S DATE OF ENTRY INTO PARENT SYSTEM
(CONTINUED)

SUBSIDIARY'S COUNTRY

SUBSIDIARY'S DATE OF ENTRY INTO PARENT SYSTEM	SINGA- PORE	INDO- NESIA	THAILAND	INDIA	OTHER ASIA + OCEANIA	TOTAL PERCENT	TOTAL NUMBER
PRE 1914	0.	0.	0.	0.	0.	100.	122
1914 - 1919	1.4	4.2	0.	0.	0.	100.	71
1920 - 1929	0.	0.3	0.	1.0	0.3	100.	299
1930 - 1938	0.	0.	0.	0.6	0.5	100.	315
1939 - 1945	0.	0.	0.	0.	0.	100.	172
1946 - 1952	0.3	0.3	0.	1.0	0.	100.	386
1953 - 1955	0.	0.	0.	0.4	0.	100.	283
1956 - 1958	0.	0.	0.5	1.6	0.5	100.	439
1959 - 1961	0.	0.	0.3	1.9	0.1	100.	901
1962 - 1964	0.2	0.	0.6	2.1	0.4	100.	959
1965 - 1967	0.6	0.1	0.4	0.9	0.6	100.	889

CROSS-TABULATION 1.17.3: PERCENTAGE BREAKDOWN OF NUMBER OF
MANUFACTURING SUBSIDIARIES OF U.K.-BASED PARENT SYSTEMS BY
SUBSIDIARY'S COUNTRY
FOR SUBSIDIARIES CLASSIFIED BY
SUBSIDIARY'S DATE OF ENTRY INTO PARENT SYSTEM

SUBSIDIARY'S COUNTRY

SUBSIDIARY'S DATE OF ENTRY INTO PARENT SYSTEM	UNITED STATES	CANADA	MEXICO	CENTRAL AMERICA + CARIB.	VENE-ZUELA	COLOMBIA	PERU
PRE 1914	3.3	12.	1.7	1.7	0.	0.	0.
1914 - 1919	0.	11.	0.	0.	0.	0.	0.
1920 - 1929	6.8	8.5	0.8	4.2	0.	0.	0.8
1930 - 1938	3.0	6.1	0.	0.	0.	0.	0.
1939 - 1945	2.9	0.	0.	2.9	0.	0.	0.
1946 - 1952	3.0	5.9	0.	1.5	0.	0.	0.5
1953 - 1955	3.6	15.	3.6	1.8	1.8	1.8	0.
1956 - 1958	3.2	38.	0.	1.1	0.	1.1	1.1
1959 - 1961	3.3	9.3	0.	2.4	0.9	0.3	0.
1962 - 1964	3.4	6.9	0.6	0.6	0.6	0.3	0.
1965 - 1967	5.4	9.2	0.9	0.7	0.2	0.7	0.2
1968 - 1970	7.4	8.2	1.1	0.8	0.1	0.	0.

TABLE CONTINUED ON NEXT PAGE

CROSS-TABULATION 1.17.3: PERCENTAGE BREAKDOWN OF NUMBER OF
MANUFACTURING SUBSIDIARIES OF U.K.-BASED PARENT SYSTEMS BY
SUBSIDIARY'S COUNTRY
FOR SUBSIDIARIES CLASSIFIED BY
SUBSIDIARY'S DATE OF ENTRY INTO PARENT SYSTEM
(CONTINUED)

SUBSIDIARY'S COUNTRY

SUBSIDIARY'S DATE OF ENTRY INTO PARENT SYSTEM	CHILE	ARGEN-TINA	BRAZIL	OTHER SOUTH AMERICA	GERMANY	FRANCE	ITALY
PRE 1914	0.	10.	1.7	1.7	8.3	3.3	1.7
1914 - 1919	0.	3.7	7.4	3.7	3.7	3.7	0.
1920 - 1929	0.8	2.5	1.7	0.8	12.	3.4	1.7
1930 - 1938	0.	2.0	2.0	2.0	8.1	3.0	1.0
1939 - 1945	0.	0.	2.9	2.9	5.9	5.9	2.9
1946 - 1952	0.	0.5	0.5	0.	1.5	1.5	1.0
1953 - 1955	0.	1.8	3.6	0.	5.5	0.	1.8
1956 - 1958	1.1	2.1	1.1	0.	3.2	0.	0.
1959 - 1961	0.	2.4	0.9	0.	5.1	3.6	3.6
1962 - 1964	0.3	0.3	0.3	0.9	3.4	6.9	2.8
1965 - 1967	0.2	0.4	0.9	0.2	6.1	3.3	2.6
1968 - 1970	0.4	0.8	1.1	0.1	5.8	5.2	2.7

TABLE CONTINUED ON NEXT PAGE

CROSS-TABULATION 1.17.3: PERCENTAGE BREAKDOWN OF NUMBER OF
MANUFACTURING SUBSIDIARIES OF U.K.-BASED PARENT SYSTEMS BY
SUBSIDIARY'S COUNTRY
FOR SUBSIDIARIES CLASSIFIED BY
SUBSIDIARY'S DATE OF ENTRY INTO PARENT SYSTEM
(CONTINUED)

SUBSIDIARY'S COUNTRY

SUBSIDIARY'S DATE OF ENTRY INTO PARENT SYSTEM	BELGIUM AND LUX-EMBURG	THE NETHER-LANDS	UNITED KINGDOM	IRELAND	DENMARK	NORWAY	SWEDEN
PRE 1914.........	3.3	0.	0.	3.3	5.0	1.7	5.0
1914 - 1919......	0.	0.	0.	3.7	0.	0.	0.
1920 - 1929......	1.7	1.7	0.	3.4	1.7	0.8	0.8
1930 - 1938......	2.0	5.1	0.	6.1	1.0	3.0	3.0
1939 - 1945......	0.	0.	0.	0.	0.	0.	0.
1946 - 1952......	1.5	0.	0.	1.5	0.5	0.	1.5
1953 - 1955......	0.	1.8	0.	1.8	0.	0.	0.
1956 - 1958......	2.1	0.	0.	1.1	0.	1.1	0.
1959 - 1961......	3.0	0.9	0.	5.4	1.5	0.3	1.5
1962 - 1964......	2.5	2.5	0.	2.5	0.6	0.	2.8
1965 - 1967......	2.0	2.8	0.	3.3	0.7	0.2	1.7
1968 - 1970......	2.2	3.3	0.	4.0	0.7	0.5	1.4

TABLE CONTINUED ON NEXT PAGE

CROSS-TABULATION 1.17.3: PERCENTAGE BREAKDOWN OF NUMBER OF
MANUFACTURING SUBSIDIARIES OF U.K.-BASED PARENT SYSTEMS BY
SUBSIDIARY'S COUNTRY

FOR SUBSIDIARIES CLASSIFIED BY
SUBSIDIARY'S DATE OF ENTRY INTO PARENT SYSTEM
(CONTINUED)

SUBSIDIARY'S COUNTRY

SUBSIDIARY'S DATE OF ENTRY INTO PARENT SYSTEM	FINLAND	SWITZ-ERLAND	AUSTRIA	PORTUGAL	SPAIN	GREECE	TURKEY
PRE 1914..........	0.	1.7	0.	1.7	5.0	0.	1.7
1914 - 1919.......	0.	3.7	0.	0.	3.7	0.	3.7
1920 - 1929.......	1.7	1.7	1.7	0.	0.8	0.	1.7
1930 - 1938.......	2.0	2.0	3.0	0.	0.	2.0	1.0
1939 - 1945.......	0.	0.	0.	0.	0.	0.	0.
1946 - 1952.......	0.	0.	0.5	0.5	0.5	0.	1.0
1953 - 1955.......	0.	0.	0.	0.	0.	0.	1.8
1956 - 1958.......	0.	0.	1.1	0.	2.1	0.	0.
1959 - 1961.......	0.	0.3	1.5	1.2	0.9	0.3	0.
1962 - 1964.......	0.	0.6	0.3	0.9	1.6	0.6	0.
1965 - 1967.......	0.	0.4	0.4	0.7	3.3	0.4	0.
1968 - 1970.......	0.	0.4	1.0	0.5	1.9	0.1	0.

TABLE CONTINUED ON NEXT PAGE

CRCSS-TABULATICN 1.17.3: PERCENTAGE BREAKDOWN CF NUMEER OF
MANUFACTURING SUBSIDIARIES OF U.K.-EASED PARENT SYSTEMS BY
SUBSIDIARY'S COUNTRY
FOR SUBSIDIARIES CLASSIFIED BY
SUBSIDIARY'S DATE OF ENTRY INTO FARENT SYSTEM
(CONTINUED)

SUBSIDIARY'S CCUNTRY

SUBSIDIARY'S DATE OF ENTRY INTO PARENT SYSTEM	OTHER EUROPE +ISRAEL	PAKISTAN	IRAN	CTHER MID EAST+LIB-YA+EGYPT	UNION OF S. AFRICA	RHODESIA	ZAMBIA
PRE 1914	3.3	0.	0.	0.	5.0	1.7	0.
1914 – 1915	0.	0.	0.	0.	3.7	0.	0.
1920 – 1929	4.2	0.	0.	0.8	5.1	2.5	0.8
1930 – 1938	0.	0.	0.	1.0	4.0	1.0	1.0
1939 – 1945	5.9	0.	0.	2.9	15.	2.9	0.
1946 – 1952	1.5	4.5	0.	0.	34.	1.5	0.
1953 – 1955	0.	3.6	1.8	1.8	13.	1.8	0.
1956 – 1958	0.	1.1	0.	0.	7.4	4.3	0.
1959 – 1961	0.	0.6	0.	0.3	7.5	5.4	0.3
1962 – 1964	0.	1.3	0.	0.	13.	1.6	6.3
1965 – 1967	0.9	1.1	0.	0.4	8.1	1.3	2.6
1968 – 1970	0.5	0.4	0.3	0.1	15.	1.2	0.5

TABLE CONTINUED CN NEXT PAGE

CROSS-TABULATION 1.17.3: PERCENTAGE BREAKDOWN OF NUMBER OF
MANUFACTURING SUBSIDIARIES OF U.K.-BASED PARENT SYSTEMS BY
SUBSIDIARY'S COUNTRY
FOR SUBSIDIARIES CLASSIFIED BY
SUBSIDIARY'S DATE OF ENTRY INTO PARENT SYSTEM
(CONTINUED)

SUBSIDIARY'S COUNTRY

SUBSIDIARY'S DATE OF ENTRY INTO PARENT SYSTEM	TANZANIA	KENYA	NIGERIA	OTHER (BRITISH) AFRICA	MOROCCO, ALGERIA + TUNISIA	OTHER (FRENCH) AFRICA	OTHER AFRICA
PRE 1914.........	0.	0.	1.7	0.	0.	0.	0.
1914 - 1919.....	0.	0.	7.4	0.	0.	0.	0.
1920 - 1929.....	0.	0.	0.8	1.7	0.	2.5	0.
1930 - 1938.....	1.0	0.	0.	2.0	0.	0.	0.
1939 - 1945.....	0.	0.	2.9	0.	0.	0.	0.
1946 - 1952.....	0.5	1.0	0.5	2.0	0.5	0.5	0.5
1953 - 1955.....	0.	1.8	3.6	3.6	0.	0.	0.
1956 - 1958.....	0.	1.1	0.	1.1	0.	0.	0.
1959 - 1961.....	0.	3.3	2.4	0.9	0.3	0.3	0.9
1962 - 1964.....	0.6	0.9	0.9	1.6	0.	0.3	0.3
1965 - 1967.....	2.2	2.8	1.3	2.2	0.	0.4	1.1
1968 - 1970.....	0.7	1.1	2.7	1.1	0.3	0.3	0.5

TABLE CONTINUED ON NEXT PAGE

CROSS-TABULATION 1.17.3: PERCENTAGE BREAKDOWN OF NUMBER OF
MANUFACTURING SUBSIDIARIES OF U.K.-BASED PARENT SYSTEMS BY
SUBSIDIARY'S COUNTRY
FOR SUBSIDIARIES CLASSIFIED BY
SUBSIDIARY'S DATE OF ENTRY INTO PARENT SYSTEM
(CONTINUED)

SUBSIDIARY'S COUNTRY

SUBSIDIARY'S DATE OF ENTRY INTO PARENT SYSTEM	AUSTRALIA	NEW ZEALAND	JAPAN	CHINA (TAIWAN)	HONG KONG	THE PHILIP- PINES	MALAYSIA
PRE 1914	6.7	1.7	3.3	0.	0.	0.	0.
1914 - 1915	22.	0.	3.7	0.	3.7	0.	0.
1920 - 1929	9.3	1.7	0.	0.	0.	0.8	0.8
1930 - 1938	15.	3.0	0.	0.	0.	0.	0.
1939 - 1945	32.	0.	0.	0.	0.	0.	0.
1946 - 1952	22.	4.0	0.	0.5	0.	0.	1.0
1953 - 1955	11.	5.5	0.	0.	0.	0.	0.
1956 - 1958	18.	1.1	0.	0.	0.	0.	2.1
1959 - 1961	14.	5.7	0.6	0.	0.3	0.3	1.8
1962 - 1964	21.	1.3	0.6	0.	0.	0.	0.6
1965 - 1967	17.	4.8	0.9	0.2	0.2	0.	1.1
1968 - 1970	14.	5.3	0.8	0.1	0.8	0.	0.5

TABLE CONTINUED ON NEXT PAGE

CROSS-TABULATICN 1.17.3: PERCENTAGE BREAKDOWN CF NUMEER OF
MANUFACTURING SUBSIDIARIES OF U.K.-BASED PARENT SYSTEMS BY
SUBSIDIARY'S COUNTRY
FCR SUBSIDIARIES CLASSIFIED BY
SUBSIDIARY'S DATE OF ENTRY INTO PARENT SYSTEM
(CONTINUED)

SUBSIDIARY'S CCUNTFY

SUBSIDIARY'S DATE OF ENTRY INTO PARENT SYSTEM	SINGA- PORE	INDO- NESIA	THAILAND	INDIA	CTHER ASIA + OCEANIA	TOTAL FERCENT	TCTAL NUMBER
PRE 1914	0.	0.	0.	1.7	1.7	100.	60
1914 - 1915	0.	0.	0.	0.	11.	100.	27
1920 - 1929	0.	1.7	0.	4.2	0.8	100.	118
1930 - 1938	1.0	2.0	1.0	8.1	2.C	100.	99
1939 - 1945	0.	0.	0.	8.8	2.9	100.	34
1946 - 1952	1.0	0.	0.	1.5	0.5	100.	202
1953 - 1955	0.	0.	0.	7.3	0.	100.	55
1956 - 1958	0.	0.	0.	3.2	1.1	100.	94
1959 - 1961	0.	0.	0.3	4.5	1.2	100.	333
1962 - 1964	0.9	0.	0.	5.0	0.9	100.	319
1965 - 1967	2.0	0.2	0.	2.6	0.	100.	459
1968 - 1970	0.4	0.	0.4	1.2	1.C	100.	729

CROSS-TABULATION 1.17.4: PERCENTAGE BREAKDOWN OF NUMBER OF
MANUFACTURING SUBSIDIARIES OF CONTINENTAL-EUROPEAN-BASED PARENT SYSTEMS BY
SUBSIDIARY'S COUNTRY
FOR SUBSIDIARIES CLASSIFIED BY
SUBSIDIARY'S DATE OF ENTRY INTO PARENT SYSTEM

SUBSIDIARY'S COUNTRY

SUBSIDIARY'S DATE OF ENTRY INTO PARENT SYSTEM	UNITED STATES	CANADA	MEXICO	CENTRAL AMERICA + CARIB.	VENE- ZUELA	COLOMBIA	PERU
PRE 1914..............	5.4	1.2	0.	0.6	0.	0.	0.
1914 - 1919..........	16.	2.0	0.	0.	0.	0.	0.
1920 - 1929..........	11.	0.	0.4	1.2	0.	0.8	0.
1930 - 1938..........	6.3	0.9	0.9	1.8	0.	0.	0.
1939 - 1945..........	4.5	2.3	0.	2.3	0.	0.	0.
1946 - 1952..........	5.4	3.1	3.9	0.	0.	0.	0.
1953 - 1955..........	4.3	10.	3.4	0.9	1.7	0.9	0.9
1956 - 1958..........	6.9	7.6	2.3	0.8	0.	0.	0.8
1959 - 1961..........	19.	2.6	3.0	1.3	0.9	0.9	1.7
1962 - 1964..........	12.	2.2	1.3	1.3	1.7	0.9	1.3
1965 - 1967..........	8.5	3.2	2.8	1.3	0.4	1.1	0.8
1968 - 1970..........	9.2	4.8	2.1	0.6	1.2	0.5	0.3

TABLE CONTINUED ON NEXT PAGE

CROSS-TABULATION 1.17.4: PERCENTAGE BREAKDOWN OF NUMBER OF
MANUFACTURING SUBSIDIARIES OF CONTINENTAL-EUROPEAN-BASED PARENT SYSTEMS BY
SUBSIDIARY'S COUNTRY
FOR SUBSIDIARIES CLASSIFIED BY
SUBSIDIARY'S DATE OF ENTRY INTO PARENT SYSTEM
(CONTINUED)

SUBSIDIARY'S COUNTRY

SUBSIDIARY'S DATE OF ENTRY INTO PARENT SYSTEM	CHILE	ARGEN- TINA	BRAZIL	OTHER SOUTH AMERICA	GERMANY	FRANCE	ITALY
PRE 1914........................	0.	0.	0.	0.6	16.	13.	7.2
1914 - 1919.....................	0.	3.9	0.	0.	12.	0.	5.9
1920 - 1929.....................	0.4	1.6	1.6	0.	12.	4.4	11.
1930 - 1938.....................	2.7	4.5	4.5	0.	6.3	6.3	1.8
1939 - 1945.....................	2.3	2.3	0.	2.3	4.5	4.5	0.
1946 - 1952.....................	0.8	7.8	11.	0.	3.9	9.3	2.3
1953 - 1955.....................	0.9	3.4	7.7	0.	3.4	9.4	1.7
1956 - 1958.....................	0.8	6.1	9.9	0.8	3.8	12.	2.3
1959 - 1961.....................	0.	3.9	1.3	0.	3.4	6.0	5.6
1962 - 1964.....................	2.2	3.1	1.3	0.4	5.2	6.6	4.4
1965 - 1967.....................	0.2	2.3	5.3	0.	8.3	11.	4.1
1968 - 1970.....................	0.9	1.8	4.7	0.5	7.2	15.	5.6

TABLE CONTINUED ON NEXT PAGE

CROSS-TABULATION 1.17.4: PERCENTAGE BREAKDOWN OF NUMBER OF
MANUFACTURING SUBSIDIARIES OF CONTINENTAL-EUROPEAN-BASED PARENT SYSTEMS BY
SUBSIDIARY'S COUNTRY
FOR SUBSIDIARIES CLASSIFIED BY
SUBSIDIARY'S DATE OF ENTRY INTO PARENT SYSTEM
(CONTINUED)

SUBSIDIARY'S DATE OF ENTRY INTO PARENT SYSTEM	SUBSIDIARY'S COUNTRY						
	BELGIUM AND LUX-EMBURG	THE NETHER-LANDS	UNITED KINGDOM	IRELAND	DENMARK	NORWAY	SWEDEN
PRE 1914...............	0.6	1.8	13.	0.	1.2	2.4	0.6
1914 – 1919...........	3.9	5.9	9.8	0.	0.	7.8	0.
1920 – 1929...........	5.2	2.0	7.2	0.	0.4	2.8	1.2
1930 – 1938...........	2.7	7.1	13.	0.	3.6	3.6	0.
1939 – 1945...........	2.3	9.1	11.	0.	9.1	4.5	0.
1946 – 1952...........	5.4	0.8	12.	0.	0.8	1.6	0.
1953 – 1955...........	3.4	1.7	9.4	0.	0.9	0.9	2.6
1956 – 1958...........	3.1	1.5	8.4	0.8	0.8	0.8	1.5
1959 – 1961...........	2.2	1.3	8.2	0.	0.	0.9	3.4
1962 – 1964...........	3.1	4.4	9.6	0.9	0.9	0.4	0.9
1965 – 1967...........	4.5	3.2	15.	0.4	0.9	0.8	0.8
1968 – 1970...........	4.2	3.8	6.5	0.4	0.6	0.6	0.8

TABLE CONTINUED ON NEXT PAGE

CROSS-TABULATION 1.17.4: PERCENTAGE BREAKDOWN OF NUMBER OF
MANUFACTURING SUBSIDIARIES OF CONTINENTAL-EUROPEAN-BASED PARENT SYSTEMS BY
SUBSIDIARY'S COUNTRY
FOR SUBSIDIARIES CLASSIFIED BY
SUBSIDIARY'S DATE OF ENTRY INTO PARENT SYSTEM
(CONTINUED)

SUBSIDIARY'S COUNTRY

SUBSIDIARY'S DATE OF ENTRY INTO PARENT SYSTEM	FINLAND	SWITZ-ERLAND	AUSTRIA	PORTUGAL	SPAIN	GREECE	TURKEY
PRE 1914...........	1.2	1.8	8.4	0.	6.0	0.	0.
1914 - 1919........	0.	2.0	9.8	2.0	9.8	0.	0.
1920 - 1929........	0.8	3.2	3.6	0.4	4.8	2.4	1.2
1930 - 1938........	1.8	2.7	5.4	0.9	7.1	0.9	0.
1939 - 1945........	4.5	0.	4.5	0.	18.	0.	0.
1946 - 1952........	0.8	2.3	4.7	1.6	5.4	0.8	0.
1953 - 1955........	0.	2.6	0.9	1.7	5.1	1.7	2.6
1956 - 1958........	0.	1.5	1.5	0.	4.6	0.	2.3
1959 - 1961........	0.4	0.	2.2	0.9	3.0	1.3	0.9
1962 - 1964........	0.	0.9	2.2	1.3	9.6	0.	2.6
1965 - 1967........	0.4	1.3	2.6	0.8	4.5	0.2	1.3
1968 - 1970........	0.8	1.7	2.8	1.8	4.8	1.1	3.4

TABLE CONTINUED ON NEXT PAGE

CROSS-TABULATION 1.17.4: PERCENTAGE BREAKDOWN OF NUMBER OF
MANUFACTURING SUBSIDIARIES OF CONTINENTAL-EUROPEAN-BASED PARENT SYSTEMS BY
SUBSIDIARY'S COUNTRY
FOR SUBSIDIARIES CLASSIFIED BY
SUBSIDIARY'S DATE OF ENTRY INTO PARENT SYSTEM
(CONTINUED)

SUBSIDIARY'S COUNTRY

SUBSIDIARY'S DATE OF ENTRY INTO PARENT SYSTEM	OTHER EUROPE +ISRAEL	PAKISTAN	IRAN	OTHER MID EAST+LIB-YA+EGYPT	UNION OF S. AFRICA	RHODESIA	ZAMBIA
PRE 1914..............	16.	0.	0.	0.	0.6	0.	0.
1914 - 1919..........	9.8	0.	0.	0.	0.	0.	0.
1920 - 1929..........	11.	0.	0.	0.	0.	0.	0.
1930 - 1938..........	7.1	0.	0.	1.8	0.	0.	0.
1939 - 1945..........	4.5	0.	0.	2.3	2.3	0.	0.
1946 - 1952..........	3.1	1.6	0.	0.	3.9	0.	0.
1953 - 1955..........	2.6	0.	0.	0.	2.6	0.	0.
1956 - 1958..........	0.	1.5	0.	1.5	3.8	0.8	0.
1959 - 1961..........	0.	0.9	0.9	0.4	3.0	1.3	0.
1962 - 1964..........	1.3	0.4	0.4	3.1	1.3	0.	0.
1965 - 1967..........	0.6	0.2	1.1	0.2	2.8	0.2	0.
1968 - 1970..........	0.6	0.1	0.7	0.3	3.6	0.1	0.

TABLE CONTINUED ON NEXT PAGE

CROSS-TABULATION 1.17.4: PERCENTAGE BREAKDOWN OF NUMBER OF
MANUFACTURING SUBSIDIARIES OF CONTINENTAL-EUROPEAN-BASED PARENT SYSTEMS BY
SUBSIDIARY'S COUNTRY
FOR SUBSIDIARIES CLASSIFIED BY
SUBSIDIARY'S DATE OF ENTRY INTO PARENT SYSTEM
(CONTINUED)

SUBSIDIARY'S COUNTRY

SUBSIDIARY'S DATE OF ENTRY INTO PARENT SYSTEM	TANZANIA	KENYA	NIGERIA	OTHER (BRITISH) AFRICA	MOROCCO, ALGERIA + TUNISIA	OTHER (FRENCH) AFRICA	OTHER AFRICA
PRE 1914	0.	0.	0.	0.	0.6	0.	0.
1914 - 1919	0.	0.	0.	0.	0.	0.	0.
1920 - 1929	0.	0.	0.	0.	0.4	0.	1.2
1930 - 1938	0.	0.	0.	0.	0.	0.	2.7
1939 - 1945	0.	0.	0.	0.	0.	0.	0.
1946 - 1952	0.	0.	0.	0.	3.9	0.	0.8
1953 - 1955	0.	0.	0.	0.	1.7	1.7	0.9
1956 - 1958	0.	0.	0.	0.	0.8	3.1	0.
1959 - 1961	0.	0.4	1.3	0.9	5.2	0.4	0.4
1962 - 1964	0.4	0.	0.	0.	1.3	1.7	0.4
1965 - 1967	0.2	0.4	0.	0.2	1.9	1.5	0.
1968 - 1970	0.1	0.1	0.	0.1	1.5	1.5	0.4

TABLE CONTINUED ON NEXT PAGE

CROSS-TABULATION 1.17.4: PERCENTAGE BREAKDOWN OF NUMBER OF
MANUFACTURING SUBSIDIARIES OF CONTINENTAL-EUROPEAN-BASED PARENT SYSTEMS BY
SUBSIDIARY'S COUNTRY
FOR SUBSIDIARIES CLASSIFIED BY
SUBSIDIARY'S DATE OF ENTRY INTO PARENT SYSTEM
(CONTINUED)

SUBSIDIARY'S COUNTRY

SUBSIDIARY'S DATE OF ENTRY INTO PARENT SYSTEM	AUSTRALIA	NEW ZEALAND	JAPAN	CHINA (TAIWAN)	HONG KONG	THE PHILIP-PINES	MALAYSIA
PRE 1914............	0.6	0.	0.	0.	0.	0.	0.
1914 – 1919.........	0.	0.	0.	0.	0.	0.	0.
1920 – 1929.........	2.0	0.8	1.2	0.8	0.	0.	0.
1930 – 1938.........	0.	0.	0.9	1.8	0.	0.9	0.
1939 – 1945.........	0.	0.	2.3	0.	0.	0.	0.
1946 – 1952.........	1.6	0.	0.8	0.	0.	0.	0.
1953 – 1955.........	2.6	0.	1.7	0.	0.	0.9	0.
1956 – 1958.........	1.5	0.	1.5	0.	0.	0.	0.
1959 – 1961.........	3.9	0.4	1.7	0.	0.	0.4	0.
1962 – 1964.........	1.7	0.4	1.3	0.	0.	1.3	0.
1965 – 1967.........	0.8	0.2	1.3	0.	0.	0.	0.6
1968 – 1970.........	1.2	0.1	2.3	0.2	0.	0.3	0.4

TABLE CONTINUED ON NEXT PAGE

CROSS-TABULATION 1.17.4: PERCENTAGE BREAKDOWN OF NUMBER OF
MANUFACTURING SUBSIDIARIES OF CONTINENTAL-EUROPEAN-BASED PARENT SYSTEMS BY
SUBSIDIARY'S COUNTRY
FOR SUBSIDIARIES CLASSIFIED BY
SUBSIDIARY'S DATE OF ENTRY INTO PARENT SYSTEM
(CONTINUED)

SUBSIDIARY'S COUNTRY

SUBSIDIARY'S DATE OF ENTRY INTO PARENT SYSTEM	SINGA-PORE	INDO-NESIA	THAILAND	INDIA	OTHER ASIA + OCEANIA	TOTAL PERCENT	TOTAL NUMBER
PRE 1914........	0.	1.8	0.	0.	0.	100.	167
1914 - 1919.....	0.	0.	0.	0.	0.	100.	51
1920 - 1929.....	0.	0.	0.	1.2	0.8	100.	249
1930 - 1938.....	0.	0.	0.	0.9	0.	100.	112
1939 - 1945.....	0.	0.	0.	0.	0.	100.	44
1946 - 1952.....	0.	0.	0.	1.6	0.	100.	129
1953 - 1955.....	0.	0.	0.	3.4	0.	100.	117
1956 - 1958.....	0.	0.	0.	4.6	0.	100.	131
1959 - 1961.....	0.4	0.	0.9	2.6	0.4	100.	232
1962 - 1964.....	0.	0.	0.	4.4	0.	100.	229
1965 - 1967.....	0.2	0.	0.6	1.3	0.4	100.	532
1968 - 1970.....	0.2	0.5	0.1	0.5	0.7	100.	1030

96

CROSS-TABULATION 1.17.5: PERCENTAGE BREAKDOWN OF NUMBER OF
MANUFACTURING SUBSIDIARIES OF JAPANESE-BASED PARENT SYSTEMS BY
SUBSIDIARY'S COUNTRY
FOR SUBSIDIARIES CLASSIFIED BY
SUBSIDIARY'S DATE OF ENTRY INTO PARENT SYSTEM

SUBSIDIARY'S COUNTRY

SUBSIDIARY'S DATE OF ENTRY INTO PARENT SYSTEM	UNITED STATES	CANADA	MEXICO	CENTRAL AMERICA + CARIB.	VENE- ZUELA	CCLOMBIA	PERU
PRE 1914........	0.	0.	0.	0.	0.	0.	0.
1914 – 1919....	0.	0.	0.	0.	0.	0.	0.
1920 – 1929....	0.	0.	0.	0.	0.	0.	0.
1930 – 1938....	0.	0.	0.	0.	0.	0.	0.
1939 – 1945....	5.0	0.	0.	0.	0.	0.	0.
1946 – 1952....	0.	0.	0.	0.	0.	0.	0.
1953 – 1955....	0.	0.	0.	0.	0.	0.	0.
1956 – 1958....	0.	0.	7.1	0.	0.	0.	0.
1959 – 1961....	2.3	0.	4.5	2.3	0.	0.	0.
1962 – 1964....	2.2	1.1	2.2	1.1	1.1	2.2	3.3
1965 – 1967....	6.2	1.8	1.8	8.8	1.8	0.	3.5
1968 – 1970....	2.9	1.0	1.0	2.4	1.0	0.	0.5

TABLE CONTINUED CN NEXT PAGE

CROSS-TABULATION 1.17.5: PERCENTAGE BREAKDOWN OF NUMBER OF
MANUFACTURING SUBSIDIARIES OF JAPANESE-BASED PARENT SYSTEMS BY
SUBSIDIARY'S COUNTRY
FOR SUBSIDIARIES CLASSIFIED BY
SUBSIDIARY'S DATE OF ENTRY INTO PARENT SYSTEM
(CONTINUED)

SUBSIDIARY'S COUNTRY

SUBSIDIARY'S DATE OF ENTRY INTO PARENT SYSTEM	CHILE	ARGEN-TINA	BRAZIL	OTHER SOUTH AMERICA	GERMANY	FRANCE	ITALY
PRE 1914	0.	0.	0.	0.	0.	0.	0.
1914 – 1919	0.	0.	0.	0.	0.	0.	0.
1920 – 1929	0.	0.	0.	0.	0.	0.	0.
1930 – 1938	0.	0.	33.	0.	0.	0.	0.
1939 – 1945	0.	0.	0.	0.	2.5	0.	0.
1946 – 1952	0.	0.	0.	0.	0.	0.	0.
1953 – 1955	0.	0.	40.	0.	0.	0.	0.
1956 – 1958	0.	7.1	57.	0.	0.	0.	0.
1959 – 1961	0.	0.	4.5	0.	0.	0.	0.
1962 – 1964	1.1	0.	4.4	0.	0.	0.	2.2
1965 – 1967	0.	0.9	7.1	0.9	0.	0.	0.
1968 – 1970	0.5	0.5	4.3	0.5	0.5	0.	0.

TABLE CONTINUED ON NEXT PAGE

Page 98

CROSS-TABULATION 1.17.5: PERCENTAGE BREAKDOWN OF NUMBER OF
MANUFACTURING SUBSIDIARIES OF JAPANESE-BASED PARENT SYSTEMS BY
SUBSIDIARY'S COUNTRY
FOR SUBSIDIARIES CLASSIFIED BY
SUBSIDIARY'S DATE OF ENTRY INTO PARENT SYSTEM
(CONTINUED)

| | | | SUBSIDIARY'S COUNTRY | | | | |
SUBSIDIARY'S DATE OF ENTRY INTO PARENT SYSTEM	BELGIUM AND LUX-EMBURG	THE NETHER-LANDS	UNITED KINGDOM	IRELAND	DENMARK	NORWAY	SWEDEN
PRE 1914........	0.	0.	0.	0.	0.	0.	0.
1914 – 1919.....	0.	0.	0.	0.	0.	0.	0.
1920 – 1929.....	0.	0.	0.	0.	0.	0.	0.
1930 – 1938.....	0.	0.	0.	0.	0.	0.	0.
1939 – 1945.....	0.	0.	0.	0.	0.	0.	0.
1946 – 1952.....	0.	0.	0.	0.	0.	0.	0.
1953 – 1955.....	0.	0.	0.	0.	0.	0.	0.
1956 – 1958.....	0.	0.	0.	0.	0.	0.	0.
1959 – 1961.....	0.	0.	2.3	2.3	0.	0.	0.
1962 – 1964.....	1.1	0.	0.	0.	0.	0.	0.
1965 – 1967.....	0.	0.	0.	0.	0.	0.	0.
1968 – 1970.....	0.5	0.	0.	0.5	0.	0.	0.

TABLE CONTINUED ON NEXT PAGE

CROSS-TABULATION 1.17.5: PERCENTAGE BREAKDOWN CF NUMBER OF
MANUFACTURING SUBSIDIARIES OF JAPANESE-BASED PARENT SYSTEMS BY
SUBSIDIARY'S COUNTRY
FCR SUBSIDIARIES CLASSIFIED BY
SUBSIDIARY'S DATE OF ENTRY INTO PARENT SYSTEM
(CONTINUED)

SUBSIDIARY'S CCUNTEY

SUBSIDIARY'S DATE OF ENTRY INTO PARENT SYSTEM	FINLAND	SWITZ- ERLAND	AUSTRIA	PCRTUGAL	SEAIN	GREECE	TURKEY
PRE 1914......	0.	0.	0.	0.	0.	0.	0.
1914 - 1919......	0.	0.	0.	0.	0.	0.	0.
1920 - 1929......	0.	0.	0.	0.	0.	0.	0.
1930 - 1938......	0.	0.	0.	0.	0.	0.	0.
1939 - 1945......	0.	0.	0.	0.	0.	0.	0.
1946 - 1952......	0.	0.	0.	0.	0.	0.	0.
1953 - 1955......	0.	0.	C.	0.	0.	0.	0.
1956 - 1958......	0.	0.	0.	0.	0.	0.	0.
1959 - 1961......	0.	0.	0.	2.3	0.	0.	0.
1962 - 1964......	0.	0.	0.	2.2	0.	0.	0.
1965 - 1967......	0.	0.	0.	0.9	0.	0.	0.
1968 - 1970......	0.	0.	0.	1.4	1.4	0.	0.

TABLE CONTINUED ON NEXT PAGE

CROSS-TABULATION 1.17.5: PERCENTAGE BREAKDOWN OF NUMBER OF
MANUFACTURING SUBSIDIARIES OF JAPANESE-BASED PARENT SYSTEMS BY
SUBSIDIARY'S COUNTRY
FOR SUBSIDIARIES CLASSIFIED BY
SUBSIDIARY'S DATE OF ENTRY INTO PARENT SYSTEM
(CONTINUED)

SUBSIDIARY'S COUNTRY

SUBSIDIARY'S DATE OF ENTRY INTO PARENT SYSTEM	OTHER EUROPE +ISRAEL	PAKISTAN	IRAN	OTHER MID EAST+LIB- YA+EGYPT	UNION OF S. AFRICA	RHODESIA	ZAMBIA
PRE 1914	0.	0.	0.	0.	0.	0.	0.
1914 - 1919	0.	0.	0.	0.	0.	0.	0.
1920 - 1929	0.	0.	0.	0.	0.	0.	0.
1930 - 1938	0.	0.	0.	0.	0.	0.	0.
1939 - 1945	0.	0.	0.	0.	0.	0.	0.
1946 - 1952	0.	0.	0.	0.	0.	0.	0.
1953 - 1955	0.	0.	0.	0.	0.	0.	0.
1956 - 1958	0.	7.1	0.	0.	0.	0.	0.
1959 - 1961	0.	6.8	0.	0.	0.	0.	0.
1962 - 1964	0.	2.2	0.	0.	0.	0.	0.
1965 - 1967	0.	0.	0.9	0.	0.9	0.	1.8
1968 - 1970	0.	0.	1.4	0.	0.	0.	0.

TABLE CONTINUED ON NEXT PAGE

CROSS-TABULATION 1.17.5: PERCENTAGE BREAKDOWN OF NUMBER OF
MANUFACTURING SUBSIDIARIES OF JAPANESE-BASED PARENT SYSTEMS BY
SUBSIDIARY'S COUNTRY
FOR SUBSIDIARIES CLASSIFIED BY
SUBSIDIARY'S DATE OF ENTRY INTO PARENT SYSTEM
(CONTINUED)

SUBSIDIARY'S COUNTRY

SUBSIDIARY'S DATE OF ENTRY INTO PARENT SYSTEM	TANZANIA	KENYA	NIGERIA	OTHER (BRITISH) AFRICA	MORCCCO, ALGERIA + TUNISIA	OTHER (FRENCH) AFRICA	OTHER AFRICA
PRE 1914.........	0.	0.	0.	0.	0.	0.	0.
1914 - 1919.....	0.	0.	0.	0.	0.	0.	0.
1920 - 1929.....	0.	0.	0.	0.	0.	0.	0.
1930 - 1938.....	0.	0.	0.	0.	0.	0.	0.
1939 - 1945.....	0.	0.	0.	0.	0.	0.	0.
1946 - 1952.....	0.	0.	0.	0.	0.	0.	0.
1953 - 1955.....	0.	0.	0.	0.	0.	0.	0.
1956 - 1958.....	0.	0.	0.	0.	0.	7.1	0.
1959 - 1961.....	0.	0.	2.3	2.3	0.	0.	0.
1962 - 1964.....	1.1	1.1	3.3	2.2	0.	0.	3.3
1965 - 1967.....	1.8	0.9	0.	1.8	0.	0.9	0.
1968 - 1970.....	0.	0.	1.9	0.5	0.5	0.5	1.0

TABLE CONTINUED CN NEXT PAGE

CROSS-TABULATION 1.17.5: PERCENTAGE BREAKDOWN OF NUMBER OF
MANUFACTURING SUBSIDIARIES OF JAPANESE-BASED PARENT SYSTEMS BY
SUBSIDIARY'S COUNTRY
FOR SUBSIDIARIES CLASSIFIED BY
SUBSIDIARY'S DATE OF ENTRY INTO PARENT SYSTEM
(CONTINUED)

SUBSIDIARY'S COUNTRY

SUBSIDIARY'S DATE OF ENTRY INTO PARENT SYSTEM	AUSTRALIA	NEW ZEALAND	JAPAN	CHINA (TAIWAN)	HONG KONG	THE PHILIPPINES	MALAYSIA
PRE 1914	0.	0.	0.	0.	0.	0.	0.
1914 - 1919	0.	0.	0.	0.	0.	0.	0.
1920 - 1929	0.	0.	0.	100.	0.	0.	0.
1930 - 1938	0.	0.	0.	67.	0.	0.	0.
1939 - 1945	0.	0.	0.	53.	0.	0.	2.5
1946 - 1952	0.	0.	0.	50.	0.	0.	0.
1953 - 1955	0.	0.	0.	20.	0.	0.	0.
1956 - 1958	0.	0.	0.	7.1	0.	0.	0.
1959 - 1961	0.	0.	0.	14.	9.1	0.	4.5
1962 - 1964	3.3	1.1	0.	10.	8.9	0.	2.2
1965 - 1967	2.7	0.	0.	19.	2.7	2.7	4.4
1968 - 1970	5.7	0.5	0.	23.	2.4	3.8	6.7

TABLE CONTINUED ON NEXT PAGE

CROSS-TABULATION 1.17.5: PERCENTAGE BREAKDOWN OF NUMBER OF
MANUFACTURING SUBSIDIARIES OF JAPANESE-BASED PARENT SYSTEMS BY
SUBSIDIARY'S COUNTRY
FOR SUBSIDIARIES CLASSIFIED BY
SUBSIDIARY'S DATE OF ENTRY INTO PARENT SYSTEM
(CONTINUED)

SUBSIDIARY'S COUNTRY

SUBSIDIARY'S DATE OF ENTRY INTO PARENT SYSTEM	SINGA- PORE	INDO- NESIA	THAILAND	INDIA	OTHER ASIA + OCEANIA	TOTAL PERCENT	TOTAL NUMBER
PRE 1914...........	0.	0.	0.	0.	0.	100.	0
1914 – 1919........	0.	0.	0.	0.	0.	100.	0
1920 – 1929........	0.	0.	0.	0.	0.	100.	1
1930 – 1938........	0.	0.	0.	0.	0.	100.	3
1939 – 1945........	0.	0.	0.	2.5	35.	100.	40
1946 – 1952........	0.	50.	0.	0.	0.	100.	2
1953 – 1955........	0.	0.	0.	0.	40.	100.	5
1956 – 1958........	0.	0.	0.	0.	7.1	100.	14
1959 – 1961........	4.5	0.	9.1	23.	4.5	100.	44
1962 – 1964........	13.	0.	14.	6.7	2.2	100.	90
1965 – 1967........	8.0	0.	9.7	6.2	2.7	100.	113
1968 – 1970........	3.3	7.2	12.	1.4	8.6	100.	209

CROSS-TABULATION 1.21.1: PERCENTAGE BREAKDOWN OF NUMBER (AS OF 1/1/71) OF
MANUFACTURING SUBSIDIARIES OF NON-U.S.-BASED PARENT SYSTEMS BY
SUBSIDIARY'S COUNTRY
FOR SUBSIDIARIES CLASSIFIED BY
NATIONAL BASE OF SUBSIDIARY'S PARENT SYSTEM

SUBSIDIARY'S COUNTRY

NATIONAL BASE OF SUBSIDIARY'S PARENT SYSTEM	UNITED STATES	CANADA	MEXICO	CENTRAL AMERICA + CARIB.	VENE-ZUELA	COLOMBIA	PERU
UNITED KINGDOM	5.1	7.8	0.8	1.4	0.4	0.3	0.2
GERMANY	6.3	3.4	3.3	1.4	0.5	0.8	1.0
FRANCE	4.9	2.1	1.6	0.7	0.5	0.5	0.2
ITALY	3.9	2.3	3.9	1.6	7.0	0.8	2.3
BELGIUM AND LUXEMBURG	8.8	12.	0.	0.	0.	0.	0.
THE NETHERLANDS	22.	0.9	2.4	1.6	0.9	0.5	0.2
SWEDEN	1.8	2.4	3.0	1.2	1.2	1.2	1.2
SWITZERLAND	7.4	3.1	2.0	1.3	1.0	0.8	0.8
JAPAN	3.8	1.0	2.1	3.8	1.3	0.4	1.9
CANADA	13.	0.	4.1	5.6	3.0	1.5	0.
OTHER NON-U.S	17.	0.	0.	0.	0.	0.	0.

TABLE CONTINUED ON NEXT PAGE

CROSS-TABULATION 1.21.1: PERCENTAGE BREAKDOWN OF NUMBER (AS OF 1/1/71) OF
MANUFACTURING SUBSIDIARIES OF NON-U.S.-BASED PARENT SYSTEMS BY
SUBSIDIARY'S COUNTRY
FOR SUBSIDIARIES CLASSIFIED BY
NATIONAL BASE OF SUBSIDIARY'S PARENT SYSTEM
(CONTINUED)

SUBSIDIARY'S COUNTRY

NATIONAL BASE OF SUBSIDIARY'S PARENT SYSTEM	CHILE	ARGEN-TINA	BRAZIL	OTHER SOUTH AMERICA	GERMANY	FRANCE	ITALY
UNITED KINGDOM................	0.3	1.3	1.2	0.5	5.5	4.4	2.5
GERMANY......................	0.8	3.9	5.9	0.2	0.2	17.	4.7
FRANCE.......................	1.0	5.5	6.6	0.5	9.7	0.	8.1
ITALY........................	1.6	7.0	8.6	0.8	2.4	8.6	0.
BELGIUM AND LUXEMBURG........	0.	0.4	4.1	0.4	9.2	18.	5.6
THE NETHERLANDS..............	0.5	1.5	1.0	0.	11.	7.8	3.1
SWEDEN.......................	1.2	1.8	3.6	0.	9.0	9.6	3.6
SWITZERLAND..................	0.8	2.8	3.4	1.1	16.	12.	6.4
JAPAN........................	0.5	0.7	7.1	0.5	0.3	0.	0.3
CANADA.......................	0.	3.1	3.1	1.1	4.1	5.1	5.1
OTHER NON-U.S................	1.1	1.1	1.1	0.	0.	54.	5.1

TABLE CONTINUED ON NEXT PAGE

CROSS-TABULATION 1.21.1: PERCENTAGE BREAKDOWN OF NUMBER (AS OF 1/1/71) OF
MANUFACTURING SUBSIDIARIES OF NON-U.S.-BASED PARENT SYSTEMS BY
SUBSIDIARY'S COUNTRY
FOR SUBSIDIARIES CLASSIFIED BY
NATIONAL BASE OF SUBSIDIARY'S PARENT SYSTEM
(CONTINUED)

SUBSIDIARY'S COUNTRY

NATIONAL BASE OF SUBSIDIARY'S PARENT SYSTEM	BELGIUM AND LUX- EMBURG	THE NETHER- LANDS	UNITED KINGDOM	IRELAND	DENMARK	NORWAY	SWEDEN
UNITED KINGDOM........................	2.3	2.4	0.	3.6	0.9	0.7	1.9
GERMANY..............................	3.1	3.1	4.7	0.2	0.6	0.5	2.6
FRANCE...............................	8.6	3.4	4.8	0.	0.3	0.3	1.0
ITALY................................	1.7	3.2	7.1	0.9	0.9	0.	0.
BELGIUM AND LUXEMBURG................	3.8	6.7	3.0	0.	0.5	0.	0.
THE NETHERLANDS......................	3.9	0.	19.	1.3	1.5	0.3	1.5
SWEDEN...............................	3.7	5.5	14.	0.	3.1	8.5	0.
SWITZERLAND..........................	2.6	3.9	12.	0.4	0.6	2.4	0.4
JAPAN................................	0.7	0.	0.3	0.3	0.	0.	0.
CANADA...............................	0.5	1.1	18.	3.7	1.6	2.1	0.6
OTHER NON-U.S........................	1.1	2.1	3.1	1.1	0.	0.	1.1

TABLE CONTINUED ON NEXT PAGE

CROSS-TABULATION 1.21.1: PERCENTAGE BREAKDOWN OF NUMBER (AS OF 1/1/71) OF
MANUFACTURING SUBSIDIARIES OF NON-U.S.-BASED PARENT SYSTEMS BY
SUBSIDIARY'S COUNTRY
FOR SUBSIDIARIES CLASSIFIED BY
NATIONAL BASE OF SUBSIDIARY'S PARENT SYSTEM
(CONTINUED)

SUBSIDIARY'S COUNTRY

NATIONAL BASE OF SUBSIDIARY'S PARENT SYSTEM	FINLAND	SWITZ-ERLAND	AUSTRIA	PORTUGAL	SPAIN	GREECE	TURKEY
UNITED KINGDOM................	0.3	0.7	1.2	0.8	2.1	0.5	0.5
GERMANY......................	0.5	2.9	4.5	1.3	5.7	1.5	2.1
FRANCE.......................	0.	1.6	1.3	2.5	9.3	0.6	0.9
ITALY........................	0.	0.9	1.7	1.7	14.	0.9	1.7
BELGIUM AND LUXEMBURG........	0.9	0.5	1.3	2.4	5.3	0.9	0.
THE NETHERLANDS..............	0.4	2.0	2.3	0.4	2.0	0.4	0.4
SWEDEN.......................	5.7	1.9	0.7	1.3	1.9	0.	0.
SWITZERLAND..................	0.4	0.	3.5	-1.2	4.0	0.7	1.2
JAPAN........................	0.	0.	0.	1.4	0.8	0.	0.
CANADA.......................	0.	0.7	0.	0.	2.2	0.	0.7
OTHER NON-U.S................	0.	1.2	1.2	0.	2.2	0.	0.

TABLE CONTINUED ON NEXT PAGE

CROSS-TABULATION 1.21.1: PERCENTAGE BREAKDOWN OF NUMBER (AS OF 1/1/71) OF
MANUFACTURING SUBSIDIARIES OF NON-U.S.-BASED PARENT SYSTEMS BY
SUBSIDIARY'S COUNTRY
FOR SUBSIDIARIES CLASSIFIED BY
NATIONAL BASE OF SUBSIDIARY'S PARENT SYSTEM
(CONTINUED)

SUBSIDIARY'S COUNTRY

NATIONAL BASE OF SUBSIDIARY'S PARENT SYSTEM	OTHER EUROPE +ISRAEL	PAKISTAN	IRAN	OTHER MID EAST+LIB-YA+EGYPT	UNION OF S. AFRICA	RHODESIA	ZAMBIA
UNITED KINGDOM	0.6	1.3	0.4	0.6	14.	2.2	1.8
GERMANY	0.7	1.0	1.1	0.8	6.3	0.	0.
FRANCE	0.	0.4	0.9	1.6	1.8	0.	0.
ITALY	2.5	0.	0.	1.8	1.8	0.	0.
BELGIUM AND LUXEMBURG	6.1	0.	0.6	0.6	3.9	1.3	0.
THE NETHERLANDS	0-	0.4	0.9	0.	1.4	0.7	0.
SWEDEN	0.8	0.8	1.4	0.8	1.4	0.	0.
SWITZERLAND	1.0	1.0	0.	0.5	2.2	0.5	0.
JAPAN	0.	1.2	1.0	0.4	0.4	0.	0.6
CANADA	0.7	0.	0.	0.	2.7	0.7	0.
OTHER NON-U.S.	0.	0.	0.	1.2	0.	1.2	0.

TABLE CONTINUED ON NEXT PAGE

CROSS-TABULATION 1.21.1: PERCENTAGE BREAKDOWN OF NUMBER (AS OF 1/1/71) OF
MANUFACTURING SUBSIDIARIES OF NON-U.S.-BASED PARENT SYSTEMS BY
SUBSIDIARY'S COUNTRY

FOR SUBSIDIARIES CLASSIFIED BY
NATIONAL BASE OF SUBSIDIARY'S PARENT SYSTEM
(CONTINUED)

SUBSIDIARY'S COUNTRY

NATIONAL BASE OF SUBSIDIARY'S PARENT SYSTEM	TANZANIA	KENYA	NIGERIA	OTHER (BRITISH) AFRICA	MOROCCO, ALGERIA + TUNISIA	OTHER (FRENCH) AFRICA	OTHER AFRICA
UNITED KINGDOM..........	1.0	1.9	2.1	2.1	0.3	0.8	0.9
GERMANY.................	0.4	0.4	0.	0.5	0.6	0.6	0.4
FRANCE..................	0.	0.	0.7	0.	7.5	7.3	0.5
ITALY...................	1.0	0.	0.	1.0	4.1	0.	1.8
BELGIUM AND LUXEMBURG...	0.	0.	0.	0.6	1.4	0.	3.9
THE NETHERLANDS.........	0.5	1.0	0.	0.	1.7	0.7	0.
SWEDEN..................	0.	0.	0.	0.	0.	0.	0.8
SWITZERLAND.............	0.	0.	0.8	0.	0.	0.5	0.
JAPAN...................	0.9	0.7	1.9	1.5	0.5	0.9	1.3
CANADA..................	0.	0.	0.8	1.3	0.8	0.	0.
OTHER NON-U.S...........	0.	0.	0.	1.3	0.	0.	1.3

TABLE CONTINUED ON NEXT PAGE

CROSS-TABULATION 1.21.1: PERCENTAGE BREAKDOWN OF NUMBER (AS OF 1/1/71) OF MANUFACTURING SUBSIDIARIES OF NON-U.S.-BASED PARENT SYSTEMS BY SUBSIDIARY'S COUNTRY FOR SUBSIDIARIES CLASSIFIED BY NATIONAL BASE OF SUBSIDIARY'S PARENT SYSTEM (CONTINUED)

NATIONAL BASE OF SUBSIDIARY'S PARENT SYSTEM	SUBSIDIARY'S COUNTRY						
	AUSTRALIA	NEW ZEALAND	JAPAN	CHINA (TAIWAN)	HONG KONG	THE PHILIPPINES	MALAYSIA
UNITED KINGDOM	18.	4.7	0.9	0.4	0.7	0.4	1.2
GERMANY	1.1	0.6	4.4	0.4	0.	0.7	0.4
FRANCE	3.1	0.	1.0	0.	0.5	0.5	0.5
ITALY	0.	0.	1.1	0.	0.	0.	1.1
BELGIUM AND LUXEMBURG	1.0	0.	0.	0.	0.	0.	0.
THE NETHERLANDS	1.9	0.5	2.4	0.5	0.	1.2	1.0
SWEDEN	3.9	0.	0.	0.	0.	0.9	1.5
SWITZERLAND	1.3	1.1	2.6	0.	0.6	0.8	0.6
JAPAN	3.6	0.7	0.	22.	3.8	2.8	5.3
CANADA	5.4	2.3	7.4	0.	0.	0.	0.8
OTHER NON-U.S.	0.	1.3	0.	1.3	0.	0.	1.3

TABLE CONTINUED ON NEXT PAGE

CROSS-TABULATION 1.21.1: PERCENTAGE BREAKDOWN OF NUMBER (AS OF 1/1/71) OF
MANUFACTURING SUBSIDIARIES OF NON-U.S.-BASED PARENT SYSTEMS BY
SUBSIDIARY'S COUNTRY
FOR SUBSIDIARIES CLASSIFIED BY
NATIONAL BASE OF SUBSIDIARY'S PARENT SYSTEM
(CONTINUED)

SUBSIDIARY'S COUNTRY

NATIONAL BASE OF SUBSIDIARY'S PARENT SYSTEM	SINGA-PORE	INDO-NESIA	THAILAND	INDIA	OTHER ASIA + OCEANIA	TOTAL PERCENT	TOTAL NUMBER
UNITED KINGDOM....................	1.2	0.6	0.5	3.7	1.3	100.	2269
GERMANY...........................	0.5	0.7	1.0	2.8	0.9	100.	792
FRANCE............................	0.	0.8	0.	1.1	1.1	100.	429
ITALY.............................	0.	0.	1.1	2.7	1.1	100.	133
BELGIUM AND LUXEMBURG.............	0.	0.	0.	0.7	0.7	100.	276
THE NETHERLANDS...................	1.1	0.6	0.6	1.5	0.8	100.	429
SWEDEN............................	0.	0.	0.	3.3	0.9	100.	171
SWITZERLAND.......................	0.6	0.	0.6	2.6	0.	100.	397
JAPAN.............................	6.0	3.5	14.	6.2	6.2	100.	483
CANADA............................	0.	0.	0.9	1.4	0.	100.	201
OTHER NON-U.S.....................	0.	0.	0.	0.	2.4	100.	100

TABULATION 2.1: PERCENTAGE BREAKDOWN OF NUMBER OF SUBSIDIARIES BY GEOGRAPHICAL REGION OF SUBSIDIARY'S COUNTRY FOR VARIOUS CATEGORIES OF SUBSIDIARIES

CATEGORY OF SUBSIDIARY	GEOGRAPHICAL REGION OF SUBSIDIARY'S COUNTRY					TOTAL PERCENT	TOTAL NUMBER
	NORTH AMERICA	LATIN AMERICA	EUROPE	AFRICA + MIDDLE EAST	OTHER ASIA + OCEANIA		
NON-U.S.-BASED SYSTEMS (AS OF 1/1/71):							
ALL SUBSIDIARIES..........	13.	16.	43.	18.	16.	100.	13774
MANUFACTURING SUBS........	12.	12.	40.	15.	21.	100.	5639
SALES SUBSIDIARIES........	13.	10.	49.	18.	11.	100.	3304
U.S.-BASED SYSTEMS (AS OF 1/1/68):							
ALL SUBSIDIARIES..........	14.	25.	41.	7.4	13.	100.	9776
MANUFACTURING SUBS........	13.	27.	39.	6.5	15.	100.	4246
SALES SUBSIDIARIES........	9.6	18.	50.	7.9	14.	100.	1664
WORLD SUBSET OF SYSTEMS (AS OF 1/1/68):							
NON-U.S.-BASED SYSTEMS:							
ALL SUBSIDIARIES..........	14.	11.	43.	16.	16.	100.	6153
MANUFACTURING SUBS........	14.	13.	40.	14.	20.	100.	2735
SALES SUBSIDIARIES........	11.	10.	50.	17.	12.	100.	1631
U.S.-BASED-SYSTEMS:							
ALL SUBSIDIARIES..........	14.	25.	40.	7.7	12.	100.	8144
MANUFACTURING SUBS........	13.	27.	38.	6.6	15.	100.	3334
SALES SUBSIDIARIES........	11.	18.	49.	8.5	14.	100.	1309

TABULATION 2.2: PERCENTAGE BREAKDOWN OF SALES OF SUBSIDIARIES IN 1970 BY
GEOGRAPHICAL REGION OF SUBSIDIARY'S COUNTRY
FOR ALL SUBSIDIARIES, MANUFACTURING SUBSIDIARIES AND SALES SUBSIDIARIES
OF NON-U.S.-BASED SYSTEMS

GEOGRAPHICAL REGION OF SUBSIDIARY'S COUNTRY

CATEGORY OF SUBSIDIARY	NORTH AMERICA	LATIN AMERICA	EUROPE	AFRICA + MIDDLE EAST	OTHER ASIA + OCEANIA	TOTAL PERCENT	TOTAL ($ MIL)
ALL SUBSIDIARIES...........	23.	8.4	44.	11.	13.	100.	132401
MANUFACTURING SUBSIDIARIES...	24.	9.8	44.	9.0	13.	100.	82412
SALES SUBSIDIARIES...........	29.	6.3	46.	9.4	9.6	100.	23243

CROSS-TABULATION 2.6.1: PERCENTAGE BREAKDOWN OF NUMBER (AS OF 1/1/71) OF MANUFACTURING SUBSIDIARIES OF NON-U.S.-BASED PARENT SYSTEMS BY GEOGRAPHICAL REGION OF SUBSIDIARY'S COUNTRY FOR SUBSIDIARIES CLASSIFIED BY PRINCIPAL INDUSTRY OF SUBSIDIARY AS OF 1/1/71

GEOGRAPHICAL REGION OF SUBSIDIARY'S COUNTRY

PRINCIPAL INDUSTRY OF SUBSIDIARY AS OF 1/1/71	NORTH AMERICA	LATIN AMERICA	EUROPE	AFRICA + MIDDLE EAST	OTHER ASIA + OCEANIA	TOTAL PERCENT	TOTAL NUMBER
ORDNANCE.................	13.	25.	50.	0.	13.	100.	8
MEAT PRODUCTS............	3.4	10.	48.	21.	17.	100.	29
DAIRY PRODUCTS...........	13.	6.7	47.	17.	16.	100.	89
CANNED FOODS.............	25.	6.8	34.	18.	16.	100.	44
GRAIN MILL PRODUCTS......	4.4	0.	22.	38.	36.	100.	45
BAKERY PRODUCTS..........	0.	0.	9.3	41.	49.	100.	75
CONFECTIONERY PRODUCTS...	13.	13.	27.	20.	27.	100.	30
BEVERAGES................	11.	11.	34.	31.	14.	100.	158
OTHER FOOD PRODUCTS......	16.	10.	35.	15.	24.	100.	143
TOBACCO PRODUCTS.........	12.	22.	21.	26.	19.	100.	58
TEXTILES.................	5.4	17.	25.	14.	39.	100.	239
APPAREL..................	2.5	0.	15.	30.	53.	100.	40
LUMBER AND WOOD..........	11.	3.8	28.	34.	23.	100.	53
FURNITURE................	17.	5.6	50.	11.	17.	100.	18
PAPER PRODUCTS...........	22.	6.5	42.	12.	19.	100.	139
PRINTED MATTER...........	16.	11.	34.	18.	20.	100.	99
INDUSTRIAL CHEMICALS.....	12.	16.	40.	14.	18.	100.	247
PLASTICS AND SYNTHETICS..	9.7	13.	56.	3.2	18.	100.	154
DRUGS....................	10.	19.	43.	12.	15.	100.	229
SOAP AND COSMETICS.......	8.2	16.	41.	18.	17.	100.	158
PAINTS...................	8.8	7.1	50.	14.	20.	100.	113
AGRICULTURAL CHEMICALS...	24.	20.	32.	13.	11.	100.	79
OTHER CHEMICALS..........	11.	9.0	44.	18.	18.	100.	155
REFINED PETROLEUM........	13.	7.3	36.	28.	16.	100.	109
OTHER PETROLEUM PRODUCTS.	6.0	1.2	53.	18.	22.	100.	83

TABLE CONTINUED ON NEXT PAGE

CROSS-TABULATION 2.6.1: PERCENTAGE BREAKDOWN OF NUMBER (AS OF 1/1/71) OF
MANUFACTURING SUBSIDIARIES OF NON-U.S.-BASED PARENT SYSTEMS BY
GEOGRAPHICAL REGION OF SUBSIDIARY'S COUNTRY
FOR SUBSIDIARIES CLASSIFIED BY
PRINCIPAL INDUSTRY OF SUBSIDIARY AS OF 1/1/71
(CONTINUED)

GEOGRAPHICAL REGION OF SUBSIDIARY'S COUNTRY

PRINCIPAL INDUSTRY OF SUBSIDIARY AS OF 1/1/71	NORTH AMERICA	LATIN AMERICA	EUROPE	AFRICA + MIDDLE EAST	OTHER ASIA + OCEANIA	TOTAL PERCENT	TOTAL NUMBER
TIRES..................	2.8	5.6	50.	19.	22.	100.	36
OTHER RUBBER PRODUCTS....	4.3	7.1	40.	17.	31.	100.	70
LEATHER PRODUCTS AND SHOES...	17.	33.	17.	17.	17.	100.	6
GLASS PRODUCTS............	6.0	4.0	86.	0.	4.0	100.	50
STONE, CLAY AND CONCRETE.....	21.	11.	44.	18.	6.3	100.	80
IRON AND STEEL PRODUCTS......	13.	14.	34.	12.	26.	100.	174
NON-FERROUS SMELTING.........	16.	4.2	35.	15.	30.	100.	96
NON-FERROUS PRODUCTS.........	9.9	7.1	30.	23.	30.	100.	141
METAL CANS.................	9.1	9.1	30.	33.	18.	100.	33
STRUCTURAL METAL PRODUCTS....	17.	17.	32.	14.	19.	100.	63
FABRICATED WIRE PRODUCTS.....	15.	13.	23.	6.4	43.	100.	47
OTHER FABRICATED METAL.......	17.	8.7	45.	8.7	21.	100.	173
ENGINES AND TURBINES.........	15.	15.	38.	10.	23.	100.	48
FARM MACHINERY............	6.1	27.	27.	18.	21.	100.	33
CONSTRUCTION MACHINERY.......	4.5	9.1	27.	23.	36.	100.	22
SPECIAL INDUSTRY MACHINERY...	14.	3.8	60.	6.3	16.	100.	80
GENERAL INDUSTRY MACHINERY...	16.	9.2	50.	13.	12.	100.	76
OFFICE MACHINES + COMPUTERS..	14.	21.	50.	7.1	7.1	100.	28
OTHER NON-ELECTR. MACHINERY..	17.	10.	48.	6.9	17.	100.	29
ELECTR. TRANSMISSION EQUIP...	6.5	15.	50.	13.	15.	100.	92
ELECTRIC LIGHTING AND WIRING.	5.5	17.	43.	11.	23.	100.	109
RADIOS, TV'S + APPLIANCES....	10.	9.4	40.	14.	27.	100.	159
COMMUNICATIONS EQUIPMENT.....	3.3	17.	37.	16.	28.	100.	90

TABLE CONTINUED ON NEXT PAGE

CROSS-TABULATION 2. 6.1: PERCENTAGE BREAKDOWN OF NUMBER (AS OF 1/1/71) OF
MANUFACTURING SUBSIDIARIES OF NON-U.S.-BASED PARENT SYSTEMS BY
GEOGRAPHICAL REGION OF SUBSIDIARY'S COUNTRY
FOR SUBSIDIARIES CLASSIFIED BY
PRINCIPAL INDUSTRY OF SUBSIDIARY AS OF 1/1/71
(CONTINUED)

GEOGRAPHICAL REGION OF SUBSIDIARY'S COUNTRY

PRINCIPAL INDUSTRY OF SUBSIDIARY AS OF 1/1/71	NORTH AMERICA	LATIN AMERICA	EUROPE	AFRICA + MIDDLE EAST	OTHER ASIA + OCEANIA	TOTAL PERCENT	TOTAL NUMBER
ELECTRONIC COMPONENTS.........	29.	7.1	43.	4.0	16.	100.	99
OTHER ELECTRICAL EQUIPMENT....	10.	10.	50.	14.	16.	100.	189
MOTOR VEHICLES AND EQUIPMENT.	3.7	22.	33.	18.	24.	100.	187
OTHER TRANSPORTATION..........	31.	10.	24.	14.	22.	100.	59
PRECISION GOODS...............	33.	5.2	53.	5.1	3.8	100.	78
MISCELLANEOUS PRODUCTS........	18.	5.1	55.	2.6	19.	100.	78

CROSS-TABULATION 2.6.2: PERCENTAGE BREAKDOWN OF NUMBER (AS OF 1/1/68) OF MANUFACTURING SUBSIDIARIES OF U.S.-BASED PARENT SYSTEMS BY GEOGRAPHICAL REGION OF SUBSIDIARY'S COUNTRY FOR SUBSIDIARIES CLASSIFIED BY PRINCIPAL INDUSTRY OF SUBSIDIARY AS OF 1/1/68

PRINCIPAL INDUSTRY OF SUBSIDIARY AS OF 1/1/68	GEOGRAPHICAL REGION OF SUBSIDIARY'S COUNTRY					TOTAL PERCENT	TOTAL NUMBER
	NORTH AMERICA	LATIN AMERICA	EUROPE	AFRICA + MIDDLE EAST	OTHER ASIA + OCEANIA		
ORDNANCE	18.	18.	27.	0.	36.	100.	11
MEAT PRODUCTS	26.	21.	26.	0.	26.	100.	38
DAIRY PRODUCTS	27.	30.	22.	6.3	15.	100.	79
CANNED FOODS	19.	30.	33.	5.6	13.	100.	54
GRAIN MILL PRODUCTS	9.2	46.	35.	3.1	7.1	100.	99
BAKERY PRODUCTS	10.	41.	38.	2.6	7.7	100.	39
CONFECTIONERY PRODUCTS	16.	23.	34.	6.6	20.	100.	61
BEVERAGES	8.3	27.	42.	10.	13.	100.	60
OTHER FOOD PRODUCTS	16.	23.	45.	3.6	13.	100.	56
TOBACCO PRODUCTS	20.	60.	10.	0.	10.	100.	10
TEXTILES	17.	38.	32.	1.1	13.	100.	88
APPAREL	14.	29.	50.	0.	7.1	100.	14
LUMBER AND WOOD	29.	19.	43.	0.	9.5	100.	21
FURNITURE	18.	24.	41.	0.	18.	100.	17
PAPER PRODUCTS	14.	30.	27.	19.	9.9	100.	161
PRINTED MATTER	7.1	14.	61.	14.	3.6	100.	28
INDUSTRIAL CHEMICALS	15.	31.	36.	2.8	15.	100.	254
PLASTICS AND SYNTHETICS	8.4	28.	40.	2.4	22.	100.	167
DRUGS	7.5	33.	32.	9.3	18.	100.	332
SOAP AND COSMETICS	8.7	25.	39.	11.	17.	100.	150
PAINTS	8.9	32.	36.	7.1	16.	100.	56
AGRICULTURAL CHEMICALS	12.	34.	30.	10.	14.	100.	50
OTHER CHEMICALS	10.	21.	43.	5.0	21.	100.	80
REFINED PETROLEUM	8.1	17.	41.	14.	20.	100.	136
OTHER PETROLEUM PRODUCTS	5.7	21.	47.	7.1	19.	100.	70

TABLE CONTINUED ON NEXT PAGE

CROSS-TABULATION 2.6.2: PERCENTAGE BREAKDOWN OF NUMBER (AS OF 1/1/68) OF MANUFACTURING SUBSIDIARIES OF U.S.-BASED PARENT SYSTEMS BY GEOGRAPHICAL REGION OF SUBSIDIARY'S COUNTRY FOR SUBSIDIARIES CLASSIFIED BY PRINCIPAL INDUSTRY OF SUBSIDIARY AS OF 1/1/68 (CONTINUED)

PRINCIPAL INDUSTRY OF SUBSIDIARY AS OF 1/1/68	GEOGRAPHICAL REGION OF SUBSIDIARY'S COUNTRY						
	NORTH AMERICA	LATIN AMERICA	EUROPE	AFRICA + MIDDLE EAST	OTHER ASIA + OCEANIA	TOTAL PERCENT	TOTAL NUMBER
TIRES	4.9	35.	32.	11.	17.	100.	81
OTHER RUBBER PRODUCTS	13.	28.	25.	13.	22.	100.	32
LEATHER PRODUCTS AND SHOES	15.	31.	38.	15.	0.	100.	13
GLASS PRODUCTS	13.	40.	30.	5.0	13.	100.	40
STONE, CLAY AND CONCRETE	8.0	28.	39.	8.0	17.	100.	75
IRON AND STEEL PRODUCTS	9.1	21.	55.	3.0	12.	100.	33
NON-FERROUS SMELTING	21.	14.	30.	14.	21.	100.	43
NON-FERROUS PRODUCTS	22.	28.	33.	5.6	11.	100.	36
METAL CANS	27.	30.	20.	6.7	17.	100.	30
STRUCTURAL METAL PRODUCTS	22.	19.	44.	7.4	7.4	100.	27
FABRICATED WIRE PRODUCTS	15.	23.	54.	0.	7.7	100.	13
OTHER FABRICATED METAL	19.	17.	46.	4.9	13.	100.	144
ENGINES AND TURBINES	35.	12.	41.	0.	12.	100.	17
FARM MACHINERY	5.9	26.	38.	12.	18.	100.	34
CONSTRUCTION MACHINERY	16.	22.	37.	6.2	19.	100.	81
SPECIAL INDUSTRY MACHINERY	9.0	12.	62.	5.1	13.	100.	78
GENERAL INDUSTRY MACHINERY	19.	19.	41.	3.4	17.	100.	58
OFFICE MACHINES + COMPUTERS	12.	22.	53.	0.	14.	100.	51
OTHER NON-ELECTR. MACHINERY	11.	21.	49.	0.	19.	100.	47
ELECTR. TRANSMISSION EQUIP.	17.	21.	54.	0.	8.3	100.	24
ELECTRIC LIGHTING AND WIRING	26.	26.	30.	0.	19.	100	27
RADIOS, TV'S + APPLIANCES	8.0	28.	41.	8.0	15.	100.	87
COMMUNICATIONS EQUIPMENT	19.	9.4	47.	3.1	22.	100.	32

TABLE CONTINUED ON NEXT PAGE

CROSS-TABULATION 2.6.2: PERCENTAGE BREAKDOWN OF NUMBER (AS OF 1/1/68) OF
MANUFACTURING SUBSIDIARIES OF U.S.-BASED PARENT SYSTEMS BY
GEOGRAPHICAL REGION OF SUBSIDIARY'S COUNTRY
FOR SUBSIDIARIES CLASSIFIED BY
PRINCIPAL INDUSTRY OF SUBSIDIARY AS OF 1/1/68
(CONTINUED)

GEOGRAPHICAL REGION OF SUBSIDIARY'S COUNTRY

PRINCIPAL INDUSTRY OF SUBSIDIARY AS OF 1/1/68	NORTH AMERICA	LATIN AMERICA	EUROPE	AFRICA + MIDDLE EAST	OTHER ASIA + OCEANIA	TOTAL PERCENT	TOTAL NUMBER
ELECTRONIC COMPONENTS	10.	18.	50.	5.0	18.	100.	40
OTHER ELECTRICAL EQUIPMENT	10.	31.	29.	3.1	28.	100.	99
MOTOR VEHICLES AND EQUIPMENT	14.	32.	36.	5.8	13.	100.	207
OTHER TRANSPORTATION	21.	5.3	63.	0.	11.	100.	19
PRECISION GOODS	9.5	22.	62.	1.4	5.4	100.	74
MISCELLANEOUS PRODUCTS	9.1	26.	41.	9.1	15.	100.	66

CROSS-TABULATION 2.8.1: PERCENTAGE BREAKDOWN OF NUMBER (AS OF 1/1/71) OF
MANUFACTURING SUBSIDIARIES OF NON-U.S.-BASED PARENT SYSTEMS BY
GEOGRAPHICAL REGION OF SUBSIDIARY'S COUNTRY
FOR SUBSIDIARIES CLASSIFIED BY
PRINCIPAL INDUSTRY-GROUP OF SUBSIDIARY AS OF 1/1/71

PRINCIPAL INDUSTRY-GROUP OF SUBSIDIARY AS OF 1/1/71	GEOGRAPHICAL REGION OF SUBSIDIARY'S COUNTRY						
	NORTH AMERICA	LATIN AMERICA	EUROPE	AFRICA + MIDDLE EAST	OTHER ASIA + OCEANIA	TOTAL PERCENT	TOTAL NUMBER
FOOD AND TOBACCO.............	12.	9.1	32.	25.	23.	100.	685
TEXTILES AND APPAREL.........	5.0	14.	24.	16.	41.	100.	279
WOOD, FURNITURE AND PAPER....	19.	5.7	39.	17.	20.	100.	210
CHEMICALS....................	11.	14.	45.	12.	17.	100.	1258
PETROLEUM....................	9.9	4.7	43.	24.	18.	100.	192
RUBBER AND TIRES.............	3.8	6.6	43.	18.	28.	100.	106
PRIMARY METALS...............	13.	9.4	33.	16.	28.	100.	413
FABR. METAL + NON-EL. MACH...	15.	11.	42.	12.	21.	100.	605
ELECTRIC AND ELECTRONIC......	11.	12.	44.	12.	20.	100.	787
TRANSPORTATION EQUIPMENT.....	10.	19.	30.	17.	24.	100.	246
PRECISION GOODS..............	33.	5.1	53.	5.1	3.8	100.	78
OTHER........................	16.	9.8	51.	11.	13.	100.	336

CROSS-TABULATION 2.8.2: PERCENTAGE BREAKDOWN OF NUMBER (AS OF 1/1/68) OF MANUFACTURING SUBSIDIARIES OF U.S.-BASED PARENT SYSTEMS BY GEOGRAPHICAL REGION OF SUBSIDIARY'S COUNTRY FOR SUBSIDIARIES CLASSIFIED BY PRINCIPAL INDUSTRY-GROUP OF SUBSIDIARY AS OF 1/1/68

PRINCIPAL INDUSTRY-GROUP OF SUBSIDIARY AS OF 1/1/68	GEOGRAPHICAL REGION OF SUBSIDIARY'S COUNTRY						
	NORTH AMERICA	LATIN AMERICA	EUROPE	AFRICA + MIDDLE EAST	OTHER ASIA + OCEANIA	TOTAL PERCENT	TOTAL NUMBER
FOOD AND TOBACCO	16.	31.	34.	4.7	14.	100.	509
TEXTILES AND APPAREL	17.	36.	34.	1.0	12.	100.	102
WOOD, FURNITURE AND PAPER	16.	29.	30.	15.	11.	100.	199
CHEMICALS	10.	29.	36.	6.6	18.	100.	1093
PETROLEUM	7.3	18.	43.	12.	19.	100.	206
RUBBER AND TIRES	7.1	33.	30.	12.	19.	100.	113
PRIMARY METALS	18.	21.	38.	8.0	15.	100.	112
FABR. METAL + NON-EL. MACH	16.	19.	45.	4.9	15.	100.	530
ELECTRIC AND ELECTRONIC	12.	24.	41.	3.6	19.	100.	359
TRANSPORTATION EQUIPMENT	14.	30.	38.	5.3	12.	100.	226
PRECISION GOODS	9.5	22.	62.	1.4	5.4	100.	74
OTHER	9.9	27.	40.	8.6	14.	100.	233

CROSS-TABULATION 2.21.1: PERCENTAGE BREAKDOWN OF NUMBER (AS OF 1/1/71) OF MANUFACTURING SUBSIDIARIES OF NON-U.S.-BASED PARENT SYSTEMS BY GEOGRAPHICAL REGION OF SUBSIDIARY'S COUNTRY FOR SUBSIDIARIES CLASSIFIED BY NATIONAL BASE OF SUBSIDIARY'S PARENT SYSTEM

GEOGRAPHICAL REGION OF SUBSIDIARY'S COUNTRY

NATIONAL BASE OF SUBSIDIARY'S PARENT SYSTEM	NORTH AMERICA	LATIN AMERICA	EUROPE	AFRICA + MIDDLE EAST	OTHER ASIA + OCEANIA	TOTAL PERCENT	TOTAL NUMBER
UNITED KINGDOM............	13.	6.1	29.	25.	27.	100.	2265
GERMANY..................	9.8	18.	53.	9.8	9.8	100.	788
FRANCE...................	7.1	17.	51.	19.	6.1	100.	425
ITALY....................	6.2	33.	45.	10.	5.4	100.	129
BELGIUM AND LUXEMBURG....	21.	4.8	62.	11.	1.5	100.	272
THE NETHERLANDS..........	23.	8.5	54.	5.4	8.7	100.	425
SWEDEN...................	4.2	14.	68.	4.2	9.0	100.	167
SWITZERLAND..............	10.	14.	64.	4.1	7.9	100.	393
JAPAN....................	4.8	18.	3.3	8.6	65.	100.	479
CANADA...................	13.	21.	44.	5.6	16.	100.	197
OTHER NON-U.S............	17.	3.0	71.	4.0	5.1	100.	99

TABULATION 3.1: PERCENTAGE BREAKDOWN OF NUMBER OF SUBSIDIARIES BY
GNP PER CAPITA IN 1970 OF SUBSIDIARY'S COUNTRY
FOR VARIOUS CATEGORIES OF SUBSIDIARIES

CATEGORY OF SUBSIDIARY	GNP PER CAPITA IN 1970 OF SUBSIDIARY'S COUNTRY						
	UNDER $200	$200-$500	$500-$1200	$1200-$2500	OVER $2500	TOTAL PERCENT	TOTAL NUMBER
NON-U.S.-BASED SYSTEMS (AS OF 1/1/71):							
ALL SUBSIDIARIES........	9.2	11.	17.	19.	43.	100.	13440
MANUFACTURING SUBS......	9.2	13.	20.	18.	40.	100.	5567
SALES SUBSIDIARIES......	10.	10.	15.	24.	41.	100.	3238
U.S.-BASED SYSTEMS (AS OF 1/1/68):							
ALL SUBSIDIARIES........	8.6	16.	17.	22.	36.	100.	9553
MANUFACTURING SUBS......	10.	15.	17.	23.	35.	100.	4203
SALES SUBSIDIARIES......	5.9	17.	18.	23.	37.	100.	1632
WORLD SUBSET OF SYSTEMS (AS OF 1/1/68):							
NON-U.S.-BASED SYSTEMS:							
ALL SUBSIDIARIES........	9.0	11.	17.	20.	44.	100.	5977
MANUFACTURING SUBS......	9.2	12.	19.	18.	42.	100.	2698
SALES SUBSIDIARIES......	11.	11.	15.	25.	39.	100.	1599
U.S.-BASED-SYSTEMS:							
ALL SUBSIDIARIES........	8.7	17.	17.	22.	36.	100.	7934
MANUFACTURING SUBS......	10.	16.	18.	22.	35.	100.	3295
SALES SUBSIDIARIES......	6.4	18.	17.	22.	37.	100.	1279

TABULATION 3.2: PERCENTAGE BREAKDOWN OF SALES OF SUBSIDIARIES IN 1970 BY
GNP PER CAPITA IN 1970 OF SUBSIDIARY'S COUNTRY
FOR ALL SUBSIDIARIES, MANUFACTURING SUBSIDIARIES AND SALES SUBSIDIARIES
OF NON-U.S.-BASED SYSTEMS

CATEGORY OF SUBSIDIARY	GNP PER CAPITA IN 1970 OF SUBSIDIARY'S COUNTRY					TOTAL PERCENT	TOTAL ($ MIL)
	UNDER $200	$200-$500	$500-$1200	$1200-$2500	OVER $2500		
ALL SUBSIDIARIES............	5.5	8.4	10.	17.	59.	100.	129959
MANUFACTURING SUBSIDIARIES...	4.8	8.6	11.	16.	60.	100.	81630
SALES SUBSIDIARIES..........	6.2	5.1	11.	19.	59.	100.	23069

CROSS-TABULATION 3. 6.1: PERCENTAGE BREAKDOWN OF NUMBER (AS OF 1/1/71) OF MANUFACTURING SUBSIDIARIES OF NON-U.S.-BASED PARENT SYSTEMS BY GNP PER CAPITA IN 1970 OF SUBSIDIARY'S COUNTRY FOR SUBSIDIARIES CLASSIFIED BY PRINCIPAL INDUSTRY OF SUBSIDIARY AS OF 1/1/71

PRINCIPAL INDUSTRY OF SUBSIDIARY AS OF 1/1/71	GNP PER CAPITA IN 1970 OF SUBSIDIARY'S COUNTRY					TOTAL PERCENT	TOTAL NUMBER
	UNDER $200	$200-$500	$500-$1200	$1200-$2500	OVER $2500		
ORDNANCE	0.	25.	13.	25.	38.	100.	8
MEAT PRODUCTS	14.	11.	7.1	36.	32.	100.	28
DAIRY PRODUCTS	9.0	2.2	21.	22.	45.	100.	89
CANNED FOODS	12.	7.3	12.	17.	51.	100.	41
GRAIN MILL PRODUCTS	4.4	4.4	31.	22.	38.	100.	45
BAKERY PRODUCTS	2.7	0.	40.	12.	45.	100.	75
CONFECTIONERY PRODUCTS	13.	10.	20.	20.	37.	100.	30
BEVERAGES	7.8	20.	18.	16.	38.	100.	153
OTHER FOOD PRODUCTS	7.1	12.	19.	13.	49.	100.	140
TOBACCO PRODUCTS	22.	22.	22.	10.	22.	100.	58
TEXTILES	17.	29.	23.	6.5	24.	100.	230
APPAREL	20.	20.	28.	5.0	28.	100.	40
LUMBER AND WOOD	5.7	15.	25.	15.	40.	100.	53
FURNITURE	0.	0.	17.	33.	50.	100.	18
PAPER PRODUCTS	3.6	8.6	10.	19.	58.	100.	139
PRINTED MATTER	13.	9.3	14.	20.	43.	100.	97
INDUSTRIAL CHEMICALS	10.	11.	25.	16.	39.	100.	240
PLASTICS AND SYNTHETICS	6.5	9.8	18.	26.	40.	100.	153
DRUGS	11.	16.	23.	19.	31.	100.	227
SOAP AND COSMETICS	8.4	14.	23.	12.	42.	100.	154
PAINTS	6.3	7.2	23.	24.	40.	100.	111
AGRICULTURAL CHEMICALS	6.4	24.	17.	14.	44.	100.	78
OTHER CHEMICALS	9.7	12.	21.	19.	39.	100.	155
REFINED PETROLEUM	15.	16.	12.	13.	43.	100.	106
OTHER PETROLEUM PRODUCTS	4.9	16.	11.	29.	40.	100.	83

TABLE CONTINUED ON NEXT PAGE

CROSS-TABULATION 3.6.1: PERCENTAGE BREAKDOWN OF NUMBER (AS OF 1/1/71) OF
MANUFACTURING SUBSIDIARIES OF NON-U.S.-BASED PARENT SYSTEMS BY
GNP PER CAPITA IN 1970 OF SUBSIDIARY'S COUNTRY
FOR SUBSIDIARIES CLASSIFIED BY
PRINCIPAL INDUSTRY OF SUBSIDIARY AS OF 1/1/71
(CONTINUED)

PRINCIPAL INDUSTRY OF SUBSIDIARY AS OF 1/1/71	GNP PER CAPITA IN 1970 OF SUBSIDIARY'S COUNTRY					TOTAL PERCENT	TOTAL NUMBER
	UNDER $200	$200-$500	$500-$1200	$1200-$2500	OVER $2500		
TIRES	22.	11.	22.	19.	25.	100.	36
OTHER RUBBER PRODUCTS	4.3	13.	31.	19.	33.	100.	70
LEATHER PRODUCTS AND SHOES	17.	33.	23.	0.	17.	100.	6
GLASS PRODUCTS	2.0	4.0	20.	20.	54.	100.	50
STONE, CLAY AND CONCRETE	2.6	18.	21.	13.	45.	100.	77
IRON AND STEEL PRODUCTS	15.	14.	16.	13.	41.	100.	173
NON-FERROUS SMELTING	7.4	3.2	16.	18.	55.	100.	94
NON-FERROUS PRODUCTS	8.6	5.8	23.	17.	45.	100.	139
METAL CANS	22.	9.4	31.	16.	22.	100.	32
STRUCTURAL METAL PRODUCTS	6.5	13.	21.	18.	42.	100.	62
FABRICATED WIRE PRODUCTS	28.	23.	8.5	13.	28.	100.	47
OTHER FABRICATED METAL	8.9	8.9	11.	23.	48.	100.	169
ENGINES AND TURBINES	8.3	15.	15.	17.	46.	100.	48
FARM MACHINERY	15.	24.	30.	9.1	21.	100.	33
CONSTRUCTION MACHINERY	14.	23.	18.	18.	27.	100.	22
SPECIAL INDUSTRY MACHINERY	6.3	7.5	14.	24.	49.	100.	80
GENERAL INDUSTRY MACHINERY	5.3	8.0	15.	24.	48.	100.	75
OFFICE MACHINES + COMPUTERS	0.	14.	29.	18.	39.	100.	28
OTHER NON-ELECTR. MACHINERY	3.4	14.	21.	24.	38.	100.	29
ELECTR. TRANSMISSION EQUIP	11.	18.	19.	15.	37.	100.	91
ELECTRIC LIGHTING AND WIRING	14.	13.	29.	17.	27.	100.	105
RADIOS, TV'S + APPLIANCES	10.	16.	18.	23.	33.	100.	159
COMMUNICATIONS EQUIPMENT	5.6	20.	24.	20.	30.	100.	89

TABLE CONTINUED ON NEXT PAGE

CROSS-TABULATION 3.6.1: PERCENTAGE BREAKDOWN OF NUMBER (AS OF 1/1/71) OF
MANUFACTURING SUBSIDIARIES OF NON-U.S.-BASED PARENT SYSTEMS BY
GNP PER CAPITA IN 1970 OF SUBSIDIARY'S COUNTRY
FOR SUBSIDIARIES CLASSIFIED BY
PRINCIPAL INDUSTRY OF SUBSIDIARY AS OF 1/1/71
(CONTINUED)

GNP PER CAPITA IN 1970 OF SUBSIDIARY'S COUNTRY

PRINCIPAL INDUSTRY OF SUBSIDIARY AS OF 1/1/71	UNDER $200	$200-$500	$500-$1200	$1200-$2500	OVER $2500	TOTAL PERCENT	TOTAL NUMBER
ELECTRONIC COMPONENTS........	1.0	12.	9.1	24.	54.	100.	99
OTHER ELECTRICAL EQUIPMENT...	6.3	11.	15.	25.	42.	100.	189
MOTOR VEHICLES AND EQUIPMENT.	17.	25.	27.	8.7	22.	100.	183
OTHER TRANSPORTATION.........	10.	15.	17.	5.8	51.	100.	59
PRECISION GOODS..............	2.6	1.3	12.	24.	60.	100.	78
MISCELLANEOUS PRODUCTS.......	3.8	6.4	10.	38.	41.	100.	78

CROSS-TABULATION 3.6.2: PERCENTAGE BREAKDOWN OF NUMBER (AS OF 1/1/68) OF MANUFACTURING SUBSIDIARIES OF U.S.-BASED PARENT SYSTEMS BY GNP PER CAPITA IN 1970 OF SUBSIDIARY'S COUNTRY FOR SUBSIDIARIES CLASSIFIED BY PRINCIPAL INDUSTRY OF SUBSIDIARY AS OF 1/1/68

PRINCIPAL INDUSTRY OF SUBSIDIARY AS OF 1/1/68	GNP PER CAPITA IN 1970 OF SUBSIDIARY'S COUNTRY					TOTAL PERCENT	TOTAL NUMBER
	UNDER $200	$200-$500	$500-$1200	$1200-$2500	OVER $2500		
ORDNANCE	9.1	18.	0.	18.	55.	100.	11
MEAT PRODUCTS	7.9	5.3	11.	34.	42.	100.	38
DAIRY PRODUCTS	7.8	23.	13.	10.	45.	100.	77
CANNED FOODS	7.7	19.	12.	25.	37.	100.	52
GRAIN MILL PRODUCTS	9.3	24.	26.	16.	25.	100.	97
BAKERY PRODUCTS	2.6	26.	26.	7.7	38.	100.	39
CONFECTIONERY PRODUCTS	8.2	15.	16.	26.	34.	100.	61
BEVERAGES	10.	22.	14.	29.	25.	100.	59
OTHER FOOD PRODUCTS	7.1	8.9	16.	32.	36.	100.	56
TOBACCO PRODUCTS	0.	0.	70.	0.	30.	100.	10
TEXTILES	11.	11.	26.	22.	30.	100.	88
APPAREL	7.1	14.	7.1	36.	36.	100.	14
LUMBER AND WOOD	4.8	14.	14.	19.	48.	100.	21
FURNITURE	5.9	0.	24.	24.	47.	100.	17
PAPER PRODUCTS	5.0	23.	29.	14.	30.	100.	159
PRINTED MATTER	3.6	3.6	29.	29.	36.	100.	28
INDUSTRIAL CHEMICALS	15.	11.	13.	25.	35.	100.	251
PLASTICS AND SYNTHETICS	12.	13.	14.	32.	30.	100.	166
DRUGS	15.	20.	21.	19.	24.	100.	329
SOAP AND COSMETICS	10.	18.	17.	19.	35.	100.	149
PAINTS	9.8	22.	16.	24.	29.	100.	51
AGRICULTURAL CHEMICALS	22.	24.	18.	6.1	29.	100.	49
OTHER CHEMICALS	7.5	15.	18.	33.	28.	100.	80
REFINED PETROLEUM	4.7	18.	12.	28.	37.	100.	129
OTHER PETROLEUM PRODUCTS	8.6	16.	11.	21.	43.	100.	70

TABLE CONTINUED ON NEXT PAGE

129

CROSS-TABULATION 3.6.2: PERCENTAGE BREAKDOWN OF NUMBER (AS OF 1/1/68) OF
MANUFACTURING SUBSIDIARIES OF U.S.-BASED PARENT SYSTEMS BY
GNP PER CAPITA IN 1970 OF SUBSIDIARY'S COUNTRY
FOR SUBSIDIARIES CLASSIFIED BY
PRINCIPAL INDUSTRY OF SUBSIDIARY AS OF 1/1/68
(CONTINUED)

GNP PER CAPITA IN 1970 OF SUBSIDIARY'S COUNTRY

PRINCIPAL INDUSTRY OF SUBSIDIARY AS OF 1/1/68	UNDER $200	$200-$500	$500-$1200	$1200-$2500	OVER $2500	TOTAL PERCENT	TOTAL NUMBER
TIRES	14.	25.	23.	15.	23.	100.	81
OTHER RUBBER PRODUCTS	19.	9.4	25.	22.	25.	100.	32
LEATHER PRODUCTS AND SHOES	7.7	15.	23.	31.	23.	100.	13
GLASS PRODUCTS	2.5	20.	25.	25.	28.	100.	40
STONE, CLAY AND CONCRETE	17.	8.0	17.	24.	33.	100.	75
IRON AND STEEL PRODUCTS	9.1	12.	15.	36.	27.	100.	33
NON-FERROUS SMELTING	9.5	12.	14.	14.	50.	100.	42
NON-FERROUS PRODUCTS	14.	11.	14.	28.	33.	100.	36
METAL CANS	13.	13.	23.	17.	33.	100.	30
STRUCTURAL METAL PRODUCTS	7.4	15.	11.	26.	41.	100.	27
FABRICATED WIRE PRODUCTS	7.7	23.	15.	23.	31.	100.	13
OTHER FABRICATED METAL	4.9	9.7	16.	28.	41.	100.	144
ENGINES AND TURBINES	0.	12.	0.	5.9	82.	100.	17
FARM MACHINERY	8.8	12.	29.9	15.	35.	100.	34
CONSTRUCTION MACHINERY	15.	7.4	9.9	20.	48.	100.	81
SPECIAL INDUSTRY MACHINERY	5.1	7.7	13.	40.	35.	100.	78
GENERAL INDUSTRY MACHINERY	12.	8.6	10.	28.	41.	100.	58
OFFICE MACHINES + COMPUTERS	12.	9.8	5.9	31.	41.	100.	51
OTHER NON-ELECTR. MACHINERY	8.5	8.5	11.	21.	51.	100.	47
ELECTR. TRANSMISSION EQUIP.	17.	8.3	4.2	38.	33.	100.	24
ELECTRIC LIGHTING AND WIRING	11.	22.	11.	19.	37.	100.	27
RADIOS, TV'S + APPLIANCES	15.	15.	17.	26.	26.	100.	87
COMMUNICATIONS EQUIPMENT	6.3	16.	9.4	25.	44.	100.	32

TABLE CONTINUED ON NEXT PAGE

CROSS-TABULATION 3.6.2: PERCENTAGE BREAKDOWN OF NUMBER (AS OF 1/1/68) OF MANUFACTURING SUBSIDIARIES OF U.S.-BASED PARENT SYSTEMS BY GNP PER CAPITA IN 1970 OF SUBSIDIARY'S COUNTRY FOR SUBSIDIARIES CLASSIFIED BY PRINCIPAL INDUSTRY OF SUBSIDIARY AS OF 1/1/68 (CONTINUED)

PRINCIPAL INDUSTRY OF SUBSIDIARY AS OF 1/1/68	GNP PER CAPITA IN 1970 OF SUBSIDIARY'S COUNTRY					TOTAL PERCENT	TOTAL NUMBER
	UNDER $200	$200-$500	$500-$1200	$1200-$2500	OVER $2500		
ELECTRONIC COMPONENTS.........	13.	10.	13.	28.	38.	100.	40
OTHER ELECTRICAL EQUIPMENT...	15.	26.	9.3	22.	28.	100.	97
MOTOR VEHICLES AND EQUIPMENT.	10.	14.	21.	22.	33.	100.	206
OTHER TRANSPORTATION.........	5.3	0.	5.3	32.	58.	100.	19
PRECISION GOODS..............	6.8	14.	5.4	27.	47.	100.	74
MISCELLANEOUS PRODUCTS.......	12.	17.	17.	21.	33.	100.	66

CROSS-TABULATION 3.8.1: PERCENTAGE BREAKDOWN OF NUMBER (AS OF 1/1/71) OF MANUFACTURING SUBSIDIARIES OF NON-U.S.-BASED PARENT SYSTEMS BY GNP PER CAPITA IN 1970 OF SUBSIDIARY'S COUNTRY FOR SUBSIDIARIES CLASSIFIED BY PRINCIPAL INDUSTRY-GROUP OF SUBSIDIARY AS OF 1/1/71

PRINCIPAL INDUSTRY-GROUP OF SUBSIDIARY AS OF 1/1/71	GNP PER CAPITA IN 1970 OF SUBSIDIARY'S COUNTRY					TOTAL PERCENT	TOTAL NUMBER
	UNDER $200	$200-$500	$500-$1200	$1200-$2500	OVER $2500		
FOOD AND TOBACCO............	8.9	11.	22.	17.	42.	100.	673
TEXTILES AND APPAREL........	18.	27.	24.	6.3	24.	100.	270
WOOD, FURNITURE AND PAPER...	3.8	9.5	14.	20.	53.	100.	210
CHEMICALS...................	8.3	13.	21.	19.	39.	100.	1238
PETROLEUM...................	11.	16.	12.	20.	42.	100.	189
RUBBER AND TIRES............	10.	12.	28.	19.	30.	100.	106
PRIMARY METALS..............	11.	9.1	19.	16.	46.	100.	408
FABR. METAL + NON-EL. MACH..	10.	12.	16.	20.	41.	100.	598
ELECTRIC AND ELECTRONIC.....	7.6	14.	19.	22.	37.	100.	781
TRANSPORTATION EQUIPMENT....	15.	22.	25.	8.3	29.	100.	242
PRECISION GOODS.............	2.6	1.3	12.	24.	60.	100.	78
OTHER.......................	6.0	11.	16.	23.	43.	100.	332

CROSS-TABULATION 3.8.2: PERCENTAGE BREAKDOWN OF NUMBER (AS OF 1/1/68) OF MANUFACTURING SUBSIDIARIES OF U.S.-BASED PARENT SYSTEMS BY GNP PER CAPITA IN 1970 OF SUBSIDIARY'S COUNTRY FOR SUBSIDIARIES CLASSIFIED BY PRINCIPAL INDUSTRY-GROUP OF SUBSIDIARY AS OF 1/1/68

PRINCIPAL INDUSTRY-GROUP OF SUBSIDIARY AS OF 1/1/68	GNP PER CAPITA IN 1970 OF SUBSIDIARY'S COUNTRY					TOTAL PERCENT	TOTAL NUMBER
	UNDER $200	$200-$500	$500-$1200	$1200-$2500	OVER $2500		
FOOD AND TOBACCO	7.8	18.	18.	21.	34.	100.	503
TEXTILES AND APPAREL	11.	12.	24.	24.	30.	100.	102
WOOD, FURNITURE AND PAPER	5.1	20.	27.	15.	33.	100.	197
CHEMICALS	13.	16.	17.	23.	30.	100.	1079
PETROLEUM	6.0	17.	12.	26.	39.	100.	199
RUBBER AND TIRES	15.	20.	24.	17.	24.	100.	113
PRIMARY METALS	11.	12.	14.	25.	38.	100.	111
FABR. METAL + NON-EL. MACH.	8.3	9.8	14.	26.	42.	100.	530
ELECTRIC AND ELECTRONIC	13.	17.	11.	26.	33.	100.	358
TRANSPORTATION EQUIPMENT	9.8	12.	20.	23.	35.	100.	225
PRECISION GOODS	6.8	14.	5.4	27.	47.	100.	74
OTHER	11.	13.	19.	24.	33.	100.	233

CROSS-TABULATION 3.21.1: PERCENTAGE BREAKDOWN OF NUMBER (AS OF 1/1/71) OF
MANUFACTURING SUBSIDIARIES OF NON-U.S.-BASED PARENT SYSTEMS BY
GNP PER CAPITA IN 1970 OF SUBSIDIARY'S COUNTRY
FOR SUBSIDIARIES CLASSIFIED BY
NATIONAL BASE OF SUBSIDIARY'S PARENT SYSTEM

NATIONAL BASE OF SUBSIDIARY'S PARENT SYSTEM	GNP PER CAPITA IN 1970 OF SUBSIDIARY'S COUNTRY						
	UNDER $200	$200-$500	$500-$1200	$1200-$2500	OVER $2500	TOTAL PERCENT	TOTAL NUMBER
UNITED KINGDOM............	12.	8.3	21.	15.	44.	100.	2243
GERMANY..................	5.1	14.	23.	22.	36.	100.	780
FRANCE...................	7.6	18.	24.	18.	31.	100.	422
ITALY....................	5.5	20.	40.	14.	20.	100.	128
BELGIUM AND LUXEMBURG....	2.0	8.4	13.	18.	58.	100.	249
THE NETHERLANDS..........	2.8	8.1	9.7	27.	52.	100.	422
SWEDEN...................	4.2	11.	12.	30.	43.	100.	166
SWITZERLAND..............	4.1	7.7	16.	28.	44.	100.	390
JAPAN....................	28.	45.	17.	1.1	9.0	100.	476
CANADA...................	2.6	9.2	18.	37.	33.	100.	195
OTHER NON-U.S............	0.	5.2	5.2	14.	76.	100.	96

134

CROSS-TABULATION 3.22.1: PERCENTAGE BREAKDOWN OF NUMBER (AS OF 1/1/71) OF MANUFACTURING SUBSIDIARIES OF NON-U.S.-BASED PARENT SYSTEMS BY GNP PER CAPITA IN 1970 OF SUBSIDIARY'S COUNTRY FOR SUBSIDIARIES CLASSIFIED BY VALUE OF SALES OF SUBSIDIARY'S PARENT SYSTEM IN 1970

VALUE OF SALES OF SUBSIDIARY'S PARENT SYSTEM IN 1970	GNP PER CAPITA IN 1970 OF SUBSIDIARY'S COUNTRY					TOTAL PERCENT	TOTAL NUMBER
	UNDER $200	$200-$500	$500-$1200	$1200-$2500	OVER $2500		
$400 - 599 MILLION..............	10.	12.	19.	18.	41.	100.	1055
$600 - 999 MILLION..............	9.0	12.	19.	20.	40.	100.	852
$1 - 2 BILLION.................	7.4	13.	21.	18.	41.	100.	1601
OVER $2 BILLION................	10.	15.	19.	18.	39.	100.	1929

CROSS-TABULATION 3.22.2: PERCENTAGE BREAKDOWN OF NUMBER (AS OF 1/1/68) OF
MANUFACTURING SUBSIDIARIES OF U.S.-BASED PARENT SYSTEMS BY
GNP PER CAPITA IN 1970 OF SUBSIDIARY'S COUNTRY
FOR SUBSIDIARIES CLASSIFIED BY
VALUE OF SALES OF SUBSIDIARY'S PARENT SYSTEM IN 1967

VALUE OF SALES OF SUBSIDIARY'S PARENT SYSTEM IN 1967	GNP PER CAPITA IN 1970 OF SUBSIDIARY'S COUNTRY					TOTAL PERCENT	TOTAL NUMBER
	UNDER $200	$200-$500	$500-$1200	$1200-$2500	OVER $2500		
$100 - 399 MILLION.........	10.	13.	15.	26.	35.	100.	823
$400 - 599 MILLION.........	13.	15.	17.	22.	33.	100.	699
$600 - 999 MILLION.........	9.0	14.	19.	22.	37.	100.	891
$1 - 2 BILLION.........	11.	17.	17.	23.	32.	100.	948
OVER $2 BILLION.........	7.9	16.	17.	22.	37.	100.	757

CROSS-TABULATION 3.23.1: PERCENTAGE BREAKDOWN OF NUMBER (AS OF 1/1/71) OF MANUFACTURING SUBSIDIARIES OF NON-U.S.-BASED PARENT SYSTEMS BY GNP PER CAPITA IN 1970 OF SUBSIDIARY'S COUNTRY FOR SUBSIDIARIES CLASSIFIED BY PRINCIPAL INDUSTRY-GROUP OF SUBSIDIARY'S PARENT SYSTEM AS OF 1/1/71

PRINCIPAL INDUSTRY-GROUP OF SUBSIDIARY'S PARENT SYSTEM AS OF 1/1/71	GNP PER CAPITA IN 1970 OF SUBSIDIARY'S COUNTRY					TOTAL PERCENT	TOTAL NUMBER
	UNDER $200	$200-$500	$500-$1200	$1200-$2500	OVER $2500		
FOOD, TOBACCO AND SOAP......	9.5	8.2	22.	17.	43.	100.	939
CHEMICALS AND DRUGS..........	7.7	12.	21.	19.	40.	100.	1253
PETROLEUM...................	9.5	15.	14.	22.	40.	100.	274
IRON AND STEEL..............	7.4	17.	17.	15.	44.	100.	216
NON-FERROUS METALS..........	7.4	6.5	23.	23.	41.	100.	417
FABR. METAL + NON-EL. MACH...	8.5	10.	17.	19.	45.	100.	437
ELECTRIC AND ELECTRONIC.....	5.8	12.	17.	22.	43.	100.	959
AUTOMOBILES.................	11.	22.	38.	5.4	23.	100.	147
OTHER.......................	16.	24.	17.	12.	32.	100.	925

CROSS-TABULATION 3.23.2: PERCENTAGE BREAKDOWN OF NUMBER (AS OF 1/1/68) OF MANUFACTURING SUBSIDIARIES OF U.S.-BASED PARENT SYSTEMS BY GNP PER CAPITA IN 1970 OF SUBSIDIARY'S COUNTRY

FOR SUBSIDIARIES CLASSIFIED BY
PRINCIPAL INDUSTRY-GROUP OF SUBSIDIARY'S PARENT SYSTEM AS OF 1/1/68

PRINCIPAL INDUSTRY-GROUP OF SUBSIDIARY'S PARENT SYSTEM AS OF 1/1/68	GNP PER CAPITA IN 1970 OF SUBSIDIARY'S COUNTRY						
	UNDER $200	$200-$500	$500-$1200	$1200-$2500	OVER $2500	TOTAL PERCENT	TOTAL NUMBER
FOOD, TOBACCO AND SOAP	9.3	19.	17.	19.	36.	100.	697
CHEMICALS AND DRUGS	13.	17.	16.	24.	31.	100.	1100
PETROLEUM	5.5	17.	16.	24.	37.	100.	330
IRON AND STEEL	4.5	9.1	27.	18.	41.	100.	22
NON-FERROUS METALS	13.	19.	12.	24.	32.	100.	123
FABR. METAL + NON-EL. MACH.	8.7	11.	18.	24.	39.	100.	462
ELECTRIC AND ELECTRONIC	11.	15.	15.	23.	37.	100.	438
AUTOMOBILES	13.	11.	18.	20.	37.	100.	239
OTHER	9.0	13.	19.	25.	33.	100.	792

CROSS-TABULATION 3.25.1: PERCENTAGE BREAKDOWN OF NUMBER (AS OF 1/1/71) OF
MANUFACTURING SUBSIDIARIES OF NON-U.S.-BASED PARENT SYSTEMS BY
GNP PER CAPITA IN 1970 OF SUBSIDIARY'S COUNTRY
FOR SUBSIDIARIES CLASSIFIED BY
NUMBER OF COUNTRIES IN WHICH SUBSIDIARY'S PARENT SYSTEM MANUFACTURED AS OF 1/1/71

NUMBER OF COUNTRIES SUB-SIDIARY'S PARENT SYSTEM MANUFACTURED IN AS OF 1/1/71	GNP PER CAPITA IN 1970 OF SUBSIDIARY'S COUNTRY						
	UNDER $200	$200-$500	$500-$1200	$1200-$2500	OVER $2500	TOTAL PERCENT	TOTAL NUMBER
TWO OR THREE.....................	14.	48.	6.9	5.2	26.	100.	58
FOUR TO SIX......................	13.	20.	25.	7.9	34.	100.	394
SEVEN TO TWELVE..................	12.	20.	23.	14.	31.	100.	621
THIRTEEN OR MORE.................	8.5	11.	19.	20.	42.	100.	4489

CROSS-TABULATION 3.25.2: PERCENTAGE BREAKDOWN OF NUMBER (AS OF 1/1/68) OF
MANUFACTURING SUBSIDIARIES OF U.S.-BASED PARENT SYSTEMS BY
GNP PER CAPITA IN 1970 OF SUBSIDIARY'S COUNTRY
FOR SUBSIDIARIES CLASSIFIED BY
NUMBER OF COUNTRIES IN WHICH SUBSIDIARY'S PARENT SYSTEM MANUFACTURED AS OF 1/1/68

NUMBER OF COUNTRIES IN WHICH SUBSIDIARY'S PARENT SYSTEM MANUFACTURED AS OF 1/1/68	GNP PER CAPITA IN 1970 OF SUBSIDIARY'S COUNTRY						
	UNDER $200	$200-$500	$500-$1200	$1200-$2500	OVER $2500	TOTAL PERCENT	TOTAL NUMBER
TWO OR THREE..........	0.	0.	0.	0.	0.	100.	0
FOUR TO SIX..........	15.	0.	15.	33.	37.	100.	27
SEVEN TO TWELVE......	11.	9.5	15.	25.	40.	100.	993
THIRTEEN OR MORE.....	9.9	17.	16.	22.	33.	100.	3156

CROSS-TABULATION 3.26.1: PERCENTAGE BREAKDOWN OF NUMBER (AS OF 1/1/71) OF
MANUFACTURING SUBSIDIARIES OF NON-U.S.-BASED PARENT SYSTEMS BY
GNP PER CAPITA IN 1970 OF SUBSIDIARY'S COUNTRY
FOR SUBSIDIARIES CLASSIFIED BY
PERCENTAGE OF PARENT SYSTEM'S EMPLOYEES OUTSIDE NATIONAL BASE AS OF 1/1/71

PERCENTAGE OF PARENT SYSTEM'S EMPLOYEES OUTSIDE NATIONAL BASE AS OF 1/1/71	GNP PER CAPITA IN 1970 OF SUBSIDIARY'S COUNTRY						
	UNDER $200	$200-$500	$500-$1200	$1200-$2500	OVER $2500	TOTAL PERCENT	TOTAL NUMBER
UNDER 10%..................	14.	24.	16.	14.	32.	100.	478
10% - 25%..................	7.9	10.	24.	17.	41.	100.	1351
25% - 50%..................	8.3	12.	20.	18.	41.	100.	989
OVER 50%..................	9.0	11.	15.	21.	43.	100.	1869

CROSS-TABULATION 3.27.1: PERCENTAGE BREAKDOWN OF NUMBER (AS OF 1/1/71) OF
MANUFACTURING SUBSIDIARIES OF NON-U.S.-BASED PARENT SYSTEMS BY
GNP PER CAPITA IN 1970 OF SUBSIDIARY'S COUNTRY
FOR SUBSIDIARIES CLASSIFIED BY
NO. OF INDUSTRIES IN WHICH PARENT SYSTEM MANUFACTURED WITHIN NATIONAL BASE AS OF 1/1/71

NO. OF INDUSTRIES IN WHICH PARENT SYSTEM MANUF. WITHIN NATIONAL BASE AS OF 1/1/71	GNP PER CAPITA IN 1970 OF SUBSIDIARY'S COUNTRY					TOTAL PERCENT	TOTAL NUMBER
	UNDER $200	$200-$500	$500-$1200	$1200-$2500	OVER $2500		
ONE TO THREE...........	20.	26.	17.	13.	25.	100.	412
FOUR TO NINE...........	9.6	17.	21.	16.	36.	100.	1697
TEN TO NINETEEN........	8.1	11.	21.	19.	40.	100.	2367
TWENTY OR MORE.........	7.2	7.1	15.	21.	50.	100.	1091

CROSS-TABULATION 3.27.2: PERCENTAGE BREAKDOWN OF NUMBER (AS OF 1/1/68) OF
MANUFACTURING SUBSIDIARIES OF U.S.-BASED PARENT SYSTEMS BY
GNP PER CAPITA IN 1970 OF SUBSIDIARY'S COUNTRY
FOR SUBSIDIARIES CLASSIFIED BY
NO. OF INDUSTRIES IN WHICH PARENT SYSTEM MANUFACTURED WITHIN NATIONAL BASE AS OF 1/1/68

NO. OF INDUSTRIES IN WHICH PARENT SYSTEM MANUF. WITHIN NATIONAL BASE AS OF 1/1/68	GNP PER CAPITA IN 1970 OF SUBSIDIARY'S COUNTRY						
	UNDER $200	$200-$500	$500-$1200	$1200-$2500	OVER $2500	TOTAL PERCENT	TOTAL NUMBER
ONE TO THREE....	11.	20.	17.	20.	32.	100.	384
FOUR TO NINE....	9.4	15.	17.	22.	37.	100.	1427
TEN TO NINETEEN....	11.	15.	18.	23.	32.	100.	1451
TWENTY OR MORE....	9.9	14.	17.	23.	35.	100.	858

CROSS-TABULATION 3.28.1: PERCENTAGE BREAKDOWN OF NUMBER (AS OF 1/1/71) OF
MANUFACTURING SUBSIDIARIES OF NON-U.S.-BASED PARENT SYSTEMS BY
GNP PER CAPITA IN 1970 OF SUBSIDIARY'S COUNTRY
FOR SUBSIDIARIES CLASSIFIED BY
NO. OF INDUSTRIES IN WHICH PARENT SYSTEM MANUFACTURED OUTSIDE NATIONAL BASE AS OF 1/1/71

NO. OF INDUSTRIES IN WHICH PARENT SYSTEM MANUF. OUTSIDE NATIONAL BASE AS OF 1/1/71	GNP PER CAPITA IN 1970 OF SUBSIDIARY'S COUNTRY						
	UNDER $200	$200- $500	$500- $1200	$1200- $2500	OVER $2500	TOTAL PERCENT	TOTAL NUMBER
ONE TO THREE................	9.1	17.	26.	16.	32.	100.	342
FOUR TO NINE................	11.	18.	20.	17.	35.	100.	1337
TEN TO NINETEEN.............	8.3	11.	24.	19.	37.	100.	1677
TWENTY OR MORE..............	9.1	11.	15.	18.	46.	100.	2211

CROSS-TABULATION 3.28.2: PERCENTAGE BREAKDOWN OF NUMBER (AS OF 1/1/68) OF
MANUFACTURING SUBSIDIARIES OF U.S.-BASED PARENT SYSTEMS BY
GNP PER CAPITA IN 1970 OF SUBSIDIARY'S COUNTRY
FOR SUBSIDIARIES CLASSIFIED BY

NO. OF INDUSTRIES IN WHICH PARENT SYSTEM MANUFACTURED OUTSIDE NATIONAL BASE AS OF 1/1/68

NO. OF INDUSTRIES IN WHICH PARENT SYSTEM MANUF. OUTSIDE NATIONAL BASE AS OF 1/1/68	GNP PER CAPITA IN 1970 OF SUBSIDIARY'S COUNTRY						
	UNDER $200	$200—$500	$500—$1200	$1200—$2500	OVER $2500	TOTAL PERCENT	TOTAL NUMBER
ONE TO THREE..........	12.	14.	15.	23.	36.	100.	576
FOUR TO NINE..........	9.8	15.	18.	23.	34.	100.	2409
TEN TO NINETEEN.......	11.	16.	17.	22.	34.	100.	889
TWENTY OR MORE........	7.3	14.	16.	27.	35.	100.	329

CROSS-TABULATION 3.29.1: PERCENTAGE BREAKDOWN OF NUMBER (AS OF 1/1/71) OF
MANUFACTURING SUBSIDIARIES OF NON-U.S.-BASED PARENT SYSTEMS BY
GNP PER CAPITA IN 1970 OF SUBSIDIARY'S COUNTRY
FOR SUBSIDIARIES CLASSIFIED BY
PARENT SYSTEM'S R&D EXPENDITURES AS A PERCENTAGE OF SALES IN 1970

PARENT SYSTEM'S R&D EXPENDITURES AS A PERCENTAGE OF SALES IN 1970	GNP PER CAPITA IN 1970 OF SUBSIDIARY'S COUNTRY						
	UNDER $200	$200-$500	$500-$1200	$1200-$2500	OVER $2500	TOTAL PERCENT	TOTAL NUMBER
LESS THAN 1%................	8.0	15.	20.	20.	37.	100.	835
1% - 4%..................	7.4	12.	21.	20.	40.	100.	1575
MORE THAN 4%............	8.3	13.	20.	19.	40.	100.	1235

CROSS-TABULATION 3.29.2: PERCENTAGE BREAKDOWN OF NUMBER (AS OF 1/1/68) OF
MANUFACTURING SUBSIDIARIES OF U.S.-BASED PARENT SYSTEMS BY
GNP PER CAPITA IN 1970 OF SUBSIDIARY'S COUNTRY
FOR SUBSIDIARIES CLASSIFIED BY
PARENT SYSTEM'S R&D EXPENDITURES AS A PERCENTAGE OF SALES IN 1967

PARENT SYSTEM'S R&D	GNP PER CAPITA IN 1970 OF SUBSIDIARY'S COUNTRY						
EXPENDITURES AS A PERCENTAGE OF SALES IN 1967	UNDER $200	$200– $500	$500– $1200	$1200– $2500	OVER $2500	TOTAL PERCENT	TOTAL NUMBER
LESS THAN 1%..............	7.2	15.	14.	25.	39.	100.	306
1% – 4%...................	12.	14.	18.	22.	34.	100.	841
MORE THAN 4%.............	13.	13.	16.	28.	30.	100.	374

TABULATION 4.1: PERCENTAGE BREAKDOWN OF NUMBER OF SUBSIDIARIES BY GNP IN 1970 OF SUBSIDIARY'S COUNTRY FOR VARIOUS CATEGORIES OF SUBSIDIARIES

CATEGORY OF SUBSIDIARY	GNP IN 1970 OF SUBSIDIARY'S COUNTRY					TOTAL PERCENT	TOTAL NUMBER
	UNDER $1 BILLION	$1-5 BILLION	$5-20 BILLION	$20-100 BILLION	OVER $100 BILLION		
NON-U.S.-BASED SYSTEMS (AS OF 1/1/71):							
ALL SUBSIDIARIES......	3.5	12.	23.	32.	29.	100.	13440
MANUFACTURING SUBS.....	2.1	11.	24.	36.	27.	100.	5567
SALES SUBSIDIARIES.....	4.4	14.	23.	27.	32.	100.	3238
U.S.-BASED SYSTEMS (AS OF 1/1/68):							
ALL SUBSIDIARIES......	3.5	8.7	20.	44.	24.	100.	9558
MANUFACTURING SUBS.....	2.9	6.4	18.	48.	25.	100.	4204
SALES SUBSIDIARIES.....	3.5	12.	24.	38.	23.	100.	1632
WORLD SUBSET OF SYSTEMS (AS OF 1/1/68):							
NON-U.S.-BASED SYSTEMS:							
ALL SUBSIDIARIES......	3.9	12.	21.	35.	29.	100.	5977
MANUFACTURING SUBS.....	2.3	11.	21.	41.	25.	100.	2698
SALES SUBSIDIARIES.....	5.4	13.	24.	27.	31.	100.	1599
U.S.-BASED-SYSTEMS:							
ALL SUBSIDIARIES......	3.9	9.0	26.	44.	23.	100.	7939
MANUFACTURING SUBS.....	3.2	6.6	19.	48.	24.	100.	3296
SALES SUBSIDIARIES.....	4.1	12.	25.	36.	22.	100.	1279

TABULATION 4.2: PERCENTAGE BREAKDOWN OF SALES OF SUBSIDIARIES IN 1970 BY
GNP IN 1970 OF SUBSIDIARY'S COUNTRY
FOR ALL SUBSIDIARIES, MANUFACTURING SUBSIDIARIES AND SALES SUBSIDIARIES
OF NON-U.S.-BASED SYSTEMS

	GNP IN 1970 OF SUBSIDIARY'S COUNTRY						
CATEGORY OF SUBSIDIARY	UNDER $1 BILLION	$1-5 BILLION	$5-20 BILLION	$20-100 BILLION	OVER $100 BILLION	TOTAL PERCENT	TOTAL ($ MIL)
ALL SUBSIDIARIES..............	2.4	7.4	13.	31.	46.	100.	129959
MANUFACTURING SUBSIDIARIES...	1.4	6.7	11.	32.	48.	100.	81630
SALES SUBSIDIARIES............	1.5	6.7	18.	24.	50.	100.	23069

CROSS-TABULATION 4.6.1: PERCENTAGE BREAKDOWN OF NUMBER (AS OF 1/1/71) OF
MANUFACTURING SUBSIDIARIES OF NON-U.S.-BASED PARENT SYSTEMS BY
GNP IN 1970 OF SUBSIDIARY'S COUNTRY
FOR SUBSIDIARIES CLASSIFIED BY
PRINCIPAL INDUSTRY OF SUBSIDIARY AS OF 1/1/71

PRINCIPAL INDUSTRY OF SUBSIDIARY AS OF 1/1/71	GNP IN 1970 OF SUBSIDIARY'S COUNTRY						
	UNDER $1 BILLION	$1-5 BILLION	$5-20 BILLION	$20-100 BILLION	OVER $100 BILLION	TOTAL PERCENT	TOTAL NUMBER
ORDNANCE	0.	0.	38.	38.	25.	100.	8
MEAT PRODUCTS	7.1	21.	21.	29.	21.	100.	28
DAIRY PRODUCTS	1.1	15.	25.	38.	21.	100.	89
CANNED FOODS	0.	20.	20.	27.	34.	100.	41
GRAIN MILL PRODUCTS	0.	24.	36.	31.	8.9	100.	45
BAKERY PRODUCTS	0.	8.0	44.	47.	1.3	100.	75
CONFECTIONERY PRODUCTS	3.3	13.	33.	40.	10.	100.	30
BEVERAGES	2.6	31.	14.	28.	24.	100.	153
OTHER FOOD PRODUCTS	1.4	13.	31.	34.	21.	100.	140
TOBACCO PRODUCTS	17.	34.	14.	28.	6.9	100.	58
TEXTILES	2.2	14.	41.	29.	14.	100.	230
APPAREL	2.5	28.	43.	20.	7.5	100.	40
LUMBER AND WOOD	3.8	15.	32.	30.	19.	100.	53
FURNITURE	0.	5.6	28.	28.	39.	100.	18
PAPER PRODUCTS	2.2	11.	14.	51.	22.	100.	139
PRINTED MATTER	1.0	20.	12.	32.	35.	100.	97
INDUSTRIAL CHEMICALS	2.9	8.3	19.	43.	27.	100.	240
PLASTICS AND SYNTHETICS	0.7	2.0	20.	44.	34.	100.	153
DRUGS	0.	8.8	28.	33.	30.	100.	227
SOAP AND COSMETICS	1.9	14.	32.	27.	25.	100.	154
PAINTS	0.9	11.	23.	37.	29.	100.	111
AGRICULTURAL CHEMICALS	0.	19.	13.	37.	31.	100.	78
OTHER CHEMICALS	1.3	8.4	25.	34.	32.	100.	155
REFINED PETROLEUM	11.	22.	17.	24.	26.	100.	106
OTHER PETROLEUM PRODUCTS	2.4	18.	19.	29.	31.	100.	83

TABLE CONTINUED ON NEXT PAGE

CROSS-TABULATION 4.6.1: PERCENTAGE BREAKDOWN OF NUMBER (AS OF 1/1/71) OF
MANUFACTURING SUBSIDIARIES OF NON-U.S.-BASED PARENT SYSTEMS BY
GNP IN 1970 OF SUBSIDIARY'S COUNTRY
FOR SUBSIDIARIES CLASSIFIED BY
PRINCIPAL INDUSTRY OF SUBSIDIARY AS OF 1/1/71
(CONTINUED)

GNP IN 1970 OF SUBSIDIARY'S COUNTRY

PRINCIPAL INDUSTRY OF SUBSIDIARY AS OF 1/1/71	UNDER $1 BILLION	$1-5 BILLION	$5-20 BILLION	$20-100 BILLION	OVER $100 BILLION	TOTAL PERCENT	TOTAL NUMBER
TIRES	2.8	17.	22.	28.	31.	100.	36
OTHER RUBBER PRODUCTS	1.4	5.7	37.	39.	17.	100.	70
LEATHER PRODUCTS AND SHOES	0.	0.	33.	50.	17.	100.	6
GLASS PRODUCTS	0.	2.0	6.0	62.	30.	100.	50
STONE, CLAY AND CONCRETE	3.9	12.	16.	51.	18.	100.	77
IRON AND STEEL PRODUCTS	5.2	8.7	22.	41.	23.	100.	173
NON-FERROUS SMELTING	3.2	6.4	23.	39.	29.	100.	94
NON-FERROUS PRODUCTS	2.2	9.4	29.	42.	17.	100.	139
METAL CANS	3.1	28.	25.	28.	16.	100.	32
STRUCTURAL METAL PRODUCTS	0.	11.	34.	27.	27.	100.	62
FABRICATED WIRE PRODUCTS	0.	17.	23.	40.	19.	100.	47
OTHER FABRICATED METAL	1.9	10.	16.	35.	37.	100.	169
ENGINES AND TURBINES	0.	8.3	6.3	50.	35.	100.	48
FARM MACHINERY	3.0	12.	15.	52.	18.	100.	33
CONSTRUCTION MACHINERY	0.	14.	27.	41.	18.	100.	22
SPECIAL INDUSTRY MACHINERY	0.	3.8	18.	30.	49.	100.	80
GENERAL INDUSTRY MACHINERY	0.	4.0	12.	43.	41.	100.	75
OFFICE MACHINES + COMPUTERS	0.	3.6	21.	39.	36.	100.	28
OTHER NON-ELECTR. MACHINERY	0.	3.4	24.	31.	41.	100.	29
ELECTR. TRANSMISSION EQUIP.	0.	2.2	31.	43.	24.	100.	91
ELECTRIC LIGHTING AND WIRING	1.9	5.7	42.	38.	12.	100.	105
RADIOS, TV'S + APPLIANCES	0.6	11.	31.	31.	26.	100.	159
COMMUNICATIONS EQUIPMENT	1.1	9.0	35.	39.	16.	100.	89

TABLE CONTINUED ON NEXT PAGE

CROSS-TABULATION 4. 6.1: PERCENTAGE BREAKDOWN OF NUMBER (AS OF 1/1/71) OF
MANUFACTURING SUBSIDIARIES OF NON-U.S.-BASED PARENT SYSTEMS BY
GNP IN 1970 OF SUBSIDIARY'S COUNTRY
FOR SUBSIDIARIES CLASSIFIED BY
PRINCIPAL INDUSTRY OF SUBSIDIARY AS OF 1/1/71
(CONTINUED)

GNP IN 1970 OF SUBSIDIARY'S COUNTRY

PRINCIPAL INDUSTRY OF SUBSIDIARY AS OF 1/1/71	UNDER $1 BILLION	$1-5 BILLION	$5-20 BILLION	$20-100 BILLION	OVER $100 BILLION	TOTAL PERCENT	TOTAL NUMBER
ELECTRONIC COMPONENTS.........	2.0	5.1	15.	24.	54.	100.	99
OTHER ELECTRICAL EQUIPMENT....	2.1	9.5	22.	33.	33.	100.	189
MOTOR VEHICLES AND EQUIPMENT.	2.2	12.	31.	45.	9.8	100.	183
OTHER TRANSPORTATION..........	0.	10.	29.	42.	19.	100.	59
PRECISION GOODS...............	0.	0.	12.	27.	62.	100.	78
MISCELLANEOUS PRODUCTS........	1.3	7.7	14.	22.	55.	100.	78

152

CROSS-TABULATION 4.6.2: PERCENTAGE BREAKDOWN OF NUMBER (AS OF 1/1/68) OF
MANUFACTURING SUBSIDIARIES OF U.S.-BASED PARENT SYSTEMS BY
GNP IN 1970 OF SUBSIDIARY'S COUNTRY
FOR SUBSIDIARIES CLASSIFIED BY
PRINCIPAL INDUSTRY OF SUBSIDIARY AS OF 1/1/68

PRINCIPAL INDUSTRY OF SUBSIDIARY AS OF 1/1/68	UNDER $1 BILLION	$1-5 BILLION	$5-20 BILLION	$20-100 BILLION	OVER $100 BILLION	TOTAL PERCENT	TOTAL NUMBER
ORDNANCE	9.1	0.	0.	64.	27.	100.	11
MEAT PRODUCTS	0.	5.3	16.	63.	16.	100.	38
DAIRY PRODUCTS	2.6	17.	23.	44.	13.	100.	77
CANNED FOODS	5.8	5.8	19.	50.	19.	100.	52
GRAIN MILL PRODUCTS	6.2	11.	25.	39.	19.	100.	97
BAKERY PRODUCTS	7.7	5.1	28.	38.	21.	100.	39
CONFECTIONERY PRODUCTS	3.3	11.	21.	44.	20.	100.	61
BEVERAGES	5.1	3.4	14.	41.	37.	100.	59
OTHER FOOD PRODUCTS	1.8	7.1	16.	52.	23.	100.	56
TOBACCO PRODUCTS	0.	0.	60.	40.	0.	100.	10
TEXTILES	2.3	3.4	28.	39.	27.	100.	88
APPAREL	0.	14.	7.1	43.	36.	100.	14
LUMBER AND WOOD	4.8	9.5	4.8	62.	19.	100.	21
FURNITURE	0.	0.	12.	47.	41.	100.	17
PAPER PRODUCTS	4.4	10.	29.	42.	14.	100.	159
PRINTED MATTER	0.	3.6	18.	46.	32.	100.	28
INDUSTRIAL CHEMICALS	1.6	3.2	12.	61.	23.	100.	251
PLASTICS AND SYNTHETICS	2.4	2.4	14.	50.	31.	100.	166
DRUGS	3.3	6.7	26.	49.	16.	100.	329
SOAP AND COSMETICS	3.4	12.	22.	38.	25.	100.	149
PAINTS	5.9	18.	16.	47.	14.	100.	51
AGRICULTURAL CHEMICALS	14.	4.1	14.	53.	14.	100.	49
OTHER CHEMICALS	3.8	3.8	15.	48.	30.	100.	80
REFINED PETROLEUM	5.4	12.	22.	38.	22.	100.	129
OTHER PETROLEUM PRODUCTS	0.	2.9	19.	49.	30.	100.	70

GNP IN 1970 OF SUBSIDIARY'S COUNTRY

TABLE CONTINUED ON NEXT PAGE

CROSS-TABULATION 4.6.2: PERCENTAGE BREAKDOWN OF NUMBER (AS OF 1/1/68) OF
MANUFACTURING SUBSIDIARIES OF U.S.-BASED PARENT SYSTEMS BY
GNP IN 1970 OF SUBSIDIARY'S COUNTRY
FOR SUBSIDIARIES CLASSIFIED BY
PRINCIPAL INDUSTRY OF SUBSIDIARY AS OF 1/1/68
(CONTINUED)

GNP IN 1970 OF SUBSIDIARY'S COUNTRY

PRINCIPAL INDUSTRY OF SUBSIDIARY AS OF 1/1/68	UNDER $1 BILLION	$1-5 BILLION	$5-20 BILLION	$20-100 BILLION	OVER $100 BILLION	TOTAL PERCENT	TOTAL NUMBER
TIRES...................	4.9	9.9	30.	40.	16.	100.	81
OTHER RUBBER PRODUCTS...	6.3	16.	13.	50.	16.	100.	32
LEATHER PRODUCTS AND SHOES...	0.	23.	23.	46.	7.7	100.	13
GLASS PRODUCTS..........	0.	2.5	25.	45.	28.	100.	40
STONE, CLAY AND CONCRETE.....	5.3	2.7	19.	49.	24.	100.	75
IRON AND STEEL PRODUCTS.......	0.	3.0	15.	45.	36.	100.	33
NON-FERROUS SMELTING......	0.	9.5	21.	50.	19.	100.	42
NON-FERROUS PRODUCTS......	0.	8.3	11.	58.	22.	100.	36
METAL CANS.............	3.3	13.	20.	53.	10.	100.	30
STRUCTURAL METAL PRODUCTS.....	3.7	7.4	11.	48.	30.	100.	27
FABRICATED WIRE PRODUCTS.....	0.	0.	15.	54.	31.	100.	13
OTHER FABRICATED METAL.......	2.8	4.2	15.	49.	28.	100.	144
ENGINES AND TURBINES.....	0.	0.	0.	59.	41.	100.	17
FARM MACHINERY...........	0.	5.9	18.	50.	26.	100.	34
CONSTRUCTION MACHINERY.......	0.	0.	6.2	65.	28.	100.	81
SPECIAL INDUSTRY MACHINERY...	1.3	2.6	13.	44.	40.	100.	78
GENERAL INDUSTRY MACHINERY...	3.4	0.	10.	59.	28.	100.	58
OFFICE MACHINES + COMPUTERS..	0.	2.0	7.8	47.	43.	100.	51
OTHER NON-ELECTR. MACHINERY..	2.1	4.3	6.4	49.	38.	100.	47
ELECTR. TRANSMISSION EQUIP...	0.	0.	13.	67.	21.	100.	24
ELECTRIC LIGHTING AND WIRING.	3.7	0.	15.	56.	26.	100.	27
RADIOS, TV'S + APPLIANCES....	4.6	5.7	17.	41.	31.	100.	87
COMMUNICATIONS EQUIPMENT.....	6.3	6.3	19.	47.	22.	100.	32

TABLE CONTINUED ON NEXT PAGE

CROSS-TABULATION 4.6.2: PERCENTAGE BREAKDOWN OF NUMBER (AS OF 1/1/68) OF
MANUFACTURING SUBSIDIARIES OF U.S.-BASED PARENT SYSTEMS BY
GNP IN 1970 OF SUBSIDIARY'S COUNTRY
FOR SUBSIDIARIES CLASSIFIED BY
PRINCIPAL INDUSTRY OF SUBSIDIARY AS OF 1/1/68
(CONTINUED)

GNP IN 1970 OF SUBSIDIARY'S COUNTRY

PRINCIPAL INDUSTRY OF SUBSIDIARY AS OF 1/1/68	UNDER $1 BILLION	$1-5 BILLION	$5-20 BILLION	$20-100 BILLION	OVER $100 BILLION	TOTAL PERCENT	TOTAL NUMBER
ELECTRONIC COMPONENTS........	0.	0.	15.	43.	43.	100.	40
OTHER ELECTRICAL EQUIPMENT...	4.1	10.	16.	45.	24.	100.	97
MOTOR VEHICLES AND EQUIPMENT.	1.5	3.9	16.	54.	25.	100.	206
OTHER TRANSPORTATION.........	0.	0.7	5.3	58.	37.	100.	19
PRECISION GOODS..............	1.4	2.7	6.8	41.	49.	100.	74
MISCELLANEOUS PRODUCTS.......	1.5	15.	20.	39.	24.	100.	66

CROSS-TABULATION 4. 8.1: PERCENTAGE BREAKDOWN OF NUMBER (AS OF 1/1/71) OF
MANUFACTURING SUBSIDIARIES OF NON-U.S.-BASED PARENT SYSTEMS BY
GNP IN 1970 OF SUBSIDIARY'S COUNTRY
FOR SUBSIDIARIES CLASSIFIED BY
PRINCIPAL INDUSTRY-GROUP OF SUBSIDIARY AS OF 1/1/71

PRINCIPAL INDUSTRY-GROUP OF SUBSIDIARY AS OF 1/1/71	GNP IN 1970 OF SUBSIDIARY'S COUNTRY						
	UNDER $1 BILLION	$1-5 BILLION	$5-20 BILLION	$20-100 BILLION	OVER $100 BILLION	TOTAL PERCENT	TOTAL NUMBER
FOOD AND TOBACCO............	3.0	20.	25.	33.	19.	100.	673
TEXTILES AND APPAREL........	2.2	16.	41.	27.	13.	100.	270
WOOD, FURNITURE AND PAPER....	2.4	11.	20.	44.	22.	100.	210
CHEMICALS...................	1.1	8.8	23.	36.	31.	100.	1238
PETROLEUM...................	7.4	20.	18.	26.	29.	100.	189
RUBBER AND TIRES............	1.9	9.4	32.	35.	22.	100.	106
PRIMARY METALS..............	3.7	8.6	25.	41.	22.	100.	408
FABR. METAL + NON-EL. MACH...	0.8	9.9	19.	37.	34.	100.	598
ELECTRIC AND ELECTRONIC......	1.3	7.8	28.	35.	28.	100.	781
TRANSPORTATION EQUIPMENT.....	1.7	12.	31.	44.	12.	100.	242
PRECISION GOODS.............	0.	0.	12.	27.	62.	100.	78
OTHER.......................	1.5	11.	14.	39.	34.	100.	332

156

CROSS-TABULATION 4.8.2: PERCENTAGE BREAKDOWN OF NUMBER (AS OF 1/1/68) OF MANUFACTURING SUBSIDIARIES OF U.S.-BASED PARENT SYSTEMS BY GNP IN 1970 OF SUBSIDIARY'S COUNTRY FOR SUBSIDIARIES CLASSIFIED BY PRINCIPAL INDUSTRY-GROUP OF SUBSIDIARY AS OF 1/1/68

PRINCIPAL INDUSTRY-GROUP OF SUBSIDIARY AS OF 1/1/68	GNP IN 1970 OF SUBSIDIARY'S COUNTRY						
	UNDER $1 BILLION	$1-5 BILLION	$5-20 BILLION	$20-100 BILLION	OVER $100 BILLION	TOTAL PERCENT	TOTAL NUMBER
FOOD AND TOBACCO..........	4.2	8.7	21.	45.	21.	100.	503
TEXTILES AND APPAREL......	2.0	4.9	25.	39.	28.	100.	102
WOOD, FURNITURE AND PAPER.....	4.1	9.1	25.	45.	17.	100.	197
CHEMICALS..........	3.4	6.1	18.	50.	22.	100.	1079
PETROLEUM..........	3.5	9.0	21.	42.	25.	100.	199
RUBBER AND TIRES..........	5.3	12.	25.	42.	16.	100.	113
PRIMARY METALS..........	0.	7.2	16.	51.	25.	100.	111
FABR. METAL + NON-EL. MACH....	1.9	3.4	14.	53.	30.	100.	530
ELECTRIC AND ELECTRONIC......	3.1	5.0	15.	47.	30.	100.	358
TRANSPORTATION EQUIPMENT......	1.3	3.6	15.	54.	26.	100.	225
PRECISION GOODS..........	1.4	2.7	6.8	41.	49.	100.	74
OTHER..........	2.6	7.3	19.	46.	25.	100.	233

CROSS-TABULATION 4.21.1: PERCENTAGE BREAKDOWN OF NUMBER (AS OF 1/1/71) OF
MANUFACTURING SUBSIDIARIES OF NON-U.S.-BASED PARENT SYSTEMS BY
GNP IN 1970 OF SUBSIDIARY'S COUNTRY
FOR SUBSIDIARIES CLASSIFIED BY
NATIONAL BASE OF SUBSIDIARY'S PARENT SYSTEM

NATIONAL BASE OF SUBSIDIARY'S PARENT SYSTEM	GNP IN 1970 OF SUBSIDIARY'S COUNTRY						
	UNDER $1 BILLION	$1-5 BILLION	$5-20 BILLION	$20-100 BILLION	OVER $100 BILLION	TOTAL PERCENT	TOTAL NUMBER
UNITED KINGDOM.............	2.1	15.	26.	41.	16.	100.	2243
GERMANY....................	1.2	2.7	26.	38.	32.	100.	780
FRANCE.....................	6.9	11.	13.	49.	20.	100.	422
ITALY......................	3.1	10.	23.	41.	23.	100.	128
BELGIUM AND LUXEMBURG......	3.2	4.0	11.	40.	42.	100.	249
THE NETHERLANDS............	0.5	6.6	13.	18.	61.	100.	422
SWEDEN.....................	0.6	3.6	30.	32.	34.	100.	166
SWITZERLAND................	0.5	3.3	17.	32.	47.	100.	390
JAPAN......................	2.1	23.	49.	22.	4.2	100.	476
CANADA.....................	1.5	11.	15.	26.	47.	100.	195
OTHER NON-U.S..............	1.0	4.2	5.2	14.	76.	100.	96

CROSS-TABULATION 4.22.1: PERCENTAGE BREAKDOWN OF NUMBER (AS OF 1/1/71) OF
MANUFACTURING SUBSIDIARIES OF NON-U.S.-BASED PARENT SYSTEMS BY
GNP IN 1970 OF SUBSIDIARY'S COUNTRY
FOR SUBSIDIARIES CLASSIFIED BY
VALUE OF SALES OF SUBSIDIARY'S PARENT SYSTEM IN 1970

VALUE OF SALES OF SUBSIDIARY'S PARENT SYSTEM IN 1970	GNP IN 1970 OF SUBSIDIARY'S COUNTRY						
	UNDER $1 BILLION	$1-5 BILLION	$5-20 BILLION	$20-100 BILLION	OVER $100 BILLION	TOTAL PERCENT	TOTAL NUMBER
$400 - 599 MILLION..............	1.7	15.	21.	33.	29.	100.	1055
$600 - 999 MILLION..............	1.6	10.	27.	38.	23.	100.	852
$1 - 2 BILLION..............	2.8	9.9	22.	43.	22.	100.	1601
OVER $2 BILLION..............	1.9	9.9	27.	30.	32.	100.	1929

CROSS-TABULATION 4.22.2: PERCENTAGE BREAKDOWN OF NUMBER (AS OF 1/1/68) OF
MANUFACTURING SUBSIDIARIES OF U.S.-BASED PARENT SYSTEMS BY
GNP IN 1970 OF SUBSIDIARY'S COUNTRY
FOR SUBSIDIARIES CLASSIFIED BY
VALUE OF SALES OF SUBSIDIARY'S PARENT SYSTEM IN 1967

VALUE OF SALES OF SUBSIDIARY'S PARENT SYSTEM IN 1967	GNP IN 1970 OF SUBSIDIARY'S COUNTRY						
	UNDER $1 BILLION	$1-5 BILLION	$5-20 BILLION	$20-100 BILLION	OVER $100 BILLION	TOTAL PERCENT	TOTAL NUMBER
$100 - 399 MILLION............	2.1	5.1	16.	48.	28.	100.	823
$400 - 599 MILLION............	2.9	5.6	18.	49.	25.	100.	699
$600 - 999 MILLION............	3.1	5.8	18.	50.	23.	100.	891
$1 - 2 BILLION............	3.2	7.4	18.	48.	24.	100.	948
OVER $2 BILLION............	3.6	7.4	21.	43.	25.	100.	758

CROSS-TABULATION 4.23.1: PERCENTAGE BREAKDOWN OF NUMBER (AS OF 1/1/71) OF
MANUFACTURING SUBSIDIARIES OF NON-U.S.-BASED PARENT SYSTEMS BY
GNP IN 1970 OF SUBSIDIARY'S COUNTRY
FOR SUBSIDIARIES CLASSIFIED BY
PRINCIPAL INDUSTRY-GROUP OF SUBSIDIARY'S PARENT SYSTEM AS OF 1/1/71

PRINCIPAL INDUSTRY-GROUP OF SUBSIDIARY'S PARENT SYSTEM AS OF 1/1/71	GNP IN 1970 OF SUBSIDIARY'S COUNTRY						
	UNDER $1 BILLION	$1-5 BILLION	$5-20 BILLION	$20-100 BILLION	OVER $100 BILLION	TOTAL PERCENT	TOTAL NUMBER
FOOD, TOBACCO AND SOAP.........	2.7	16.	26.	35.	20.	100.	939
CHEMICALS AND DRUGS............	1.4	8.1	22.	36.	32.	100.	1253
PETROLEUM......................	5.5	18.	20.	30.	27.	100.	274
IRON AND STEEL.................	2.3	8.3	27.	36.	27.	100.	216
NON-FERROUS METALS.............	4.3	8.2	22.	38.	28.	100.	417
FABR. METAL + NON-EL. MACH.....	1.6	6.6	20.	43.	29.	100.	437
ELECTRIC AND ELECTRONIC........	0.7	5.6	23.	33.	38.	100.	959
AUTOMOBILES....................	2.0	8.2	38.	44.	7.5	100.	147
OTHER..........................	1.8	19.	28.	35.	16.	100.	925

CROSS-TABULATION 4.23.2: PERCENTAGE BREAKDOWN OF NUMBER (AS OF 1/1/68) OF
MANUFACTURING SUBSIDIARIES OF U.S.-BASED PARENT SYSTEMS BY
GNP IN 1970 OF SUBSIDIARY'S COUNTRY
FOR SUBSIDIARIES CLASSIFIED BY
PRINCIPAL INDUSTRY-GROUP OF SUBSIDIARY'S PARENT SYSTEM AS OF 1/1/68

GNP IN 1970 OF SUBSIDIARY'S COUNTRY

PRINCIPAL INDUSTRY-GROUP OF SUBSIDIARY'S PARENT SYSTEM AS OF 1/1/68	UNDER $1 BILLION	$1-5 BILLION	$5-20 BILLION	$20-100 BILLION	OVER $100 BILLION	TOTAL PERCENT	TOTAL NUMBER
FOOD, TOBACCO AND SOAP........	3.6	9.6	20.	46.	20.	100.	697
CHEMICALS AND DRUGS...........	3.5	5.7	18.	50.	23.	100.	1100
PETROLEUM.....................	3.9	9.7	22.	39.	26.	100.	331
IRON AND STEEL................	0.	4.5	18.	59.	18.	100.	22
NON-FERROUS METALS............	1.6	8.9	20.	45.	24.	100.	123
FABR. METAL + NON-EL. MACH....	1.9	4.5	16.	49.	28.	100.	462
ELECTRIC AND ELECTRONIC.......	2.7	5.0	14.	47.	31.	100.	438
AUTOMOBILES...................	1.3	2.9	18.	54.	24.	100.	239
OTHER.........................	2.7	5.6	19.	47.	27.	100.	792

CROSS-TABULATION 4.25.1: PERCENTAGE BREAKDOWN OF NUMBER (AS OF 1/1/71) OF
MANUFACTURING SUBSIDIARIES OF NON-U.S.-BASED PARENT SYSTEMS BY
GNP IN 1970 OF SUBSIDIARY'S COUNTRY
FOR SUBSIDIARIES CLASSIFIED BY
NUMBER OF COUNTRIES IN WHICH SUBSIDIARY'S PARENT SYSTEM MANUFACTURED AS OF 1/1/71

NUMBER OF COUNTRIES SUB-SIDIARY'S PARENT SYSTEM MANUFACTURED IN AS OF 1/1/71	GNP IN 1970 OF SUBSIDIARY'S COUNTRY						
	UNDER $1 BILLION	$1-5 BILLION	$5-20 BILLION	$20-100 BILLION	OVER $100 BILLION	TOTAL PERCENT	TOTAL NUMBER
TWO OR THREE..................	0.	22.	45.	14.	19.	100.	58
FOUR TO SIX...................	2.0	10.	41.	31.	15.	100.	394
SEVEN TO TWELVE...............	2.4	12.	30.	41.	14.	100.	621
THIRTEEN OR MORE..............	2.0	11.	22.	36.	30.	100.	4489

CROSS-TABULATION 4.25.2: PERCENTAGE BREAKDOWN OF NUMBER (AS OF 1/1/68) OF
MANUFACTURING SUBSIDIARIES OF U.S.-BASED PARENT SYSTEMS BY
GNP IN 1970 OF SUBSIDIARY'S COUNTRY
FOR SUBSIDIARIES CLASSIFIED BY
NUMBER OF COUNTRIES IN WHICH SUBSIDIARY'S PARENT SYSTEM MANUFACTURED AS OF 1/1/68

GNP IN 1970 OF SUBSIDIARY'S COUNTRY

NUMBER OF COUNTRIES IN WHICH SUBSIDIARY'S PARENT SYSTEM MANUFACTURED AS OF 1/1/68	UNDER $1 BILLION	$1-5 BILLION	$5-20 BILLION	$20-100 BILLION	OVER $100 BILLION	TOTAL PERCENT	TOTAL NUMBER
TWO OR THREE........	0.	0.	0.	0.	0.	100.	0
FOUR TO SIX........	0.	0.	3.7	52.	44.	100.	27
SEVEN TO TWELVE....	1.0	2.3	13.	54.	29.	100.	993
THIRTEEN OR MORE...	3.6	7.7	20.	45.	23.	100.	3157

164

CROSS-TABULATION 4.26.1: PERCENTAGE BREAKDOWN OF NUMBER (AS OF 1/1/71) OF
MANUFACTURING SUBSIDIARIES OF NON-U.S.-BASED PARENT SYSTEMS BY
GNP IN 1970 OF SUBSIDIARY'S COUNTRY
FOR SUBSIDIARIES CLASSIFIED BY
PERCENTAGE OF PARENT SYSTEM'S EMPLOYEES OUTSIDE NATIONAL BASE AS OF 1/1/71

GNP IN 1970 OF SUBSIDIARY'S COUNTRY

PERCENTAGE OF PARENT SYSTEM'S EMPLOYEES OUTSIDE NATIONAL BASE AS OF 1/1/71	UNDER $1 BILLION	$1-5 BILLION	$5-20 BILLION	$20-100 BILLION	OVER $100 BILLION	TOTAL PERCENT	TOTAL NUMBER
UNDER 10%................	2.1	14.	30.	36.	18.	100.	478
10% - 25%................	1.3	7.0	28.	46.	18.	100.	1351
25% - 50%................	0.9	8.7	24.	37.	30.	100.	989
OVER 50%................	2.6	14.	19.	28.	37.	100.	1869

CROSS-TABULATION 4.27.1: PERCENTAGE BREAKDOWN OF NUMBER (AS OF 1/1/71) OF
MANUFACTURING SUBSIDIARIES OF NON-U.S.-BASED PARENT SYSTEMS BY
GNP IN 1970 OF SUBSIDIARY'S COUNTRY
FOR SUBSIDIARIES CLASSIFIED BY
NO. OF INDUSTRIES IN WHICH PARENT SYSTEM MANUFACTURED WITHIN NATIONAL BASE AS OF 1/1/71

NO. OF INDUSTRIES IN WHICH PARENT SYSTEM MANUF. WITHIN NATIONAL BASE AS OF 1/1/71	GNP IN 1970 OF SUBSIDIARY'S COUNTRY						
	UNDER $1 BILLION	$1-5 BILLION	$5-20 BILLION	$20-100 BILLION	OVER $100 BILLION	TOTAL PERCENT	TOTAL NUMBER
ONE TO THREE...............	1.5	19.	33.	30.	16.	100.	412
FOUR TO NINE...............	2.0	14.	26.	35.	23.	100.	1697
TEN TO NINETEEN............	2.4	9.2	24.	38.	27.	100.	2367
TWENTY OR MORE.............	1.7	8.2	20.	35.	36.	100.	1091

CROSS-TABULATION 4.27.2: PERCENTAGE BREAKDOWN OF NUMBER (AS OF 1/1/68) OF MANUFACTURING SUBSIDIARIES OF U.S.-BASED PARENT SYSTEMS BY GNP IN 1970 OF SUBSIDIARY'S COUNTRY FOR SUBSIDIARIES CLASSIFIED BY NO. OF INDUSTRIES IN WHICH PARENT SYSTEM MANUFACTURED WITHIN NATIONAL BASE AS OF 1/1/68

	GNP IN 1970 OF SUBSIDIARY'S COUNTRY						
NO. OF INDUSTRIES IN WHICH PARENT SYSTEM MANUF. WITHIN NATIONAL BASE AS OF 1/1/68	UNDER $1 BILLION	$1-5 BILLION	$5-20 BILLION	$20-100 BILLION	OVER $100 BILLION	TOTAL PERCENT	TOTAL NUMBER
ONE TO THREE.........	4.2	9.1	20.	41.	26.	100.	384
FOUR TO NINE.........	2.7	6.4	19.	47.	25.	100.	1428
TEN TO NINETEEN......	3.0	6.3	18.	49.	24.	100.	1451
TWENTY OR MORE.......	2.8	5.6	17.	48.	26.	100.	858

CROSS-TABULATION 4.28.1: PERCENTAGE BREAKDOWN OF NUMBER (AS OF 1/1/71) OF
MANUFACTURING SUBSIDIARIES OF NON-U.S.-BASED PARENT SYSTEMS BY
GNP IN 1970 OF SUBSIDIARY'S COUNTRY
FOR SUBSIDIARIES CLASSIFIED BY
NO. OF INDUSTRIES IN WHICH PARENT SYSTEM MANUFACTURED OUTSIDE NATIONAL BASE AS OF 1/1/71

NO. OF INDUSTRIES IN WHICH PARENT SYSTEM MANUF. OUTSIDE NATIONAL BASE AS OF 1/1/71	GNP IN 1970 OF SUBSIDIARY'S COUNTRY						
	UNDER $1 BILLION	$1-5 BILLION	$5-20 BILLION	$20-100 BILLION	OVER $100 BILLION	TOTAL PERCENT	TOTAL NUMBER
ONE TO THREE..............	4.1	17.	26.	34.	19.	100.	342
FOUR TO NINE..............	2.5	13.	27.	38.	20.	100.	1337
TEN TO NINETEEN..........	1.8	8.0	25.	40.	25.	100.	1677
TWENTY OR MORE...........	1.7	12.	22.	31.	34.	100.	2211

CROSS-TABULATION 4.28.2: PERCENTAGE BREAKDOWN OF NUMBER (AS CF 1/1/68) OF
MANUFACTURING SUBSIDIARIES OF U.S.-BASED PARENT SYSTEMS BY
GNP IN 1970 OF SUBSIDIARY'S COUNTRY
FOR SUBSIDIARIES CLASSIFIED BY
NO. OF INDUSTRIES IN WHICH PARENT SYSTEM MANUFACTURED OUTSIDE NATIONAL BASE AS QF 1/1/68

NO. OF INDUSTRIES IN WHICH PARENT SYSTEM MANUF. OUTSIDE NATIONAL BASE AS OF 1/1/68	GNP IN 1970 OF SUBSIDIARY'S CCUNTRY						
	UNDER $1 BILLION	$1-5 BILLION	$5-20 BILLION	$20-100 BILLION	CVER $100 BILLION	TOTAL PERCENT	TCTAL NUMBER
ONE TO THREE..........	2.3	4.0	15.	51.	27.	100.	576
FOUR TO NINE..........	2.9	6.8	18.	48.	24.	100.	2409
TEN TO NINETEEN.......	3.4	6.5	18.	47.	25.	100.	889
TWENTY OR MORE........	2.7	7.3	23.	42.	25.	100.	330

CROSS-TABULATION 4.29.1: PERCENTAGE BREAKDOWN OF NUMBER (AS OF 1/1/71) OF
MANUFACTURING SUBSIDIARIES OF NON-U.S.-BASED PARENT SYSTEMS BY
GNP IN 1970 OF SUBSIDIARY'S COUNTRY
FOR SUBSIDIARIES CLASSIFIED BY
PARENT SYSTEM'S R&D EXPENDITURES AS A PERCENTAGE OF SALES IN 1970

| | GNP IN 1970 OF SUBSIDIARY'S COUNTRY | | | | | | |
PARENT SYSTEM'S R&D EXPENDITURES AS A PERCENTAGE OF SALES IN 1970	UNDER $1 BILLION	$1-5 BILLION	$5-20 BILLION	$20-100 BILLION	OVER $100 BILLION	TOTAL PERCENT	TOTAL NUMBER
LESS THAN 1%...................	1.9	14.	21.	38.	25.	100.	835
1% - 4%.......................	2.1	8.7	22.	35.	31.	100.	1575
MORE THAN 4%..................	1.6	8.0	25.	33.	33.	100.	1235

CROSS-TABULATION 4.29.2: PERCENTAGE BREAKDOWN OF NUMBER (AS OF 1/1/68) OF
MANUFACTURING SUBSIDIARIES OF U.S.-BASED PARENT SYSTEMS BY
GNP IN 1970 OF SUBSIDIARY'S COUNTRY
FOR SUBSIDIARIES CLASSIFIED BY
PARENT SYSTEM'S R&D EXPENDITURES AS A PERCENTAGE OF SALES IN 1967

| | GNP IN 1970 OF SUBSIDIARY'S COUNTRY | | | | | | |
PARENT SYSTEM'S R&D EXPENDITURES AS A PERCENTAGE OF SALES IN 1967	UNDER $1 BILLION	$1-5 BILLION	$5-20 BILLION	$20-100 BILLION	OVER $100 BILLION	TOTAL PERCENT	TOTAL NUMBER
LESS THAN 1%..............	3.3	7.5	19.	42.	29.	100.	306
1% - 4%..............	2.9	7.6	20.	45.	24.	100.	841
MORE THAN 4%..............	2.1	2.7	14.	52.	29.	100.	374

CROSS-TABULATION 5.17.1: PERCENTAGE BREAKDOWN OF NUMBER OF
MANUFACTURING SUBSIDIARIES OF NON-U.S.-BASED PARENT SYSTEMS BY
PRINCIPAL INDUSTRY OF SUBSIDIARY AT DATE OF ENTRY
FOR SUBSIDIARIES CLASSIFIED BY
SUBSIDIARY'S DATE OF ENTRY INTO PARENT SYSTEM

SUBSIDIARY'S DATE OF ENTRY INTO PARENT SYSTEM	PRINCIPAL INDUSTRY OF SUBSIDIARY AT DATE OF ENTRY						
	ORDNANCE	MEAT PRODUCTS	DAIRY PRODUCTS	CANNED FOODS	GRAIN MILL PRODUCTS	BAKERY PRODUCTS	CONFECTIONERY PRODUCTS
PRE 1914.....	1.4	1.4	6.2	0.	0.	0.	0.5
1914 - 1919...	2.7	5.5	6.8	2.7	0.	0.	1.4
1920 - 1929...	2.3	0.9	2.3	0.	0.3	0.	1.4
1930 - 1938...	0.5	1.9	3.4	1.0	0.5	0.	2.9
1939 - 1945...	0.	0.	1.9	0.9	0.	0.	0.
1946 - 1952...	0.	0.6	0.6	0.	3.5	16.	0.6
1953 - 1955...	0.	1.2	0.	0.6	0.	4.1	0.6
1956 - 1958...	0.5	0.	0.9	0.	0.	0.5	0.5
1959 - 1961...	0.5	1.2	3.3	1.2	0.3	0.	0.7
1962 - 1964...	0.	0.3	1.6	1.3	2.6	0.5	0.2
1965 - 1967...	0.2	0.1	1.0	1.2	0.5	0.1	0.4
1968 - 1970...	0.1	0.7	2.1	1.0	0.3	0.3	0.2

TABLE CONTINUED ON NEXT PAGE

CROSS-TABULATION 5.17.1: PERCENTAGE BREAKDOWN OF NUMBER OF
MANUFACTURING SUBSIDIARIES OF NON-U.S.-BASED PARENT SYSTEMS BY
PRINCIPAL INDUSTRY OF SUBSIDIARY AT DATE OF ENTRY
FOR SUBSIDIARIES CLASSIFIED BY
SUBSIDIARY'S DATE OF ENTRY INTO PARENT SYSTEM
(CONTINUED)

PRINCIPAL INDUSTRY OF SUBSIDIARY AT DATE OF ENTRY

SUBSIDIARY'S DATE OF ENTRY INTO PARENT SYSTEM	BEVER-AGES	OTHER FOOD PRODUCTS	TOBACCO PRODUCTS	TEXTILES	APPAREL	LUMBER AND WOOD	FURNI-TURE
PRE 1914	0.5	2.8	2.8	8.5	0.	0.	0.
1914 - 1919	1.4	4.1	2.7	1.4	0.	0.	0.
1920 - 1929	0.3	4.9	6.0	6.0	0.3	0.3	0.
1930 - 1938	2.9	1.9	3.9	3.4	0.5	0.	0.5
1939 - 1945	1.9	2.8	0.9	7.5	0.	1.9	0.
1946 - 1952	2.4	3.5	2.4	3.5	0.	0.3	0.3
1953 - 1955	4.7	0.	1.2	1.8	0.6	0.	0.
1956 - 1958	1.8	2.8	1.4	5.5	0.	1.8	0.
1959 - 1961	5.5	2.5	0.7	2.7	0.2	2.2	0.3
1962 - 1964	5.5	3.2	0.5	7.3	0.8	0.8	0.5
1965 - 1967	3.4	1.9	0.4	4.2	0.9	0.7	0.3
1968 - 1970	2.2	3.9	0.2	4.7	1.3	1.4	0.5

TABLE CONTINUED ON NEXT PAGE

CROSS-TABULATION 5.17.1: PERCENTAGE BREAKDOWN OF NUMBER OF
MANUFACTURING SUBSIDIARIES OF NON-U.S.-BASED PARENT SYSTEMS BY
PRINCIPAL INDUSTRY OF SUBSIDIARY AT DATE OF ENTRY
FOR SUBSIDIARIES CLASSIFIED BY
SUBSIDIARY'S DATE OF ENTRY INTO PARENT SYSTEM
(CONTINUED)

SUBSIDIARY'S DATE OF ENTRY INTO PARENT SYSTEM	PRINCIPAL INDUSTRY OF SUBSIDIARY AT DATE OF ENTRY						
	PAPER PRODUCTS	PRINTED MATTER	INDUSTRIAL CHEMICALS	PLASTICS AND SYNTHETICS	DRUGS	SOAP AND COSMETICS	PAINTS
PRE 1914...............	0.	0.5	10.	0.	0.9	9.5	0.
1914 - 1919...........	0.	0.	1.4	0.	0.	14.	1.4
1920 - 1929...........	2.3	2.0	2.9	1.1	1.1	4.3	0.3
1930 - 1938...........	2.9	1.0	6.3	1.0	3.9	5.3	0.5
1939 - 1945...........	0.	0.9	6.6	0.9	9.4	7.5	0.9
1946 - 1952...........	2.4	0.3	5.0	0.9	4.4	2.9	0.6
1953 - 1955...........	0.	1.2	5.3	1.2	5.9	3.6	0.
1956 - 1958...........	3.2	0.5	6.0	3.2	6.5	0.9	0.9
1959 - 1961...........	3.3	1.2	4.1	2.3	2.7	1.2	3.0
1962 - 1964...........	5.5	2.3	4.5	5.3	3.9	3.1	1.3
1965 - 1967...........	4.0	2.5	4.3	2.0	5.8	4.1	2.9
1968 - 1970...........	2.0	3.1	5.2	4.4	3.6	2.0	3.5

TABLE CONTINUED ON NEXT PAGE

CROSS-TABULATION 5.17.1: PERCENTAGE BREAKDOWN OF NUMBER OF
MANUFACTURING SUBSIDIARIES OF NON-U.S.-BASED PARENT SYSTEMS BY
PRINCIPAL INDUSTRY OF SUBSIDIARY AT DATE OF ENTRY
FOR SUBSIDIARIES CLASSIFIED BY
SUBSIDIARY'S DATE OF ENTRY INTO PARENT SYSTEM
(CONTINUED)

PRINCIPAL INDUSTRY OF SUBSIDIARY AT DATE OF ENTRY

SUBSIDIARY'S DATE OF ENTRY INTO PARENT SYSTEM	AGRICULTURAL CHEMICALS	OTHER CHEMICALS	REFINED PETROLEUM	OTHER PETROLEUM PRODUCTS	TIRES	OTHER RUBBER PRODUCTS	LEATHER PRODUCTS + SHOES
PRE 1914	0.	1.4	5.7	0.5	2.4	1.4	0.
1914 - 1919	0.	2.7	1.4	1.4	0.	1.4	0.
1920 - 1929	0.3	5.2	2.3	1.4	0.9	1.1	0.
1930 - 1938	0.5	4.4	0.	2.9	1.9	1.5	0.
1939 - 1945	0.9	3.8	1.9	0.	2.8	0.9	0.
1946 - 1952	1.5	2.6	1.8	0.	0.3	2.1	0.
1953 - 1955	2.4	1.8	4.7	3.6	0.6	1.8	0.
1956 - 1958	0.	4.6	1.8	0.9	0.5	1.4	0.
1959 - 1961	1.3	3.0	1.8	1.2	1.8	0.8	0.
1962 - 1964	1.9	2.7	2.3	1.0	0.5	1.6	0.
1965 - 1967	2.5	2.9	1.5	2.2	0.3	1.1	0.
1968 - 1970	1.3	2.9	0.9	1.5	0.2	1.8	0.5

TABLE CONTINUED ON NEXT PAGE

CROSS-TABULATION 5.17.1: PERCENTAGE BREAKDOWN OF NUMBER OF
MANUFACTURING SUBSIDIARIES OF NON-U.S.-BASED PARENT SYSTEMS BY
PRINCIPAL INDUSTRY OF SUBSIDIARY AT DATE OF ENTRY
FOR SUBSIDIARIES CLASSIFIED BY
SUBSIDIARY'S DATE OF ENTRY INTO PARENT SYSTEM
(CONTINUED)

SUBSIDIARY'S DATE OF ENTRY INTO PARENT SYSTEM	PRINCIPAL INDUSTRY OF SUBSIDIARY AT DATE OF ENTRY						
	GLASS PRODUCTS	STONE, CLAY + CONCRETE	IRON AND STEEL	NON-FERROUS SMELTING	NON-FERROUS PRODUCTS	METAL CANS	STRUCTURAL METAL PRODUCTS
PRE 1914	1.4	0.	2.8	1.9	0.5	0.	0.5
1914 - 1919	0.	0.	4.1	2.7	2.7	0.	1.4
1920 - 1929	1.4	1.4	2.9	1.1	1.7	0.	0.
1930 - 1938	0.	0.5	3.9	1.9	2.4	1.9	0.5
1939 - 1945	3.8	0.	1.9	3.8	9.4	0.9	2.8
1946 - 1952	0.3	1.2	1.5	1.5	1.8	2.9	1.8
1953 - 1955	3.0	2.4	3.6	3.0	2.4	0.6	2.4
1956 - 1958	0.5	1.9	5.1	0.5	3.2	0.	3.7
1959 - 1961	0.5	0.8	2.8	2.3	4.8	1.0	1.5
1962 - 1964	0.	0.6	3.2	1.1	1.8	0.6	0.8
1965 - 1967	1.6	1.1	3.6	1.9	2.8	0.6	1.0
1968 - 1970	1.4	2.5	3.7	1.7	2.9	0.4	1.2

TABLE CONTINUED ON NEXT PAGE

CROSS-TABULATION 5.17.1: PERCENTAGE BREAKDOWN OF NUMBER OF
MANUFACTURING SUBSIDIARIES OF NON-U.S.-BASED PARENT SYSTEMS BY
PRINCIPAL INDUSTRY OF SUBSIDIARY AT DATE OF ENTRY
FOR SUBSIDIARIES CLASSIFIED BY
SUBSIDIARY'S DATE OF ENTRY INTO PARENT SYSTEM
(CONTINUED)

PRINCIPAL INDUSTRY OF SUBSIDIARY AT DATE OF ENTRY

SUBSIDIARY'S DATE OF ENTRY INTO PARENT SYSTEM	FABRICATED WIRE PRODUCTS	OTHER FABRICATED METAL PRODUCTS	ENGINES AND TURBINES	FARM MACHINERY	CONSTRUCTION MACHINERY	SPECIAL INDUSTRY MACHINERY	GENERAL INDUSTRY MACHINERY
PRE 1914	0.5	6.6	2.4	0.5	0.	0.	0.9
1914 - 1919	2.7	0.	0.	0.	0.	0.	5.5
1920 - 1929	0.3	3.2	0.3	0.6	0.6	0.6	2.9
1930 - 1938	0.5	4.9	1.5	1.0	0.	1.0	2.4
1939 - 1945	0.	0.9	0.	2.8	0.9	0.	2.8
1946 - 1952	1.2	3.2	1.2	0.6	0.3	0.9	1.8
1953 - 1955	0.	2.4	1.8	0.6	0.6	0.6	1.8
1956 - 1958	1.4	4.6	3.2	2.3	0.5	1.8	0.9
1959 - 1961	1.5	4.6	2.0	1.2	0.2	1.0	0.5
1962 - 1964	1.8	2.7	0.6	0.3	0.5	2.9	1.3
1965 - 1967	0.7	3.0	1.2	1.2	0.4	2.6	1.6
1968 - 1970	0.9	4.3	0.6	0.4	0.6	1.2	1.3

TABLE CONTINUED ON NEXT PAGE

CROSS-TABULATION 5.17.1: PERCENTAGE BREAKDOWN OF NUMBER OF
MANUFACTURING SUBSIDIARIES OF NON-U.S.-BASED PARENT SYSTEMS BY
PRINCIPAL INDUSTRY OF SUBSIDIARY AT DATE OF ENTRY
FOR SUBSIDIARIES CLASSIFIED BY
SUBSIDIARY'S DATE OF ENTRY INTO PARENT SYSTEM
(CONTINUED)

PRINCIPAL INDUSTRY OF SUBSIDIARY AT DATE OF ENTRY

SUBSIDIARY'S DATE OF ENTRY INTO PARENT SYSTEM	OFFICE MACHINES+ COMPUTERS	OTHER NON-EL. MACHINERY	ELECTRIC TRANSMIS. EQUIPMENT + MACHINERY	ELECTRIC LIGHTING + WIRING	RADIOS, TV'S+AP- PLIANCES	COMMUNI- CATIONS EQUIPMENT	ELECTRON- IC COM- PONENTS
PRE 1914	0.	0.	10.	1.4	0.	0.5	0.5
1914 - 1919	0.	0.	8.2	8.2	0.	0.	1.4
1920 - 1929	0.	0.3	7.2	8.0	2.6	3.7	2.3
1930 - 1938	0.	0.	1.5	3.9	6.3	2.4	1.9
1939 - 1945	0.	0.9	4.7	2.8	0.9	0.	0.9
1946 - 1952	1.2	0.	2.1	2.1	3.8	2.9	0.6
1953 - 1955	0.6	2.4	3.6	3.6	2.4	2.4	0.
1956 - 1958	0.5	0.	2.8	1.4	1.4	0.9	0.9
1959 - 1961	0.8	0.5	2.5	1.8	2.8	2.0	1.7
1962 - 1964	0.6	0.3	1.8	1.1	1.8	1.5	1.0
1965 - 1967	0.5	0.7	1.7	2.8	3.4	2.0	1.8
1968 - 1970	0.5	0.6	1.6	1.2	3.7	2.1	2.6

TABLE CONTINUED ON NEXT PAGE

CROSS-TABULATION 5.17.1: PERCENTAGE BREAKDOWN OF NUMBER OF
MANUFACTURING SUBSIDIARIES OF NON-U.S.-BASED PARENT SYSTEMS BY
PRINCIPAL INDUSTRY OF SUBSIDIARY AT DATE OF ENTRY
FOR SUBSIDIARIES CLASSIFIED BY
SUBSIDIARY'S DATE OF ENTRY INTO PARENT SYSTEM
(CONTINUED)

PRINCIPAL INDUSTRY OF SUBSIDIARY AT DATE OF ENTRY

SUBSIDIARY'S DATE OF ENTRY INTO PARENT SYSTEM	OTHER ELECTRIC EQUIPMENT	MOTOR VEHICLES + EQUIP.	OTHER TRANS-PORTATION	PRECISION GOODS	MISC. PRODUCTS	TOTAL PERCENT	TOTAL NUMBER
PRE 1914	4.7	5.2	2.4	0.9	0.	100.	211
1914 - 1919	5.5	1.4	2.7	0.	1.4	100.	73
1920 - 1929	2.9	2.3	0.9	2.3	0.3	100.	348
1930 - 1938	1.9	1.0	0.5	1.5	1.5	100.	206
1939 - 1945	2.8	0.9	0.	0.	0.9	100.	106
1946 - 1952	1.8	3.5	3.2	0.	0.	100.	340
1953 - 1955	7.7	4.1	1.2	0.	0.6	100.	169
1956 - 1958	5.1	4.1	5.1	1.4	0.9	100.	217
1959 - 1961	4.6	3.5	3.0	1.0	2.3	100.	603
1962 - 1964	1.9	5.8	1.5	2.3	1.3	100.	620
1965 - 1967	4.5	4.2	1.0	1.7	1.5	100.	1045
1968 - 1970	4.0	3.8	1.0	2.4	2.1	100.	1776

CROSS-TABULATION 5.17.2: PERCENTAGE BREAKDOWN OF NUMBER OF
MANUFACTURING SUBSIDIARIES OF U.S.-BASED PARENT SYSTEMS BY
PRINCIPAL INDUSTRY OF SUBSIDIARY AT DATE OF ENTRY
FOR SUBSIDIARIES CLASSIFIED BY
SUBSIDIARY'S DATE OF ENTRY INTO PARENT SYSTEM

PRINCIPAL INDUSTRY OF SUBSIDIARY AT DATE OF ENTRY

SUBSIDIARY'S DATE OF ENTRY INTO PARENT SYSTEM	ORDNANCE	MEAT PRODUCTS	DAIRY PRODUCTS	CANNED FOODS	GRAIN MILL PRODUCTS	BAKERY PRODUCTS	CONFECTIONERY PRODUCTS
PRE 1914	0.9	6.5	2.8	0.9	0.9	0.9	0.9
1914 - 1919	0.	10.	1.4	0.	1.4	0.	2.9
1920 - 1929	0.	0.4	7.2	1.5	4.2	1.5	1.5
1930 - 1938	0.3	0.7	7.2	0.3	2.8	3.1	0.3
1939 - 1945	0.	0.6	5.5	0.6	2.4	1.8	1.2
1946 - 1952	0.5	3.0	1.4	0.3	1.6	1.4	0.8
1953 - 1955	0.4	0.7	2.2	0.4	3.0	1.1	1.1
1956 - 1958	0.	1.4	3.1	1.9	1.7	0.2	0.7
1959 - 1961	0.5	0.5	2.5	1.4	3.8	0.8	1.3
1962 - 1964	0.4	1.2	1.4	2.9	2.4	0.9	3.0
1965 - 1967	0.1	1.8	2.0	1.3	3.2	1.6	3.3

TABLE CONTINUED ON NEXT PAGE

CROSS-TABULATION 5.17.2: PERCENTAGE BREAKDOWN OF NUMBER OF
MANUFACTURING SUBSIDIARIES OF U.S.-BASED PARENT SYSTEMS BY
PRINCIPAL INDUSTRY OF SUBSIDIARY AT DATE OF ENTRY
FOR SUBSIDIARIES CLASSIFIED BY
SUBSIDIARY'S DATE OF ENTRY INTO PARENT SYSTEM
(CONTINUED)

PRINCIPAL INDUSTRY OF SUBSIDIARY AT DATE OF ENTRY

SUBSIDIARY'S DATE OF ENTRY INTO PARENT SYSTEM	BEVER-AGES	OTHER FOOD PRODUCTS	TOBACCO PRODUCTS	TEXTILES	APPAREL	LUMBER AND WOOD	FURNI-TURE
PRE 1914	0.	0.0	0.	0.0	0.	0.	0.
1914 – 1919	0.	0.	0.	0.	1.4	0.	1.4
1920 – 1929	1.9	3.0	0.	1.1	0.	1.5	0.4
1930 – 1938	4.8	2.8	0.3	1.0	0.	0.	0.
1939 – 1945	5.5	0.	0.	3.7	0.	0.6	0.
1946 – 1952	1.9	0.3	0.	3.3	0.3	0.	0.
1953 – 1955	1.5	2.2	0.4	1.9	0.4	0.	0.4
1956 – 1958	2.1	2.6	0.2	1.4	0.2	0.2	0.7
1959 – 1961	0.6	1.6	0.7	1.9	1.4	0.6	0.1
1962 – 1964	1.3	2.0	0.2	1.9	0.8	0.3	0.4
1965 – 1967	1.9	2.3	0.7	2.2	0.5	0.9	0.4

TABLE CONTINUED ON NEXT PAGE

CROSS-TABULATION 5.17.2: PERCENTAGE BREAKDOWN OF NUMBER OF MANUFACTURING SUBSIDIARIES OF U.S.-BASED PARENT SYSTEMS BY PRINCIPAL INDUSTRY OF SUBSIDIARY AT DATE OF ENTRY FOR SUBSIDIARIES CLASSIFIED BY SUBSIDIARY'S DATE OF ENTRY INTO PARENT SYSTEM

(CONTINUED)

PRINCIPAL INDUSTRY OF SUBSIDIARY AT DATE OF ENTRY

SUBSIDIARY'S DATE OF ENTRY INTO PARENT SYSTEM	PAPER PRODUCTS	PRINTED MATTER	INDUS- TRIAL CHEMICALS	PLASTICS AND SYN- THETICS	DRUGS	SOAP AND COSMETICS	PAINTS
PRE 1914	0.	2.8	4.7	0.	0.	0.9	0.
1914 - 1919	1.4	0.	1.4	1.4	2.9	4.3	0.
1920 - 1929	1.9	0.	5.7	0.8	4.5	4.9	0.8
1930 - 1938	3.4	0.	4.1	2.1	10.	5.5	0.3
1939 - 1945	4.3	0.6	9.1	2.4	12.	6.7	0.6
1946 - 1952	1.9	3.5	8.7	2.4	10.	3.5	0.3
1953 - 1955	10.	0.7	7.1	7.1	8.9	2.2	1.9
1956 - 1958	6.4	1.4	9.3	3.6	9.8	4.3	1.0
1959 - 1961	4.2	0.1	7.3	5.1	10.	4.9	0.9
1962 - 1964	5.4	1.2	5.2	6.5	6.4	2.8	0.9
1965 - 1967	5.0	0.8	5.4	5.0	5.2	3.9	2.2

TABLE CONTINUED ON NEXT PAGE

182

CROSS-TABULATION 5.17.2: PERCENTAGE BREAKDOWN OF NUMBER OF
MANUFACTURING SUBSIDIARIES OF U.S.-BASED PARENT SYSTEMS BY
PRINCIPAL INDUSTRY OF SUBSIDIARY AT DATE OF ENTRY
FOR SUBSIDIARIES CLASSIFIED BY
SUBSIDIARY'S DATE OF ENTRY INTO PARENT SYSTEM
(CONTINUED)

PRINCIPAL INDUSTRY OF SUBSIDIARY AT DATE OF ENTRY

SUBSIDIARY'S DATE OF ENTRY INTO PARENT SYSTEM	AGRI-CULTURAL CHEMICALS	OTHER CHEMICALS	REFINED PETRO-LEUM	OTHER PETROLEUM PRODUCTS	TIRES	OTHER RUBBER PRODUCTS	LEATHER PRODUCTS + SHOES
PRE 1914	0.	4.7	12.	2.8	0.9	0.	0.
1914 - 1919	1.4	2.9	2.9	0.	2.9	5.7	2.9
1920 - 1929	0.9	4.5	6.0	2.3	1.5	1.1	0.4
1930 - 1938	0.3	1.7	4.5	2.1	5.9	0.7	0.3
1939 - 1945	0.	1.2	4.3	0.6	6.1	3.0	0.6
1946 - 1953	1.9	3.0	6.5	1.1	4.1	1.1	0.5
1954 - 1955	0.7	1.5	1.5	1.5	1.1	1.9	0.
1956 - 1958	1.2	2.6	3.1	0.7	1.7	0.2	0.
1959 - 1961	1.0	1.3	2.4	1.5	1.3	0.7	0.5
1962 - 1964	1.3	2.2	2.7	2.0	0.9	0.8	0.4
1965 - 1967	2.1	2.7	2.0	1.9	0.7	1.4	0.

TABLE CONTINUED ON NEXT PAGE

CROSS-TABULATION 5.17.2: PERCENTAGE BREAKDOWN OF NUMBER OF
MANUFACTURING SUBSIDIARIES OF U.S.-BASED PARENT SYSTEMS BY
PRINCIPAL INDUSTRY OF SUBSIDIARY AT DATE OF ENTRY
FOR SUBSIDIARIES CLASSIFIED BY
SUBSIDIARY'S DATE OF ENTRY INTO PARENT SYSTEM
(CONTINUED)

PRINCIPAL INDUSTRY OF SUBSIDIARY AT DATE OF ENTRY

SUBSIDIARY'S DATE OF ENTRY INTO PARENT SYSTEM	GLASS PRODUCTS	STONE, CLAY + CONCRETE	IRON AND STEEL	NON-FERROUS SMELTING	NON-FERROUS PRODUCTS	METAL CANS	STRUCTURAL METAL PRODUCTS
PRE 1914.........	0.9	2.8	0.	1.9	0.	0.	0.
1914 - 1919.....	0.	1.4	0.	2.9	1.4	0.	1.4
1920 - 1929.....	0.8	1.9	0.8	2.6	0.	0.4	0.
1930 - 1938.....	0.3	1.4	1.7	1.4	0.	1.7	0.3
1939 - 1945.....	5.5	0.6	0.6	0.	0.	0.6	1.2
1946 - 1952.....	1.1	3.5	0.8	0.8	0.9	0.8	1.6
1953 - 1955.....	0.7	3.7	0.4	0.4	0.7	0.7	0.7
1956 - 1958.....	0.7	2.6	0.	1.0	1.2	2.4	1.2
1959 - 1961.....	1.0	2.1	1.2	2.3	1.6	0.5	0.3
1962 - 1964.....	0.7	2.0	0.9	0.9	1.2	1.0	0.7
1965 - 1967.....	1.8	2.3	1.1	1.1	1.1	0.8	0.6

TABLE CONTINUED ON NEXT PAGE

CROSS-TABULATION 5.17.2: PERCENTAGE BREAKDOWN OF NUMBER OF
MANUFACTURING SUBSIDIARIES OF U.S.-BASED PARENT SYSTEMS BY
PRINCIPAL INDUSTRY OF SUBSIDIARY AT DATE OF ENTRY
FOR SUBSIDIARIES CLASSIFIED BY
SUBSIDIARY'S DATE OF ENTRY INTO PARENT SYSTEM
(CONTINUED)

SUBSIDIARY'S DATE OF ENTRY INTO PARENT SYSTEM	PRINCIPAL INDUSTRY OF SUBSIDIARY AT DATE OF ENTRY						
	FABRICATED WIRE PRODUCTS	OTHER FABRICATED METAL	ENGINES AND TURBINES	FARM MACHINERY	CONSTRUCTION MACHINERY	SPECIAL INDUSTRY MACHINERY	GENERAL INDUSTRY MACHINERY
PRE 1914	0.	5.6	0.	3.7	4.7	8.4	4.7
1914 - 1919	0.	4.3	0.	0.	5.7	4.3	1.4
1920 - 1929	0.4	2.6	0.8	0.	0.8	1.5	3.4
1930 - 1938	0.	2.4	0.3	0.3	0.3	0.	2.1
1939 - 1945	0.	3.0	0.	0.	1.2	0.	1.2
1946 - 1952	0.	5.1	0.5	0.3	3.5	1.4	2.2
1953 - 1955	1.1	2.6	0.4	1.5	3.3	2.6	3.0
1956 - 1958	0.5	3.3	0.2	0.7	3.1	1.9	1.2
1959 - 1961	0.3	5.3	1.2	0.9	1.7	2.0	1.4
1962 - 1964	0.6	4.2	0.9	0.9	1.5	1.4	1.4
1965 - 1967	0.1	3.8	0.2	0.2	2.1	2.7	1.6

TABLE CONTINUED ON NEXT PAGE

CROSS-TABULATION 5.17.2: PERCENTAGE BREAKDOWN OF NUMBER OF
MANUFACTURING SUBSIDIARIES OF U.S.-BASED PARENT SYSTEMS BY
PRINCIPAL INDUSTRY OF SUBSIDIARY AT DATE OF ENTRY
FOR SUBSIDIARIES CLASSIFIED BY
SUBSIDIARY'S DATE OF ENTRY INTO PARENT SYSTEM
(CONTINUED)

PRINCIPAL INDUSTRY OF SUBSIDIARY AT DATE OF ENTRY

SUBSIDIARY'S DATE OF ENTRY INTO PARENT SYSTEM	OFFICE MACHINES+ COMPUTERS	OTHER NON-EL. MACHINERY	ELECTRIC TRANSMTS. EQUIPMENT	ELECTRIC LIGHTING + WIRING	RADIOS, TV'S+AP- PLIANCES	COMMUNI- CATIONS EQUIPMENT	ELECTRON- IC COM- PONENTS
PRE 1914..................	2.8	0.9	0.	4.7	2.8	0.	0.
1914 - 1919..............	8.6	2.9	0.	1.4	1.4	0.	0.
1920 - 1929..............	2.6	0.8	0.4	0.	2.6	3.8	0.
1930 - 1938..............	4.9	1.0	0.	0.3	1.4	2.4	0.
1939 - 1945..............	3.7	1.8	0.	0.6	0.6	1.8	0.
1946 - 1952..............	3.0	0.	0.	0.3	1.4	0.8	0.8
1953 - 1955..............	1.5	0.4	0.	0.	1.5	2.2	1.1
1956 - 1958..............	1.0	0.7	1.7	0.2	1.7	0.5	0.5
1959 - 1961..............	0.8	0.6	1.4	1.2	2.7	1.0	1.7
1962 - 1964..............	0.4	2.4	0.4	0.8	2.7	0.7	0.9
1965 - 1967..............	0.8	1.5	0.2	0.8	2.5	0.5	1.2

TABLE CONTINUED ON NEXT PAGE

CROSS-TABULATION 5.17.2: PERCENTAGE BREAKDOWN OF NUMBER OF
MANUFACTURING SUBSIDIARIES OF U.S.-BASED PARENT SYSTEMS BY
PRINCIPAL INDUSTRY OF SUBSIDIARY AT DATE OF ENTRY
FOR SUBSIDIARIES CLASSIFIED BY
SUBSIDIARY'S DATE OF ENTRY INTO PARENT SYSTEM
(CONTINUED)

PRINCIPAL INDUSTRY OF SUBSIDIARY AT DATE OF ENTRY

SUBSIDIARY'S DATE OF ENTRY INTO PARENT SYSTEM	OTHER ELECTRIC EQUIPMENT	MOTOR VEHICLES + EQUIP.	OTHER TRANS-PORTATION	PRECI-SION GOODS	MISC. PRODUCTS	TOTAL PERCENT	TOTAL NUMBER
PRE 1914............	1.9	2.9	0.	3.7	2.8	100.	107
1914 - 1919.........	5.7	7.1	0.	0.	1.4	100.	70
1920 - 1929.........	3.0	7.5	0.8	1.5	1.9	100.	265
1930 - 1938.........	4.1	4.1	0.	1.7	2.4	100.	290
1939 - 1945.........	1.2	0.6	0.	0.6	1.2	100.	164
1946 - 1952.........	4.1	2.4	0.5	1.6	2.4	100.	369
1953 - 1955.........	3.3	3.7	0.7	0.7	0.7	100.	269
1956 - 1958.........	3.1	6.0	1.0	1.0	0.7	100.	419
1959 - 1961.........	1.2	4.9	0.7	0.7	2.5	100.	863
1962 - 1964.........	1.8	7.6	0.3	4.1	1.7	100.	904
1965 - 1967.........	2.6	5.6	0.1	3.0	1.6	100.	853

TABULATION 6.1: PERCENTAGE BREAKDOWN OF NUMBER OF MANUFACTURING SUBSIDIARIES BY PRINCIPAL INDUSTRY OF SUBSIDIARY FOR VARIOUS CATEGORIES OF SUBSIDIARIES

PRINCIPAL INDUSTRY OF SUBSIDIARY

CATEGORY OF SUBSIDIARY	ORDNANCE	MEAT PRODUCTS	DAIRY PRODUCTS	CANNED FOODS	GRAIN MILL PRODUCTS	BAKERY PRODUCTS	CONFECTIONERY PRODUCTS
SUBSIDIARIES OF:							
NON-U.S.-BASED SYSTEMS (AS OF 1/1/71)	0.2	0.6	1.8	0.9	0.9	1.5	0.6
U.S.-BASED SYSTEMS (AS OF 1/1/68)	0.3	1.0	2.1	1.4	2.6	1.0	1.6
NON-U.S.-BASED SYSTEMS IN WORLD SUBSET OF SYSTEMS (AS OF 1/1/68)	0.2	0.1	2.3	0.6	0.1	0.1	1.0
U.S.-BASED SYSTEMS IN WORLD SUBSET OF SYSTEMS (AS OF 1/1/68)	0.4	0.7	2.2	1.6	3.1	1.3	0.9

(TABLE CONTINUED ON NEXT PAGE)

TABULATION 6.1: PERCENTAGE BREAKDOWN OF NUMBER OF MANUFACTURING SUBSIDIARIES BY PRINCIPAL INDUSTRY OF SUBSIDIARY FOR VARIOUS CATEGORIES OF SUBSIDIARIES (CONTINUED)

CATEGORY OF SUBSIDIARY	PRINCIPAL INDUSTRY OF SUBSIDIARY						
	BEVER- AGES	OTHER FOOD PRODUCTS	TOBACCO PRODUCTS	TEXTILES	APPAREL	LUMBER AND WOOD	FURN- TURE
SUBSIDIARIES OF:							
NON-U.S.-BASED SYSTEMS (AS OF 1/1/71)..........	3.1	2.8	1.2	4.8	0.8	1.1	0.4
U.S.-BASED SYSTEMS (AS OF 1/1/68)..........	1.6	1.5	0.3	2.4	0.4	0.6	0.5
NON-U.S.-BASED SYSTEMS IN WORLD SUBSET OF SYSTEMS (AS OF 1/1/68)..........	3.6	3.3	2.5	4.9	0.4	0.6	0.3
U.S.-BASED SYSTEMS IN WORLD SUBSET OF SYSTEMS (AS OF 1/1/68)..........	1.9	1.7	0.3	2.7	0.4	0.7	0.1

(TABLE CONTINUED ON NEXT PAGE)

189

TABULATION 6.1: PERCENTAGE BREAKDOWN OF NUMBER OF MANUFACTURING SUBSIDIARIES BY
PRINCIPAL INDUSTRY OF SUBSIDIARY
FOR VARIOUS CATEGORIES OF SUBSIDIARIES
(CONTINUED)

CATEGORY OF SUBSIDIARY	PRINCIPAL INDUSTRY OF SUBSIDIARY						
	PAPER PRODUCTS	PRINTED MATTER	INDUS-TRIAL CHEMICALS	PLASTICS AND SYN-THETICS	DRUGS	SOAP AND COSMETICS	PAINTS
SUBSIDIARIES OF:							
NON-U.S.-BASED SYSTEMS (AS OF 1/1/71)........	2.8	2.6	4.9	3.1	4.6	3.2	2.2
U.S.-BASED SYSTEMS (AS OF 1/1/68)........	4.3	3.7	6.8	4.5	8.9	4.0	1.5
NON-U.S.-BASED SYSTEMS IN WORLD SUBSET OF SYSTEMS (AS OF 1/1/68)........	3.1	3.7	4.2	2.7	4.7	3.3	1.8
U.S.-BASED SYSTEMS IN WORLD SUBSET OF SYSTEMS (AS OF 1/1/68)........	5.5	1.8	7.3	5.4	7.5	3.1	1.9

(TABLE CONTINUED ON NEXT PAGE)

TABULATION 6.1: PERCENTAGE BREAKDOWN OF NUMBER OF MANUFACTURING SUBSIDIARIES BY PRINCIPAL INDUSTRY OF SUBSIDIARY FOR VARIOUS CATEGORIES OF SUBSIDIARIES (CONTINUED)

CATEGORY OF SUBSIDIARY	PRINCIPAL INDUSTRY OF SUBSIDIARY						
	AGRI-CULTURAL CHEMICALS	OTHER CHEMICALS	REFINED PETRO-LEUM	OTHER PETROLEUM PRODUCTS	TIRES	OTHER RUBBER PRODUCTS	LEATHER PRODUCTS + SHOES
SUBSIDIARIES OF:							
NON-U.S.-BASED SYSTEMS (AS OF 1/1/71)............	1.6	3.1	2.2	1.7	0.7	1.4	0.1
U.S.-BASED SYSTEMS (AS OF 1/1/68)............	1.3	2.1	3.0	1.9	2.2	0.9	0.3
NON-U.S.-BASED SYSTEMS IN WORLD SUBSET OF SYSTEMS (AS OF 1/1/68)............	1.8	2.9	3.7	1.6	1.2	1.4	0.
U.S.-BASED SYSTEMS IN WORLD SUBSET OF SYSTEMS (AS OF 1/1/68)............	1.7	1.5	4.7	2.3	2.8	1.6	0.3

(TABLE CONTINUED ON NEXT PAGE)

TABULATION 6.1: PERCENTAGE BREAKDOWN OF NUMBER OF MANUFACTURING SUBSIDIARIES BY PRINCIPAL INDUSTRY OF SUBSIDIARY FOR VARIOUS CATEGORIES OF SUBSIDIARIES (CONTINUED)

CATEGORY OF SUBSIDIARY	PRINCIPAL INDUSTRY OF SUBSIDIARY						
	GLASS PRODUCTS	STONE, CLAY + CONCRETE	IRON AND STEEL	NON-FERROUS SMELTING	NON-FERROUS PRODUCTS	METAL CANS	STRUCTURAL METAL PRODUCTS
SUBSIDIARIES OF:							
NON-U.S.-BASED SYSTEMS (AS OF 1/1/71)............	1.0	1.6	3.5	1.9	2.8	0.7	1.3
U.S.-BASED SYSTEMS (AS OF 1/1/68)............	1.1	2.0	0.9	1.2	1.0	0.8	0.7
NON-U.S.-BASED SYSTEMS IN WORLD SUBSET OF SYSTEMS (AS OF 1/1/68)............	1.2	1.4	2.8	1.9	3.2	0.9	1.1
U.S.-BASED SYSTEMS IN WORLD SUBSET OF SYSTEMS (AS OF 1/1/68)............	1.4	1.5	0.7	1.5	1.0	0.9	0.7

(TABLE CONTINUED ON NEXT PAGE)

TABULATION 6.1: PERCENTAGE BREAKDOWN OF NUMBER OF MANUFACTURING SUBSIDIARIES BY PRINCIPAL INDUSTRY OF SUBSIDIARY FOR VARIOUS CATEGORIES OF SUBSIDIARIES (CONTINUED)

CATEGORY OF SUBSIDIARY	PRINCIPAL INDUSTRY OF SUBSIDIARY						
	FABRICATED WIRE PRODUCTS	OTHER FABRICATED METAL	ENGINES AND TURBINES	FARM MACHINERY	CONSTRUCTION MACHINERY	SPECIAL INDUSTRY MACHINERY	GENERAL INDUSTRY MACHINERY
SUBSIDIARIES OF:							
NON-U.S.-BASED SYSTEMS (AS OF 1/1/71)...............	0.9	3.5	1.0	0.7	0.4	1.6	1.5
U.S.-BASED SYSTEMS (AS OF 1/1/68)...............	1.3	3.9	0.5	0.9	2.2	2.1	1.6
NON-U.S.-BASED SYSTEMS IN WORLD SUBSET OF SYSTEMS (AS OF 1/1/68)...............	0.9	2.8	1.2	1.0	0.2	1.4	1.7
U.S.-BASED SYSTEMS IN WORLD SUBSET OF SYSTEMS (AS OF 1/1/68)...............	0.4	3.1	0.3	1.0	2.3	1.2	1.8

(TABLE CONTINUED ON NEXT PAGE)

TABULATION 6.1: PERCENTAGE BREAKDOWN OF NUMBER OF MANUFACTURING SUBSIDIARIES BY PRINCIPAL INDUSTRY OF SUBSIDIARY FOR VARIOUS CATEGORIES OF SUBSIDIARIES (CONTINUED)

PRINCIPAL INDUSTRY OF SUBSIDIARY

CATEGORY OF SUBSIDIARY	OFFICE MACHINES+ COMPUTERS	OTHER NON-EL. MACHINERY	ELECTRIC TRANSMIS. EQUIPMENT	ELECTRIC LIGHTING +WIRING	RADIOS, TV'S+AP- PLIANCES	COMMUNI- CATIONS EQUIPMENT	ELECTRON- IC COM- PONENTS
SUBSIDIARIES OF:							
NON-U.S.-BASED SYSTEMS (AS OF 1/1/71)............	0.6	0.6	1.8	2.2	3.2	1.8	2.0
U.S.-BASED SYSTEMS (AS OF 1/1/68)............	1.4	1.3	0.5	0.7	2.3	0.9	1.1
NON-U.S.-BASED SYSTEMS IN WORLD SUBSET OF SYSTEMS (AS OF 1/1/68)............	0.7	0.5	2.5	3.4	2.3	2.3	1.8
U.S.-BASED SYSTEMS IN WORLD SUBSET OF SYSTEMS (AS OF 1/1/68)............	1.7	1.0	0.4	0.8	2.3	1.1	1.2

(TABLE CONTINUED ON NEXT PAGE)

TABULATION 6.1: PERCENTAGE BREAKDOWN OF NUMBER OF MANUFACTURING SUBSIDIARIES BY PRINCIPAL INDUSTRY OF SUBSIDIARY FOR VARIOUS CATEGORIES OF SUBSIDIARIES (CONTINUED)

	PRINCIPAL INDUSTRY OF SUBSIDIARY						
CATEGORY OF SUBSIDIARY	OTHER ELECTRIC EQUIPMENT	MOTOR VEHICLES + EQUIP.	OTHER TRANS-PORTATION	PREC-SION GOODS	MISC. PRODUCTS	TOTAL PERCENT	TOTAL NUMBER
SUBSIDIARIES OF:							
NON-U.S.-BASED SYSTEMS (AS OF 1/1/71)............	3.8	3.7	1.2	1.6	1.6	100.	5023
U.S.-BASED SYSTEMS (AS OF 1/1/68)............	2.6	5.5	0.5	2.0	1.8	100.	3737
NON-U.S.-BASED SYSTEMS IN WORLD SUBSET OF SYSTEMS (AS OF 1/1/68)............	4.1	3.4	1.4	0.8	1.4	100.	2220
U.S.-BASED SYSTEMS IN WORLD SUBSET OF SYSTEMS (AS OF 1/1/68)............	2.0	5.6	0.3	1.1	0.9	100.	2922

TABULATION 6.2: PERCENTAGE BREAKDOWN OF SALES OF SUBSIDIARIES IN 1970 BY PRINCIPAL INDUSTRY OF SUBSIDIARY AS OF 1/1/71 FOR MANUFACTURING SUBSIDIARIES OF NON-U.S.-BASED SYSTEMS

PRINCIPAL INDUSTRY OF SUBSIDIARY AS OF 1/1/71	PERCENTAGE
ORDNANCE	0.1
MEAT PRODUCTS	0.3
DAIRY PRODUCTS	0.8
CANNED FOODS	0.9
GRAIN MILL PRODUCTS	0.4
BAKERY PRODUCTS	0.1
CONFECTIONERY PRODUCTS	0.2
BEVERAGES	1.3
OTHER FOOD PRODUCTS	3.0
TOBACCO PRODUCTS	4.9
TEXTILES	3.0
APPAREL	0.1
LUMBER AND WOOD	0.2
FURNITURE	0.1
PAPER PRODUCTS	2.3
PRINTED MATTER	1.2
INDUSTRIAL CHEMICALS	6.1
PLASTICS AND SYNTHETICS	1.9
DRUGS	2.7
SOAP AND COSMETICS	1.6
PAINTS	0.6
AGRICULTURAL CHEMICALS	1.0
OTHER CHEMICALS	1.9
REFINED PETROLEUM	25.
OTHER PETROLEUM PRODUCTS	2.2
TIRES	1.4
OTHER RUBBER PRODUCTS	0.4
LEATHER PRODUCTS + SHOES	0.1

(TABLE CONTINUED ON NEXT PAGE)

TABULATION 6.2: PERCENTAGE BREAKDOWN OF SALES OF SUBSIDIARIES IN 1970 BY PRINCIPAL INDUSTRY OF SUBSIDIARY AS OF 1/1/71 FOR MANUFACTURING SUBSIDIARIES OF NON-U.S.-BASED SYSTEMS (CONTINUED)

PRINCIPAL INDUSTRY OF SUBSIDIARY AS OF 1/1/71	PERCENTAGE
GLASS PRODUCTS.........	0.7
STONE, CLAY + CONCRETE PROD...	0.8
IRON AND STEEL.........	5.8
NON-FERROUS SMELTING........	3.1
NON-FERROUS PRODUCTS........	2.1
METAL CANS.........	0.4
STRUCTURAL METAL PRODUCTS.....	0.5
FABRICATED WIRE PRODUCTS......	0.8
OTHER FABRICATED METAL.......	2.2
ENGINES AND TURBINES........	0.5
FARM MACHINERY.........	0.8
CONSTRUCTION MACHINERY.......	0.1
SPECIAL INDUSTRY MACHINERY....	0.5
GENERAL INDUSTRY MACHINERY....	1.2
OFFICE MACHINES + COMPUTERS...	0.6
OTHER NON-EL. MACHINERY......	0.2
ELECTRIC TRANSMIS. EQUIPMENT..	2.3
ELECTRIC LIGHTING + WIRING....	0.6
RADIOS, TV'S + APPLIANCES.....	1.3
COMMUNICATIONS EQUIPMENT......	1.7
ELECTRONIC COMPONENTS........	1.3
OTHER ELECTRIC EQUIPMENT......	1.7
MOTOR VEHICLES + EQUIPMENT....	6.4
OTHER TRANSPORTATION EQUIP....	0.5
PRECISION GOODS.........	0.4
MISC. PRODUCTS.........	0.3
TOTAL PERCENTAGE.........	100.
TOTAL VALUE OF SALES IN $ BIL.	74.9

CROSS-TABULATION 6. 1.1: PERCENTAGE BREAKDOWN OF NUMBER (AS OF 1/1/71) OF
MANUFACTURING SUBSIDIARIES OF NON-U.S.-BASED PARENT SYSTEMS BY
PRINCIPAL INDUSTRY OF SUBSIDIARY AS OF 1/1/71
FOR SUBSIDIARIES CLASSIFIED BY
SUBSIDIARY'S COUNTRY

PRINCIPAL INDUSTRY OF SUBSIDIARY AS OF 1/1/71

SUBSIDIARY'S COUNTRY	ORDNANCE	MEAT PRODUCTS	DAIRY PRODUCTS	CANNED FOODS	GRAIN MILL PRODUCTS	BAKERY PRODUCTS	CONFEC-TIONERY PRODUCTS
UNITED STATES	0.	0.	1.1	2.3	0.6	0.	0.3
CANADA	0.4	0.4	3.2	1.2	0.	0.	1.2
MEXICO	0.	0.	2.4	1.2	0.	0.	0.
CENTRAL AMERICA AND CARIB.	0.	0.	2.4	1.2	0.	0.	1.2
VENEZUELA	0.	0.	0.	0.	0.	0.	2.6
COLOMBIA	0.	0.	0.	0.	0.	0.	0.
PERU	0.	0.	0.	3.6	0.	0.	0.
CHILE	0.	0.	3.8	0.	0.	0.	0.
ARGENTINA	0.9	0.9	0.9	0.	0.	0.	0.
BRAZIL	0.6	0.6	0.	0.	0.	0.	0.6
OTHER SOUTH AMERICA	0.	5.3	0.	0.	0.	0.	5.3
GERMANY	0.6	1.1	1.8	1.4	0.4	0.	0.
FRANCE	0.	0.6	1.9	0.3	0.	0.3	0.
ITALY	0.	0.6	2.8	0.6	0.	0.	0.
BELGIUM AND LUXEMBURG	0.	1.4	3.5	0.	0.	0.	0.7
THE NETHERLANDS	0.	0.8	1.7	0.	0.	0.8	0.
UNITED KINGDOM	0.	0.4	1.3	0.4	0.4	0.	0.9
IRELAND	0.	3.4	6.7	5.6	9.0	5.6	2.2
DENMARK	0.	0.	2.6	2.6	0.	0.	2.6
NORWAY	0.	0.	4.5	0.5	0.	0.	0.
SWEDEN	0.	0.	1.5	1.5	0.	0.	0.
FINLAND	0.	0.	0.	0.	0.	0.	0.

TABLE CONTINUED ON NEXT PAGE

CROSS-TABULATION 6. 1.1: PERCENTAGE BREAKDOWN OF NUMBER (AS OF 1/1/71) OF
MANUFACTURING SUBSIDIARIES OF NON-U.S.-BASED PARENT SYSTEMS BY
PRINCIPAL INDUSTRY OF SUBSIDIARY AS OF 1/1/71
FOR SUBSIDIARIES CLASSIFIED BY
SUBSIDIARY'S COUNTRY
(CONTINUED)

PRINCIPAL INDUSTRY OF SUBSIDIARY AS OF 1/1/71

SUBSIDIARY'S COUNTRY	ORDNANCE	MEAT PRODUCTS	DAIRY PRODUCTS	CANNED FOODS	GRAIN MILL PRODUCTS	BAKERY PRODUCTS	CONFEC- TIONERY PRODUCTS
SWITZERLAND	0.	0.	0.	0.	0.	0.	0.
AUSTRIA	2.6	0.	1.3	0.	0.	0.	0.
PORTUGAL	0.	0.	4.2	0.	0.	0.	0.
SPAIN	0.	0.	1.2	0.6	0.	0.	0.6
GREECE	0.	0.	0.	0.	0.	0.	0.3
TURKEY	0.	0.	0.	0.	0.	0.	3.3
OTHER EUROPE + ISRAEL	0.	2.9	0.	0.	0.	0.	0.
PAKISTAN	0.	0.	2.7	0.	2.7	0.	0.
IRAN	0.	0.	0.	0.	0.	0.	0.
OTHER MID EAST+EGYPT+LIBYA	0.	0.	0.	0.	0.	0.	0.
UNION OF SOUTH AFRICA	0.	0.	2.5	1.2	4.3	9.2	0.9
RHODESIA	0.	2.0	2.0	2.0	2.0	0.	0.
ZAMBIA	0.	0.	0.	0.	0.	0.	0.
TANZANIA	0.	9.1	0.	0.	0.	0.	0.
KENYA	0.	0.	7.5	2.5	0.	0.	0.
NIGERIA	0.	4.0	2.0	2.0	0.	0.	4.0
OTHER (BRITISH) AFRICA	0.	0.	0.	1.9	1.9	1.9	0.
MOROCCO, ALGERIA + TUNISIA	0.	0.	0.	0.	0.	0.	0.
OTHER (FRENCH) AFRICA	0.	0.	2.2	0.	0.	0.	2.2
OTHER AFRICA	0.	3.2	0.	0.	0.	0.	0.
AUSTRALIA	0.	0.3	1.8	0.8	3.7	8.7	1.3
NEW ZEALAND	0.	4.0	3.0	0.	1.0	3.0	2.0

TABLE CONTINUED ON NEXT PAGE

CROSS-TABULATION 6. 1.1: PERCENTAGE BREAKDOWN OF NUMBER (AS OF 1/1/71) OF
MANUFACTURING SUBSIDIARIES OF NON-U.S.-BASED PARENT SYSTEMS BY
PRINCIPAL INDUSTRY OF SUBSIDIARY AS OF 1/1/71
FOR SUBSIDIARIES CLASSIFIED BY
SUBSIDIARY'S COUNTRY
(CONTINUED)

PRINCIPAL INDUSTRY OF SUBSIDIARY AS OF 1/1/71

SUBSIDIARY'S COUNTRY	ORDNANCE	MEAT PRODUCTS	DAIRY PRODUCTS	CANNED FOODS	GRAIN MILL PRODUCTS	BAKERY PRODUCTS	CONFEC-TIONERY PRODUCTS
JAPAN...............	0.	0.	0.	0.	0.	0.	0.
CHINA (TAIWAN)......	0.	0.	0.	1.1	0.	0.	0.
HONG KONG...........	0.	0.	0.	0.	0.	0.	0.
THE PHILIPPINES.....	4.5	0.	4.5	0.	0.	0.	0.
MALAYSIA............	0.	0.	0.	0.	1.9	0.	0.
SINGAPORE...........	0.	0.	2.1	0.	0.	0.	0.
INDONESIA...........	0.	0.	0.	4.3	0.	0.	0.
THAILAND............	0.	0.	1.6	0.	0.	0.	0.
INDIA...............	0.	0.	0.7	0.7	0.	0.7	0.7
OTHER ASIA AND OCEANIA.....	0.	0.	0.	1.7	0.	0.	0.

TABLE CONTINUED ON NEXT PAGE

CROSS-TABULATION 6.1.1: PERCENTAGE BREAKDOWN OF NUMBER (AS OF 1/1/71) OF MANUFACTURING SUBSIDIARIES OF NON-U.S.-BASED PARENT SYSTEMS BY PRINCIPAL INDUSTRY OF SUBSIDIARY AS OF 1/1/71 FOR SUBSIDIARIES CLASSIFIED BY SUBSIDIARY'S COUNTRY (CONTINUED)

SUBSIDIARY'S COUNTRY	PRINCIPAL INDUSTRY OF SUBSIDIARY AS OF 1/1/71						
	BEVER-AGES	OTHER FOOD PRODUCTS	TOBACCO PRODUCTS	TEXTILES	APPAREL	LUMBER AND WOOD	FURNI-TURE
UNITED STATES	3.4	3.1	0.6	1.4	0.	0.3	0.6
CANADA	2.0	4.8	2.0	3.2	0.4	2.0	0.4
MEXICO	2.4	0.	1.2	3.6	0.	0.	0.
CENTRAL AMERICA AND CARIB.	7.1	3.6	9.5	8.3	0.	0.	0.
VENEZUELA	5.3	0.	0.	11.	0.	0.	0.
COLOMBIA	0.	3.8	0.	12.	0.	3.8	0.
PERU	3.6	7.1	0.	7.1	0.	0.	0.
CHILE	0.	0.	0.	7.7	0.	3.8	0.
ARGENTINA	2.8	2.8	0.9	4.6	0.	0.	0.9
BRAZIL	1.2	2.5	1.2	7.4	0.	0.	0.
OTHER SOUTH AMERICA	5.3	11.	5.3	11.	0.	0.	0.
GERMANY	1.4	2.5	0.7	4.6	0.7	0.7	0.4
FRANCE	4.5	2.8	0.	2.5	0.	0.8	0.3
ITALY	2.2	0.	0.	2.2	0.	0.6	0.
BELGIUM AND LUXEMBURG	3.5	2.1	0.7	2.1	0.	0.	0.
THE NETHERLANDS	2.5	2.5	2.5	1.7	0.	0.8	0.8
UNITED KINGDOM	2.1	0.	0.	1.7	0.4	1.7	1.3
IRELAND	6.7	3.4	1.1	0.	1.1	1.1	1.1
DENMARK	0.	7.9	2.6	0.	0.	0.	2.6
NORWAY	0.	2.3	0.	0.	0.	2.3	2.3
SWEDEN	1.5	9.2	0.	3.1	0.	5.3	0.
FINLAND	0.	5.3	5.3	0.	0.	5.3	0.

TABLE CONTINUED ON NEXT PAGE

CROSS-TABULATION 6.1.1: PERCENTAGE BREAKDOWN OF NUMBER (AS OF 1/1/71) OF MANUFACTURING SUBSIDIARIES OF NON-U.S.-BASED PARENT SYSTEMS BY PRINCIPAL INDUSTRY OF SUBSIDIARY AS OF 1/1/71 FOR SUBSIDIARIES CLASSIFIED BY SUBSIDIARY'S COUNTRY (CONTINUED)

PRINCIPAL INDUSTRY OF SUBSIDIARY AS OF 1/1/71

SUBSIDIARY'S COUNTRY	BEVER-AGES	OTHER FOOD PRODUCTS	TOBACCO PRODUCTS	TEXTILES	APPAREL	LUMBER AND WOOD	FURNI-TURE
SWITZERLAND	2.2	8.7	2.2	4.3	2.2	0.	0.
AUSTRIA	0.	2.6	0.	2.6	0.	0.	0.
PORTUGAL	4.2	2.1	0.	8.3	0.	2.1	0.
SPAIN	2.4	2.4	0.	6.0	0.	0.	0.
GREECE	4.3	0.	0.	0.	0.	0.	0.
TURKEY	0.	3.3	0.	3.3	0.	0.	0.
OTHER EUROPE + ISRAEL	5.9	2.9	5.9	12.	2.9	0.	0.
PAKISTAN	0.	0.	2.7	5.4	0.	0.	0.
IRAN	0.	0.	0.	4.8	0.	0.	0.
OTHER MID EAST+EGYPT+LIBYA	0.	0.	0.	0.	0.	0.	0.
UNION OF SOUTH AFRICA	1.8	4.0	0.3	2.8	1.8	3.1	0.6
RHODESIA	24.	0.	8.0	2.0	0.	2.0	0.
ZAMBIA	38.	2.7	2.7	0.	0.	2.7	0.
TANZANIA	9.1	0.	4.5	9.1	9.1	0.	0.
KENYA	10.	0.	2.5	2.5	2.5	0.	0.
NIGERIA	4.0	2.0	2.0	12.	2.0	4.0	0.
OTHER (BRITISH) AFRICA	11.	5.7	7.5	3.8	3.8	7.5	0.
MOROCCO, ALGERIA + TUNISIA	0.	0.	0.	0.	0.	0.	0.
OTHER (FRENCH) AFRICA	2.2	2.2	0.	2.2	0.	0.	0.
OTHER AFRICA	3.2	6.5	3.2	26.	3.2	0.	0.
AUSTRALIA	3.7	3.2	0.3	3.4	1.8	2.4	0.5

TABLE CONTINUED ON NEXT PAGE

202

CROSS-TABULATION 6. 1.1: PERCENTAGE BREAKDOWN OF NUMBER (AS OF 1/1/71) OF
MANUFACTURING SUBSIDIARIES OF NON-U.S.-BASED PARENT SYSTEMS BY
PRINCIPAL INDUSTRY OF SUBSIDIARY AS OF 1/1/71
FOR SUBSIDIARIES CLASSIFIED BY
SUBSIDIARY'S COUNTRY
(CONTINUED)

PRINCIPAL INDUSTRY OF SUBSIDIARY AS OF 1/1/71

SUBSIDIARY'S COUNTRY	BEVER-AGES	OTHER FOOD PRODUCTS	TOBACCO PRODUCTS	TEXTILES	APPAREL	LUMBER AND WOOD	FURNI-TURE
NEW ZEALAND.........	6.1	8.1	1.0	1.0	0.	0.	1.0
JAPAN...........	0.	1.4	0.	2.9	0.	0.	0.
CHINA (TAIWAN).....	0.	0.	0.	36.	6.4	0.	0.
HONG KONG.........	0.	0.	3.8	38.	12.	0.	0.
THE PHILIPPINES.....	0.	4.5	0.	4.5	0.	0.	0.
MALAYSIA........	0.	5.6	1.9	1.9	0.	3.7	0.
SINGAPORE......	4.3	4.3	4.3	6.4	2.1	2.1	0.
INDONESIA......	0.	8.7	4.3	17.	0.	0.	0.
THAILAND......	0.	3.2	0.	21.	3.2	0.	0.
INDIA.........	0.	0.7	1.5	2.9	0.	0.	0.
OTHER ASIA AND OCEANIA.......	0.	3.4	3.4	12.	3.4	0.	0.

TABLE CONTINUED ON NEXT PAGE

CROSS-TABULATION 6.1.1: PERCENTAGE BREAKDOWN OF NUMBER (AS OF 1/1/71) OF
MANUFACTURING SUBSIDIARIES OF NON-U.S.-BASED PARENT SYSTEMS BY
PRINCIPAL INDUSTRY OF SUBSIDIARY AS OF 1/1/71
FOR SUBSIDIARIES CLASSIFIED BY
SUBSIDIARY'S COUNTRY
(CONTINUED)

PRINCIPAL INDUSTRY OF SUBSIDIARY AS OF 1/1/71

SUBSIDIARY'S COUNTRY	PAPER PRODUCTS	PRINTED MATTER	INDUSTRIAL CHEMICALS	PLASTICS AND SYNTHETICS	DRUGS	SOAP AND COSMETICS	PAINTS
UNITED STATES	2.5	4.2	5.1	2.8	5.1	2.3	0.9
CANADA	8.4	0.4	4.4	2.0	2.4	2.0	2.8
MEXICO	1.2	1.2	7.1	4.8	15.	3.6	2.4
CENTRAL AMERICA AND CARIB.	3.6	4.8	2.4	1.2	1.2	3.6	2.4
VENEZUELA	0.	2.6	5.3	5.3	7.9	7.9	2.6
COLOMBIA	3.8	0.	3.8	3.8	12.	12.	0.
PERU	0.	0.	3.6	0.	14.	3.6	0.
CHILE	0.	3.8	23.	3.8	7.7	7.7	0.
ARGENTINA	1.9	1.9	8.3	3.7	8.3	2.8	0.9
BRAZIL	1.2	1.2	7.4	4.3	3.7	3.1	1.2
OTHER SOUTH AMERICA	0.	0.	5.3	0.	11.	11.	0.
GERMANY	2.5	0.4	6.7	2.8	4.2	5.7	2.5
FRANCE	1.9	2.5	4.2	6.7	5.8	3.6	3.9
ITALY	2.8	1.7	5.6	5.6	3.9	3.4	4.5
BELGIUM AND LUXEMBURG	4.9	3.5	5.6	2.1	2.8	0.7	2.1
THE NETHERLANDS	5.0	4.2	4.2	8.4	3.4	0.	2.5
UNITED KINGDOM	3.0	3.0	2.1	2.6	5.2	0.	2.1
IRELAND	5.6	0.	2.2	1.1	4.5	4.5	2.2
DENMARK	2.6	0.	0.	5.3	2.6	7.9	5.3
NORWAY	9.1	0.	2.3	2.3	2.3	0.	2.3
SWEDEN	6.2	1.5	3.1	3.1	3.1	6.2	1.5
FINLAND	0.	0.	5.3	0.	0.	5.3	5.3

TABLE CONTINUED ON NEXT PAGE

CROSS-TABULATION 6.1.1: PERCENTAGE BREAKDOWN OF NUMBER (AS OF 1/1/71) OF MANUFACTURING SUBSIDIARIES OF NON-U.S.-BASED PARENT SYSTEMS BY PRINCIPAL INDUSTRY OF SUBSIDIARY AS OF 1/1/71 FOR SUBSIDIARIES CLASSIFIED BY SUBSIDIARY'S COUNTRY (CONTINUED)

PRINCIPAL INDUSTRY OF SUBSIDIARY AS OF 1/1/71

SUBSIDIARY'S COUNTRY	PAPER PRODUCTS	PRINTED MATTER	INDUSTRIAL CHEMICALS	PLASTICS AND SYNTHETICS	DRUGS	SOAP AND COSMETICS	PAINTS
SWITZERLAND	2.2	2.2	4.3	0.	2.2	6.5	0.
AUSTRIA	2.6	0.	9.1	9.1	9.1	5.2	0.
PORTUGAL	0.	0.	6.3	8.3	6.3	4.2	4.2
SPAIN	1.2	0.	11.	4.8	6.6	1.2	3.0
GREECE	0.	4.3	0.	0.	8.7	4.3	8.7
TURKEY	0.	0.	3.3	0.	17.	13.	0.
OTHER EUROPE + ISRAEL	0.	0.	2.9	2.9	5.9	2.9	0.
PAKISTAN	0.	0.	11.	0.	16.	5.4	0.
IRAN	4.8	0.	4.8	0.	14.	0.	0.
OTHER MID EAST+EGYPT+LIBYA	0.	0.	0.	0.	18.	0.	0.
UNION OF SOUTH AFRICA	1.8	1.2	3.4	1.2	2.1	3.4	2.5
RHODESIA	2.0	0.	4.0	2.0	0.	4.0	4.0
ZAMBIA	0.	8.1	5.4	0.	0.	2.7	5.4
TANZANIA	0.	4.5	4.5	0.	0.	0.	0.
KENYA	2.5	13.	7.5	0.	0.	2.5	2.5
NIGERIA	4.0	2.0	4.0	0.	2.0	8.0	4.0
OTHER (BRITISH) AFRICA	1.9	3.8	7.5	0.	3.8	7.5	1.9
MOROCCO, ALGERIA + TUNISIA	5.4	2.7	2.7	0.	8.1	0.	0.
OTHER (FRENCH) AFRICA	2.2	2.2	6.7	0.	2.2	2.2	0.
OTHER AFRICA	3.2	0.	0.	0.	3.2	6.5	0.
AUSTRALIA	5.3	2.4	4.5	1.6	1.3	3.2	1.6

TABLE CONTINUED ON NEXT PAGE

CROSS-TABULATION 6.1.1: PERCENTAGE BREAKDOWN OF NUMBER (AS OF 1/1/71) OF MANUFACTURING SUBSIDIARIES OF NON-U.S.-BASED PARENT SYSTEMS BY PRINCIPAL INDUSTRY OF SUBSIDIARY AS OF 1/1/71 FOR SUBSIDIARIES CLASSIFIED BY SUBSIDIARY'S COUNTRY (CONTINUED)

PRINCIPAL INDUSTRY OF SUBSIDIARY AS OF 1/1/71

SUBSIDIARY'S COUNTRY	PAPER PRODUCTS	PRINTED MATTER	INDUS-TRIAL CHEMICALS	PLASTICS AND SYN-THETICS	DRUGS	SOAP AND COSMETICS	PAINTS
NEW ZEALAND	2.0	2.0	1.0	2.0	2.0	2.0	5.1
JAPAN	0.	2.9	10.	5.7	7.1	2.9	4.3
CHINA (TAIWAN)	0.	0.	0.	3.2	2.1	0.	1.1
HONG KONG	0.	3.8	7.7	0.	0.	3.8	3.8
THE PHILIPPINES	0.	0.	0.	4.5	14.	0.	0.
MALAYSIA	3.7	1.9	5.6	1.9	1.9	3.7	1.9
SINGAPORE	2.1	2.1	2.1	0.	2.1	6.4	2.1
INDONESIA	0.	4.3	4.3	4.3	8.7	8.7	0.
THAILAND	0.	0.	1.6	1.6	3.2	1.6	0.
INDIA	0.7	1.5	4.4	5.9	6.6	0.7	2.2
OTHER ASIA AND OCEANIA	0.	1.7	8.5	0.	5.1	1.7	3.4

TABLE CONTINUED ON NEXT PAGE

CROSS-TABULATION 6. 1.1: PERCENTAGE BREAKDOWN OF NUMBER (AS OF 1/1/71) OF MANUFACTURING SUBSIDIARIES OF NON-U.S.-BASED PARENT SYSTEMS BY PRINCIPAL INDUSTRY OF SUBSIDIARY AS OF 1/1/71 FOR SUBSIDIARIES CLASSIFIED BY SUBSIDIARY'S COUNTRY (CONTINUED)

PRINCIPAL INDUSTRY OF SUBSIDIARY AS OF 1/1/71

SUBSIDIARY'S COUNTRY	AGRI-CULTURAL CHEMICALS	OTHER CHEMICALS	REFINED PETRO-LEUM	OTHER PETROLEUM PRODUCTS	TIRES	OTHER RUBBER PRODUCTS	LEATHER PRODUCTS + SHOES
UNITED STATES	3.4	3.4	2.5	0.8	0.3	0.3	0.3
CANADA	2.8	2.0	2.0	0.8	0.	0.8	0.
MEXICO	1.2	0.	0.	0.	0.	0.	0.
CENTRAL AMERICA AND CARIB.	3.6	1.2	6.0	0.	1.2	1.2	0.
VENEZUELA	2.6	0.	2.6	0.	0.	2.6	0.
COLOMBIA	3.8	0.	0.	0.	0.	0.	0.
PERU	3.6	3.6	0.	0.	0.	0.	0.
CHILE	0.	7.7	0.	0.	0.	0.	0.
ARGENTINA	1.9	2.8	0.9	0.	0.9	1.9	0.9
BRAZIL	4.3	3.7	0.	0.	0.	0.6	0.6
OTHER SOUTH AMERICA	0.	5.3	5.3	5.3	0.	0.	0.
GERMANY	0.7	2.5	3.2	2.5	1.1	1.4	0.
FRANCE	1.7	3.6	1.9	1.4	0.8	1.1	0.
ITALY	1.1	1.7	2.8	1.7	0.6	1.1	0.
BELGIUM AND LUXEMBURG	0.7	5.6	2.1	2.8	0.7	2.1	0.
THE NETHERLANDS	1.7	4.2	0.8	3.4	0.8	2.5	0.
UNITED KINGDOM	1.7	6.0	0.	4.7	1.3	0.4	0.
IRELAND	2.2	0.	1.1	2.2	1.1	1.1	0.
DENMARK	0.	2.6	5.3	2.6	0.	0.	0.
NORWAY	0.	2.3	2.3	0.	0.	0.	0.
SWEDEN	0.	1.5	3.1	3.1	0.	1.5	0.
FINLAND	0.	5.3	0.	0.	0.	0.	0.

TABLE CONTINUED ON NEXT PAGE

CROSS-TABULATION 6. 1. 1: PERCENTAGE BREAKDOWN OF NUMBER (AS OF 1/1/71) OF MANUFACTURING SUBSIDIARIES OF NON-U.S.-BASED PARENT SYSTEMS BY PRINCIPAL INDUSTRY OF SUBSIDIARY AS OF 1/1/71 FOR SUBSIDIARIES CLASSIFIED BY SUBSIDIARY'S COUNTRY (CONTINUED)

PRINCIPAL INDUSTRY OF SUBSIDIARY AS OF 1/1/71

SUBSIDIARY'S COUNTRY	AGRI-CULTURAL CHEMICALS	OTHER CHEMICALS	REFINED PETRO-LEUM	OTHER PETROLEUM PRODUCTS	TIRES	OTHER RUBBER PRODUCTS	LEATHER PRODUCTS + SHOES
SWITZERLAND	0.	8.7	6.5	2.2	0.	2.2	0.
AUSTRIA	0.	1.3	2.6	2.6	0.	1.3	0.
PORTUGAL	2.1	2.1	0.	2.1	0.	2.1	0.
SPAIN	1.2	4.2	1.2	0.6	1.8	3.0	0.6
GREECE	4.3	0.	0.	0.	4.3	4.3	0.
TURKEY	6.7	3.3	3.3	0.	3.3	0.	0.
OTHER EUROPE + ISRAEL	0.	0.	0.	0.	0.	0.	0.
PAKISTAN	0.	5.4	2.7	5.4	0.	0.	0.
IRAN	0.	0.	4.8	4.8	0.	0.	0.
OTHER MID EAST+EGYPT+LIBYA	4.5	4.5	18.	0.	0.	0.	0.
UNION OF SOUTH AFRICA	0.	4.9	0.6	1.2	0.6	3.4	0.
RHODESIA	4.0	0.	0.	2.0	2.0	0.	0.
ZAMBIA	2.7	2.7	0.	0.	2.7	0.	0.
TANZANIA	4.5	4.5	4.5	0.	0.	0.	0.
KENYA	5.0	5.0	2.5	0.	0.	2.5	0.
NIGERIA	2.0	0.	2.0	0.	4.0	0.	2.0
OTHER (BRITISH) AFRICA	0.	0.	5.7	0.	1.9	0.	0.
MOROCCO, ALGERIA + TUNISIA	2.7	2.7	11.	11.	0.	0.	0.
OTHER (FRENCH) AFRICA	0.	6.7	22.	6.7	0.	0.	0.
OTHER AFRICA	3.2	3.2	9.7	0.	0.	0.	0.
AUSTRALIA	1.3	2.4	1.1	2.1	0.3	1.8	0.

TABLE CONTINUED ON NEXT PAGE

CROSS-TABULATION 6. 1.1: PERCENTAGE BREAKDOWN OF NUMBER (AS OF 1/1/71) OF
MANUFACTURING SUBSIDIARIES OF NON-U.S.-BASED PARENT SYSTEMS BY
PRINCIPAL INDUSTRY OF SUBSIDIARY AS OF 1/1/71
FOR SUBSIDIARIES CLASSIFIED BY
SUBSIDIARY'S COUNTRY
(CONTINUED)

PRINCIPAL INDUSTRY OF SUBSIDIARY AS OF 1/1/71

SUBSIDIARY'S COUNTRY	AGRI-CULTURAL CHEMICALS	OTHER CHEMICALS	REFINED PETRO-LEUM	OTHER PETROLEUM PRODUCTS	TIRES	OTHER RUBBER PRODUCTS	LEATHER PRODUCTS + SHOES
NEW ZEALAND........	1.0	1.0	1.0	2.0	0.	3.0	0.
JAPAN..............	0.	5.7	4.3	0.	1.4	2.9	0.
CHINA (TAIWAN).....	0.	4.3	0.	0.	0.	7.4	1.1
HONG KONG..........	0.	0.	0.	0.	0.	0.	0.
THE PHILIPPINES....	4.5	4.5	4.5	3.7	0.9	0.	0.
MALAYSIA...........	1.9	1.9	3.7	3.7	1.9	0.	0.
SINGAPORE..........	0.	2.1	4.3	6.4	0.	2.1	0.
INDONESIA..........	0.	4.3	0.	0.	0.	0.	0.
THAILAND...........	0.	0.	0.	0.	3.2	0.	0.
INDIA..............	0.	3.7	1.5	0.7	1.5	0.7	0.
OTHER ASIA AND OCEANIA.....	1.7	1.7	3.4	3.4	1.7	1.7	0.

TABLE CONTINUED ON NEXT PAGE

CROSS-TABULATION 6. 1.1: PERCENTAGE BREAKDOWN OF NUMBER (AS OF 1/1/71) OF MANUFACTURING SUBSIDIARIES OF NON-U.S.-BASED PARENT SYSTEMS BY PRINCIPAL INDUSTRY OF SUBSIDIARY AS OF 1/1/71 FOR SUBSIDIARIES CLASSIFIED BY SUBSIDIARY'S COUNTRY (CONTINUED)

SUBSIDIARY'S COUNTRY	PRINCIPAL INDUSTRY OF SUBSIDIARY AS OF 1/1/71						
	GLASS PRODUCTS	STONE, CLAY + CONCRETE	IRON AND STEEL	NON-FERROUS SMELTING PRODUCTS	NON-FERROUS PRODUCTS	METAL CANS	STRUCTURAL METAL PRODUCTS
UNITED STATES	0.6	0.3	3.1	2.3	1.1	0.6	2.3
CANADA	0.4	6.4	4.8	2.8	4.0	0.4	1.2
MEXICO	0.	2.4	1.2	0.	0.	0.	1.2
CENTRAL AMERICA AND CARIB.	0.	0.	6.0	2.4	1.2	2.4	3.6
VENEZUELA	0.	2.6	0.	2.6	2.6	0.	2.6
COLOMBIA	0.	3.8	0.	0.	3.8	0.	3.8
PERU	0.	0.	3.6	0.	0.	0.	3.6
CHILE	0.	0.	0.	0.	0.	0.	0.
ARGENTINA	0.	0.9	5.6	0.	5.6	0.	1.9
BRAZIL	1.2	2.5	5.6	0.6	0.6	0.6	1.2
OTHER SOUTH AMERICA	0.	0.	11.	0.	0.	0.	0.
GERMANY	3.5	3.2	2.1	2.1	3.2	0.4	1.1
FRANCE	0.6	0.8	5.6	1.1	1.4	0.6	0.8
ITALY	4.5	1.1	2.2	1.1	1.1	1.1	1.1
BELGIUM AND LUXEMBURG	4.9	2.8	3.5	2.1	2.1	0.	0.7
THE NETHERLANDS	0.8	4.2	5.0	1.7	2.5	1.7	1.7
UNITED KINGDOM	0.4	0.4	1.3	2.1	2.1	0.	1.3
IRELAND	0.	1.1	0.	1.1	1.1	0.	0.
DENMARK	2.6	0.	0.	5.3	2.6	0.	0.
NORWAY	2.3	0.	2.3	6.8	4.5	0.	4.5
SWEDEN	3.1	0.	1.5	3.1	0.	0.	0.
FINLAND	0.	0.	5.3	0.	16.	0.	0.

TABLE CONTINUED ON NEXT PAGE

CROSS-TABULATION 6.1.1: PERCENTAGE BREAKDOWN OF NUMBER (AS OF 1/1/71) OF MANUFACTURING SUBSIDIARIES OF NON-U.S.-BASED PARENT SYSTEMS BY PRINCIPAL INDUSTRY OF SUBSIDIARY AS OF 1/1/71 FOR SUBSIDIARIES CLASSIFIED BY SUBSIDIARY'S COUNTRY (CONTINUED)

PRINCIPAL INDUSTRY OF SUBSIDIARY AS OF 1/1/71

SUBSIDIARY'S COUNTRY	GLASS PRODUCTS	STONE, CLAY + CONCRETE	IRON AND STEEL	NON-FERROUS SMELTING	NON-FERROUS PRODUCTS	METAL CANS	STRUCTURAL METAL PRODUCTS
SWITZERLAND	0.	2.2	2.2	0.	2.2	0.	4.3
AUSTRIA	0.	0.	5.2	1.3	2.6	0.	1.3
PORTUGAL	2.1	2.1	2.1	4.2	4.2	2.1	0.
SPAIN	5.4	3.0	3.0	0.6	1.8	0.6	0.
GREECE	0.	0.	0.	0.	4.3	4.3	4.3
TURKEY	0.	0.	3.3	0.	0.	0.	0.
OTHER EUROPE + ISRAEL	0.	8.8	2.9	0.	0.	2.9	0.
PAKISTAN	0.	2.7	0.	0.	5.4	2.7	0.
IRAN	0.	9.5	0.	4.8	0.	0.	0.
OTHER MID EAST+EGYPT+LIBYA	0.	0.	0.	4.5	9.1	0.	0.
UNION OF SOUTH AFRICA	0.	1.2	3.1	2.5	4.9	0.9	2.1
RHODESIA	0.	0.	4.0	0.	8.0	2.0	0.
ZAMBIA	0.	14.	0.	0.	2.7	0.	0.
TANZANIA	0.	0.	0.	0.	4.5	4.5	0.
KENYA	0.	0.	0.	0.	5.0	5.0	0.
NIGERIA	0.	0.	6.0	2.0	0.	2.0	0.
OTHER (BRITISH) AFRICA	0.	0.	1.9	1.9	0.	0.	1.9
MOROCCO, ALGERIA + TUNISIA	0.	2.7	0.	0.	0.	0.	2.7
OTHER (FRENCH) AFRICA	0.	2.2	8.9	4.4	4.4	0.	0.
OTHER AFRICA	0.	0.	3.2	0.	6.5	3.2	0.
AUSTRALIA	0.3	0.3	3.7	4.5	7.4	0.3	1.1

TABLE CONTINUED ON NEXT PAGE

CROSS-TABULATION 6.1.1: PERCENTAGE BREAKDOWN OF NUMBER (AS OF 1/1/71) OF MANUFACTURING SUBSIDIARIES OF NON-U.S.-BASED PARENT SYSTEMS BY PRINCIPAL INDUSTRY OF SUBSIDIARY AS OF 1/1/71 FOR SUBSIDIARIES CLASSIFIED BY SUBSIDIARY'S COUNTRY (CONTINUED)

SUBSIDIARY'S COUNTRY	PRINCIPAL INDUSTRY OF SUBSIDIARY AS OF 1/1/71						
	GLASS PRODUCTS	STONE, CLAY + CONCRETE	IRON AND STEEL	NON-FERROUS SMELTING	NON-FERROUS PRODUCTS	METAL CANS	STRUCTURAL METAL PRODUCTS
NEW ZEALAND.	0.	1.0	4.0	3.0	7.1	0.	3.0
JAPAN.	0.	0.	0.	4.3	1.4	0.	0.
CHINA (TAIWAN).	0.	0.	0.	0.	0.	0.	0.
HONG KONG.	0.	0.	7.7	7.7	0.	3.8	0.
THE PHILIPPINES.	0.	0.	9.1	0.	0.	0.	0.
MALAYSIA.	0.	1.9	3.7	1.9	1.9	1.9	0.
SINGAPORE.	0.	2.1	4.3	0.	0.	2.1	0.
INDONESIA.	0.	0.	8.7	0.	0.	0.	4.3
THAILAND.	0.	0.	11.	0.	1.6	1.6	1.6
INDIA.	0.	0.7	7.4	2.2	2.2	0.7	0.
OTHER ASIA AND OCEANIA.	1.7	0.	1.7	0.	1.7	0.	5.1

TABLE CONTINUED ON NEXT PAGE

CROSS-TABULATION 6.1.1: PERCENTAGE BREAKDOWN OF NUMBER (AS OF 1/1/71) OF MANUFACTURING SUBSIDIARIES OF NON-U.S.-BASED PARENT SYSTEMS BY PRINCIPAL INDUSTRY OF SUBSIDIARY AS OF 1/1/71 FOR SUBSIDIARIES CLASSIFIED BY SUBSIDIARY'S COUNTRY (CONTINUED)

PRINCIPAL INDUSTRY OF SUBSIDIARY AS OF 1/1/71

SUBSIDIARY'S COUNTRY	FABRICA-TED WIRE PRODUCTS	OTHER FABRICA-TED METAL	ENGINES AND TURBINES	FARM MACHIN-ERY	CONSTRUC-TION MA-CHINERY	SPECIAL INDUSTRY MACHINERY	GENERAL INDUSTRY MACHINERY
UNITED STATES	1.4	5.6	0.8	0.6	0.3	1.7	2.0
CANADA	0.8	3.6	1.6	0.	0.	2.0	2.0
MEXICO	0.	6.0	1.2	4.8	0.	0.	1.2
CENTRAL AMERICA AND CARIB	1.2	2.4	0.	0.	0.	0.	0.
VENEZUELA	0.	2.6	0.	0.	0.	2.6	0.
COLOMBIA	3.8	0.	0.	0.	0.	0.	0.
PERU	0.	0.	0.	0.	0.	0.	0.
CHILE	0.	0.	0.	0.	0.	0.	0.
ARGENTINA	0.9	1.9	2.8	1.9	0.	0.	1.9
BRAZIL	1.9	2.5	1.9	1.9	1.2	1.2	2.5
OTHER SOUTH AMERICA	0.	5.3	0.	0.	0.	0.	0.
GERMANY	0.7	3.2	1.4	0.7	0.4	4.2	2.1
FRANCE	0.3	5.0	1.4	0.3	0.	2.5	3.1
ITALY	0.	3.9	1.1	1.1	0.6	1.1	4.5
BELGIUM AND LUXEMBURG	2.1	4.9	2.1	0.	0.7	0.	0.
THE NETHERLANDS	0.	4.2	0.8	0.	0.7	2.5	1.7
UNITED KINGDOM	0.4	4.3	0.4	0.4	0.9	5.2	2.1
IRELAND	1.1	4.5	0.	0.	0.	1.1	0.
DENMARK	0.	0.	0.	2.6	0.	0.	0.
NORWAY	0.	4.5	0.	0.	0.	2.3	2.3
SWEDEN	0.	9.2	0.	0.	0.	0.	1.5
FINLAND	5.3	0.	0.	0.	5.3	0.	0.

TABLE CONTINUED ON NEXT PAGE

CROSS-TABULATION 6.1.1: PERCENTAGE BREAKDOWN OF NUMBER (AS OF 1/1/71) OF
MANUFACTURING SUBSIDIARIES OF NON-U.S.-BASED PARENT SYSTEMS BY
PRINCIPAL INDUSTRY OF SUBSIDIARY AS OF 1/1/71
FOR SUBSIDIARIES CLASSIFIED BY
SUBSIDIARY'S COUNTRY
(CONTINUED)

PRINCIPAL INDUSTRY OF SUBSIDIARY AS OF 1/1/71

SUBSIDIARY'S COUNTRY	FABRICATED WIRE PRODUCTS	OTHER FABRICATED METAL	ENGINES AND TURBINES	FARM MACHINERY	CONSTRUCTION MACHINERY	SPECIAL INDUSTRY MACHINERY	GENERAL INDUSTRY MACHINERY
SWITZERLAND	0.	4.3	0.	0.	0.	4.3	0.
AUSTRIA	1.3	3.9	0.	0.	0.	1.3	1.3
PORTUGAL	0.	2.1	0.	0.	0.	2.1	0.
SPAIN	0.	0.6	1.2	1.2	0.	1.8	1.2
GREECE	0.	0.	0.	0.	0.	0.	0.
TURKEY	3.3	0.	0.	0.	0.	3.3	0.
OTHER EUROPE + ISRAEL	0.	8.8	0.	0.	0.	0.	2.9
PAKISTAN	0.	5.4	2.7	0.	0.	0.	0.
IRAN	0.	0.	9.5	0.	0.	0.	4.8
OTHER MID EAST+EGYPT+LIBYA	0.	0.	4.5	0.	9.1	0.	0.
UNION OF SOUTH AFRICA	0.3	1.2	0.	0.6	0.6	1.5	1.8
RHODESIA	0.	0.	0.	2.0	0.	0.	0.
ZAMBIA	0.	2.7	0.	0.	0.	0.	2.7
TANZANIA	0.	0.	0.	0.	0.	0.	4.5
KENYA	0.	0.	2.5	2.5	2.5	0.	0.
NIGERIA	0.	4.0	0.	0.	0.	0.	0.
OTHER (BRITISH) AFRICA	0.	1.9	0.	1.9	0.	0.	1.9
MOROCCO, ALGERIA + TUNISIA	5.4	5.4	0.	2.7	0.	0.	0.
OTHER (FRENCH) AFRICA	0.	2.2	0.	0.	0.	0.	0.
OTHER AFRICA	0.	6.5	0.	0.	0.	0.	0.
AUSTRALIA	0.	2.1	0.8	0.3	0.8	1.1	1.3

TABLE CONTINUED ON NEXT PAGE

CROSS-TABULATION 6.1.1: PERCENTAGE BREAKDOWN OF NUMBER (AS OF 1/1/71) OF
MANUFACTURING SUBSIDIARIES OF NON-U.S.-BASED PARENT SYSTEMS BY
PRINCIPAL INDUSTRY OF SUBSIDIARY AS OF 1/1/71
FOR SUBSIDIARIES CLASSIFIED BY
SUBSIDIARY'S COUNTRY
(CONTINUED)

SUBSIDIARY'S COUNTRY	FABRICATED WIRE PRODUCTS	OTHER FABRICATED METAL	ENGINES AND TURBINES	FARM MACHINERY	CONSTRUCTION MACHINERY	SPECIAL INDUSTRY MACHINERY	GENERAL INDUSTRY MACHINERY
NEW ZEALAND......	2.0	4.0	0.	0.	0.	0.	0.
JAPAN......	0.	8.6	5.7	0.	0.	0.	2.9
CHINA (TAIWAN)......	1.1	3.2	0.	2.1	2.1	1.1	0.
HONG KONG......	0.	0.	0.	0.	0.	3.8	0.
THE PHILIPPINES......	0.	0.	0.	0.	4.5	0.	0.
MALAYSIA......	3.7	3.7	1.9	1.9	0.	1.9	0.
SINGAPORE......	4.3	6.4	2.1	0.	0.	0.	0.
INDONESIA......	0.	0.	0.	0.	0.	0.	0.
THAILAND......	4.8	3.2	0.	0.	0.	0.	0.
INDIA......	7.4	3.7	1.5	2.2	1.5	3.7	1.5
OTHER ASIA AND OCEANIA......	0.	5.1	0.	0.	0.	1.7	0.

PRINCIPAL INDUSTRY OF SUBSIDIARY AS OF 1/1/71

TABLE CONTINUED ON NEXT PAGE

CROSS-TABULATION 6.1.1: PERCENTAGE BREAKDOWN OF NUMBER (AS OF 1/1/71) OF MANUFACTURING SUBSIDIARIES OF NON-U.S.-BASED PARENT SYSTEMS BY PRINCIPAL INDUSTRY OF SUBSIDIARY AS OF 1/1/71 FOR SUBSIDIARIES CLASSIFIED BY SUBSIDIARY'S COUNTRY (CONTINUED)

PRINCIPAL INDUSTRY OF SUBSIDIARY AS OF 1/1/71

SUBSIDIARY'S COUNTRY	OFFICE MACHINES+ COMPUTERS	OTHER NON-EL. MACHINERY	ELECTRIC TRANSMIS. EQUIPMENT	ELECTRIC LIGHTING + WIRING	RADIOS, TV'S+AP-PLIANCES	COMMUNI-CATIONS EQUIPMENT	ELECTRON-IC COM-PONENTS
UNITED STATES	0.8	0.6	0.8	1.4	3.9	0.6	7.9
CANADA	0.4	1.2	1.2	0.4	0.8	0.4	0.4
MEXICO	2.4	0.	2.4	6.0	6.0	4.8	2.4
CENTRAL AMERICA AND CARIB.	0.	0.	1.2	1.2	1.2	0.	2.4
VENEZUELA	0.	2.6	0.	7.9	2.6	2.6	0.
COLOMBIA	3.8	0.	7.7	0.	0.	3.8	0.
PERU	0.	0.	3.6	7.1	0.	0.	0.
CHILE	3.8	0.	0.	3.8	0.	0.	0.
ARGENTINA	0.9	0.	0.	3.7	2.8	3.7	0.9
BRAZIL	0.6	1.2	4.9	1.9	3.1	3.1	1.2
OTHER SOUTH AMERICA	0.	0.	0.	0.	0.	0.	0.
GERMANY	0.7	1.1	1.1	1.1	3.2	0.4	1.1
FRANCE	0.6	0.3	3.3	0.8	1.7	0.3	2.5
ITALY	0.	0.6	3.4	3.4	3.4	1.1	3.4
BELGIUM AND LUXEMBURG	1.4	0.7	2.1	2.8	2.1	0.7	2.1
THE NETHERLANDS	0.8	0.	0.8	0.	1.7	0.8	0.8
UNITED KINGDOM	0.9	1.7	0.	0.9	3.9	3.4	5.2
IRELAND	0.	0.	0.	1.1	4.5	2.2	0.
DENMARK	2.6	0.	2.6	2.6	7.9	5.3	5.3
NORWAY	0.	0.	4.5	6.8	0.	9.1	0.
SWEDEN	0.	0.	6.2	3.1	9.2	1.5	3.1
FINLAND	0.	0.	5.3	11.	0.	5.3	0.

TABLE CONTINUED ON NEXT PAGE

CROSS-TABULATION 6.1.1: PERCENTAGE BREAKDOWN OF NUMBER (AS OF 1/1/71) OF MANUFACTURING SUBSIDIARIES OF NON-U.S.-BASED PARENT SYSTEMS BY PRINCIPAL INDUSTRY OF SUBSIDIARY AS OF 1/1/71 FOR SUBSIDIARIES CLASSIFIED BY SUBSIDIARY'S COUNTRY (CONTINUED)

SUBSIDIARY'S COUNTRY	PRINCIPAL INDUSTRY OF SUBSIDIARY AS OF 1/1/71						
	OFFICE MACHINES+ COMPUTERS	OTHER NON-EL. MACHINERY	ELECTRIC TRANSMIS. EQUIPMENT	ELECTRIC LIGHTING + WIRING	RADIOS, TV'S+AP- PLIANCES	COMMUNI- CATIONS EQUIPMENT	ELECTRON- IC COM- PONENTS
SWITZERLAND................	0.	2.2	4.3	6.5	0.	2.2	2.2
AUSTRIA....................	1.3	0.	2.6	1.3	7.8	1.3	2.6
PORTUGAL...................	0.	2.1	0.	4.2	0.	2.1	0.
SPAIN......................	1.8	1.2	2.4	3.0	4.2	1.2	0.6
GREECE.....................	0.	0.	8.7	22.	4.3	8.7	0.
TURKEY.....................	0.	0.	6.7	0.	3.3	6.7	0.
OTHER EUROPE + ISRAEL......	0.	0.	2.9	12.	0.	0.	2.9
PAKISTAN...................	0.	0.	5.4	5.4	2.7	0.	0.
IRAN.......................	0.	0.	0.	9.5	4.8	4.8	0.
OTHER MID EAST+EGYPT+LIBYA..	0.	0.	0.	9.1	9.1	0.	0.
UNION OF SOUTH AFRICA.......	0.3	0.6	2.8	1.2	2.1	1.8	0.6
RHODESIA...................	0.	0.	0.	0.	0.	0.	0.
ZAMBIA.....................	0.	0.	0.	0.	0.	0.	0.
TANZANIA...................	0.	0.	0.	0.	4.5	0.	0.
KENYA......................	0.	0.	0.	2.5	5.0	0.	0.
NIGERIA....................	0.	0.	0.	0.	6.0	4.0	0.
OTHER (BRITISH) AFRICA......	0.	0.	0.	1.9	0.	1.9	0.
MOROCCO, ALGERIA + TUNISIA..	2.7	0.	0.	0.	14.	8.1	5.4
OTHER (FRENCH) AFRICA......	0.	0.	2.2	0.	0.	2.2	0.
OTHER AFRICA...............	0.	0.	0.	0.	0.	0.	0.
AUSTRALIA..................	0.	0.	0.3	0.8	2.4	3.4	1.1

TABLE CONTINUED ON NEXT PAGE

CROSS-TABULATION 6.1.1: PERCENTAGE BREAKDOWN OF NUMBER (AS OF 1/1/71) OF
MANUFACTURING SUBSIDIARIES OF NON-U.S.-BASED PARENT SYSTEMS BY
PRINCIPAL INDUSTRY OF SUBSIDIARY AS OF 1/1/71
FOR SUBSIDIARIES CLASSIFIED BY
SUBSIDIARY'S COUNTRY
(CONTINUED)

SUBSIDIARY'S COUNTRY	PRINCIPAL INDUSTRY OF SUBSIDIARY AS OF 1/1/71						
	OFFICE MACHINES+ COMPUTERS	OTHER NON-EL. MACHINERY	ELECTRIC TRANSMIS. EQUIPMENT	ELECTRIC LIGHTING + WIRING	RADIOS, TV'S+AP-PLIANCES	COMMUNI-CATIONS EQUIPMENT	ELECTRON-IC COM-PONENTS
NEW ZEALAND	0.	0.	0.	5.1	7.1	1.0	2.0
JAPAN	1.4	2.9	5.7	0.	4.3	2.9	1.4
CHINA (TAIWAN)	1.1	1.1	1.1	4.3	8.5	3.2	0.
HONG KONG	0.	0.	0.	0.	3.8	0.	0.
THE PHILIPPINES	0.	0.	0.	0.	14.	0.	0.
MALAYSIA	0.	1.9	0.	1.9	3.7	1.9	1.9
SINGAPORE	0.	0.	0.	0.	2.1	2.1	2.1
INDONESIA	0.	0.	4.3	0.	13.	0.	0.
THAILAND	0.	1.6	0.	4.8	6.5	1.6	0.
INDIA	0.	0.	5.1	5.9	1.5	0.7	0.7
OTHER ASIA AND OCEANIA	0.	0.	0.	1.7	0.	3.4	10.

TABLE CONTINUED ON NEXT PAGE

CROSS-TABULATION 5.1.1: PERCENTAGE BREAKDOWN OF NUMBER (AS OF 1/1/71) OF MANUFACTURING SUBSIDIARIES OF NON-U.S.-BASED PARENT SYSTEMS BY PRINCIPAL INDUSTRY OF SUBSIDIARY AS OF 1/1/71 FOR SUBSIDIARIES CLASSIFIED BY SUBSIDIARY'S COUNTRY (CONTINUED)

SUBSIDIARY'S COUNTRY	PRINCIPAL INDUSTRY OF SUBSIDIARY AS OF 1/1/71						
	OTHER ELECTRIC EQUIPMENT + EQUIP.	MOTOR VEHICLES + EQUIP.	OTHER TRANS-PORTATION	PRECI-SION GOODS	MISC. PRODUCTS	TOTAL PERCENT	TOTAL NUMBER
UNITED STATES	3.9	0.6	1.1	6.8	1.7	100.	355
CANADA	2.0	2.0	5.6	0.8	3.2	100.	251
MEXICO	3.6	6.0	0.	0.	1.2	100.	84
CENTRAL AMERICA AND CARIB.	4.8	3.6	0.	0.	1.2	100.	84
VENEZUELA	2.6	5.3	2.6	0.	0.	100.	38
COLOMBIA	0.	7.7	3.8	0.	0.	100.	26
PERU	7.1	21.	3.6	0.	0.	100.	28
CHILE	3.8	15.	0.	3.8	0.	100.	26
ARGENTINA	2.8	7.4	0.	1.9	0.9	100.	108
BRAZIL	3.1	6.8	1.9	0.6	0.6	100.	162
OTHER SOUTH AMERICA	0.	0.	0.	0.	0.	100.	19
GERMANY	5.7	1.8	0.7	1.4	2.1	100.	283
FRANCE	3.9	2.2	1.4	3.6	2.2	100.	359
ITALY	7.3	2.8	0.	5.0	0.	100.	179
BELGIUM AND LUXEMBURG	5.6	6.3	0.7	0.	0.	100.	143
THE NETHERLANDS	5.0	4.2	0.8	1.7	0.8	100.	119
UNITED KINGDOM	6.0	0.9	0.	3.0	9.9	100.	233
IRELAND	3.4	1.1	1.1	0.	1.1	100.	89
DENMARK	2.6	0.	0.	2.6	0.	100.	38
NORWAY	11.	0.	2.3	2.3	0.	100.	44
SWEDEN	4.6	1.5	0.	0.	1.5	100.	65
FINLAND	0.	5.3	5.3	0.	0.	100.	19

TABLE CONTINUED ON NEXT PAGE

CROSS-TABULATION 6. 1.1: PERCENTAGE BREAKDOWN OF NUMBER (AS OF 1/1/71) OF
MANUFACTURING SUBSIDIARIES OF NON-U.S.-BASED PARENT SYSTEMS BY
PRINCIPAL INDUSTRY OF SUBSIDIARY AS OF 1/1/71
FOR SUBSIDIARIES CLASSIFIED BY
SUBSIDIARY'S COUNTRY
(CONTINUED)

SUBSIDIARY'S COUNTRY	PRINCIPAL INDUSTRY OF SUBSIDIARY AS OF 1/1/71						
	OTHER ELECTRIC EQUIPMENT + EQUIP.	MOTOR VEHICLES + EQUIP.	OTHER TRANS- PORTATION	PRECI- SION GOODS	MISC. PRODUCTS	TOTAL PERCENT	TOTAL NUMBER
SWITZERLAND........................	4.3	0.	0.	2.2	0.	100.	46
AUSTRIA........................	7.8	0.	1.3	1.3	2.6	100.	77
PORTUGAL........................	2.1	10.	0.	0.	0.	100.	48
SPAIN........................	1.8	7.8	0.6	1.2	0.	100.	166
GREECE........................	0.	0.	0.	0.	0.	100.	23
TURKEY........................	0.	13.	0.	0.	0.	100.	30
OTHER EUROPE + ISRAEL...........	0.	5.9	0.	0.	2.9	100.	34
PAKISTAN........................	5.4	2.7	0.	0.	0.	100.	37
IRAN........................	4.8	9.5	0.	0.	0.	100.	21
OTHER MID EAST+EGYPT+LIBYA...	0.	9.1	0.	0.	0.	100.	22
UNION OF SOUTH AFRICA...........	3.7	3.7	1.8	1.2	0.3	100.	326
RHODESIA........................	3.0	6.0	0.	0.	2.0	100.	50
ZAMBIA........................	2.7	0.	0.	0.	0.	100.	37
TANZANIA........................	4.5	14.	0.	0.	3.	100.	22
KENYA........................	2.5	2.5	0.	0.	0.	100.	40
NIGERIA........................	2.0	2.0	2.0	0.	0.	100.	50
OTHER (BRITISH) AFRICA........	1.9	3.8	0.	0.	0.	100.	53
MOROCCO, ALGERIA + TUNISIA...	2.7	0.	2.7	0.	0.	100.	37
OTHER (FRENCH) AFRICA.........	2.2	8.9	0.	0.	0.	100.	45
OTHER AFRICA.................	0.	6.5	0.	0.	0.	100.	31
AUSTRALIA........................	2.9	2.9	0.8	0.3	0.8	100.	379

TABLE CONTINUED ON NEXT PAGE

CROSS-TABULATION 6.1.1: PERCENTAGE BREAKDOWN OF NUMBER (AS OF 1/1/71) OF
MANUFACTURING SUBSIDIARIES OF NON-U.S.-BASED PARENT SYSTEMS BY
PRINCIPAL INDUSTRY OF SUBSIDIARY AS OF 1/1/71
FOR SUBSIDIARIES CLASSIFIED BY
SUBSIDIARY'S COUNTRY
(CONTINUED)

SUBSIDIARY'S COUNTRY	OTHER ELECTRIC EQUIPMENT + EQUIP.	MOTOR VEHICLES + EQUIP.	OTHER TRANS-PORTATION	PRECI-SION GOODS	MISC. PRODUCTS	TOTAL PERCENT	TOTAL NUMBER
	PRINCIPAL INDUSTRY OF SUBSIDIARY AS OF 1/1/71						
NEW ZEALAND	2.0	1.0	0.	0.	3.0	100.	99
JAPAN	5.7	1.4	0.	0.	0.	100.	70
CHINA (TAIWAN)	3.2	1.1	2.1	0.	2.1	100.	94
HONG KONG	0.	0.	0.	0.	0.	100.	26
THE PHILIPPINES	0.	18.	0.	0.	4.5	100.	22
MALAYSIA	5.6	9.3	1.9	0.	0.	100.	54
SINGAPORE	2.1	2.1	4.3	0.	6.4	100.	47
INDONESIA	0.	0.	0.	0.	0.	100.	23
THAILAND	1.6	13.	3.2	0.	3.2	100.	62
INDIA	2.2	7.4	1.5	1.5	0.7	100.	136
OTHER ASIA AND OCEANIA	3.4	5.1	1.7	0.	0.	100.	59

221

CROSS-TABULATION 6.1.2: PERCENTAGE BREAKDOWN OF NUMBER (AS OF 1/1/68) OF
MANUFACTURING SUBSIDIARIES OF U.S.-BASED PARENT SYSTEMS BY
PRINCIPAL INDUSTRY OF SUBSIDIARY AS OF 1/1/68
FOR SUBSIDIARIES CLASSIFIED BY
SUBSIDIARY'S COUNTRY

PRINCIPAL INDUSTRY OF SUBSIDIARY AS OF 1/1/68

SUBSIDIARY'S COUNTRY	ORDNANCE	MEAT PRODUCTS	DAIRY PRODUCTS	CANNED FOODS	GRAIN MILL PRODUCTS	BAKERY PRODUCTS	CONFEC-TIONERY PRODUCTS
CANADA	0.4	2.1	4.4	2.1	1.9	0.8	2.1
MEXICO	0.4	1.2	1.2	1.6	2.4	0.4	1.6
CENTRAL AMERICA AND CARIB	0.	0.	7.4	1.6	11.	1.6	1.6
VENEZUELA	0.	0.8	3.3	1.7	5.0	2.5	1.7
COLOMBIA	0.	0.	4.8	1.0	3.8	2.9	1.9
PERU	0.	0.	4.3	8.5	4.3	4.3	0.
CHILE	0.	0.	0.	0.	13.	0.	6.5
ARGENTINA	0.6	1.6	0.8	0.	3.2	0.8	0.
BRAZIL	0.6	1.2	0.	0.6	2.5	1.2	1.2
OTHER SOUTH AMERICA	0.	0.	0.	5.0	5.0	5.0	0.
GERMANY	0.5	0.5	1.9	0.9	2.3	0.9	1.4
FRANCE	0.5	0.	0.5	1.0	1.5	2.4	1.5
ITALY	0.6	0.6	0.	2.3	1.7	0.6	0.6
BELGIUM AND LUXEMBURG	0.	0.	3.5	1.2	1.2	2.4	1.2
THE NETHERLANDS	0.	0.	1.3	1.3	3.8	0.	5.0
UNITED KINGDOM	0.	1.4	1.1	1.7	2.5	0.3	1.1
IRELAND	0.	7.1	7.1	3.6	0.	0.	7.1
DENMARK	0.	0.	8.0	0.	12.	0.	0.
NORWAY	0.	0.	0.	0.	0.	0.	0.
SWEDEN	0.	0.	0.	0.	0.	2.9	0.
FINLAND	0.	0.	0.	0.	0.	0.	0.

TABLE CONTINUED ON NEXT PAGE

222

CROSS-TABULATION 6.1.2: PERCENTAGE BREAKDOWN OF NUMBER (AS OF 1/1/68) OF
MANUFACTURING SUBSIDIARIES OF U.S.-BASED PARENT SYSTEMS BY
PRINCIPAL INDUSTRY OF SUBSIDIARY AS OF 1/1/68
FOR SUBSIDIARIES CLASSIFIED BY
SUBSIDIARY'S COUNTRY
(CONTINUED)

PRINCIPAL INDUSTRY OF SUBSIDIARY AS OF 1/1/68

SUBSIDIARY'S COUNTRY	ORDNANCE	MEAT PRODUCTS	DAIRY PRODUCTS	CANNED FOODS	GRAIN MILL PRODUCTS	BAKERY PRODUCTS	CONFEC- TIONERY PRODUCTS
SWITZERLAND	0.	0.	0.	0.	4.0	4.0	0.
AUSTRIA	0.	0.	0.	0.	0.	0.	5.9
PORTUGAL	0.	0.	0.	0.	12.	0.	0.
SPAIN	0.	1.0	0.	1.0	3.8	1.9	1.0
GREECE	0.	0.	0.	0.	0.	0.	5.9
TURKEY	0.	0.	0.	0.	0.	0.	0.
OTHER EUROPE + ISRAEL	0.	0.	0.	0.	0.	0.	0.
PAKISTAN	0.	0.	6.3	0.	0.	0.	0.
IRAN	0.	0.	6.3	0.	0.	0.	0.
OTHER MID EAST+EGYPT+LIBYA	0.	0.	4.8	4.8	0.	0.	4.8
UNION OF SOUTH AFRICA	0.	0.	0.9	1.7	0.9	0.9	1.7
RHODESIA	0.	0.	0.	0.	0.	0.	0.
ZAMBIA	0.	0.	0.	0.	0.	0.	0.
TANZANIA	0.	0.	0.	0.	0.	0.	0.
KENYA	0.	0.	0.	0.	0.	0.	0.
NIGERIA	0.	0.	9.1	0.	9.1	0.	0.
OTHER (BRITISH) AFRICA	0.	0.	0.	0.	0.	0.	0.
MOROCCO, ALGERIA + TUNISIA	0.	0.	0.	0.	6.7	0.	6.7
OTHER (FRENCH) AFRICA	0.	0.	0.	0.	0.	0.	0.
OTHER AFRICA	0.	0.	0.	0.	0.	0.	0.
AUSTRALIA	1.0	2.4	1.9	1.9	1.4	0.5	1.9
NEW ZEALAND	0.	11.	0.	2.2	0.	2.2	4.4

TABLE CONTINUED ON NEXT PAGE

CROSS-TABULATION 6.1.2: PERCENTAGE BREAKDOWN OF NUMBER (AS OF 1/1/68) OF MANUFACTURING SUBSIDIARIES OF U.S.-BASED PARENT SYSTEMS BY PRINCIPAL INDUSTRY OF SUBSIDIARY AS OF 1/1/68 FOR SUBSIDIARIES CLASSIFIED BY SUBSIDIARY'S COUNTRY

(CONTINUED)

SUBSIDIARY'S COUNTRY	PRINCIPAL INDUSTRY OF SUBSIDIARY AS OF 1/1/68						
	ORDNANCE	MEAT PRODUCTS	DAIRY PRODUCTS	CANNED FOODS	GRAIN MILL PRODUCTS	BAKERY PRODUCTS	CONFEC-TIONERY PRODUCTS
JAPAN................	0.7	0.	0.7	0.	0.7	0.	1.4
CHINA (TAIWAN).......	0.	0.	7.7	0.	0.	0.	0.
HONG KONG............	0.	0.	0.	0.	0.	0.	0.
THE PHILIPPINES......	1.9	0.	3.8	3.8	3.8	1.9	1.9
MALAYSIA.............	0.	0.	14.	0.	0.	0.	14.
SINGAPORE............	0.	0.	10.	0.	0.	0.	0.
INDONESIA............	0.	0.	0.	0.	0.	0.	0.
THAILAND.............	0.	0.	7.1	0.	0.	0.	7.1
INDIA................	0.	0.	0.	0.	1.5	0.	0.
OTHER ASIA AND OCEANIA..	0.	0.	0.	0.	0.	0.	0.

TABLE CONTINUED ON NEXT PAGE

CROSS-TABULATION 6.1.2: PERCENTAGE BREAKDOWN OF NUMBER (AS OF 1/1/68) OF
MANUFACTURING SUBSIDIARIES OF U.S.-BASED PARENT SYSTEMS BY
PRINCIPAL INDUSTRY OF SUBSIDIARY AS OF 1/1/68
FOR SUBSIDIARIES CLASSIFIED BY
SUBSIDIARY'S COUNTRY
(CONTINUED)

PRINCIPAL INDUSTRY OF SUBSIDIARY AS OF 1/1/68

SUBSIDIARY'S COUNTRY	BEVER-AGES	OTHER FOOD PRODUCTS	TOBACCO PRODUCTS	TEXTILES	APPAREL	LUMBER AND WOOD	FURNI-TURE
CANADA	1.1	1.9	0.4	3.2	0.4	1.3	0.6
MEXICO	1.6	1.6	0.	3.5	0.4	0.4	0.4
CENTRAL AMERICA AND CARIB	0.8	1.6	0.	0.	1.6	1.6	0.
VENEZUELA	0.	0.	4.1	9.1	0.	0.	1.7
COLOMBIA	2.9	1.0	0.	4.8	1.0	0.	0.
PERU	2.1	6.4	0.	4.3	0.	2.1	0.
CHILE	0.	6.5	0.	0.	0.	0.	0.
ARGENTINA	2.4	0.8	0.8	0.8	0.	0.	0.8
BRAZIL	2.5	0.	0.	1.2	0.	0.	0.
OTHER SOUTH AMERICA	0.	0.	0.	7.5	0.	0.	0.
GERMANY	2.3	0.9	0.	1.4	0.	0.5	0.9
FRANCE	1.0	1.0	0.	2.0	1.0	0.5	0.5
ITALY	1.1	1.7	0.	1.1	1.1	1.1	0.
BELGIUM AND LUXEMBURG	1.2	0.	0.	3.5	0.	1.2	0.
THE NETHERLANDS	0.	2.5	0.	0.	0.	0.	0.
UNITED KINGDOM	3.4	1.7	0.	2.2	0.8	0.3	0.8
IRELAND	0.	7.1	0.	0.	0.	0.	0.
DENMARK	0.	0.	0.	0.	0.	0.	0.
NORWAY	0.	5.9	0.	0.	0.	0.	0.
SWEDEN	0.	5.7	0.	2.9	0.	2.9	0.
FINLAND	0.	0.	0.	0.	0.	0.	0.

TABLE CONTINUED ON NEXT PAGE

CROSS-TABULATION 6.1.2: PERCENTAGE BREAKDOWN OF NUMBER (AS OF 1/1/68) OF
MANUFACTURING SUBSIDIARIES OF U.S.-BASED PARENT SYSTEMS BY
PRINCIPAL INDUSTRY OF SUBSIDIARY AS OF 1/1/68
FOR SUBSIDIARIES CLASSIFIED BY
SUBSIDIARY'S COUNTRY
(CONTINUED)

PRINCIPAL INDUSTRY OF SUBSIDIARY AS OF 1/1/68

SUBSIDIARY'S COUNTRY	BEVER-AGES	OTHER FOOD PRODUCTS	TOBACCO PRODUCTS	TEXTILES	APPAREL	LUMBER AND WOOD	FURNI-TURE
SWITZERLAND	0.	0.	4.0	16.	0.	0.	0.
AUSTRIA	0.	5.9	0.	0.	0.	0.	0.
PORTUGAL	0.	0.	0.	5.9	0.	0.	0.
SPAIN	1.9	3.8	0.	1.9	0.	1.9	1.0
GREECE	0.	0.	0.	0.	0.	0.	0.
TURKEY	6.3	0.	0.	0.	0.	0.	0.
OTHER EUROPE + ISRAEL	0.	9.1	0.	0.	0.	0.	0.
PAKISTAN	6.3	0.	0.	0.	0.	0.	0.
IRAN	0.	0.	3.	0.	0.	0.	0.
OTHER MID EAST+EGYPT+LIBYA	0.	0.	0.	0.	0.	0.	0.
UNION OF SOUTH AFRICA	2.6	0.9	0.	0.9	0.	0.	0.
RHODESIA	0.	0.	0.	0.	0.	0.	0.
ZAMBIA	17.	0.	0.	0.	0.	0.	0.
TANZANIA	0.	0.	0.	0.	0.	0.	0.
KENYA	13.	0.	0.	0.	0.	0.	0.
NIGERIA	0.	0.	0.	0.	0.	0.	0.
OTHER (BRITISH) AFRICA	0.	0.	0.	0.	0.	0.	0.
MOROCCO, ALGERIA + TUNISIA	0.	0.	0.	0.	0.	0.	0.
OTHER (FRENCH) AFRICA	0.	0.	0.	0.	0.	0.	0.
OTHER AFRICA	0.	0.	0.	0.	0.	0.	0.
AUSTRALIA	1.0	1.9	0.5	0.	0.5	0.	1.0

TABLE CONTINUED ON NEXT PAGE

CROSS-TABULATION 6.1.2: PERCENTAGE BREAKDOWN OF NUMBER (AS OF 1/1/68) OF MANUFACTURING SUBSIDIARIES OF U.S.-BASED PARENT SYSTEMS BY PRINCIPAL INDUSTRY OF SUBSIDIARY AS OF 1/1/68 FOR SUBSIDIARIES CLASSIFIED BY SUBSIDIARY'S COUNTRY (CONTINUED)

SUBSIDIARY'S COUNTRY	PRINCIPAL INDUSTRY OF SUBSIDIARY AS OF 1/1/68						
	BEVERAGES	OTHER FOOD PRODUCTS	TOBACCO PRODUCTS	TEXTILES	APPAREL	LUMBER AND WOOD	FURNITURE
NEW ZEALAND........	0.	0.	0.	0.	0.	0.	0.
JAPAN.............	2.2	2.2	0.	6.5	0.	0.7	0.7
CHINA (TAIWAN)....	0.	0.	0.	0.	0.	0.	0.
HONG KONG.........	0.	0.	0.	0.	0.	0.	0.
THE PHILIPPINES...	5.7	0.	0.	0.	0.	1.9	0.
MALAYSIA..........	0.	0.	0.	0.	0.	0.	0.
SINGAPORE.........	0.	0.	0.	0.	0.	0.	0.
INDONESIA.........	0.	0.	0.	0.	0.	0.	0.
THAILAND..........	0.	0.	0.	0.	0.	0.	0.
INDIA.............	0.	0.	0.	1.5	0.	0.	0.
OTHER ASIA AND OCEANIA......	0.	0.	0.	7.7	0.	0.	0.

TABLE CONTINUED ON NEXT PAGE

CROSS-TABULATION 6.1.2: PERCENTAGE BREAKDOWN OF NUMBER (AS OF 1/1/68) OF MANUFACTURING SUBSIDIARIES OF U.S.-BASED PARENT SYSTEMS BY PRINCIPAL INDUSTRY OF SUBSIDIARY AS OF 1/1/68 FOR SUBSIDIARIES CLASSIFIED BY SUBSIDIARY'S COUNTRY (CONTINUED)

PRINCIPAL INDUSTRY OF SUBSIDIARY AS OF 1/1/68

SUBSIDIARY'S COUNTRY	PAPER PRODUCTS	PRINTED MATTER	INDUSTRIAL CHEMICALS	PLASTICS AND SYNTHETICS	DRUGS	SOAP AND COSMETICS	PAINTS
CANADA	4.8	0.4	8.2	2.9	5.3	2.7	1.1
MEXICO	1.6	0.4	14.	5.9	9.0	3.5	1.2
CENTRAL AMERICA AND CARIB.	8.2	0.	5.7	3.3	14.	6.6	4.1
VENEZUELA	9.9	0.	4.1	3.3	9.1	3.3	1.7
COLOMBIA	4.8	0.	6.7	5.7	12.	3.8	1.9
PERU	6.4	0.	6.4	0.	13.	6.4	0.
CHILE	0.	0.	6.5	0.	13.	0.	0.
ARGENTINA	2.4	2.4	5.6	8.0	11.	3.2	0.
BRAZIL	5.6	0.	6.2	3.7	10.	2.5	0.6
OTHER SOUTH AMERICA	7.5	0.	2.5	2.5	10.	2.5	13.
GERMANY	2.3	0.9	5.6	2.8	4.2	3.3	0.5
FRANCE	3.9	2.0	6.3	4.4	5.9	6.3	1.0
ITALY	4.0	2.3	6.3	3.4	12.	1.7	1.1
BELGIUM AND LUXEMBURG	3.5	0.	5.9	8.2	12.	5.9	4.7
THE NETHERLANDS	3.8	1.3	14.	7.5	3.8	1.3	5.0
UNITED KINGDOM	2.0	0.6	4.2	6.2	6.7	3.9	0.6
IRELAND	0.	0.	3.6	0.	7.1	7.1	3.6
DENMARK	4.0	4.0	4.0	4.0	4.0	12.	0.
NORWAY	0.9	0.9	5.9	5.9	0.	0.	5.9
SWEDEN	2.9	2.9	11.	2.9	11.	8.6	2.9
FINLAND	0.	0.	17.	0.	0.	0.	0.

TABLE CONTINUED ON NEXT PAGE

CROSS-TABULATION 6.1.2: PERCENTAGE BREAKDOWN OF NUMBER (AS OF 1/1/68) OF MANUFACTURING SUBSIDIARIES OF U.S.-BASED PARENT SYSTEMS BY PRINCIPAL INDUSTRY OF SUBSIDIARY AS OF 1/1/68 FOR SUBSIDIARIES CLASSIFIED BY SUBSIDIARY'S COUNTRY (CONTINUED)

PRINCIPAL INDUSTRY OF SUBSIDIARY AS OF 1/1/68

SUBSIDIARY'S COUNTRY	PAPER PRODUCTS	PRINTED MATTER	INDUS-TRIAL CHEMICALS	PLASTICS AND SYN-THETICS	DRUGS	SOAP AND COSMETICS	PAINTS
SWITZERLAND	0.	4.0	0.	0.	12.	0.	0.
AUSTRIA	0.	0.	5.9	0.	5.9	5.9	0.
PORTUGAL	5.9	0.	5.9	5.9	24.	5.9	0.
SPAIN	5.8	1.0	13.	3.8	4.8	3.8	1.9
GREECE	5.9	0.	0.	12.	29.	5.9	0.
TURKEY	5.9	0.	0.	0.	19.	0.	0.
OTHER EUROPE + ISRAEL	9.1	0.	9.1	9.1	0.	9.1	0.
PAKISTAN	6.3	0.	6.3	0.	44.	6.3	0.
IRAN	0.	0.	6.3	0.	25.	6.3	0.
OTHER MID EAST+EGYPT+LIBYA	0.	0.	9.5	0.	4.8	4.8	0.
UNION OF SOUTH AFRICA	18.	2.6	1.7	1.7	15.	6.1	0.9
RHODESIA	23.	7.7	0.	0.	0.	7.7	7.7
ZAMBIA	33.	0.	0.	0.	17.	0.	17.
TANZANIA	0.	0.	0.	0.	0.	0.	0.
KENYA	0.	0.	0.	0.	0.	13.	0.
NIGERIA	0.	0.	0.	9.1	9.1	9.1	9.1
OTHER (BRITISH) AFRICA	0.	0.	0.	0.	0.	25.	0.
MOROCCO, ALGERIA + TUNISIA	6.7	0.	6.7	0.	0.	13.	0.
OTHER (FRENCH) AFRICA	11.	0.	0.	0.	0.	0.	0.
OTHER AFRICA	0.	0.	0.	0.	0.	0.	0.
AUSTRALIA	2.9	0.	6.7	4.8	9.1	3.8	0.5

TABLE CONTINUED ON NEXT PAGE

CROSS-TABULATION 6. 1.2: PERCENTAGE BREAKDOWN OF NUMBER (AS OF 1/1/68) OF
MANUFACTURING SUBSIDIARIES OF U.S.-BASED PARENT SYSTEMS BY
PRINCIPAL INDUSTRY OF SUBSIDIARY AS OF 1/1/68
FOR SUBSIDIARIES CLASSIFIED BY
SUBSIDIARY'S COUNTRY
(CONTINUED)

	PRINCIPAL INDUSTRY OF SUBSIDIARY AS OF 1/1/68						
SUBSIDIARY'S COUNTRY	PAPER PRODUCTS	PRINTED MATTER	INDUS-TRIAL CHEMICALS	PLASTICS AND SYN-THETICS	DRUGS	SOAP AND COSMETICS	PAINTS
NEW ZEALAND	2.2	0.	11.	6.7	16.	8.9	2.2
JAPAN	2.2	0.7	12.	11.	4.3	2.2	1.4
CHINA (TAIWAN)	0.	0.	0.	15.	23.	7.7	0.
HONG KONG	0.	0.	0.	14.	0.	14.	0.
THE PHILIPPINES	5.7	0.	3.8	3.8	13.	5.7	1.9
MALAYSIA	7.1	0.	0.	0.	14.	7.1	0.
SINGAPORE	0.	0.	0.	0.	0.	10.	10.
INDONESIA	0.	0.	0.	0.	0.	0.	0.
THAILAND	7.1	0.	0.	0.	14.	14.	0.
INDIA	1.5	0.	1.5	6.2	18.	1.5	1.5
OTHER ASIA AND OCEANIA	0.	0.	0.	0.	15.	0.	15.

TABLE CONTINUED ON NEXT PAGE

CROSS-TABULATION 6.1.2: PERCENTAGE BREAKDOWN OF NUMBER (AS OF 1/1/68) OF
MANUFACTURING SUBSIDIARIES OF U.S.-BASED PARENT SYSTEMS BY
PRINCIPAL INDUSTRY OF SUBSIDIARY AS OF 1/1/68
FOR SUBSIDIARIES CLASSIFIED BY
SUBSIDIARY'S COUNTRY
(CONTINUED)

PRINCIPAL INDUSTRY OF SUBSIDIARY AS OF 1/1/68

SUBSIDIARY'S COUNTRY	AGRI-CULTURAL CHEMICALS	OTHER CHEMICALS	REFINED PETRO-LEUM	OTHER PETROLEUM PRODUCTS	TIRES	OTHER RUBBER PRODUCTS	LEATHER PRODUCTS + SHOES
CANADA	1.3	1.7	2.3	0.8	0.8	0.8	0.4
MEXICO	1.2	2.0	0.	1.2	2.4	1.2	0.4
CENTRAL AMERICA AND CARIB	3.3	1.6	5.7	0.	3.3	0.8	0.
VENEZUELA	0.8	0.8	5.0	0.8	2.5	1.7	0.
COLOMBIA	2.9	1.9	4.8	1.9	2.9	0.	0.
PERU	2.1	0.	2.1	2.1	4.3	0.	2.1
CHILE	0.	3.2	0.	3.2	0.	0.	3.2
ARGENTINA	0.	2.4	1.6	1.6	3.2	1.6	0.
BRAZIL	2.5	1.9	0.	3.1	2.5	0.6	0.6
OTHER SOUTH AMERICA	2.5	0.	5.0	0.	5.0	0.	0.
GERMANY	0.5	2.3	7.0	2.8	1.9	0.	0.
FRANCE	2.0	2.0	1.0	2.4	1.5	0.5	0.
ITALY	0.	3.4	6.9	1.1	1.1	0.6	0.
BELGIUM AND LUXEMBURG	1.2	0.	1.2	3.5	2.4	0.	1.2
THE NETHERLANDS	0.	3.8	5.0	1.3	2.5	0.	0.
UNITED KINGDOM	0.6	2.8	2.0	1.7	0.8	0.6	0.3
IRELAND	0.	3.6	0.	0.	0.	7.1	7.1
DENMARK	0.	0.	8.0	16.	0.	0.	0.
NORWAY	0.	0.	18.	0.	5.9	0.	0.
SWEDEN	2.9	0.	5.7	8.6	2.9	2.9	0.
FINLAND	17.	0.	0.	0.	0.	0.	0.

TABLE CONTINUED ON NEXT PAGE

CROSS-TABULATION 6.1.2: PERCENTAGE BREAKDOWN OF NUMBER (AS OF 1/1/68) OF
MANUFACTURING SUBSIDIARIES OF U.S.-BASED PARENT SYSTEMS BY
PRINCIPAL INDUSTRY OF SUBSIDIARY AS OF 1/1/68
FOR SUBSIDIARIES CLASSIFIED BY
SUBSIDIARY'S COUNTRY
(CONTINUED)

PRINCIPAL INDUSTRY OF SUBSIDIARY AS OF 1/1/68

SUBSIDIARY'S COUNTRY	AGRI- CULTURAL CHEMICALS	OTHER CHEMICALS	REFINED PETRO- LEUM	OTHER PETROLEUM PRODUCTS	TIRES	OTHER RUBBER PRODUCTS	LEATHER PRODUCTS + SHOES
SWITZERLAND	0.	4.0	0.	0.	4.0	0.	0.
AUSTRIA	0.	0.	18.	0.	0.	0.	0.
PORTUGAL	0.	0.	0.	0.	18.	0.	0.
SPAIN	4.8	3.8	2.9	2.9	1.9	1.0	1.0
GREECE	0.	0.	5.9	0.	0.	0.	0.
TURKEY	0.	0.	6.3	0.	13.	0.	0.
CTHER EUROPE + ISRAEL	0.	0.	0.	0.	0.	0.	9.1
PAKISTAN	6.3	0.	6.3	0.	6.3	0.	0.
IRAN	0.	0.	13.	13.	13.	0.	0.
CTHER MID EAST+EGYPT+LIBYA	4.8	0.	38.	9.5	0.	4.8	0.
UNION OF SOUTH AFRICA	0.	3.5	0.	0.9	2.6	0.9	0.9
RHODESIA	0.	0.	15.	0.	0.	0.	0.
ZAMBIA	0.	0.	0.	0.	0.	0.	0.
TANZANIA	0.	0.	0.	0.	0.	0.	0.
KENYA	13.	0.	13.	0.	13.	13.	0.
NIGERIA	0.	0.	0.	0.	0.	0.	0.
CTHER (BRITISH) AFRICA	0.	0.	0.	0.	0.	0.	0.
MOROCCO, ALGERIA + TUNISIA	0.	0.	6.7	0.	13.	0.	0.
OTHER (FRENCH) AFRICA	22.	0.	33.	0.	0.	0.	0.
CTHER AFRICA	0.	0.	33.	0.	0.	33.	0.
AUSTRALIA	0.5	2.4	5.7	2.4	1.9	1.0	0.

TABLE CONTINUED ON NEXT PAGE

CROSS-TABULATION 6. 1.2: PERCENTAGE BREAKDOWN OF NUMBER (AS OF 1/1/68) OF
MANUFACTURING SUBSIDIARIES OF U.S.-BASED PARENT SYSTEMS BY
PRINCIPAL INDUSTRY OF SUBSIDIARY AS OF 1/1/68
FOR SUBSIDIARIES CLASSIFIED BY
SUBSIDIARY'S COUNTRY
(CONTINUED)

PRINCIPAL INDUSTRY OF SUBSIDIARY AS OF 1/1/68

SUBSIDIARY'S COUNTRY	AGRI-CULTURAL CHEMICALS	OTHER CHEMICALS	REFINED PETRO-LEUM	OTHER PETROLEUM PRODUCTS	TIRES	OTHER RUBBER PRODUCTS	LEATHER PRODUCTS + SHOES
NEW ZEALAND.................	0.	2.2	6.7	0.	4.4	0.	0.
JAPAN.......................	0.	3.6	3.6	2.9	2.2	1.4	0.
CHINA (TAIWAN)..............	0.	15.	0.	7.7	0.	0.	0.
HONG KONG...................	0.	14.	0.	0.	0.	0.	0.
THE PHILIPPINES.............	1.9	3.8	3.8	0.	3.8	0.	0.
MALAYSIA....................	0.	0.	7.1	0.	0.	7.1	0.
SINGAPORE...................	0.	0.	0.	0.	0.	0.	0.
INDONESIA...................	0.	0.	0.	0.	33.	33.	0.
THAILAND....................	0.	0.	0.	0.	7.1	0.	0.
INDIA.......................	6.2	1.5	1.5	4.6	1.5	1.5	0.
OTHER ASIA AND OCEANIA......	7.7	0.	23.	0.	0.	0.	0.

TABLE CONTINUED ON NEXT PAGE

CROSS-TABULATION 6. 1.2: PERCENTAGE BREAKDOWN OF NUMBER (AS OF 1/1/68) OF
MANUFACTURING SUBSIDIARIES OF U.S.-BASED PARENT SYSTEMS BY
PRINCIPAL INDUSTRY OF SUBSIDIARY AS OF 1/1/68
FOR SUBSIDIARIES CLASSIFIED BY
SUBSIDIARY'S COUNTRY
(CONTINUED)

PRINCIPAL INDUSTRY OF SUBSIDIARY AS OF 1/1/68

SUBSIDIARY'S COUNTRY	GLASS PRODUCTS	STONE, CLAY + CONCRETE	IRON AND STEEL	NON-FERROUS SMELTING	NON-FERROUS PRODUCTS	METAL CANS	STRUCTURAL METAL PRODUCTS
CANADA	1.1	1.3	0.6	1.9	1.7	1.7	1.3
MEXICO	0.	3.1	0.8	0.4	1.6	1.2	0.8
CENTRAL AMERICA AND CARIB	0.	0.	0.	0.	0.8	0.8	0.8
VENEZUELA	4.1	0.8	0.	0.8	0.8	1.7	0.8
COLOMBIA	1.9	0.	1.0	0.	1.0	1.0	1.0
PERU	0.	2.1	0.	0.	0.	0.	0.
CHILE	6.5	6.5	3.2	0.	0.	0.	0.
ARGENTINA	1.6	3.2	0.8	1.6	1.6	0.	0.
BRAZIL	3.1	1.9	1.2	0.6	0.6	0.6	0.
OTHER SOUTH AMERICA	0.	5.0	0.	2.5	0.	2.5	0.
GERMANY	1.4	0.9	0.5	0.9	0.5	0.	0.9
FRANCE	0.5	2.4	1.5	0.	0.5	0.	0.5
ITALY	1.7	1.7	0.6	0.	0.6	0.	1.1
BELGIUM AND LUXEMBURG	1.2	4.7	1.2	1.2	0.	0.	2.4
THE NETHERLANDS	0.	1.3	3.8	0.	2.5	1.3	0.
UNITED KINGDOM	1.1	2.0	2.0	1.4	1.4	0.3	1.1
IRELAND	0.	3.6	0.	0.	0.	0.	0.
DENMARK	0.	0.	0.	0.	0.	4.0	0.
NORWAY	0.	18.	0.	24.	0.	0.	0.
SWEDEN	0.	0.	0.	0.	0.	0.	0.
FINLAND	0.	0.	0.	0.	0.	0.	0.

TABLE CONTINUED ON NEXT PAGE

CROSS-TABULATION 6.1.2: PERCENTAGE BREAKDOWN OF NUMBER (AS OF 1/1/68) OF MANUFACTURING SUBSIDIARIES OF U.S.-BASED PARENT SYSTEMS BY PRINCIPAL INDUSTRY OF SUBSIDIARY AS OF 1/1/68 FOR SUBSIDIARIES CLASSIFIED BY SUBSIDIARY'S COUNTRY (CONTINUED)

PRINCIPAL INDUSTRY OF SUBSIDIARY AS OF 1/1/68

SUBSIDIARY'S COUNTRY	GLASS PRODUCTS	STONE, CLAY + CONCRETE	IRON AND STEEL	NON-FERROUS SMELTING	NON-FERROUS PRODUCTS	METAL CANS	STRUCTURAL METAL PRODUCTS
SWITZERLAND	0.	0.	0.	0.	4.0	0.	0.
AUSTRIA	0.	0.	0.	0.	0.	0.	0.
PORTUGAL	0.	0.	0.	0.	0.	0.	0.
SPAIN	0.	1.0	0.	1.0	0.	1.9	1.0
GREECE	0.	5.9	5.9	0.	5.9	5.9	0.
TURKEY	0.	0.	6.3	0.	0.	0.	0.
OTHER EUROPE + ISRAEL	0.	9.1	0.	0.	0.	9.1	0.
PAKISTAN	0.	0.	0.	0.	0.	0.	0.
IRAN	0.	6.3	0.	0.	0.	0.	0.
OTHER MID EAST+EGYPT+LIBYA	0.	4.8	0.	0.	4.8	0.	0.
UNION OF SOUTH AFRICA	0.9	2.6	0.9	1.7	0.	0.9	0.9
RHODESIA	7.7	0.	0.	7.7	0.	0.	0.
ZAMBIA	0.	0.	0.	17.	0.	0.	0.
TANZANIA	0.	0.	0.	0.	0.	0.	0.
KENYA	0.	0.	0.	0.	0.	0.	0.
NIGERIA	0.	9.1	0.	0.	0.	0.	0.
OTHER (BRITISH) AFRICA	0.	0.	0.	50.	0.	0.	0.
MOROCCO, ALGERIA + TUNISIA	0.	0.	0.	0.	6.7	0.	6.7
OTHER (FRENCH) AFRICA	0.	0.	0.	0.	0.	0.	0.
OTHER AFRICA	0.	0.	0.	0.	0.	0.	0.
AUSTRALIA	0.5	2.4	0.5	2.4	1.0	0.5	0.

TABLE CONTINUED ON NEXT PAGE

CROSS-TABULATION 6.1.2: PERCENTAGE BREAKDOWN OF NUMBER (AS OF 1/1/68) OF
MANUFACTURING SUBSIDIARIES OF U.S.-BASED PARENT SYSTEMS BY
PRINCIPAL INDUSTRY OF SUBSIDIARY AS OF 1/1/68
FOR SUBSIDIARIES CLASSIFIED BY
SUBSIDIARY'S COUNTRY
(CONTINUED)

PRINCIPAL INDUSTRY OF SUBSIDIARY AS OF 1/1/68

SUBSIDIARY'S COUNTRY	GLASS PRODUCTS	STONE, CLAY + CONCRETE	IRON AND STEEL	NON-FERROUS SMELTING	NON-FERROUS PRODUCTS	METAL CANS	STRUCTURAL METAL PRODUCTS
NEW ZEALAND	0.	0.	0.	0.	0.	0.	0.
JAPAN	2.2	2.9	0.7	0.7	0.7	1.4	0.7
CHINA (TAIWAN)	0.	0.	0.	0.	0.	0.	0.
HONG KONG	0.	0.	0.	0.	0.	0.	0.
THE PHILIPPINES	0.	1.9	0.	0.	0.	1.9	1.9
MALAYSIA	0.	0.	0.	0.	0.	0.	0.
SINGAPORE	0.	0.	12.	0.	0.	0.	0.
INDONESIA	0.	0.	0.	0.	0.	0.	0.
THAILAND	0.	7.1	0.	14.	0.	0.	0.
INDIA	1.5	3.1	1.5	1.5	1.5	0.	0.
OTHER ASIA AND OCEANIA	0.	0.	0.	0.	0.	7.7	0.

TABLE CONTINUED ON NEXT PAGE

CROSS-TABULATION 6.1.2: PERCENTAGE BREAKDOWN OF NUMBER (AS OF 1/1/68) OF
MANUFACTURING SUBSIDIARIES OF U.S.-BASED PARENT SYSTEMS BY
PRINCIPAL INDUSTRY OF SUBSIDIARY AS OF 1/1/68
FOR SUBSIDIARIES CLASSIFIED BY
SUBSIDIARY'S COUNTRY
(CONTINUED)

SUBSIDIARY'S COUNTRY	PRINCIPAL INDUSTRY OF SUBSIDIARY AS OF 1/1/68						
	FABRICA-TED WIRE PRODUCTS	OTHER FABRICA-TED METAL	ENGINES AND TURBINES	FARM MACHIN-ERY	CONSTRUC-TION MA-CHINERY	SPECIAL INDUSTRY MACHINERY	GENERAL INDUSTRY MACHINERY
CANADA	0.4	5.7	1.3	0.4	2.7	1.5	2.3
MEXICO	0.	1.6	0.	0.8	3.9	1.2	2.4
CENTRAL AMERICA AND CARIB.	0.	0.8	0.	0.	0.	0.8	0.
VENEZUELA	0.	3.3	0.	0.	0.	0.8	0.
COLOMBIA	1.0	2.9	0.	1.0	0.	1.0	1.0
PERU	2.1	2.1	0.	0.	0.	0.	0.
CHILE	0.	6.5	0.	0.	0.	0.	0.
ARGENTINA	0.6	4.0	0.	3.2	1.6	0.	1.6
BRAZIL	0.6	2.5	1.2	0.6	3.7	1.2	1.2
OTHER SOUTH AMERICA	0.	2.5	0.	2.5	0.	2.5	0.
GERMANY	0.9	5.6	1.4	0.5	2.8	4.2	2.3
FRANCE	0.6	3.4	1.5	2.0	3.4	1.5	1.0
ITALY	0.6	5.2	0.	0.	2.3	5.2	2.3
BELGIUM AND LUXEMBURG	0.	3.5	1.2	1.2	4.7	2.4	2.4
THE NETHERLANDS	0.	6.3	0.	0.	2.5	1.3	1.3
UNITED KINGDOM	0.6	5.3	0.	1.1	1.7	4.5	1.7
IRELAND	0.	7.1	0.	0.	0.	0.	0.
DENMARK	0.	4.0	0.	0.	0.	0.	0.
NORWAY	0.	0.	0.	0.	0.	0.	0.
SWEDEN	0.	0.	0.	0.	0.	5.7	0.
FINLAND	0.	0.	0.	0.	0.	0.	0.

TABLE CONTINUED ON NEXT PAGE

CROSS-TABULATION 6.1.2: PERCENTAGE BREAKDOWN OF NUMBER (AS OF 1/1/68) OF MANUFACTURING SUBSIDIARIES OF U.S.-BASED PARENT SYSTEMS BY PRINCIPAL INDUSTRY OF SUBSIDIARY AS OF 1/1/68 FOR SUBSIDIARIES CLASSIFIED BY SUBSIDIARY'S COUNTRY (CONTINUED)

PRINCIPAL INDUSTRY OF SUBSIDIARY AS OF 1/1/68

SUBSIDIARY'S COUNTRY	FABRICATED WIRE PRODUCTS	OTHER FABRICATED METAL	ENGINES AND TURBINES	FARM MACHINERY	CONSTRUCTION MACHINERY	SPECIAL INDUSTRY MACHINERY	GENERAL INDUSTRY MACHINERY
SWITZERLAND	0.	4.0	0.	0.	0.	4.0	4.0
AUSTRIA	0.	12.	0.	0.	0.	5.9	5.9
PORTUGAL	0.	5.9	0.	0.	0.	0.	0.
SPAIN	1.9	2.9	0.	1.9	1.0	2.9	1.9
GREECE	0.	0.	0.	0.	0.	5.9	0.
TURKEY	0.	6.3	0.	6.3	0.	0.	0.
OTHER EUROPE + ISRAEL	0.	0.	0.	0.	0.	0.	0.
PAKISTAN	0.	0.	0.	0.	0.	0.	0.
IRAN	0.	0.	0.	0.	0.	0.	6.3
OTHER MID EAST+EGYPT+LIBYA	0.	0.	0.	0.	0.	0.	0.
UNION OF SOUTH AFRICA	0.	4.3	0.	2.6	4.3	3.5	0.9
RHODESIA	0.	0.	0.	0.	0.	0.	0.
ZAMBIA	0.	0.	0.	0.	0.	0.	0.
TANZANIA	0.	0.	0.	0.	0.	0.	0.
KENYA	0.	0.	0.	0.	0.	0.	0.
NIGERIA	0.	0.	0.	0.	0.	0.	0.
OTHER (BRITISH) AFRICA	0.	0.	0.	0.	0.	0.	0.
MOROCCO, ALGERIA + TUNISIA	0.	0.	0.	6.7	0.	0.	0.
OTHER (FRENCH) AFRICA	0.	22.	0.	0.	0.	0.	0.
OTHER AFRICA	0.	0.	0.	0.	0.	0.	0.
AUSTRALIA	0.	4.3	0.5	1.9	4.3	1.9	1.9

TABLE CONTINUED ON NEXT PAGE

CROSS-TABULATION 6.1.2: PERCENTAGE BREAKDOWN OF NUMBER (AS OF 1/1/68) OF
MANUFACTURING SUBSIDIARIES OF U.S.-BASED PARENT SYSTEMS BY
PRINCIPAL INDUSTRY OF SUBSIDIARY AS OF 1/1/68
FOR SUBSIDIARIES CLASSIFIED BY
SUBSIDIARY'S COUNTRY
(CONTINUED)

PRINCIPAL INDUSTRY OF SUBSIDIARY AS OF 1/1/68

SUBSIDIARY'S COUNTRY	FABRICA-TED WIRE PRODUCTS	OTHER FABRICA-TED METAL	ENGINES AND TURBINES	FARM MACHIN-ERY	CONSTRUC-TION MA-CHINERY	SPECIAL INDUSTRY MACHINERY	GENERAL INDUSTRY MACHINERY
NEW ZEALAND	0.	2.2	0.	2.2	0.	2.2	2.2
JAPAN	0.	2.2	0.7	0.	2.9	2.2	2.2
CHINA (TAIWAN)	0.	0.	0.	0.	0.	0.	0.
HONG KONG	0.	0.	0.	0.	0.	0.	0.
THE PHILIPPINES	0.	1.9	0.	0.	0.	1.9	1.9
MALAYSIA	0.	7.1	0.	0.	0.	0.	0.
SINGAPORE	0.	10.	0.	0.	0.	0.	0.
INDONESIA	0.	0.	0.	0.	0.	0.	0.
THAILAND	0.	0.	0.	0.	0.	0.	0.
INDIA	1.5	3.1	0.	1.5	3.1	1.5	1.5
OTHER ASIA AND OCEANIA	0.	7.7	0.	0.	0.	0.	0.

TABLE CONTINUED ON NEXT PAGE

CROSS-TABULATION 6.1.2: PERCENTAGE BREAKDOWN OF NUMBER (AS OF 1/1/68) OF
MANUFACTURING SUBSIDIARIES OF U.S.-BASED PARENT SYSTEMS BY
PRINCIPAL INDUSTRY OF SUBSIDIARY AS OF 1/1/68
FOR SUBSIDIARIES CLASSIFIED BY
SUBSIDIARY'S COUNTRY
(CONTINUED)

PRINCIPAL INDUSTRY OF SUBSIDIARY AS OF 1/1/68

SUBSIDIARY'S COUNTRY	OFFICE MACHINES+ COMPUTERS	OTHER NON-EL. MACHINERY	ELECTRIC TRANSMIS. EQUIPMENT	ELECTRIC LIGHTING +WIRING	RADIOS, TV'S+AP-PLIANCES	COMMUNI-CATIONS EQUIPMENT	ELECTRON-IC COM-PONENTS
CANADA	1.3	1.1	0.8	1.5	1.5	1.3	0.8
MEXICO	1.6	1.2	1.6	0.4	2.7	0.8	1.2
CENTRAL AMERICA AND CARIB	0.	2.5	0.	0.	0.8	0.	0.
VENEZUELA	0.8	0.8	0.	0.8	0.8	0.	0.
COLOMBIA	1.0	0.	0.	0.	1.9	0.	0.
PERU	0.	0.	0.	0.	2.1	0.	0.
CHILE	3.2	0.	0.	3.2	6.5	0.	0.
ARGENTINA	0.	0.8	0.	0.8	4.0	0.8	0.8
BRAZIL	2.5	1.2	0.6	1.9	2.5	0.	1.9
OTHER SOUTH AMERICA	0.	0.	0.	0.	2.5	0.	0.
GERMANY	3.3	2.3	0.5	0.9	2.3	0.5	2.3
FRANCE	2.4	3.4	0.5	0.5	2.9	1.0	2.0
ITALY	0.6	0.6	2.3	0.6	2.9	0.	1.7
BELGIUM AND LUXEMBURG	1.2	0.	0.	0.	0.	1.2	0.
THE NETHERLANDS	5.0	2.5	1.3	0.	0.	1.3	0.
UNITED KINGDOM	1.4	1.4	0.8	0.8	4.2	0.6	1.4
IRELAND	3.6	0.	0.	0.	0.	0.	0.
DENMARK	0.	0.	0.	0.	0.	4.0	0.
NORWAY	0.	0.	0.	0.	0.	5.9	0.
SWEDEN	5.7	0.	0.	0.	0.	2.9	0.
FINLAND	0.	0.	0.	0.	17.	17.	0.

TABLE CONTINUED ON NEXT PAGE

CROSS-TABULATION 6. 1.2: PERCENTAGE BREAKDOWN OF NUMBER (AS OF 1/1/68) OF MANUFACTURING SUBSIDIARIES OF U.S.-BASED PARENT SYSTEMS BY PRINCIPAL INDUSTRY OF SUBSIDIARY AS OF 1/1/68 FOR SUBSIDIARIES CLASSIFIED BY SUBSIDIARY'S COUNTRY (CONTINUED)

SUBSIDIARY'S COUNTRY	PRINCIPAL INDUSTRY OF SUBSIDIARY AS OF 1/1/68						
	OFFICE MACHINES+ COMPUTERS	OTHER NON-EL. MACHINERY EQUIPMENT	ELECTRIC TRANSMIS. EQUIPMENT	ELECTRIC LIGHTING +WIRING	RADIOS, TV'S+AP- PLIANCES	COMMUNI- CATIONS EQUIPMENT	ELECTRON- IC COM- PONENTS
SWITZERLAND	4.0	4.0	4.0	0.	0.	0.	12.
AUSTRIA	0.	5.9	5.9	5.9	0.	5.9	0.
PORTUGAL	0.	0.	0.	0.	0.	0.	0.
SPAIN	0.	1.0	0.	0.	1.9	1.9	0.
GREECE	0.	0.	0.	0.	5.9	0.	0.
TURKEY	0.	0.	6.3	6.3	6.3	6.3	0.
OTHER EUROPE + ISRAEL	0.	0.	0.	0.	0.	0.	0.
PAKISTAN	0.	0.	0.	0.	6.3	0.	0.
IRAN	0.	0.	0.	0.	0.	0.	0.
OTHER MID EAST+EGYPT+LIBYA	0.	0.	0.	0.	0.	0.	0.
UNION OF SOUTH AFRICA	0.	0.	3.	0.	1.7	0.	0.9
RHODESIA	0.	0.	0.	0.	0.	7.7	0.
ZAMBIA	0.	0.	0.	0.	0.	0.	0.
TANZANIA	0.	0.	0.	0.	0.	0.	0.
KENYA	0.	0.	0.	0.	13.	0.	0.
NIGERIA	0.	0.	3.	0.	9.1	0.	9.1
OTHER (BRITISH) AFRICA	0.	0.	0.	0.	0.	0.	0.
MOROCCO, ALGERIA + TUNISIA	0.	0.	0.	0.	6.7	0.	0.
OTHER (FRENCH) AFRICA	0.	0.	0.	0.	11.	0.	0.
OTHER AFRICA	0.	0.	0.	0.	0.	0.	0.
AUSTRALIA	0.	3.3	1.0	0.	2.4	0.5	1.0

TABLE CONTINUED ON NEXT PAGE

CROSS-TABULATION 6. 1.2: PERCENTAGE BREAKDOWN OF NUMBER (AS OF 1/1/68) OF
MANUFACTURING SUBSIDIARIES OF U.S.-BASED PARENT SYSTEMS BY
PRINCIPAL INDUSTRY OF SUBSIDIARY AS OF 1/1/68
FOR SUBSIDIARIES CLASSIFIED BY
SUBSIDIARY'S COUNTRY
(CONTINUED)

PRINCIPAL INDUSTRY OF SUBSIDIARY AS OF 1/1/68

SUBSIDIARY'S COUNTRY	OFFICE MACHINES+ COMPUTERS	OTHER NON-EL. MACHINERY	ELECTRIC TRANSMIS. EQUIPMENT	ELECTRIC LIGHTING +WIRING	RADIOS, TV'S+AP- PLIANCES	COMMUNI- CATIONS EQUIPMENT	ELECTRON- IC CCM- PONENTS
NEW ZEALAND.	0.	0.	0.	0.	2.2	2.2	0.
JAPAN.	3.6	0.7	0.	0.7	0.7	1.4	2.2
CHINA (TAIWAN).	0.	0.	3.	0.	7.7	0.	7.7
HONG KONG.	0.	0.	0.	0.	0.	14.	0.
THE PHILIPPINES.	0.	0.	0.	1.9	3.8	3.8	0.
MALAYSIA.	0.	0.	0.	0.	7.1	0.	0.
SINGAPORE.	0.	0.	0.	0.	0.	0.	0.
INDONESIA.	0.	0.	0.	0.	0.	0.	0.
THAILAND.	0.	0.	0.	0.	7.1	0.	0.
INDIA.	3.1	1.5	0.	3.1	0.	0.	1.5
OTHER ASIA AND OCEANIA.	0.	0.	0.	7.7	7.7	0.	0.

TABLE CONTINUED ON NEXT PAGE

CROSS-TABULATION 6.1.2: PERCENTAGE BREAKDOWN OF NUMBER (AS OF 1/1/68) OF
MANUFACTURING SUBSIDIARIES OF U.S.-BASED PARENT SYSTEMS BY
PRINCIPAL INDUSTRY OF SUBSIDIARY AS OF 1/1/68
FOR SUBSIDIARIES CLASSIFIED BY
SUBSIDIARY'S COUNTRY
(CONTINUED)

SUBSIDIARY'S COUNTRY	PRINCIPAL INDUSTRY OF SUBSIDIARY AS OF 1/1/68						
	OTHER ELECTRIC EQUIPMENT + EQUIP.	MOTOR VEHICLES + EQUIP.	OTHER TRANS-PORTATION	PRECI-SION GOODS	MISC. PRODUCTS	TOTAL PERCENT	TOTAL NUMBER
CANADA	2.1	5.9	0.8	1.5	1.3	100.	475
MEXICO	3.1	6.3	0.4	1.2	1.6	100.	255
CENTRAL AMERICA AND CARIB.	4.9	1.6	0.	0.8	0.	100.	122
VENEZUELA	2.5	5.8	0.	0.	2.5	100.	121
COLOMBIA	2.9	3.8	0.	1.9	2.9	100.	105
PERU	2.1	4.3	0.	2.1	2.1	100.	47
CHILE	0.	3.2	0.	3.2	3.2	100.	31
ARGENTINA	0.8	14.	0.	2.4	0.8	100.	125
BRAZIL	4.9	9.9	0.	3.1	1.2	100.	162
OTHER SOUTH AMERICA	0.	2.5	0.	0.	5.0	100.	40
GERMANY	1.4	4.2	1.4	6.5	2.8	100.	214
FRANCE	3.4	6.3	1.0	4.4	2.0	100.	205
ITALY	3.4	2.9	2.3	2.3	2.3	100.	174
BELGIUM AND LUXEMBURG	0.	2.4	0.	3.5	1.2	100.	85
THE NETHERLANDS	1.3	2.5	0.	2.5	1.3	100.	80
UNITED KINGDOM	2.0	7.3	0.6	3.6	1.7	100.	357
IRELAND	0.	11.	0.	0.	3.6	100.	28
DENMARK	0.	12.	0.	0.	0.	100.	25
NORWAY	5.9	0.	0.	0.	0.	100.	17
SWEDEN	2.9	2.9	0.	0.	0.	100.	35
FINLAND	0.	17.	0.	0.	17.	100.	6

TABLE CONTINUED ON NEXT PAGE

CROSS-TABULATION 6.1.2: PERCENTAGE BREAKDOWN OF NUMBER (AS OF 1/1/68) OF MANUFACTURING SUBSIDIARIES OF U.S.-BASED PARENT SYSTEMS BY PRINCIPAL INDUSTRY OF SUBSIDIARY AS OF 1/1/68 FOR SUBSIDIARIES CLASSIFIED BY SUBSIDIARY'S COUNTRY (CONTINUED)

PRINCIPAL INDUSTRY OF SUBSIDIARY AS OF 1/1/68

SUBSIDIARY'S COUNTRY	OTHER ELECTRIC EQUIPMENT + EQUIP.	MOTOR VEHICLES + EQUIP.	OTHER TRANS-PORTATION	PRECI-SION GOODS	MISC. PRODUCTS	TOTAL PERCENT	TOTAL NUMBER
SWITZERLAND	4.0	0.	0.	0.	4.0	100.	25
AUSTRIA	0.	5.9	0.	5.9	0.	100.	17
PORTUGAL	0.	0.	5.9	0.	5.9	100.	17
SPAIN	0.	5.8	0.	0.	1.0	100.	104
GREECE	0.	0.	0.	0.	0.	100.	17
TURKEY + ISRAEL	0.	13.	0.	0.	0.	100.	16
OTHER EUROPE + ISRAEL	9.1	9.1	0.	0.	9.1	100.	11
PAKISTAN	0.	0.	0.	0.	0.	100.	16
IRAN	6.3	0.	0.	0.	0.	100.	16
OTHER MID EAST+EGYPT+LIBYA	0.	0.	0.	0.	0.	100.	21
UNION OF SOUTH AFRICA	0.9	7.8	0.	0.	0.	100.	115
RHODESIA	7.7	0.	0.	0.	7.7	100.	13
ZAMBIA	0.	0.	0.	0.	0.	100.	6
TANZANIA	0.	0.	0.	0.	0.	100.	0
KENYA	0.	0.	0.	0.	13.	100.	8
NIGERIA	0.	0.	0.	0.	18.	100.	11
OTHER (BRITISH) AFRICA	0.	0.	0.	25.	0.	100.	4
MOROCCO, ALGERIA + TUNISIA	0.	6.7	0.	0.	6.7	100.	15
OTHER (FRENCH) AFRICA	0.	0.	0.	0.	0.	100.	9
OTHER AFRICA	0.	33.	0.	0.	0.	100.	3
AUSTRALIA	2.4	5.7	1.0	1.0	2.4	100.	209

TABLE CONTINUED ON NEXT PAGE

CROSS-TABULATION 6.1.2: PERCENTAGE BREAKDOWN OF NUMBER (AS OF 1/1/68) OF MANUFACTURING SUBSIDIARIES OF U.S.-BASED PARENT SYSTEMS BY PRINCIPAL INDUSTRY OF SUBSIDIARY AS OF 1/1/68 FOR SUBSIDIARIES CLASSIFIED BY SUBSIDIARY'S COUNTRY (CONTINUED)

SUBSIDIARY'S COUNTRY	PRINCIPAL INDUSTRY OF SUBSIDIARY AS OF 1/1/68					TOTAL PERCENT	TOTAL NUMBER
	OTHER ELECTRIC EQUIPMENT + EQUIP.	MOTOR VEHICLES + EQUIP.	OTHER TRANS-PORTATION	PRECISION GOODS	MISC. PRODUCTS		
NEW ZEALAND	2.2	4.4	0.	0.	0.	100.	45
JAPAN	4.3	2.9	0.	0.	0.	100.	138
CHINA (TAIWAN)	7.7	0.	0.	0.	0.	100.	13
HONG KONG	29.	0.	0.	0.	14.	100.	7
THE PHILIPPINES	3.8	3.8	0.	0.	0.	100.	53
MALAYSIA	7.1	0.	0.	0.	7.1	100.	14
SINGAPORE	20.	10.	0.	0.	20.	100.	10
INDONESIA	33.	0.	0.	0.	0.	100.	3
THAILAND	14.	0.	0.	0.	0.	100.	14
INDIA	6.2	7.7	0.	3.1	1.5	100.	65
OTHER ASIA AND OCEANIA	0.	0.	0.	0.	0.	100.	13

245

CROSS-TABULATION 6.21.1: PERCENTAGE BREAKDOWN OF NUMBER (AS OF 1/1/71) OF
MANUFACTURING SUBSIDIARIES OF NON-U.S.-BASED PARENT SYSTEMS BY
PRINCIPAL INDUSTRY OF SUBSIDIARY AS OF 1/1/71
FOR SUBSIDIARIES CLASSIFIED BY
NATIONAL BASE OF SUBSIDIARY'S PARENT SYSTEM

PRINCIPAL INDUSTRY OF SUBSIDIARY AS OF 1/1/71

NATIONAL BASE OF SUBSIDIARY'S PARENT SYSTEM	ORDNANCE	MEAT PRODUCTS	DAIRY PRODUCTS	CANNED FOODS	GRAIN MILL PRODUCTS	BAKERY PRODUCTS	CONFEC- TIONERY PRODUCTS
UNITED KINGDOM..............	0.1	1.2	2.4	1.3	2.0	3.5	0.9
GERMANY....................	0.3	0.	0.	0.	0.	0.	0.
FRANCE.....................	0.	0.	0.	0.	0.	0.	0.3
ITALY......................	0.	0.	0.	0.	0.	0.	0.
BELGIUM AND LUXEMBURG......	0.4	0.	0.	0.	0.	0.	0.
THE NETHERLANDS............	0.	0.	0.	0.	0.	0.	0.
SWEDEN.....................	0.	0.	0.	0.	0.	0.	0.
SWITZERLAND................	0.3	0.	11.	2.3	0.6	0.3	2.6
JAPAN......................	0.2	0.2	0.2	1.8	0.	0.	0.2
CANADA.....................	0.	1.1	0.	0.5	0.	0.	0.
OTHER NON-U.S..............	0.	0.	0.	0.	0.	0.	0.

TABLE CONTINUED ON NEXT PAGE

CROSS-TABULATION 6.21.1: PERCENTAGE BREAKDOWN OF NUMBER (AS OF 1/1/71) OF
MANUFACTURING SUBSIDIARIES OF NON-U.S.-BASED PARENT SYSTEMS BY
PRINCIPAL INDUSTRY OF SUBSIDIARY AS OF 1/1/71
FOR SUBSIDIARIES CLASSIFIED BY
NATIONAL BASE OF SUBSIDIARY'S PARENT SYSTEM
(CONTINUED)

PRINCIPAL INDUSTRY OF SUBSIDIARY AS OF 1/1/71

NATIONAL BASE OF SUBSIDIARY'S PARENT SYSTEM	BEVER-AGES	OTHER FOOD PRODUCTS	TOBACCO PRODUCTS	TEXTILES	APPAREL	LUMBER AND WOOD	FURNI-TURE
UNITED KINGDOM..........	5.7	5.4	2.6	3.4	0.8	0.7	0.5
GERMANY................	0.	0.2	0.	1.2	0.	0.	0.
FRANCE.................	0.	0.3	0.	7.0	0.3	0.	0.6
ITALY..................	0.	0.	0.	4.0	1.0	0.	0.
BELGIUM AND LUXEMBURG..	0.4	1.6	0.	6.8	0.	6.4	0.
THE NETHERLANDS........	0.	0.5	0.	3.1	0.3	0.	0.5
SWEDEN.................	0.	0.	0.	0.	0.	7.0	0.6
SWITZERLAND............	1.4	2.3	0.	5.4	0.	0.	0.
JAPAN..................	0.	2.3	0.5	23.	4.6	1.4	0.
CANADA.................	17.	0.	0.	0.	0.	2.7	0.5
OTHER NON-U.S	0.	2.5	0.	0.	0.	0.	2.5

TABLE CONTINUED ON NEXT PAGE

CROSS-TABULATION 6.21.1: PERCENTAGE BREAKDOWN OF NUMBER (AS OF 1/1/71) OF
MANUFACTURING SUBSIDIARIES OF NON-U.S.-BASED PARENT SYSTEMS BY
PRINCIPAL INDUSTRY OF SUBSIDIARY AS OF 1/1/71
FOR SUBSIDIARIES CLASSIFIED BY
NATIONAL BASE OF SUBSIDIARY'S PARENT SYSTEM
(CONTINUED)

PRINCIPAL INDUSTRY OF SUBSIDIARY AS OF 1/1/71

NATIONAL BASE OF SUBSIDIARY'S PARENT SYSTEM	PAPER PRODUCTS	PRINTED MATTER	INDUSTRIAL CHEMICALS	PLASTICS AND SYNTHETICS	DRUGS	SOAP AND COSMETICS	PAINTS
UNITED KINGDOM..........	4.6	2.8	4.0	2.1	1.8	6.7	3.1
GERMANY................	2.0	0.3	10.	6.3	9.5	1.5	4.8
FRANCE.................	0.8	1.1	10.	2.0	5.3	0.	0.
ITALY..................	0.	0.	2.0	13.	1.0	0.	1.0
BELGIUM AND LUXEMBURG..	0.8	0.	10.	6.4	1.2	0.	2.8
THE NETHERLANDS........	0.3	4.1	7.6	1.8	8.7	0.3	2.5
SWEDEN.................	5.1	1.3	0.	1.3	0.	0.	0.
SWITZERLAND............	0.9	0.6	1.4	3.7	21.	1.7	0.3
JAPAN..................	1.1	0.7	0.7	3.0	1.1	0.	0.2
CANADA.................	4.3	4.8	0.	0.	0.	0.	0.
OTHER NON-U.S..........	0.	0.	0.	2.5	0.	1.3	0.

TABLE CONTINUED ON NEXT PAGE

CROSS-TABULATION 6.21.1: PERCENTAGE BREAKDOWN OF NUMBER (AS OF 1/1/71) OF
MANUFACTURING SUBSIDIARIES OF NON-U.S.-BASED PARENT SYSTEMS BY
PRINCIPAL INDUSTRY OF SUBSIDIARY AS OF 1/1/71
FOR SUBSIDIARIES CLASSIFIED BY
NATIONAL BASE OF SUBSIDIARY'S PARENT SYSTEM
(CONTINUED)

PRINCIPAL INDUSTRY OF SUBSIDIARY AS OF 1/1/71

NATIONAL BASE OF SUBSIDIARY'S PARENT SYSTEM	AGRI-CULTURAL CHEMICALS	OTHER CHEMICALS	REFINED PETRO-LEUM	OTHER PETROLEUM PRODUCTS	TIRES	OTHER RUBBER PRODUCTS	LEATHER PRODUCTS + SHOES
UNITED KINGDOM.........	0.8	2.3	2.0	1.5	0.8	1.7	0.1
GERMANY................	2.2	5.6	0.2	1.2	0.5	1.9	0.2
FRANCE.................	2.5	4.2	3.6	6.4	2.5	1.1	0.6
ITALY..................	2.0	1.0	11.	1.0	5.0	5.0	0.
BELGIUM AND LUXEMBURG..	2.0	1.2	4.0	2.4	0.	0.	0.
THE NETHERLANDS........	3.6	4.8	7.9	2.8	0.	0.3	0.
SWEDEN.................	0.	13.	0.	0.	0.	0.	0.
SWITZERLAND............	3.7	2.0	0.	0.3	0.	0.9	0.
JAPAN..................	1.1	1.8	0.2	0.	0.5	2.3	0.2
CANADA.................	0.	0.	0.	0.	0.	0.	0.
OTHER NON-U.S.........	2.5	0.	0.	2.5	0.	1.3	1.3

TABLE CONTINUED ON NEXT PAGE

CROSS-TABULATION 6.21.1: PERCENTAGE BREAKDOWN OF NUMBER (AS OF 1/1/71) OF MANUFACTURING SUBSIDIARIES OF NON-U.S.-BASED PARENT SYSTEMS BY PRINCIPAL INDUSTRY OF SUBSIDIARY AS OF 1/1/71 FOR SUBSIDIARIES CLASSIFIED BY NATIONAL BASE OF SUBSIDIARY'S PARENT SYSTEM (CONTINUED)

PRINCIPAL INDUSTRY OF SUBSIDIARY AS OF 1/1/71

NATIONAL BASE OF SUBSIDIARY'S PARENT SYSTEM	GLASS PRODUCTS	STONE, CLAY + CONCRETE	IRON AND STEEL	NON-FERROUS SMELTING	NON-FERROUS PRODUCTS	METAL CANS	STRUCTURAL METAL PRODUCTS
UNITED KINGDOM............	0.1	0.8	1.9	2.2	4.4	1.3	0.7
GERMANY..................	0.3	1.0	5.9	1.0	0.3	0.	2.9
FRANCE...................	11.	5.6	5.3	1.4	4.2	0.	0.6
ITALY....................	0.	1.0	2.0	1.0	0.	0.	0.
BELGIUM AND LUXEMBURG....	2.0	12.	10.	4.4	0.8	0.	0.4
THE NETHERLANDS..........	0.	0.3	1.0	0.3	0.5	0.	0.8
SWEDEN...................	0.6	0.6	1.3	0.	5.1	0.	0.6
SWITZERLAND..............	0.	0.	2.0	0.6	1.1	1.7	0.6
JAPAN....................	0.2	1.1	8.0	1.4	0.	0.	1.6
CANADA...................	0.	0.5	1.6	9.6	7.0	0.	7.5
OTHER NON-U.S............	0.	0.	1.3	0.	1.3	0.	1.3

TABLE CONTINUED ON NEXT PAGE

CROSS-TABULATION 6.21.1: PERCENTAGE BREAKDOWN OF NUMBER (AS OF 1/1/71) OF
MANUFACTURING SUBSIDIARIES OF NON-U.S.-BASED PARENT SYSTEMS BY
PRINCIPAL INDUSTRY OF SUBSIDIARY AS OF 1/1/71
FOR SUBSIDIARIES CLASSIFIED BY
NATIONAL BASE OF SUBSIDIARY'S PARENT SYSTEM
(CONTINUED)

PRINCIPAL INDUSTRY OF SUBSIDIARY AS OF 1/1/71

NATIONAL BASE OF SUBSIDIARY'S PARENT SYSTEM	FABRICATED WIRE PRODUCTS	OTHER FABRICATED METAL	ENGINES AND TURBINES	FARM MACHINERY	CONSTRUCTION MACHINERY	SPECIAL INDUSTRY MACHINERY	GENERAL INDUSTRY MACHINERY
UNITED KINGDOM	0.2	1.8	0.8	0.1	0.3	1.4	1.2
GERMANY	1.0	4.9	1.0	0.	0.5	0.8	1.2
FRANCE	1.1	3.6	0.3	0.3	0.	0.8	0.8
ITALY	4.0	4.0	0.	0.	1.0	2.0	0.
BELGIUM AND LUXEMBURG	1.6	4.0	0.4	0.	0.	2.4	0.4
THE NETHERLANDS	0.8	1.3	0.3	0.	0.	1.8	0.3
SWEDEN	0.	0.6	0.6	0.	0.6	7.0	17.
SWITZERLAND	0.	5.4	3.4	0.	0.	3.4	3.1
JAPAN	3.4	3.4	0.7	1.8	1.4	0.9	0.2
CANADA	2.1	16.	3.2	11.	1.1	0.5	0.
OTHER NON-U.S	3.8	11.	0.	0.	2.5	0.	1.3

TABLE CONTINUED ON NEXT PAGE

CROSS-TABULATION 6.21.1: PERCENTAGE BREAKDOWN OF NUMBER (AS OF 1/1/71) OF MANUFACTURING SUBSIDIARIES OF NON-U.S.-BASED PARENT SYSTEMS BY PRINCIPAL INDUSTRY OF SUBSIDIARY AS OF 1/1/71 FOR SUBSIDIARIES CLASSIFIED BY NATIONAL BASE OF SUBSIDIARY'S PARENT SYSTEM (CONTINUED)

PRINCIPAL INDUSTRY OF SUBSIDIARY AS OF 1/1/71

NATIONAL BASE OF SUBSIDIARY'S PARENT SYSTEM	OFFICE MACHINES+ COMPUTERS	OTHER NON-EL. MACHINERY	ELECTRIC TRANSMIS. EQUIPMENT	ELECTRIC LIGHTING + WIRING	RADIOS, TV'S+AP- PLIANCES	COMMUNI- CATIONS EQUIPMENT	ELECTRON- IC COM- PONENTS
UNITED KINGDOM.............	0.1	0.4	0.6	1.3	3.7	1.0	0.8
GERMANY....................	0.3	0.8	4.4	3.9	1.4	2.9	1.4
FRANCE.....................	0.	0.3	0.8	1.7	0.3	1.4	2.5
ITALY......................	13.	0.	2.0	4.0	0.	2.0	0.
BELGIUM AND LUXEMBURG......	0.	0.4	0.4	4.4	0.8	0.	3.6
THE NETHERLANDS............	1.3	0.8	0.5	6.1	8.4	2.8	10.
SWEDEN.....................	0.6	0.6	3.8	0.	0.	15.	0.
SWITZERLAND................	0.	1.4	5.4	0.6	1.7	0.3	1.1
JAPAN......................	0.5	0.9	1.1	1.4	6.6	1.8	2.1
CANADA.....................	0.	0.	1.6	3.2	0.	1.1	0.
OTHER NON-U.S..............	2.5	1.3	16.	0.	1.3	0.	2.5

TABLE CONTINUED ON NEXT PAGE

CROSS-TABULATION 6.21.1: PERCENTAGE BREAKDOWN OF NUMBER (AS OF 1/1/71) OF MANUFACTURING SUBSIDIARIES OF NON-U.S.-BASED PARENT SYSTEMS BY PRINCIPAL INDUSTRY OF SUBSIDIARY AS OF 1/1/71 FOR SUBSIDIARIES CLASSIFIED BY NATIONAL BASE OF SUBSIDIARY'S PARENT SYSTEM (CONTINUED)

PRINCIPAL INDUSTRY OF SUBSIDIARY AS OF 1/1/71

NATIONAL BASE OF SUBSIDIARY'S PARENT SYSTEM	OTHER ELECTRIC EQUIPMENT + EQUIP.	MOTOR VEHICLES + EQUIP.	OTHER TRANS-PORTATION	PRECI-SION GOODS	MISC. PRODUCTS	TOTAL PERCENT	TOTAL NUMBER
UNITED KINGDOM............	3.4	3.2	1.6	0.6	1.4	100.	2121
GERMANY..................	5.1	5.6	0.8	3.7	0.5	100.	589
FRANCE...................	3.4	8.7	0.3	1.1	0.6	100.	357
ITALY....................	0.	17.	0.	0.	1.0	100.	101
BELGIUM AND LUXEMBURG....	0.	0.	0.8	1.6	3.2	100.	250
THE NETHERLANDS..........	6.6	0.3	0.	3.1	4.1	100.	393
SWEDEN...................	6.4	6.4	1.3	0.6	3.8	100.	157
SWITZERLAND..............	3.4	0.3	0.3	1.7	0.3	100.	350
JAPAN....................	3.4	5.7	2.7	0.2	1.6	100.	438
CANADA...................	1.6	1.1	0.5	0.	0.	100.	187
OTHER NON-U.S............	11.	0.	1.3	19.	6.3	100.	80

TABULATION 8.1: PERCENTAGE BREAKDOWN OF NUMBER OF MANUFACTURING SUBSIDIARIES BY PRINCIPAL INDUSTRY-GROUP OF SUBSIDIARY FOR VARIOUS CATEGORIES OF SUBSIDIARIES

CATEGORY OF SUBSIDIARY	PRINCIPAL INDUSTRY-GROUP OF SUBSIDIARY						
	FOOD AND TOBACCO	TEXTILES AND APPAREL	WOOD, PAPER+ FURNITURE	CHEMICALS	PETROLEUM	RUBBER AND TIRES	PRIMARY METALS
SUBSIDIARIES OF:							
NON-U.S.-BASED SYSTEMS (AS OF 1/1/71).............	13.	5.4	4.0	24.	3.7	2.0	7.9
U.S.-BASED SYSTEMS (AS OF 1/1/68).............	14.	2.7	5.3	29.	5.5	3.0	3.0
NON-U.S.-BASED SYSTEMS IN WORLD SUBSET OF SYSTEMS (AS OF 1/1/68).............	13.	5.1	4.4	23.	5.1	2.5	7.6
U.S.-BASED SYSTEMS IN WORLD SUBSET OF SYSTEMS (AS OF 1/1/68).............	14.	3.1	6.3	28.	6.9	3.8	3.2

(TABLE CONTINUED ON NEXT PAGE)

TABULATION 8.1: PERCENTAGE BREAKDOWN OF NUMBER OF MANUFACTURING SUBSIDIARIES BY PRINCIPAL INDUSTRY-GROUP OF SUBSIDIARY FOR VARIOUS CATEGORIES OF SUBSIDIARIES (CONTINUED)

CATEGORY OF SUBSIDIARY	PRINCIPAL INDUSTRY-GROUP OF SUBSIDIARY						
	FABRICAT. METAL+NON EL. MACH.	ELECTRIC AND ELEC-TRONIC	TRANS-PORTATION EQUIPMENT	PRECI-SION GOODS	OTHER	TOTAL PERCENT	TOTAL NUMBER
SUBSIDIARIES OF:							
NON-U.S.-BASED SYSTEMS (AS OF 1/1/71)............	12.	15.	4.7	1.5	6.5	100.	5290
U.S.-BASED SYSTEMS (AS OF 1/1/68)............	14.	9.6	6.9	2.0	6.2	100.	3756
NON-U.S.-BASED SYSTEMS IN WORLD SUPSET OF SYSTEMS (AS OF 1/1/68)............	11.	17.	4.6	0.7	5.2	100.	2306
U.S.-BASED SYSTEMS IN WORLD SUBSET OF SYSTEMS (AS OF 1/1/68)............	13.	9.5	5.9	1.1	5.3	100.	2941

CROSS-TABULATION 8.21.1: PERCENTAGE BREAKDOWN OF NUMBER (AS OF 1/1/71) OF
MANUFACTURING SUBSIDIARIES OF NON-U.S.-BASED PARENT SYSTEMS BY
PRINCIPAL INDUSTRY-GROUP OF SUBSIDIARY AS OF 1/1/71
FOR SUBSIDIARIES CLASSIFIED BY
NATIONAL BASE OF SUBSIDIARY'S PARENT SYSTEM

PRINCIPAL INDUSTRY-GROUP OF SUBSIDIARY AS OF 1/1/71

NATIONAL BASE OF SUBSIDIARY'S PARENT SYSTEM	FOOD AND TOBACCO	TEXTILES AND APPAREL	WOOD, PAPER+ FURNITURE	CHEMI-CALS	PETRO-LEUM	RUBBER AND TIRES	PRIMARY METALS
UNITED KINGDOM	25.	4.1	5.6	21.	3.4	2.4	8.4
GERMANY	0.3	1.1	1.8	46.	1.2	2.1	6.6
FRANCE	0.5	2.1	1.3	24.	9.6	3.5	11.
ITALY	0.	5.0	0.	20.	12.	9.9	3.0
BELGIUM AND LUXEMBURG	2.0	6.7	7.1	25.	6.3	0.	15.
THE NETHERLANDS	0.5	3.2	0.7	32.	10.	0.2	1.7
SWEDEN	0.	0.	13.	14.	0.	0.	6.4
SWITZERLAND	21.	5.1	0.8	35.	0.3	0.8	3.5
JAPAN	5.3	28.	2.5	8.0	0.2	2.7	9.4
CANADA	18.	0.	7.4	0.	0.	0.	18.
OTHER NON-U.S.	2.5	0.	2.5	6.3	2.5	1.3	2.5

TABLE CONTINUED ON NEXT PAGE

CROSS-TABULATION 8.21.1: PERCENTAGE BREAKDOWN OF NUMBER (AS OF 1/1/71) OF MANUFACTURING SUBSIDIARIES OF NON-U.S.-BASED PARENT SYSTEMS BY PRINCIPAL INDUSTRY-GROUP OF SUBSIDIARY AS OF 1/1/71 FOR SUBSIDIARIES CLASSIFIED BY NATIONAL BASE OF SUBSIDIARY'S PARENT SYSTEM (CONTINUED)

NATIONAL BASE OF SUBSIDIARY'S PARENT SYSTEM	PRINCIPAL INDUSTRY-GROUP OF SUBSIDIARY AS OF 1/1/71						
	FABRICAT. METAL+NON EL. MACH.	ELECTRIC AND ELEC- TRONIC	TRANS- PORTATION EQUIPMENT	PRECI- SION GOODS	OTHER	TOTAL PERCENT	TOTAL NUMBER
UNITED KINGDOM............	8.1	11.	4.7	0.6	5.2	100.	2160
GERMANY..................	12.	18.	5.7	3.3	2.4	100.	666
FRANCE...................	7.4	9.6	8.5	1.1	21.	100.	376
ITALY....................	11.	21.	17.	0.	2.0	100.	101
BELGIUM AND LUXEMBURG....	9.5	9.1	0.8	1.6	17.	100.	253
THE NETHERLANDS..........	5.6	34.	0.2	2.9	8.0	100.	410
SWEDEN...................	27.	25.	7.6	0.6	6.4	100.	157
SWITZERLAND..............	18.	12.	0.5	1.6	1.1	100.	371
JAPAN....................	14.	17.	8.4	0.2	4.1	100.	438
CANADA...................	41.	7.4	1.6	0.	5.9	100.	188
OTHER NON-U.S............	21.	34.	1.3	19.	7.5	100.	80

CROSS-TABULATION 8.23.1: PERCENTAGE BREAKDOWN OF NUMBER (AS OF 1/1/71) OF MANUFACTURING SUBSIDIARIES OF NON-U.S.-BASED PARENT SYSTEMS BY PRINCIPAL INDUSTRY-GROUP OF SUBSIDIARY AS OF 1/1/71

FOR SUBSIDIARIES CLASSIFIED BY PRINCIPAL INDUSTRY-GROUP OF SUBSIDIARY'S PARENT SYSTEM AS OF 1/1/71

PRINCIPAL INDUSTRY-GROUP OF SUBSIDIARY'S PARENT SYSTEM AS OF 1/1/71	PRINCIPAL INDUSTRY-GROUP OF SUBSIDIARY AS OF 1/1/71						
	FOOD AND TOBACCO	TEXTILES AND APPAREL	WOOD, PAPER+ FURNITURE	CHEMICALS	PETRO-LEUM	RUBBER AND TIRES	PRIMARY METALS
FOOD, TOBACCO AND SOAP.........	67.	0.8	4.1	23.	0.	0.4	0.1
CHEMICALS AND DRUGS...........	1.6	11.	2.3	66.	0.5	1.5	1.9
PETROLEUM.....................	0.	0.4	0.	23.	67.	0.4	0.8
IRON AND STEEL................	0.5	1.6	0.5	5.2	1.6	0.	43.
NON-FERROUS METALS............	0.3	0.	0.8	16.	2.4	0.5	47.
FABR. METAL + NON-EL. MACH....	0.	0.2	2.2	1.5	0.	1.0	18.
ELECTRIC AND ELECTRONIC.......	0.	0.2	0.8	6.2	0.2	0.5	0.9
AUTOMOBILES...................	0.	0.	0.8	2.5	0.	0.	4.2
OTHER.........................	6.3	15.	14.	8.8	0.	8.2	4.4

TABLE CONTINUED ON NEXT PAGE

CROSS-TABULATION 8.23.1: PERCENTAGE BREAKDOWN OF NUMBER (AS OF 1/1/71) OF MANUFACTURING SUBSIDIARIES OF NON-U.S.-BASED PARENT SYSTEMS BY PRINCIPAL INDUSTRY-GROUP OF SUBSIDIARY AS OF 1/1/71
FOR SUBSIDIARIES CLASSIFIED BY
PRINCIPAL INDUSTRY-GROUP OF SUBSIDIARY'S PARENT SYSTEM AS OF 1/1/71
(CONTINUED)

PRINCIPAL INDUSTRY-GROUP OF SUBSIDIARY AS OF 1/1/71

PRINCIPAL INDUSTRY-GROUP OF SUBSIDIARY'S PARENT SYSTEM AS OF 1/1/71	FABRICAT. METAL+NON EL. MACH.	ELECTRIC AND ELEC-TRONIC	TRANS-PORTATION EQUIPMENT	PRECI-SION GOODS	OTHER	TOTAL PERCENT	TOTAL NUMBER
FOOD, TOBACCO AND SOAP.........	1.9	0.1	0.4	0.	1.9	100.	907
CHEMICALS AND DRUGS...........	2.8	4.3	0.2	1.4	6.3	100.	1176
PETROLEUM......................	6.6	0.8	0.4	0.4	0.	100.	256
IRON AND STEEL.................	33.	2.1	7.9	0.5	4.2	100.	191
NON-FERROUS METALS............	26.	3.7	1.6	0.	1.9	100.	377
FABR. METAL + NON-EL. MACH....	43.	16.	16.	1.2	1.9	100.	412
ELECTRIC AND ELECTRONIC.......	8.1	68.	1.7	5.1	7.9	100.	874
AUTOMOBILES...................	9.2	0.8	82.	0.	0.8	100.	120
OTHER.........................	14.	6.1	4.7	1.1	17.	100.	887

CROSS-TABULATION 8.23.2: PERCENTAGE BREAKDOWN OF NUMBER (AS OF 1/1/68) OF
MANUFACTURING SUBSIDIARIES OF U.S.-BASED PARENT SYSTEMS BY
PRINCIPAL INDUSTRY-GROUP OF SUBSIDIARY AS OF 1/1/68
FOR SUBSIDIARIES CLASSIFIED BY
PRINCIPAL INDUSTRY-GROUP OF SUBSIDIARY'S PARENT SYSTEM AS OF 1/1/68

PRINCIPAL INDUSTRY-GROUP OF SUBSIDIARY'S PARENT SYSTEM AS OF 1/1/68	PRINCIPAL INDUSTRY-GROUP OF SUBSIDIARY AS OF 1/1/68						
	FOOD AND TOBACCO	TEXTILES AND APPAREL	WOOD, PAPER+ FURNITURE	CHEMICALS	PETRO-LEUM	RUBBER AND TIRES	PRIMARY METALS
FOOD, TOBACCO AND SOAP	70.	0.	0.5	25.	0.2	0.	0.2
CHEMICALS AND DRUGS	6.7	3.1	1.4	71.	0.	0.1	2.8
PETROLEUM	0.3	2.0	1.0	23.	68.	5.0	0.
IRON AND STEEL	0.	0.	0.	0.	0.	0.	9.5
NON-FERROUS METALS	0.9	0.	0.	1.8	1.8	0.	38.
FABR. METAL + NON-EL. MACH.	0.	0.5	5.0	6.9	0.2	0.2	2.0
ELECTRIC AND ELECTRONIC	0.6	0.6	0.6	4.2	0.	0.	0.3
AUTOMOBILES	0.	0.	0.	1.3	0.	0.	9.4
OTHER	0.3	8.5	22.	14.	0.	14.	1.3

TABLE CONTINUED ON NEXT PAGE

CROSS-TABULATION 8.23.2: PERCENTAGE BREAKDOWN OF NUMBER (AS OF 1/1/68) OF
MANUFACTURING SUBSIDIARIES OF U.S.-BASED PARENT SYSTEMS BY
PRINCIPAL INDUSTRY-GROUP OF SUBSIDIARY AS OF 1/1/68
FOR SUBSIDIARIES CLASSIFIED BY
PRINCIPAL INDUSTRY-GROUP OF SUBSIDIARY'S PARENT SYSTEM AS OF 1/1/68
(CONTINUED)

PRINCIPAL INDUSTRY-GROUP OF SUBSIDIARY'S PARENT SYSTEM AS OF 1/1/68	PRINCIPAL INDUSTRY-GROUP OF SUBSIDIARY AS OF 1/1/68						
	FABRICAT. METAL+NON-EL. MACH.	ELECTRIC AND ELEC-TRONIC	TRANS-PORTATION EQUIPMENT	PRECI-SION GOODS	OTHER	TOTAL PERCENT	TOTAL NUMBER
FOOD, TOBACCO AND SOAP.........	3.1	0.5	0.	0.2	0.3	100.	621
CHEMICALS AND DRUGS...........	4.8	3.6	0.2	3.8	2.6	100.	1018
PETROLEUM....................	1.0	0.	0.	0.	0.3	100.	299
IRON AND STEEL...............	90.	0.	0.	0.	0.	100.	21
NON-FERROUS METALS...........	41.	2.7	3.6	0.	10.	100.	110
FABR. METAL + NON-EL. MACH...	69.	0.7	5.0	0.2	11.	100.	404
ELECTRIC AND ELECTRONIC......	7.3	73.	9.9	0.6	2.8	100.	355
AUTOMOBILES..................	17.	9.8	58.	0.9	3.1	100.	224
OTHER........................	7.7	4.4	4.8	4.1	19.	100.	704

CROSS-TABULATION 9.13.1: PERCENTAGE BREAKDOWN OF NUMBER OF
MANUFACTURING SUBSIDIARIES OF NON-U.S.-BASED PARENT SYSTEMS BY
PERCENTAGE OF SUBSIDIARY'S EQUITY OWNED BY PARENT SYSTEM AT DATE OF ENTRY
FOR SUBSIDIARIES CLASSIFIED BY
SUBSIDIARY'S METHOD OF ENTRY INTO PARENT SYSTEM

SUBSIDIARY'S METHOD OF ENTRY INTO PARENT SYSTEM	PERCENTAGE OF SUBSIDIARY'S EQUITY OWNED BY PARENT SYSTEM AT DATE OF ENTRY						
	95% OR MORE	OVER 50% BUT UNDER 95%	EXACTLY 50%	AT LEAST 25% BUT UNDER 50%	OVER 5% BUT UNDER 25%	TOTAL PERCENT	TOTAL NUMBER
NEWLY FORMED............	41.	20.	11.	15.	12.	100.	2006
REORGANIZATION.........	46.	30.	8.8	8.8	6.2	100.	227
ACQUIRED DIRECTLY......	43.	23.	7.3	16.	9.8	100.	1290
ACQUIRED THRU ACQUISITION....	64.	18.	6.4	8.4	3.1	100.	1133

CROSS-TABULATION 9.13.2: PERCENTAGE BREAKDOWN OF NUMBER OF
MANUFACTURING SUBSIDIARIES OF U.S.-BASED PARENT SYSTEMS BY
PERCENTAGE OF SUBSIDIARY'S EQUITY OWNED BY PARENT SYSTEM AT DATE OF ENTRY
FOR SUBSIDIARIES CLASSIFIED BY
SUBSIDIARY'S METHOD OF ENTRY INTO PARENT SYSTEM

PERCENTAGE OF SUBSIDIARY'S EQUITY OWNED
BY PARENT SYSTEM AT DATE OF ENTRY

SUBSIDIARY'S METHOD OF ENTRY INTO PARENT SYSTEM	95% OR MORE	OVER 50% BUT UNDER 95%	EXACTLY 50%	AT LEAST 25% BUT UNDER 50%	OVER 5% BUT UNDER 25%	TOTAL PERCENT	TOTAL NUMBER
NEWLY FORMED.............	61.	14.	13.	10.	1.9	100.	2004
REORGANIZATION...........	71.	16.	6.6	5.3	1.3	100.	76
ACQUIRED DIRECTLY........	59.	17.	8.0	8.8	7.2	100.	1960
ACQUIRED THRU ACQUISITION....	0.	0.	0.	0.	0.	100.	0

CROSS-TABULATION 9.17.1: PERCENTAGE BREAKDOWN OF NUMBER OF
MANUFACTURING SUBSIDIARIES OF NON-U.S.-BASED PARENT SYSTEMS BY
PERCENTAGE OF SUBSIDIARY'S EQUITY OWNED BY PARENT SYSTEM AT DATE OF ENTRY
FOR SUBSIDIARIES CLASSIFIED BY
SUBSIDIARY'S DATE OF ENTRY INTO PARENT SYSTEM

SUBSIDIARY'S DATE OF ENTRY INTO PARENT SYSTEM	PERCENTAGE OF SUBSIDIARY'S EQUITY OWNED BY PARENT SYSTEM AT DATE OF ENTRY						
	95% OR MORE	OVER 50% BUT UNDER 95%	EXACTLY 50%	AT LEAST 25% BUT UNDER 50%	OVER 5% BUT UNDER 25%	TOTAL PERCENT	TOTAL NUMBER
PRE 1914........	53.	28.	3.3	13.	2.8	100.	180
1914 - 1919.....	57.	23.	8.3	10.	1.7	100.	60
1920 - 1929.....	50.	31.	4.8	11.	3.5	100.	312
1930 - 1938.....	57.	24.	2.1	9.5	6.8	100.	190
1939 - 1945.....	61.	19.	10.	6.5	3.7	100.	107
1946 - 1952.....	54.	21.	8.8	11.	5.6	100.	250
1953 - 1955.....	42.	24.	11.	16.	8.2	100.	159
1956 - 1958.....	49.	22.	9.1	11.	8.7	100.	219
1959 - 1961.....	51.	20.	9.4	12.	6.9	100.	554
1962 - 1964.....	41.	16.	12.	17.	13.	100.	547
1965 - 1967.....	47.	20.	9.1	13.	11.	100.	1003
1968 - 1970.....	45.	21.	9.1	15.	11.	100.	1427

CROSS-TABULATION 9.17.**2**: PERCENTAGE BREAKDOWN OF NUMBER OF
MANUFACTURING SUBSIDIARIES OF U.S.-BASED PARENT SYSTEMS BY
PERCENTAGE OF SUBSIDIARY'S EQUITY OWNED BY PARENT SYSTEM AT DATE OF ENTRY
FOR SUBSIDIARIES CLASSIFIED BY
SUBSIDIARY'S DATE OF ENTRY INTO PARENT SYSTEM

SUBSIDIARY'S DATE OF ENTRY INTO PARENT SYSTEM	PERCENTAGE OF SUBSIDIARY'S EQUITY OWNED BY PARENT SYSTEM AT DATE OF ENTRY						
	95% OR MORE	OVER 50% BUT UNDER 95%	EXACTLY 50%	AT LEAST 25% BUT UNDER 50%	OVER 5% BUT UNDER 25%	TOTAL PERCENT	TOTAL NUMBER
PRE 1914............	79.	17.	1.0	2.9	0.	100.	104
1914 - 1919........	92.	4.8	0.	3.2	0.	100.	63
1920 - 1929........	75.	12.	5.8	5.4	2.3	100.	259
1930 - 1938........	76.	12.	4.7	3.9	2.9	100.	279
1939 - 1945........	66.	8.2	8.8	10.	6.8	100.	147
1946 - 1952........	65.	14.	9.0	7.2	5.1	100.	334
1953 - 1955........	66.	14.	6.3	9.0	4.3	100.	255
1956 - 1958........	64.	15.	8.4	8.4	4.1	100.	391
1959 - 1961........	56.	15.	13.	11.	4.8	100.	795
1962 - 1964........	54.	17.	14.	11.	4.9	100.	855
1965 - 1967........	51.	21.	13.	10.	4.6	100.	801

CROSS-TABULATION 9.24.1: PERCENTAGE BREAKDOWN OF NUMBER OF
MANUFACTURING SUBSIDIARIES OF NON-U.S.-BASED PARENT SYSTEMS BY
PERCENTAGE OF SUBSIDIARY'S EQUITY OWNED BY PARENT SYSTEM AT DATE OF ENTRY
FOR SUBSIDIARIES CLASSIFIED BY
NUMBER OF COUNTRIES IN WHICH PARENT SYSTEM MANUFACTURED AT SUBSIDIARY'S DATE OF ENTRY

| | PERCENTAGE OF SUBSIDIARY'S EQUITY OWNED BY PARENT SYSTEM AT DATE OF ENTRY | | | | | | |
NUMBER OF COUNTRIES PARENT SYSTEM MANUFACTURED IN AT SUB'S DATE OF ENTRY	95% OR MORE	OVER 50% BUT UNDER 95%	EXACTLY 50%	AT LEAST 25% BUT UNDER 50%	OVER 5% BUT UNDER 25%	TOTAL PERCENT	TOTAL NUMBER
ONE..........................	37.	17.	8.3	15.	22.	100.	300
TWO OR THREE.................	44.	17.	9.3	15.	14.	100.	538
FOUR TO SIX..................	40.	22.	7.5	17.	13.	100.	702
SEVEN TO TWELVE..............	45.	23.	8.6	16.	6.9	100.	1109
THIRTEEN OR MORE.............	53.	21.	9.5	11.	6.0	100.	2283

CROSS-TABULATION 9.24.2: PERCENTAGE BREAKDOWN OF NUMBER OF
MANUFACTURING SUBSIDIARIES OF U.S.-BASED PARENT SYSTEMS BY
PERCENTAGE OF SUBSIDIARY'S EQUITY OWNED BY PARENT SYSTEM AT DATE OF ENTRY
FOR SUBSIDIARIES CLASSIFIED BY
NUMBER OF COUNTRIES IN WHICH PARENT SYSTEM MANUFACTURED AT SUBSIDIARY'S DATE OF ENTRY

PERCENTAGE OF SUBSIDIARY'S EQUITY OWNED
BY PARENT SYSTEM AT DATE OF ENTRY

NUMBER OF COUNTRIES PARENT SYSTEM MANUFACTURED IN AT SUB'S DATE OF ENTRY	95% OR MORE	OVER 50% BUT UNDER 95%	EXACTLY 50%	AT LEAST 25% BUT UNDER 50%	OVER 5% BUT UNDER 25%	TOTAL PERCENT	TOTAL NUMBER
ONE............	72.	14.	4.4	5.6	3.8	100.	339
TWO OR THREE...	67.	12.	9.7	6.4	4.7	100.	485
FOUR TO SIX....	60.	13.	9.8	12.	4.7	100.	774
SEVEN TO TWELVE.	57.	15.	12.	10.	5.4	100.	1413
THIRTEEN OR MORE.	59.	19.	11.	8.2	3.1	100.	1313

TABULATION 10.1: PERCENTAGE BREAKDOWN OF NUMBER OF SUBSIDIARIES BY
PERCENTAGE OF SUBSIDIARY'S EQUITY OWNED BY PARENT SYSTEM
FOR VARIOUS CATEGORIES OF SUBSIDIARIES

CATEGORY OF SUBSIDIARY	PERCENTAGE OF SUBSIDIARY'S EQUITY OWNED BY PARENT SYSTEM						
	95% OR MORE	OVER 50% BUT UNDER 95%	EXACTLY 50%	AT LEAST 25% BUT UNDER 50%	OVER 5% BUT UNDER 25%	TOTAL PERCENT	TOTAL NUMBER
NON-U.S.-BASED SYSTEMS (AS OF 1/1/71):							
ALL SUBSIDIARIES.........	61.	17.	6.2	9.8	6.8	100.	12197
MANUFACTURING SUBS.......	50.	21.	7.7	13.	8.7	100.	5178
SALES SUBSIDIARIES.......	76.	11.	5.0	4.7	2.8	100.	3075
U.S.-BASED SYSTEMS (AS OF 1/1/68):							
ALL SUBSIDIARIES.........	75.	11.	6.2	5.6	2.9	100.	8285
MANUFACTURING SUBS.......	63.	15.	9.2	8.5	3.9	100.	3720
SALES SUBSIDIARIES.......	89.	5.4	3.3	1.9	0.5	100.	1506
WORLD SUBSET OF SYSTEMS (AS OF 1/1/68):							
NON-U.S.-BASED SYSTEMS:							
ALL SUBSIDIARIES........	63.	16.	6.4	8.9	5.1	100.	4922
MANUFACTURING SUBS.......	51.	22.	8.5	12.	6.7	100.	2278
SALES SUBSIDIARIES.......	80.	11.	4.3	3.4	1.4	100.	1386
U.S.-BASED-SYSTEMS:							
ALL SUBSIDIARIES........	74.	11.	6.5	5.7	3.1	100.	6821
MANUFACTURING SUBS.......	60.	16.	10.	8.9	4.3	100.	2877
SALES SUBSIDIARIES.......	88.	5.6	3.4	2.3	0.5	100.	1178

TABULATION 10.2: PERCENTAGE BREAKDOWN OF SALES OF SUBSIDIARIES IN 1970 BY
PERCENTAGE OF SUBSIDIARY'S EQUITY OWNED BY PARENT SYSTEM AS OF 1/1/71
FOR ALL SUBSIDIARIES, MANUFACTURING SUBSIDIARIES AND SALES SUBSIDIARIES
OF NON-U.S.-BASED SYSTEMS

CATEGORY OF SUBSIDIARY	PERCENTAGE OF SUBSIDIARY'S EQUITY OWNED BY PARENT SYSTEM AS OF 1/1/71						
	95% OR MORE	OVER 50% BUT UNDER 95%	EXACTLY 50%	AT LEAST 25% BUT UNDER 50%	OVER 5% BUT UNDER 25%	TOTAL PERCENT	TOTAL ($ MIL)
ALL SUBSIDIARIES............	50.	24.	6.1	11.	8.8	100.	128135
MANUFACTURING SUBSIDIARIES...	40.	31.	7.5	11.	9.4	100.	80644
SALES SUBSIDIARIES..........	81.	8.6	3.7	4.6	2.0	100.	22588

CROSS-TABULATION 10. 1.1: PERCENTAGE BREAKDOWN OF NUMBER (AS OF 1/1/71) OF MANUFACTURING SUBSIDIARIES OF NON-U.S.-BASED PARENT SYSTEMS BY PERCENTAGE OF SUBSIDIARY'S EQUITY OWNED BY PARENT SYSTEM AS OF 1/1/71 FOR SUBSIDIARIES CLASSIFIED BY SUBSIDIARY'S COUNTRY

	PERCENTAGE OF SUBSIDIARY'S EQUITY OWNED BY PARENT SYSTEM AS OF 1/1/71						
SUBSIDIARY'S COUNTRY	95% OR MORE	OVER 50% BUT UNDER 95%	EXACTLY 50%	AT LEAST 25% BUT UNDER 50%	OVER 5% BUT UNDER 25%	TOTAL PERCENT	TOTAL NUMBER
UNITED STATES	70.	10.	6.7	4.7	8.7	100.	358
CANADA	73.	14.	3.8	6.1	2.7	100.	261
MEXICO	38.	20.	4.4	29.	8.9	100.	90
CENTRAL AMERICA AND CARIB.	36.	24.	7.5	16.	16.	100.	80
VENEZUELA	38.	20.	10.	23.	10.	100.	40
COLOMBIA	41.	19.	15.	19.	7.4	100.	27
PERU	50.	14.	14.	11.	11.	100.	28
CHILE	35.	35.	7.7	15.	7.7	100.	26
ARGENTINA	46.	25.	9.4	13.	5.7	100.	106
BRAZIL	49.	30.	4.3	13.	3.7	100.	164
OTHER SOUTH AMERICA	63.	21.	11.	0.	5.3	100.	19
GERMANY	60.	20.	8.7	7.3	4.5	100.	289
FRANCE	42.	28.	9.2	14.	7.4	100.	380
ITALY	51.	27.	8.5	9.1	4.0	100.	176
BELGIUM AND LUXEMBURG	53.	18.	10.	9.1	9.1	100.	143
THE NETHERLANDS	56.	21.	7.2	14.	1.6	100.	125
UNITED KINGDOM	71.	14.	5.3	4.9	4.9	100.	244
IRELAND	57.	24.	5.3	9.5	4.2	100.	95
DENMARK	69.	13.	5.1	7.7	5.1	100.	39
NORWAY	59.	13.	10.	10.	7.7	100.	39
SWEDEN	63.	15.	8.3	11.	2.8	100.	72
FINLAND	58.	5.3	11.	21.	5.3	100.	19

TABLE CONTINUED ON NEXT PAGE

CROSS-TABULATION 10. 1.1: PERCENTAGE BREAKDOWN OF NUMBER (AS OF 1/1/71) OF MANUFACTURING SUBSIDIARIES OF NON-U.S.-BASED PARENT SYSTEMS BY PERCENTAGE OF SUBSIDIARY'S EQUITY OWNED BY PARENT SYSTEM AS OF 1/1/71 FOR SUBSIDIARIES CLASSIFIED BY SUBSIDIARY'S COUNTRY (CONTINUED)

SUBSIDIARY'S COUNTRY	PERCENTAGE OF SUBSIDIARY'S EQUITY OWNED BY PARENT SYSTEM AS OF 1/1/71						
	95% OR MORE	OVER 50% BUT UNDER 95%	EXACTLY 50%	AT LEAST 25% BUT UNDER 50%	OVER 5% BUT UNDER 25%	TOTAL PERCENT	TOTAL NUMBER
SWITZERLAND	42.	29.	7.7	13.	7.7	100.	52
AUSTRIA	48.	33.	6.7	10.	2.2	100.	89
PORTUGAL	36.	32.	8.0	16.	8.0	100.	50
SPAIN	20.	35.	13.	23.	7.9	100.	178
GREECE	38.	43.	0.	9.5	9.5	100.	21
TURKEY	21.	45.	6.9	24.	3.4	100.	29
OTHER EUROPE + ISRAEL	40.	20.	0.	25.	15.	100.	20
PAKISTAN	17.	40.	7.1	9.5	26.	100.	42
IRAN	4.5	9.1	14.	55.	18.	100.	22
OTHER MID EAST+EGYPT+LIBYA	25.	25.	5.0	20.	25.	100.	20
UNION OF SOUTH AFRICA	62.	19.	7.5	9.7	1.9	100.	359
RHODESIA	73.	17.	5.8	1.9	1.9	100.	52
ZAMBIA	68.	16.	2.7	11.	2.7	100.	37
TANZANIA	55.	18.	4.5	14.	9.1	100.	22
KENYA	56.	19.	4.7	9.3	12.	100.	43
NIGERIA	34.	25.	7.5	25.	9.4	100.	53
OTHER (BRITISH) AFRICA	55.	23.	7.5	1.9	13.	100.	53
MOROCCO, ALGERIA + TUNISIA	14.	38.	14.	19.	16.	100.	37
OTHER (FRENCH) AFRICA	21.	28.	7.0	19.	26.	100.	43
OTHER AFRICA	46.	31.	3.8	7.7	12.	100.	26
AUSTRALIA	69.	16.	4.3	6.8	3.8	100.	396
NEW ZEALAND	62.	18.	5.5	8.2	6.4	100.	110

TABLE CONTINUED ON NEXT PAGE

CROSS-TABULATION 10. 1.1: PERCENTAGE BREAKDOWN OF NUMBER (AS OF 1/1/71) OF
MANUFACTURING SUBSIDIARIES OF NON-U.S.-BASED PARENT SYSTEMS BY
PERCENTAGE OF SUBSIDIARY'S EQUITY OWNED BY PARENT SYSTEM AS OF 1/1/71
FOR SUBSIDIARIES CLASSIFIED BY
SUBSIDIARY'S COUNTRY
(CONTINUED)

PERCENTAGE OF SUBSIDIARY'S EQUITY OWNED
BY PARENT SYSTEM AS OF 1/1/71

SUBSIDIARY'S COUNTRY	95% OR MORE	OVER 50% BUT UNDER 95%	EXACTLY 50%	AT LEAST 25% BUT UNDER 50%	OVER 5% BUT UNDER 25%	TOTAL PERCENT	TOTAL NUMBER
JAPAN....................	19.	16.	37.	25.	2.5	100.	79
CHINA (TAIWAN)...........	5.6	7.8	8.9	33.	44.	100.	90
HONG KONG................	21.	18.	21.	18.	21.	100.	28
THE PHILIPPINES..........	16.	28.	4.0	28.	24.	100.	25
MALAYSIA.................	25.	25.	5.8	12.	33.	100.	52
SINGAPORE................	33.	24.	2.0	12.	29.	100.	51
INDONESIA................	17.	26.	0.	30.	26.	100.	23
THAILAND.................	6.7	13.	10.	30.	40.	100.	60
INDIA....................	9.5	38.	6.6	26.	20.	100.	136
OTHER ASIA AND OCEANIA...	23.	16.	8.9	21.	30.	100.	56

CROSS-TABULATION 10. 1.2: PERCENTAGE BREAKDOWN OF NUMBER (AS OF 1/1/68) OF MANUFACTURING SUBSIDIARIES OF U.S.-BASED PARENT SYSTEMS BY PERCENTAGE OF SUBSIDIARY'S EQUITY OWNED BY PARENT SYSTEM AS OF 1/1/68 FOR SUBSIDIARIES CLASSIFIED BY SUBSIDIARY'S COUNTRY

PERCENTAGE OF SUBSIDIARY'S EQUITY OWNED BY PARENT SYSTEM AS OF 1/1/68

SUBSIDIARY'S COUNTRY	95% OR MORE	OVER 50% BUT UNDER 95%	EXACTLY 50%	AT LEAST 25% BUT UNDER 50%	OVER 5% BUT UNDER 25%	TOTAL PERCENT	TOTAL NUMBER
UNITED STATES.........	0.	0.	0.	0.	0.	100.	0
CANADA...............	85.	9.0	2.5	2.7	0.8	100.	480
MEXICO...............	55.	17.	8.0	18.	1.6	100.	249
CENTRAL AMERICA AND CARIB....	43.	28.	11.	11.	6.5	100.	123
VENEZUELA............	54.	25.	6.1	7.9	7.0	100.	114
COLOMBIA.............	60.	16.	12.	12.	1.0	100.	102
PERU.................	65.	15.	6.3	10.	4.2	100.	48
CHILE................	49.	22.	12.	4.9	12.	100.	41
ARGENTINA............	69.	7.4	7.4	9.9	6.6	100.	121
BRAZIL...............	75.	14.	4.6	6.6	0.	100.	151
OTHER SOUTH AMERICA....	61.	17.	2.4	17.	2.4	100.	41
GERMANY..............	67.	13.	11.	7.0	0.9	100.	215
FRANCE...............	57.	22.	6.7	7.7	6.7	100.	209
ITALY................	64.	18.	10.	4.8	2.4	100.	166
BELGIUM AND LUXEMBURG....	73.	9.8	8.7	6.5	2.2	100.	92
THE NETHERLANDS......	64.	14.	13.	3.9	5.2	100.	77
UNITED KINGDOM.......	75.	8.9	8.6	5.3	2.7	100.	338
IRELAND..............	75.	7.1	7.1	11.	0.	100.	28
DENMARK..............	88.	4.0	4.0	0.	4.0	100.	25
NORWAY...............	63.	19.	19.	0.	0.8	100.	16
SWEDEN...............	72.	8.3	14.	2.8	2.8	100.	36
FINLAND..............	80.	20.	0.	0.	0.	100.	5

TABLE CONTINUED ON NEXT PAGE

CROSS-TABULATION 10.1.2: PERCENTAGE BREAKDOWN OF NUMBER (AS OF 1/1/68) OF
MANUFACTURING SUBSIDIARIES OF U.S.-BASED PARENT SYSTEMS BY
PERCENTAGE OF SUBSIDIARY'S EQUITY OWNED BY PARENT SYSTEM AS OF 1/1/68
FOR SUBSIDIARIES CLASSIFIED BY
SUBSIDIARY'S COUNTRY
(CONTINUED)

SUBSIDIARY'S COUNTRY	PERCENTAGE OF SUBSIDIARY'S EQUITY OWNED BY PARENT SYSTEM AS OF 1/1/68						
	95% OR MORE	OVER 50% BUT UNDER 95%	EXACTLY 50%	AT LEAST 25% BUT UNDER 50%	OVER 5% BUT UNDER 25%	TOTAL PERCENT	TOTAL NUMBER
SWITZERLAND	87.	3.3	6.7	0.	3.3	100.	30
AUSTRIA	76.	5.9	12.	5.9	0.	100.	17
PORTUGAL	71.	18.	5.9	5.9	0.	100.	17
SPAIN	32.	28.	24.	9.5	6.9	100.	116
GREECE	40.	25.	10.	15.	10.	100.	20
TURKEY	38.	38.	0.	15.	7.7	100.	13
OTHER EUROPE + ISRAEL	38.	15.	7.7	23.	15.	100.	13
PAKISTAN	13.	67.	0.	6.7	13.	100.	15
IRAN	28.	28.	22.	11.	11.	100.	18
OTHER MID EAST+EGYPT+LIBYA	58.	12.	3.8	15.	12.	100.	26
UNION OF SOUTH AFRICA	81.	10.	5.0	1.7	2.5	100.	119
RHODESIA	83.	8.3	0.	0.	8.3	100.	12
ZAMBIA	67.	17.	0.	17.	0.	100.	6
TANZANIA	0.	0.	0.	0.	0.	100.	0
KENYA	67.	11.	11.	11.	0.	100.	9
NIGERIA	70.	20.	0.	0.	10.	100.	10
OTHER (BRITISH) AFRICA	17.	67.	0.	0.	17.	100.	6
MOROCCO, ALGERIA + TUNISIA	50.	14.	7.1	14.	14.	100.	14
OTHER (FRENCH) AFRICA	50.	0.	13.	0.	38.	100.	8
OTHER AFRICA	100.	0.	0.	0.	0.	100.	3
AUSTRALIA	62.	15.	12.	8.0	2.3	100.	213
NEW ZEALAND	70.	21.	7.0	0.	2.3	100.	43

TABLE CONTINUED ON NEXT PAGE

CROSS-TABULATION 10. 1.2: PERCENTAGE BREAKDOWN OF NUMBER (AS OF 1/1/68) OF
MANUFACTURING SUBSIDIARIES OF U.S.-BASED PARENT SYSTEMS BY
PERCENTAGE OF SUBSIDIARY'S EQUITY OWNED BY PARENT SYSTEM AS OF 1/1/68
FOR SUBSIDIARIES CLASSIFIED BY
SUBSIDIARY'S COUNTRY
(CONTINUED)

SUBSIDIARY'S COUNTRY	PERCENTAGE OF SUBSIDIARY'S EQUITY OWNED BY PARENT SYSTEM AS OF 1/1/68						
	95% OR MORE	OVER 50% BUT UNDER 95%	EXACTLY 50%	AT LEAST 25% BUT UNDER 50%	OVER 5% BUT UNDER 25%	TOTAL PERCENT	TOTAL NUMBER
JAPAN.	14.	7.0	32.	30.	16.	100.	128
CHINA (TAIWAN).	58.	25.	8.3	8.3	0.	100.	12
HONG KONG.	50.	50.	0.	0.	0.	100.	6
THE PHILIPPINES.	56.	29.	3.6	5.5	5.5	100.	55
MALAYSIA.	57.	29.	0.	14.	0.	100.	14
SINGAPORE.	33.	33.	11.	22.	0.	100.	9
INDONESIA.	100.	0.	0.	0.	0.	100.	2
THAILAND.	38.	46.	0.	15.	0.	100.	13
INDIA.	26.	16.	21.	27.	9.7	100.	62
OTHER ASIA AND OCEANIA.	43.	29.	7.1	21.	0.	100.	14

CROSS-TABULATION 10. 2.1: PERCENTAGE BREAKDOWN OF NUMBER (AS OF 1/1/71) OF MANUFACTURING SUBSIDIARIES OF NON-U.S.-BASED PARENT SYSTEMS BY PERCENTAGE OF SUBSIDIARY'S EQUITY OWNED BY PARENT SYSTEM AS OF 1/1/71 FOR SUBSIDIARIES CLASSIFIED BY GEOGRAPHICAL REGION OF SUBSIDIARY'S COUNTRY

PERCENTAGE OF SUBSIDIARY'S EQUITY OWNED BY PARENT SYSTEM AS OF 1/1/71

GEOGRAPHICAL REGION OF SUBSIDIARY'S COUNTRY	95% OR MORE	OVER 50% BUT UNDER 95%	EXACTLY 50%	AT LEAST 25% BUT UNDER 50%	OVER 5% BUT UNDER 25%	TOTAL PERCENT	TOTAL NUMBER
NORTH AMERICA.........	71.	12.	5.5	5.3	6.1	100.	619
LATIN AMERICA.........	44.	25.	7.4	16.	7.8	100.	580
EUROPE................	51.	24.	8.3	12.	5.7	100.	2058
AFRICA AND MIDDLE EAST.......	50.	22.	7.1	12.	8.4	100.	812
OTHER ASIA AND OCEANIA.......	39.	19.	8.2	17.	16.	100.	1105

CROSS-TABULATION 10.2.2: PERCENTAGE BREAKDOWN OF NUMBER (AS OF 1/1/68) OF
MANUFACTURING SUBSIDIARIES OF U.S.-BASED PARENT SYSTEMS BY
PERCENTAGE OF SUBSIDIARY'S EQUITY OWNED BY PARENT SYSTEM AS OF 1/1/68
FOR SUBSIDIARIES CLASSIFIED BY
GEOGRAPHICAL REGION OF SUBSIDIARY'S COUNTRY

GEOGRAPHICAL REGION OF SUBSIDIARY'S COUNTRY	PERCENTAGE OF SUBSIDIARY'S EQUITY OWNED BY PARENT SYSTEM AS OF 1/1/68						
	95% OR MORE	OVER 50% BUT UNDER 95%	EXACTLY 50%	AT LEAST 25% BUT UNDER 50%	OVER 5% BUT UNDER 25%	TOTAL PERCENT	TOTAL NUMBER
NORTH AMERICA.........	85.	9.0	2.5	2.7	0.8	100.	480
LATIN AMERICA.........	59.	18.	7.9	12.	3.7	100.	990
EUROPE................	65.	15.	10.	6.3	3.4	100.	1424
AFRICA AND MIDDLE EAST.......	64.	17.	5.9	5.5	7.8	100.	255
OTHER ASIA AND OCEANIA......	46.	17.	15.	15.	6.3	100.	571

CROSS-TABULATION 10. 3.1: PERCENTAGE BREAKDOWN OF NUMBER (AS OF 1/1/71) OF
MANUFACTURING SUBSIDIARIES OF NON-U.S.-BASED PARENT SYSTEMS BY
PERCENTAGE OF SUBSIDIARY'S EQUITY OWNED BY PARENT SYSTEM AS OF 1/1/71
FOR SUBSIDIARIES CLASSIFIED BY
GNP PER CAPITA IN 1970 OF SUBSIDIARY'S COUNTRY

GNP PER CAPITA IN 1970 OF SUBSIDIARY'S COUNTRY	PERCENTAGE OF SUBSIDIARY'S EQUITY OWNED BY PARENT SYSTEM AS OF 1/1/71						
	95% OR MORE	OVER 50% BUT UNDER 95%	EXACTLY 50%	AT LEAST 25% BUT UNDER 50%	OVER 5% BUT UNDER 25%	TOTAL PERCENT	TOTAL NUMBER
UNDER $200............	24.	28.	6.5	20.	22.	100.	476
$200 - $500...........	35.	23.	7.5	18.	17.	100.	664
$500 - $1200..........	44.	25.	8.3	16.	7.3	100.	1016
$1200 - $2500.........	56.	21.	9.0	10.	4.0	100.	943
OVER $2500............	61.	18.	7.0	8.3	5.9	100.	2031

CROSS-TABULATION 10.3.2: PERCENTAGE BREAKDOWN OF NUMBER (AS OF 1/1/68) OF
MANUFACTURING SUBSIDIARIES OF U.S.-BASED PARENT SYSTEMS BY
PERCENTAGE OF SUBSIDIARY'S EQUITY OWNED BY PARENT SYSTEM AS OF 1/1/68
FOR SUBSIDIARIES CLASSIFIED BY
GNP PER CAPITA IN 1970 OF SUBSIDIARY'S COUNTRY

GNP PER CAPITA IN 1970 OF SUBSIDIARY'S COUNTRY	PERCENTAGE OF SUBSIDIARY'S EQUITY OWNED BY PARENT SYSTEM AS OF 1/1/68					TOTAL PERCENT	TOTAL NUMBER
	95% OR MORE	OVER 50% BUT UNDER 95%	EXACTLY 50%	AT LEAST 25% BUT UNDER 50%	OVER 5% BUT UNDER 25%		
UNDER $200...............	49.	20.	9.3	18.	3.7	100.	376
$200 - $500..............	59.	21.	7.5	9.3	3.4	100.	561
$500 - $1200.............	59.	17.	10.	7.7	6.0	100.	646
$1200 - $2500...........	61.	12.	13.	9.3	5.2	100.	820
OVER $2500...............	72.	13.	7.2	5.3	2.3	100.	1286

CROSS-TABULATION 10.4.1: PERCENTAGE BREAKDOWN OF NUMBER (AS OF 1/1/71) OF
MANUFACTURING SURSIDIARIES OF NON-U.S.-BASED PARENT SYSTEMS BY
PERCENTAGE OF SUBSIDIARY'S EQUITY OWNED BY PARENT SYSTEM AS OF 1/1/71
FOR SUBSIDIARIES CLASSIFIED BY
GNP IN 1970 OF SUBSIDIARY'S COUNTRY

PERCENTAGE OF SUBSIDIARY'S EQUITY OWNED
BY PARENT SYSTEM AS OF 1/1/71

GNP IN 1970 OF SUBSIDIARY'S COUNTRY	95% OR MORE	OVER 50% BUT UNDER 95%	EXACTLY 50%	AT LEAST 25% BUT UNDER 50%	OVER 5% BUT UNDER 25%	TOTAL PERCENT	TOTAL NUMBER
UNDER $1 BILLION..............	41.	28.	5.0	10.	16.	100.	100
$1 - $5 BILLION..............	44.	22.	6.6	12.	15.	100.	578
$5 - $20 BILLION..............	43.	21.	7.8	17.	12.	100.	1266
$20 - $100 BILLION..............	52.	23.	6.8	13.	5.7	100.	1836
OVER $100 BILLION..............	57.	18.	9.3	9.0	6.4	100.	1350

CROSS-TABULATION 10. 4.2: PERCENTAGE BREAKDOWN OF NUMBER (AS OF 1/1/68) OF
MANUFACTURING SUBSIDIARIES OF U.S.-BASED PARENT SYSTEMS BY
PERCENTAGE OF SUBSIDIARY'S EQUITY OWNED BY PARENT SYSTEM AS OF 1/1/68
FOR SUBSIDIARIES CLASSIFIED BY
GNP IN 1970 OF SUBSIDIARY'S COUNTRY

GNP IN 1970 OF SUBSIDIARY'S COUNTRY	PERCENTAGE OF SUBSIDIARY'S EQUITY OWNED BY PARENT SYSTEM AS OF 1/1/68						
	95% OR MORE	OVER 50% BUT UNDER 95%	EXACTLY 50%	AT LEAST 25% BUT UNDER 50%	OVER 5% BUT UNDER 25%	TOTAL PERCENT	TOTAL NUMBER
UNDER $1 BILLION.............	50.	30.	6.1	7.9	6.1	100.	114
$1 - $5 BILLION.............	54.	21.	6.7	12.	6.3	100.	238
$5 - $20 BILLION.............	64.	17.	8.0	6.5	4.1	100.	675
$20 - $100 BILLION.............	66.	14.	8.7	8.1	2.7	100.	1773
OVER $100 BILLION.............	60.	13.	12.	9.9	5.2	100.	890

CROSS-TABULATION 10. 6.1: PERCENTAGE BREAKDOWN OF NUMBER (AS OF 1/1/71) OF
MANUFACTURING SUBSIDIARIES OF NON-U.S.-BASED PARENT SYSTEMS BY
PERCENTAGE OF SUBSIDIARY'S EQUITY OWNED BY PARENT SYSTEM AS OF 1/1/71
FOR SUBSIDIARIES CLASSIFIED BY
PRINCIPAL INDUSTRY OF SUBSIDIARY AS OF 1/1/71

PRINCIPAL INDUSTRY OF SUBSIDIARY AS OF 1/1/71	PERCENTAGE OF SUBSIDIARY'S EQUITY OWNED BY PARENT SYSTEM AS OF 1/1/71						
	95% OR MORE	OVER 50% BUT UNDER 95%	EXACTLY 50%	AT LEAST 25% BUT UNDER 50%	OVER 5% BUT UNDER 25%	TOTAL PERCENT	TOTAL NUMBER
ORDNANCE	50.	13.	38.	0.	0.	100.	8
MEAT PRODUCTS	62.	28.	3.4	6.9	0.	100.	29
DAIRY PRODUCTS	58.	25.	6.3	7.8	3.1	100.	64
CANNED FOODS	56.	20.	2.4	7.3	15.	100.	41
GRAIN MILL PRODUCTS	51.	31.	8.9	6.7	2.2	100.	45
BAKERY PRODUCTS	86.	11.	1.4	1.4	0.	100.	74
CONFECTIONERY PRODUCTS	58.	29.	0.	13.	0.	100.	24
BEVERAGES	68.	15.	2.7	10.	4.7	100.	149
OTHER FOOD PRODUCTS	73.	12.	5.8	4.3	5.8	100.	139
TOBACCO PRODUCTS	50.	40.	0.	8.6	1.7	100.	58
TEXTILES	30.	18.	9.3	18.	26.	100.	216
APPAREL	31.	13.	7.7	18.	31.	100.	39
LUMBER AND WOOD	65.	13.	2.2	15.	4.3	100.	46
FURNITURE	81.	6.3	13.	0.	0.	100.	16
PAPER PRODUCTS	53.	18.	8.1	15.	5.9	100.	136
PRINTED MATTER	59.	13.	9.3	12.	6.2	100.	97
INDUSTRIAL CHEMICALS	41.	26.	17.	11.	5.6	100.	234
PLASTICS AND SYNTHETICS	32.	28.	12.	18.	10.	100.	146
DRUGS	59.	26.	7.5	7.0	0.	100.	199
SOAP AND COSMETICS	81.	14.	3.2	1.9	0.	100.	154
PAINTS	50.	35.	6.4	5.5	3.7	100.	109
AGRICULTURAL CHEMICALS	44.	16.	15.	15.	10.	100.	68
OTHER CHEMICALS	44.	20.	17.	12.	6.8	100.	146
REFINED PETROLEUM	34.	23.	8.3	13.	21.	100.	108
OTHER PETROLEUM PRODUCTS	61.	2.6	9.1	9.1	18.	100.	77

TABLE CONTINUED ON NEXT PAGE

CROSS-TABULATION 10.6.1: PERCENTAGE BREAKDOWN OF NUMBER (AS OF 1/1/71) OF MANUFACTURING SUBSIDIARIES OF NON-U.S.-BASED PARENT SYSTEMS BY PERCENTAGE OF SUBSIDIARY'S EQUITY OWNED BY PARENT SYSTEM AS OF 1/1/71 FOR SUBSIDIARIES CLASSIFIED BY PRINCIPAL INDUSTRY OF SUBSIDIARY AS OF 1/1/71 (CONTINUED)

PRINCIPAL INDUSTRY OF SUBSIDIARY AS OF 1/1/71	PERCENTAGE OF SUBSIDIARY'S EQUITY OWNED BY PARENT SYSTEM AS OF 1/1/71						
	95% OR MORE	OVER 50% BUT UNDER 95%	EXACTLY 50%	AT LEAST 25% BUT UNDER 50%	OVER 5% BUT UNDER 25%	TOTAL PERCENT	TOTAL NUMBER
TIRES..........	52.	39.	0.	6.1	3.0	100.	33
OTHER RUBBER PRODUCTS.....	43.	16.	9.0	16.	15.	100.	67
LEATHER PRODUCTS AND SHOES....	20.	40.	0.	20.	20.	100.	5
GLASS PRODUCTS......	20.	41.	0.	24.	15.	100.	41
STONE, CLAY AND CONCRETE.....	50.	31.	0.	13.	5.9	100.	68
IRON AND STEEL PRODUCTS.......	30.	24.	4.4	18.	24.	100.	160
NON-FERROUS SMELTING..........	35.	17.	11.	18.	19.	100.	94
NON-FERROUS PRODUCTS.........	47.	26.	8.2	16.	3.0	100.	134
METAL CANS.........	38.	31.	3.1	16.	13.	100.	32
STRUCTURAL METAL PRODUCTS.....	41.	23.	15.	6.6	15.	100.	61
FABRICATED WIRE PRODUCTS......	24.	26.	0.	14.	36.	100.	42
OTHER FABRICATED METAL........	45.	28.	7.4	11.	8.6	100.	163
ENGINES AND TURBINES..........	43.	16.	11.	18.	11.	100.	44
FARM MACHINERY........	44.	16.	3.1	31.	6.3	100.	32
CONSTRUCTION MACHINERY.......	43.	9.5	0.	14.	33.	100.	21
SPECIAL INDUSTRY MACHINERY...	58.	18.	11.	7.0	5.6	100.	71
GENERAL INDUSTRY MACHINERY...	44.	25.	15.	11.	4.2	100.	71
OFFICE MACHINES + COMPUTERS..	61.	21.	3.6	14.	0.	100.	28
OTHER NON-ELECTR. MACHINERY..	59.	0.	10.	10.	21.	100.	29
ELECTR. TRANSMISSION EQUIP...	44.	34.	3.5	16.	2.3	100.	86
ELECTRIC LIGHTING AND WIRING.	39.	21.	9.0	17.	13.	100.	89
RADIOS, TV'S + APPLIANCES....	54.	20.	7.3	17.	2.6	100.	151
COMMUNICATIONS EQUIPMENT.....	58.	18.	5.9	14.	4.7	100.	85

TABLE CONTINUED ON NEXT PAGE

CROSS-TABULATION 10.6.1: PERCENTAGE BREAKDOWN OF NUMBER (AS OF 1/1/71) OF
MANUFACTURING SUBSIDIARIES OF NON-U.S.-BASED PARENT SYSTEMS BY
PERCENTAGE OF SUBSIDIARY'S EQUITY OWNED BY PARENT SYSTEM AS OF 1/1/71
FOR SUBSIDIARIES CLASSIFIED BY
PRINCIPAL INDUSTRY OF SUBSIDIARY AS OF 1/1/71
(CONTINUED)

PERCENTAGE OF SUBSIDIARY'S EQUITY OWNED
BY PARENT SYSTEM AS OF 1/1/71

PRINCIPAL INDUSTRY OF SUBSIDIARY AS OF 1/1/71	95% OR MORE	OVER 50% BUT UNDER 95%	EXACTLY 50%	AT LEAST 25% BUT UNDER 50%	OVER 5% BUT UNDER 25%	TOTAL PERCENT	TOTAL NUMBER
ELECTRONIC COMPONENTS........	53.	13.	8.7	9.8	15.	100.	92
OTHER ELECTRICAL EQUIPMENT...	60.	24.	4.0	11.	1.7	100.	176
MOTOR VEHICLES AND EQUIPMENT.	40.	19.	9.3	23.	9.9	100.	172
OTHER TRANSPORTATION.........	50.	20.	9.3	17.	3.7	100.	54
PRECISION GOODS..............	58.	32.	1.4	4.1	5.5	100.	73
MISCELLANEOUS PRODUCTS.......	60.	16.	11.	6.8	5.5	100.	73

CROSS-TABULATION 10.6.2: PERCENTAGE BREAKDOWN OF NUMBER (AS OF 1/1/68) OF MANUFACTURING SUBSIDIARIES OF U.S.-BASED PARENT SYSTEMS BY PERCENTAGE OF SUBSIDIARY'S EQUITY OWNED BY PARENT SYSTEM AS OF 1/1/68 FOR SUBSIDIARIES CLASSIFIED BY PRINCIPAL INDUSTRY OF SUBSIDIARY AS OF 1/1/68

PRINCIPAL INDUSTRY OF SUBSIDIARY AS OF 1/1/68	PERCENTAGE OF SUBSIDIARY'S EQUITY OWNED BY PARENT SYSTEM AS OF 1/1/68						
	95% OR MORE	OVER 50% BUT UNDER 95%	EXACTLY 50%	AT LEAST 25% BUT UNDER 50%	OVER 5% BUT UNDER 25%	TOTAL PERCENT	TOTAL NUMBER
ORDNANCE	33.	11.	22.	33.	0.	100.	9
MEAT PRODUCTS	79.	3.0	12.	6.1	0.	100.	33
DAIRY PRODUCTS	58.	17.	2.6	19.	2.6	100.	77
CANNED FOODS	74.	17.	7.5	0.	1.9	100.	53
GRAIN MILL PRODUCTS	64.	14.	12.	5.3	5.3	100.	94
BAKERY PRODUCTS	64.	28.	5.6	2.8	0.	100.	36
CONFECTIONERY PRODUCTS	68.	17.	14.	0.	1.7	100.	59
BEVERAGES	81.	15.	4.3	0.	0.	100.	47
OTHER FOOD PRODUCTS	70.	20.	9.3	0.	0.	100.	54
TOBACCO PRODUCTS	56.	44.	0.	0.	0.	100.	9
TEXTILES	61.	9.4	16.	13.	1.6	100.	64
APPAREL	54.	23.	23.	0.	0.	100.	13
LUMBER AND WOOD	52.	14.	14.	9.5	9.5	100.	21
FURNITURE	81.	6.3	6.3	6.3	0.	100.	16
PAPER PRODUCTS	47.	21.	13.	9.0	10.	100.	156
PRINTED MATTER	64.	12.	8.0	8.0	8.0	100.	25
INDUSTRIAL CHEMICALS	51.	17.	17.	12.	2.3	100.	219
PLASTICS AND SYNTHETICS	51.	16.	14.	16.	3.4	100.	146
DRUGS	82.	11.	6.3	0.3	0.3	100.	302
SOAP AND COSMETICS	93.	2.8	2.1	1.4	0.7	100.	144
PAINTS	57.	29.	2.9	8.6	2.9	100.	35
AGRICULTURAL CHEMICALS	52.	23.	14.	9.1	2.3	100.	44
OTHER CHEMICALS	60.	13.	11.	11.	5.3	100.	75
REFINED PETROLEUM	57.	14.	11.	13.	5.8	100.	120
OTHER PETROLEUM PRODUCTS	54.	5.1	25.	14.	1.7	100.	59

TABLE CONTINUED ON NEXT PAGE

CROSS-TABULATION 10.6.2: PERCENTAGE BREAKDOWN OF NUMBER (AS OF 1/1/68) OF MANUFACTURING SUBSIDIARIES OF U.S.-BASED PARENT SYSTEMS BY PERCENTAGE OF SUBSIDIARY'S EQUITY OWNED BY PARENT SYSTEM AS OF 1/1/68 FOR SUBSIDIARIES CLASSIFIED BY PRINCIPAL INDUSTRY OF SUBSIDIARY AS OF 1/1/68 (CONTINUED)

PERCENTAGE OF SUBSIDIARY'S EQUITY OWNED BY PARENT SYSTEM AS OF 1/1/68

PRINCIPAL INDUSTRY OF SUBSIDIARY AS OF 1/1/68	95% OR MORE	OVER 50% BUT UNDER 95%	EXACTLY 50%	AT LEAST 25% BUT UNDER 50%	OVER 5% BUT UNDER 25%	TOTAL PERCENT	TOTAL NUMBER
TIRES	55.	26.	1.7	12.	5.2	100.	58
OTHER RUBBER PRODUCTS	41.	9.1	23.	23.	4.5	100.	22
LEATHER PRODUCTS AND SHOES	67.	17.	0.	8.3	8.3	100.	12
GLASS PRODUCTS	38.	24.	11.	14.	14.	100.	37
STONE, CLAY AND CONCRETE	52.	8.5	5.6	24.	9.9	100.	71
IRON AND STEEL PRODUCTS	59.	16.	6.3	16.	3.1	100.	32
NON-FERROUS SMELTING	38.	21.	19.	17.	4.8	100.	42
NON-FERROUS PRODUCTS	49.	14.	8.6	23.	5.7	100.	35
METAL CANS	41.	11.	7.4	22.	19.	100.	27
STRUCTURAL METAL PRODUCTS	67.	22.	3.7	7.4	0.	100.	27
FABRICATED WIRE PRODUCTS	33.	0.	22.	33.	11.	100.	9
OTHER FABRICATED METAL	64.	11.	9.9	9.9	5.8	100.	121
ENGINES AND TURBINES	73.	13.	6.7	0.	6.7	100.	15
FARM MACHINERY	64.	18.	6.1	6.1	6.1	100.	33
CONSTRUCTION MACHINERY	71.	7.7	10.	7.7	3.8	100.	78
SPECIAL INDUSTRY MACHINERY	74.	10.	4.3	8.7	2.9	100.	69
GENERAL INDUSTRY MACHINERY	73.	12.	3.9	5.9	5.9	100.	51
OFFICE MACHINES + COMPUTERS	84.	10.	0.	6.1	0.	100.	49
OTHER NON-ELECTR. MACHINERY	63.	7.3	9.8	9.8	9.8	100.	41
ELECTR. TRANSMISSION EQUIP	70.	15.	10.	5.0	0.	100.	20
ELECTRIC LIGHTING AND WIRING	61.	22.	4.3	8.7	4.3	100.	23
RADIOS, TV'S + APPLIANCES	78.	16.	4.8	1.2	0.	100.	83
COMMUNICATIONS EQUIPMENT	76.	10.	3.4	3.4	6.9	100.	29

TABLE CONTINUED ON NEXT PAGE

CROSS-TABULATION 10.6.2: PERCENTAGE BREAKDOWN OF NUMBER (AS OF 1/1/68) OF
MANUFACTURING SUBSIDIARIES OF U.S.-BASED PARENT SYSTEMS BY
PERCENTAGE OF SUBSIDIARY'S EQUITY OWNED BY PARENT SYSTEM AS OF 1/1/68
FOR SUBSIDIARIES CLASSIFIED BY
PRINCIPAL INDUSTRY OF SUBSIDIARY AS OF 1/1/68
(CONTINUED)

PRINCIPAL INDUSTRY OF SUBSIDIARY AS OF 1/1/68	PERCENTAGE OF SUBSIDIARY'S EQUITY OWNED BY PARENT SYSTEM AS OF 1/1/68					TOTAL PERCENT	TOTAL NUMBER
	95% OR MORE	OVER 50% BUT UNDER 95%	EXACTLY 50%	AT LEAST 25% BUT UNDER 50%	OVER 5% BUT UNDER 25%		
ELECTRONIC COMPONENTS........	61.	16.	2.6	13.	7.9	100.	38
OTHER ELECTRICAL EQUIPMENT...	50.	24.	11.	9.8	4.9	100.	82
MOTOR VEHICLES AND EQUIPMENT.	57.	21.	6.0	10.	6.0	100.	182
OTHER TRANSPORTATION.........	50.	13.	6.3	19.	13.	100.	16
PRECISION GOODS..............	91.	4.3	1.4	2.9	0.	100.	69
MISCELLANEOUS PRODUCTS.......	75.	20.	3.6	1.8	0.	100.	56

CROSS-TABULATION 10.8.1: PERCENTAGE BREAKDOWN OF NUMBER (AS OF 1/1/71) OF MANUFACTURING SUBSIDIARIES OF NON-U.S.-BASED PARENT SYSTEMS BY PERCENTAGE OF SUBSIDIARY'S EQUITY OWNED BY PARENT SYSTEM AS OF 1/1/71 FOR SUBSIDIARIES CLASSIFIED BY PRINCIPAL INDUSTRY-GROUP OF SUBSIDIARY AS OF 1/1/71

PRINCIPAL INDUSTRY-GROUP OF SUBSIDIARY AS OF 1/1/71	PERCENTAGE OF SUBSIDIARY'S EQUITY OWNED BY PARENT SYSTEM AS OF 1/1/71						
	95% OR MORE	OVER 50% BUT UNDER 95%	EXACTLY 50%	AT LEAST 25% BUT UNDER 50%	OVER 5% BUT UNDER 25%	TOTAL PERCENT	TOTAL NUMBER
FOOD AND TOBACCO..........	66.	20.	3.8	6.8	3.9	100.	634
TEXTILES AND APPAREL.........	30.	17.	9.0	18.	27.	100.	255
WOOD, FURNITURE AND PAPER.....	58.	16.	7.1	14.	5.1	100.	198
CHEMICALS......................	49.	25.	11.	10.	4.6	100.	1166
PETROLEUM.....................	45.	15.	8.6	11.	20.	100.	185
RUBBER AND TIRES..............	46.	24.	6.0	13.	11.	100.	100
PRIMARY METALS................	37.	23.	7.2	17.	16.	100.	390
FABR. METAL + NON-EL. MACH....	44.	22.	8.8	12.	12.	100.	567
ELECTRIC AND ELECTRONIC.......	53.	22.	5.9	14.	5.6	100.	728
TRANSPORTATION EQUIPMENT......	42.	19.	9.3	21.	8.4	100.	226
PRECISION GOODS...............	58.	32.	1.4	4.1	5.5	100.	73
OTHER.........................	50.	22.	6.8	14.	7.5	100.	307

288

CROSS-TABULATION 10.8.4: PERCENTAGE BREAKDOWN OF NUMBER (AS OF 1/1/68) OF MANUFACTURING SUBSIDIARIES OF U.S.-BASED PARENT SYSTEMS BY PERCENTAGE OF SUBSIDIARY'S EQUITY OWNED BY PARENT SYSTEM AS OF 1/1/68 FOR SUBSIDIARIES CLASSIFIED BY PRINCIPAL INDUSTRY-GROUP OF SUBSIDIARY AS OF 1/1/68

PERCENTAGE OF SUBSIDIARY'S EQUITY OWNED BY PARENT SYSTEM AS OF 1/1/68

PRINCIPAL INDUSTRY-GROUP OF SUBSIDIARY AS OF 1/1/68	95% OR MORE	OVER 50% BUT UNDER 95%	EXACTLY 50%	AT LEAST 25% BUT UNDER 50%	OVER 5% BUT UNDER 25%	TOTAL PERCENT	TOTAL NUMBER
FOOD AND TOBACCO..........	67.	17.	8.4	5.0	2.1	100.	476
TEXTILES AND APPAREL......	60.	12.	17.	10.	1.3	100.	77
WOOD, FURNITURE AND PAPER....	50.	19.	13.	8.8	9.3	100.	193
CHEMICALS.................	68.	13.	9.8	7.0	2.0	100.	968
PETROLEUM.................	56.	11.	16.	13.	4.5	100.	179
RUBBER AND TIRES..........	51.	21.	7.5	15.	5.0	100.	80
PRIMARY METALS............	48.	17.	12.	18.	4.6	100.	109
FABR. METAL + NON-EL. MACH...	66.	11.	7.9	9.3	5.9	100.	471
ELECTRIC AND ELECTRONIC...	68.	17.	5.6	6.5	3.1	100.	324
TRANSPORTATION EQUIPMENT...	56.	20.	6.1	11.	6.6	100.	198
PRECISION GOODS...........	91.	4.3	1.4	2.9	0.	100.	69
OTHER.....................	57.	15.	6.7	14.	7.1	100.	210

289

CROSS-TABULATION 10.12.1: PERCENTAGE BREAKDOWN OF NUMBER (AS OF 1/1/71) OF
MANUFACTURING SUBSIDIARIES OF NON-U.S.-BASED PARENT SYSTEMS BY
PERCENTAGE OF SUBSIDIARY'S EQUITY OWNED BY PARENT SYSTEM AS OF 1/1/71
FOR SUBSIDIARIES CLASSIFIED BY
CATEGORY OF SUBSIDIARY'S PRINCIPAL OUTSIDE OWNER (IF ANY) AS OF 1/1/71

CATEGORY OF SUBSIDIARY'S PRINCIPAL OUTSIDE OWNER (IF ANY) AS OF 1/1/71	PERCENTAGE OF SUBSIDIARY'S EQUITY OWNED BY PARENT SYSTEM AS OF 1/1/71					
	OVER 50% BUT UNDER 95%	EXACTLY 50%	AT LEAST 25% BUT UNDER 50%	OVER 5% BUT UNDER 25%	TOTAL PERCENT	TOTAL NUMBER
LOCAL PRIVATE............	29.	22.	28.	21.	100.	839
LOCAL STATE.............	28.	13.	35.	23.	100.	137
FOREIGN PRIVATE.........	26.	25.	29.	20.	100.	373
STOCK WIDELY DISPERSED...	73.	2.2	16.	8.6	100.	93

290

CROSS-TABULATION 10.12.2: PERCENTAGE BREAKDOWN OF NUMBER (AS OF 1/1/68) OF
MANUFACTURING SUBSIDIARIES OF U.S.-BASED PARENT SYSTEMS BY
PERCENTAGE OF SUBSIDIARY'S EQUITY OWNED BY PARENT SYSTEM AS OF 1/1/68
FOR SUBSIDIARIES CLASSIFIED BY
CATEGORY OF SUBSIDIARY'S PRINCIPAL OUTSIDE OWNER (IF ANY) AS OF 1/1/68

CATEGORY OF SUBSIDIARY'S PRINCIPAL OUTSIDE OWNER (IF ANY) AS OF 1/1/68	PERCENTAGE OF SUBSIDIARY'S EQUITY OWNED BY PARENT SYSTEM AS OF 1/1/68					
	OVER 50% BUT UNDER 95%	EXACTLY 50%	AT LEAST 25% BUT UNDER 50%	OVER 5% BUT UNDER 25%	TOTAL PERCENT	TOTAL NUMBER
LOCAL PRIVATE.........	30.	37.	26.	7.3	100.	490
LOCAL STATE..........	27.	18.	45.	9.1	100.	11
FOREIGN PRIVATE......	34.	25.	29.	12.	100.	121
STOCK WIDELY DISPERSED.......	53.	16.	21.	10.	100.	227

CROSS-TABULATION 10.15.1: PERCENTAGE BREAKDOWN OF NUMBER (AS OF 1/1/71) OF
MANUFACTURING SUBSIDIARIES OF NON-U.S.-BASED PARENT SYSTEMS BY
PERCENTAGE OF SUBSIDIARY'S EQUITY OWNED BY PARENT SYSTEM AS OF 1/1/71
FOR SUBSIDIARIES CLASSIFIED BY
SUBSIDIARY'S PRINCIPAL MARKET AS OF 1/1/71

SUBSIDIARY'S PRINCIPAL MARKET AS OF 1/1/71	PERCENTAGE OF SUBSIDIARY'S EQUITY OWNED BY PARENT SYSTEM AS OF 1/1/71						
	95% OR MORE	OVER 50% BUT UNDER 95%	EXACTLY 50%	AT LEAST 25% BUT UNDER 50%	OVER 5% BUT UNDER 25%	TOTAL PERCENT	TOTAL NUMBER
LOCAL COUNTRY............	52.	21.	7.4	12.	7.5	100.	3830
EXPORT MARKETS..........	44.	17.	7.8	15.	17.	100.	309

CROSS-TABULATION 10.16.1: PERCENTAGE BREAKDOWN OF NUMBER (AS OF 1/1/71) OF
MANUFACTURING SUBSIDIARIES OF NON-U.S.-BASED PARENT SYSTEMS BY
PERCENTAGE OF SUBSIDIARY'S EQUITY OWNED BY PARENT SYSTEM AS OF 1/1/71
FOR SUBSIDIARIES CLASSIFIED BY
SUBSIDIARY'S PRINCIPAL CUSTOMER AS OF 1/1/71

				PERCENTAGE OF SUBSIDIARY'S EQUITY OWNED BY PARENT SYSTEM AS OF 1/1/71			
SUBSIDIARY'S PRINCIPAL CUSTOMER AS OF 1/1/71	95% OR MORE	OVER 50% BUT UNDER 95%	EXACTLY 50%	AT LEAST 25% BUT UNDER 50%	OVER 5% BUT UNDER 25%	TOTAL PERCENT	TOTAL NUMBER
PARENT SYSTEM............	53.	19.	11.	13.	4.8	100.	357
OUTSIDE CUSTOMERS........	50.	21.	7.3	13.	8.9	100.	3654

CROSS-TABULATION 10.18.1: PERCENTAGE BREAKDOWN OF NUMBER (AS OF 1/1/71) OF
MANUFACTURING SUBSIDIARIES OF NON-U.S.-BASED PARENT SYSTEMS BY
PERCENTAGE OF SUBSIDIARY'S EQUITY OWNED BY PARENT SYSTEM AS OF 1/1/71
FOR SUBSIDIARIES CLASSIFIED BY
VALUE OF SUBSIDIARY'S SALES IN 1970

VALUE OF SUBSIDIARY'S SALES AS OF 1/1/71	PERCENTAGE OF SUBSIDIARY'S EQUITY OWNED BY PARENT SYSTEM AS OF 1/1/71						
	95% OR MORE	OVER 50% BUT UNDER 95%	EXACTLY 50%	AT LEAST 25% BUT UNDER 50%	OVER 5% BUT UNDER 25%	TOTAL PERCENT	TOTAL NUMBER
UNDER $1 MILLION..............	58.	19.	5.8	9.7	7.2	100.	891
$1 - $10 MILLION..............	53.	19.	8.2	12.	7.5	100.	1574
$10 - $25 MILLION..............	53.	22.	6.7	11.	6.9	100.	507
$25 - $100 MILLION..............	43.	30.	4.5	13.	9.4	100.	331
OVER $100 MILLION..............	47.	23.	8.3	13.	8.3	100.	132

CROSS-TABULATION 10.18.2: PERCENTAGE BREAKDOWN OF NUMBER (AS OF 1/1/68) OF MANUFACTURING SUBSIDIARIES OF U.S.-BASED PARENT SYSTEMS BY PERCENTAGE OF SUBSIDIARY'S EQUITY OWNED BY PARENT SYSTEM AS OF 1/1/68 FOR SUBSIDIARIES CLASSIFIED BY VALUE OF SUBSIDIARY'S SALES IN 1967

VALUE OF SUBSIDIARY'S SALES IN 1967	PERCENTAGE OF SUBSIDIARY'S EQUITY OWNED BY PARENT SYSTEM AS OF 1/1/68						
	95% OR MORE	OVER 50% BUT UNDER 95%	EXACTLY 50%	AT LEAST 25% BUT UNDER 50%	OVER 5% BUT UNDER 25%	TOTAL PERCENT	TOTAL NUMBER
UNDER $1 MILLION..............	54.	20.	10.	13.	3.2	100.	185
$1 - $10 MILLION..............	55.	17.	11.	14.	2.7	100.	376
$10 - $25 MILLION............	58.	13.	13.	6.3	10.	100.	96
$25 - $100 MILLION...........	53.	26.	1.8	5.3	14.	100.	57
OVER $100 MILLION............	64.	29.	0.	0.	7.1	100.	14

CROSS-TABULATION 10.21.1: PERCENTAGE BREAKDOWN OF NUMBER (AS OF 1/1/71) OF MANUFACTURING SUBSIDIARIES OF NON-U.S.-BASED PARENT SYSTEMS BY PERCENTAGE OF SUBSIDIARY'S EQUITY OWNED BY PARENT SYSTEM AS OF 1/1/71 FOR SUBSIDIARIES CLASSIFIED BY NATIONAL BASE OF SUBSIDIARY'S PARENT SYSTEM

PERCENTAGE OF SUBSIDIARY'S EQUITY OWNED BY PARENT SYSTEM AS OF 1/1/71

NATIONAL BASE OF SUBSIDIARY'S PARENT SYSTEM	95% OR MORE	OVER 50% BUT UNDER 95%	EXACTLY 50%	AT LEAST 25% BUT UNDER 50%	OVER 5% BUT UNDER 25%	TOTAL PERCENT	TOTAL NUMBER
UNITED KINGDOM	61.	19.	6.6	8.8	4.2	100.	2236
GERMANY	42.	28.	11.	14.	4.4	100.	753
FRANCE	24.	29.	11.	22.	14.	100.	333
ITALY	42.	24.	8.5	21.	5.7	100.	106
BELGIUM AND LUXEMBURG	37.	34.	3.8	9.2	16.	100.	184
THE NETHERLANDS	61.	18.	10.	8.5	2.0	100.	401
SWEDEN	64.	17.	6.5	9.7	2.6	100.	155
SWITZERLAND	59.	29.	5.8	4.8	2.1	100.	292
JAPAN	9.0	9.0	5.9	29.	47.	100.	445
CANADA	51.	19.	9.1	16.	4.8	100.	186
OTHER NON-U.S.	55.	24.	4.6	10.	5.7	100.	87

CROSS-TABULATION 10.22.1: PERCENTAGE BREAKDOWN OF NUMBER (AS OF 1/1/71) OF
MANUFACTURING SUBSIDIARIES OF NON-U.S.-BASED PARENT SYSTEMS BY
PERCENTAGE OF SUBSIDIARY'S EQUITY OWNED BY PARENT SYSTEM AS OF 1/1/71
FOR SUBSIDIARIES CLASSIFIED BY
VALUE OF SALES OF SUBSIDIARY'S PARENT SYSTEM IN 1970

VALUE OF SALES OF SUBSIDIARY'S PARENT SYSTEM IN 1970	PERCENTAGE OF SUBSIDIARY'S EQUITY OWNED BY PARENT SYSTEM AS OF 1/1/71					TOTAL PERCENT	TOTAL NUMBER
	95% OR MORE	OVER 50% BUT UNDER 95%	EXACTLY 50%	AT LEAST 25% BUT UNDER 50%	OVER 5% BUT UNDER 25%		
$400 - 599 MILLION..............	59.	19.	6.1	9.8	5.6	100.	1023
$600 - 999 MILLION..............	49.	24.	6.3	13.	8.1	100.	805
$1 - 2 BILLION..............	47.	24.	7.9	13.	8.6	100.	1466
OVER $2 BILLION..............	46.	19.	8.5	15.	11.	100.	1757

CROSS-TABULATION 10.22.2: PERCENTAGE BREAKDOWN OF NUMBER (AS OF 1/1/68) OF
MANUFACTURING SUBSIDIARIES OF U.S.-BASED PARENT SYSTEMS BY
PERCENTAGE OF SUBSIDIARY'S EQUITY OWNED BY PARENT SYSTEM AS OF 1/1/68
FOR SUBSIDIARIES CLASSIFIED BY
VALUE OF SALES OF SUBSIDIARY'S PARENT SYSTEM IN 1967

VALUE OF SALES OF SUBSIDIARY'S PARENT SYSTEM IN 1967	PERCENTAGE OF SUBSIDIARY'S EQUITY OWNED BY PARENT SYSTEM AS OF 1/1/68						
	95% OR MORE	OVER 50% BUT UNDER 95%	EXACTLY 50%	AT LEAST 25% BUT UNDER 50%	OVER 5% BUT UNDER 25%	TOTAL PERCENT	TOTAL NUMBER
$100 - 399 MILLION..........	71.	12.	6.5	7.7	2.7	100.	764
$400 - 599 MILLION..........	64.	14.	7.5	9.4	4.6	100.	584
$600 - 999 MILLION..........	57.	18.	12.	8.2	5.5	100.	784
$1 - 2 BILLION..........	58.	17.	9.2	11.	4.4	100.	834
OVER $2 BILLION..........	64.	16.	11.	6.7	2.7	100.	675

CROSS-TABULATION 10.23.1: PERCENTAGE BREAKDOWN OF NUMBER (AS OF 1/1/71) OF MANUFACTURING SUBSIDIARIES OF NON-U.S.-BASED PARENT SYSTEMS BY PERCENTAGE OF SUBSIDIARY'S EQUITY OWNED BY PARENT SYSTEM AS OF 1/1/71 FOR SUBSIDIARIES CLASSIFIED BY PRINCIPAL INDUSTRY-GROUP OF SUBSIDIARY'S PARENT SYSTEM AS OF 1/1/71

PRINCIPAL INDUSTRY-GROUP OF SUBSIDIARY'S PARENT SYSTEM AS OF 1/1/71	PERCENTAGE OF SUBSIDIARY'S EQUITY OWNED BY PARENT SYSTEM AS OF 1/1/71						
	95% OR MORE	OVER 50% BUT UNDER 95%	EXACTLY 50%	AT LEAST 25% BUT UNDER 50%	OVER 5% BUT UNDER 25%	TOTAL PERCENT	TOTAL NUMBER
FOOD, TOBACCO AND SOAP.......	69.	19.	4.2	5.2	2.0	100.	887
CHEMICALS AND DRUGS..........	43.	27.	12.	12.	5.9	100.	1094
PETROLEUM....................	48.	14.	14.	11.	14.	100.	274
IRON AND STEEL...............	32.	22.	10.	18.	18.	100.	197
NON-FERROUS METALS...........	44.	21.	11.	14.	9.6	100.	408
FABR. METAL + NON-EL. MACH...	48.	25.	5.9	15.	5.6	100.	408
ELECTRIC AND ELECTRONIC......	58.	21.	5.1	12.	4.0	100.	900
AUTOMOBILES..................	37.	17.	7.9	29.	8.7	100.	126
OTHER........................	40.	18.	5.1	16.	21.	100.	884

CROSS-TABULATION 10.23.2: PERCENTAGE BREAKDOWN OF NUMBER (AS OF 1/1/68) OF MANUFACTURING SUBSIDIARIES OF U.S.-BASED PARENT SYSTEMS BY PERCENTAGE OF SUBSIDIARY'S EQUITY OWNED BY PARENT SYSTEM AS OF 1/1/68 FOR SUBSIDIARIES CLASSIFIED BY PRINCIPAL INDUSTRY-GROUP OF SUBSIDIARY'S PARENT SYSTEM AS OF 1/1/68

PRINCIPAL INDUSTRY-GROUP OF SUBSIDIARY'S PARENT SYSTEM AS OF 1/1/68	PERCENTAGE OF SUBSIDIARY'S EQUITY OWNED BY PARENT SYSTEM AS OF 1/1/68					TOTAL PERCENT	TOTAL NUMBER
	95% OR MORE	OVER 50% BUT UNDER 95%	EXACTLY 50%	AT LEAST 25% BUT UNDER 50%	OVER 5% BUT UNDER 25%		
FOOD, TOBACCO AND SOAP.........	69.	14.	8.9	5.3	2.3	100.	655
CHEMICALS AND DRUGS...........	66.	17.	9.2	5.9	1.4	100.	945
PETROLEUM.....................	50.	13.	18.	14.	5.7	100.	282
IRON AND STEEL................	71.	9.5	19.	0.	0.	100.	21
NON-FERROUS METALS............	43.	18.	15.	18.	5.7	100.	122
FABR. METAL + NON-EL. MACH....	66.	14.	4.6	9.2	6.3	100.	411
ELECTRIC AND ELECTRONIC.......	68.	17.	3.6	7.4	3.8	100.	392
AUTOMOBILES...................	58.	14.	8.9	14.	5.6	100.	213
OTHER.........................	58.	15.	11.	10.	6.2	100.	679

CROSS-TABULATION 10.25.1: PERCENTAGE BREAKDOWN OF NUMBER (AS OF 1/1/71) OF
MANUFACTURING SUBSIDIARIES OF NON-U.S.-BASED PARENT SYSTEMS BY
PERCENTAGE OF SUBSIDIARY'S EQUITY OWNED BY PARENT SYSTEM AS OF 1/1/71
FOR SUBSIDIARIES CLASSIFIED BY
NUMBER OF COUNTRIES IN WHICH SUBSIDIARY'S PARENT SYSTEM MANUFACTURED AS OF 1/1/71

NUMBER OF COUNTRIES SUB-SIDIARY'S PARENT SYSTEM MANUFACTURED IN AS OF 1/1/71	PERCENTAGE OF SUBSIDIARY'S EQUITY OWNED BY PARENT SYSTEM AS OF 1/1/71						
	95% OR MORE	OVER 50% BUT UNDER 95%	EXACTLY 50%	AT LEAST 25% BUT UNDER 50%	OVER 5% BUT UNDER 25%	TOTAL PERCENT	TOTAL NUMBER
TWO OR THREE..................	23.	13.	5.8	19.	38.	100.	52
FOUR TO SIX...................	40.	11.	6.5	16.	25.	100.	370
SEVEN TO TWELVE...............	35.	20.	7.1	22.	16.	100.	588
THIRTEEN OR MORE..............	53.	22.	7.9	11.	5.7	100.	4163

CROSS-TABULATION 10.25.2: PERCENTAGE BREAKDOWN OF NUMBER (AS OF 1/1/68) OF
MANUFACTURING SUBSIDIARIES OF U.S.-BASED PARENT SYSTEMS BY
PERCENTAGE OF SUBSIDIARY'S EQUITY OWNED BY PARENT SYSTEM AS OF 1/1/68
FOR SUBSIDIARIES CLASSIFIED BY
NUMBER OF COUNTRIES IN WHICH SUBSIDIARY'S PARENT SYSTEM MANUFACTURED AS OF 1/1/68

| | | PERCENTAGE OF SUBSIDIARY'S EQUITY OWNED BY PARENT SYSTEM AS OF 1/1/68 | | | | | |
NUMBER OF COUNTRIES IN WHICH SUBSIDIARY'S PARENT SYSTEM MANUFACTURED AS OF 1/1/68	95% OR MORE	OVER 50% BUT UNDER 95%	EXACTLY 50%	AT LEAST 25% BUT UNDER 50%	OVER 5% BUT UNDER 25%	TOTAL PERCENT	TOTAL NUMBER
TWO OR THREE............	0.	0.	0.	0.	0.	100.	0
FOUR TO SIX.............	71.	9.5	14.	0.	4.8	100.	21
SEVEN TO TWELVE.........	62.	12.	9.0	11.	5.7	100.	876
THIRTEEN OR MORE........	63.	16.	5.2	8.0	3.4	100.	2802

CROSS-TABULATION 10.26.1: PERCENTAGE BREAKDOWN OF NUMBER (AS OF 1/1/71) OF
MANUFACTURING SUBSIDIARIES OF NON-U.S.-BASED PARENT SYSTEMS BY
PERCENTAGE OF SUBSIDIARY'S EQUITY OWNED BY PARENT SYSTEM AS OF 1/1/71
FOR SUBSIDIARIES CLASSIFIED BY
PERCENTAGE OF PARENT SYSTEM'S EMPLOYEES OUTSIDE NATIONAL BASE AS OF 1/1/71

PERCENTAGE OF PARENT SYSTEM'S EMPLOYEES OUTSIDE NATIONAL BASE AS OF 1/1/71	PERCENTAGE OF SUBSIDIARY'S EQUITY OWNED BY PARENT SYSTEM AS OF 1/1/71						
	95% OR MORE	OVER 50% BUT UNDER 95%	EXACTLY 50%	AT LEAST 25% BUT UNDER 50%	OVER 5% BUT UNDER 25%	TOTAL PERCENT	TOTAL NUMBER
UNDER 10%............	35.	19.	6.8	22.	17.	100.	426
10% - 25%............	52.	21.	7.9	14.	5.7	100.	1323
25% - 50%............	46.	25.	11.	14.	4.3	100.	903
OVER 50%.............	62.	21.	6.5	6.5	4.7	100.	1757

CROSS-TABULATION 10.27.1: PERCENTAGE BREAKDOWN OF NUMBER (AS OF 1/1/71) OF
MANUFACTURING SUBSIDIARIES OF NON-U.S.-BASED PARENT SYSTEMS BY
PERCENTAGE OF SUBSIDIARY'S EQUITY OWNED BY PARENT SYSTEM AS OF 1/1/71
FOR SUBSIDIARIES CLASSIFIED BY
NO. OF INDUSTRIES IN WHICH PARENT SYSTEM MANUFACTURED WITHIN NATIONAL BASE AS OF 1/1/71

PERCENTAGE OF SUBSIDIARY'S EQUITY OWNED
BY PARENT SYSTEM AS OF 1/1/71

NO. OF INDUSTRIES IN WHICH PARENT SYSTEM MANUF. WITHIN NATIONAL BASE AS OF 1/1/71	95% OR MORE	OVER 50% BUT UNDER 95%	EXACTLY 50%	AT LEAST 25% BUT UNDER 50%	OVER 5% BUT UNDER 25%	TOTAL PERCENT	TOTAL NUMBER
ONE TO THREE..................	32.	13.	5.8	17.	32.	100.	379
FOUR TO NINE..................	48.	22.	6.4	14.	10.	100.	1627
TEN TO NINETEEN..................	49.	23.	9.5	13.	5.3	100.	2188
TWENTY OR MORE..................	62.	19.	6.5	7.0	5.2	100.	984

CROSS-TABULATION 10.27.2: PERCENTAGE BREAKDOWN OF NUMBER (AS OF 1/1/68) OF
MANUFACTURING SUBSIDIARIES OF U.S.-BASED PARENT SYSTEMS BY
PERCENTAGE OF SUBSIDIARY'S EQUITY OWNED BY PARENT SYSTEM AS OF 1/1/68
FOR SUBSIDIARIES CLASSIFIED BY
NO. OF INDUSTRIES IN WHICH PARENT SYSTEM MANUFACTURED WITHIN NATIONAL BASE AS OF 1/1/68

NO. OF INDUSTRIES IN WHICH PARENT SYSTEM MANUF. WITHIN NATIONAL BASE AS OF 1/1/68	PERCENTAGE OF SUBSIDIARY'S EQUITY OWNED BY PARENT SYSTEM AS OF 1/1/68						
	95% OR MORE	OVER 50% BUT UNDER 95%	EXACTLY 50%	AT LEAST 25% BUT UNDER 50%	OVER 5% BUT UNDER 25%	TOTAL PERCENT	TOTAL NUMBER
ONE TO THREE........	76.	14.	4.9	3.3	2.2	100.	368
FOUR TO NINE........	66.	12.	9.4	8.7	3.7	100.	1272
TEN TO NINETEEN.....	58.	17.	10.	9.6	5.1	100.	1266
TWENTY OR MORE......	62.	19.	7.8	8.4	3.5	100.	752

CROSS-TABULATION 10.28.1: PERCENTAGE BREAKDOWN OF NUMBER (AS OF 1/1/71) OF
MANUFACTURING SUBSIDIARIES OF NON-U.S.-BASED PARENT SYSTEMS BY
PERCENTAGE OF SUBSIDIARY'S EQUITY OWNED BY PARENT SYSTEM AS OF 1/1/71
FOR SUBSIDIARIES CLASSIFIED BY
NO. OF INDUSTRIES IN WHICH PARENT SYSTEM MANUFACTURED OUTSIDE NATIONAL BASE AS OF 1/1/71

NO. OF INDUSTRIES IN WHICH PARENT SYSTEM MANUF. OUTSIDE NATIONAL BASE AS OF 1/1/71	PERCENTAGE OF SUBSIDIARY'S EQUITY OWNED BY PARENT SYSTEM AS OF 1/1/71						
	95% OR MORE	OVER 50% BUT UNDER 95%	EXACTLY 50%	AT LEAST 25% BUT UNDER 50%	OVER 5% BUT UNDER 25%	TOTAL PERCENT	TOTAL NUMBER
ONE TO THREE............	48.	18.	7.3	16.	11.	100.	316
FOUR TO NINE............	43.	21.	7.5	18.	11.	100.	1263
TEN TO NINETEEN.........	51.	25.	9.3	9.3	5.7	100.	1545
TWENTY OR MORE..........	53.	19.	6.6	11.	9.4	100.	2054

CROSS-TABULATION 10.28.2: PERCENTAGE BREAKDOWN OF NUMBER (AS OF 1/1/68) OF
MANUFACTURING SUBSIDIARIES OF U.S.-BASED PARENT SYSTEMS BY
PERCENTAGE OF SUBSIDIARY'S EQUITY OWNED BY PARENT SYSTEM AS OF 1/1/68
FOR SUBSIDIARIES CLASSIFIED BY
NO. OF INDUSTRIES IN WHICH PARENT SYSTEM MANUFACTURED OUTSIDE NATIONAL BASE AS OF 1/1/68

		PERCENTAGE OF SUBSIDIARY'S EQUITY OWNED BY PARENT SYSTEM AS OF 1/1/68					
NO. OF INDUSTRIES IN WHICH PARENT SYSTEM MANUF. OUTSIDE NATIONAL BASE AS OF 1/1/68	95% OR MORE	OVER 50% BUT UNDER 95%	EXACTLY 50%	AT LEAST 25% BUT UNDER 50%	OVER 5% BUT UNDER 25%	TOTAL PERCENT	TOTAL NUMBER
ONE TO THREE............	72.	14.	7.7	3.8	2.2	100.	495
FOUR TO NINE............	63.	14.	10.	8.8	4.2	100.	2198
TEN TO NINETEEN.........	54.	19.	9.2	13.	5.0	100.	742
TWENTY OR MORE..........	72.	18.	4.6	3.9	1.8	100.	285

CROSS-TABULATION 10.29.1: PERCENTAGE BREAKDOWN OF NUMBER (AS OF 1/1/71) OF
MANUFACTURING SUBSIDIARIES OF NON-U.S.-BASED PARENT SYSTEMS BY
PERCENTAGE OF SUBSIDIARY'S EQUITY OWNED BY PARENT SYSTEM AS OF 1/1/71
FOR SUBSIDIARIES CLASSIFIED BY
PARENT SYSTEM'S R&D EXPENDITURES AS A PERCENTAGE OF SALES IN 1970

PARENT SYSTEM'S R&D EXPENDITURES AS A PERCENTAGE OF SALES IN 1970	PERCENTAGE OF SUBSIDIARY'S EQUITY OWNED BY PARENT SYSTEM AS OF 1/1/71						
	95% OR MORE	OVER 50% BUT UNDER 95%	EXACTLY 50%	AT LEAST 25% BUT UNDER 50%	OVER 5% BUT UNDER 25%	TOTAL PERCENT	TOTAL NUMBER
LESS THAN 1%..........	40.	25.	7.1	16.	11.	100.	760
1% - 4%..........	50.	21.	11.	13.	5.3	100.	1478
MORE THAN 4%..........	46.	24.	7.3	14.	9.0	100.	1134

CROSS-TABULATION 10.29.2: PERCENTAGE BREAKDOWN OF NUMBER (AS OF 1/1/68) OF
MANUFACTURING SUBSIDIARIES OF U.S.-BASED PARENT SYSTEMS BY
PERCENTAGE OF SUBSIDIARY'S EQUITY OWNED BY PARENT SYSTEM AS OF 1/1/68
FOR SUBSIDIARIES CLASSIFIED BY
PARENT SYSTEM'S R&D EXPENDITURES AS A PERCENTAGE OF SALES IN 1967

	PERCENTAGE OF SUBSIDIARY'S EQUITY OWNED BY PARENT SYSTEM AS OF 1/1/68						
PARENT SYSTEM'S R&D EXPENDITURES AS A PERCENTAGE OF SALES IN 1967	95% OR MORE	OVER 50% BUT UNDER 95%	EXACTLY 50%	AT LEAST 25% BUT UNDER 50%	OVER 5% BUT UNDER 25%	TOTAL PERCENT	TOTAL NUMBER
LESS THAN 1%..........	52.	13.	20.	11.	3.8	100.	287
1% - 4%..............	60.	14.	8.8	11.	6.9	100.	750
MORE THAN 4%.........	72.	11.	7.7	6.5	2.7	100.	339

CROSS-TABULATION 11.17.1: PERCENTAGE BREAKDOWN OF NUMBER OF
MANUFACTURING SUBSIDIARIES OF NON-U.S.-BASED PARENT SYSTEMS BY
CATEGORY OF SUBSIDIARY'S PRINCIPAL OUTSIDE OWNER (IF ANY) AT DATE OF ENTRY
FOR SUBSIDIARIES CLASSIFIED BY
SUBSIDIARY'S DATE OF ENTRY INTO PARENT SYSTEM

SUBSIDIARY'S DATE OF ENTRY INTO PARENT SYSTEM	CATEGORY OF SUBSIDIARY'S PRINCIPAL OUTSIDE OWNER (IF ANY) AT DATE OF ENTRY					
	LOCAL PRIVATE	LOCAL STATE	FOREIGN PRIVATE	STOCK WIDELY DISPERSED	TOTAL PERCENT	TOTAL NUMBER
PRE 1914.........	75.	5.0	20.	0.	100.	20
1914 - 1919......	78.	0.	22.	0.	100.	9
1920 - 1929......	45.	6.9	36.	12.	100.	58
1930 - 1938......	39.	0.	45.	15.	100.	33
1939 - 1945......	73.	0.	27.	0.	100.	11
1946 - 1952......	59.	13.	14.	14.	100.	70
1953 - 1955......	69.	7.8	20.	3.9	100.	51
1956 - 1958......	55.	6.5	31.	8.1	100.	62
1959 - 1961......	63.	8.7	23.	4.9	100.	184
1962 - 1964......	57.	8.5	30.	4.0	100.	224
1965 - 1967......	66.	8.2	23.	2.9	100.	340
1968 - 1970......	66.	5.2	25.	3.4	100.	465

CROSS-TABULATION 11.17.2: PERCENTAGE BREAKDOWN OF NUMBER OF
MANUFACTURING SUBSIDIARIES OF U.S.-BASED PARENT SYSTEMS BY
CATEGORY OF SUBSIDIARY'S PRINCIPAL OUTSIDE OWNER (IF ANY) AT DATE OF ENTRY
FOR SUBSIDIARIES CLASSIFIED BY
SUBSIDIARY'S DATE OF ENTRY INTO PARENT SYSTEM

SUBSIDIARY'S DATE OF ENTRY INTO PARENT SYSTEM	CATEGORY OF SUBSIDIARY'S PRINCIPAL OUTSIDE OWNER (IF ANY) AT DATE OF ENTRY					
	LOCAL PRIVATE	LOCAL STATE	FOREIGN PRIVATE	STOCK WIDELY DISPERSED	TOTAL PERCENT	TOTAL NUMBER
PRE 1914..............	43.	0.	14.	43.	100.	7
1914 - 1919..........	0.	0.	0.	100.	100.	1
1920 - 1929..........	66.	0.	17.	17.	100.	41
1930 - 1938..........	19.	0.	53.	28.	100.	36
1939 - 1945..........	34.	2.6	21.	42.	100.	38
1946 - 1952..........	64.	2.4	8.2	26.	100.	85
1953 - 1955..........	56.	1.6	16.	26.	100.	61
1956 - 1958..........	54.	1.8	16.	28.	100.	111
1959 - 1961..........	60.	0.7	16.	23.	100.	269
1962 - 1964..........	64.	1.7	15.	19.	100.	293
1965 - 1967..........	57.	1.4	14.	27.	100.	282
1968 - 1970..........	0.	0.	0.	0.	100.	0

TABULATION 12.1: PERCENTAGE BREAKDOWN OF NUMBER OF SUBSIDIARIES BY
CATEGORY OF SUBSIDIARY'S PRINCIPAL OUTSIDE OWNER (IF ANY)
FOR VARIOUS CATEGORIES OF SUBSIDIARIES

CATEGORY OF SUBSIDIARY	CATEGORY OF SUBSIDIARY'S PRINCIPAL OUTSIDE OWNER (IF ANY)					
	LOCAL PRIVATE	LOCAL STATE	FOREIGN PRIVATE	STOCK WIDELY DISPERSED	TOTAL PERCENT	TOTAL NUMBER
NON-U.S.-BASED SYSTEMS (AS OF 1/1/71):						
ALL SUBSIDIARIES.........	57.	9.2	28.	5.5	100.	2324
MANUFACTURING SUBS......	58.	9.6	26.	6.4	100.	1455
SALES SUBSIDIARIES......	62.	5.4	31.	2.0	100.	351
U.S.-BASED SYSTEMS (AS OF 1/1/68):						
ALL SUBSIDIARIES.........	56.	1.7	18.	25.	100.	1229
MANUFACTURING SUBS......	58.	1.4	14.	26.	100.	930
SALES SUBSIDIARIES......	60.	0.	12.	28.	100.	98
WORLD SUBSET OF SYSTEMS (AS OF 1/1/68):						
NON-U.S.-BASED SYSTEMS:						
ALL SUBSIDIARIES.......	53.	9.8	29.	7.8	100.	1003
MANUFACTURING SUBS.....	54.	14.	27.	9.6	100.	646
SALES SUBSIDIARIES.....	65.	7.5	67.	0.7	100.	147
U.S.-BASED-SYSTEMS:						
ALL SUBSIDIARIES.......	57.	1.8	18.	23.	100.	1028
MANUFACTURING SUBS.....	59.	1.4	14.	25.	100.	780
SALES SUBSIDIARIES.....	58.	0.	15.	27.	100.	73

TABULATION 12 .2: PERCENTAGE BREAKDOWN OF SALES OF SUBSIDIARIES IN 1970 BY
CATEGORY OF SUBSIDIARY'S PRINCIPAL OUTSIDE OWNER (IF ANY) AS OF 1/1/71
FOR ALL SUBSIDIARIES, MANUFACTURING SUBSIDIARIES AND SALES SUBSIDIARIES
OF NON-U.S.-BASED SYSTEMS

CATEGORY OF SUBSIDIARY			CATEGORY OF SUBSIDIARY'S PRINCIPAL OUTSIDE OWNER (IF ANY) AS OF 1/1/71			
	LOCAL PRIVATE	LOCAL STATE	FOREIGN PRIVATE	STOCK WIDELY DISPERSED	TOTAL PERCENT	TOTAL ($ MIL)
ALL SUBSIDIARIES............	36.	5.5	28.	30.	100.	40981
MANUFACTURING SUBSIDIARIES...	35.	5.0	26.	34.	100.	31530
SALES SUBSIDIARIES...........	63.	4.0	27.	5.9	100.	2857

CROSS-TABULATION 12. 1.1: PERCENTAGE BREAKDOWN OF NUMBER (AS OF 1/1/71) OF MANUFACTURING SUBSIDIARIES OF NON-U.S.-BASED PARENT SYSTEMS BY CATEGORY OF SUBSIDIARY'S PRINCIPAL OUTSIDE OWNER (IF ANY) AS OF 1/1/71 FOR SUBSIDIARIES CLASSIFIED BY SUBSIDIARY'S COUNTRY

SUBSIDIARY'S COUNTRY	CATEGORY OF SUBSIDIARY'S PRINCIPAL OUTSIDE OWNER (IF ANY) AS OF 1/1/71					
	LOCAL PRIVATE	LOCAL STATE	FOREIGN PRIVATE	STOCK WIDELY DISPERSED	TOTAL PERCENT	TOTAL NUMBER
UNITED STATES	75.	0.	18.	6.1	100.	49
CANADA	47.	0.	32.	21.	100.	38
MEXICO	72.	3.1	22.	3.1	100.	32
CENTRAL AMERICA AND CARIB	51.	8.1	38.	2.7	100.	37
VENEZUELA	75.	6.3	13.	6.3	100.	16
COLOMBIA	56.	22.	11.	11.	100.	9
PERU	33.	0.	67.	0.	100.	9
CHILE	44.	11.	33.	11.	100.	9
ARGENTINA	54.	0.	42.	4.2	100.	24
BRAZIL	30.	13.	46.	11.	100.	46
OTHER SOUTH AMERICA	20.	0.	60.	20.	100.	5
GERMANY	68.	5.1	25.	1.7	100.	59
FRANCE	70.	3.0	19.	7.5	100.	67
ITALY	49.	9.8	39.	2.4	100.	41
BELGIUM AND LUXEMBURG	45.	3.2	45.	6.5	100.	31
THE NETHERLANDS	67.	0.	30.	3.3	100.	30
UNITED KINGDOM	64.	2.0	26.	8.0	100.	50
IRELAND	77.	9.1	14.	0.	100.	22
DENMARK	83.	0.	17.	0.	100.	6
NORWAY	67.	17.	17.	0.	100.	6
SWEDEN	67.	8.3	25.	0.	100.	12
FINLAND	50.	17.	33.	0.	100.	6

TABLE CONTINUED ON NEXT PAGE

CROSS-TABULATION 12. 1.1: PERCENTAGE BREAKDOWN OF NUMBER (AS OF 1/1/71) OF MANUFACTURING SUBSIDIARIES OF NON-U.S.-BASED PARENT SYSTEMS BY CATEGORY OF SUBSIDIARY'S PRINCIPAL OUTSIDE OWNER (IF ANY) AS OF 1/1/71 FOR SUBSIDIARIES CLASSIFIED BY SUBSIDIARY'S COUNTRY (CONTINUED)

SUBSIDIARY'S COUNTRY	CATEGORY OF SUBSIDIARY'S PRINCIPAL OUTSIDE OWNER (IF ANY) AS OF 1/1/71				TOTAL PERCENT	TOTAL NUMBER
	LOCAL PRIVATE	LOCAL STATE	FOREIGN PRIVATE	STOCK WIDELY DISPERSED		
SWITZERLAND	73.	0.	27.	0.	100.	11
AUSTRIA	68.	16.	11.	5.3	100.	19
PORTUGAL	77.	7.7	0.	15.	100.	13
SPAIN	68.	14.	14.	3.2	100.	63
GREECE	43.	43.	14.	0.	100.	7
TURKEY	50.	28.	22.	0.	100.	18
OTHER EUROPE + ISRAEL	63.	25.	13.	0.	100.	8
PAKISTAN	50.	17.	13.	21.	100.	24
IRAN	63.	25.	6.3	6.3	100.	16
OTHER MID EAST+EGYPT+LIBYA	50.	25.	25.	0.	100.	8
UNION OF SOUTH AFRICA	57.	2.9	31.	8.8	100.	68
RHODESIA	60.	0.	40.	0.	100.	5
ZAMBIA	29.	57.	14.	0.	100.	7
TANZANIA	43.	57.	0.	0.	100.	7
KENYA	33.	33.	22.	11.	100.	9
NIGERIA	18.	45.	27.	9.1	100.	22
OTHER (BRITISH) AFRICA	21.	58.	21.	0.	100.	19
MOROCCO, ALGERIA + TUNISIA	22.	56.	11.	11.	100.	9
OTHER (FRENCH) AFRICA	5.3	37.	58.	0.	100.	19
OTHER AFRICA	27.	64.	9.1	0.	100.	11
AUSTRALIA	53.	2.6	36.	9.2	100.	76
NEW ZEALAND	64.	0.	27.	9.1	100.	22

TABLE CONTINUED ON NEXT PAGE

CROSS-TABULATION 12. 1.1: PERCENTAGE BREAKDOWN OF NUMBER (AS OF 1/1/71) OF
MANUFACTURING SUBSIDIARIES OF NON-U.S.-BASED PARENT SYSTEMS BY
CATEGORY OF SUBSIDIARY'S PRINCIPAL OUTSIDE OWNER (IF ANY) AS OF 1/1/71
FOR SUBSIDIARIES CLASSIFIED BY
SUBSIDIARY'S COUNTRY
(CONTINUED)

SUBSIDIARY'S COUNTRY	CATEGORY OF SUBSIDIARY'S PRINCIPAL OUTSIDE OWNER (IF ANY) AS OF 1/1/71					
	LOCAL PRIVATE	LOCAL STATE	FOREIGN PRIVATE	STOCK WIDELY DISPERSED	TOTAL PERCENT	TOTAL NUMBER
JAPAN..........	88.	0.	6.1	6.1	100.	49
CHINA (TAIWAN).....	65.	1.3	31.	2.7	100.	75
HONG KONG..........	57.	0.	33.	0.	100.	18
THE PHILIPPINES.....	47.	0.	33.	20.	100.	15
MALAYSIA..........	54.	3.6	29.	14.	100.	28
SINGAPORE..........	52.	15.	30.	3.7	100.	27
INDONESIA..........	32.	11.	58.	0.	100.	19
THAILAND..........	61.	0.	37.	2.0	100.	49
INDIA..........	64.	9.6	11.	15.	100.	73
OTHER ASIA AND OCEANIA........	71.	21.	5.9	2.9	100.	34

CROSS-TABULATION 12.1.2: PERCENTAGE BREAKDOWN OF NUMBER (AS OF 1/1/68) OF MANUFACTURING SUBSIDIARIES OF U.S.-BASED PARENT SYSTEMS BY CATEGORY OF SUBSIDIARY'S PRINCIPAL OUTSIDE OWNER (IF ANY) AS OF 1/1/68 FOR SUBSIDIARIES CLASSIFIED BY SUBSIDIARY'S COUNTRY

SUBSIDIARY'S COUNTRY	CATEGORY OF SUBSIDIARY'S PRINCIPAL OUTSIDE OWNER (IF ANY) AS OF 1/1/68					
	LOCAL PRIVATE	LOCAL STATE	FOREIGN PRIVATE	STOCK WIDELY DISPERSED	TOTAL PERCENT	TOTAL NUMBER
UNITED STATES	0.	0.	0.	0.	100.	0
CANADA	53.	2.2	18.	27.	100.	45
MEXICO	44.	0.	8.8	48.	100.	80
CENTRAL AMERICA AND CARIB	38.	0.	23.	40.	100.	40
VENEZUELA	20.	3.3	23.	53.	100.	30
COLOMBIA	38.	0.	25.	38.	100.	24
PERU	25.	0.	0.	75.	100.	4
CHILE	73.	9.1	0.	18.	100.	11
ARGENTINA	52.	0.	24.	24.	100.	29
BRAZIL	41.	0.	29.	29.	100.	34
OTHER SOUTH AMERICA	13.	0.	88.	0.	100.	8
GERMANY	63.	0.	17.	20.	100.	46
FRANCE	68.	0.	9.4	23.	100.	53
ITALY	76.	0.	4.0	20.	100.	50
BELGIUM AND LUXEMBURG	45.	0.	27.	27.	100.	22
THE NETHERLANDS	68.	0.	5.3	26.	100.	19
UNITED KINGDOM	86.	0.	3.1	11.	100.	64
IRELAND	67.	0.	0.	33.	100.	6
DENMARK	80.	0.	0.	20.	100.	5
NORWAY	67.	0.	33.	0.	100.	3
SWEDEN	88.	0.	0.	13.	100.	8
FINLAND	0.	0.	0.	100.	100.	1

TABLE CONTINUED ON NEXT PAGE

CROSS-TABULATION 12. 1.2: PERCENTAGE BREAKDOWN OF NUMBER (AS OF 1/1/68) OF MANUFACTURING SUBSIDIARIES OF U.S.-BASED PARENT SYSTEMS BY CATEGORY OF SUBSIDIARY'S PRINCIPAL OUTSIDE OWNER (IF ANY) AS OF 1/1/68 FOR SUBSIDIARIES CLASSIFIED BY SUBSIDIARY'S COUNTRY (CONTINUED)

SUBSIDIARY'S COUNTRY	CATEGORY OF SUBSIDIARY'S PRINCIPAL OUTSIDE OWNER (IF ANY) AS OF 1/1/68					
	LOCAL PRIVATE	LOCAL STATE	FOREIGN PRIVATE	STOCK WIDELY DISPERSED	TOTAL PERCENT	TOTAL NUMBER
SWITZERLAND	33.	0.	33.	33.	100.	3
AUSTRIA	0.	0.	100.	0.	100.	1
PORTUGAL	20.	20.	20.	40.	100.	5
SPAIN	52.	1.9	15.	31.	100.	52
GREECE	11.	0.	22.	67.	100.	9
TURKEY	40.	0.	0.	60.	100.	5
OTHER EUROPE + ISRAEL	60.	20.	20.	0.	100.	5
PAKISTAN	38.	0.	0.	63.	100.	8
IRAN	27.	18.	36.	18.	100.	11
OTHER MID EAST+EGYPT+LIBYA	0.	0.	33.	67.	100.	3
UNION OF SOUTH AFRICA	76.	0.	12.	12.	100.	17
RHODESIA	0.	0.	0.	0.	100.	0
ZAMBIA	0.	0.	100.	0.	100.	2
TANZANIA	0.	0.	0.	0.	100.	0
KENYA	100.	0.	0.	0.	100.	1
NIGERIA	0.	0.	0.	100.	100.	1
OTHER (BRITISH) AFRICA	0.	0.	100.	0.	100.	2
MOROCCO, ALGERIA + TUNISIA	25.	25.	25.	25.	100.	4
OTHER (FRENCH) AFRICA	0.	0.	100.	0.	100.	2
OTHER AFRICA	0.	0.	0.	0.	100.	0
AUSTRALIA	67.	0.	16.	16.	100.	49
NEW ZEALAND	86.	0.	0.	14.	100.	7

TABLE CONTINUED ON NEXT PAGE

CROSS-TABULATION 12. 1.2: PERCENTAGE BREAKDOWN OF NUMBER (AS OF 1/1/68) OF
MANUFACTURING SUBSIDIARIES OF U.S.-BASED PARENT SYSTEMS BY
CATEGORY OF SUBSIDIARY'S PRINCIPAL OUTSIDE OWNER (IF ANY) AS OF 1/1/68
FOR SUBSIDIARIES CLASSIFIED BY
SUBSIDIARY'S COUNTRY
(CONTINUED)

| SUBSIDIARY'S COUNTRY | CATEGORY OF SUBSIDIARY'S PRINCIPAL OUTSIDE OWNER (IF ANY) AS OF 1/1/68 | | | | | |
	LOCAL PRIVATE	LOCAL STATE	FOREIGN PRIVATE	STOCK WIDELY DISPERSED	TOTAL PERCENT	TOTAL NUMBER
JAPAN..............	91.	0.	1.0	8.2	100.	97
CHINA (TAIWAN).....	60.	20.	0.	20.	100.	5
HONG KONG..........	0.	0.	0.	0.	100.	0
THE PHILIPPINES....	64.	0.	9.1	27.	100.	11
MALAYSIA...........	0.	0.	100.	0.	100.	3
SINGAPORE..........	0.	0.	0.	0.	100.	0
INDONESIA..........	0.	0.	0.	0.	100.	0
THAILAND...........	33.	0.	33.	33.	100.	6
INDIA..............	54.	5.7	8.6	31.	100.	35
OTHER ASIA AND OCEANIA.....	25.	25.	0.	50.	100.	4

CROSS-TABULATION 12.6.1: PERCENTAGE BREAKDOWN OF NUMBER (AS OF 1/1/71) OF MANUFACTURING SUBSIDIARIES OF NON-U.S.-BASED PARENT SYSTEMS BY CATEGORY OF SUBSIDIARY'S PRINCIPAL OUTSIDE OWNER (IF ANY) AS OF 1/1/71 FOR SUBSIDIARIES CLASSIFIED BY PRINCIPAL INDUSTRY OF SUBSIDIARY AS OF 1/1/71

PRINCIPAL INDUSTRY OF SUBSIDIARY AS OF 1/1/71	CATEGORY OF SUBSIDIARY'S PRINCIPAL OUTSIDE OWNER (IF ANY) AS OF 1/1/71					
	LOCAL PRIVATE	LOCAL STATE	FOREIGN PRIVATE	STOCK WIDELY DISPERSED	TOTAL PERCENT	TOTAL NUMBER
ORDNANCE	0.	0.	100.	0.	100.	2
MEAT PRODUCTS	45.	18.	36.	0.	100.	11
DAIRY PRODUCTS	75.	8.3	17.	0.	100.	12
CANNED FOODS	92.	0.	7.7	0.	100.	13
GRAIN MILL PRODUCTS	57.	0.	43.	0.	100.	7
BAKERY PRODUCTS	67.	0.	33.	0.	100.	3
CONFECTIONERY PRODUCTS	71.	14.	0.	14.	100.	7
BEVERAGES	85.	9.1	3.0	3.0	100.	33
OTHER FOOD PRODUCTS	59.	21.	21.	0.	100.	19
TOBACCO PRODUCTS	14.	9.1	64.	14.	100.	22
TEXTILES	53.	11.	31.	4.6	100.	109
APPAREL	76.	4.8	19.	0.	100.	21
LUMBER AND WOOD	73.	18.	9.1	0.	100.	11
FURNITURE	100.	0.	0.	0.	100.	1
PAPER PRODUCTS	71.	12.	16.	2.0	100.	51
PRINTED MATTER	59.	0.	34.	6.9	100.	29
INDUSTRIAL CHEMICALS	53.	10.	25.	12.	100.	68
PLASTICS AND SYNTHETICS	69.	4.1	24.	2.0	100.	49
DRUGS	73.	5.0	18.	5.0	100.	40
SOAP AND COSMETICS	60.	10.	20.	10.	100.	20
PAINTS	64.	0.	29.	7.1	100.	14
AGRICULTURAL CHEMICALS	40.	25.	30.	5.0	100.	20
OTHER CHEMICALS	62.	13.	17.	8.5	100.	47
REFINED PETROLEUM	11.	17.	62.	11.	100.	47
OTHER PETROLEUM PRODUCTS	61.	5.6	28.	5.6	100.	18

TABLE CONTINUED ON NEXT PAGE

CROSS-TABULATION 12. 6.1: PERCENTAGE BREAKDOWN OF NUMBER (AS OF 1/1/71) OF MANUFACTURING SUBSIDIARIES OF NON-U.S.-BASED PARENT SYSTEMS BY CATEGORY OF SUBSIDIARY'S PRINCIPAL OUTSIDE OWNER (IF ANY) AS OF 1/1/71 FOR SUBSIDIARIES CLASSIFIED BY PRINCIPAL INDUSTRY OF SUBSIDIARY AS OF 1/1/71 (CONTINUED)

PRINCIPAL INDUSTRY OF SUBSIDIARY AS OF 1/1/71	CATEGORY OF SUBSIDIARY'S PRINCIPAL OUTSIDE OWNER (IF ANY) AS OF 1/1/71					
	LOCAL PRIVATE	LOCAL STATE	FOREIGN PRIVATE	STOCK WIDELY DISPERSED	TOTAL PERCENT	TOTAL NUMBER
TIRES................	67.	33.	0.	0.	100.	6
OTHER RUBBER PRODUCTS.....	64.	0.	27.	9.1	100.	22
LEATHER PRODUCTS AND SHOES...	0.	0.	100.	0.	100.	1
GLASS PRODUCTS..........	67.	33.	0.	0.	100.	3
STONE, CLAY AND CONCRETE.....	80.	0.	10.	10.	100.	10
IRON AND STEEL PRODUCTS......	57.	11.	25.	7.7	100.	65
NON-FERROUS SMELTING.......	47.	11.	34.	7.9	100.	38
NON-FERROUS PRODUCTS.......	47.	5.3	42.	5.3	100.	38
METAL CANS............	17.	11.	17.	56.	100.	18
STRUCTURAL METAL PRODUCTS.....	67.	15.	11.	7.4	100.	27
FABRICATED WIRE PRODUCTS.....	63.	4.2	29.	4.2	100.	24
OTHER FABRICATED METAL......	53.	1.8	37.	8.8	100.	57
ENGINES AND TURBINES.......	67.	5.6	17.	11.	100.	18
FARM MACHINERY..........	54.	23.	23.	0.	100.	13
CONSTRUCTION MACHINERY......	63.	0.	38.	0.	100.	8
SPECIAL INDUSTRY MACHINERY...	72.	0.	22.	5.6	100.	18
GENERAL INDUSTRY MACHINERY..	57.	11.	32.	0.	100.	28
OFFICE MACHINES + COMPUTERS..	40.	0.	40.	20.	100.	5
OTHER NON-ELECTR. MACHINERY..	70.	0.	30.	0.	100.	10
ELECTR. TRANSMISSION EQUIP...	56.	25.	0.	19.	100.	16
ELECTRIC LIGHTING AND WIRING.	59.	18.	18.	5.9	100.	17
RADIOS, TV'S + APPLIANCES....	71.	9.5	12.	7.1	100.	42
COMMUNICATIONS EQUIPMENT.....	60.	25.	15.	0.	100.	20

TABLE CONTINUED ON NEXT PAGE

CROSS-TABULATION 12. 6.1: PERCENTAGE BREAKDOWN OF NUMBER (AS OF 1/1/71) OF
MANUFACTURING SUBSIDIARIES OF NON-U.S.-BASED PARENT SYSTEMS BY
CATEGORY OF SUBSIDIARY'S PRINCIPAL OUTSIDE OWNER (IF ANY) AS OF 1/1/71
FOR SUBSIDIARIES CLASSIFIED BY
PRINCIPAL INDUSTRY OF SUBSIDIARY AS OF 1/1/71
(CONTINUED)

PRINCIPAL INDUSTRY OF SUBSIDIARY AS OF 1/1/71	CATEGORY OF SUBSIDIARY'S PRINCIPAL OUTSIDE OWNER (IF ANY) AS OF 1/1/71					
	LOCAL PRIVATE	LOCAL STATE	FOREIGN PRIVATE	STOCK WIDELY DISPERSED	TOTAL PERCENT	TOTAL NUMBER
ELECTRONIC COMPONENTS........	79.	0.	21.	0.	100.	19
OTHER ELECTRICAL EQUIPMENT...	83.	2.9	11.	2.9	100.	35
MOTOR VEHICLES AND EQUIPMENT.	50.	13.	32.	5.3	100.	76
OTHER TRANSPORTATION.........	57.	14.	21.	7.1	100.	14
PRECISION GOODS..............	55.	0.	36.	9.1	100.	11
MISCELLANEOUS PRODUCTS.......	58.	0.	42.	0.	100.	19

CROSS-TABULATION 12.6.2: PERCENTAGE BREAKDOWN OF NUMBER (AS OF 1/1/68) OF MANUFACTURING SUBSIDIARIES OF U.S.-BASED PARENT SYSTEMS BY CATEGORY OF SUBSIDIARY'S PRINCIPAL OUTSIDE OWNER (IF ANY) AS OF 1/1/68 FOR SUBSIDIARIES CLASSIFIED BY PRINCIPAL INDUSTRY OF SUBSIDIARY AS OF 1/1/68

PRINCIPAL INDUSTRY OF SUBSIDIARY AS OF 1/1/68	CATEGORY OF SUBSIDIARY'S PRINCIPAL OUTSIDE OWNER (IF ANY) AS OF 1/1/68					
	LOCAL PRIVATE	LOCAL STATE	FOREIGN PRIVATE	STOCK WIDELY DISPERSED	TOTAL PERCENT	TOTAL NUMBER
ORDNANCE	50.	0.	17.	33.	100.	6
MEAT PRODUCTS	83.	0.	0.	17.	100.	6
DAIRY PRODUCTS	13.	6.3	31.	50.	100.	16
CANNED FOODS	30.	0.	30.	40.	100.	10
GRAIN MILL PRODUCTS	50.	0.	19.	31.	100.	26
BAKERY PRODUCTS	50.	0.	17.	33.	100.	6
CONFECTIONERY PRODUCTS	47.	0.	6.7	47.	100.	15
BEVERAGES	80.	0.	0.	20.	100.	5
OTHER FOOD PRODUCTS	64.	0.	9.1	27.	100.	11
TOBACCO PRODUCTS	0.	0.	0.	100.	100.	4
TEXTILES	82.	0.	14.	4.5	100.	22
APPAREL	83.	0.	0.	17.	100.	6
LUMBER AND WOOD	25.	0.	13.	63.	100.	8
FURNITURE	100.	0.	0.	0.	100.	2
PAPER PRODUCTS	53.	0.	16.	32.	100.	57
PRINTED MATTER	80.	0.	0.	20.	100.	5
INDUSTRIAL CHEMICALS	73.	1.1	5.4	21.	100.	92
PLASTICS AND SYNTHETICS	70.	0.	15.	15.	100.	61
DRUGS	52.	0.	16.	32.	100.	44
SOAP AND COSMETICS	50.	0.	25.	25.	100.	4
PAINTS	30.	0.	30.	40.	100.	10
AGRICULTURAL CHEMICALS	55.	0.	18.	27.	100.	11
OTHER CHEMICALS	54.	4.2	21.	21.	100.	24
REFINED PETROLEUM	53.	3.3	33.	10.	100.	30
OTHER PETROLEUM PRODUCTS	79.	8.3	13.	0.	100.	24

TABLE CONTINUED ON NEXT PAGE

CROSS-TABULATION 12. 6.2: PERCENTAGE BREAKDOWN OF NUMBER (AS OF 1/1/68) OF MANUFACTURING SUBSIDIARIES OF U.S.-BASED PARENT SYSTEMS BY CATEGORY OF SUBSIDIARY'S PRINCIPAL OUTSIDE OWNER (IF ANY) AS OF 1/1/68 FOR SUBSIDIARIES CLASSIFIED BY PRINCIPAL INDUSTRY OF SUBSIDIARY AS OF 1/1/68 (CONTINUED)

PRINCIPAL INDUSTRY OF SUBSIDIARY AS OF 1/1/68	CATEGORY OF SUBSIDIARY'S PRINCIPAL OUTSIDE OWNER (IF ANY) AS OF 1/1/68				TOTAL PERCENT	TOTAL NUMBER
	LOCAL PRIVATE	LOCAL STATE	FOREIGN PRIVATE	STOCK WIDELY DISPERSED		
TIRES........................	59.	0.	9.1	32.	100.	22
OTHER RUBBER PRODUCTS........	75.	0.	0.	25.	100.	12
LEATHER PRODUCTS AND SHOES...	50.	0.	0.	50.	100.	4
GLASS PRODUCTS...............	62.	0.	24.	14.	100.	21
STONE, CLAY AND CONCRETE.....	50.	11.	11.	28.	100.	18
IRON AND STEEL PRODUCTS......	25.	13.	25.	38.	100.	8
NON-FERROUS SMELTING.........	46.	4.2	42.	8.3	100.	24
NON-FERROUS PRODUCTS.........	60.	0.	13.	27.	100.	15
METAL CANS...................	25.	0.	25.	50.	100.	8
STRUCTURAL METAL PRODUCTS....	33.	0.	0.	67.	100.	9
FABRICATED WIRE PRODUCTS.....	38.	0.	25.	38.	100.	8
OTHER FABRICATED METAL.......	78.	0.	3.7	19.	100.	27
ENGINES AND TURBINES.........	75.	0.	0.	25.	100.	4
FARM MACHINERY...............	44.	11.	11.	33.	100.	9
CONSTRUCTION MACHINERY.......	67.	0.	0.	33.	100.	21
SPECIAL INDUSTRY MACHINERY...	47.	0.	33.	20.	100.	15
GENERAL INDUSTRY MACHINERY...	36.	0.	18.	45.	100.	11
OFFICE MACHINES + COMPUTERS..	57.	0.	14.	29.	100.	7
OTHER NON-ELECTR. MACHINERY..	67.	0.	22.	11.	100.	9
ELECTR. TRANSMISSION EQUIP...	100.	0.	0.	0.	100.	7
ELECTRIC LIGHTING AND WIRING.	33.	0.	33.	33.	100.	3
RADIOS, TV'S + APPLIANCES....	57.	0.	0.	43.	100.	7
COMMUNICATIONS EQUIPMENT.....	100.	0.	0.	0.	100.	1

TABLE CONTINUED CN NEXT PAGE

CROSS-TABULATION 12.6.2: PERCENTAGE BREAKDOWN OF NUMBER (AS OF 1/1/68) OF
MANUFACTURING SUBSIDIARIES OF U.S.-BASED PARENT SYSTEMS BY
CATEGORY OF SUBSIDIARY'S PRINCIPAL OUTSIDE OWNER (IF ANY) AS OF 1/1/68
FOR SUBSIDIARIES CLASSIFIED BY
PRINCIPAL INDUSTRY OF SUBSIDIARY AS OF 1/1/68
(CONTINUED)

PRINCIPAL INDUSTRY OF SUBSIDIARY AS OF 1/1/68	CATEGORY OF SUBSIDIARY'S PRINCIPAL OUTSIDE OWNER (IF ANY) AS OF 1/1/68					
	LOCAL PRIVATE	LOCAL STATE	FOREIGN PRIVATE	STOCK WIDELY DISPERSED	TOTAL PERCENT	TOTAL NUMBER
ELECTRONIC COMPONENTS........	91.	0.	0.	9.1	100.	11
OTHER ELECTRICAL EQUIPMENT...	73.	0.	4.5	23.	100.	22
MOTOR VEHICLES AND EQUIPMENT.	49.	0.	15.	36.	100.	72
OTHER TRANSPORTATION.........	25.	13.	0.	63.	100.	8
PRECISION GOODS.............	100.	0.	0.	0.	100.	4
MISCELLANEOUS PRODUCTS.......	67.	0.	0.	33.	100.	6

325

CROSS-TABULATION 12.15.1: PERCENTAGE BREAKDOWN OF NUMBER (AS OF 1/1/71) OF
MANUFACTURING SUBSIDIARIES OF NON-U.S.-BASED PARENT SYSTEMS BY
CATEGORY OF SUBSIDIARY'S PRINCIPAL OUTSIDE OWNER (IF ANY) AS OF 1/1/71
FOR SUBSIDIARIES CLASSIFIED BY
SUBSIDIARY'S PRINCIPAL MARKET AS OF 1/1/71

SUBSIDIARY'S PRINCIPAL MARKET AS OF 1/1/71	CATEGORY OF SUBSIDIARY'S PRINCIPAL OUTSIDE OWNER (IF ANY) AS OF 1/1/71					
	LOCAL PRIVATE	LOCAL STATE	FOREIGN PRIVATE	STOCK WIDELY DISPERSED	TOTAL PERCENT	TOTAL NUMBER
LOCAL COUNTRY............	59.	8.9	24.	7.8	100.	1103
EXPORT MARKETS..........	61.	7.4	31.	0.7	100.	148

CROSS-TABULATION 12.16.1: PERCENTAGE BREAKDOWN OF NUMBER (AS OF 1/1/71) OF
MANUFACTURING SUBSIDIARIES OF NON-U.S.-BASED PARENT SYSTEMS BY
CATEGORY OF SUBSIDIARY'S PRINCIPAL OUTSIDE OWNER (IF ANY) AS OF 1/1/71
FOR SUBSIDIARIES CLASSIFIED BY
SUBSIDIARY'S PRINCIPAL CUSTOMER AS OF 1/1/71

SUBSIDIARY'S PRINCIPAL CUSTOMER AS OF 1/1/71	CATEGORY OF SUBSIDIARY'S PRINCIPAL OUTSIDE OWNER (IF ANY) AS OF 1/1/71					
	LOCAL PRIVATE	LOCAL STATE	FOREIGN PRIVATE	STOCK WIDELY DISPERSED	TOTAL PERCENT	TOTAL NUMBER
PARENT SYSTEM............	57.	11.	28.	4.2	100.	120
OUTSIDE CUSTOMERS........	59.	8.9	25.	7.2	100.	1119

CROSS-TABULATION 12.18.1: PERCENTAGE BREAKDOWN OF NUMBER (AS OF 1/1/71) OF
MANUFACTURING SUBSIDIARIES OF NON-U.S.-BASED PARENT SYSTEMS BY
CATEGORY OF SUBSIDIARY'S PRINCIPAL OUTSIDE OWNER (IF ANY) AS OF 1/1/71
FOR SUBSIDIARIES CLASSIFIED BY
VALUE OF SUBSIDIARY'S SALES IN 1970

VALUE OF SUBSIDIARY'S SALES AS OF 1/1/71	CATEGORY OF SUBSIDIARY'S PRINCIPAL OUTSIDE OWNER (IF ANY) AS OF 1/1/71					
	LOCAL PRIVATE	LOCAL STATE	FOREIGN PRIVATE	STOCK WIDELY DISPERSED	TOTAL PERCENT	TOTAL NUMBER
UNDER $1 MILLION..........	69.	6.7	21.	2.8	100.	252
$1 - $10 MILLION..........	63.	7.7	26.	4.0	100.	521
$10 - $25 MILLION.........	56.	11.	23.	9.8	100.	163
$25 - $100 MILLION........	50.	8.5	24.	18.	100.	117
OVER $100 MILLION.........	33.	2.0	35.	31.	100.	49

328

CROSS-TABULATION 12.21.1: PERCENTAGE BREAKDOWN OF NUMBER (AS OF 1/1/71) OF
MANUFACTURING SUBSIDIARIES OF NON-U.S.-BASED PARENT SYSTEMS BY
CATEGORY OF SUBSIDIARY'S PRINCIPAL OUTSIDE OWNER (IF ANY) AS OF 1/1/71
FOR SUBSIDIARIES CLASSIFIED BY
NATIONAL BASE OF SUBSIDIARY'S PARENT SYSTEM

NATIONAL BASE OF SUBSIDIARY'S PARENT SYSTEM	CATEGORY OF SUBSIDIARY'S PRINCIPAL OUTSIDE OWNER (IF ANY) AS OF 1/1/71					
	LOCAL PRIVATE	LOCAL STATE	FOREIGN PRIVATE	STOCK WIDELY DISPERSED	TOTAL PERCENT	TOTAL NUMBER
UNITED KINGDOM.............	56.	8.4	27.	8.6	100.	498
GERMANY...................	70.	8.0	19.	3.2	100.	187
FRANCE....................	37.	20.	37.	6.2	100.	81
ITALY.....................	50.	27.	20.	3.3	100.	30
BELGIUM AND LUXEMBURG.....	42.	3.0	39.	15.	100.	33
THE NETHERLANDS...........	58.	6.6	22.	13.	100.	91
SWEDEN....................	51.	20.	20.	8.6	100.	35
SWITZERLAND...............	72.	3.8	21.	3.8	100.	53
JAPAN.....................	62.	8.8	28.	1.1	100.	362
CANADA....................	49.	15.	24.	12.	100.	75
OTHER NON-U.S.............	50.	0.	20.	30.	100.	10

CROSS-TABULATION 12.26.1: PERCENTAGE BREAKDOWN OF NUMBER (AS OF 1/1/71) OF
MANUFACTURING SUBSIDIARIES OF NON-U.S.-BASED PARENT SYSTEMS BY
CATEGORY OF SUBSIDIARY'S PRINCIPAL OUTSIDE OWNER (IF ANY) AS OF 1/1/71
FOR SUBSIDIARIES CLASSIFIED BY
PERCENTAGE OF PARENT SYSTEM'S EMPLOYEES OUTSIDE NATIONAL BASE AS OF 1/1/71

PERCENTAGE OF PARENT SYSTEM'S EMPLOYEES OUTSIDE NATIONAL BASE AS OF 1/1/71	CATEGORY OF SUBSIDIARY'S PRINCIPAL OUTSIDE OWNER (IF ANY) AS OF 1/1/71					
	LOCAL PRIVATE	LOCAL STATE	FOREIGN PRIVATE	STOCK WIDELY DISPERSED	TOTAL PERCENT	TOTAL NUMBER
UNDER 10%.............	63.	11.	23.	3.1	100.	194
10% - 25%.............	66.	8.2	18.	7.4	100.	364
25% - 50%.............	62.	6.3	24.	8.4	100.	239
OVER 50%.............	47.	12.	31.	9.7	100.	352

TABULATION 13.1: PERCENTAGE BREAKDOWN OF NUMBER OF SUBSIDIARIES BY
SUBSIDIARY'S METHOD OF ENTRY INTO PARENT SYSTEM
FOR VARIOUS CATEGORIES OF SUBSIDIARIES

CATEGORY OF SUBSIDIARY	SUBSIDIARY'S METHOD OF ENTRY INTO PARENT SYSTEM					
	NEWLY FORMED	REORGAN- IZATION	ACQUIRED DIRECTLY	ACQUIRED THRU AC- QUISITION	TOTAL PERCENT	TOTAL NUMBER
NON-U.S.-BASED SYSTEMS:						
ALL SUBSIDIARIES........	48.	4.2	22.	26.	100.	12690
MANUFACTURING SUBS......	41.	4.7	29.	26.	100.	5628
SALES SUBSIDIARIES......	60.	4.3	13.	23.	100.	3480
U.S.-BASED SYSTEMS:						
ALL SUBSIDIARIES........	58.	1.3	41.	*	100.	9119
MANUFACTURING SUBS......	49.	1.9	49.	*	100.	4512
SALES SUBSIDIARIES......	71.	0.8	28.	*	100.	2007
WORLD SUBSET OF SYSTEMS:						
NON-U.S.-BASED SYSTEMS:						
ALL SUBSIDIARIES........	54.	4.7	20.	21.	100.	6136
MANUFACTURING SUBS......	46.	5.2	27.	22.	100.	2761
SALES SUBSIDIARIES......	63.	5.1	12.	20.	100.	1816
U.S.-BASED SYSTEMS:						
ALL SUBSIDIARIES........	58.	1.3	41.	*	100.	7363
MANUFACTURING SUBS......	49.	1.7	49.	*	100.	3511
SALES SUBSIDIARIES......	72.	0.9	27.	*	100.	1537

*FOR SUBSIDIARIES OF U.S.-BASED SYSTEMS, 'ACQUIRED DIRECTLY' INCLUDES 'ACQUIRED THRU ACQUISITION'

CROSS-TABULATION 13. 1.1: PERCENTAGE BREAKDOWN OF NUMBER OF
MANUFACTURING SUBSIDIARIES OF NON-U.S.-BASED PARENT SYSTEMS BY
SUBSIDIARY'S METHOD OF ENTRY INTO PARENT SYSTEM
FOR SUBSIDIARIES CLASSIFIED BY
SUBSIDIARY'S COUNTRY

SUBSIDIARY'S COUNTRY	SUBSIDIARY'S METHOD OF ENTRY INTO PARENT SYSTEM					
	NEWLY FORMED	REORGAN- IZATION	ACQUIRED DIRECTLY	ACQUIRED THRU AC- QUISITION	TOTAL PERCENT	TOTAL NUMBER
UNITED STATES.........	26.	5.1	44.	25.	100.	450
CANADA................	26.	4.4	34.	36.	100.	315
MEXICO................	62.	1.2	16.	21.	100.	86
CENTRAL AMERICA AND CARIB....	68.	0.	24.	8.3	100.	84
VENEZUELA.............	69.	0.	23.	8.6	100.	35
COLOMBIA..............	68.	0.	25.	7.1	100.	28
PERU..................	74.	0.	26.	0.	100.	27
CHILE.................	61.	3.6	29.	7.1	100.	28
ARGENTINA.............	48.	7.0	22.	23.	100.	100
BRAZIL................	51.	5.4	21.	23.	100.	168
OTHER SOUTH AMERICA...	65.	0.	10.	25.	100.	20
GERMANY...............	32.	7.7	34.	26.	100.	312
FRANCE................	21.	5.3	29.	44.	100.	433
ITALY.................	39.	4.8	28.	28.	100.	188
BELGIUM AND LUXEMBURG.	43.	4.6	24.	29.	100.	152
THE NETHERLANDS.......	28.	1.5	43.	28.	100.	137
UNITED KINGDOM........	30.	7.4	35.	28.	100.	337
IRELAND...............	30.	3.4	18.	49.	100.	88
DENMARK...............	38.	6.4	32.	23.	100.	47
NORWAY................	27.	8.9	44.	20.	100.	45
SWEDEN................	25.	6.6	46.	23.	100.	61
FINLAND...............	55.	0.	27.	18.	100.	22

TABLE CONTINUED ON NEXT PAGE

CROSS-TABULATION 13.1.1: PERCENTAGE BREAKDOWN OF NUMBER OF
MANUFACTURING SUBSIDIARIES OF NON-U.S.-BASED PARENT SYSTEMS BY
SUBSIDIARY'S METHOD OF ENTRY INTO PARENT SYSTEM
FOR SUBSIDIARIES CLASSIFIED BY
SUBSIDIARY'S COUNTRY
(CONTINUED)

SUBSIDIARY'S COUNTRY	SUBSIDIARY'S METHOD OF ENTRY INTO PARENT SYSTEM					
	NEWLY FORMED	REORGAN-IZATION	ACQUIRED DIRECTLY	ACQUIRED THRU AC-QUISITION	TOTAL PERCENT	TOTAL NUMBER
SWITZERLAND	38.	5.4	30.	27.	100.	56
AUSTRIA	37.	10.	29.	24.	100.	105
PORTUGAL	51.	4.7	16.	28.	100.	43
SPAIN	43.	4.7	29.	23.	100.	191
GREECE	54.	14.	18.	14.	100.	28
TURKEY	72.	6.3	19.	3.1	100.	32
OTHER EUROPE + ISRAEL	70.	3.0	26.	1.0	100.	101
PAKISTAN	70.	0.	12.	18.	100.	33
IRAN	76.	0.	9.5	14.	100.	21
OTHER MID EAST+EGYPT+LIBYA	75.	8.3	8.3	8.3	100.	24
UNION OF SOUTH AFRICA	28.	5.3	38.	29.	100.	318
RHODESIA	42.	3.8	15.	38.	100.	52
ZAMBIA	25.	5.6	19.	50.	100.	36
TANZANIA	59.	9.1	4.5	27.	100.	22
KENYA	48.	2.5	20.	30.	100.	40
NIGERIA	63.	0.	5.6	31.	100.	54
OTHER (BRITISH) AFRICA	74.	4.3	6.5	15.	100.	46
MOROCCO, ALGERIA + TUNISIA	75.	0.	7.5	18.	100.	40
OTHER (FRENCH) AFRICA	66.	0.	13.	21.	100.	38
OTHER AFRICA	73.	3.3	13.	10.	100.	30
AUSTRALIA	23.	6.6	41.	30.	100.	422
NEW ZEALAND	43.	3.3	29.	25.	100.	91

TABLE CONTINUED ON NEXT PAGE

CROSS-TABULATION 13. 1.1: PERCENTAGE-BREAKDOWN OF NUMBER OF
MANUFACTURING SUBSIDIARIES OF NON-U.S.-BASED PARENT SYSTEMS BY
SUBSIDIARY'S METHOD OF ENTRY INTO PARENT SYSTEM
FOR SUBSIDIARIES CLASSIFIED BY
SUBSIDIARY'S COUNTRY
(CONTINUED)

SUBSIDIARY'S METHOD OF ENTRY INTO PARENT SYSTEM

SUBSIDIARY'S COUNTRY	NEWLY FORMED	REORGAN- IZATION	ACQUIRED DIRECTLY	ACQUIRED THRU AC- QUISITION	TOTAL PERCENT	TOTAL NUMBER
JAPAN................	52.	0.	10.	38.	100.	77
CHINA (TAIWAN).......	84.	0.9	9.7	5.3	100.	113
HONG KONG............	81.	0.	12.	7.7	100.	26
THE PHILIPPINES......	64.	0.	32.	4.5	100.	22
MALAYSIA.............	78.	4.0	4.0	14.	100.	50
SINGAPORE............	72.	2.1	17.	8.5	100.	47
INDONESIA............	100.	0.	0.	0.	100.	26
THAILAND.............	95.	0.	3.1	1.5	100.	65
INDIA................	61.	4.3	13.	21.	100.	141
OTHER ASIA AND OCEANIA.......	66.	1.5	19.	13.	100.	68

CROSS-TABULATION 13. 1.2: PERCENTAGE BREAKDOWN OF NUMBER OF
MANUFACTURING SUBSIDIARIES OF U.S.-BASED PARENT SYSTEMS BY
SUBSIDIARY'S METHOD OF ENTRY INTO PARENT SYSTEM
FOR SUBSIDIARIES CLASSIFIED BY
SUBSIDIARY'S COUNTRY

SUBSIDIARY'S COUNTRY	SUBSIDIARY'S METHOD OF ENTRY INTO PARENT SYSTEM					
	NEWLY FORMED	REORGAN-IZATION	ACQUIRED DIRECTLY	ACQUIRED THRU AC-QUISITION	TOTAL PERCENT	TOTAL NUMBER
UNITED STATES	0.	0.	0.	0.	100.	0
CANADA	35.	2.8	62.	0.	100.	703
MEXICO	50.	1.3	48.	0.	100.	320
CENTRAL AMERICA AND CARIB.	59.	4.8	36.	0.	100.	165
VENEZUELA	74.	0.8	26.	0.	100.	129
COLOMBIA	57.	0.9	42.	0.	100.	109
PERU	64.	0.	36.	0.	100.	50
CHILE	58.	0.	42.	0.	100.	38
ARGENTINA	50.	2.8	47.	0.	100.	145
BRAZIL	58.	1.6	41.	0.	100.	184
OTHER SOUTH AMERICA	63.	0.	37.	0.	100.	38
GERMANY	42.	2.3	56.	0.	100.	259
FRANCE	39.	3.5	57.	0.	100.	286
ITALY	50.	0.5	50.	0.	100.	200
BELGIUM AND LUXEMBURG	49.	0.	51.	0.	100.	103
THE NETHERLANDS	53.	1.1	46.	0.	100.	91
UNITED KINGDOM	35.	3.3	62.	0.	100.	452
IRELAND	45.	3.2	52.	0.	100.	31
DENMARK	48.	0.	52.	0.	100.	29
NORWAY	50.	0.	50.	0.	100.	18
SWEDEN	62.	0.	38.	0.	100.	39
FINLAND	60.	0.	40.	0.	100.	5

TABLE CONTINUED ON NEXT PAGE

CROSS-TABULATION 13. 1.2: PERCENTAGE BREAKDOWN OF NUMBER OF
MANUFACTURING SUBSIDIARIES OF U.S.-BASED PARENT SYSTEMS BY
SUBSIDIARY'S METHOD OF ENTRY INTO PARENT SYSTEM
FOR SUBSIDIARIES CLASSIFIED BY
SUBSIDIARY'S COUNTRY
(CONTINUED)

SUBSIDIARY'S COUNTRY	SUBSIDIARY'S METHOD OF ENTRY INTO PARENT SYSTEM					
	NEWLY FORMED	REORGAN-IZATION	ACQUIRED DIRECTLY	ACQUIRED THRU AC-QUISITION	TOTAL PERCENT	TOTAL NUMBER
SWITZERLAND	48.	0.	52.	0.	100.	25
AUSTRIA	59.	0.	41.	0.	100.	22
PORTUGAL	81.	0.	19.	0.	100.	21
SPAIN	43.	0.8	57.	0.	100.	129
GREECE	78.	0.	22.	0.	100.	23
TURKEY	86.	0.	14.	0.	100.	14
OTHER EUROPE + ISRAEL	71.	0.	29.	0.	100.	24
PAKISTAN	73.	0.	27.	0.	100.	15
IRAN	94.	0.	6.3	0.	100.	16
OTHER MID EAST+EGYPT+LIBY	75.	0.	25.	0.	100.	20
UNION OF SOUTH AFRICA	52.	0.8	47.	0.	100.	126
RHODESIA	40.	0.	60.	0.	100.	10
ZAMBIA	67.	0.	33.	0.	100.	6
TANZANIA	0.	0.	0.	0.	100.	0
KENYA	86.	0.	14.	0.	100.	7
NIGERIA	55.	0.	45.	0.	100.	11
OTHER (BRITISH) AFRICA	71.	0.	29.	0.	100.	7
MOROCCO, ALGERIA + TUNISIA	82.	0.	18.	0.	100.	17
OTHER (FRENCH) AFRICA	67.	0.	33.	0.	100.	6
OTHER AFRICA	50.	0.	50.	0.	100.	2
AUSTRALIA	47.	2.1	50.	0.	100.	236
NEW ZEALAND	68.	2.3	30.	0.	100.	44

TABLE CONTINUED ON NEXT PAGE

CROSS-TABULATION 13. 1.2: PERCENTAGE BREAKDOWN OF NUMBER OF
MANUFACTURING SUBSIDIARIES OF U.S.-BASED PARENT SYSTEMS BY
SUBSIDIARY'S METHOD OF ENTRY INTO PARENT SYSTEM
FOR SUBSIDIARIES CLASSIFIED BY
SUBSIDIARY'S COUNTRY
(CONTINUED)

SUBSIDIARY'S COUNTRY	SUBSIDIARY'S METHOD OF ENTRY INTO PARENT SYSTEM					
	NEWLY FORMED	REORGAN-IZATION	ACQUIRED DIRECTLY	ACQUIRED THRU AC-QUISITION	TOTAL PERCENT	TOTAL NUMBER
JAPAN..........	64.	0.7	35.	0.	100.	142
CHINA (TAIWAN)....	88.	0.	13.	0.	100.	16
HONG KONG........	30.	0.	70.	0.	100.	10
THE PHILIPPINES...	67.	2.0	31.	0.	100.	51
MALAYSIA.........	71.	0.	29.	0.	100.	14
SINGAPORE........	67.	0.	33.	0.	100.	9
INDONESIA........	67.	0.	33.	0.	100.	3
THAILAND........	85.	0.	15.	0.	100.	13
INDIA..........	66.	0.	34.	0.	100.	62
OTHER ASIA AND OCEANIA......	76.	0.	24.	0.	100.	17

CROSS-TABULATION 13. 3. 1: PERCENTAGE BREAKDOWN OF NUMBER OF
MANUFACTURING SUBSIDIARIES OF NON-U.S.-BASED PARENT SYSTEMS BY
SUBSIDIARY'S METHOD OF ENTRY INTO PARENT SYSTEM
FOR SUBSIDIARIES CLASSIFIED BY
GNP PER CAPITA IN 1970 OF SUBSIDIARY'S COUNTRY

GNP PER CAPITA IN 1970 OF SUBSIDIARY'S COUNTRY	SUBSIDIARY'S METHOD OF ENTRY INTO PARENT SYSTEM					
	NEWLY FORMED	REORGAN-IZATION	ACQUIRED DIRECTLY	ACQUIRED THRU AC-QUISITION	TOTAL PERCENT	TOTAL NUMBER
UNDER $200...........	59.	2.1	9.4	19.	100.	477
$200 - $500.........	64.	3.0	17.	16.	100.	670
$500 - $1200........	47.	4.3	28.	22.	100.	967
$1200 - $2500.......	36.	5.0	30.	29.	100.	1053
OVER $2500..........	27.	5.8	36.	31.	100.	2293

CROSS-TABULATION 13.3.2: PERCENTAGE BREAKDOWN OF NUMBER OF
MANUFACTURING SUBSIDIARIES OF U.S.-BASED PARENT SYSTEMS BY
SUBSIDIARY'S METHOD OF ENTRY INTO PARENT SYSTEM
FOR SUBSIDIARIES CLASSIFIED BY
GNP PER CAPITA IN 1970 OF SUBSIDIARY'S COUNTRY

SUBSIDIARY'S METHOD OF ENTRY INTO PARENT SYSTEM

GNP PER CAPITA IN 1970 OF SUBSIDIARY'S COUNTRY	NEWLY FORMED	REORGAN- IZATION	ACQUIRED DIRECTLY	ACQUIRED THRU AC- QUISITION	TOTAL PERCENT	TOTAL NUMBER
UNDER $200............	55.	1.1	44.	0.	100.	444
$200 - $500...........	62.	1.5	37.	0.	100.	610
$500 - $1200..........	57.	1.0	42.	0.	100.	700
$1200 - $2500.........	47.	2.0	51.	0.	100.	1006
OVER $2500............	40.	2.5	57.	0.	100.	1673

CROSS-TABULATION 13. 4.1: PERCENTAGE BREAKDOWN OF NUMBER OF
MANUFACTURING SUBSIDIARIES OF NON-U.S.-BASED PARENT SYSTEMS BY
SUBSIDIARY'S METHOD OF ENTRY INTO PARENT SYSTEM
FOR SUBSIDIARIES CLASSIFIED BY
GNP IN 1970 OF SUBSIDIARY'S COUNTRY

	SUBSIDIARY'S METHOD OF ENTRY INTO PARENT SYSTEM					
GNP IN 1970 OF SUBSIDIARY'S COUNTRY	NEWLY FORMED	REORGAN- IZATION	ACQUIRED DIRECTLY	ACQUIRED THRU AC- QUISITION	TOTAL PERCENT	TOTAL NUMBER
UNDER $1 BILLION.............	63.	2.1	13.	23.	100.	96
$1 - $5 BILLION.............	59.	2.7	14.	25.	100.	561
$5 - $20 BILLION.............	52.	4.1	26.	19.	100.	1247
$20 - $100 BILLION...........	37.	4.9	31.	27.	100.	1947
OVER $100 BILLION............	28.	5.9	35.	32.	100.	1609

CROSS-TABULATION 13. 4.2: PERCENTAGE BREAKDOWN OF NUMBER OF
MANUFACTURING SUBSIDIARIES OF U.S.-BASED PARENT SYSTEMS BY
SUBSIDIARY'S METHOD OF ENTRY INTO PARENT SYSTEM
FOR SUBSIDIARIES CLASSIFIED BY
GNP IN 1970 OF SUBSIDIARY'S COUNTRY

	SUBSIDIARY'S METHOD OF ENTRY INTO PARENT SYSTEM					
GNP IN 1970 OF SUBSIDIARY'S COUNTRY	NEWLY FORMED	REORGAN-IZATION	ACQUIRED DIRECTLY	ACQUIRED THRU AC-QUISITION	TOTAL PERCENT	TOTAL NUMBER
UNDER $1 BILLION............	63.	1.9	35.	0.	100.	104
$1 - $5 BILLION............	60.	2.0	38.	0.	100.	251
$5 - $20 BILLION............	64.	0.6	36.	0.	100.	718
$20 - $100 BILLION............	46.	1.8	52.	0.	100.	2222
OVER $100 BILLION............	41.	2.8	56.	0.	100.	1139

CROSS-TABULATION 13.5.1: PERCENTAGE BREAKDOWN OF NUMBER OF
MANUFACTURING SUBSIDIARIES OF NON-U.S.-BASED PARENT SYSTEMS BY
SUBSIDIARY'S METHOD OF ENTRY INTO PARENT SYSTEM
FOR SUBSIDIARIES CLASSIFIED BY
PRINCIPAL INDUSTRY OF SUBSIDIARY AT DATE OF ENTRY

PRINCIPAL INDUSTRY OF SUBSIDIARY AT DATE OF ENTRY	SUBSIDIARY'S METHOD OF ENTR. INTO PARENT SYSTEM				TOTAL PERCENT	TOTAL NUMBER
	NEWLY FORMED	REORGAN-IZATION	ACQUIRED DIRECTLY	ACQUIRED THRU AC-QUISITION		
ORDNANCE	26.	5.3	53.	16.	100.	19
MEAT PRODUCTS	59.	11.	22.	8.1	100.	37
DAIRY PRODUCTS	21.	6.6	66.	6.6	100.	106
CANNED FOODS	35.	2.1	40.	23.	100.	48
GRAIN MILL PRODUCTS	7.9	5.3	76.	11.	100.	38
BAKERY PRODUCTS	7.7	0.	91.	1.5	100.	65
CONFECTIONERY PRODUCTS	41.	10.	24.	24.	100.	29
BEVERAGES	29.	3.1	44.	24.	100.	161
OTHER FOOD PRODUCTS	35.	2.5	30.	32.	100.	161
TOBACCO PRODUCTS	81.	1.7	14.	3.4	100.	58
TEXTILES	65.	4.2	19.	11.	100.	236
APPAREL	61.	0.	17.	22.	100.	36
LUMBER AND WOOD	45.	0.	40.	15.	100.	47
FURNITURE	13.	0.	40.	47.	100.	15
PAPER PRODUCTS	26.	3.2	44.	26.	100.	156
PRINTED MATTER	22.	2.1	28.	48.	100.	96
INDUSTRIAL CHEMICALS	51.	4.1	27.	18.	100.	242
PLASTICS AND SYNTHETICS	50.	1.6	24.	24.	100.	129
DRUGS	52.	3.6	19.	26.	100.	192
SOAP AND COSMETICS	41.	2.9	23.	33.	100.	172
PAINTS	15.	1.8	17.	67.	100.	114
AGRICULTURAL CHEMICALS	48.	1.4	35.	16.	100.	69
OTHER CHEMICALS	39.	5.7	27.	28.	100.	158
REFINED PETROLEUM	58.	5.0	29.	8.8	100.	80
OTHER, PETROLEUM PRODUCTS	33.	2.7	24.	40.	100.	75

TABLE CONTINUED ON NEXT PAGE

CROSS-TABULATION 13.5.1: PERCENTAGE BREAKDOWN OF NUMBER OF MANUFACTURING SUBSIDIARIES OF NON-U.S.-BASED PARENT SYSTEMS BY SUBSIDIARY'S METHOD OF ENTRY INTO PARENT SYSTEM FOR SUBSIDIARIES CLASSIFIED BY PRINCIPAL INDUSTRY OF SUBSIDIARY AT DATE OF ENTRY (CONTINUED)

PRINCIPAL INDUSTRY OF SUBSIDIARY AT DATE OF ENTRY	SUBSIDIARY'S METHOD OF ENTRY INTO PARENT SYSTEM					
	NEWLY FORMED	REORGAN- IZATION	ACQUIRED DIRECTLY	ACQUIRED THRU AC- QUISITION	TOTAL PERCENT	TOTAL NUMBER
TIRES...................	72.	9.4	16.	3.1	100.	32
OTHER RUBBER PRODUCTS....	45.	3.9	27.	23.	100.	77
LEATHER PRODUCTS AND SHOES...	14.	14.	29.	43.	100.	7
GLASS PRODUCTS...........	38.	14.	8.1	41.	100.	37
STONE, CLAY AND CONCRETE....	33.	1.4	24.	42.	100.	72
IRON AND STEEL PRODUCTS....	45.	4.8	27.	23.	100.	168
NON-FERROUS SMELTING.....	40.	6.5	33.	20.	100.	93
NON-FERROUS PRODUCTS.....	31.	6.5	28.	35.	100.	124
METAL CANS...............	51.	5.4	32.	11.	100.	37
STRUCTURAL METAL PRODUCTS....	43.	4.8	27.	25.	100.	63
FABRICATED WIRE PRODUCTS....	56.	6.3	31.	6.3	100.	48
OTHER FABRICATED METAL....	42.	5.3	26.	27.	100.	190
ENGINES AND TURBINES.....	36.	9.1	20.	35.	100.	55
FARM MACHINERY...........	51.	2.3	40.	7.0	100.	43
CONSTRUCTION MACHINERY....	24.	4.8	33.	38.	100.	21
SPECIAL INDUSTRY MACHINERY...	19.	6.5	32.	42.	100.	77
GENERAL INDUSTRY MACHINERY...	24.	6.3	42.	28.	100.	79
OFFICE MACHINES + COMPUTERS...	46.	0.	39.	14.	100.	28
OTHER NON-ELECTR. MACHINERY...	48.	4.0	24.	24.	100.	25
ELECTR. TRANSMISSION EQUIP...	40.	12.	29.	19.	100.	142
ELECTRIC LIGHTING AND WIRING.	67.	6.9	16.	9.5	100.	116
RADIOS, TV'S + APPLIANCES....	50.	5.7	23.	21.	100.	141
COMMUNICATIONS EQUIPMENT.....	34.	10.	34.	23.	100.	110

TABLE CONTINUED ON NEXT PAGE

CROSS-TABULATION 13.5.1: PERCENTAGE BREAKDOWN OF NUMBER OF
MANUFACTURING SUBSIDIARIES OF NON-U.S.-BASED PARENT SYSTEMS BY
SUBSIDIARY'S METHOD OF ENTRY INTO PARENT SYSTEM
FOR SUBSIDIARIES CLASSIFIED BY
PRINCIPAL INDUSTRY OF SUBSIDIARY AT DATE OF ENTRY
(CONTINUED)

SUBSIDIARY'S METHOD OF ENTRY INTO PARENT SYSTEM

PRINCIPAL INDUSTRY OF SUBSIDIARY AT DATE OF ENTRY	NEWLY FORMED	REORGAN- IZATION	ACQUIRED DIRECTLY	ACQUIRED THRU AC- QUISITION	TOTAL PERCENT	TOTAL NUMBER
ELECTRONIC COMPONENTS........	43.	1.1	16.	40.	100.	91
OTHER ELECTRICAL EQUIPMENT...	33.	7.4	24.	35.	100.	203
MOTOR VEHICLES AND EQUIPMENT.	59.	4.0	23.	14.	100.	201
OTHER TRANSPORTATION.........	47.	3.7	21.	28.	100.	81
PRECISION GOODS.............	18.	4.7	38.	40.	100.	85
MISCELLANEOUS PRODUCTS.......	22.	1.4	31.	46.	100.	72

CROSS-TABULATION 13.5.2: PERCENTAGE BREAKDOWN OF NUMBER OF
MANUFACTURING SUBSIDIARIES OF U.S.-BASED PARENT SYSTEMS BY
SUBSIDIARY'S METHOD OF ENTRY INTO PARENT SYSTEM
FOR SUBSIDIARIES CLASSIFIED BY
PRINCIPAL INDUSTRY OF SUBSIDIARY AT DATE OF ENTRY

PRINCIPAL INDUSTRY OF SUBSIDIARY AT DATE OF ENTRY	SUBSIDIARY'S METHOD OF ENTRY INTO PARENT SYSTEM					
	NEWLY FORMED	REORGANIZATION	ACQUIRED DIRECTLY	ACQUIRED THRU ACQUISITION	TOTAL PERCENT	TOTAL NUMBER
ORDNANCE................	77.	0.	23.	0.	100.	13
MEAT PRODUCTS...........	28.	1.5	70.	0.	100.	67
DAIRY PRODUCTS..........	43.	1.6	55.	0.	100.	127
CANNED FOODS............	27.	3.0	70.	0.	100.	66
GRAIN MILL PRODUCTS.....	37.	0.9	62.	0.	100.	113
BAKERY PRODUCTS.........	28.	0.	72.	0.	100.	53
CONFECTIONERY PRODUCTS..	34.	2.4	63.	0.	100.	82
BEVERAGES...............	47.	0.7	53.	0.	100.	76
OTHER FOOD PRODUCTS.....	30.	2.7	68.	0.	100.	74
TOBACCO PRODUCTS........	23.	0.	77.	0.	100.	13
TEXTILES................	63.	0.	37.	0.	100.	87
APPAREL.................	73.	0.8	27.	0.	100.	26
LUMBER AND WOOD.........	29.	4.8	67.	0.	100.	21
FURNITURE...............	43.	0.	57.	0.	100.	14
PAPER PRODUCTS..........	30.	0.5	70.	0.	100.	205
PRINTED MATTER..........	44.	2.9	53.	0.	100.	34
INDUSTRIAL CHEMICALS....	61.	1.5	37.	0.	100.	269
PLASTICS AND SYNTHETICS.	61.	2.1	37.	0.	100.	188
DRUGS...................	66.	1.2	33.	0.	100.	326
SOAP AND COSMETICS......	58.	0.	42.	0.	100.	170
PAINTS..................	33.	0.	67.	0.	100.	45
AGRICULTURAL CHEMICALS..	67.	0.	33.	0.	100.	52
OTHER CHEMICALS.........	50.	5.9	44.	0.	100.	102
REFINED PETROLEUM.......	67.	0.8	33.	0.	100.	123
OTHER PETROLEUM PRODUCTS.	72.	1.5	26.	0.	100.	68

TABLE CONTINUED ON NEXT PAGE

CROSS-TABULATION 13.5.2: PERCENTAGE BREAKDOWN OF NUMBER OF
MANUFACTURING SUBSIDIARIES OF U.S.-BASED PARENT SYSTEMS BY
SUBSIDIARY'S METHOD OF ENTRY INTO PARENT SYSTEM
FOR SUBSIDIARIES CLASSIFIED BY
PRINCIPAL INDUSTRY OF SUBSIDIARY AT DATE OF ENTRY
(CONTINUED)

SUBSIDIARY'S METHOD OF ENTRY INTO PARENT SYSTEM

PRINCIPAL INDUSTRY OF SUBSIDIARY AT DATE OF ENTRY	NEWLY FORMED	REORGAN- IZATION	ACQUIRED DIRECTLY	ACQUIRED THRU AC- QUISITION	TOTAL PERCENT	TOTAL NUMBER
TIRES..................	68.	2.5	29.	0.	100.	79
OTHER RUBBER PRODUCTS...	50.	0.	50.	0.	100.	40
LEATHER PRODUCTS AND SHOES...	47.	0.	53.	0.	100.	15
GLASS PRODUCTS........	31.	0.	69.	0.	100.	52
STONE, CLAY AND CONCRETE.....	51.	1.0	48.	0.	100.	101
IRON AND STEEL PRODUCTS.......	53.	0.	47.	0.	100.	34
NON-FERROUS SMELTING..........	55.	0.	45.	0.	100.	53
NON-FERROUS PRODUCTS..........	47.	2.3	51.	0.	100.	43
METAL CANS............	35.	13.	53.	0.	100.	40
STRUCTURAL METAL PRODUCTS.....	59.	6.9	34.	0.	100.	29
FABRICATED WIRE PRODUCTS......	6.7	6.7	87.	0.	100.	15
OTHER FABRICATED METAL........	44.	2.9	53.	0.	100.	170
ENGINES AND TURBINES..........	38.	7.7	54.	0.	100.	26
FARM MACHINERY........	52.	3.2	45.	0.	100.	31
CONSTRUCTION MACHINERY........	50.	3.2	47.	0.	100.	94
SPECIAL INDUSTRY MACHINERY...	39.	0.	61.	0.	100.	84
GENERAL INDUSTRY MACHINERY...	55.	1.3	44.	0.	100.	77
OFFICE MACHINES + COMPUTERS...	47.	4.3	49.	0.	100.	70
OTHER NON-ELECTR. MACHINERY...	34.	0.	66.	0.	100.	56
ELECTR. TRANSMISSION EQUIP....	58.	0.	42.	0.	100.	26
ELECTRIC LIGHTING AND WIRING.	29.	2.9	68.	0.	100.	34
RADIOS, TV'S + APPLIANCES....	58.	2.1	40.	0.	100.	95
COMMUNICATIONS EQUIPMENT......	35.	0.	65.	0.	100.	49

TABLE CONTINUED ON NEXT PAGE

CROSS-TABULATION 13.5.2: PERCENTAGE BREAKDOWN OF NUMBER OF
MANUFACTURING SUBSIDIARIES OF U.S.-BASED PARENT SYSTEMS BY
SUBSIDIARY'S METHOD OF ENTRY INTO PARENT SYSTEM
FOR SUBSIDIARIES CLASSIFIED BY
PRINCIPAL INDUSTRY OF SUBSIDIARY AT DATE OF ENTRY
(CONTINUED)

PRINCIPAL INDUSTRY OF SUBSIDIARY AT DATE OF ENTRY	SUBSIDIARY'S METHOD OF ENTRY INTO PARENT SYSTEM					
	NEWLY FORMED	REORGAN-IZATION	ACQUIRED DIRECTLY	ACQUIRED THRU AC-QUISITION	TOTAL PERCENT	TOTAL NUMBER
ELECTRONIC COMPONENTS........	35.	0.	65.	0.	100.	40
OTHER ELECTRICAL EQUIPMENT...	53.	4.3	43.	0.	100.	93
MOTOR VEHICLES AND EQUIPMENT.	40.	2.5	57.	0.	100.	239
OTHER TRANSPORTATION.........	58.	5.3	37.	0.	100.	19
PRECISION GOODS.............	26.	6.3	67.	0.	100.	95
MISCELLANEOUS PRODUCTS.......	69.	0.	31.	0.	100.	74

CROSS-TABULATION 13.17.1: PERCENTAGE BREAKDOWN OF NUMBER OF
MANUFACTURING SUBSIDIARIES OF NON-U.S.-BASED PARENT SYSTEMS BY
SUBSIDIARY'S METHOD OF ENTRY INTO PARENT SYSTEM
FOR SUBSIDIARIES CLASSIFIED BY
SUBSIDIARY'S DATE OF ENTRY INTO PARENT SYSTEM

SUBSIDIARY'S DATE OF ENTRY INTO PARENT SYSTEM	SUBSIDIARY'S METHOD OF ENTRY INTO PARENT SYSTEM					
	NEWLY FORMED	REORGAN- IZATION	ACQUIRED DIRECTLY	ACQUIRED THRU AC- QUISITION	TOTAL PERCENT	TOTAL NUMBER
PRE 1914............	66.	3.7	26.	4.1	100.	217
1914 - 1919.........	37.	15.	27.	22.	100.	79
1920 - 1929.........	54.	7.4	32.	6.6	100.	364
1930 - 1938.........	52.	7.8	34.	6.9	100.	217
1939 - 1945.........	58.	5.5	20.	17.	100.	109
1946 - 1952.........	46.	6.8	38.	9.0	100.	323
1953 - 1955.........	52.	9.7	33.	6.1	100.	165
1956 - 1958.........	51.	4.0	26.	19.	100.	225
1959 - 1961.........	45.	3.0	29.	24.	100.	597
1962 - 1964.........	43.	4.4	33.	19.	100.	619
1965 - 1967.........	37.	3.2	23.	38.	100.	1073
1968 - 1970.........	30.	4.2	28.	38.	100.	1636

CROSS-TABULATION 13.17.2: PERCENTAGE BREAKDOWN OF NUMBER OF
MANUFACTURING SUBSIDIARIES OF U.S.-BASED PARENT SYSTEMS BY
SUBSIDIARY'S METHOD OF ENTRY INTO PARENT SYSTEM
FOR SUBSIDIARIES CLASSIFIED BY
SUBSIDIARY'S DATE OF ENTRY INTO PARENT SYSTEM

	SUBSIDIARY'S METHOD OF ENTRY INTO PARENT SYSTEM					
SUBSIDIARY'S DATE OF ENTRY INTO PARENT SYSTEM	NEWLY FORMED	REORGAN- IZATION	ACQUIRED DIRECTLY	ACQUIRED THRU AC- QUISITION	TOTAL PERCENT	TOTAL NUMBER
PRE 1914.........	70.	1.8	28.	0.	100.	114
1914 - 1919.....	78.	1.6	21.	0.	100.	63
1920 - 1929.....	54.	4.1	42.	0.	100.	271
1930 - 1938.....	59.	1.9	39.	0.	100.	270
1939 - 1945.....	70.	2.0	28.	0.	100.	149
1946 - 1952.....	63.	2.0	35.	0.	100.	352
1953 - 1955.....	49.	1.2	50.	0.	100.	260
1956 - 1958.....	51.	2.4	47.	0.	100.	410
1959 - 1961.....	49.	2.0	49.	0.	100.	848
1962 - 1964.....	42.	1.9	56.	0.	100.	894
1965 - 1967.....	38.	1.1	61.	0.	100.	845
1968 - 1970.....	0.	0.	0.	0.	100.	0

CROSS-TABULATION 13.21.1: PERCENTAGE BREAKDOWN OF NUMBER OF
MANUFACTURING SUBSIDIARIES OF NON-U.S.-BASED PARENT SYSTEMS BY
SUBSIDIARY'S METHOD OF ENTRY INTO PARENT SYSTEM
FOR SUBSIDIARIES CLASSIFIED BY
NATIONAL BASE OF SUBSIDIARY'S PARENT SYSTEM

SUBSIDIARY'S METHOD OF ENTRY INTO PARENT SYSTEM

NATIONAL BASE OF SUBSIDIARY'S PARENT SYSTEM	NEWLY FORMED	REORGANIZATION	ACQUIRED DIRECTLY	ACQUIRED THRU ACQUISITION	TOTAL PERCENT	TOTAL NUMBER
UNITED KINGDOM	31.	4.5	30.	34.	100.	2153
GERMANY	40.	8.0	26.	26.	100.	937
FRANCE	51.	3.7	21.	25.	100.	297
ITALY	72.	2.9	21.	4.9	100.	102
BELGIUM AND LUXEMBURG	40.	2.7	32.	25.	100.	255
THE NETHERLANDS	40.	3.6	24.	32.	100.	413
SWEDEN	39.	5.1	46.	9.7	100.	195
SWITZERLAND	39.	6.6	37.	17.	100.	411
JAPAN	85.	0.4	13.	1.0	100.	503
CANADA	41.	5.6	40.	13.	100.	268
OTHER NON-U.S.	3.2	3.2	23.	70.	100.	94

CROSS-TABULATION 13.22.1: PERCENTAGE BREAKDOWN OF NUMBER OF
MANUFACTURING SUBSIDIARIES OF NON-U.S.-BASED PARENT SYSTEMS BY
SUBSIDIARY'S METHOD OF ENTRY INTO PARENT SYSTEM
FOR SUBSIDIARIES CLASSIFIED BY
VALUE OF SALES OF SUBSIDIARY'S PARENT SYSTEM IN 1970

VALUE OF SALES OF SUBSIDIARY'S-PARENT SYSTEM IN 1970	SUBSIDIARY'S METHOD OF ENTRY INTO PARENT SYSTEM					
	NEWLY FORMED	REORGAN- IZATION	ACQUIRED DIRECTLY	ACQUIRED THRU AC- QUISITION	TOTAL PERCENT	TOTAL NUMBER
$400 - 599 MILLION.............	36.	4.5	30.	30.	100.	1105
$600 - 999 MILLION.............	39.	5.4	29.	27.	100.	859
$1 - 2 BILLION.................	40.	3.8	30.	26.	100.	1530
OVER $2 BILLION................	47.	5.0	26.	22.	100.	1956

CROSS-TABULATION 13.22.2: PERCENTAGE BREAKDOWN OF NUMBER OF
MANUFACTURING SUBSIDIARIES OF U.S.-BASED PARENT SYSTEMS BY
SUBSIDIARY'S METHOD OF ENTRY INTO PARENT SYSTEM
FOR SUBSIDIARIES CLASSIFIED BY
VALUE OF SALES OF SUBSIDIARY'S PARENT SYSTEM IN 1970

SUBSIDIARY'S METHOD OF ENTRY INTO PARENT SYSTEM

VALUE OF SALES OF SUBSIDIARY'S PARENT SYSTEM IN 1970	NEWLY FORMED	REORGAN- IZATION	ACQUIRED DIRECTLY	ACQUIRED THRU AC- QUISITION	TOTAL PERCENT	TOTAL NUMBER
$100 - 399 MILLION............	47.	2.2	50.	0.	100.	912
$400 - 599 MILLION............	45.	2.3	53.	0.	100.	754
$600 - 999 MILLION............	46.	0.9	53.	0.	100.	989
$1 - 2 BILLION............	49.	1.1	50.	0.	100.	1010
OVER $2 BILLION............	50.	3.2	38.	0.	100.	758

CROSS-TABULATION 13.24.1: PERCENTAGE BREAKDOWN OF NUMBER OF
MANUFACTURING SUBSIDIARIES OF NON-U.S.-BASED PARENT SYSTEMS BY
SUBSIDIARY'S METHOD OF ENTRY INTO PARENT SYSTEM
FOR SUBSIDIARIES CLASSIFIED BY
NUMBER OF COUNTRIES IN WHICH PARENT SYSTEM MANUFACTURED AT SUBSIDIARY'S DATE OF ENTRY

	SUBSIDIARY'S METHOD OF ENTRY INTO PARENT SYSTEM					
NUMBER OF COUNTRIES PARENT SYSTEM MANUFACTURED IN AT SUB'S DATE OF ENTRY	NEWLY FORMED	REORGAN- IZATION	ACQUIRED DIRECTLY	ACQUIRED THRU AC- QUISITION	TOTAL PERCENT	TOTAL NUMBER
ONE........................	47.	2.0	35.	16.	100.	397
TWO OR THREE................	49.	4.1	25.	21.	100.	580
FOUR TO SIX.................	45.	5.7	26.	23.	100.	870
SEVEN TO TWELVE.............	40.	5.8	27.	27.	100.	1228
THIRTEEN OR MORE............	36.	4.4	30.	29.	100.	2450

CROSS-TABULATION 13.24.2: PERCENTAGE BREAKDOWN OF NUMBER OF
MANUFACTURING SUBSIDIARIES OF U.S.-BASED PARENT SYSTEMS BY
SUBSIDIARY'S METHOD OF ENTRY INTO PARENT SYSTEM
FOR SUBSIDIARIES CLASSIFIED BY
NUMBER OF COUNTRIES IN WHICH PARENT SYSTEM MANUFACTURED AT SUBSIDIARY'S DATE OF ENTRY

SUBSIDIARY'S METHOD OF ENTRY INTO PARENT SYSTEM

NUMBER OF COUNTRIES PARENT SYSTEM MANUFACTURED IN AT SUB'S DATE OF ENTRY	NEWLY FORMED	REORGAN- IZATION	ACQUIRED DIRECTLY	ACQUIRED THRU AC- QUISITION	TOTAL PERCENT	TOTAL NUMBER
ONE......................	58.	0.9	41.	0.	100.	349
TWO OR THREE.............	50.	2.0	48.	0.	100.	503
FOUR TO SIX..............	50.	2.6	48.	0.	100.	832
SEVEN TO TWELVE..........	48.	2.0	50.	0.	100.	1483
THIRTEEN OR MORE.........	47.	1.5	51.	0.	100.	1345

TABULATION 14.1: PERCENTAGE BREAKDOWN OF NUMBER OF SUBSIDIARIES BY
SUBSIDIARY'S METHOD OF EXIT FROM PARENT SYSTEM
FOR VARIOUS CATEGORIES OF SUBSIDIARIES

SUBSIDIARY'S METHOD OF EXIT FROM PARENT SYSTEM

CATEGORY OF SUBSIDIARY	SOLD	CONFIS-CATED OR EXPROPRL.	LIQUIDAT. FUNCTION ENDED	LIQUIDAT. FUNCTION CONTINUED	DID NOT EXIT	TOTAL PERCENT	TOTAL NUMBER
NON-U.S.-BASED SYSTEMS (UNTIL 1/1/71):							
ALL SUBSIDIARIES............	3.5	4.0	7.4	5.4	85.	100.	16576
MANUFACTURING SUBS..........	3.9	4.0	1.4	6.3	84.	100.	6508
SALES SUBSIDIARIES..........	2.7	4.5	1.8	5.3	86.	100.	4038
U.S.-BASED SYSTEMS (UNTIL 1/1/68):							
ALL SUBSIDIARIES............	2.0	1.4	5.4	6.5	84.	100.	11657
MANUFACTURING SUBS..........	4.0	1.3	3.7	7.7	83.	100.	5111
SALES SUBSIDIARIES..........	1.7	1.5	4.3	5.2	84.	100.	1991
WORLD SUBSET OF SYSTEMS (UNTIL 1/1/68):							
NON-U.S.-BASED SYSTEMS:							
ALL SUBSIDIARIES............	4.5	5.9	2.7	7.3	79.	100.	7226
MANUFACTURING SUBS..........	5.6	5.3	2.3	8.7	78.	100.	3046
SALES SUBSIDIARIES..........	3.6	6.5	2.1	6.6	81.	100.	1981
U.S.-BASED SYSTEMS:							
ALL SUBSIDIARIES............	6.9	1.5	5.3	6.5	84.	100.	9725
MANUFACTURING SUBS..........	4.3	1.4	3.7	7.9	83.	100.	4035
SALES SUBSIDIARIES..........	1.8	1.5	6.1	5.7	83.	100.	1580

CROSS-TABULATION 14. 1.1: PERCENTAGE BREAKDOWN OF NUMBER OF
MANUFACTURING SUBSIDIARIES OF NON-U.S.-BASED PARENT SYSTEMS BY
SUBSIDIARY'S METHOD OF EXIT FROM PARENT SYSTEM
FOR SUBSIDIARIES CLASSIFIED BY
SUBSIDIARY'S COUNTRY

SUBSIDIARY'S COUNTRY	SUBSIDIARY'S METHOD OF EXIT FROM PARENT SYSTEM						
	SOLD	CONFIS-CATED OR EXPROPRI.	LIQUIDAT. FUNCTION ENDED	LIQUIDAT. FUNCTION CONTINUED	DID NOT EXIT	TOTAL PERCENT	TOTAL NUMBER
UNITED STATES	6.5	3.4	1.6	13.	75.	100.	506
CANADA	8.5	0.9	2.0	12.	76.	100.	352
MEXICO	1.0	1.0	0.	4.1	94.	100.	97
CENTRAL AMERICA AND CARIB	4.4	3.3	0.	0.	92.	100.	91
VENEZUELA	0.	0.	0.	0.	100.	100.	42
COLOMBIA	0.	6.7	6.7	3.3	83.	100.	30
PERU	0.	0.	0.	0.	100.	100.	29
CHILE	0.	0.	0.	6.1	94.	100.	33
ARGENTINA	3.1	3.1	1.6	6.3	86.	100.	127
BRAZIL	3.9	1.0	1.5	5.4	88.	100.	203
OTHER SOUTH AMERICA	0.	0.	8.7	0.	91.	100.	23
GERMANY	3.2	0.8	2.7	7.2	86.	100.	373
FRANCE	2.8	2.4	0.8	8.3	86.	100.	494
ITALY	5.6	4.7	0.9	6.8	82.	100.	234
BELGIUM AND LUXEMBURG	3.4	2.3	1.7	4.5	88.	100.	176
THE NETHERLANDS	3.8	7.0	0.	2.5	87.	100.	158
UNITED KINGDOM	4.0	4.2	3.7	5.9	82.	100.	354
IRELAND	2.8	0.	0.9	5.6	91.	100.	107
DENMARK	5.7	3.8	0.	15.	75.	100.	53
NORWAY	7.4	7.4	1.9	9.3	74.	100.	54
SWEDEN	3.8	2.6	0.	10.	83.	100.	78
FINLAND	0.	4.2	0.	4.2	92.	100.	24

TABLE CONTINUED ON NEXT PAGE

CROSS-TABULATION 14.1.1: PERCENTAGE BREAKDOWN OF NUMBER OF
MANUFACTURING SUBSIDIARIES OF NON-U.S.-BASED PARENT SYSTEMS BY
SUBSIDIARY'S METHOD OF EXIT FROM PARENT SYSTEM
FOR SUBSIDIARIES CLASSIFIED BY
SUBSIDIARY'S COUNTRY
(CONTINUED)

SUBSIDIARY'S COUNTRY	SUBSIDIARY'S METHOD OF EXIT FROM PARENT SYSTEM						
	SOLD	CONFIS-CATED OR EXPROPRI.	LIQUIDAT. FUNCTION ENDED	LIQUIDAT. FUNCTION CONTINUED	DID NOT EXIT	TOTAL PERCENT	TOTAL NUMBER
SWITZERLAND	0.	12.	1.5	0.	86.	100.	66
AUSTRIA	4.1	20.	0.	3.3	72.	100.	122
PORTUGAL	3.4	0.	3.4	3.4	90.	100.	59
SPAIN	2.7	8.1	3.2	4.1	82.	100.	221
GREECE	0.	9.1	3.0	6.1	82.	100.	33
TURKEY	2.7	5.4	5.4	2.7	84.	100.	37
OTHER EUROPE + ISRAEL	4.5	52.	2.7	1.8	39.	100.	112
PAKISTAN	0.	0.	2.4	2.4	95.	100.	41
IRAN	4.2	0.	0.	0.	96.	100.	24
OTHER MID EAST+EGYPT+LIBYA	0.	15.	0.	0.	85.	100.	26
UNION OF SOUTH AFRICA	2.3	0.3	0.5	5.3	92.	100.	397
RHODESIA	0.	0.	3.3	6.6	90.	100.	61
ZAMBIA	9.8	0.	0.	0.	90.	100.	41
TANZANIA	12.	0.	0.	4.0	84.	100.	25
KENYA	0.	0.	0.	8.9	91.	100.	45
NIGERIA	6.7	0.	3.3	1.7	88.	100.	60
OTHER (BRITISH) AFRICA	2.0	0.	0.	0.	99.	100.	50
MOROCCO, ALGERIA + TUNISIA	1.8	11.	1.8	0.	86.	100.	57
OTHER (FRENCH) AFRICA	0.	0.	0.	0.	100.	100.	47
OTHER AFRICA	0.	0.	0.	0.	100.	100.	34
AUSTRALIA	6.3	0.	0.8	12.	81.	100.	491
NEW ZEALAND	2.6	0.	1.7	5.2	90.	100.	115

TABLE CONTINUED ON NEXT PAGE

CROSS-TABULATION 14.1.1: PERCENTAGE BREAKDOWN OF NUMBER OF
MANUFACTURING SUBSIDIARIES OF NON-U.S.-BASED PARENT SYSTEMS BY
SUBSIDIARY'S METHOD OF EXIT FROM PARENT SYSTEM
FOR SUBSIDIARIES CLASSIFIED BY
SUBSIDIARY'S COUNTRY
(CONTINUED)

SUBSIDIARY'S COUNTRY	SUBSIDIARY'S METHOD OF EXIT FROM PARENT SYSTEM						
	SOLD	CONFIS-CATED OR EXPROPRI.	LIQUIDAT. FUNCTION ENDED	LIQUIDAT. FUNCTION CONTINUED	DID NOT EXIT	TOTAL PERCENT	TOTAL NUMBER
JAPAN.	3.7	3.7	0.	0.	93.	100.	82
CHINA (TAIWAN).	0.	24.	0.	0.8	75.	100.	124
HONG KONG.	3.4	0.	6.9	0.	90.	100.	29
THE PHILIPPINES.	0.	0.	0.	0.	100.	100.	23
MALAYSIA.	3.6	1.8	1.8	1.8	91.	100.	55
SINGAPORE.	5.8	0.	0.	0.	94.	100.	52
INDONESIA.	6.7	6.7	0.	0.	87.	100.	30
THAILAND.	1.5	0.	0.	0.	99.	100.	66
INDIA.	4.5	0.6	0.	5.2	90.	100.	155
OTHER ASIA AND OCEANIA.	2.5	17.	0.	1.2	79.	100.	81

CROSS-TABULATION 14. 1.2: PERCENTAGE BREAKDOWN OF NUMBER OF MANUFACTURING SUBSIDIARIES OF U.S.-BASED PARENT SYSTEMS BY SUBSIDIARY'S METHOD OF EXIT FROM PARENT SYSTEM FOR SUBSIDIARIES CLASSIFIED BY SUBSIDIARY'S COUNTRY

SUBSIDIARY'S COUNTRY	SUBSIDIARY'S METHOD OF EXIT FROM PARENT SYSTEM						
	SOLD	CONFIS-CATED OR EXPROPRI.	LIQUIDAT. FUNCTION ENDED	LIQUIDAT. FUNCTION CONTINUED	DID NOT EXIT	TOTAL PERCENT	TOTAL NUMBER
UNITED STATES	0.	0.	0.	0.	0.	100.	0
CANADA	4.1	0.	5.8	19.	72.	100.	776
MEXICO	3.3	0.9	3.6	13.	79.	100.	338
CENTRAL AMERICA AND CARIB.	3.7	17.	5.3	3.7	71.	100.	190
VENEZUELA	3.5	0.	3.5	0.	93.	100.	141
COLOMBIA	1.7	0.	4.2	2.5	92.	100.	119
PERU	3.6	0.	1.8	3.6	91.	100.	56
CHILE	2.4	0.	0.	0.	98.	100.	42
ARGENTINA	1.3	0.	3.3	9.8	86.	100.	153
BRAZIL	5.6	0.	4.1	5.6	85.	100.	195
OTHER SOUTH AMERICA	2.2	0.	2.2	0.	96.	100.	45
GERMANY	6.0	0.7	3.9	6.7	83.	100.	283
FRANCE	4.2	0.	4.9	16.	75.	100.	308
ITALY	3.8	0.5	2.8	4.7	88.	100.	212
BELGIUM AND LUXEMBURG	5.4	0.	1.8	1.8	91.	100.	111
THE NETHERLANDS	8.9	0.	5.0	4.0	82.	100.	101
UNITED KINGDOM	8.1	0.2	4.7	11.	76.	100.	507
IRELAND	8.8	0.	0.	2.9	88.	100.	34
DENMARK	0.	0.	6.1	0.	94.	100.	33
NORWAY	0.	0.	8.7	0.	91.	100.	23
SWEDEN	4.9	0.	9.8	2.4	83.	100.	41
FINLAND	0.	0.	0.	0.	100.	100.	5

TABLE CONTINUED ON NEXT PAGE

CROSS-TABULATION 14. 1.2: PERCENTAGE BREAKDOWN OF NUMBER OF
MANUFACTURING SUBSIDIARIES OF U.S.-BASED PARENT SYSTEMS BY
SUBSIDIARY'S METHOD OF EXIT FROM PARENT SYSTEM
FOR SUBSIDIARIES CLASSIFIED BY
SUBSIDIARY'S COUNTRY
(CONTINUED)

SUBSIDIARY'S METHOD OF EXIT FROM PARENT SYSTEM

SUBSIDIARY'S COUNTRY	SOLD	CONFIS-CATED OR EXPROPRI.	LIQUIDAT. FUNCTION ENDED	LIQUIDAT. FUNCTION CONTINUED	DID NOT EXIT	TOTAL PERCENT	TOTAL NUMBER
SWITZERLAND	0.	0.	6.9	0.	93.	100.	29
AUSTRIA	4.3	4.3	4.3	0.	87.	100.	23
PORTUGAL	0.	0.	4.3	0.	96.	100.	23
SPAIN	3.0	2.2	0.	2.2	93.	100.	135
GREECE	4.0	0.	8.0	0.	88.	100.	25
TURKEY	0.	0.	5.9	0.	94.	100.	17
OTHER EUROPE + ISRAEL	3.6	18.	11.	7.1	61.	100.	28
PAKISTAN	6.3	0.	0.	0.	94.	100.	16
IRAN	0.	0.	0.	0.	100.	100.	17
OTHER MID EAST+EGYPT+LIBYA	4.3	0.	4.3	0.	91.	100.	23
UNION OF SOUTH AFRICA	0.8	0.	5.4	3.1	91.	100.	130
RHODESIA	0.	0.	0.	0.	100.	100.	14
ZAMBIA	0.	0.	13.	0.	88.	100.	8
TANZANIA	0.	0.	0.	0.	0.	100.	0
KENYA	0.	0.	0.	0.	100.	100.	9
NIGERIA	0.	0.	0.	0.	100.	100.	13
OTHER (BRITISH) AFRICA	0.	0.	13.	0.	88.	100.	8
MOROCCO, ALGERIA + TUNISIA	0.	12.	0.	0.	88.	100.	17
OTHER (FRENCH) AFRICA	0.	0.	0.	0.	100.	100.	9
OTHER AFRICA	0.	0.	0.	0.	100.	100.	2
AUSTRALIA	3.8	0.	1.5	8.0	87.	100.	261
NEW ZEALAND	0.	0.	0.	8.5	91.	100.	47

TABLE CONTINUED ON NEXT PAGE

CROSS-TABULATION 14. 1.2: PERCENTAGE BREAKDOWN OF NUMBER OF
MANUFACTURING SUBSIDIARIES OF U.S.-BASED PARENT SYSTEMS BY
SUBSIDIARY'S METHOD OF EXIT FROM PARENT SYSTEM
FOR SUBSIDIARIES CLASSIFIED BY
SUBSIDIARY'S COUNTRY
(CONTINUED)

SUBSIDIARY'S COUNTRY	SUBSIDIARY'S METHOD OF EXIT FROM PARENT SYSTEM						
	SOLD	CONFIS-CATED OR EXPROPRI.	LIQUIDAT. FUNCTION ENDED	LIQUIDAT. FUNCTION CONTINUED	DID NOT EXIT	TOTAL PERCENT	TOTAL NUMBER
JAPAN....................	1.2	1.2	0.6	1.2	96.	100.	161
CHINA (TAIWAN)...........	5.3	11.	0.	0.	84.	100.	19
HONG KONG................	0.	0.	27.	0.	73.	100.	11
THE PHILIPPINES..........	3.6	0.	1.8	0.	95.	100.	56
MALAYSIA.................	11.	0.	0.	0.	89.	100.	19
SINGAPORE................	8.3	0.	0.	0.	92.	100.	12
INDONESIA................	0.	33.	17.	0.	50.	100.	6
THAILAND.................	0.	0.	0.	0.	100.	100.	15
INDIA....................	1.5	0.	3.1	0.	95.	100.	65
OTHER ASIA AND OCEANIA...	4.5	0.	0.	0.	95.	100.	22

CROSS-TABULATION 14.5.1: PERCENTAGE BREAKDOWN OF NUMBER OF
MANUFACTURING SUBSIDIARIES OF NON-U.S.-BASED PARENT SYSTEMS BY
SUBSIDIARY'S METHOD OF EXIT FROM PARENT SYSTEM
FOR SUBSIDIARIES CLASSIFIED BY
PRINCIPAL INDUSTRY OF SUBSIDIARY AT DATE OF ENTRY

PRINCIPAL INDUSTRY OF SUBSIDIARY AT DATE OF ENTRY	SUBSIDIARY'S METHOD OF EXIT FROM PARENT SYSTEM						
	SOLD	CONFIS-CATED OR EXPROPRI.	LIQUIDAT. FUNCTION ENDED	LIQUIDAT. FUNCTION CONTINUED	DID NOT EXIT	TOTAL PERCENT	TOTAL NUMBER
ORDNANCE	18.	27.	4.5	14.	36.	100.	22
MEAT PRODUCTS	0.	0.	2.5	18.	80.	100.	40
DAIRY PRODUCTS	0.9	1.7	0.	19.	78.	100.	116
CANNED FOODS	3.8	1.9	1.9	5.8	87.	100.	52
GRAIN MILL PRODUCTS	2.4	0.	4.8	2.4	90.	100.	42
BAKERY PRODUCTS	0.	0.	1.4	5.5	93.	100.	73
CONFECTIONERY PRODUCTS	3.3	3.3	0.	3.3	90.	100.	30
BEVERAGES	2.3	0.	0.	7.5	90.	100.	173
OTHER FOOD PRODUCTS	1.7	0.	2.3	7.4	89.	100.	176
TOBACCO PRODUCTS	6.2	0.	0.	4.6	89.	100.	65
TEXTILES	3.0	2.6	1.5	4.8	88.	100.	270
APPAREL	2.4	0.	2.4	2.4	93.	100.	41
LUMBER AND WOOD	3.5	0.	0.	0.	96.	100.	57
FURNITURE	5.6	0.	0.	0.	94.	100.	18
PAPER PRODUCTS	6.3	0.	1.3	4.4	88.	100.	160
PRINTED MATTER	2.6	0.9	1.7	6.8	88.	100.	117
INDUSTRIAL CHEMICALS	3.9	6.4	1.1	9.2	79.	100.	282
PLASTICS AND SYNTHETICS	3.6	1.2	0.9	3.6	92.	100.	165
DRUGS	2.2	4.4	0.9	1.8	91.	100.	228
SOAP AND COSMETICS	4.8	1.6	2.2	2.7	89.	100.	186
PAINTS	6.3	0.	0.8	4.0	89.	100.	126
AGRICULTURAL CHEMICALS	6.2	2.5	0.	3.7	88.	100.	81
OTHER CHEMICALS	1.7	2.9	1.1	3.4	91.	100.	174
REFINED PETROLEUM	8.2	6.2	1.0	11.	73.	100.	97
OTHER PETROLEUM PRODUCTS	0.	1.2	1.2	1.2	96.	100.	83

TABLE CONTINUED ON NEXT PAGE

CROSS-TABULATION 14.5.1: PERCENTAGE BREAKDOWN OF NUMBER OF
MANUFACTURING SUBSIDIARIES OF NON-U.S.-BASED PARENT SYSTEMS BY
SUBSIDIARY'S METHOD OF EXIT FROM PARENT SYSTEM
FOR SUBSIDIARIES CLASSIFIED BY
PRINCIPAL INDUSTRY OF SUBSIDIARY AT DATE OF ENTRY
(CONTINUED)

PRINCIPAL INDUSTRY OF SUBSIDIARY AT DATE OF ENTRY	SUBSIDIARY'S METHOD OF EXIT FROM PARENT SYSTEM						
	SOLD	CONFIS- CATED OR EXPROPRI.	LIQUIDAT. FUNCTION ENDED	LIQUIDAT. FUNCTION CONTINUED	DID NOT EXIT	TOTAL PERCENT	TOTAL NUMBER
TIRES.........................	5.1	10.	0.	0.	85.	100.	39
OTHER RUBBER PRODUCTS.........	4.8	7.1	2.4	2.4	83.	100.	84
LEATHER PRODUCTS AND SHOES....	0.	0.	0.	25.	75.	100.	8
GLASS PRODUCTS................	7.9	4.8	1.6	1.6	84.	100.	63
STONE, CLAY AND CONCRETE......	4.9	1.2	0.	2.4	91.	100.	82
IRON AND STEEL PRODUCTS.......	6.3	5.2	2.1	2.1	84.	100.	191
NON-FERROUS SMELTING..........	6.9	1.0	1.0	5.0	86.	100.	101
NON-FERROUS PRODUCTS..........	4.9	1.2	0.6	3.7	90.	100.	162
METAL CANS....................	7.7	0.	0.	10.	82.	100.	39
STRUCTURAL METAL PRODUCTS.....	4.3	4.3	2.9	7.2	81.	100.	69
FABRICATED WIRE PRODUCTS......	0.	3.6	0.	11.	85.	100.	55
OTHER FABRICATED METAL........	3.7	6.1	2.3	11.	77.	100.	214
ENGINES AND TURBINES..........	3.2	3.2	1.6	11.	81.	100.	62
FARM MACHINERY................	4.4	0.	4.4	18.	73.	100.	45
CONSTRUCTION MACHINERY........	0.	13.	4.2	0.	83.	100.	24
SPECIAL INDUSTRY MACHINERY....	5.9	0.	0.	4.7	89.	100.	85
GENERAL INDUSTRY MACHINERY....	5.8	2.3	0.	14.	78.	100.	86
OFFICE MACHINES + COMPUTERS...	7.1	0.	0.	11.	82.	100.	28
OTHER NON-ELECTR. MACHINERY...	3.6	3.6	0.	3.6	89.	100.	28
ELECTR. TRANSMISSION EQUIP....	4.0	28.	0.7	9.3	58.	100.	151
ELECTRIC LIGHTING AND WIRING..	0.	9.8	6.8	4.5	79.	100.	132
RADIOS, TV'S + APPLIANCES.....	2.3	0.6	1.2	4.7	91.	100.	172
COMMUNICATIONS EQUIPMENT......	7.0	9.6	1.7	4.3	77.	100.	115

TABLE CONTINUED ON NEXT PAGE

CROSS-TABULATION 14. 5.1: PERCENTAGE BREAKDOWN OF NUMBER OF
MANUFACTURING SUBSIDIARIES OF NON-U.S.-BASED PARENT SYSTEMS BY
SUBSIDIARY'S METHOD OF EXIT FROM PARENT SYSTEM
FOR SUBSIDIARIES CLASSIFIED BY
PRINCIPAL INDUSTRY OF SUBSIDIARY AT DATE OF ENTRY
(CONTINUED)

SUBSIDIARY'S METHOD OF EXIT FROM PARENT SYSTEM

PRINCIPAL INDUSTRY OF SUBSIDIARY AT DATE OF ENTRY	SOLD	CONFIS-CATED OR EXPROPRI.	LIQUIDAT. FUNCTION ENDED	LIQUIDAT. FUNCTION CONTINUED	DID NOT EXIT	TOTAL PERCENT	TOTAL NUMBER
ELECTRONIC COMPONENTS........	1.0	3.0	2.0	1.0	93.	100.	101
OTHER ELECTRICAL EQUIPMENT...	2.7	5.5	1.8	5.5	84.	100.	219
MOTOR VEHICLES AND EQUIPMENT.	2.3	6.8	0.9	7.3	83.	100.	220
OTHER TRANSPORTATION.........	7.9	6.7	3.4	4.5	78.	100.	89
PRECISION GOODS..............	5.4	8.7	1.1	5.4	79.	100.	92
MISCELLANEOUS PRODUCTS.......	1.2	0.	0.	2.4	96.	100.	84

CROSS-TABULATION 14. 5.2: PERCENTAGE BREAKDOWN OF NUMBER OF
MANUFACTURING SUBSIDIARIES OF U.S.-BASED PARENT SYSTEMS BY
SUBSIDIARY'S METHOD OF EXIT FROM PARENT SYSTEM
FOR SUBSIDIARIES CLASSIFIED BY
PRINCIPAL INDUSTRY OF SUBSIDIARY AT DATE OF ENTRY

PRINCIPAL INDUSTRY OF SUBSIDIARY AT DATE OF ENTRY	SUBSIDIARY'S METHOD OF EXIT FROM PARENT SYSTEM						
	SOLD	CONFIS-CATED OR EXPROPRI.	LIQUIDAT. FUNCTION ENDED	LIQUIDAT. FUNCTION CONTINUED	DID NOT EXIT	TOTAL PERCENT	TOTAL NUMBER
ORDNANCE	13.	0.	0.	13.	73.	100.	15
MEAT PRODUCTS	16.	2.9	7.1	7.1	67.	100.	70
DAIRY PRODUCTS	16.	1.5	9.2	5.3	68.	100.	131
CANNED FOODS	4.5	4.5	3.0	16.	72.	100.	67
GRAIN MILL PRODUCTS	2.4	0.8	5.5	8.7	83.	100.	127
BAKERY PRODUCTS	0.	1.8	7.3	9.1	82.	100.	55
CONFECTIONERY PRODUCTS	0.	0.	3.5	12.	85.	100.	85
BEVERAGES	4.8	1.2	8.4	1.2	84.	100.	83
OTHER FOOD PRODUCTS	9.2	2.3	10.	10.	68.	100.	87
TOBACCO PRODUCTS	0.	0.	10.	0.	100.	100.	13
TEXTILES	1.9	0.	1.9	2.8	93.	100.	106
APPAREL	3.6	3.6	3.6	3.6	86.	100.	28
LUMBER AND WOOD	4.5	0.	9.1	0.	86.	100.	22
FURNITURE	0.	0.	0.	0.	100.	100.	14
PAPER PRODUCTS	3.7	0.5	4.7	11.	80.	100.	215
PRINTED MATTER	0.	0.	0.	11.	89.	100.	35
INDUSTRIAL CHEMICALS	4.9	0.7	3.6	5.9	85.	100.	307
PLASTICS AND SYNTHETICS	9.8	0.	2.5	6.4	81.	100.	204
DRUGS	0.3	0.3	2.8	5.6	91.	100.	357
SOAP AND COSMETICS	2.7	1.1	4.4	7.1	85.	100.	182
PAINTS	7.5	1.5	1.5	3.0	87.	100.	67
AGRICULTURAL CHEMICALS	3.2	1.6	1.6	3.2	90.	100.	63
OTHER CHEMICALS	4.7	0.	3.7	11.	80.	100.	107
REFINED PETROLEUM	3.8	8.8	2.5	3.8	81.	100.	159
OTHER PETROLEUM PRODUCTS	2.7	1.3	4.0	1.3	91.	100.	75

TABLE CONTINUED ON NEXT PAGE

CROSS-TABULATION 14. 5.2: PERCENTAGE BREAKDOWN OF NUMBER OF
MANUFACTURING SUBSIDIARIES OF U.S.-BASED PARENT SYSTEMS BY
SUBSIDIARY'S METHOD OF EXIT FROM PARENT SYSTEM
FOR SUBSIDIARIES CLASSIFIED BY
PRINCIPAL INDUSTRY OF SUBSIDIARY AT DATE OF ENTRY
(CONTINUED)

PRINCIPAL INDUSTRY OF SUBSIDIARY AT DATE OF ENTRY	SUBSIDIARY'S METHOD OF EXIT FROM PARENT SYSTEM					TOTAL PERCENT	TOTAL NUMBER
	SOLD	CONFIS-CATED OR EXPROPRI.	LIQUIDAT. FUNCTION ENDED	LIQUIDAT. FUNCTION CONTINUED	DID NOT EXIT		
TIRES.................	2.4	3.6	1.2	2.4	90.	100.	84
OTHER RUBBER PRODUCTS.....	5.9	5.9	9.8	3.9	75.	100.	51
LEATHER PRODUCTS AND SHOES...	0.	0.	0.	6.7	93.	100.	15
GLASS PRODUCTS...........	3.8	1.9	1.9	3.8	89.	100.	53
STONE, CLAY AND CONCRETE.....	2.9	0.	1.9	15.	81.	100.	103
IRON AND STEEL PRODUCTS.......	6.8	0.	6.8	9.1	77.	100.	44
NON-FERROUS SMELTING.........	3.3	0.	3.3	10.	83.	100.	60
NON-FERROUS PRODUCTS.........	4.3	0.	0.	6.5	89.	100.	46
METAL CANS...............	2.4	7.1	4.8	9.5	76.	100.	42
STRUCTURAL METAL PRODUCTS.....	3.2	0.	3.2	9.7	84.	100.	31
FABRICATED WIRE PRODUCTS.....	0.	0.	6.7	6.7	87.	100.	15
OTHER FABRICATED METAL.......	3.3	1.1	4.3	9.8	82.	100.	184
ENGINES AND TURBINES.........	3.7	0.	3.7	22.	70.	100.	27
FARM MACHINERY.............	0.	0.	3.2	13.	84.	100.	31
CONSTRUCTION MACHINERY.......	0.	1.0	3.1	10.	85.	100.	96
SPECIAL INDUSTRY MACHINERY...	2.2	1.1	2.2	4.5	90.	100.	89
GENERAL INDUSTRY MACHINERY...	2.4	0.	2.4	20.	75.	100.	84
OFFICE MACHINES + COMPUTERS..	1.4	0.	9.7	22.	67.	100.	72
OTHER NON-ELECTR. MACHINERY..	3.4	0.	1.7	6.9	88.	100.	58
ELECTR. TRANSMISSION EQUIP...	0.	0.	3.8	0.	96.	100.	26
ELECTRIC LIGHTING AND WIRING.	2.8	2.8	0.	8.3	86.	100.	36
RADIOS, TV'S + APPLIANCES....	1.0	1.0	2.0	8.1	88.	100.	99
COMMUNICATIONS EQUIPMENT.....	4.1	2.0	4.1	2.0	88.	100.	49

TABLE CONTINUED ON NEXT PAGE

CROSS-TABULATION 14. 5.2: PERCENTAGE BREAKDOWN OF NUMBER OF
MANUFACTURING SUBSIDIARIES OF U.S.-BASED PARENT SYSTEMS BY
SUBSIDIARY'S METHOD OF EXIT FROM PARENT SYSTEM
FOR SUBSIDIARIES CLASSIFIED BY
PRINCIPAL INDUSTRY OF SUBSIDIARY AT DATE OF ENTRY
(CONTINUED)

PRINCIPAL INDUSTRY OF SUBSIDIARY AT DATE OF ENTRY	SUBSIDIARY'S METHOD OF EXIT FROM PARENT SYSTEM						
	SOLD	CONFIS-CATED OR EXPROPRI.	LIQUIDAT. FUNCTION ENDED	LIQUIDAT. FUNCTION CONTINUED	DID NOT EXIT	TOTAL PERCENT	TOTAL NUMBER
ELECTRONIC COMPONENTS.........	4.8	0.	2.4	0.	93.	100.	42
OTHER ELECTRICAL EQUIPMENT...	0.	0.9	0.9	11.	88.	100.	114
MOTOR VEHICLES AND EQUIPMENT.	6.3	0.	3.9	11.	79.	100.	254
OTHER TRANSPORTATION.........	4.8	0.	0.	0.	95.	100.	21
PRECISION GOODS.............	2.1	0.	2.1	18.	78.	100.	95
MISCELLANEOUS PRODUCTS.......	2.4	0.	6.0	4.8	87.	100.	83

IHE806I DATA INTERRUPT IN STATEMENT 00189 AT OFFSET +0023C FROM ENTRY POINT CROSS

CROSS-TABULATION 14.9.1: PERCENTAGE BREAKDOWN OF NUMBER OF
MANUFACTURING SUBSIDIARIES OF NON-U.S.-BASED PARENT SYSTEMS BY
SUBSIDIARY'S METHOD OF EXIT FROM PARENT SYSTEM
FOR SUBSIDIARIES CLASSIFIED BY
PERCENTAGE OF SUBSIDIARY'S EQUITY OWNED BY PARENT SYSTEM AT DATE OF ENTRY

SUBSIDIARY'S METHOD OF EXIT FROM PARENT SYSTEM

PERCENTAGE OF SUBSIDIARY'S EQUITY OWNED BY PARENT SYSTEM AT DATE OF ENTRY	SOLD	CONFIS- CATED OR EXPROPRI.	LIQUIDAT. FUNCTION ENDED	LIQUIDAT. FUNCTION CONTINUED	DID NOT EXIT	TOTAL PERCENT	TOTAL NUMBER
95% OR MORE..............	3.8	2.4	1.9	8.6	83.	100.	2384
OVER 50% BUT UNDER 95%.......	3.2	8.9	1.7	6.3	80.	100.	1059
EXACTLY 50%..............	6.8	4.3	0.2	2.7	86.	100.	441
AT LEAST 25% BUT UNDER 50%...	6.2	7.3	0.9	3.6	82.	100.	675
OVER 5% BUT UNDER 25%........	6.3	3.1	0.9	3.5	86.	100.	457

CROSS-TABULATION 14. 9.2: PERCENTAGE BREAKDOWN OF NUMBER OF
MANUFACTURING SUBSIDIARIES OF U.S.-BASED PARENT SYSTEMS BY
SUBSIDIARY'S METHOD OF EXIT FROM PARENT SYSTEM
FOR SUBSIDIARIES CLASSIFIED BY
PERCENTAGE OF SUBSIDIARY'S EQUITY OWNED BY PARENT SYSTEM AT DATE OF ENTRY

SUBSIDIARY'S METHOD OF EXIT FROM PARENT SYSTEM

PERCENTAGE OF SUBSIDIARY'S EQUITY OWNED BY PARENT SYSTEM AT DATE OF ENTRY	SOLD	CONFIS-CATED OR EXPROPRI.	LIQUIDAT. FUNCTION ENDED	LIQUIDAT. FUNCTION CONTINUED	DID NOT EXIT	TOTAL PERCENT	TOTAL NUMBER
95% OR MORE..............	1.9	1.0	5.2	11.	81.	100.	2609
OVER 50% BUT UNDER 95%....	1.5	1.2	3.1	5.9	88.	100.	677
EXACTLY 50%..............	4.3	0.4	2.7	3.8	89.	100.	446
AT LEAST 25% BUT UNDER 50%...	5.6	0.5	1.5	2.8	90.	100.	395
OVER 5% BUT UNDER 25%.........	6.9	3.7	1.6	1.1	87.	100.	189

CROSS-TABULATION 14.11.1: PERCENTAGE BREAKDOWN OF NUMBER OF
MANUFACTURING SUBSIDIARIES OF NON-U.S.-BASEL PARENT SYSTEMS BY
SUBSIDIARY'S METHOD OF EXIT FROM PARENT SYSTEM
FOR SUBSIDIARIES CLASSIFIED BY
CATEGORY OF SUBSIDIARY'S PRINCIPAL OUTSIDE OWNER (IF ANY) AT DATE OF ENTRY

SUBSIDIARY'S METHOD OF EXIT FROM PARENT SYSTEM

CATEGORY OF SUBSIDIARY'S PRINCIPAL OUTSIDE OWNER (IF ANY) AT DATE OF ENTRY	SOLD	CONFIS-CATED OR EXPROPRI.	LIQUIDAT. FUNCTION ENDED	LIQUIDAT. FUNCTION CONTINUED	DID NOT EXIT	TOTAL PERCENT	TOTAL NUMBER
LOCAL PRIVATE.........	4.8	1.4	0.9	3.2	90.	100.	955
LOCAL STATE..........	3.6	0.9	0.	2.7	93.	100.	111
FOREIGN PRIVATE......	5.6	3.1	0.3	3.3	88.	100.	391
STOCK WIDELY DISPERSED......	4.1	0.	0.	4.1	92.	100.	73

370

CROSS-TABULATION 14.11.2: PERCENTAGE BREAKDOWN OF NUMBER OF
MANUFACTURING SUBSIDIARIES OF U.S.-BASED PARENT SYSTEMS BY
SUBSIDIARY'S METHOD OF EXIT FROM PARENT SYSTEM
FOR SUBSIDIARIES CLASSIFIED BY
CATEGORY OF SUBSIDIARY'S PRINCIPAL OUTSIDE OWNER (IF ANY) AT DATE OF ENTRY

CATEGORY OF SUBSIDIARY'S PRINCIPAL OUTSIDE OWNER (IF ANY) AT DATE OF ENTRY	SUBSIDIARY'S METHOD OF EXIT FROM PARENT SYSTEM						
	SOLD	CONFIS- CATED OR EXPROPRI.	LIQUIDAT. FUNCTION ENDED	LIQUIDAT. FUNCTION CONTINUED	DID NOT EXIT	TOTAL PERCENT	TOTAL NUMBER
LOCAL PRIVATE...........	4.6	0.4	2.3	4.1	89.	100.	710
LOCAL STATE............	0.	5.9	5.9	0.	88.	100.	17
FOREIGN PRIVATE........	9.5	2.0	3.0	2.5	83.	100.	200
STOCK WIDELY DISPERSED..	8.3	1.3	0.7	3.0	87.	100.	303

CROSS-TABULATION 14.13.1: PERCENTAGE BREAKDOWN OF NUMBER OF
MANUFACTURING SUBSIDIARIES OF NON-U.S.-BASED PARENT SYSTEMS BY
SUBSIDIARY'S METHOD OF EXIT FROM PARENT SYSTEM
FOR SUBSIDIARIES CLASSIFIED BY
SUBSIDIARY'S METHOD OF ENTRY INTO PARENT SYSTEM

SUBSIDIARY'S METHOD OF ENTRY INTO PARENT SYSTEM	SUBSIDIARY'S METHOD OF EXIT FROM PARENT SYSTEM						
	SOLD	CONFIS-CATED OR EXPROPRI.	LIQUIDAT. FUNCTION ENDED	LIQUIDAT. FUNCTION CONTINUED	DID NOT EXIT	TOTAL PERCENT	TOTAL NUMBER
NEWLY FORMED..........	3.0	6.0	1.3	5.0	85.	100.	2317
REORGANIZATION........	3.0	7.6	1.5	5.3	83.	100.	264
ACQUIRED DIRECTLY.....	4.5	4.0	1.4	10.	80.	100.	1602
ACQUIRED THRU ACQUISITION.....	4.4	1.1	1.7	4.3	89.	100.	1445

CROSS-TABULATION 14.13.2: PERCENTAGE BREAKDOWN OF NUMBER OF
MANUFACTURING SUBSIDIARIES OF U.S.-BASED PARENT SYSTEMS BY
SUBSIDIARY'S METHOD OF EXIT FROM PARENT SYSTEM
    FOR SUBSIDIARIES CLASSIFIED BY
SUBSIDIARY'S METHOD OF ENTRY INTO PARENT SYSTEM

SUBSIDIARY'S METHOD OF ENTRY INTO PARENT SYSTEM	SUBSIDIARY'S METHOD OF EXIT FROM PARENT SYSTEM						
	SOLD	CONFIS-CATED OR EXPROPRI.	LIQUIDAT. FUNCTION ENDED	LIQUIDAT. FUNCTION CONTINUED	DID NOT EXIT	TOTAL PERCENT	TOTAL NUMBER
NEWLY FORMED............	3.6	1.5	3.5	5.2	86.	100.	2216
REORGANIZATION.........	7.1	1.2	1.2	8.2	82.	100.	85
ACQUIRED DIRECTLY......	4.0	0.5	4.4	11.	80.	100.	2203
ACQUIRED THRU ACQUISITION....	0.	0.	0.	0.	0.	100.	0

CROSS-TABULATION 14.21.1: PERCENTAGE BREAKDOWN OF NUMBER OF
MANUFACTURING SUBSIDIARIES OF NON-U.S.-BASED PARENT SYSTEMS BY
SUBSIDIARY'S METHOD OF EXIT FROM PARENT SYSTEM
FOR SUBSIDIARIES CLASSIFIED BY
NATIONAL BASE OF SUBSIDIARY'S PARENT SYSTEM

NATIONAL BASE OF SUBSIDIARY'S PARENT SYSTEM	SUBSIDIARY'S METHOD OF EXIT FROM PARENT SYSTEM						
	SOLD	CONFIS-CATED OR EXPROPRI.	LIQUIDAT. FUNCTION ENDED	LIQUIDAT. FUNCTION CONTINUED	DID NOT EXIT	TOTAL PERCENT	TOTAL NUMBER
UNITED KINGDOM	5.0	0.6	1.6	6.9	86.	100.	2533
GERMANY	4.0	17.	0.7	5.3	73.	100.	1030
FRANCE	1.8	1.1	0.4	2.6	94.	100.	454
ITALY	0.8	0.	0.8	7.1	91.	100.	126
BELGIUM AND LUXEMBURG	2.9	2.9	0.3	3.8	90.	100.	312
THE NETHERLANDS	2.4	2.4	3.9	4.8	87.	100.	460
SWEDEN	2.9	3.3	1.0	9.1	84.	100.	209
SWITZERLAND	5.9	2.6	2.0	12.	77.	100.	460
JAPAN	2.0	8.1	0.7	0.6	89.	100.	543
CANADA	5.0	0.4	2.5	16.	76.	100.	282
OTHER NON-U.S.	0.	0.	0.	1.0	99.	100.	99

CROSS-TABULATION 14.22.1: PERCENTAGE BREAKDOWN OF NUMBER OF
MANUFACTURING SUBSIDIARIES OF NON-U.S.-BASED PARENT SYSTEMS BY
SUBSIDIARY'S METHOD OF EXIT FROM PARENT SYSTEM
FOR SUBSIDIARIES CLASSIFIED BY
VALUE OF SALES OF SUBSIDIARY'S PARENT SYSTEM IN 1970

VALUE OF SALES OF SUBSIDIARY'S PARENT SYSTEM IN 1970	SUBSIDIARY'S METHOD OF EXIT FROM PARENT SYSTEM						
	SOLD	CONFIS-CATED OR EXPROPRI.	LIQUIDAT. FUNCTION ENDED	LIQUIDAT. FUNCTION CONTINUED	DID NOT EXIT	TOTAL PERCENT	TOTAL NUMBER
$400 - 599 MILLION........	4.3	2.1	1.7	5.7	86.	100.	1254
$600 - 999 MILLION........	4.6	1.7	0.5	7.5	86.	100.	1014
$1 - 2 BILLION........	4.5	2.3	1.8	6.8	85.	100.	1818
OVER $2 BILLION........	3.0	5.7	1.5	5.2	85.	100.	2210

CROSS-TABULATION 14.22.2: PERCENTAGE BREAKDOWN OF NUMBER OF
MANUFACTURING SUBSIDIARIES OF U.S.-BASED PARENT SYSTEMS BY
SUBSIDIARY'S METHOD OF EXIT FROM PARENT SYSTEM
FOR SUBSIDIARIES CLASSIFIED BY
VALUE OF SALES OF SUBSIDIARY'S PARENT SYSTEM IN 1970

VALUE OF SALES OF SUBSIDIARY'S PARENT SYSTEM IN 1970	SUBSIDIARY'S METHOD OF EXIT FROM PARENT SYSTEM						
	SOLD	CONFIS-CATED OR EXPROPRI.	LIQUIDAT. FUNCTION ENDED	LIQUIDAT. FUNCTION CONTINUED	DID NOT EXIT	TOTAL PERCENT	TOTAL NUMBER
$100 - 399 MILLION............	3.0	0.6	4.3	8.8	83.	100.	955
$400 - 599 MILLION............	8.3	0.5	3.1	6.6	82.	100.	834
$600 - 999 MILLION............	2.0	0.8	4.1	9.1	84.	100.	1061
$1 - 2 BILLION...............	2.8	1.1	3.9	8.7	83.	100.	1133
OVER $2 BILLION..............	5.8	2.5	4.7	7.2	80.	100.	878

TABULATION 15.1: PERCENTAGE BREAKDOWN OF NUMBER OF SUBSIDIARIES BY SUBSIDIARY'S PRINCIPAL MARKET FOR VARIOUS CATEGORIES OF SUBSIDIARIES

CATEGORY OF SUBSIDIARY	SUBSIDIARY'S PRINCIPAL MARKET			
	LOCAL COUNTRY	EXPORT MARKETS	TOTAL PERCENT	TOTAL NUMBER
NON-U.S.-BASED SYSTEMS (AS OF 1/1/71):				
ALL SUBSIDIARIES..........	92.	8.2	100.	7446
MANUFACTURING SUBS........	93.	7.5	100.	4259
SALES SUBSIDIARIES........	95.	4.9	100.	2487
U.S.-BASED SYSTEMS (AS OF 1/1/68):				
ALL SUBSIDIARIES..........	91.	9.3	100.	1426
MANUFACTURING SUBS........	94.	5.7	100.	958
SALES SUBSIDIARIES........	85.	15.	100.	353
WORLD SUBSET OF SYSTEMS (AS OF 1/1/68):				
NON-U.S.-BASED SYSTEMS:				
ALL SUBSIDIARIES..........	93.	7.1	100.	3297
MANUFACTURING SUBS........	93.	7.1	100.	1899
SALES SUBSIDIARIES........	97.	3.2	100.	1130
U.S.-BASED-SYSTEMS:				
ALL SUBSIDIARIES..........	91.	9.0	100.	1053
MANUFACTURING SUBS........	95.	5.0	100.	683
SALES SURSIDIARIES........	86.	14.	100.	267

TABULATION 15.2: PERCENTAGE BREAKDOWN OF SALES OF SUBSIDIARIES IN 1970 BY
SUBSIDIARY'S PRINCIPAL MARKET AS OF 1/1/71
FOR ALL SUBSIDIARIES, MANUFACTURING SUBSIDIARIES AND SALES SUBSIDIARIES
OF NON-U.S.-BASED SYSTEMS

CATEGORY OF SUBSIDIARY	SUBSIDIARY'S PRINCIPAL MARKET AS OF 1/1/71			
	LOCAL COUNTRY	EXPORT MARKETS	TOTAL PERCENT	TOTAL ($ MIL)
ALL SUBSIDIARIES.............	86.	14.	100.	94984
MANUFACTURING SUBSIDIARIES...	87.	13.	100.	66346
SALES SUBSIDIARIES...........	94.	5.7	100.	19682

CROSS-TABULATION 15. 1.1: PERCENTAGE BREAKDOWN OF NUMBER (AS OF 1/1/71) OF
MANUFACTURING SUBSIDIARIES OF NON-U.S.-BASED PARENT SYSTEMS BY
SUBSIDIARY'S PRINCIPAL MARKET AS OF 1/1/71
FOR SUBSIDIARIES CLASSIFIED BY
SUBSIDIARY'S COUNTRY

SUBSIDIARY'S COUNTRY	SUBSIDIARY'S PRINCIPAL MARKET AS OF 1/1/71			
	LOCAL COUNTRY	EXPORT MARKETS	TOTAL PERCENT	TOTAL NUMBER
UNITED STATES	98.	2.4	100.	287
CANADA	94.	5.9	100.	222
MEXICO	99.	1.3	100.	75
CENTRAL AMERICA AND CARIB	75.	25.	100.	69
VENEZUELA	97.	2.9	100.	34
COLOMBIA	96.	4.2	100.	24
PERU	93.	7.4	100.	27
CHILE	100.	0.	100.	21
ARGENTINA	98.	2.4	100.	82
BRAZIL	95.	4.7	100.	129
OTHER SOUTH AMERICA	87.	13.	100.	15
GERMANY	94.	5.8	100.	225
FRANCE	94.	5.8	100.	292
ITALY	95.	5.1	100.	136
BELGIUM AND LUXEMBURG	77.	23.	100.	107
THE NETHERLANDS	81.	19.	100.	107
UNITED KINGDOM	95.	5.4	100.	203
IRELAND	89.	11.	100.	79
DENMARK	97.	2.9	100.	34
NORWAY	74.	26.	100.	35
SWEDEN	96.	3.6	100.	55
FINLAND	88.	12.	100.	17

TABLE CONTINUED ON NEXT PAGE

CROSS-TABULATION 15. 1.1: PERCENTAGE BREAKDOWN OF NUMBER (AS OF 1/1/71) OF MANUFACTURING SUBSIDIARIES OF NON-U.S.-BASED PARENT SYSTEMS BY SUBSIDIARY'S PRINCIPAL MARKET AS OF 1/1/71 FOR SUBSIDIARIES CLASSIFIED BY SUBSIDIARY'S COUNTRY (CONTINUED)

SUBSIDIARY'S COUNTRY	SUBSIDIARY'S PRINCIPAL MARKET AS OF 1/1/71			
	LOCAL COUNTRY	EXPORT MARKETS	TOTAL PERCENT	TOTAL NUMBER
SWITZERLAND	92.	8.3	100.	36
AUSTRIA	97.	2.9	100.	70
PORTUGAL	90.	10.	100.	39
SPAIN	97.	3.0	100.	134
GREECE	90.	10.	100.	20
TURKEY	100.	0.	100.	25
OTHER EUROPE + ISRAEL	53.	47.	100.	17
PAKISTAN	100.	0.	100.	34
IRAN	94.	6.3	100.	16
OTHER MID EAST+EGYPT+LIBYA	72.	28.	100.	18
UNION OF SOUTH AFRICA	99.	1.7	100.	290
RHODESIA	93.	6.8	100.	44
ZAMBIA	100.	0.	100.	35
TANZANIA	81.	19.	100.	21
KENYA	95.	5.1	100.	39
NIGERIA	100.	0.	100.	48
OTHER (BRITISH) AFRICA	89.	11.	100.	46
MOROCCO, ALGERIA + TUNISIA	69.	31.	100.	13
OTHER (FRENCH) AFRICA	72.	28.	100.	25
OTHER AFRICA	95.	5.0	100.	20
AUSTRALIA	96.	4.4	100.	344
NEW ZEALAND	94.	5.6	100.	90

TABLE CONTINUED ON NEXT PAGE

CROSS-TABULATION 15. 1.1: PERCENTAGE BREAKDOWN OF NUMBER (AS OF 1/1/71) OF
MANUFACTURING SUBSIDIARIES OF NON-U.S.-BASED PARENT SYSTEMS BY
SUBSIDIARY'S PRINCIPAL MARKET AS OF 1/1/71
FOR SUBSIDIARIES CLASSIFIED BY
SUBSIDIARY'S COUNTRY
(CONTINUED)

SUBSIDIARY'S COUNTRY	SUBSIDIARY'S PRINCIPAL MARKET AS OF 1/1/71			
	LOCAL COUNTRY	EXPORT MARKETS	TOTAL PERCENT	TOTAL NUMBER
JAPAN..........	99.	1.4	100.	71
CHINA (TAIWAN)....	51.	49.	100.	84
HONG KONG......	68.	32.	100.	22
THE PHILIPPINES.....	95.	4.5	100.	22
MALAYSIA.......	88.	12.	100.	51
SINGAPORE......	91.	8.7	100.	46
INDONESIA......	100.	0.	100.	23
THAILAND.......	100.	0.	100.	59
INDIA.........	100.	0.	100.	130
OTHER ASIA AND OCEANIA.......	73.	27.	100.	49

CROSS-TABULATION 15. 2.1: PERCENTAGE BREAKDOWN OF NUMBER (AS OF 1/1/71) OF
MANUFACTURING SUBSIDIARIES OF NON-U.S.-BASED PARENT SYSTEMS BY
SUBSIDIARY'S PRINCIPAL MARKET AS OF 1/1/71
FOR SUBSIDIARIES CLASSIFIED BY
GEOGRAPHICAL REGION OF SUBSIDIARY'S COUNTRY

GEOGRAPHICAL REGION OF SUBSIDIARY'S COUNTRY	SUBSIDIARY'S PRINCIPAL MARKET AS OF 1/1/71			
	LOCAL COUNTRY	EXPORT MARKETS	TOTAL PERCENT	TOTAL NUMBER
NORTH AMERICA................	96.	3.9	100.	509
LATIN AMERICA................	93.	6.7	100.	476
EUROPE.......................	92.	8.5	100.	1629
AFRICA AND MIDDLE EAST.......	94.	5.8	100.	651
OTHER ASIA AND OCEANIA.......	91.	9.4	100.	991

382

CROSS-TABULATION 15. 2.2: PERCENTAGE BREAKDOWN OF NUMBER (AS OF 1/1/68) OF
MANUFACTURING SUBSIDIARIES OF U.S.-BASED PARENT SYSTEMS BY
SUBSIDIARY'S PRINCIPAL MARKET AS OF 1/1/68
FOR SUBSIDIARIES CLASSIFIED BY
GEOGRAPHICAL REGION OF SUBSIDIARY'S COUNTRY

GEOGRAPHICAL REGION OF SUBSIDIARY'S COUNTRY	SUBSIDIARY'S PRINCIPAL MARKET AS OF 1/1/68			
	LOCAL COUNTRY	EXPORT MARKETS	TOTAL PERCENT	TOTAL NUMBER
NORTH AMERICA................	97.	2.7	100.	112
LATIN AMERICA................	97.	2.9	100.	274
EUROPE.......................	92.	7.6	100.	355
AFRICA AND MIDDLE EAST.......	95.	4.9	100.	61
OTHER ASIA AND OCEANIA.......	91.	9.0	100.	156

CROSS-TABULATION 15. 3.1: PERCENTAGE BREAKDOWN OF NUMBER (AS OF 1/1/71) OF
MANUFACTURING SUBSIDIARIES OF NON-U.S.-BASED PARENT SYSTEMS BY
SUBSIDIARY'S PRINCIPAL MARKET AS OF 1/1/71
FOR SUBSIDIARIES CLASSIFIED BY
GNP PER CAPITA IN 1970 OF SUBSIDIARY'S COUNTRY

GNP PER CAPITA IN 1970 OF SUBSIDIARY'S COUNTRY	SUBSIDIARY'S PRINCIPAL MARKET AS OF 1/1/71			
	LOCAL COUNTRY	EXPORT MARKETS	TOTAL PERCENT	TOTAL NUMBER
UNDER $200............................	97.	3.5	100.	430
$200 - $500............................	85.	15.	100.	557
$500 - $1200...........................	94.	5.6	100.	818
$1200 - $2500..........................	92.	7.6	100.	778
OVER $2500.............................	94.	6.5	100.	1638

384

CROSS-TABULATION 15. 4.1: PERCENTAGE BREAKDOWN OF NUMBER (AS OF 1/1/71) OF
MANUFACTURING SUBSIDIARIES OF NON-U.S.-BASED PARENT SYSTEMS BY
SUBSIDIARY'S PRINCIPAL MARKET AS OF 1/1/71
FOR SUBSIDIARIES CLASSIFIED BY
GNP IN 1970 OF SUBSIDIARY'S COUNTRY

| GNP IN 1970 OF SUBSIDIARY'S COUNTRY | SUBSIDIARY'S PRINCIPAL MARKET AS OF 1/1/71 | | | |
	LOCAL COUNTRY	EXPORT MARKETS	TOTAL PERCENT	TOTAL NUMBER
UNDER $1 BILLION.............	68.	32.	100.	72
$1 - $5 BILLION.............	89.	11.	100.	486
$5 - $20 BILLION.............	92.	8.3	100.	1071
$20 - $100 BILLION.............	94.	6.3	100.	1514
OVER $100 BILLION.............	95.	4.5	100.	1078

CROSS-TABULATION 15. 6.1: PERCENTAGE BREAKDOWN OF NUMBER (AS OF 1/1/71) OF MANUFACTURING SUBSIDIARIES OF NON-U.S.-BASED PARENT SYSTEMS BY SUBSIDIARY'S PRINCIPAL MARKET AS OF 1/1/71 FOR SUBSIDIARIES CLASSIFIED BY PRINCIPAL INDUSTRY OF SUBSIDIARY AS OF 1/1/71

PRINCIPAL INDUSTRY OF SUBSIDIARY AS OF 1/1/71	SUBSIDIARY'S PRINCIPAL MARKET AS OF 1/1/71			
	LOCAL COUNTRY	EXPORT MARKETS	TOTAL PERCENT	TOTAL NUMBER
ORDNANCE	80.	20.	100.	5
MEAT PRODUCTS	67.	33.	100.	24
DAIRY PRODUCTS	91.	8.9	100.	45
CANNED FOODS	79.	21.	100.	39
GRAIN MILL PRODUCTS	100.	0.	100.	42
BAKERY PRODUCTS	100.	0.	100.	63
CONFECTIONERY PRODUCTS	91.	8.7	100.	23
BEVERAGES	87.	13.	100.	145
OTHER FOOD PRODUCTS	93.	7.1	100.	127
TOBACCO PRODUCTS	88.	13.	100.	56
TEXTILES	82.	18.	100.	205
APPAREL	71.	29.	100.	34
LUMBER AND WOOD	78.	23.	100.	40
FURNITURE	100.	0.	100.	12
PAPER PRODUCTS	81.	19.	100.	130
PRINTED MATTER	92.	8.1	100.	86
INDUSTRIAL CHEMICALS	96.	4.3	100.	161
PLASTICS AND SYNTHETICS	97.	3.0	100.	100
DRUGS	96.	3.5	100.	170
SOAP AND COSMETICS	98.	2.1	100.	146
PAINTS	99.	2.0	100.	102
AGRICULTURAL CHEMICALS	100.	0.	100.	50
OTHER CHEMICALS	93.	6.8	100.	117
REFINED PETROLEUM	85.	15.	100.	71
OTHER PETROLEUM PRODUCTS	94.	6.5	100.	62

TABLE CONTINUED ON NEXT PAGE

CROSS-TABULATION 15. 6.1: PERCENTAGE BREAKDOWN OF NUMBER (AS OF 1/1/71) OF MANUFACTURING SUBSIDIARIES OF NON-U.S.-BASED PARENT SYSTEMS BY SUBSIDIARY'S PRINCIPAL MARKET AS OF 1/1/71 FOR SUBSIDIARIES CLASSIFIED BY PRINCIPAL INDUSTRY OF SUBSIDIARY AS OF 1/1/71 (CONTINUED)

PRINCIPAL INDUSTRY OF SUBSIDIARY AS OF 1/1/71	SUBSIDIARY'S PRINCIPAL MARKET AS OF 1/1/71			
	LOCAL COUNTRY	EXPORT MARKETS	TOTAL PERCENT	TOTAL NUMBER
TIRES........................	96.	3.7	100.	27
OTHER RUBBER PRODUCTS........	91.	9.1	100.	55
LEATHER PRODUCTS AND SHOES...	100.	0.	100.	3
GLASS PRODUCTS...............	96.	3.6	100.	28
STONE, CLAY AND CONCRETE.....	95.	5.0	100.	60
IRON AND STEEL PRODUCTS......	94.	6.3	100.	142
NON-FERROUS SMELTING.........	71.	29.	100.	69
NON-FERROUS PRODUCTS.........	95.	5.2	100.	115
METAL CANS...................	100.	0.	100.	29
STRUCTURAL METAL PRODUCTS....	99.	1.9	100.	53
FABRICATED WIRE PRODUCTS.....	94.	5.7	100.	35
OTHER FABRICATED METAL.......	94.	5.8	100.	139
ENGINES AND TURBINES.........	97.	2.8	100.	36
FARM MACHINERY...............	97.	3.0	100.	33
CONSTRUCTION MACHINERY.......	87.	13.	100.	15
SPECIAL INDUSTRY MACHINERY...	92.	8.1	100.	62
GENERAL INDUSTRY MACHINERY...	100.	0.	100.	50
OFFICE MACHINES + COMPUTERS..	88.	13.	100.	24
OTHER NON-ELECTR. MACHINERY..	100.	0.	100.	25
ELECTR. TRANSMISSION EQUIP...	100.	0.	100.	68
ELECTRIC LIGHTING AND WIRING.	100.	0.	100.	77
RADIOS, TV'S + APPLIANCES....	93.	6.9	100.	130
COMMUNICATIONS EQUIPMENT.....	95.	5.5	100.	73

TABLE CONTINUED ON NEXT PAGE

387

CROSS-TABULATION 15. 6.1: PERCENTAGE BREAKDOWN OF NUMBER (AS OF 1/1/71) OF
MANUFACTURING SUBSIDIARIES OF NON-U.S.-BASED PARENT SYSTEMS BY
SUBSIDIARY'S PRINCIPAL MARKET AS OF 1/1/71
FOR SUBSIDIARIES CLASSIFIED BY
PRINCIPAL INDUSTRY OF SUBSIDIARY AS OF 1/1/71
(CONTINUED)

SUBSIDIARY'S PRINCIPAL MARKET AS OF 1/1/71

PRINCIPAL INDUSTRY OF SUBSIDIARY AS OF 1/1/71	LOCAL COUNTRY	EXPORT MARKETS	TOTAL PERCENT	TOTAL NUMBER
ELECTRONIC COMPONENTS............	89.	11.	100.	70
OTHER ELECTRICAL EQUIPMENT.......	94.	5.8	100.	139
MOTOR VEHICLES AND EQUIPMENT.	93.	6.6	100.	151
OTHER TRANSPORTATION.............	89.	11.	100.	47
PRECISION GOODS..................	90.	10.	100.	48
MISCELLANEOUS PRODUCTS...........	97.	3.3	100.	60

CROSS-TABULATION 15.10.1: PERCENTAGE BREAKDOWN OF NUMBER (AS OF 1/1/71) OF
MANUFACTURING SUBSIDIARIES OF NON-U.S.-BASED PARENT SYSTEMS BY
SUBSIDIARY'S PRINCIPAL MARKET AS OF 1/1/71
FOR SUBSIDIARIES CLASSIFIED BY
PERCENTAGE OF SUBSIDIARY'S EQUITY OWNED BY PARENT SYSTEM AS OF 1/1/71

PERCENTAGE OF SUBSIDIARY'S EQUITY OWNED BY PARENT SYSTEM AS OF 1/1/71	SUBSIDIARY'S PRINCIPAL MARKET AS OF 1/1/71			
	LOCAL COUNTRY	EXPORT MARKETS	TOTAL PERCENT	TOTAL NUMBER
95% OR MORE.................	94.	6.3	100.	2126
OVER 50% BUT UNDER 95%.......	94.	6.0	100.	857
EXACTLY 50%................	92.	7.8	100.	309
AT LEAST 25% BUT UNDER 50%...	91.	9.3	100.	506
OVER 5% BUT UNDER 25%........	85.	15.	100.	341

CROSS-TABULATION 15.12.1: PERCENTAGE BREAKDOWN OF NUMBER (AS OF 1/1/71) OF
MANUFACTURING SUBSIDIARIES OF NON-U.S.-BASED PARENT SYSTEMS BY
SUBSIDIARY'S PRINCIPAL MARKET AS OF 1/1/71
FOR SUBSIDIARIES CLASSIFIED BY
CATEGORY OF SUBSIDIARY'S PRINCIPAL OUTSIDE OWNER (IF ANY) AS OF 1/1/71

CATEGORY OF SUBSIDIARY'S PRINCIPAL OUTSIDE OWNER (IF ANY) AS OF 1/1/71	SUBSIDIARY'S PRINCIPAL MARKET AS OF 1/1/71			
	LOCAL COUNTRY	EXPORT MARKETS	TOTAL PERCENT	TOTAL NUMBER
LOCAL PRIVATE............	88.	12.	100.	740
LOCAL STATE.............	90.	10.	100.	109
FOREIGN PRIVATE.........	85.	15.	100.	315
STOCK WIDELY DISPERSED...	99.	1.1	100.	87

CROSS-TABULATION 15.16.1: PERCENTAGE BREAKDOWN OF NUMBER (AS OF 1/1/71) OF
MANUFACTURING SUBSIDIARIES OF NON-U.S.-BASED PARENT SYSTEMS BY
SUBSIDIARY'S PRINCIPAL MARKET AS OF 1/1/71
FOR SUBSIDIARIES CLASSIFIED BY
SUBSIDIARY'S PRINCIPAL CUSTOMER AS OF 1/1/71

SUBSIDIARY'S PRINCIPAL CUSTOMER AS OF 1/1/71	SUBSIDIARY'S PRINCIPAL MARKET AS OF 1/1/71			
	LOCAL COUNTRY	EXPORT MARKETS	TOTAL PERCENT	TOTAL NUMBER
PARENT SYSTEM.............	71.	29.	100.	352
OUTSIDE CUSTOMERS.........	95.	5.4	100.	3637

CROSS-TABULATION 15.18.1: PERCENTAGE BREAKDOWN OF NUMBER (AS OF 1/1/71) OF
MANUFACTURING SUBSIDIARIES OF NON-U.S.-BASED PARENT SYSTEMS BY
SUBSIDIARY'S PRINCIPAL MARKET AS OF 1/1/71
FOR SUBSIDIARIES CLASSIFIED BY
VALUE OF SUBSIDIARY'S SALES IN 1970

VALUE OF SUBSIDIARY'S SALES AS OF 1/1/71	SUBSIDIARY'S PRINCIPAL MARKET AS OF 1/1/71			
	LOCAL COUNTRY	EXPORT MARKETS	TOTAL PERCENT	TOTAL NUMBER
UNDER $1 MILLION............	94.	6.4	100.	829
$1 - $10 MILLION............	92.	7.8	100.	1474
$10 - $25 MILLION...........	90.	9.7	100.	465
$25 - $100 MILLION..........	90.	10.	100.	289
OVER $100 MILLION...........	86.	14.	100.	118

CROSS-TABULATION 15.21.1: PERCENTAGE BREAKDOWN OF NUMBER (AS OF 1/1/71) OF
MANUFACTURING SUBSIDIARIES OF NON-U.S.-BASED PARENT SYSTEMS BY
SUBSIDIARY'S PRINCIPAL MARKET AS OF 1/1/71
FOR SUBSIDIARIES CLASSIFIED BY
NATIONAL BASE OF SUBSIDIARY'S PARENT SYSTEM

NATIONAL BASE OF SUBSIDIARY'S PARENT SYSTEM	SUBSIDIARY'S PRINCIPAL MARKET AS OF 1/1/71			
	LOCAL COUNTRY	EXPORT MARKETS	TOTAL PERCENT	TOTAL NUMBER
UNITED KINGDOM...................	94.	5.8	100.	1962
GERMANY..........................	96.	3.7	100.	645
FRANCE...........................	90.	10.	100.	153
ITALY............................	95.	4.6	100.	65
BELGIUM AND LUXEMBURG............	93.	6.8	100.	132
THE NETHERLANDS..................	96.	4.0	100.	326
SWEDEN...........................	92.	7.9	100.	114
SWITZERLAND......................	92.	7.9	100.	229
JAPAN............................	79.	21.	100.	435
CANADA...........................	39.	11.	100.	178
OTHER NON-U.S....................	85.	15.	100.	20

CROSS-TABULATION 15.22.1: PERCENTAGE BREAKDOWN OF NUMBER (AS OF 1/1/71) OF
MANUFACTURING SUBSIDIARIES OF NON-U.S.-BASED PARENT SYSTEMS BY
SUBSIDIARY'S PRINCIPAL MARKET AS OF 1/1/71
FOR SUBSIDIARIES CLASSIFIED BY
VALUE OF SALES OF SUBSIDIARY'S PARENT SYSTEM IN 1970

VALUE OF SALES OF SUBSIDIARY'S PARENT SYSTEM IN 1970	SUBSIDIARY'S PRINCIPAL MARKET AS OF 1/1/71			
	LOCAL COUNTRY	EXPORT MARKETS	TOTAL PERCENT	TOTAL NUMBER
$400 - 599 MILLION................	92.	8.4	100.	846
$600 - 999 MILLION................	89.	11.	100.	667
$1 - 2 BILLION....................	93.	7.3	100.	1168
OVER $2 BILLION...................	94.	6.2	100.	1465

CROSS-TABULATION 15.25.1: PERCENTAGE BREAKDOWN OF NUMBER (AS OF 1/1/71) OF
MANUFACTURING SUBSIDIARIES OF NON-U.S.-BASED PARENT SYSTEMS BY
SUBSIDIARY'S PRINCIPAL MARKET AS OF 1/1/71
FOR SUBSIDIARIES CLASSIFIED BY
NUMBER OF COUNTRIES IN WHICH SUBSIDIARY'S PARENT SYSTEM MANUFACTURED AS OF 1/1/71

NUMBER OF COUNTRIES SUB-SIDIARY'S PARENT SYSTEM MANUFACTURED IN AS OF 1/1/71	SUBSIDIARY'S PRINCIPAL MARKET AS OF 1/1/71			
	LOCAL COUNTRY	EXPORT MARKETS	TOTAL PERCENT	TOTAL NUMBER
TWO OR THREE........................	82.	18.	100.	51
FOUR TO SIX.........................	86.	14.	100.	315
SEVEN TO TWELVE.....................	85.	15.	100.	485
THIRTEEN OR MORE....................	94.	5.8	100.	3404

CROSS-TABULATION 15.26.1: PERCENTAGE BREAKDOWN OF NUMBER (AS OF 1/1/71) OF
MANUFACTURING SUBSIDIARIES OF NON-U.S.-BASED PARENT SYSTEMS BY
SUBSIDIARY'S PRINCIPAL MARKET AS OF 1/1/71
FOR SUBSIDIARIES CLASSIFIED BY
PERCENTAGE OF PARENT SYSTEM'S EMPLOYEES OUTSIDE NATIONAL BASE AS OF 1/1/71

PERCENTAGE OF PARENT SYSTEM'S EMPLOYEES OUTSIDE NATIONAL BASE AS OF 1/1/71	SUBSIDIARY'S PRINCIPAL MARKET AS OF 1/1/71			
	LOCAL COUNTRY	EXPORT MARKETS	TOTAL PERCENT	TOTAL NUMBER
UNDER 10%......................	88.	12.	100.	385
10% - 25%......................	94.	6.4	100.	1157
25% - 50%......................	95.	4.9	100.	736
OVER 50%.......................	94.	6.4	100.	1388

CROSS-TABULATION 15.27.1: PERCENTAGE BREAKDOWN OF NUMBER (AS OF 1/1/71) OF
MANUFACTURING SUBSIDIARIES OF NON-U.S.-BASED PARENT SYSTEMS BY
SUBSIDIARY'S PRINCIPAL MARKET AS OF 1/1/71
FOR SUBSIDIARIES CLASSIFIED BY
NO. OF INDUSTRIES IN WHICH PARENT SYSTEM MANUFACTURED WITHIN NATIONAL BASE AS OF 1/1/71

| | SUBSIDIARY'S PRINCIPAL MARKET AS OF 1/1/71 | | | |
NO. OF INDUSTRIES IN WHICH PARENT SYSTEM MANUF. WITHIN NATIONAL BASE AS OF 1/1/71	LOCAL COUNTRY	EXPORT MARKETS	TOTAL PERCENT	TOTAL NUMBER
ONE TO THREE......	83.	17.	100.	362
FOUR TO NINE......	92.	8.1	100.	1267
TEN TO NINETEEN......	93.	6.9	100.	1798
TWENTY OR MORE......	96.	3.8	100.	832

CROSS-TABULATION 15.28.1: PERCENTAGE BREAKDOWN OF NUMBER (AS OF 1/1/71) OF
MANUFACTURING SUBSIDIARIES OF NON-U.S.-BASED PARENT SYSTEMS BY
SUBSIDIARY'S PRINCIPAL MARKET AS OF 1/1/71
FOR SUBSIDIARIES CLASSIFIED BY
NO. OF INDUSTRIES IN WHICH PARENT SYSTEM MANUFACTURED OUTSIDE NATIONAL BASE AS OF 1/1/71

NO. OF INDUSTRIES IN WHICH PARENT SYSTEM MANUF. OUTSIDE NATIONAL BASE AS OF 1/1/71	SUBSIDIARY'S PRINCIPAL MARKET AS OF 1/1/71			
	LOCAL COUNTRY	EXPORT MARKETS	TOTAL PERCENT	TOTAL NUMBER
ONE TO THREE................	84.	16.	100.	228
FOUR TO NINE................	90.	9.6	100.	1051
TEN TO NINETEEN.............	94.	6.2	100.	1245
TWENTY OR MORE..............	94.	6.2	100.	1735

CROSS-TABULATION 15.29.1: PERCENTAGE BREAKDOWN OF NUMBER (AS OF 1/1/71) OF
MANUFACTURING SUBSIDIARIES OF NON-U.S.-BASED PARENT SYSTEMS BY
SUBSIDIARY'S PRINCIPAL MARKET AS OF 1/1/71
FOR SUBSIDIARIES CLASSIFIED BY
PARENT SYSTEM'S R&D EXPENDITURES AS A PERCENTAGE OF SALES IN 1970

PARENT SYSTEM'S R&D EXPENDITURES AS A PERCENTAGE OF SALES IN 1970	SUBSIDIARY'S PRINCIPAL MARKET AS OF 1/1/71			
	LOCAL COUNTRY	EXPORT MARKETS	TOTAL PERCENT	TOTAL NUMBER
LESS THAN 1%....................	91.	8.7	100.	598
1% - 4%........................	94.	6.2	100.	1142
MORE THAN 4%...................	95.	5.3	100.	907

TABULATION 16.1: PERCENTAGE BREAKDOWN OF NUMBER OF SUBSIDIARIES BY SUBSIDIARY'S PRINCIPAL CUSTOMER FOR VARIOUS CATEGORIES OF SUBSIDIARIES

CATEGORY OF SUBSIDIARY	SUBSIDIARY'S PRINCIPAL CUSTOMER			
	PARENT SYSTEM	OUTSIDE CUSTOMERS	TOTAL PERCENT	TOTAL NUMBER
NON-U.S.-BASED SYSTEMS (AS OF 1/1/71):				
ALL SUBSIDIARIES........	8.9	91.	100.	7244
MANUFACTURING SUBS......	8.9	91.	100.	4122
SALES SUBSIDIARIES......	3.1	97.	100.	2406
U.S.-BASED SYSTEMS (AS OF 1/1/68):				
ALL SUBSIDIARIES........	3.4	97.	100.	1426
MANUFACTURING SURS......	2.2	98.	100.	958
SALES SUBSIDIARIES......	5.1	95.	100.	353
WORLD SUBSET OF SYSTEMS (AS OF 1/1/68):				
NON-U.S.-BASED SYSTEMS:				
ALL SUBSIDIARIES.......	8.9	91.	100.	3177
MANUFACTURING SUBS.....	8.8	91.	100.	1826
SALES SUBSIDIARIES.....	3.2	97.	100.	1089
U.S.-BASED-SYSTEMS:				
ALL SUBSIDIARIES.......	2.6	97.	100.	1053
MANUFACTURING SUBS.....	1.6	98.	100.	683
SALES SUBSIDIARIES.....	2.2	98.	100.	267

TABULATION 16.2: PERCENTAGE BREAKDOWN OF SALES OF SUBSIDIARIES IN 1970 BY
SUBSIDIARY'S PRINCIPAL CUSTOMER AS OF 1/1/71
FOR ALL SUBSIDIARIES, MANUFACTURING SUBSIDIARIES AND SALES SUBSIDIARIES
OF NON-U.S.-BASED SYSTEMS

CATEGORY OF SUBSIDIARY	SUBSIDIARY'S PRINCIPAL CUSTOMER AS OF 1/1/71			
	PARENT ENTER-PRISE	OUTSIDE CUSTOMERS	TOTAL PERCENT	TOTAL ($ MIL)
ALL SUBSIDIARIES..............	9.9	90.	100.	95267
MANUFACTURING SUBSIDIARIES....	8.2	92.	100.	68085
SALES SUBSIDIARIES............	4.0	96.	100.	19202

CROSS-TABULATION 16. 1.1: PERCENTAGE BREAKDOWN OF NUMBER (AS OF 1/1/71) OF MANUFACTURING SUBSIDIARIES OF NON-U.S.-BASED PARENT SYSTEMS BY SUBSIDIARY'S PRINCIPAL CUSTOMER AS OF 1/1/71 FOR SUBSIDIARIES CLASSIFIED BY SUBSIDIARY'S COUNTRY

SUBSIDIARY'S COUNTRY	SUBSIDIARY'S PRINCIPAL CUSTOMER AS OF 1/1/71			
	PARENT ENTER-PRISE	OUTSIDE CUSTOMERS	TOTAL PERCENT	TOTAL NUMBER
UNITED STATES.............	9.0	91.	100.	266
CANADA....................	8.3	91.	100.	216
MEXICO....................	4.1	96.	100.	74
CENTRAL AMERICA AND CARIB..	15.	85.	100.	68
VENEZUELA.................	9.1	91.	100.	33
COLOMBIA..................	8.3	92.	100.	24
PERU.....................	15.	85.	100.	26
CHILE....................	9.5	90.	100.	21
ARGENTINA.................	5.2	95.	100.	77
BRAZIL...................	6.3	94.	100.	126
OTHER SOUTH AMERICA.......	27.	73.	100.	15
GERMANY..................	9.5	90.	100.	221
FRANCE...................	4.5	96.	100.	289
ITALY....................	9.4	91.	100.	128
BELGIUM AND LUXEMBURG.....	12.	88.	100.	113
THE NETHERLANDS...........	9.3	91.	100.	108
UNITED KINGDOM............	13.	87.	100.	137
IRELAND..................	11.	89.	100.	79
DENMARK..................	12.	88.	100.	33
NORWAY...................	34.	66.	100.	32
SWEDEN...................	9.4	91.	100.	53
FINLAND..................	12.	88.	100.	17

TABLE CONTINUED ON NEXT PAGE

CROSS-TABULATION 16. 1.1: PERCENTAGE BREAKDOWN OF NUMBER (AS OF 1/1/71) OF MANUFACTURING SUBSIDIARIES OF NON-U.S.-BASED PARENT SYSTEMS BY SUBSIDIARY'S PRINCIPAL CUSTOMER AS OF 1/1/71 FOR SUBSIDIARIES CLASSIFIED BY SUBSIDIARY'S COUNTRY (CONTINUED)

SUBSIDIARY'S COUNTRY	SUBSIDIARY'S PRINCIPAL CUSTOMER AS OF 1/1/71			
	PARENT ENTER-PRISE	OUTSIDE CUSTOMERS	TOTAL PERCENT	TOTAL NUMBER
SWITZERLAND.............	17.	83.	100.	36
AUSTRIA.................	0.	100.	100.	69
PORTUGAL................	10.	90.	100.	40
SPAIN...................	7.6	92.	100.	131
GREECE..................	5.3	95.	100.	19
TURKEY..................	0.	100.	100.	25
OTHER EUROPE + ISRAEL...	18.	82.	100.	17
PAKISTAN................	2.9	97.	100.	35
IRAN....................	6.3	94.	100.	16
OTHER MID EAST+EGYPT+LIBYA...	5.3	95.	100.	19
UNION OF SOUTH AFRICA...	8.0	92.	100.	288
RHODESIA................	6.7	93.	100.	45
ZAMBIA..................	0.	100.	100.	36
TANZANIA................	5.3	95.	100.	19
KENYA...................	7.5	93.	100.	40
NIGERIA.................	6.3	94.	100.	48
OTHER (BRITISH) AFRICA..	8.9	91.	100.	45
MOROCCO, ALGERIA + TUNISIA...	27.	73.	100.	11
OTHER (FRENCH) AFRICA...	12.	88.	100.	25
OTHER AFRICA............	9.5	90.	100.	21
AUSTRALIA...............	9.4	91.	100.	341
NEW ZEALAND.............	6.7	93.	100.	90

TABLE CONTINUED ON NEXT PAGE

403

CROSS-TABULATION 16. 1.1: PERCENTAGE BREAKDOWN OF NUMBER (AS OF 1/1/71) OF
MANUFACTURING SUBSIDIARIES OF NON-U.S.-BASED PARENT SYSTEMS BY
SUBSIDIARY'S PRINCIPAL CUSTOMER AS OF 1/1/71
FOR SUBSIDIARIES CLASSIFIED BY
SUBSIDIARY'S COUNTRY
(CONTINUED)

SUBSIDIARY'S COUNTRY	SUBSIDIARY'S PRINCIPAL CUSTOMER AS OF 1/1/71			
	PARENT ENTER-PRISE	OUTSIDE CUSTOMERS	TOTAL PERCENT	TOTAL NUMBER
JAPAN	8.8	91.	100.	68
CHINA (TAIWAN)	11.	89.	100.	88
HONG KONG	17.	83.	100.	23
THE PHILIPPINES	13.	87.	100.	23
MALAYSIA	14.	86.	100.	51
SINGAPORE	2.2	98.	100.	45
INDONESIA	0.	100.	100.	22
THAILAND	8.8	91.	100.	57
INDIA	9.7	90.	100.	124
OTHER ASIA AND OCEANIA	13.	87.	100.	47

404

CROSS-TABULATION 16. 2.1: PERCENTAGE BREAKDOWN OF NUMBER (AS OF 1/1/71) OF
MANUFACTURING SUBSIDIARIES OF NON-U.S.-BASED PARENT SYSTEMS BY
SUBSIDIARY'S PRINCIPAL CUSTOMER AS OF 1/1/71
FOR SUBSIDIARIES CLASSIFIED BY
GEOGRAPHICAL REGION OF SUBSIDIARY'S COUNTRY

GEOGRAPHICAL REGION OF SUBSIDIARY'S COUNTRY	SUBSIDIARY'S PRINCIPAL CUSTOMER AS OF 1/1/71			
	PARENT ENTER- PRISE	OUTSIDE CUSTOMERS	TOTAL PERCENT	TOTAL NUMBER
NORTH AMERICA................	8.9	91.	100.	482
LATIN AMERICA................	8.6	91.	100.	464
EUROPE.......................	9.2	91.	100.	1546
AFRICA AND MIDDLE EAST........	7.4	93.	100.	649
OTHER ASIA AND OCEANIA........	9.4	91.	100.	979

CROSS-TABULATION 16. 3.1: PERCENTAGE BREAKDOWN OF NUMBER (AS OF 1/1/71) OF MANUFACTURING SUBSIDIARIES OF NON-U.S.-BASED PARENT SYSTEMS BY SUBSIDIARY'S PRINCIPAL CUSTOMER AS OF 1/1/71 FOR SUBSIDIARIES C-ASSIFIED BY GNP PER CAPITA IN 1970 OF SUBSIDIARY'S COUNTRY

GNP PER CAPITA IN 1970 OF SUBSIDIARY'S COUNTRY	SUBSIDIARY'S PRINCIPAL CUSTOMER AS OF 1/1/71			
	PARENT ENTER- PRISE	OUTSIDE CUSTOMERS	TOTAL PERCENT	TOTAL NUMBER
UNDER $200..............	7.3	93.	100.	422
$200 - $500.............	10.	90.	100.	558
$500 - $1200............	8.0	92.	100.	805
$1200 - $2500...........	9.1	91.	100.	700
OVER $2500..............	9.3	91.	100.	1602

CROSS-TABULATION 16. 4.1: PERCENTAGE BREAKDOWN OF NUMBER (AS OF 1/1/71) OF
MANUFACTURING SUBSIDIARIES OF NON-U.S.-BASED PARENT SYSTEMS BY
SUBSIDIARY'S PRINCIPAL CUSTOMER AS OF 1/1/71
FOR SUBSIDIARIES CLASSIFIED BY
GNP IN 1970 OF SUBSIDIARY'S COUNTRY

GNP IN 1970 OF SUBSIDIARY'S COUNTRY	SUBSIDIARY'S PRINCIPAL CUSTOMER AS OF 1/1/71			
	PARENT ENTER-PRISE	OUTSIDE CUSTOMERS	TOTAL PERCENT	TOTAL NUMBER
UNDER $1 BILLION................	19.	81.	100.	74
$1 - $5 BILLION................	8.7	91.	100.	484
$5 - $20 BILLION................	9.1	91.	100.	1064
$20 - $100 BILLION................	8.7	91.	100.	1484
OVER $100 BILLION................	9.4	92.	100.	981

CROSS-TABULATION 16.6.1: PERCENTAGE BREAKDOWN OF NUMBER (AS OF 1/1/71) OF MANUFACTURING SUBSIDIARIES OF NON-U.S.-BASED PARENT SYSTEMS BY SUBSIDIARY'S PRINCIPAL CUSTOMER AS OF 1/1/71 FOR SUBSIDIARIES CLASSIFIED BY PRINCIPAL INDUSTRY OF SUBSIDIARY AS OF 1/1/71

PRINCIPAL INDUSTRY OF SUBSIDIARY AS OF 1/1/71	SUBSIDIARY'S PRINCIPAL CUSTOMER AS OF 1/1/71			
	PARENT ENTERPRISE	OUTSIDE CUSTOMERS	TOTAL PERCENT	TOTAL NUMBER
ORDNANCE	20.	80.	100.	5
MEAT PRODUCTS	21.	79.	100.	24
DAIRY PRODUCTS	2.1	98.	100.	47
CANNED FOODS	8.3	92.	100.	36
GRAIN MILL PRODUCTS	41.	59.	100.	41
BAKERY PRODUCTS	0.	100.	100.	63
CONFECTIONERY PRODUCTS	4.3	96.	100.	23
BEVERAGES	11.	89.	100.	129
OTHER FOOD PRODUCTS	3.2	97.	100.	125
TOBACCO PRODUCTS	7.1	93.	100.	56
TEXTILES	8.8	91.	100.	205
APPAREL	9.1	91.	100.	33
LUMBER AND WOOD	38.	62.	100.	39
FURNITURE	9.1	91.	100.	11
PAPER PRODUCTS	21.	79.	100.	126
PRINTED MATTER	3.5	96.	100.	85
INDUSTRIAL CHEMICALS	8.6	91.	100.	151
PLASTICS AND SYNTHETICS	5.2	95.	100.	97
DRUGS	8.3	92.	100.	169
SOAP AND COSMETICS	3.4	97.	100.	147
PAINTS	2.0	99.	100.	100
AGRICULTURAL CHEMICALS	4.0	96.	100.	50
OTHER CHEMICALS	6.3	94.	100.	112
REFINED PETROLEUM	29.	71.	100.	78
OTHER PETROLEUM PRODUCTS	13.	87.	100.	62

TABLE CONTINUED ON NEXT PAGE

CROSS-TABULATION 16.6.1: PERCENTAGE BREAKDOWN OF NUMBER (AS OF 1/1/71) OF MANUFACTURING SUBSIDIARIES OF NON-U.S.-BASED PARENT SYSTEMS BY SUBSIDIARY'S PRINCIPAL CUSTOMER AS OF 1/1/71 FOR SUBSIDIARIES CLASSIFIED BY PRINCIPAL INDUSTRY OF SUBSIDIARY AS OF 1/1/71 (CONTINUED)

PRINCIPAL INDUSTRY OF SUBSIDIARY AS OF 1/1/71	SUBSIDIARY'S PRINCIPAL CUSTOMER AS OF 1/1/71			
	PARENT ENTER-PRISE	OUTSIDE CUSTOMERS	TOTAL PERCENT	TOTAL NUMBER
TIRES........................	4.2	96.	100.	24
OTHER RUBBER PRODUCTS........	3.5	96.	100.	57
LEATHER PRODUCTS AND SHOES...	0.	100.	100.	3
GLASS PRODUCTS...............	6.1	94.	100.	33
STONE, CLAY AND CONCRETE.....	4.1	96.	100.	49
IRON AND STEEL PRODUCTS......	11.	89.	100.	141
NON-FERROUS SMELTING.........	29.	71.	100.	72
NON-FERROUS PRODUCTS.........	5.2	95.	100.	115
METAL CANS...................	9.7	90.	100.	31
STRUCTURAL METAL PRODUCTS....	5.7	94.	100.	53
FABRICATED WIRE PRODUCTS.....	15.	85.	100.	34
OTHER FABRICATED METAL.......	8.1	92.	100.	135
ENGINES AND TURBINES.........	9.1	91.	100.	33
FARM MACHINERY...............	0.	100.	100.	32
CONSTRUCTION MACHINERY.......	0.	100.	100.	14
SPECIAL INDUSTRY MACHINERY...	7.0	93.	100.	57
GENERAL INDUSTRY MACHINERY...	4.5	95.	100.	44
OFFICE MACHINES + COMPUTERS..	17.	83.	100.	24
OTHER NON-ELECTR. MACHINERY..	4.3	96.	100.	23
ELECTR. TRANSMISSION EQUIP...	3.0	97.	100.	67
ELECTRIC LIGHTING AND WIRING.	5.4	95.	100.	74
RADIOS, TV'S + APPLIANCES....	8.4	92.	100.	131
COMMUNICATIONS EQUIPMENT.....	4.7	95.	100.	64

TABLE CONTINUED ON NEXT PAGE

CROSS-TABULATION 16.6.1: PERCENTAGE BREAKDOWN OF NUMBER (AS OF 1/1/71) OF
MANUFACTURING SUBSIDIARIES OF NON-U.S.-BASED PARENT SYSTEMS BY
SUBSIDIARY'S PRINCIPAL CUSTOMER AS OF 1/1/71
FOR SUBSIDIARIES CLASSIFIED BY
PPINCIPAL INDUSTRY OF SUBSIDIARY AS OF 1/1/71
(CONTINUED)

PRINCIPAL INDUSTRY OF SUBSIDIARY AS OF 1/1/71	SUBSIDIARY'S PRINCIPAL CUSTOMER AS OF 1/1/71			
	PARENT ENTER- PRISE	OUTSIDE CUSTOMERS	TOTAL PERCENT	TOTAL NUMBER
ELECTRONIC COMPONENTS.....	21.	79.	100.	48
OTHER ELECTRICAL EQUIPMENT...	7.6	92.	100.	131
MOTOR VEHICLES AND EQUIPMENT.	9.2	91.	100.	152
OTHER TRANSPORTATION.........	3.8	96.	100.	52
PRECISION GOODS.............	12.	88.	100.	43
MISCELLANEOUS PRODUCTS......	4.3	96.	100.	47

CROSS-TABULATION 16.10.1: PERCENTAGE BREAKDOWN OF NUMBER (AS OF 1/1/71) OF
MANUFACTURING SUBSIDIARIES OF NON-U.S.-BASED PARENT SYSTEMS BY
SUBSIDIARY'S PRINCIPAL CUSTOMER AS OF 1/1/71
FOR SUBSIDIARIES CLASSIFIED BY
PERCENTAGE OF SUBSIDIARY'S EQUITY OWNED BY PARENT SYSTEM AS OF 1/1/71

PERCENTAGE OF SUBSIDIARY'S EQUITY OWNED BY PARENT SYSTEM AS OF 1/1/71	SUBSIDIARY'S PRINCIPAL CUSTOMER AS OF 1/1/71			
	PARENT ENTER- PRISE	OUTSIDE CUSTOMERS	TOTAL PERCENT	TOTAL NUMBER
95% OR MORE....................	9.3	91.	100.	2028
OVER 50% BUT UNDER 95%........	8.2	92.	100.	822
EXACTLY 50%...................	12.	88.	100.	305
AT LEAST 25% BUT UNDER 50%....	8.9	91.	100.	514
OVER 5% BUT UNDER 25%.........	5.0	95.	100.	342

CROSS-TABULATION 16.12.1: PERCENTAGE BREAKDOWN OF NUMBER (AS OF 1/1/71) OF
MANUFACTURING SUBSIDIARIES OF NON-U.S.-BASED PARENT SYSTEMS BY
SUBSIDIARY'S PRINCIPAL CUSTOMER AS OF 1/1/71
FOR SUBSIDIARIES CLASSIFIED BY
CATEGORY OF SUBSIDIARY'S PRINCIPAL OUTSIDE OWNER (IF ANY) AS OF 1/1/71

	SUBSIDIARY'S PRINCIPAL CUSTOMER AS OF 1/1/71			
CATEGORY OF SUBSIDIARY'S PRINCIPAL OUTSIDE OWNER (IF ANY) AS OF 1/1/71	PARENT ENTER- PRISE	OUTSIDE CUSTOMERS	TOTAL PERCENT	TOTAL NUMBER
LOCAL PRIVATE............	9.3	91.	100.	731
LOCAL STATE.............	12.	88.	100.	113
FOREIGN PRIVATE.........	11.	89.	100.	309
STOCK WIDELY DISPERSED...	5.8	94.	100.	86

CROSS-TABULATION 16.15.1: PERCENTAGE BREAKDOWN OF NUMBER (AS OF 1/1/71) OF
MANUFACTURING SUBSIDIARIES OF NON-U.S.-BASED PARENT SYSTEMS BY
SUBSIDIARY'S PRINCIPAL CUSTOMER AS OF 1/1/71
FOR SUBSIDIARIES CLASSIFIED BY
SUBSIDIARY'S PRINCIPAL MARKET AS OF 1/1/71

| SUBSIDIARY'S PRINCIPAL
MARKET AS OF 1/1/71 | SUBSIDIARY'S PRINCIPAL CUSTOMER AS OF 1/1/71 | | | |
	PARENT ENTER- PRISE	OUTSIDE CUSTOMERS	TOTAL PERCENT	TOTAL NUMBER
LOCAL COUNTRY.....................	6.7	93.	100.	3691
EXPORT MARKETS....................	35.	65.	100.	298

CROSS-TABULATION 16.18.1: PERCENTAGE BREAKDOWN OF NUMBER (AS OF 1/1/71) OF
MANUFACTURING SUBSIDIARIES OF NON-U.S.-BASED PARENT SYSTEMS BY
SUBSIDIARY'S PRINCIPAL CUSTOMER AS OF 1/1/71
FOR SUBSIDIARIES CLASSIFIED BY
VALUE OF SUBSIDIARY'S SALES IN 1970

VALUE OF SUBSIDIARY'S SALES AS OF 1/1/71	SUBSIDIARY'S PRINCIPAL CUSTOMER AS OF 1/1/71			
	PARENT ENTER- PRISE	OUTSIDE CUSTOMERS	TOTAL PERCENT	TOTAL NUMBER
UNDER $1 MILLION............	8.3	92.	100.	796
$1 - $10 MILLION............	9.1	91.	100.	1418
$10 - $25 MILLION...........	12.	88.	100.	451
$25 - $100 MILLION..........	9.8	90.	100.	276
OVER $100 MILLION...........	11.	89.	100.	117

CROSS-TABULATION 16.21.1: PERCENTAGE BREAKDOWN OF NUMBER (AS OF 1/1/71) OF MANUFACTURING SUBSIDIARIES OF NON-U.S.-BASED PARENT SYSTEMS BY SUBSIDIARY'S PRINCIPAL CUSTOMER AS OF 1/1/71 FOR SUBSIDIARIES CLASSIFIED BY NATIONAL BASE OF SUBSIDIARY'S PARENT SYSTEM

NATIONAL BASE OF SUBSIDIARY'S PARENT SYSTEM	SUBSIDIARY'S PRINCIPAL CUSTOMER AS OF 1/1/71			
	PARENT ENTERPRISE	OUTSIDE CUSTOMERS	TOTAL PERCENT	TOTAL NUMBER
UNITED KINGDOM....................	7.2	93.	100.	1973
GERMANY..........................	6.0	94.	100.	600
FRANCE...........................	21.	79.	100.	160
ITALY............................	6.0	94.	100.	67
BELGIUM AND LUXEMBURG............	7.1	93.	100.	112
THE NETHERLANDS..................	10.	90.	100.	272
SWEDEN...........................	12.	88.	100.	103
SWITZERLAND......................	13.	87.	100.	230
JAPAN............................	10.	90.	100.	429
CANADA...........................	17.	83.	100.	158
OTHER NON-U.S....................	5.6	94.	100.	18

CROSS-TABULATION 16.22.1: PERCENTAGE BREAKDOWN OF NUMBER (AS OF 1/1/71) OF
MANUFACTURING SUBSIDIARIES OF NON-U.S.-BASED PARENT SYSTEMS BY
SUBSIDIARY'S PRINCIPAL CUSTOMER AS OF 1/1/71
FOR SUBSIDIARIES CLASSIFIED BY
VALUE OF SALES OF SUBSIDIARY'S PARENT SYSTEM IN 1970

VALUE OF SALES OF SUBSIDIARY'S PARENT SYSTEM IN 1970	SUBSIDIARY'S PRINCIPAL CUSTOMER AS OF 1/1/71			
	PARENT ENTER- PRISE	OUTSIDE CUSTOMERS	TOTAL PERCENT	TOTAL NUMBER
$400 - 599 MILLION.............	9.8	90.	100.	851
$600 - 999 MILLION.............	9.2	91.	100.	633
$1 - 2 BILLION................	11.	89.	100.	1158
OVER $2 BILLION..............	7.1	93.	100.	1379

CROSS-TABULATION 16.23.1: PERCENTAGE BREAKDOWN OF NUMBER (AS OF 1/1/71) OF
MANUFACTURING SUBSIDIARIES OF NON-U.S.-BASED PARENT SYSTEMS BY
SUBSIDIARY'S PRINCIPAL CUSTOMER AS OF 1/1/71
FOR SUBSIDIARIES CLASSIFIED BY
PRINCIPAL INDUSTRY-GROUP OF SUBSIDIARY'S PARENT SYSTEM AS OF 1/1/71

PRINCIPAL INDUSTRY-GROUP OF SUBSIDIARY'S PARENT SYSTEM AS OF 1/1/71	SUBSIDIARY'S PRINCIPAL CUSTOMER AS OF 1/1/71			
	PARENT ENTER-PRISE	OUTSIDE CUSTOMERS	TOTAL PERCENT	TOTAL NUMBER
FOOD, TOBACCO AND SOAP.........	8.3	92.	100.	779
CHEMICALS AND DRUGS............	5.7	94.	100.	831
PETROLEUM......................	17.	83.	100.	216
IRON AND STEEL.................	7.3	93.	100.	165
NON-FERROUS METALS.............	16.	84.	100.	307
FABR. METAL + NON-EL. MACH....	4.3	96.	100.	346
ELECTRIC AND ELECTRONIC.......	8.8	91.	100.	592
AUTOMOBILES....................	17.	83.	100.	93
OTHER..........................	9.3	91.	100.	793

CROSS-TABULATION 16.25.1: PERCENTAGE BREAKDOWN OF NUMBER (AS OF 1/1/71) OF
MANUFACTURING SUBSIDIARIES OF NON-U.S.-BASED PARENT SYSTEMS BY
SUBSIDIARY'S PRINCIPAL CUSTOMER AS OF 1/1/71 .
FOR SUBSIDIARIES CLASSIFIED BY
NUMBER OF COUNTRIES IN WHICH SUBSIDIARY'S PARENT SYSTEM MANUFACTURED AS OF 1/1/71

| | SUBSIDIARY'S PRINCIPAL CUSTOMER AS OF 1/1/71 | | | |
NUMBER OF COUNTRIES SUB- SIDIARY'S PARENT SYSTEM MANUFACTURED IN AS OF 1/1/71	PARENT ENTER- PRISE	OUTSIDE CUSTOMERS	TOTAL PERCENT	TOTAL NUMBER
TWO OR THREE......................	21.	79.	100.	48
FOUR TO SIX.......................	13.	87.	100.	309
SEVEN TO TWELVE...................	12.	88.	100.	490
THIRTEEN OR MORE..................	7.9	92.	100.	3271

CROSS-TABULATION 16.26.1: PERCENTAGE BREAKDOWN OF NUMBER (AS OF 1/1/71) OF MANUFACTURING SUBSIDIARIES OF NON-U.S.-BASED PARENT SYSTEMS BY SUBSIDIARY'S PRINCIPAL CUSTOMER AS OF 1/1/71 FOR SUBSIDIARIES CLASSIFIED BY PERCENTAGE OF PARENT SYSTEM'S EMPLOYEES OUTSIDE NATIONAL BASE AS OF 1/1/71

PERCENTAGE OF PARENT SYSTEM'S EMPLOYEES OUTSIDE NATIONAL BASE AS OF 1/1/71	SUBSIDIARY'S PRINCIPAL CUSTOMER AS OF 1/1/71			
	PARENT ENTER-PRISE	OUTSIDE CUSTOMERS	TOTAL PERCENT	TOTAL NUMBER
UNDER 10%.........................	13.	87.	100.	381
10% - 25%.........................	7.8	92.	100.	1124
25% - 50%.........................	7.3	93.	100.	730
OVER 50%..........................	9.7	90.	100.	1318

CROSS-TABULATION 16.27.1: PERCENTAGE BREAKDOWN OF NUMBER (AS OF 1/1/71) OF
MANUFACTURING SUBSIDIARIES OF NON-U.S.-BASED PARENT SYSTEMS BY
SUBSIDIARY'S PRINCIPAL CUSTOMER AS OF 1/1/71
FOR SUBSIDIARIES CLASSIFIED BY
NO. OF INDUSTRIES IN WHICH PARENT SYSTEM MANUFACTURED WITHIN NATIONAL BASE AS OF 1/1/71

| | SUBSIDIARY'S PRINCIPAL CUSTOMER AS OF 1/1/71 | | | |
NO. OF INDUSTRIES IN WHICH PARENT SYSTEM MANUF. WITHIN NATIONAL BASE AS OF 1/1/71	PARENT ENTER- PRISE	OUTSIDE CUSTOMERS	TOTAL PERCENT	TOTAL NUMBER
ONE TO THREE..................	12.	88.	100.	335
FOUR TO NINE..................	11.	89.	100.	1281
TEN TO NINETEEN..............	8.2	92.	100.	1734
TWENTY OR MORE...............	4.9	95.	100.	772

420

CROSS-TABULATION 16.28.1: PERCENTAGE BREAKDOWN OF NUMBER (AS OF 1/1/71) OF
MANUFACTURING SUBSIDIARIES OF NON-U.S.-BASED PARENT SYSTEMS BY
SUBSIDIARY'S PRINCIPAL CUSTOMER AS OF 1/1/71
FOR SUBSIDIARIES CLASSIFIED BY
NO. OF INDUSTRIES IN WHICH PARENT SYSTEM MANUFACTURED OUTSIDE NATIONAL BASE AS OF 1/1/71

NO. OF INDUSTRIES IN WHICH PARENT SYSTEM MANUF. OUTSIDE NATIONAL BASE AS OF 1/1/71	SUBSIDIARY'S PRINCIPAL CUSTOMER AS OF 1/1/71			
	PARENT ENTER- PRISE	OUTSIDE CUSTOMERS	TOTAL PERCENT	TOTAL NUMBER
ONE TO THREE................	16.	84.	100.	204
FOUR TO NINE................	9.2	91.	100.	1031
TEN TO NINETEEN.............	10.	90.	100.	1212
TWENTY OR MORE..............	6.7	93.	100.	1675

CROSS-TABULATION 16.29.1: PERCENTAGE BREAKDOWN OF NUMBER (AS OF 1/1/71) OF
MANUFACTURING SUBSIDIARIES OF NON-U.S.-BASED PARENT SYSTEMS BY
SUBSIDIARY'S PRINCIPAL CUSTOMER AS OF 1/1/71
FOR SUBSIDIARIES CLASSIFIED BY
PARENT SYSTEM'S R&D EXPENDITURES AS A PERCENTAGE OF SALES IN 1970

	SUBSIDIARY'S PRINCIPAL CUSTOMER AS OF 1/1/71			
PARENT SYSTEM'S R&D EXPENDITURES AS A PERCENTAGE OF SALES IN 1970	PARENT ENTER- PRISE	OUTSIDE CUSTOMERS	TOTAL PERCENT	TOTAL NUMBER
LESS THAN 1%...............	10.	90.	100.	598
1% - 4%...............	9.7	90.	100.	1075
MORE THAN 4%...............	8.3	91.	100.	880

TABULATION 17.1: PERCENTAGE BREAKDOWN OF NUMBER OF SUBSIDIARIES BY
SUBSIDIARY'S DATE OF ENTRY INTO PARENT SYSTEM
FOR VARIOUS CATEGORIES OF SUBSIDIARIES

CATEGORY OF SUBSIDIARY	SUBSIDIARY'S DATE OF ENTRY INTO PARENT SYSTEM						
	PRE-1914	1914-1919	1920-1929	1930-1938	1939-1945	1946-1952	1953-1955
NON-U.S.-BASED SYSTEMS (UNTIL 1/1/71):							
ALL SUBSIDIARIES........	3.6	1.2	5.2	4.2	2.3	5.3	3.2
MANUFACTURING SUBS......	3.6	1.3	6.1	3.6	2.1	5.6	2.9
SALES SUBSIDIARIES......	3.4	1.2	6.0	3.7	2.8	5.8	4.1
U.S.-BASED SYSTEMS (UNTIL 1/1/68):							
ALL SUBSIDIARIES........	2.5	1.4	6.5	8.9	3.6	9.7	6.3
MANUFACTURING SUBS......	2.5	1.5	6.2	6.5	3.6	8.0	5.9
SALES SUBSIDIARIES......	4.5	1.6	8.3	9.1	3.2	8.9	5.8
WORLD SUBSET OF SYSTEMS (UNTIL 1/1/68):							
NON-U.S.-BASED SYSTEMS:							
ALL SUBSIDIARIES........	5.0	2.2	9.1	5.8	2.5	7.1	5.4
MANUFACTURING SUBS......	5.5	2.4	10.	4.7	2.4	7.0	4.5
SALES SUBSIDIARIES......	4.9	1.8	19.	6.0	2.6	8.2	6.1
U.S.-BASED SYSTEMS:							
ALL SUBSIDIARIES........	2.6	1.4	7.3	9.5	3.9	10.	6.2
MANUFACTURING SUBS......	2.4	1.3	6.5	6.8	3.8	7.9	6.0
SALES SUBSIDIARIES......	5.5	1.7	9.4	10.	3.5	9.3	5.5

(TABLE CONTINUED ON NEXT PAGE)

TABULATION 17.1: PERCENTAGE BREAKDOWN OF NUMBER OF SUBSIDIARIES BY
SUBSIDIARY'S DATE OF ENTRY INTO PARENT SYSTEM
FOR VARIOUS CATEGORIES OF SUBSIDIARIES
(CONTINUED)

CATEGORY OF SUBSIDIARY	SUBSIDIARY'S DATE OF ENTRY INTO PARENT SYSTEM					TOTAL PERCENT	TOTAL NUMBER
	1956-1958	1959-1961	1962-1964	1965-1967	1968-1970		
NON-U.S.-BASED SYSTEMS (UNTIL 1/1/71):							
ALL SUBSIDIARIES..........	4.1	9.6	16.	17.	34.	100.	15896
MANUFACTURING SUBS........	3.9	9.9	11.	18.	32.	100.	6461
SALES SUBSIDIARIES........	4.8	9.9	12.	19.	28.	100.	3894
U.S.-BASED SYSTEMS (UNTIL 1/1/68):							
ALL SUBSIDIARIES..........	9.5	16.	19.	17.	0.	100.	11076
MANUFACTURING SUBS........	9.1	19.	20.	18.	0.	100.	4836
SALES SUBSIDIARIES........	8.8	14.	19.	17.	0.	100.	2205
WORLD SUBSET OF SYSTEMS (UNTIL 1/1/68):							
NON-U.S.-BASED SYSTEMS:							
ALL SUBSIDIARIES..........	7.3	16.	14.	26.	0.	100.	6871
MANUFACTURING SUBS........	6.7	17.	14.	26.	0.	100.	3026
SALES SUBSIDIARIES........	6.7	14.	14.	26.	0.	100.	1969
U.S.-BASED SYSTEMS:							
ALL SUBSIDIARIES..........	9.3	15.	18.	17.	0.	100.	9184
MANUFACTURING SUBS........	8.9	19.	19.	18.	0.	100.	3797
SALES SUBSIDIARIES........	7.8	14.	19.	15.	0.	100.	1719

CROSS-TABULATION 17.21.1: PERCENTAGE BREAKDOWN OF NUMBER OF MANUFACTURING SUBSIDIARIES OF NON-U.S.-BASED PARENT SYSTEMS BY SUBSIDIARY'S DATE OF ENTRY INTO PARENT SYSTEM FOR SUBSIDIARIES CLASSIFIED BY NATIONAL BASE OF SUBSIDIARY'S PARENT SYSTEM

NATIONAL BASE OF SUBSIDIARY'S PARENT SYSTEM	SUBSIDIARY'S DATE OF ENTRY INTO PARENT SYSTEM						
	PRE-1914	1914-1919	1920-1929	1930-1938	1939-1945	1946-1952	1953-1955
UNITED KINGDOM..................	3.4	1.1	4.7	3.9	1.3	8.0	2.2
GERMANY........................	5.7	1.5	7.4	3.0	1.2	2.5	5.6
FRANCE.........................	1.8	0.2	2.2	2.5	1.6	3.3	3.8
ITALY..........................	1.6	1.6	2.4	1.6	3.3	14.	4.1
BELGIUM AND LUXEMBURG..........	7.7	1.6	13.	4.2	0.	4.5	3.9
THE NETHERLANDS................	2.9	0.7	9.9	2.4	1.3	4.6	1.5
SWEDEN.........................	2.9	6.2	13.	7.2	2.4	7.7	3.3
SWITZERLAND....................	12.	2.6	10.	6.6	2.2	4.4	2.6
JAPAN..........................	0.	0.	0.2	0.6	7.8	0.4	1.0
CANADA.........................	1.1	1.8	9.5	6.0	5.7	8.5	3.9
OTHER NON-U.S..................	1.0	0.	0.	0.	0.	2.0	0.

TABLE CONTINUED ON NEXT PAGE

CROSS-TABULATION 17.21.1: PERCENTAGE BREAKDOWN OF NUMBER OF
MANUFACTURING SUBSIDIARIES OF NON-U.S.-BASED PARENT SYSTEMS BY
SUBSIDIARY'S DATE OF ENTRY INTO PARENT SYSTEM
FOR SUBSIDIARIES CLASSIFIED BY
NATIONAL BASE OF SUBSIDIARY'S PARENT SYSTEM
(CONTINUED)

SUBSIDIARY'S DATE OF ENTRY INTO PARENT SYSTEM

NATIONAL BASE OF SUBSIDIARY'S PARENT SYSTEM	1956-1958	1959-1961	1962-1964	1965-1967	1968-1970	TOTAL PERCENT	TOTAL NUMBER
UNITED KINGDOM....................	3.7	13.	13.	18.	29.	100.	2530
GERMANY....................	5.9	6.5	7.8	14.	39.	100.	1024
FRANCE....................	3.1	7.4	7.1	18.	49.	100.	448
ITALY....................	4.1	15.	15.	14.	23.	100.	123
BELGIUM AND LUXEMBURG....................	3.5	4.5	3.9	9.6	43.	100.	311
THE NETHERLANDS....................	3.3	12.	6.2	30.	25.	100.	455
SWEDEN....................	1.9	6.2	7.2	16.	25.	100.	209
SWITZERLAND....................	4.8	7.0	9.4	19.	19.	100.	458
JAPAN....................	2.7	8.4	17.	22.	40.	100.	523
CANADA....................	3.9	16.	8.9	18.	17.	100.	281
OTHER NON-U.S.....................	1.0	11.	13.	5.1	67.	100.	99

TABULATION 16.1: PERCENTAGE BREAKDOWN OF NUMBER OF SUBSIDIARIES BY
SUBSIDIARY'S SALES
FOR VARIOUS CATEGORIES OF SUBSIDIARIES

CATEGORY OF SUBSIDIARY	SUBSIDIARY'S SALES					TOTAL PERCENT	TOTAL NUMBER
	UNDER $1 MILLION	$1-10 MILLION	$10-25 MILLION	$25-100 MILLION	OVER $100 MILLION		
NON-U.S.-BASED SYSTEMS (AS OF 1/1/71):							
ALL SUBSIDIARIES......	33.	42.	13.	8.3	3.1	100.	6324
MANUFACTURING SUBS...	26.	46.	15.	9.5	3.8	100.	3488
SALES SUBSIDIARIES...	39.	45.	12.	7.1	1.8	100.	2050
U.S.-BASED SYSTEMS (AS OF 1/1/68):							
ALL SUBSIDIARIES......	32.	48.	11.	6.6	2.1	100.	1052
MANUFACTURING SUBS...	25.	52.	14.	7.0	1.9	100.	750
SALES SUBSIDIARIES...	47.	43.	6.3	1.0	3.4	100.	206
WORLD SUBSET OF SYSTEMS (AS OF 1/1/68):							
NON-U.S.-BASED SYSTEMS:							
ALL SUBSIDIARIES......	24.	43.	17.	11.	5.1	100.	2859
MANUFACTURING SUBS...	17.	45.	18.	13.	6.4	100.	1593
SALES SUBSIDIARIES...	36.	44.	15.	8.2	2.3	100.	987
U.S.-BASED SYSTEMS:							
ALL SUBSIDIARIES......	30.	47.	14.	7.8	2.1	100.	752
MANUFACTURING SUBS...	24.	49.	16.	9.0	2.5	100.	556
SALES SUBSIDIARIES...	46.	42.	11.	9.9	0.9	100.	113

TABULATION 18.2: PERCENTAGE BREAKDOWN OF SALES OF SUBSIDIARIES IN 1970 BY
VALUE OF SUBSIDIARY'S SALES IN 1970
FOR ALL SUBSIDIARIES, MANUFACTURING SUBSIDIARIES AND SALES SUBSIDIARIES
OF NON-U.S.-BASED SYSTEMS

VALUE OF SUBSIDIARY'S SALES IN 1970

CATEGORY OF SUBSIDIARY	UNDER $1 MILLION	$1-10 MILLION	$10-25 MILLION	$25-100 MILLION	OVER $100 MILLION	TOTAL PERCENT	TOTAL ($ MIL)
ALL SUBSIDIARIES............	0.6	7.9	12.	26.	54.	100.	101910
MANUFACTURING SUBSIDIARIES...	0.4	6.6	11.	23.	59.	100.	72119
SALES SUBSIDIARIES..........	1.2	13.	18.	37.	31.	100.	19743

CROSS-TABULATION 18.21.1: PERCENTAGE BREAKDOWN OF NUMBER (AS OF 1/1/71) OF
MANUFACTURING SUBSIDIARIES OF NON-U.S.-BASED PARENT SYSTEMS BY
VALUE OF SUBSIDIARY'S SALES IN 1970
FOR SUBSIDIARIES CLASSIFIED BY
NATIONAL BASE OF SUBSIDIARY'S PARENT SYSTEM

VALUE OF SUBSIDIARY'S SALES IN 1970

NATIONAL BASE OF SUBSIDIARY'S PARENT SYSTEM	UNDER $1 MILLION	$1-10 MILLION	$10-25 MILLION	$25-100 MILLION	OVER $100 MILLION	TOTAL PERCENT	TOTAL NUMBER
UNITED KINGDOM........	33.	42.	14.	7.4	3.2	100.	1709
GERMANY..............	19.	50.	17.	11.	3.3	100.	484
FRANCE...............	13.	42.	19.	21.	4.7	100.	149
ITALY................	15.	28.	26.	23.	8.5	100.	47
BELGIUM AND LUXEMBURG.	13.	48.	13.	13.	12.	100.	52
THE NETHERLANDS......	12.	50.	14.	14.	9.6	100.	240
SWEDEN...............	15.	51.	18.	13.	2.4	100.	125
SWITZERLAND..........	15.	48.	19.	14.	4.0	100.	198
JAPAN................	33.	56.	8.2	2.3	0.3	100.	341
CANADA...............	19.	44.	16.	13.	8.1	100.	123
OTHER NON-U.S........	15.	45.	15.	20.	5.0	100.	20

TABULATION 20.1: PERCENTAGE BREAKDOWN OF NUMBER OF SUBSIDIARIES BY
SUBSIDIARY'S PRINCIPAL ACTIVITY
FOR VARIOUS CATEGORIES OF SUBSIDIARIES

CATEGORY OF SUBSIDIARY	SUBSIDIARY'S PRINCIPAL ACTIVITY					TOTAL PERCENT	TOTAL NUMBER
	SOME MANUFAC-TURING	SALES OR SERVICE	EXTRAC-TION	OTHER	INACTIVE		
SUBSIDIARIES OF:							
NON-U.S.-BASED SYSTEMS (AS OF 1/1/71)............	48.	28.	4.3	15.	5.5	100.	11849
U.S.-BASED SYSTEMS (AS OF 1/1/68)............	54.	21.	3.3	15.	7.4	100.	7927
NON-U.S.-BASED SYSTEMS IN WORLD SUBSET OF SYSTEMS (AS OF 1/1/68)............	63.	16.	6.4	8.9	5.1	100.	4922
U.S.-BASED SYSTEMS IN WORLD SUBSET OF SYSTEMS (AS OF 1/1/68)............	52.	20.	4.0	16.	7.4	100.	6430

TABULATION 20.2: PERCENTAGE BREAKDOWN OF SALES OF SUBSIDIARIES IN 1970 BY
SUBSIDIARY'S PRINCIPAL ACTIVITY AS OF 1/1/71
FOR ALL SUBSIDIARIES, MANUFACTURING SUBSIDIARIES AND SALES SUBSIDIARIES
OF NON-U.S.-BASED SYSTEMS

	SUBSIDIARY'S PRINCIPAL ACTIVITY AS OF 1/1/71						
CATEGORY OF SUBSIDIARY	SOME MANUFAC-TURING	SALES OR SERVICE	EXTRAC-TION	OTHER	INACTIVE	TOTAL PERCENT	TOTAL ($ MIL)
ALL SUBSIDIARIES............	65.	18.	4.0	12.	0.0	100.	127786
MANUFACTURING SUBSIDIARIES...	100.	0.0	0.0	0.0	0.0	100.	82434
SALES SUBSIDIARIES..........	0.0	100.	0.0	0.0	0.0	100.	23262

TABULATION 21.1: PERCENTAGE BREAKDOWN OF NUMBER OF SUBSIDIARIES BY
NATIONAL BASE OF SUBSIDIARY'S PARENT SYSTEM
FOR VARIOUS CATEGORIES OF SUBSIDIARIES

NATIONAL BASE OF SUBSIDIARY'S PARENT SYSTEM

CATEGORY OF SUBSIDIARY	UNITED KINGDOM	GERMANY	FRANCE	ITALY	BELGIUM AND LUXEMBURG	THE NETHER- LANDS	SWEDEN
NON-U.S.-BASED SYSTEMS (AS OF 1/1/71):							
ALL SUBSIDIARIES.........	30.	15.	9.8	4.2	4.9	7.7	4.5
MANUFACTURING SUBS.......	43.	14.	7.6	2.3	4.8	7.5	3.0
SALES SUBSIDIARIES.......	28.	17.	12.	5.1	3.7	8.7	8.0
NON-U.S.-BASED SYSTEMS IN WORLD SUBSET OF SYSTEMS (AS OF 1/1/68):							
ALL SUBSIDIARIES.........	37.	14.	9.1	6.3	4.9	12.	3.2
MANUFACTURING SUBS.......	45.	13.	6.6	3.4	3.6	11.	2.1
SALES SUBSIDIARIES.......	31.	17.	12.	7.2	2.9	14.	6.2

(TABLE CONTINUED ON NEXT PAGE)

TABULATION 21.1: PERCENTAGE BREAKDOWN OF NUMBER OF SUBSIDIARIES BY
NATIONAL BASE OF SUBSIDIARY'S PARENT SYSTEM
FOR VARIOUS CATEGORIES OF SUBSIDIARIES
(CONTINUED)

CATEGORY OF SUBSIDIARY	NATIONAL BASE OF SUBSIDIARY'S PARENT SYSTEM					
	SWITZ-ERLAND	JAPAN	CANADA	OTHER NON-U.S.	TOTAL PERCENT	TOTAL NUMBER
NON-U.S.-BASED SYSTEMS (AS OF 1/1/71):						
ALL SUBSIDIARIES............	5.4	7.0	3.9	1.4	100.	13800
MANUFACTURING SUBS..........	7.0	8.5	3.5	1.8	100.	5645
SALES SUBSIDIARIES..........	4.2	9.5	2.6	0.7	100.	3311
NON-U.S.-BASED SYSTEMS IN WORLD SUBSET OF SYSTEMS (AS OF 1/1/68):						
ALL SUBSIDIARIES............	5.3	2.9	5.3	0.	100.	6153
MANUFACTURING SUBS..........	6.8	3.7	4.9	0.	100.	2737
SALES SUBSIDIARIES..........	3.6	2.9	3.2	0.	100.	1634

TABULATION 21.2: PERCENTAGE BREAKDOWN OF SALES OF SUBSIDIARIES IN 1970 BY
NATIONAL BASE OF SUBSIDIARY'S PARENT SYSTEM
FOR ALL SUBSIDIARIES, MANUFACTURING SUBSIDIARIES AND SALES SUBSIDIARIES
OF NON-U.S.-BASED SYSTEMS

NATIONAL BASE OF SUBSIDIARY'S PARENT SYSTEM

CATEGORY OF SUBSIDIARY	UNITED KINGDOM	GERMANY	FRANCE	ITALY	BELGIUM AND LUXEMBURG	THE NETHER-LANDS	SWEDEN
ALL SUBSIDIARIES............	32.	14.	8.2	4.6	3.9	18.	3.0
MANUFACTURING SUBSIDIARIES...	35.	10.	6.7	4.5	3.3	21.	2.5
SALES SUBSIDIARIES..........	18.	22.	12.	4.0	4.6	10.	5.2

TABLE CONTINUED ON NEXT PAGE

TABULATION 21.2: PERCENTAGE BREAKDOWN OF SALES OF SUBSIDIARIES IN 1970 BY
NATIONAL BASE OF SUBSIDIARY'S PARENT SYSTEM
FOR ALL SUBSIDIARIES, MANUFACTURING SUBSIDIARIES AND SALES SUBSIDIARIES
OF NON-U.S.-BASED SYSTEMS
(CONTINUED)

NATIONAL BASE OF SUBSIDIARY'S PARENT SYSTEM

CATEGORY OF SUBSIDIARY	SWITZ-ERLAND	JAPAN	CANADA	OTHER NON-U.S.	TOTAL PERCENT	TOTAL ($ MIL)
ALL SUBSIDIARIES............	5.9	5.9	3.9	0.8	100.	132500
MANUFACTURING SUBSIDIARIES...	7.5	3.1	4.8	0.7	100.	82434
SALES SUBSIDIARIES..........	2.2	18.	3.0	0.7	100.	23262

CROSS-TABULATION 21. 1.1: PERCENTAGE BREAKDOWN OF NUMBER (AS OF 1/1/71) OF MANUFACTURING SUBSIDIARIES OF NON-U.S.-BASED PARENT SYSTEMS BY NATIONAL BASE OF SUBSIDIARY'S PARENT SYSTEM FOR SUBSIDIARIES CLASSIFIED BY SUBSIDIARY'S COUNTRY

NATIONAL BASE OF SUBSIDIARY'S PARENT SYSTEM

SUBSIDIARY'S COUNTRY	UNITED KINGDOM	GERMANY	FRANCE	ITALY	BELGIUM AND LUXEMBURG	THE NETHER-LANDS	SWEDEN
UNITED STATES	29.	12.	5.2	1.2	6.0	24.	0.7
CANADA	64.	9.9	3.3	1.1	12.	1.5	1.5
MEXICO	19.	27.	7.2	5.2	0.	10.	5.2
CENTRAL AMERICA AND CARIB.	34.	12.	3.3	2.2	0.	7.8	2.2
VENEZUELA	20.	8.7	4.3	20.	0.	8.7	4.3
COLOMBIA	25.	21.	7.1	3.6	0.	7.1	7.1
PERU	13.	26.	3.2	9.7	0.	3.2	6.5
CHILE	21.	21.	14.	7.1	0.	7.1	7.1
ARGENTINA	23.	25.	19.	7.4	0.8	5.0	2.5
BRAZIL	14.	25.	15.	5.9	5.9	2.2	3.2
OTHER SOUTH AMERICA	43.	4.3	8.7	4.3	4.3	0.	0.
GERMANY	39.	0.3	13.	0.9	7.8	13.	4.7
FRANCE	22.	29.	0.	2.5	11.	7.5	3.6
ITALY	28.	18.	17.	0.	7.4	6.4	3.0
BELGIUM AND LUXEMBURG	31.	15.	23.	1.3	6.3	10.	3.8
THE NETHERLANDS	37.	17.	10.	2.9	13.	0.	6.5
UNITED KINGDOM	0.	14.	7.9	3.6	3.2	31.	8.7
IRELAND	82.	1.0	0.	1.0	0.	5.2	0.
DENMARK	43.	10.	2.5	2.5	2.5	15.	13.
NORWAY	29.	6.7	2.2	0.	0.	2.2	31.
SWEDEN	55.	27.	5.4	0.	0.	8.1	0.
FINLAND	18.	14.	0.	0.	9.1	4.5	50.

TABLE CONTINUED ON NEXT PAGE

CROSS-TABULATION 21. 1.1: PERCENTAGE BREAKDOWN OF NUMBER (AS OF 1/1/71) OF
MANUFACTURING SUBSIDIARIES OF NON-U.S.-BASED PARENT SYSTEMS BY
NATIONAL BASE OF SUBSIDIARY'S PARENT SYSTEM
FOR SUBSIDIARIES CLASSIFIED BY
SUBSIDIARY'S COUNTRY
(CONTINUED)

NATIONAL BASE OF SUBSIDIARY'S PARENT SYSTEM

SUBSIDIARY'S COUNTRY	UNITED KINGDOM	GERMANY	FRANCE	ITALY	BELGIUM AND LUXEMBURG	THE NETHERLANDS	SWEDEN
SWITZERLAND..........	23.	39.	11.	1.8	1.8	14.	5.4
AUSTRIA..............	25.	37.	5.5	2.2	3.3	9.9	1.1
PORTUGAL.............	26.	17.	19.	3.7	11.	1.9	3.7
SPAIN................	23.	23.	20.	8.3	7.3	4.1	1.6
GREECE...............	27.	42.	7.7	3.8	7.7	3.8	0.
TURKEY...............	21.	45.	9.1	6.1	0.	3.0	0.
OTHER EUROPE + ISRAEL	24.	11.	0.	8.1	43.	0.	2.7
PAKISTAN.............	60.	14.	2.4	0.	0.	2.4	2.4
IRAN.................	17.	29.	13.	0.	4.2	13.	8.3
OTHER MID EAST+EGYPT+LIBYA...	33.	19.	22.	7.4	3.7	0.	3.7
UNION OF SOUTH AFRICA........	76.	13.	1.9	0.5	2.7	1.3	0.5
RHODESIA.............	85.	0.	0.	0.	5.6	3.7	0.
ZAMBIA...............	95.	0.	0.	0.	0.	0.	0.
TANZANIA.............	73.	4.5	0.	4.5	0.	4.5	0.
KENYA................	86.	2.3	0.	0.	0.	6.8	0.
NIGERIA..............	76.	0.	3.7	0.	0.	0.	0.
OTHER (BRITISH) AFRICA.......	76.	3.7	0.	1.9	1.9	0.	0.
MOROCCO, ALGERIA + TUNISIA...	2.0	5.9	61.	9.8	5.9	12.	0.
OTHER (FRENCH) AFRICA........	25.	5.8	58.	0.	0.	3.8	0.
OTHER AFRICA.........	40.	2.9	2.9	5.7	29.	0.	2.9
AUSTRALIA............	85.	1.5	2.9	0.	0.5	1.7	1.5
NEW ZEALAND..........	88.	1.8	0.	0.	0.	0.9	0.

TABLE CONTINUED ON NEXT PAGE

CROSS-TABULATION 21.1.1: PERCENTAGE BREAKDOWN OF NUMBER (AS OF 1/1/71) OF
MANUFACTURING SUBSIDIARIES OF NON-U.S.-BASED PARENT SYSTEMS BY
NATIONAL BASE OF SUBSIDIARY'S PARENT SYSTEM
FOR SUBSIDIARIES CLASSIFIED BY
SUBSIDIARY'S COUNTRY
(CONTINUED)

NATIONAL BASE OF SUBSIDIARY'S PARENT SYSTEM

SUBSIDIARY'S COUNTRY	UNITED KINGDOM	GERMANY	FRANCE	ITALY	BELGIUM AND LUXEMBURG	THE NETHER- LANDS	SWEDEN
JAPAN	17.	39.	3.7	1.2	0.	11.	0.
CHINA (TAIWAN)	2.1	1.0	0.	0.	0.	1.0	0.
HONG KONG	32.	0.	3.6	0.	0.	0.	0.
THE PHILIPPINES	8.0	12.	4.0	0.	0.	16.	4.0
MALAYSIA	36.	1.8	1.8	1.8	0.	5.5	3.6
SINGAPORE	38.	1.9	0.	0.	0.	5.8	0.
INDONESIA	19.	12.	7.7	0.	0.	3.8	0.
THAILAND	6.2	7.7	0.	1.5	0.	1.5	0.
INDIA	51.	13.	2.0	2.0	0.7	3.3	3.3
OTHER ASIA AND OCEANIA	33.	6.3	4.8	1.6	1.6	3.2	1.6

TABLE CONTINUED ON NEXT PAGE

438

CROSS-TABULATION 21. 1.1: PERCENTAGE BREAKDOWN OF NUMBER (AS OF 1/1/71) OF
MANUFACTURING SUBSIDIARIES OF NON-U.S.-BASED PARENT SYSTEMS BY
NATIONAL BASE OF SUBSIDIARY'S PARENT SYSTEM
FOR SUBSIDIARIES CLASSIFIED BY
SUBSIDIARY'S COUNTRY
(CONTINUED)

NATIONAL BASE OF SUBSIDIARY'S PARENT SYSTEM

SUBSIDIARY'S COUNTRY	SWITZ-ERLAND	JAPAN	CANADA	OTHER NON-U.S.	TOTAL PERCENT	TOTAL NUMBER
UNITED STATES............	7.2	4.5	6.5	4.2	100.	403
CANADA..................	4.4	1.8	0.	0.	100.	273
MEXICO..................	8.2	10.	8.2	0.	100.	97
CENTRAL AMERICA AND CARIB.	5.6	20.	12.	0.	100.	90
VENEZUELA...............	8.7	13.	13.	0.	100.	46
COLOMBIA................	11.	7.1	11.	0.	100.	28
PERU....................	9.7	29.	0.	0.	100.	31
CHILE...................	11.	7.1	0.	3.6	100.	28
ARGENTINA...............	9.1	2.5	5.0	0.8	100.	121
BRAZIL..................	7.0	18.	3.2	0.5	100.	186
OTHER SOUTH AMERICA.....	17.	8.7	8.7	0.	100.	23
GERMANY.................	18.	0.3	2.5	0.	100.	320
FRANCE..................	10.	0.	2.3	12.	100.	441
ITALY...................	12.	0.5	5.0	2.5	100.	202
BELGIUM AND LUXEMBURG...	6.3	1.9	0.6	0.6	100.	158
THE NETHERLANDS.........	11.	0.	1.4	1.4	100.	139
UNITED KINGDOM..........	17.	0.4	13.	1.2	100.	253
IRELAND.................	1.0	1.0	7.2	1.0	100.	97
DENMARK.................	5.0	0.	7.5	0.	100.	40
NORWAY..................	20.	0.	8.9	0.	100.	45
SWEDEN..................	1.4	0.	1.4	1.4	100.	74
FINLAND.................	4.5	0.	0.	0.	100.	22

TABLE CONTINUED ON NEXT PAGE

CROSS-TABULATION 21. 1.1: PERCENTAGE BREAKDOWN OF NUMBER (AS OF 1/1/71) OF
MANUFACTURING SUBSIDIARIES OF NON-U.S.-BASED PARENT SYSTEMS BY
NATIONAL BASE OF SUBSIDIARY'S PARENT SYSTEM
FOR SUBSIDIARIES CLASSIFIED BY
SUBSIDIARY'S COUNTRY
(CONTINUED)

SUBSIDIARY'S COUNTRY	NATIONAL BASE OF SUBSIDIARY'S PARENT SYSTEM					
	SWITZ- ERLAND	JAPAN	CANADA	OTHER NON-U.S.	TOTAL PERCENT	TOTAL NUMBER
SWITZERLAND	0.	0.	1.8	1.8	100.	56
AUSTRIA	14.	0.	0.	1.1	100.	91
PORTUGAL	7.4	11.	0.	0.	100.	54
SPAIN	7.8	1.6	2.1	1.0	100.	193
GREECE	7.7	0.	0.	0.	100.	26
TURKEY	12.	0.	3.0	0.	100.	33
OTHER EUROPE + ISRAEL	8.1	0.	2.7	0.	100.	37
PAKISTAN	7.1	12.	0.	0.	100.	42
IRAN	0.	17.	0.	0.	100.	24
OTHER MID EAST+EGYPT+LIBYA	3.7	3.7	0.	3.7	100.	27
UNION OF SOUTH AFRICA	2.2	0.3	1.3	0.	100.	371
RHODESIA	1.9	0.	1.9	1.9	100.	54
ZAMBIA	0.	5.3	0.	0.	100.	38
TANZANIA	0.	14.	0.	0.	100.	22
KENYA	0.	4.5	0.	0.	100.	44
NIGERIA	3.7	15.	1.9	0.	100.	54
OTHER (BRITISH) AFRICA	0.	11.	3.7	1.9	100.	54
MOROCCO, ALGERIA + TUNISIA	0.	2.0	2.0	0.	100.	51
OTHER (FRENCH) AFRICA	1.9	5.8	0.	0.	100.	52
OTHER AFRICA	0.	14.	0.	2.9	100.	35
AUSTRALIA	1.0	3.9	2.5	0.	100.	407

TABLE CONTINUED ON NEXT PAGE

CROSS-TABULATION 21. 1.1: PERCENTAGE BREAKDOWN OF NUMBER (AS OF 1/1/71) OF MANUFACTURING SUBSIDIARIES OF NON-U.S.-BASED PARENT SYSTEMS BY NATIONAL BASE OF SUBSIDIARY'S PARENT SYSTEM FOR SUBSIDIARIES CLASSIFIED BY SUBSIDIARY'S COUNTRY (CONTINUED)

SUBSIDIARY'S COUNTRY	NATIONAL BASE OF SUBSIDIARY'S PARENT SYSTEM					
	SWITZERLAND	JAPAN	CANADA	OTHER NON-U.S.	TOTAL PERCENT	TOTAL NUMBER
NEW ZEALAND	2.7	1.8	3.6	0.9	100.	112
JAPAN	11.	0.	17.	0.	100.	82
CHINA (TAIWAN)	0.	95.	0.	1.0	100.	97
HONG KONG	3.6	61.	0.	0.	100.	28
THE PHILIPPINES	8.0	48.	0.	0.	100.	25
MALAYSIA	1.8	44.	1.8	1.8	100.	55
SINGAPORE	1.9	52.	0.	0.	100.	52
INDONESIA	0.	58.	0.	0.	100.	26
THAILAND	1.5	80.	1.5	0.	100.	65
INDIA	5.9	18.	1.3	0.	100.	152
OTHER ASIA AND OCEANIA	0.	44.	0.	3.2	100.	63

CROSS-TABULATION 21. 6.1: PERCENTAGE BREAKDOWN OF NUMBER (AS OF 1/1/71) OF
MANUFACTURING SUBSIDIARIES OF NON-U.S.-BASED PARENT SYSTEMS BY
NATIONAL BASE OF SUBSIDIARY'S PARENT SYSTEM
FOR SUBSIDIARIES CLASSIFIED BY
PRINCIPAL INDUSTRY OF SUBSIDIARY AS OF 1/1/71

NATIONAL BASE OF SUBSIDIARY'S PARENT SYSTEM

PRINCIPAL INDUSTRY OF SUBSIDIARY AS OF 1/1/71	UNITED KINGDOM	GERMANY	FRANCE	ITALY	BELGIUM AND LUXEMBURG	THE NETHER-LANDS	SWEDEN
ORDNANCE................	38.	25.	0.	0.	13.	0.	0.
MEAT PRODUCTS...........	90.	0.	0.	0.	0.	0.	0.
DAIRY PRODUCTS..........	56.	0.	0.	0.	0.	0.	0.
CANNED FOODS............	61.	0.	0.	0.	0.	0.	0.
GRAIN MILL PRODUCTS.....	96.	0.	0.	0.	0.	0.	0.
BAKERY PRODUCTS.........	99.	0.	0.	0.	0.	0.	0.
CONFECTIONERY PRODUCTS..	63.	0.	3.3	0.	0.	0.	0.
BEVERAGES...............	77.	0.	0.	0.	0.6	0.	0.
OTHER FOOD PRODUCTS.....	80.	0.7	0.7	0.	2.8	1.4	0.
TOBACCO PRODUCTS........	97.	0.	0.	0.	0.	0.	0.
TEXTILES................	30.	2.9	2.9	1.7	7.1	5.0	0.
APPAREL.................	43.	0.	2.5	2.5	0.	2.5	0.
LUMBER AND WOOD.........	28.	0.	0.	0.	30.	0.	21.
FURNITURE...............	56.	0.	11.	0.	0.	11.	5.6
PAPER PRODUCTS..........	70.	8.6	2.2	0.	1.4	0.7	5.8
PRINTED MATTER..........	61.	2.0	4.1	0.	0.	16.	2.0
INDUSTRIAL CHEMICALS....	34.	24.	15.	0.8	11.	12.	0.3
PLASTICS AND SYNTHETICS.	29.	24.	4.5	8.4	10.	4.5	1.3
DRUGS...................	17.	24.	8.3	0.4	1.3	15.	0.
SOAP AND COSMETICS......	89.	5.7	0.	0.	0.	0.6	0.
PAINTS..................	58.	25.	0.	0.9	6.2	8.8	0.
AGRICULTURAL CHEMICALS..	20.	16.	11.	2.5	6.3	18.	0.
OTHER CHEMICALS.........	32.	21.	9.7	0.6	1.9	12.	13.
REFINED PETROLEUM.......	39.	0.9	12.	10.	9.2	28.	0.
OTHER PETROLEUM PRODUCTS	39.	8.4	28.	1.2	7.2	13.	0.

TABLE CONTINUED ON NEXT PAGE

CROSS-TABULATION 21.6.1: PERCENTAGE BREAKDOWN OF NUMBER (AS OF 1/1/71) OF
MANUFACTURING SUBSIDIARIES OF NON-U.S.-BASED PARENT SYSTEMS BY
NATIONAL BASE OF SUBSIDIARY'S PARENT SYSTEM
FOR SUBSIDIARIES CLASSIFIED BY
PRINCIPAL INDUSTRY OF SUBSIDIARY AS OF 1/1/71
(CONTINUED)

NATIONAL BASE OF SUBSIDIARY'S PARENT SYSTEM

PRINCIPAL INDUSTRY OF SUBSIDIARY AS OF 1/1/71	UNITED KINGDOM	GERMANY	FRANCE	ITALY	BELGIUM AND LUXEMBURG	THE NETHER-LANDS	SWEDEN
TIRES............................	47.	8.3	25.	14.	0.	0.	0.
OTHER RUBBER PRODUCTS........	50.	16.	5.7	7.1	0.	1.4	0.
LEATHER PRODUCTS AND SHOES...	17.	17.	33.	0.	0.	0.	0.
GLASS PRODUCTS...............	4.0	4.0	78.	0.	10.	0.	2.0
STONE, CLAY AND CONCRETE.....	20.	7.5	25.	1.3	36.	1.3	1.3
IRON AND STEEL PRODUCTS......	24.	20.	11.	1.1	14.	2.3	1.1
NON-FERROUS SMELTING.........	48.	6.3	5.2	1.0	11.	1.0	0.
NON-FERROUS PRODUCTS.........	67.	1.4	11.	0.	1.4	1.4	5.7
METAL CANS...................	82.	0.	0.	0.	0.	0.	0.
STRUCTURAL METAL PRODUCTS....	24.	27.	3.2	0.	1.6	4.8	1.6
FABRICATED WIRE PRODUCTS.....	8.5	13.	8.5	8.5	8.5	6.4	0.
OTHER FABRICATED METAL.......	22.	17.	7.5	2.3	5.7	2.9	0.6
ENGINES AND TURBINES.........	35.	13.	2.1	0.	2.1	2.1	2.1
FARM MACHINERY...............	9.1	0.	3.0	0.	0.	0.	0.
CONSTRUCTION MACHINERY.......	32.	14.	0.	4.5	0.	0.	4.5
SPECIAL INDUSTRY MACHINERY...	36.	6.3	3.8	2.5	7.5	8.8	14.
GENERAL INDUSTRY MACHINERY...	33.	9.2	3.9	0.	1.3	1.3	34.
OFFICE MACHINES + COMPUTERS..	11.	7.1	0.	46.	0.	18.	3.6
OTHER NON-ELECTR. MACHINERY..	28.	17.	3.4	0.	3.4	10.	3.4
ELECTR. TRANSMISSION EQUIP...	13.	28.	3.3	2.2	1.1	2.2	6.5
ELECTRIC LIGHTING AND WIRING.	25.	21.	5.5	3.7	10.	22.	0.
RADIOS, TV'S + APPLIANCES....	50.	5.0	0.6	0.	1.3	21.	0.
COMMUNICATIONS EQUIPMENT.....	23.	19.	5.6	2.2	0.	12.	26.

TABLE CONTINUED ON NEXT PAGE

CROSS-TABULATION 21. 6.1: PERCENTAGE BREAKDOWN OF NUMBER (AS OF 1/1/71) OF
MANUFACTURING SUBSIDIARIES OF NON-U.S.-BASED PARENT SYSTEMS BY
NATIONAL BASE OF SUBSIDIARY'S PARENT SYSTEM
FOR SUBSIDIARIES CLASSIFIED BY
PRINCIPAL INDUSTRY OF SUBSIDIARY AS OF 1/1/71
(CONTINUED)

NATIONAL BASE OF SUBSIDIARY'S PARENT SYSTEM

PRINCIPAL INDUSTRY OF SUBSIDIARY AS OF 1/1/71	UNITED KINGDOM	GERMANY	FRANCE	ITALY	BELGIUM AND LUXEMBURG	THE NETHER-LANDS	SWEDEN
ELECTRONIC COMPONENTS.........	18.	8.1	9.1	0.	9.1	40.	0.
OTHER ELECTRICAL EQUIPMENT....	38.	16.	6.3	0.	0.	14.	5.3
MOTOR VEHICLES AND EQUIPMENT.	36.	18.	16.	9.0	0.	0.5	5.3
OTHER TRANSPORTATION..........	58.	8.5	1.7	0.	3.4	0.	3.4
PRECISION GOODS..............	17.	28.	5.1	0.	5.1	15.	1.3
MISCELLANEOUS PRODUCTS........	37.	3.8	2.6	1.3	10.	21.	7.7

TABLE CONTINUED ON NEXT PAGE

CROSS-TABULATION 21. 6.1: PERCENTAGE BREAKDOWN OF NUMBER (AS OF 1/1/71) OF
MANUFACTURING SUBSIDIARIES OF NON-U.S.-BASED PARENT SYSTEMS BY
NATIONAL BASE OF SUBSIDIARY'S PARENT SYSTEM
FOR SUBSIDIARIES CLASSIFIED BY
PRINCIPAL INDUSTRY OF SUBSIDIARY AS OF 1/1/71
(CONTINUED)

NATIONAL BASE OF SUBSIDIARY'S PARENT SYSTEM

PRINCIPAL INDUSTRY OF SUBSIDIARY AS OF 1/1/71	SWITZ- ERLAND	JAPAN	CANADA	OTHER NON-U.S.	TOTAL PERCENT	TOTAL NUMBER
ORDNANCE................	13.	13.	0.	0.	100.	8
MEAT PRODUCTS...........	0.	3.4	6.9	0.	100.	29
DAIRY PRODUCTS..........	43.	1.1	0.	0.	100.	89
CANNED FOODS............	18.	18.	2.3	0.	100.	44
GRAIN MILL PRODUCTS.....	4.4	0.	0.	0.	100.	45
BAKERY PRODUCTS.........	1.3	0.	0.	0.	100.	75
CONFECTIONERY PRODUCTS..	30.	3.3	0.	0.	100.	30
BEVERAGES..............	3.2	0.	20.	0.	100.	158
OTHER FOOD PRODUCTS.....	5.6	7.0	0.	1.4	100.	143
TOBACCO PRODUCTS........	0.	3.4	0.	0.	100.	58
TEXTILES...............	7.9	43.	0.	0.	100.	240
APPAREL................	0.	50.	0.	0.	100.	40
LUMBER AND WOOD........	0.	11.	9.4	0.	100.	53
FURNITURE..............	0.	0.	5.6	11.	100.	18
PAPER PRODUCTS.........	2.2	3.6	5.8	0.	100.	139
PRINTED MATTER.........	2.0	3.1	9.2	0.	100.	99
INDUSTRIAL CHEMICALS...	2.0	1.2	0.	0.	100.	247
PLASTICS AND SYNTHETICS..	8.4	8.4	0.	1.3	100.	155
DRUGS.................	31.	2.2	0.	0.	100.	229
SOAP AND COSMETICS.....	3.8	0.	0.	0.6	100.	159
PAINTS................	0.9	0.9	0.	0.	100.	113
AGRICULTURAL CHEMICALS..	16.	6.3	0.	2.5	100.	79
OTHER CHEMICALS........	4.5	5.2	0.	0.	100.	155
REFINED PETROLEUM......	0.	0.9	0.	0.	100.	109

TABLE CONTINUED ON NEXT PAGE

CROSS-TABULATION 21. 6.1: PERCENTAGE BREAKDOWN OF NUMBER (AS OF 1/1/71) OF MANUFACTURING SUBSIDIARIES OF NON-U.S.-BASED PARENT SYSTEMS BY NATIONAL BASE OF SUBSIDIARY'S PARENT SYSTEM FOR SUBSIDIARIES CLASSIFIED BY PRINCIPAL INDUSTRY OF SUBSIDIARY AS OF 1/1/71 (CONTINUED)

NATIONAL BASE OF SUBSIDIARY'S PARENT SYSTEM

PRINCIPAL INDUSTRY OF SUBSIDIARY AS OF 1/1/71	SWITZ- ERLAND	JAPAN	CANADA	OTHER NON-U.S.	TOTAL PERCENT	TOTAL NUMBER
OTHER PETROLEUM PRODUCTS......	1.2	0.	0.	2.4	100.	83
TIRES........................	0.	5.6	0.	0.	100.	36
OTHER RUBBER PRODUCTS........	4.3	14.	0.	1.4	100.	70
LEATHER PRODUCTS AND SHOES...	0.	17.	0.	17.	100.	6
GLASS PRODUCTS...............	0.	2.0	0.	0.	100.	50
STONE, CLAY AND CONCRETE.....	0.	6.3	1.3	0.	100.	80
IRON AND STEEL PRODUCTS......	4.0	20.	1.7	0.6	100.	174
NON-FERROUS SMELTING.........	2.1	6.3	19.	0.7	100.	96
NON-FERROUS PRODUCTS.........	2.8	0.	9.2	0.7	100.	141
METAL CANS...................	18.	0.	0.	0.	100.	33
STRUCTURAL METAL PRODUCTS....	3.2	11.	22.	1.6	100.	63
FABRICATED WIRE PRODUCTS.....	0.	32.	8.5	6.4	100.	47
OTHER FABRICATED METAL.......	11.	8.6	17.	5.2	100.	174
ENGINES AND TURBINES.........	25.	6.3	13.	0.	100.	48
FARM MACHINERY...............	0.	24.	64.	0.	100.	33
CONSTRUCTION MACHINERY.......	0.	27.	9.1	9.1	100.	22
SPECIAL INDUSTRY MACHINERY...	15.	5.0	1.3	0.	100.	80
GENERAL INDUSTRY MACHINERY...	14.	1.3	0.	1.3	100.	76
OFFICE MACHINES + COMPUTERS..	0.	7.1	0.	7.1	100.	28
OTHER NON-ELECTR. MACHINERY..	17.	14.	0.	3.4	100.	29
ELECTR. TRANSMISSION EQUIP...	21.	5.4	3.3	14.	100.	92
ELECTRIC LIGHTING AND WIRING.	1.8	5.5	5.5	0.	100.	109
RADIOS, TV'S + APPLIANCES....	3.8	18.	0.	0.6	100.	159

TABLE CONTINUED ON NEXT PAGE

CROSS-TABULATION 21.6.1: PERCENTAGE BREAKDOWN OF NUMBER (AS OF 1/1/71) OF
MANUFACTURING SUBSIDIARIES OF NON-U.S.-BASED PARENT SYSTEMS BY
NATIONAL BASE OF SUBSIDIARY'S PARENT SYSTEM
FOR SUBSIDIARIES CLASSIFIED BY
PRINCIPAL INDUSTRY OF SUBSIDIARY AS OF 1/1/71
(CONTINUED)

NATIONAL BASE OF SUBSIDIARY'S PARENT SYSTEM

PRINCIPAL INDUSTRY OF SUBSIDIARY AS OF 1/1/71	SWITZ-ERLAND	JAPAN	CANADA	OTHER NON-U.S.	TOTAL PERCENT	TOTAL NUMBER
COMMUNICATIONS EQUIPMENT.....	1.1	8.9	2.2	0.	100.	90
ELECTRONIC COMPONENTS........	4.0	9.1	0.	2.0	100.	99
OTHER ELECTRICAL EQUIPMENT...	6.3	7.9	1.6	4.8	100.	189
MOTOR VEHICLES AND EQUIPMENT.	0.5	13.	1.1	0.	100.	188
OTHER TRANSPORTATION.........	1.7	20.	1.7	1.7	100.	59
PRECISION GOODS..............	7.7	1.3	0.	19.	100.	78
MISCELLANEOUS PRODUCTS.......	1.3	9.0	0.	6.4	100.	78

CROSS-TABULATION 21.17.1: PERCENTAGE BREAKDOWN OF NUMBER (AS OF 1/1/71) OF
MANUFACTURING SUBSIDIARIES OF NON-U.S.-BASED PARENT SYSTEMS BY
NATIONAL BASE OF SUBSIDIARY'S PARENT SYSTEM
FOR SUBSIDIARIES CLASSIFIED BY
SUBSIDIARY'S DATE OF ENTRY INTO PARENT SYSTEM

NATIONAL BASE OF SUBSIDIARY'S PARENT SYSTEM

SUBSIDIARY'S DATE OF ENTRY INTO PARENT SYSTEM	UNITED KINGDOM	GERMANY	FRANCE	ITALY	BELGIUM AND LUXEMBURG	THE NETHER- LANDS	SWEDEN
PRE 1914..................	42.	0.	6.3	2.1	7.3	5.2	2.1
1914 - 1919..............	38.	2.1	2.1	2.1	6.4	4.3	13.
1920 - 1929..............	41.	0.5	2.7	1.8	13.	15.	7.8
1930 - 1938..............	50.	1.2	6.7	1.8	7.9	4.9	6.1
1939 - 1945..............	40.	3.0	9.0	3.0	0.	4.5	9.0
1946 - 1952..............	55.	7.1	4.6	5.9	4.6	5.3	4.3
1953 - 1955..............	32.	33.	8.9	4.7	5.3	3.6	2.4
1956 - 1958..............	34.	25.	6.5	2.8	4.2	6.5	0.9
1959 - 1961..............	48.	10.	5.6	3.2	2.5	8.2	2.2
1962 - 1964..............	48.	11.	4.7	3.4	1.8	4.6	2.1
1965 - 1967..............	39.	13.	7.1	1.4	2.4	12.	3.1
1968 - 1970..............	35.	19.	10.	1.4	6.5	6.3	2.3

TABLE CONTINUED ON NEXT PAGE

CROSS-TABULATION 21.17.1: PERCENTAGE BREAKDOWN OF NUMBER (AS OF 1/1/71) OF
MANUFACTURING SUBSIDIARIES OF NON-U.S.-BASED PARENT SYSTEMS BY
NATIONAL BASE OF SUBSIDIARY'S PARENT SYSTEM
FOR SUBSIDIARIES CLASSIFIED BY
SUBSIDIARY'S DATE OF ENTRY INTO PARENT SYSTEM
(CONTINUED)

NATIONAL BASE OF SUBSIDIARY'S PARENT SYSTEM

SUBSIDIARY'S DATE OF ENTRY INTO PARENT SYSTEM	SWITZ-ERLAND	JAPAN	CANADA	OTHER NON-U.S.	TOTAL PERCENT	TOTAL NUMBER
PRE 1914	31.	0.	3.1	1.0	100.	96
1914 - 1919	23.	0.	8.5	0.	100.	47
1920 - 1929	15.	0.	3.7	0.	100.	219
1930 - 1938	13.	0.6	7.3	0.	100.	164
1939 - 1945	13.	0.	18.	0.	100.	67
1946 - 1952	7.7	0.	5.0	0.6	100.	323
1953 - 1955	4.7	3.0	2.4	0.	100.	169
1956 - 1958	11.	6.0	2.3	0.5	100.	215
1959 - 1961	5.2	7.0	5.4	2.0	100.	558
1962 - 1964	6.4	14.	2.6	1.8	100.	613
1965 - 1967	7.6	10.	3.9	0.5	100.	1063
1968 - 1970	3.9	10.	2.2	3.3	100.	2067

TABULATION 22.1: PERCENTAGE BREAKDOWN OF NUMBER OF SUBSIDIARIES BY
VALUE OF SALES OF SUBSIDIARY'S PARENT SYSTEM IN YEAR PRIOR TO TERMINAL DATE
FOR VARIOUS CATEGORIES OF SUBSIDIARIES

CATEGORY OF SUBSIDIARY	VALUE OF SALES OF SUBSIDIARY'S PARENT SYSTEM IN YEAR PRIOR TO TERMINAL DATE					TOTAL PERCENT	TOTAL NUMBER
	$100-399 MILLION	$400-599 MILLION	$600-999 MILLION	$1-2 BILLION	OVER $2 BILLION		
NON-U.S.-BASED SYSTEMS (AS OF 1/1/71):							
ALL SUBSIDIARIES	0.	20.	16.	28.	36.	100.	13541
MANUFACTURING SUBS	0.	19.	16.	29.	36.	100.	5511
SALES SUBSIDIARIES	0.	18.	19.	25.	38.	100.	3267
U.S.-BASED SYSTEMS (AS OF 1/1/68):							
ALL SUBSIDIARIES	15.	15.	17.	22.	32.	100.	9632
MANUFACTURING SUBS	20.	17.	22.	23.	19.	100.	4160
SALES SUBSIDIARIES	20.	13.	12.	21.	34.	100.	1645
WORLD SUBSET OF SYSTEMS (AS OF 1/1/68):							
NON-U.S.-BASED SYSTEMS:							
ALL SUBSIDIARIES	0.	19.	26.	26.	29.	100.	6153
MANUFACTURING SUBS	0.	19.	29.	24.	28.	100.	2737
SALES SUBSIDIARIES	0.	19.	26.	27.	28.	100.	1634
U.S.-BASED SYSTEMS:							
ALL SUBSIDIARIES	0.	17.	20.	26.	38.	100.	8144
MANUFACTURING SUBS	0.	21.	27.	29.	23.	100.	3334
SALES SUBSIDIARIES	0.	17.	15.	26.	43.	100.	1309

TABULATION 22.2: PERCENTAGE BREAKDOWN OF SALES OF SUBSIDIARIES IN 1970 BY VALUE OF SALES OF SUBSIDIARY'S PARENT SYSTEM IN 1970 FOR ALL SUBSIDIARIES, MANUFACTURING SUBSIDIARIES AND SALES SUBSIDIARIES OF NON-U.S.-BASED SYSTEMS

CATEGORY OF SUBSIDIARY	VALUE OF SALES OF SUBSIDIARY'S PARENT SYSTEM IN 1970					
	$400-$599 MILLION	$600-$999 MILLION	$1-$2 BILLION	OVER $2 BILLION	TOTAL PERCENT	TOTAL ($ MIL)
ALL SUBSIDIARIES............	11.	12.	26.	51.	100.	131027
MANUFACTURING SUBSIDIARIES...	10.	11.	27.	51.	100.	81387
SALES SUBSIDIARIES...........	13.	14.	24.	49.	100.	23164

CROSS-TABULATION 22.1.1: PERCENTAGE BREAKDOWN OF NUMBER (AS OF 1/1/71) OF MANUFACTURING SUBSIDIARIES OF NON-U.S.-BASED PARENT SYSTEMS BY VALUE OF SALES OF SUBSIDIARY'S PARENT SYSTEM IN 1970 FOR SUBSIDIARIES CLASSIFIED BY SUBSIDIARY'S COUNTRY

SUBSIDIARY'S COUNTRY	VALUE OF SALES OF SUBSIDIARY'S PARENT SYSTEM IN 1970				TOTAL PERCENT	TOTAL NUMBER
	$400-$599 MILLION	$600-$999 MILLION	$1-$2 BILLION	OVER $2 BILLION		
UNITED STATES	22.	11.	21.	46.	100.	391
CANADA	11.	16.	41.	32.	100.	262
MEXICO	15.	20.	19.	45.	100.	94
CENTRAL AMERICA AND CARIB.	15.	14.	32.	40.	100.	88
VENEZUELA	15.	17.	22.	46.	100.	46
COLOMBIA	19.	19.	33.	30.	100.	27
PERU	6.5	26.	26.	42.	100.	31
CHILE	25.	13.	21.	42.	100.	24
ARGENTINA	13.	14.	39.	34.	100.	119
BRAZIL	13.	23.	36.	28.	100.	179
OTHER SOUTH AMERICA	26.	22.	26.	26.	100.	23
GERMANY	18.	15.	36.	30.	100.	316
FRANCE	25.	18.	15.	42.	100.	433
ITALY	21.	16.	32.	32.	100.	198
BELGIUM AND LUXEMBURG	23.	16.	32.	29.	100.	154
THE NETHERLANDS	29.	18.	27.	25.	100.	136
UNITED KINGDOM	16.	9.2	29.	46.	100.	249
IRELAND	24.	33.	22.	21.	100.	95
DENMARK	20.	20.	20.	40.	100.	40
NORWAY	14.	39.	32.	16.	100.	44
SWEDEN	14.	2.7	26.	58.	100.	74
FINLAND	9.1	41.	18.	32.	100.	22

TABLE CONTINUED ON NEXT PAGE

452

CROSS-TABULATION 22. 1.1: PERCENTAGE BREAKDOWN OF NUMBER (AS OF 1/1/71) OF MANUFACTURING SUBSIDIARIES OF NON-U.S.-BASED PARENT SYSTEMS BY VALUE OF SALES OF SUBSIDIARY'S PARENT SYSTEM IN 1970 FOR SUBSIDIARIES CLASSIFIED BY SUBSIDIARY'S COUNTRY (CONTINUED)

SUBSIDIARY'S COUNTRY	VALUE OF SALES OF SUBSIDIARY'S PARENT SYSTEM IN 1970					
	$400-$599 MILLION	$600-$999 MILLION	$1-$2 BILLION	OVER $2 BILLION	TOTAL PERCENT	TOTAL NUMBER
SWITZERLAND	15.	20.	25.	40.	100.	55
AUSTRIA	13.	18.	19.	49.	100.	89
PORTUGAL	19.	22.	22.	37.	100.	54
SPAIN	17.	19.	33.	31.	100.	189
GREECE	15.	7.7	23.	54.	100.	26
TURKEY	9.4	16.	16.	59.	100.	32
OTHER EUROPE + ISRAEL	22.	11.	14.	54.	100.	37
PAKISTAN	29.	12.	22.	37.	100.	41
IRAN	4.2	13.	25.	58.	100.	24
OTHER MID EAST+EGYPT+LIBYA	27.	7.4	22.	48.	100.	27
UNION OF SOUTH AFRICA	23.	11.	39.	27.	100.	359
RHODESIA	44.	7.7	29.	19.	100.	52
ZAMBIA	67.	2.8	19.	11.	100.	36
TANZANIA	52.	9.5	9.5	29.	100.	21
KENYA	55.	12.	4.8	29.	100.	42
NIGERIA	23.	19.	19.	40.	100.	53
OTHER (BRITISH) AFRICA	32.	8.0	28.	32.	100.	50
MOROCCO, ALGERIA + TUNISIA	12.	3.9	63.	22.	100.	51
OTHER (FRENCH) AFRICA	9.6	5.8	48.	37.	100.	52
OTHER AFRICA	20.	20.	26.	34.	100.	35
AUSTRALIA	21.	17.	45.	17.	100.	398
NEW ZEALAND	16.	26.	34.	24.	100.	110

TABLE CONTINUED ON NEXT PAGE

CROSS-TABULATION 22. 1.1: PERCENTAGE BREAKDOWN OF NUMBER (AS OF 1/1/71) OF
MANUFACTURING SUBSIDIARIES OF NON-U.S.-BASED PARENT SYSTEMS BY
VALUE OF SALES OF SUBSIDIARIES' PARENT SYSTEM IN 1970
FOR SUBSIDIARIES CLASSIFIED BY
SUBSIDIARY'S COUNTRY
(CONTINUED)

VALUE OF SALES OF SUBSIDIARY'S PARENT SYSTEM IN 1970

SUBSIDIARY'S COUNTRY	$400-$599 MILLION	$600-$999 MILLION	$1-$2 BILLION	OVER $2 BILLION	TOTAL PERCENT	TOTAL NUMBER
JAPAN	10.	6.3	37.	47.	100.	79
CHINA (TAIWAN)	14.	13.	19.	54.	100.	97
HONG KONG	11.	26.	30.	33.	100.	27
THE PHILIPPINES	8.0	12.	8.0	72.	100.	25
MALAYSIA	13.	13.	28.	45.	100.	53
SINGAPORE	16.	8.0	20.	56.	100.	50
INDONESIA	4.0	16.	16.	64.	100.	25
THAILAND	7.8	19.	20.	53.	100.	64
INDIA	19.	16.	28.	37.	100.	149
OTHER ASIA AND OCEANIA	10.	19.	26.	45.	100.	58

CROSS-TABULATION 22.1.2: PERCENTAGE BREAKDOWN OF NUMBER (AS OF 1/1/68) OF MANUFACTURING SUBSIDIARIES OF U.S.-BASED PARENT SYSTEMS BY VALUE OF SALES OF SUBSIDIARY'S PARENT SYSTEM IN 1967 FOR SUBSIDIARIES CLASSIFIED BY SUBSIDIARY'S COUNTRY

SUBSIDIARY'S COUNTRY	VALUE OF SALES OF SUBSIDIARY'S PARENT SYSTEM IN 1967						
	$100-399 MILLION	$400-599 MILLION	$600-999 MILLION	$1-$2 BILLION	OVER $2 BILLION	TOTAL PERCENT	TOTAL NUMBER
UNITED STATES	0.	0.	0.	0.	0.	100.	0
CANADA	18.	17.	27.	22.	15.	100.	532
MEXICO	23.	20.	20.	25.	12.	100.	283
CENTRAL AMERICA AND CARIB.	13.	24.	26.	20.	16.	100.	135
VENEZUELA	11.	23.	21.	21.	24.	100.	133
COLOMBIA	14.	19.	18.	33.	17.	100.	113
PERU	20.	16.	12.	37.	16.	100.	51
CHILE	20.	29.	4.9	24.	22.	100.	41
ARGENTINA	21.	20.	24.	21.	14.	100.	134
BRAZIL	23.	17.	18.	23.	18.	100.	174
OTHER SOUTH AMERICA	11.	4.5	27.	41.	16.	100.	44
GERMANY	21.	16.	21.	19.	23.	100.	244
FRANCE	24.	17.	18.	22.	20.	100.	234
ITALY	22.	15.	23.	22.	18.	100.	187
BELGIUM AND LUXEMBURG	17.	15.	24.	25.	20.	100.	102
THE NETHERLANDS	13.	21.	22.	28.	16.	100.	86
UNITED KINGDOM	25.	19.	22.	19.	16.	100.	393
IRELAND	31.	6.9	6.9	45.	10.	100.	29
DENMARK	13.	16.	9.4	22.	41.	100.	32
NORWAY	15.	10.	20.	20.	35.	100.	20
SWEDEN	16.	16.	11.	24.	32.	100.	37
FINLAND	33.	0.	33.	0.	33.	100.	6

TABLE CONTINUED ON NEXT PAGE

CROSS-TABULATION 22. 1.2: PERCENTAGE BREAKDOWN OF NUMBER (AS OF 1/1/68) OF
MANUFACTURING SUBSIDIARIES OF U.S.-BASED PARENT SYSTEMS BY
VALUE OF SALES OF SUBSIDIARY'S PARENT SYSTEM IN 1967
FOR SUBSIDIARIES CLASSIFIED BY
SUBSIDIARY'S COUNTRY
(CONTINUED)

VALUE OF SALES OF SUBSIDIARY'S
PARENT SYSTEM IN 1967

SUBSIDIARY'S COUNTRY	$100-399 MILLION	$400-599 MILLION	$600-999 MILLION	$1-$2 BILLION	OVER $2 BILLION	TOTAL PERCENT	TOTAL NUMBER
SWITZERLAND	16.	9.4	19.	31.	25.	100.	32
AUSTRIA	28.	5.6	11.	17.	39.	100.	18
PORTUGAL	22.	13.	30.	22.	13.	100.	23
SPAIN	16.	13.	20.	31.	19.	100.	124
GREECE	27.	14.	18.	23.	18.	100.	22
TURKEY	19.	6.3	31.	13.	31.	100.	16
OTHER EUROPE + ISRAEL	38.	6.3	25.	19.	13.	100.	16
PAKISTAN	25.	25.	25.	13.	13.	100.	16
IRAN	11.	15.	21.	26.	26.	100.	19
OTHER MID EAST+EGYPT+LIBYA	0.	14.	6.9	10.	69.	100.	29
UNION OF SOUTH AFRICA	25.	12.	39.	13.	10.	100.	119
RHODESIA	21.	7.1	36.	14.	21.	100.	14
ZAMBIA	0.	29.	29.	43.	0.	100.	7
TANZANIA	0.	0.	0.	0.	0.	100.	0
KENYA	11.	11.	0.	44.	33.	100.	9
NIGERIA	7.7	54.	7.7	23.	7.7	100.	13
OTHER (BRITISH) AFRICA	17.	0.	33.	17.	33.	100.	6
MOROCCO, ALGERIA + TUNISIA	13.	0.	6.7	47.	33.	100.	15
OTHER (FRENCH) AFRICA	22.	22.	11.	11.	33.	100.	9
OTHER AFRICA	0.	0.	0.	50.	50.	100.	4
AUSTRALIA	26.	15.	23.	18.	18.	100.	229
NEW ZEALAND	37.	9.3	19.	16.	19.	100.	43

TABLE CONTINUED ON NEXT PAGE

CROSS-TABULATION 22.1.2: PERCENTAGE BREAKDOWN OF NUMBER (AS OF 1/1/68) OF
MANUFACTURING SUBSIDIARIES OF U.S.-BASED PARENT SYSTEMS BY
VALUE OF SALES OF SUBSIDIARY'S PARENT SYSTEM IN 1967
FOR SUBSIDIARIES CLASSIFIED BY
SUBSIDIARY'S COUNTRY
(CONTINUED)

VALUE OF SALES OF SUBSIDIARY'S
PARENT SYSTEM IN 1967

SUBSIDIARY'S COUNTRY	$100-399 MILLION	$400-599 MILLION	$600-999 MILLION	$1-$2 BILLION	OVER $2 BILLION	TOTAL PERCENT	TOTAL NUMBER
JAPAN	17.	13.	18.	34.	17.	100.	157
CHINA (TAIWAN)	13.	38.	13.	13.	25.	100.	16
HONG KONG	38.	13.	0.	0.	50.	100.	8
THE PHILIPPINES	13.	16.	27.	20.	25.	100.	56
MALAYSIA	6.7	13.	13.	40.	27.	100.	15
SINGAPORE	27.	0.	9.1	27.	36.	100.	11
INDONESIA	0.	0.	0.	25.	75.	100.	4
THAILAND	7.1	14.	36.	21.	21.	100.	14
INDIA	21.	21.	18.	24.	15.	100.	66
OTHER ASIA AND OCEANIA	0.	35.	5.0	35.	25.	100.	20

CROSS-TABULATION 22. 6.1: PERCENTAGE BREAKDOWN OF NUMBER (AS OF 1/1/71) OF
MANUFACTURING SUBSIDIARIES OF NON-U.S.-BASED PARENT SYSTEMS BY
VALUE OF SALES OF SUBSIDIARY'S PARENT SYSTEM IN 1970
FOR SUBSIDIARIES CLASSIFIED BY
PRINCIPAL INDUSTRY OF SUBSIDIARY AS OF 1/1/71

PRINCIPAL INDUSTRY OF SUBSIDIARY AS OF 1/1/71	VALUE OF SALES OF SUBSIDIARY'S PARENT SYSTEM IN 1970				TOTAL PERCENT	TOTAL NUMBER
	$400-$599 MILLION	$600-$999 MILLION	$1-$2 BILLION	OVER $2 BILLION		
ORDNANCE	13.	0.	38.	50.	100.	8
MEAT PRODUCTS	69.	17.	3.4	10.	100.	29
DAIRY PRODUCTS	10.	17.	1.1	72.	100.	89
CANNED FOODS	28.	21.	21.	30.	100.	43
GRAIN MILL PRODUCTS	20.	20.	56.	4.4	100.	45
BAKERY PRODUCTS	4.0	8.0	88.	0.	100.	75
CONFECTIONERY PRODUCTS	5.7	50.	10.	33.	100.	30
BEVERAGES	29.	61.	3.8	5.7	100.	158
OTHER FOOD PRODUCTS	11.	24.	4.2	60.	100.	143
TOBACCO PRODUCTS	0.	0.	97.	3.4	100.	58
TEXTILES	8.8	33.	25.	34.	100.	240
APPAREL	2.5	20.	38.	40.	100.	40
LUMBER AND WOOD	32.	1.9	15.	51.	100.	53
FURNITURE	22.	5.6	56.	17.	100.	18
PAPER PRODUCTS	21.	19.	48.	12.	100.	139
PRINTED MATTER	50.	2.0	28.	20.	100.	99
INDUSTRIAL CHEMICALS	15.	18.	22.	45.	100.	176
PLASTICS AND SYNTHETICS	18.	16.	20.	46.	100.	150
DRUGS	19.	17.	25.	39.	100.	229
SOAP AND COSMETICS	30.	3.8	24.	42.	100.	159
PAINTS	11.	0.	50.	38.	100.	105
AGRICULTURAL CHEMICALS	12.	5.5	25.	57.	100.	77
OTHER CHEMICALS	28.	4.5	22.	45.	100.	152
REFINED PETROLEUM	10.	0.	31.	58.	100.	108
OTHER PETROLEUM PRODUCTS	29.	8.5	35.	27.	100.	82

TABLE CONTINUED ON NEXT PAGE

458

CROSS-TABULATION 22.6.1: PERCENTAGE BREAKDOWN OF NUMBER (AS OF 1/1/71) OF MANUFACTURING SUBSIDIARIES OF NON-U.S.-BASED PARENT SYSTEMS BY VALUE OF SALES OF SUBSIDIARY'S PARENT SYSTEM IN 1970 FOR SUBSIDIARIES CLASSIFIED BY PRINCIPAL INDUSTRY OF SUBSIDIARY AS OF 1/1/71 (CONTINUED)

PRINCIPAL INDUSTRY OF SUBSIDIARY AS OF 1/1/71	VALUE OF SALES OF SUBSIDIARY'S PARENT SYSTEM IN 1970				TOTAL PERCENT	TOTAL NUMBER
	$400-$599 MILLION	$600-$999 MILLION	$1-$2 BILLION	OVER $2 BILLION		
TIRES	11.	0.	86.	2.8	100.	36
OTHER RUBBER PRODUCTS	26.	1.4	47.	26.	100.	70
LEATHER PRODUCTS AND SHOES	40.	0.	40.	20.	100.	5
GLASS PRODUCTS	0.	22.	58.	20.	100.	50
STONE, CLAY AND CONCRETE	10.	0.	41.	49.	100.	80
IRON AND STEEL PRODUCTS	13.	16.	35.	36.	100.	172
NON-FERROUS SMELTING	23.	19.	48.	9.5	100.	95
NON-FERROUS PRODUCTS	23.	9.2	61.	7.1	100.	141
METAL CANS	85.	3.0	6.1	6.1	100.	33
STRUCTURAL METAL PRODUCTS	22.	0.	65.	13.	100.	63
FABRICATED WIRE PRODUCTS	17.	2.1	45.	36.	100.	47
OTHER FABRICATED METAL	24.	7.6	46.	22.	100.	172
ENGINES AND TURBINES	10.	17.	40.	33.	100.	48
FARM MACHINERY	3.0	76.	6.1	15.	100.	33
CONSTRUCTION MACHINERY	27.	14.	27.	32.	100.	22
SPECIAL INDUSTRY MACHINERY	35.	6.4	31.	28.	100.	78
GENERAL INDUSTRY MACHINERY	25.	43.	21.	11.	100.	76
OFFICE MACHINES + COMPUTERS	18.	50.	0.	32.	100.	28
OTHER NON-ELECTR. MACHINERY	24.	17.	34.	24.	100.	29
ELECTR. TRANSMISSION EQUIP.	20.	8.7	37.	35.	100.	92
ELECTRIC LIGHTING AND WIRING	6.4	10.	15.	69.	100.	109
RADIOS, TV'S + APPLIANCES	32.	14.	7.0	47.	100.	158
COMMUNICATIONS EQUIPMENT	17.	30.	12.	41.	100.	90

TABLE CONTINUED ON NEXT PAGE

CROSS-TABULATION 22.6.1: PERCENTAGE BREAKDOWN OF NUMBER (AS OF 1/1/71) OF
MANUFACTURING SUBSIDIARIES OF NON-U.S.-BASED PARENT SYSTEMS BY
VALUE OF SALES OF SUBSIDIARY'S PARENT SYSTEM IN 1970
FOR SUBSIDIARIES CLASSIFIED BY
PRINCIPAL INDUSTRY OF SUBSIDIARY AS OF 1/1/71
(CONTINUED)

VALUE OF SALES OF SUBSIDIARY'S PARENT SYSTEM IN 1970

PRINCIPAL INDUSTRY OF SUBSIDIARY AS OF 1/1/71	$400-$599 MILLION	$600-$999 MILLION	$1-$2 BILLION	OVER $2 BILLION	TOTAL PERCENT	TOTAL NUMBER
ELECTRONIC COMPONENTS........	18.	7.1	10.	64.	100.	99
OTHER ELECTRICAL EQUIPMENT...	15.	18.	27.	40.	100.	174
MOTOR VEHICLES AND EQUIPMENT.	17.	16.	28.	39.	100.	188
OTHER TRANSPORTATION.........	10.	31.	44.	15.	100.	59
PRECISION GOODS.............	40.	6.7	17.	36.	100.	75
MISCELLANEOUS PRODUCTS.......	22.	2.6	30.	45.	100.	77

CROSS-TABULATION 22.6.2: PERCENTAGE BREAKDOWN OF NUMBER (AS OF 1/1/68) OF
MANUFACTURING SUBSIDIARIES OF U.S.-BASED PARENT SYSTEMS BY
VALUE OF SALES OF SUBSIDIARY'S PARENT SYSTEM IN 1967
FOR SUBSIDIARIES CLASSIFIED BY
PRINCIPAL INDUSTRY OF SUBSIDIARY AS OF 1/1/68

PRINCIPAL INDUSTRY OF SUBSIDIARY AS OF 1/1/68	VALUE OF SALES OF SUBSIDIARY'S PARENT SYSTEM IN 1967						
	$100-399 MILLION	$400-$599 MILLION	$600-$999 MILLION	$1-$2 BILLION	OVER $2 BILLION	TOTAL PERCENT	TOTAL NUMBER
ORDNANCE	0.	0.	73.	9.1	18.	100.	11
MEAT PRODUCTS	45.	7.9	0.	29.	18.	100.	38
DAIRY PRODUCTS	1.6	25.	9.4	42.	22.	100.	64
CANNED FOODS	13.	28.	25.	30.	3.8	100.	53
GRAIN MILL PRODUCTS	8.2	30.	19.	41.	2.0	100.	99
BAKERY PRODUCTS	0.	18.	72.	10.	0.	100.	39
CONFECTIONERY PRODUCTS	37.	9.3	23.	30.	0.	100.	43
BEVERAGES	8.3	25.	40.	27.	0.	100.	60
OTHER FOOD PRODUCTS	8.9	7.1	36.	41.	7.1	100.	56
TOBACCO PRODUCTS	0.	100.	0.	0.	0.	100.	10
TEXTILES	10.	3.4	18.	58.	10.	100.	88
APPAREL	14.	0.	79.	7.1	0.	100.	14
LUMBER AND WOOD	4.8	14.	48.	29.	4.8	100.	21
FURNITURE	76.	5.9	0.	12.	5.9	100.	17
PAPER PRODUCTS	0.6	11.	63.	24.	1.9	100.	161
PRINTED MATTER	0.	75.	21.	0.	3.6	100.	28
INDUSTRIAL CHEMICALS	16.	13.	17.	33.	20.	100.	254
PLASTICS AND SYNTHETICS	5.4	16.	15.	49.	15.	100.	167
DRUGS	27.	41.	28.	2.3	1.7	100.	301
SOAP AND COSMETICS	34.	13.	14.	25.	14.	100.	138
PAINTS	0.	1.8	43.	39.	16.	100.	56
AGRICULTURAL CHEMICALS	2.0	20.	22.	20.	36.	100.	50
OTHER CHEMICALS	46.	1.3	10.	31.	11.	100.	80
REFINED PETROLEUM	0.	0.	0.	4.4	96.	100.	136
OTHER PETROLEUM PRODUCTS	4.3	1.4	0.	26.	69.	100.	70

TABLE CONTINUED ON NEXT PAGE

CROSS-TABULATION 22.6.2: PERCENTAGE BREAKDOWN OF NUMBER (AS OF 1/1/68) OF
MANUFACTURING SUBSIDIARIES OF U.S.-BASED PARENT SYSTEMS BY
VALUE OF SALES OF SUBSIDIARY'S PARENT SYSTEM IN 1967
FOR SUBSIDIARIES CLASSIFIED BY
PRINCIPAL INDUSTRY OF SUBSIDIARY AS OF 1/1/68
(CONTINUED)

PRINCIPAL INDUSTRY OF SUBSIDIARY AS OF 1/1/68	VALUE OF SALES OF SUBSIDIARY'S PARENT SYSTEM IN 1967					TOTAL PERCENT	TOTAL NUMBER
	$100-399 MILLION	$400-$599 MILLION	$600-$999 MILLION	$1-$2 BILLION	OVER $2 BILLION		
TIRES...............................	0.	0.	17.	59.	23.	100.	81
OTHER RUBBER PRODUCTS...............	6.3	0.	19.	63.	13.	100.	32
LEATHER PRODUCTS AND SHOES..........	38.	0.	54.	7.7	0.	100.	13
GLASS PRODUCTS......................	0.	30.	65.	5.0	0.	100.	40
STONE, CLAY AND CONCRETE............	43.	32.	21.	2.7	1.3	100.	75
IRON AND STEEL PRODUCTS.............	36.	9.1	18.	24.	12.	100.	33
NON-FERROUS SMELTING................	0.	21.	63.	7.0	9.3	100.	43
NON-FERROUS PRODUCTS................	19.	11.	39.	28.	2.8	100.	36
METAL CANS..........................	3.7	11.	3.7	78.	3.7	100.	27
STRUCTURAL METAL PRODUCTS...........	30.	0.	52.	19.	0.	100.	27
FABRICATED WIRE PRODUCTS............	15.	38.	38.	0.	7.7	100.	13
OTHER FABRICATED METAL..............	36.	21.	26.	15.	2.1	100.	144
ENGINES AND TURBINES................	47.	5.9	12.	18.	18.	100.	17
FARM MACHINERY......................	12.	0.	18.	29.	41.	100.	34
CONSTRUCTION MACHINERY..............	19.	37.	14.	26.	4.9	100.	81
SPECIAL INDUSTRY MACHINERY..........	56.	26.	3.8	13.	1.3	100.	78
GENERAL INDUSTRY MACHINERY..........	10.	21.	59.	8.6	1.7	100.	58
OFFICE MACHINES + COMPUTERS.........	0.	14.	25.	35.	25.	100.	51
OTHER NON-ELECTR. MACHINERY.........	38.	26.	28.	2.1	6.4	100.	47
ELECTR. TRANSMISSION EQUIP..........	46.	25.	4.2	17.	8.3	100.	24
ELECTRIC LIGHTING AND WIRING........	15.	7.4	7.4	3.7	67.	100.	27
RADIOS, TV'S + APPLIANCES...........	23.	1.1	4.6	30.	41.	100.	87
COMMUNICATIONS EQUIPMENT............	3.1	0.	0.	13.	84.	100.	32

TABLE CONTINUED ON NEXT PAGE

CROSS-TABULATION 22.6.2: PERCENTAGE BREAKDOWN OF NUMBER (AS OF 1/1/68) OF
MANUFACTURING SUBSIDIARIES OF U.S.-BASED PARENT SYSTEMS BY
VALUE OF SALES OF SUBSIDIARY'S PARENT SYSTEM IN 1967
FOR SUBSIDIARIES CLASSIFIED BY
PRINCIPAL INDUSTRY OF SUBSIDIARY AS OF 1/1/68
(CONTINUED)

PRINCIPAL INDUSTRY OF SUBSIDIARY AS OF 1/1/68	VALUE OF SALES OF SUBSIDIARY'S PARENT SYSTEM IN 1967						
	$100-399 MILLION	$400-599 MILLION	$600-999 MILLION	$1-$2 BILLION	OVER $2 BILLION	TOTAL PERCENT	TOTAL NUMBER
ELECTRONIC COMPONENTS........	13.	18.	2.5	23.	45.	100.	40
OTHER ELECTRICAL EQUIPMENT...	40.	7.1	4.1	6.1	43.	100.	99
MOTOR VEHICLES AND EQUIPMENT.	20.	14.	20.	18.	28.	100.	207
OTHER TRANSPORTATION.........	53.	5.3	5.3	26.	11.	100.	19
PRECISION GOODS.............	55.	15.	1.4	7.0	21.	100.	71
MISCELLANEOUS PRODUCTS.......	62.	14.	12.	9.1	3.0	100.	66

CROSS-TABULATION 22.21.1: PERCENTAGE BREAKDOWN OF NUMBER (AS OF 1/1/71) OF
MANUFACTURING SUBSIDIARIES OF NON-U.S.-BASED PARENT SYSTEMS BY
VALUE OF SALES OF SUBSIDIARY'S PARENT SYSTEM IN 1970
FOR SUBSIDIARIES CLASSIFIED BY
NATIONAL BASE OF SUBSIDIARY'S PARENT SYSTEM

VALUE OF SALES OF SUBSIDIARY'S PARENT SYSTEM IN 1970

NATIONAL BASE OF SUBSIDIARY'S PARENT SYSTEM	$400-$599 MILLION	$600-$999 MILLION	$1-$2 BILLION	OVER $2 BILLION	TOTAL PERCENT	TOTAL NUMBER
UNITED KINGDOM............	27.	17.	33.	23.	100.	2200
GERMANY..................	13.	6.1	15.	66.	100.	723
FRANCE...................	10.	8.4	75.	6.1	100.	427
ITALY....................	8.5	13.	33.	45.	100.	130
BELGIUM AND LUXEMBURG....	0.	32.	16.	52.	100.	272
THE NETHERLANDS..........	4.5	0.	0.	96.	100.	425
SWEDEN...................	37.	57.	6.0	0.	100.	167
SWITZERLAND..............	18.	14.	47.	21.	100.	393
JAPAN....................	8.8	18.	18.	55.	100.	478
CANADA...................	17.	37.	46.	0.	100.	197
OTHER NON-U.S............	95.	2.0	3.0	0.	100.	99

TABULATION 23.1: PERCENTAGE BREAKDOWN OF NUMBER OF SUBSIDIARIES BY
PRINCIPAL INDUSTRY OF PARENT SYSTEM
FOR VARIOUS CATEGORIES OF SUBSIDIARIES

CATEGORY OF SUBSIDIARY	PRINCIPAL INDUSTRY OF PARENT SYSTEM						
	FOOD, TOBACCO + SOAP	CHEMICALS AND DRUGS	PETRO-LEUM	IRON AND STEEL	NON-FERROUS METALS	FABRICAT. METAL+NON EL. MACH.	ELECTRIC AND ELEC-TRONIC
NON-U.S.-BASED SYSTEMS (AS OF 1/1/71):							
ALL SUBSIDIARIES..........	14.	19.	8.7	5.0	8.1	7.2	16.
MANUFACTURING SUBS........	17.	23.	4.9	3.9	7.5	7.8	17.
SALES SUBSIDIARIES........	8.6	13.	12.	6.0	4.4	7.8	20.
U.S.-BASED SYSTEMS (AS OF 1/1/68):							
ALL SUBSIDIARIES..........	14.	21.	26.	0.4	3.7	8.6	12.
MANUFACTURING SUBS........	17.	26.	8.0	0.5	2.9	11.	10.
SALES SUBSIDIARIES........	10.	16.	22.	0.2	4.2	10.	14.
WORLD SUBSET OF SYSTEMS (AS OF 1/1/68):							
NON-U.S.-BASED SYSTEMS:							
ALL SUBSIDIARIES..........	15.	18.	13.	3.4	8.0	10.	16.
MANUFACTURING SUBS........	20.	21.	6.3	2.0	7.1	11.	16.
SALES SUBSIDIARIES........	8.7	13.	18.	3.7	5.1	11.	23.
U.S.-BASED SYSTEMS:							
ALL SUBSIDIARIES..........	13.	18.	24.	0.4	3.6	6.3	12.
MANUFACTURING SUBS........	18.	25.	10.	0.7	3.1	8.0	10.
SALES SUBSIDIARIES........	8.9	12.	28.	0.3	2.4	8.0	16.

(TABLE CONTINUED ON NEXT PAGE)

TABULATION 23.1: PERCENTAGE BREAKDOWN OF NUMBER OF SUBSIDIARIES BY PRINCIPAL INDUSTRY OF PARENT SYSTEM FOR VARIOUS CATEGORIES OF SUBSIDIARIES (CONTINUED)

CATEGORY OF SUBSIDIARY	PRINCIPAL INDUSTRY OF PARENT SYSTEM			
	AUTO-MOBILES	OTHER	TOTAL PERCENT	TOTAL NUMBER
NON-U.S.-BASED SYSTEMS (AS OF 1/1/71):				
ALL SUBSIDIARIES........	4.9	17.	100.	13800
MANUFACTURING SUBS......	2.7	17.	100.	5645
SALES SUBSIDIARIES......	8.9	20.	100.	3311
U.S.-BASED SYSTEMS (AS OF 1/1/68):				
ALL SUBSIDIARIES........	4.5	17.	100.	9776
MANUFACTURING SUBS......	5.7	19.	100.	4246
SALES SUBSIDIARIES......	5.5	18.	100.	1664
WORLD SUBSET OF SYSTEMS (AS OF 1/1/68):				
NON-U.S.-BASED SYSTEMS:				
ALL SUBSIDIARIES........	4.7	12.	100.	6153
MANUFACTURING SUBS......	2.3	15.	100.	2737
SALES SUBSIDIARIES......	6.9	12.	100.	1634
U.S.-BASED SYSTEMS:				
ALL SUBSIDIARIES........	4.8	17.	100.	8144
MANUFACTURING SUBS......	6.1	20.	100.	3334
SALES SUBSIDIARIES......	6.6	18.	100.	1309

TABULATION 23.2: PERCENTAGE BREAKDOWN OF SALES OF SUBSIDIARIES IN 1970 BY
PRINCIPAL INDUSTRY-GROUP OF SUBSIDIARY'S PARENT SYSTEM AS OF 1/1/71
FOR ALL SUBSIDIARIES, MANUFACTURING SUBSIDIARIES AND SALES SUBSIDIARIES
OF NON-U.S.-BASED SYSTEMS

PRINCIPAL INDUSTRY-GROUP OF SUBSIDIARY'S
PARENT SYSTEM AS OF 1/1/71

CATEGORY OF SUBSIDIARY	FOOD, TOBACCO + SOAP	CHEMICALS AND DRUGS	PETRO-LEUM	IRON AND STEEL	NON-FERROUS METALS	FABRICAT. METAL+NON EL. MACH	ELECTRIC AND ELECTRONIC
ALL SUBSIDIARIES............	12.	14.	27.	5.1	6.0	6.4	11.
MANUFACTURING SUBSIDIARIES...	13.	16.	29.	4.7	5.7	7.5	8.7
SALES SUBSIDIARIES..........	4.0	8.3	20.	5.8	3.0	5.8	17.

TABLE CONTINUED ON NEXT PAGE

TABULATION 23.2: PERCENTAGE BREAKDOWN OF SALES OF SUBSIDIARIES IN 1970 BY
PRINCIPAL INDUSTRY-GROUP OF SUBSIDIARY'S PARENT SYSTEM AS OF 1/1/71
FOR ALL SUBSIDIARIES, MANUFACTURING SUBSIDIARIES AND SALES SUBSIDIARIES
OF NON-U.S.-BASED SYSTEMS
(CONTINUED)

CATEGORY OF SUBSIDIARY	PRINCIPAL INDUSTRY-GROUP OF SUBSIDIARY'S PARENT SYSTEM AS OF 1/1/71			
	AUTO-MOBILES	OTHER	TOTAL PERCENT	TOTAL ($ MIL)
ALL SUBSIDIARIES............	8.0	11.	100.	132474
MANUFACTURING SUBSIDIARIES...	5.8	9.4	100.	82434
SALES SUBSIDIARIES..........	22.	14.	100.	23262

TABULATION 25.1: PERCENTAGE BREAKDOWN OF NUMBER OF SUBSIDIARIES BY
NUMBER OF COUNTRIES IN WHICH SUBSIDIARY'S PARENT SYSTEM MANUFACTURED
FOR VARIOUS CATEGORIES OF SUBSIDIARIES

CATEGORY OF SUBSIDIARY	NUMBER OF COUNTRIES IN WHICH SUBSIDIARY'S PARENT SYSTEM MANUFACTURED					
	TWO OR THREE	FOUR TO SIX	SEVEN TO TWELVE	THIRTEEN OR MORE	TOTAL PERCENT	TOTAL NUMBER
NON-U.S.-BASED SYSTEMS (AS OF 1/1/71):						
ALL SUBSIDIARIES........	20.	16.	28.	36.	100.	13541
MANUFACTURING SUBS......	19.	16.	29.	36.	100.	5511
SALES SUBSIDIARIES......	18.	19.	25.	38.	100.	3267
U.S.-BASED SYSTEMS (AS OF 1/1/68):						
ALL SUBSIDIARIES........	0.	1.1	24.	75.	100.	9727
MANUFACTURING SUBS......	0.	0.6	24.	76.	100.	4219
SALES SUBSIDIARIES......	0.	2.2	33.	64.	100.	1651
WORLD SUBSET OF SYSTEMS (AS OF 1/1/68):						
NON-U.S.-BASED SYSTEMS:						
ALL SUBSIDIARIES.......	0.	0.	23.	77.	100.	6153
MANUFACTURING SUBS.....	0.	0.	18.	82.	100.	2737
SALES SUBSIDIARIES.....	0.	0.	27.	73.	100.	1634
U.S.-BASED SYSTEMS:						
ALL SUBSIDIARIES.......	0.	0.	20.	80.	100.	8144
MANUFACTURING SUBS.....	0.	0.	19.	81.	100.	3334
SALES SUBSIDIARIES.....	0.	0.	28.	72.	100.	1309

TABULATION 25.2: PERCENTAGE BREAKDOWN OF SALES OF SUBSIDIARIES IN 1970 BY
NUMBER OF COUNTRIES IN WHICH SUBSIDIARY'S PARENT SYSTEM MANUFACTURED AS OF 1/1/71
FOR ALL SUBSIDIARIES, MANUFACTURING SUBSIDIARIES AND SALES SUBSIDIARIES
OF NON-U.S.-BASED SYSTEMS

CATEGORY OF SUBSIDIARY	NUMBER OF COUNTRIES IN WHICH SUBSIDIARY'S PARENT SYSTEM MANUFACTURED AS OF 1/1/71					
	TWO OR THREE	FOUR TO SIX	SEVEN TO TWELVE	THIRTEEN OR MORE	TOTAL PERCENT	TOTAL ($ MIL)
ALL SUBSIDIARIES..............	1.1	5.5	13.	81.	100.	131915
MANUFACTURING SUBSIDIARIES...	0.5	4.0	8.8	87.	100.	82250
SALES SUBSIDIARIES...........	3.6	12.	21.	63.	100.	23095

CROSS-TABULATION 25. 1.1: PERCENTAGE BREAKDOWN OF NUMBER (AS OF 1/1/71) OF MANUFACTURING SUBSIDIARIES OF NON-U.S.-BASED PARENT SYSTEMS BY NUMBER OF COUNTRIES IN WHICH SUBSIDIARY'S PARENT SYSTEM MANUFACTURED AS OF 1/1/71 FOR SUBSIDIARIES CLASSIFIED BY SUBSIDIARY'S COUNTRY

SUBSIDIARY'S COUNTRY	NUMBER OF COUNTRIES IN WHICH SUBSIDIARY'S PARENT SYSTEM MANUFACTURED AS OF 1/1/71					
	TWO OR THREE	FOUR TO SIX	SEVEN TO TWELVE	THIRTEEN OR MORE	TOTAL PERCENT	TOTAL NUMBER
UNITED STATES	0.7	4.5	9.2	86.	100.	402
CANADA	0.4	1.1	12.	86.	100.	273
MEXICO	0.	2.1	19.	79.	100.	97
CENTRAL AMERICA AND CARIB.	5.6	2.2	13.	79.	100.	90
VENEZUELA	2.2	2.2	20.	76.	100.	46
COLOMBIA	0.	7.1	18.	75.	100.	28
PERU	9.7	9.7	16.	65.	100.	31
CHILE	0.	0.	7.1	93.	100.	28
ARGENTINA	0.	1.7	14.	84.	100.	121
BRAZIL	0.5	5.9	24.	69.	100.	185
OTHER SOUTH AMERICA	0.	4.3	8.7	87.	100.	23
GERMANY	1.9	2.2	4.4	92.	100.	320
FRANCE	0.	5.4	5.2	89.	100.	441
ITALY	0.	2.0	5.9	92.	100.	202
BELGIUM AND LUXEMBURG	2.5	10.	16.	71.	100.	158
THE NETHERLANDS	0.	5.8	14.	80.	100.	139
UNITED KINGDOM	0.8	2.8	4.3	92.	100.	253
IRELAND	0.	3.1	15.	81.	100.	97
DENMARK	0.	0.	5.0	95.	100.	40
NORWAY	0.	2.2	20.	78.	100.	45
SWEDEN	0.	1.4	4.1	95.	100.	74
FINLAND	0.	9.1	18.	73.	100.	22

TABLE CONTINUED ON NEXT PAGE

CROSS-TABULATION 25. 1.1: PERCENTAGE BREAKDOWN OF NUMBER (AS OF 1/1/71) OF MANUFACTURING SUBSIDIARIES OF NON-U.S.-BASED PARENT SYSTEMS BY NUMBER OF COUNTRIES IN WHICH SUBSIDIARY'S PARENT SYSTEM MANUFACTURED AS OF 1/1/71 FOR SUBSIDIARIES CLASSIFIED BY SUBSIDIARY'S COUNTRY
(CONTINUED)

NUMBER OF COUNTRIES IN WHICH SUBSIDIARY'S PARENT SYSTEM MANUFACTURED AS OF 1/1/71

SUBSIDIARY'S COUNTRY	TWO OR THREE	FOUR TO SIX	SEVEN TO TWELVE	THIRTEEN OR MORE	TOTAL PERCENT	TOTAL NUMBER
SWITZERLAND	0.	7.1	11.	82.	100.	56
AUSTRIA	0.	1.1	11.	88.	100.	91
PORTUGAL	0.	5.6	11.	83.	100.	54
SPAIN	0.	2.1	15.	83.	100.	191
GREECE	0.	0.	0.	100.	100.	26
TURKEY	3.0	0.	3.0	94.	100.	33
OTHER EUROPE + ISRAEL	0.	5.4	11.	84.	100.	37
PAKISTAN	0.	4.8	2.4	93.	100.	42
IRAN	0.	8.3	17.	75.	100.	24
OTHER MID EAST+EGYPT+LIBYA	0.	3.8	7.7	88.	100.	26
UNION OF SOUTH AFRICA	0.3	20.	10.	70.	100.	371
RHODESIA	0.	3.7	5.6	91.	100.	54
ZAMBIA	0.	5.3	0.	95.	100.	38
TANZANIA	0.	0.	14.	86.	100.	22
KENYA	2.3	0.	11.	86.	100.	44
NIGERIA	0.	3.7	17.	80.	100.	54
OTHER (BRITISH) AFRICA	0.	11.	13.	76.	100.	54
MOROCCO, ALGERIA + TUNISIA	2.0	5.9	2.0	90.	100.	51
OTHER (FRENCH) AFRICA	0.	1.9	15.	83.	100.	52
OTHER AFRICA	0.	14.	14.	71.	100.	35
AUSTRALIA	0.2	15.	9.6	75.	100.	407
NEW ZEALAND	0.9	3.6	12.	84.	100.	112

TABLE CONTINUED ON NEXT PAGE

CROSS-TABULATION 25. 1.1: PERCENTAGE BREAKDOWN OF NUMBER (AS OF 1/1/71) OF
MANUFACTURING SUBSIDIARIES OF NON-U.S.-BASED PARENT SYSTEMS BY
NUMBER OF COUNTRIES IN WHICH SUBSIDIARY'S PARENT SYSTEM MANUFACTURED AS OF 1/1/71
FOR SUBSIDIARIES CLASSIFIED BY
SUBSIDIARY'S COUNTRY
(CONTINUED)

	NUMBER OF COUNTRIES IN WHICH SUBSIDIARY'S PARENT SYSTEM MANUFACTURED AS OF 1/1/71					
SUBSIDIARY'S COUNTRY	TWO OR THREE	FOUR TO SIX	SEVEN TO TWELVE	THIRTEEN OR MORE	TOTAL PERCENT	TOTAL NUMBER
JAPAN..................	0.	2.4	3.7	94.	100.	82
CHINA (TAIWAN)........	10.	35.	27.	28.	100.	97
HONG KONG.............	0.	11.	29.	61.	100.	28
THE PHILIPPINES.......	8.0	8.0	24.	60.	100.	25
MALAYSIA..............	5.5	15.	16.	64.	100.	55
SINGAPORE.............	3.8	17.	12.	67.	100.	52
INDONESIA.............	0.	23.	19.	58.	100.	26
THAILAND..............	7.7	23.	34.	35.	100.	65
INDIA.................	0.7	11.	9.9	78.	100.	152
OTHER ASIA AND OCEANIA..	7.9	13.	17.	62.	100.	63

473

CROSS-TABULATION 25.1.2: PERCENTAGE BREAKDOWN OF NUMBER (AS OF 1/1/68) OF MANUFACTURING SUBSIDIARIES OF U.S.-BASED PARENT SYSTEMS BY NUMBER OF COUNTRIES IN WHICH SUBSIDIARY'S PARENT SYSTEM MANUFACTURED AS OF 1/1/68 FOR SUBSIDIARIES CLASSIFIED BY SUBSIDIARY'S COUNTRY

SUBSIDIARY'S COUNTRY	NUMBER OF COUNTRIES IN WHICH SUBSIDIARY'S PARENT SYSTEM MANUFACTURED AS OF 1/1/68				TOTAL PERCENT	TOTAL NUMBER
	TWO OR THREE	FOUR TO SIX	SEVEN TO TWELVE	THIRTEEN OR MORE		
UNITED STATES	0.	0.	0.	0.	100.	0
CANADA	0.	0.7	29.	70.	100.	538
MEXICO	0.	0.7	32.	67.	100.	286
CENTRAL AMERICA AND CARIB.	0.	0.	14.	86.	100.	139
VENEZUELA	0.	0.	20.	80.	100.	135
COLOMBIA	0.	0.	19.	81.	100.	114
PERU	0.	0.	9.8	90.	100.	51
CHILE	0.	0.	19.	81.	100.	42
ARGENTINA	0.	0.8	27.	72.	100.	133
BRAZIL	0.	0.	23.	77.	100.	177
OTHER SOUTH AMERICA	0.	0.	6.8	93.	100.	44
GERMANY	0.	1.2	27.	72.	100.	247
FRANCE	0.	0.9	29.	70.	100.	235
ITALY	0.	0.5	26.	74.	100.	187
BELGIUM AND LUXEMBURG	0.	0.	19.	81.	100.	103
THE NETHERLANDS	0.	1.1	25.	74.	100.	89
UNITED KINGDOM	0.	1.2	30.	69.	100.	404
IRELAND	0.	0.	10.	90.	100.	30
DENMARK	0.	0.	16.	84.	100.	31
NORWAY	0.	0.	5.0	95.	100.	20
SWEDEN	0.	0.	19.	81.	100.	36
FINLAND	0.	0.	33.	67.	100.	6

TABLE CONTINUED ON NEXT PAGE

CROSS-TABULATION 25. 1.2: PERCENTAGE BREAKDOWN OF NUMBER (AS OF 1/1/68) OF
MANUFACTURING SUBSIDIARIES OF U.S.-BASED PARENT SYSTEMS BY
NUMBER OF COUNTRIES IN WHICH SUBSIDIARY'S PARENT SYSTEM MANUFACTURED AS OF 1/1/68
FOR SUBSIDIARIES CLASSIFIED BY
SUBSIDIARY'S COUNTRY
(CONTINUED)

SUBSIDIARY'S COUNTRY	NUMBER OF COUNTRIES IN WHICH SUBSIDIARY'S PARENT SYSTEM MANUFACTURED AS OF 1/1/68					
	TWO OR THREE	FOUR TO SIX	SEVEN TO TWELVE	THIRTEEN OR MORE	TOTAL PERCENT	TOTAL NUMBER
SWITZERLAND	0.	0.	36.	64.	100.	33
AUSTRIA	0.	0.	35.	65.	100.	20
PORTUGAL	0.	0.	13.	87.	100.	23
SPAIN	0.	1.6	24.	74.	100.	124
GREECE	0.	0.	13.	87.	100.	23
TURKEY	0.	0.	13.	88.	100.	16
OTHER EUROPE + ISRAEL	0.	0.	33.	67.	100.	15
PAKISTAN	0.	0.	13.	88.	100.	16
IRAN	0.	0.	0.	100.	100.	19
OTHER MID EAST+EGYPT+LIBYA	0.	0.	0.	100.	100.	30
UNION OF SOUTH AFRICA	0.	0.8	19.	81.	100.	124
RHODESIA	0.	0.	0.	100.	100.	14
ZAMBIA	0.	0.	14.	86.	100.	7
TANZANIA	0.	0.	0.	0.	100.	0
KENYA	0.	0.	0.	100.	100.	9
NIGERIA	0.	0.	15.	85.	100.	13
OTHER (BRITISH) AFRICA	0.	0.	0.	100.	100.	6
MOROCCO, ALGERIA + TUNISIA	0.	0.	19.	81.	100.	16
OTHER (FRENCH) AFRICA	0.	0.	0.	100.	100.	9
OTHER AFRICA	0.	0.	0.	100.	100.	4
AUSTRALIA	0.	0.4	32.	68.	100.	234
NEW ZEALAND	0.	0.	17.	83.	100.	47

TABLE CONTINUED ON NEXT PAGE

CROSS-TABULATION 25. 1.2: PERCENTAGE BREAKDOWN OF NUMBER (AS OF 1/1/68) OF MANUFACTURING SUBSIDIARIES OF U.S.-BASED PARENT SYSTEMS BY NUMBER OF COUNTRIES IN WHICH SUBSIDIARY'S PARENT SYSTEM MANUFACTURED AS OF 1/1/68 FOR SUBSIDIARIES CLASSIFIED BY SUBSIDIARY'S COUNTRY (CONTINUED)

SUBSIDIARY'S COUNTRY	NUMBER OF COUNTRIES IN WHICH SUBSIDIARY'S PARENT SYSTEM MANUFACTURED AS OF 1/1/68					
	TWO OR THREE	FOUR TO SIX	SEVEN TO TWELVE	THIRTEEN OR MORE	TOTAL PERCENT	TOTAL NUMBER
JAPAN............	0.	1.3	22.	76.	100.	157
CHINA (TAIWAN)...	0.	0.	13.	88.	100.	16
HONG KONG........	0.	0.	0.	100.	100.	6
THE PHILIPPINES..	0.	0.	5.3	95.	100.	57
MALAYSIA.........	0.	0.	0.	100.	100.	16
SINGAPORE........	0.	0.	0.	100.	100.	12
INDONESIA........	0.	0.	0.	100.	100.	4
THAILAND.........	0.	0.	0.	100.	100.	15
INDIA............	0.	3.0	20.	77.	100.	66
OTHER ASIA AND OCEANIA......	0.	0.	4.8	95.	100.	21

CROSS-TABULATION 25.21.1: PERCENTAGE BREAKDOWN OF NUMBER (AS OF 1/1/71) OF
MANUFACTURING SUBSIDIARIES OF NON-U.S.-BASED PARENT SYSTEMS BY
NUMBER OF COUNTRIES IN WHICH SUBSIDIARY'S PARENT SYSTEM MANUFACTURED AS OF 1/1/71
FOR SUBSIDIARIES CLASSIFIED BY
NATIONAL BASE OF SUBSIDIARY'S PARENT SYSTEM

NATIONAL BASE OF SUBSIDIARY'S PARENT SYSTEM	NUMBER OF COUNTRIES IN WHICH SUBSIDIARY'S PARENT SYSTEM MANUFACTURED AS OF 1/1/71					
	TWO OR THREE	FOUR TO SIX	SEVEN TO TWELVE	THIRTEEN OR MORE	TOTAL PERCENT	TOTAL NUMBER
UNITED KINGDOM.	0.1	5.5	7.7	87.	100.	2265
GERMANY.	0.3	4.9	15.	80.	100.	789
FRANCE.	1.9	3.0	14.	81.	100.	427
ITALY.	0.	0.	33.	67.	100.	130
BELGIUM AND LUXEMBURG.	0.	13.	6.6	80.	100.	272
THE NETHERLANDS.	0.	1.6	2.8	96.	100.	425
SWEDEN.	1.2	4.8	13.	81.	100.	167
SWITZERLAND.	0.	0.	0.	100.	100.	393
JAPAN.	8.4	32.	32.	28.	100.	477
CANADA.	0.5	8.2	14.	77.	100.	196
OTHER NON-U.S.	5.1	5.1	0.	90.	100.	99

TABULATION 26.1: PERCENTAGE BREAKDOWN OF NUMBER OF SUBSIDIARIES BY
PERCENTAGE OF PARENT SYSTEM'S EMPLOYEES OUTSIDE PARENT SYSTEM'S NATIONAL BASE
FOR VARIOUS CATEGORIES OF SUBSIDIARIES

CATEGORY OF SUBSIDIARY	PERCENTAGE OF PARENT SYSTEM'S EMPLOYEES OUTSIDE PARENT SYSTEM'S NATIONAL BASE					
	UNDER 10%	10% - 25%	25% - 50%	OVER 50%	TOTAL PERCENT	TOTAL NUMBER
NON-U.S.-BASED SYSTEMS (AS OF 1/1/71):						
ALL SUBSIDIARIES........	10.	28.	19.	43.	100.	11103
MANUFACTURING SUBS......	10.	29.	21.	40.	100.	4734
SALES SUBSIDIARIES......	14.	33.	16.	37.	100.	2670

TABULATION 26.2: PERCENTAGE BREAKDOWN OF SALES OF SUBSIDIARIES IN 1970 BY
PERCENTAGE OF PARENT SYSTEM'S EMPLOYEES OUTSIDE PARENT SYSTEM'S NATIONAL BASE AS OF 1/1/71
FOR ALL SUBSIDIARIES, MANUFACTURING SUBSIDIARIES AND SALES SUBSIDIARIES
OF NON-U.S.-BASED SYSTEMS

CATEGORY OF SUBSIDIARY	PERCENTAGE OF PARENT SYSTEM'S EMPLOYEES OUTSIDE PARENT SYSTEM'S NATIONAL BASE AS OF 1/1/71					
	UNDER 10%	10% - 25%	25% - 50%	OVER 50%	TOTAL PERCENT	TOTAL ($ MIL)
ALL SUBSIDIARIES............	8.2	21.	15.	56.	100.	114150
MANUFACTURING SUBSIDIARIES...	7.0	18.	15.	60.	100.	72530
SALES SUBSIDIARIES...........	16.	37.	12.	35.	100.	19608

CROSS-TABULATION 26. 1.1: PERCENTAGE BREAKDOWN OF NUMBER (AS OF 1/1/71) OF MANUFACTURING SUBSIDIARIES OF NON-U.S.-BASED PARENT SYSTEMS BY PERCENTAGE OF PARENT SYSTEM'S EMPLOYEES OUTSIDE NATIONAL BASE AS OF 1/1/71 FOR SUBSIDIARIES CLASSIFIED BY SUBSIDIARY'S COUNTRY

SUBSIDIARY'S COUNTRY	PERCENTAGE OF PARENT SYSTEM'S EMPLOYEES OUTSIDE NATIONAL BASE AS OF 1/1/71					
	UNDER 10%	10% - 25%	25% - 50%	OVER 50%	TOTAL PERCENT	TOTAL NUMBER
UNITED STATES	4.9	21.	18.	56.	100.	346
CANADA	8.3	45.	12.	35.	100.	217
MEXICO	11.	35.	26.	28.	100.	80
CENTRAL AMERICA AND CARIB	4.0	20.	21.	55.	100.	75
VENEZUELA	0.	29.	26.	46.	100.	35
COLOMBIA	13.	25.	25.	38.	100.	24
PERU	24.	24.	28.	24.	100.	25
CHILE	4.3	26.	17.	52.	100.	23
ARGENTINA	7.2	28.	31.	34.	100.	97
BRAZIL	20.	31.	29.	21.	100.	150
OTHER SOUTH AMERICA	5.3	0.	26.	68.	100.	19
GERMANY	12.	24.	15.	50.	100.	274
FRANCE	6.8	15.	35.	43.	100.	385
ITALY	8.0	28.	26.	38.	100.	162
BELGIUM AND LUXEMBURG	19.	32.	19.	31.	100.	129
THE NETHERLANDS	12.	35.	18.	35.	100.	117
UNITED KINGDOM	3.0	9.9	17.	70.	100.	232
IRELAND	16.	28.	15.	41.	100.	75
DENMARK	0.	22.	30.	49.	100.	37
NORWAY	19.	24.	29.	29.	100.	42
SWEDEN	1.4	44.	17.	37.	100.	70
FINLAND	15.	20.	30.	35.	100.	20

TABLE CONTINUED ON NEXT PAGE

CROSS-TABULATION 26. 1.1: PERCENTAGE BREAKDOWN OF NUMBER (AS OF 1/1/71) OF MANUFACTURING SUBSIDIARIES OF NON-U.S.-BASED PARENT SYSTEMS BY PERCENTAGE OF PARENT SYSTEM'S EMPLOYEES OUTSIDE NATIONAL BASE AS OF 1/1/71 FOR SUBSIDIARIES CLASSIFIED BY SUBSIDIARY'S COUNTRY (CONTINUED)

PERCENTAGE OF PARENT SYSTEM'S EMPLOYEES OUTSIDE NATIONAL BASE AS OF 1/1/71

SUBSIDIARY'S COUNTRY	UNDER 10%	10% - 25%	25% - 50%	OVER 50%	TOTAL PERCENT	TOTAL NUMBER
SWITZERLAND	4.4	27.	20.	49.	100.	45
AUSTRIA	7.1	32.	25.	36.	100.	84
PORTUGAL	15.	28.	30.	28.	100.	40
SPAIN	8.3	34.	31.	26.	100.	145
GREECE	0.	43.	35.	22.	100.	23
TURKEY	3.4	34.	28.	34.	100.	29
OTHER EUROPE + ISRAEL	4.8	29.	24.	43.	100.	21
PAKISTAN	5.1	31.	26.	38.	100.	39
IRAN	23.	45.	14.	18.	100.	22
OTHER MID EAST+EGYPT+LIBYA	18.	14.	18.	50.	100.	22
UNION OF SOUTH AFRICA	7.4	48.	14.	31.	100.	324
RHODESIA	6.1	24.	10.	59.	100.	49
ZAMBIA	5.3	7.9	7.9	79.	100.	38
TANZANIA	4.8	24.	9.5	62.	100.	21
KENYA	9.8	15.	24.	51.	100.	41
NIGERIA	8.9	18.	13.	60.	100.	45
OTHER (BRITISH) AFRICA	8.7	15.	2.2	74.	100.	46
MOROCCO, ALGERIA + TUNISIA	23.	21.	15.	41.	100.	39
OTHER (FRENCH) AFRICA	6.3	9.4	13.	72.	100.	32
OTHER AFRICA	9.5	14.	33.	43.	100.	21
AUSTRALIA	6.1	43.	19.	32.	100.	376
NEW ZEALAND	9.4	39.	22.	30.	100.	96

TABLE CONTINUED ON NEXT PAGE

481

CROSS-TABULATION 26. 1.1: PERCENTAGE BREAKDOWN OF NUMBER (AS OF 1/1/71) OF MANUFACTURING SUBSIDIARIES OF NON-U.S.-BASED PARENT SYSTEMS BY PERCENTAGE OF PARENT SYSTEM'S EMPLOYEES OUTSIDE NATIONAL BASE AS OF 1/1/71 FOR SUBSIDIARIES CLASSIFIED BY SUBSIDIARY'S COUNTRY (CONTINUED)

PERCENTAGE OF PARENT SYSTEM'S EMPLOYEES OUTSIDE NATIONAL BASE AS OF 1/1/71

SUBSIDIARY'S COUNTRY	UNDER 10%	10% - 25%	25% - 50%	OVER 50%	TOTAL PERCENT	TOTAL NUMBER
JAPAN	2.5	33.	21.	43.	100.	81
CHINA (TAIWAN)	52.	25.	21.	1.6	100.	61
HONG KONG	16.	16.	32.	37.	100.	19
THE PHILIPPINES	20.	25.	20.	35.	100.	20
MALAYSIA	25.	18.	20.	38.	100.	40
SINGAPORE	22.	27.	19.	32.	100.	37
INDONESIA	24.	12.	29.	35.	100.	17
THAILAND	40.	19.	26.	14.	100.	42
INDIA	18.	38.	20.	24.	100.	137
OTHER ASIA AND OCEANIA	30.	15.	20.	35.	100.	46

482

CROSS-TABULATION 26.21.1: PERCENTAGE BREAKDOWN OF NUMBER (AS OF 1/1/71) OF
MANUFACTURING SUBSIDIARIES OF NON-U.S.-BASED PARENT SYSTEMS BY
PERCENTAGE OF PARENT SYSTEM'S EMPLOYEES OUTSIDE NATIONAL BASE AS OF 1/1/71
FOR SUBSIDIARIES CLASSIFIED BY
NATIONAL BASE OF SUBSIDIARY'S PARENT SYSTEM

NATIONAL BASE OF SUBSIDIARY'S PARENT SYSTEM	PERCENTAGE OF PARENT SYSTEM'S EMPLOYEES OUTSIDE NATIONAL BASE AS OF 1/1/71					
	UNDER 10%	10% - 25%	25% - 50%	OVER 50%	TOTAL PERCENT	TOTAL NUMBER
UNITED KINGDOM................	5.5	34.	18.	42.	100.	2119
GERMANY.......................	5.5	49.	45.	0.	100.	713
FRANCE........................	22.	19.	27.	32.	100.	194
ITALY.........................	0.	46.	54.	0.	100.	81
BELGIUM AND LUXEMBURG.........	17.	22.	61.	0.	100.	83
THE NETHERLANDS...............	0.	21.	0.	79.	100.	406
SWEDEN........................	4.8	15.	24.	56.	100.	165
SWITZERLAND...................	17.	0.	14.	68.	100.	393
JAPAN.........................	62.	24.	13.	0.	100.	289
CANADA........................	3.6	3.6	11.	82.	100.	197
OTHER NON-U.S.................	5.3	0.	0.	95.	100.	94

TABULATION 27.1: PERCENTAGE BREAKDOWN OF NUMBER OF SUBSIDIARIES BY
NO. OF INDUSTRIES IN WHICH PARENT SYSTEM MANUFACTURED WITHIN NATIONAL BASE
FOR VARIOUS CATEGORIES OF SUBSIDIARIES

CATEGORY OF SUBSIDIARY	NO. OF INDUSTRIES IN WHICH PARENT SYSTEM MANUFACTURED WITHIN NATIONAL BASE					
	ONE TO THREE	FOUR TO NINE	TEN TO NINETEEN	TWENTY OR MORE	TOTAL PERCENT	TOTAL NUMBER
NON-U.S.-BASED SYSTEMS (AS OF 1/1/71):						
ALL SUBSIDIARIES.........	8.6	31.	42.	19.	100.	13800
MANUFACTURING SUBS.......	7.4	31.	42.	20.	100.	5645
SALES SUBSIDIARIES.......	12.	30.	42.	16.	100.	3311
U.S.-BASED SYSTEMS (AS OF 1/1/68):						
ALL SUBSIDIARIES.........	9.4	40.	30.	20.	100.	9586
MANUFACTURING SUBS.......	9.3	35.	35.	21.	100.	4162
SALES SUBSIDIARIES.......	8.7	46.	29.	17.	100.	1632
WORLD SUBSET OF SYSTEMS (AS OF 1/1/68):						
NON-U.S.-BASED SYSTEMS:						
ALL SUBSIDIARIES.........	4.6	24.	45.	27.	100.	6153
MANUFACTURING SUBS.......	2.7	24.	44.	30.	100.	2737
SALES SUBSIDIARIES.......	4.0	25.	49.	22.	100.	1634
U.S.-BASED-SYSTEMS:						
ALL SUBSIDIARIES.........	8.6	38.	31.	22.	100.	8059
MANUFACTURING SUBS.......	8.2	31.	37.	24.	100.	3298
SALES SUBSIDIARIES.......	8.6	44.	28.	19.	100.	1297

TABULATION 27.2: PERCENTAGE BREAKDOWN OF SALES OF SUBSIDIARIES IN 1970 BY
NO. OF INDUSTRIES IN WHICH PARENT SYSTEM MANUFACTURED WITHIN NATIONAL BASE AS OF 1/1/71
FOR ALL SUBSIDIARIES, MANUFACTURING SUBSIDIARIES AND SALES SUBSIDIARIES
OF NON-U.S.-BASED SYSTEMS

CATEGORY OF SUBSIDIARY	NO. OF INDUSTRIES IN WHICH PARENT SYSTEM MANUFACTURED WITHIN NATIONAL BASE AS OF 1/1/71				TOTAL PERCENT	TOTAL ($ MIL)
	ONE TO THREE	FOUR TO NINE	TEN TO NINETEEN	TWENTY OR MORE		
ALL SUBSIDIARIES............	6.2	26.	54.	14.	100.	132500
MANUFACTURING SUBSIDIARIES...	4.1	23.	60.	13.	100.	82434
SALES SUBSIDIARIES..........	13.	37.	40.	10.	100.	23262

CROSS-TABULATION 27.21.1: PERCENTAGE BREAKDOWN OF NUMBER (AS OF 1/1/71) OF
MANUFACTURING SUBSIDIARIES OF NON-U.S.-BASED PARENT SYSTEMS BY
NO. OF INDUSTRIES IN WHICH PARENT SYSTEM MANUFACTURED WITHIN NATIONAL BASE AS OF 1/1/71
FOR SUBSIDIARIES CLASSIFIED BY
NATIONAL BASE OF SUBSIDIARY'S PARENT SYSTEM

NATIONAL BASE OF SUBSIDIARY'S PARENT SYSTEM	NO. OF INDUSTRIES IN WHICH PARENT SYSTEM MANUFACTURED WITHIN NATIONAL BASE AS OF 1/1/71					
	ONE TO THREE	FOUR TO NINE	TEN TO NINETEEN	TWENTY OR MORE	TOTAL PERCENT	TOTAL NUMBER
UNITED KINGDOM...........	4.7	30.	42.	24.	100.	2265
GERMANY..............	2.8	11.	85.	1.3	100.	789
FRANCE............	7.5	54.	32.	6.3	100.	427
ITALY..............	0.	34.	29.	37.	100.	130
BELGIUM AND LUXEMBURG........	0.	36.	12.	52.	100.	272
THE NETHERLANDS.........	0.	4.5	37.	59.	100.	425
SWEDEN..........	0.	19.	80.	1.2	100.	167
SWITZERLAND........	0.	23.	51.	27.	100.	393
JAPAN..........	43.	48.	8.7	0.	100.	481
CANADA.........	25.	60.	15.	0.	100.	197
OTHER NON-U.S..............	0.	95.	5.1	0.	100.	99

TABULATION 28.1: PERCENTAGE BREAKDOWN OF NUMBER OF SUBSIDIARIES BY NO. OF INDUSTRIES IN WHICH PARENT SYSTEM MANUFACTURED OUTSIDE NATIONAL BASE FOR VARIOUS CATEGORIES OF SUBSIDIARIES

CATEGORY OF SUBSIDIARY	NO. OF INDUSTRIES IN WHICH PARENT SYSTEM MANUFACTURED OUTSIDE NATIONAL BASE					
	ONE TO THREE	FOUR TO NINE	TEN TO NINETEEN	TWENTY OR MORE	TOTAL PERCENT	TOTAL NUMBER
NON-U.S.-BASED SYSTEMS (AS OF 1/1/71):						
ALL SUBSIDIARIES........:	9.5	30.	26.	34.	100.	13800
MANUFACTURING SUBS......:	6.2	24.	30.	40.	100.	5645
SALES SUBSIDIARIES......:	13.	36.	25.	26.	100.	3311
U.S.-BASED SYSTEMS (AS OF 1/1/68):						
ALL SUBSIDIARIES........:	12.	59.	20.	9.3	100.	9776
MANUFACTURING SUBS......:	14.	57.	21.	7.9	100.	4246
SALES SUBSIDIARIES......:	14.	63.	13.	10.	100.	1664
WORLD SUBSET OF SYSTEMS (AS OF 1/1/68):						
NON-U.S.-BASED SYSTEMS:						
ALL SUBSIDIARIES........:	7.1	30.	25.	38.	100.	6153
MANUFACTURING SUBS......:	4.6	22.	28.	45.	100.	2737
SALES SUBSIDIARIES......:	7.5	38.	25.	30.	100.	1634
U.S.-BASED-SYSTEMS:						
ALL SUBSIDIARIES........:	9.2	57.	24.	10.	100.	8144
MANUFACTURING SUBS......:	10.	55.	27.	8.3	100.	3334
SALES SUBSIDIARIES......:	11.	61.	17.	11.	100.	1309

TABULATION 28.2: PERCENTAGE BREAKDOWN OF SALES OF SUBSIDIARIES IN 1970 BY
NO. OF INDUSTRIES IN WHICH PARENT SYSTEM MANUFACTURED OUTSIDE NATIONAL BASE AS OF 1/1/71
FOR ALL SUBSIDIARIES, MANUFACTURING SUBSIDIARIES AND SALES SUBSIDIARIES
OF NON-U.S.-BASED SYSTEMS

CATEGORY OF SUBSIDIARY	NO. OF INDUSTRIES IN WHICH PARENT SYSTEM MANUFACTURED OUTSIDE NATIONAL BASE AS OF 1/1/71					
	ONE TO THREE	FOUR TO NINE	TEN TO NINETEEN	TWENTY OR MORE	TOTAL PERCENT	TOTAL ($ MIL)
ALL SUBSIDIARIES............	8.0	45.	23.	24.	100.	132500
MANUFACTURING SUBSIDIARIES...	4.4	47.	24.	24.	100.	82434
SALES SUBSIDIARIES..........	20.	45.	21.	14.	100.	23262

CROSS-TABULATION 28. 1.1: PERCENTAGE BREAKDOWN OF NUMBER (AS OF 1/1/71) OF
MANUFACTURING SUBSIDIARIES OF NON-U.S.-BASED PARENT SYSTEMS BY
NO. OF INDUSTRIES IN WHICH PARENT SYSTEM MANUFACTURED OUTSIDE NATIONAL BASE AS OF 1/1/71
FOR SUBSIDIARIES CLASSIFIED BY
SUBSIDIARY'S COUNTRY

SUBSIDIARY'S COUNTRY	NO. OF INDUSTRIES IN WHICH PARENT SYSTEM MANUFACTURED OUTSIDE NATIONAL BASE AS OF 1/1/71					
	ONE TO THREE	FOUR TO NINE	TEN TO NINETEEN	TWENTY OR MORE	TOTAL PERCENT	TOTAL NUMBER
UNITED STATES........	6.7	17.	27.	50.	100.	403
CANADA...............	3.7	21.	25.	51.	100.	273
MEXICO...............	9.3	30.	35.	26.	100.	97
CENTRAL AMERICA AND CARIB....	7.8	32.	28.	32.	100.	90
VENEZUELA............	2.2	41.	26.	30.	100.	46
COLOMBIA.............	7.1	25.	32.	36.	100.	28
PERU.................	19.	23.	29.	29.	100.	31
CHILE................	11.	18.	43.	29.	100.	28
ARGENTINA............	9.9	26.	40.	23.	100.	121
BRAZIL...............	9.1	31.	37.	23.	100.	186
OTHER SOUTH AMERICA..	4.3	26.	39.	30.	100.	23
GERMANY..............	2.5	22.	27.	49.	100.	320
FRANCE...............	3.6	18.	27.	52.	100.	441
ITALY................	3.5	23.	37.	36.	100.	202
BELGIUM AND LUXEMBURG..........	14.	25.	29.	32.	100.	158
THE NETHERLANDS......	6.5	24.	39.	30.	100.	139
UNITED KINGDOM.......	4.3	16.	27.	53.	100.	253
IRELAND..............	13.	32.	14.	40.	100.	97
DENMARK..............	5.0	33.	23.	40.	100.	40
NORWAY...............	4.4	31.	24.	40.	100.	45
SWEDEN...............	0.	14.	35.	51.	100.	74
FINLAND..............	9.1	41.	18.	32.	100.	22

TABLE CONTINUED ON NEXT PAGE

CROSS-TABULATION 28. 1.1: PERCENTAGE BREAKDOWN OF NUMBER (AS OF 1/1/71) OF MANUFACTURING SUBSIDIARIES OF NON-U.S.-BASED PARENT SYSTEMS BY NO. OF INDUSTRIES IN WHICH PARENT SYSTEM MANUFACTURED OUTSIDE NATIONAL BASE AS OF 1/1/71 FOR SUBSIDIARIES CLASSIFIED BY SUBSIDIARY'S COUNTRY (CONTINUED)

SUBSIDIARY'S COUNTRY	NO. OF INDUSTRIES IN WHICH PARENT SYSTEM MANUFACTURED OUTSIDE NATIONAL BASE AS OF 1/1/71					
	ONE TO THREE	FOUR TO NINE	TEN TO NINETEEN	TWENTY OR MORE	TOTAL PERCENT	TOTAL NUMBER
SWITZERLAND	13.	18.	29.	41.	100.	56
AUSTRIA	2.2	19.	41.	38.	100.	91
PORTUGAL	11.	28.	35.	26.	100.	54
SPAIN	8.8	26.	36.	29.	100.	193
GREECE	0.	12.	54.	35.	100.	26
TURKEY	3.0	27.	52.	18.	100.	33
OTHER EUROPE + ISRAEL	11.	14.	24.	51.	100.	37
PAKISTAN	0.	19.	43.	38.	100.	42
IRAN	17.	29.	29.	25.	100.	24
OTHER MID EAST+EGYPT+LIBYA	11.	37.	26.	26.	100.	27
UNION OF SOUTH AFRICA	6.7	20.	39.	34.	100.	371
RHODESIA	1.9	31.	13.	54.	100.	54
ZAMBIA	0.	13.	16.	71.	100.	38
TANZANIA	9.1	27.	18.	45.	100.	22
KENYA	6.8	32.	16.	45.	100.	44
NIGERIA	1.9	28.	17.	54.	100.	54
OTHER (BRITISH) AFRICA	7.4	20.	17.	56.	100.	54
MOROCCO, ALGERIA + TUNISIA	12.	37.	24.	27.	100.	51
OTHER (FRENCH) AFRICA	9.6	35.	29.	27.	100.	52
OTHER AFRICA	14.	31.	11.	43.	100.	35
AUSTRALIA	3.7	25.	34.	37.	100.	407
NEW ZEALAND	7.1	28.	26.	39.	100.	112

TABLE CONTINUED ON NEXT PAGE

CROSS-TABULATION 28. 1.1: PERCENTAGE BREAKDOWN OF NUMBER (AS OF 1/1/71) OF
MANUFACTURING SUBSIDIARIES OF NON-U.S.-BASED PARENT SYSTEMS BY
NO. OF INDUSTRIES IN WHICH PARENT SYSTEM MANUFACTURED OUTSIDE NATIONAL BASE AS OF 1/1/71
FOR SUBSIDIARIES CLASSIFIED BY
SUBSIDIARY'S COUNTRY
(CONTINUED)

| SUBSIDIARY'S COUNTRY | NO. OF INDUSTRIES IN WHICH PARENT SYSTEM MANUFACTURED OUTSIDE NATIONAL BASE AS OF 1/1/71 | | | | | |
	ONE TO THREE	FOUR TO NINE	TEN TO NINETEEN	TWENTY OR MORE	TOTAL PERCENT	TOTAL NUMBER
JAPAN................	2.4	17.	48.	33.	100.	82
CHINA (TAIWAN).......	5.2	51.	5.2	39.	100.	97
HONG KONG............	7.1	14.	36.	43.	100.	28
THE PHILIPPINES......	4.0	44.	24.	28.	100.	25
MALAYSIA.............	13.	33.	22.	33.	100.	55
SINGAPORE............	12.	23.	27.	38.	100.	52
INDONESIA............	3.8	15.	42.	38.	100.	26
THAILAND.............	11.	28.	17.	45.	100.	65
INDIA................	3.3	33.	34.	30.	100.	152
OTHER ASIA AND OCEANIA......	13.	22.	29.	37.	100.	63

CROSS-TABULATION 28. 1.2: PERCENTAGE BREAKDOWN OF NUMBER (AS OF 1/1/68) OF
MANUFACTURING SUBSIDIARIES OF U.S.-BASED PARENT SYSTEMS BY
NO. OF INDUSTRIES IN WHICH PARENT SYSTEM MANUFACTURED OUTSIDE NATIONAL BASE AS OF 1/1/68
FOR SUBSIDIARIES CLASSIFIED BY
SUBSIDIARY'S COUNTRY

SUBSIDIARY'S COUNTRY	NO. OF INDUSTRIES IN WHICH PARENT SYSTEM MANUFACTURED OUTSIDE NATIONAL BASE AS OF 1/1/68				TOTAL PERCENT	TOTAL NUMBER
	ONE TO THREE	FOUR TO NINE	TEN TO NINETEEN	TWENTY OR MORE		
UNITED STATES	0.	0.	0.	0.	100.	0
CANADA	13.	58.	24.	5.3	100.	543
MEXICO	17.	57.	21.	4.9	100.	288
CENTRAL AMERICA AND CARIB	10.	70.	14.	5.8	100.	139
VENEZUELA	12.	58.	21.	9.6	100.	135
COLOMBIA	11.	56.	21.	11.	100.	114
PERU	9.6	60.	12.	19.	100.	52
CHILE	4.7	65.	19.	12.	100.	43
ARGENTINA	16.	61.	18.	4.4	100.	135
BRAZIL	16.	50.	28.	5.1	100.	177
OTHER SOUTH AMERICA	2.3	57.	25.	16.	100.	44
GERMANY	16.	56.	20.	7.3	100.	248
FRANCE	17.	54.	22.	7.1	100.	238
ITALY	15.	60.	18.	7.4	100.	188
BELGIUM AND LUXEMBURG	13.	59.	22.	6.7	100.	104
THE NETHERLANDS	13.	57.	21.	7.9	100.	89
UNITED KINGDOM	13.	59.	18.	9.9	100.	404
IRELAND	10.	37.	27.	27.	100.	30
DENMARK	13.	53.	19.	16.	100.	32
NORWAY	0.	40.	40.	20.	100.	20
SWEDEN	2.7	46.	27.	24.	100.	37
FINLAND	17.	33.	33.	17.	100.	6

TABLE CONTINUED ON NEXT PAGE

CROSS-TABULATION 28.1.2: PERCENTAGE BREAKDOWN OF NUMBER (AS OF 1/1/68) OF MANUFACTURING SUBSIDIARIES OF U.S.-BASED PARENT SYSTEMS BY NO. OF INDUSTRIES IN WHICH PARENT SYSTEM MANUFACTURED OUTSIDE NATIONAL BASE AS OF 1/1/68 FOR SUBSIDIARIES CLASSIFIED BY SUBSIDIARY'S COUNTRY (CONTINUED)

SUBSIDIARY'S COUNTRY	NO. OF INDUSTRIES IN WHICH PARENT SYSTEM MANUFACTURED OUTSIDE NATIONAL BASE AS OF 1/1/68					
	ONE TO THREE	FOUR TO NINE	TEN TO NINETEEN	TWENTY OR MORE	TOTAL PERCENT	TOTAL NUMBER
SWITZERLAND........	6.1	55.	36.	3.0	100.	33
AUSTRIA............	10.	70.	20.	0.	100.	20
PORTUGAL...........	0.	48.	30.	22.	100.	23
SPAIN..............	13.	58.	22.	7.2	100.	125
GREECE.............	4.3	70.	17.	8.7	100.	23
TURKEY.............	6.3	50.	38.	6.3	100.	16
OTHER EUROPE + ISRAEL........	13.	63.	25.	0.	100.	16
PAKISTAN...........	25.	44.	13.	19.	100.	16
IRAN...............	16.	68.	16.	0.	100.	19
OTHER MID EAST+EGYPT+LIBYA...	6.7	70.	6.7	17.	100.	30
UNION OF SOUTH AFRICA........	20.	58.	15.	6.4	100.	125
RHODESIA...........	14.	57.	29.	0.	100.	14
ZAMBIA.............	14.	71.	14.	0.	100.	7
TANZANIA...........	0.	0.	0.	0.	100.	0
KENYA..............	11.	44.	33.	11.	100.	9
NIGERIA............	0.	77.	23.	0.	100.	13
OTHER (BRITISH) AFRICA.......	17.	0.	83.	0.	100.	6
MOROCCO, ALGERIA + TUNISIA...	6.3	63.	25.	6.3	100.	16
OTHER (FRENCH) AFRICA........	0.	89.	11.	0.	100.	9
OTHER AFRICA.......	0.	25.	50.	25.	100.	4
AUSTRALIA..........	16.	61.	12.	11.	100.	235
NEW ZEALAND........	13.	57.	13.	17.	100.	47

TABLE CONTINUED ON NEXT PAGE

CROSS-TABULATION 28. 1.2: PERCENTAGE BREAKDOWN OF NUMBER (AS OF 1/1/68) OF MANUFACTURING SUBSIDIARIES OF U.S.-BASED PARENT SYSTEMS BY NO. OF INDUSTRIES IN WHICH PARENT SYSTEM MANUFACTURED OUTSIDE NATIONAL BASE AS OF 1/1/68 FOR SUBSIDIARIES CLASSIFIED BY SUBSIDIARY'S COUNTRY (CONTINUED)

SUBSIDIARY'S COUNTRY	NO. OF INDUSTRIES IN WHICH PARENT SYSTEM MANUFACTURED OUTSIDE NATIONAL BASE AS OF 1/1/68					
	ONE TO THREE	FOUR TO NINE	TEN TO NINETEEN	TWENTY OR MORE	TOTAL PERCENT	TOTAL NUMBER
JAPAN	15.	50.	30.	5.1	100.	158
CHINA (TAIWAN)	19.	69.	13.	0.	100.	16
HONG KONG	0.	63.	38.	0.	100.	8
THE PHILIPPINES	18.	54.	25.	3.5	100.	57
MALAYSIA	6.3	44.	25.	25.	100.	16
SINGAPORE	0.	58.	42.	0.	100.	12
INDONESIA	0.	25.	75.	0.	100.	4
THAILAND	27.	33.	40.	0.	100.	15
INDIA	16.	52.	25.	6.0	100.	67
OTHER ASIA AND OCEANIA	4.8	57.	38.	0.	100.	21

CROSS-TABULATION 28.21.1: PERCENTAGE BREAKDOWN OF NUMBER (AS OF 1/1/71) OF
MANUFACTURING SUBSIDIARIES OF NON-U.S.-BASED PARENT SYSTEMS BY
NO. OF INDUSTRIES IN WHICH PARENT SYSTEM MANUFACTURED OUTSIDE NATIONAL BASE AS OF 1/1/71
FOR SUBSIDIARIES CLASSIFIED BY
NATIONAL BASE OF SUBSIDIARY'S PARENT SYSTEM

NATIONAL BASE OF SUBSIDIARY'S PARENT SYSTEM	NO. OF INDUSTRIES IN WHICH PARENT SYSTEM MANUFACTURED OUTSIDE NATIONAL BASE AS OF 1/1/71					
	ONE TO THREE	FOUR TO NINE	TEN TO NINETEEN	TWENTY OR MORE	TOTAL PERCENT	TOTAL NUMBER
UNITED KINGDOM................	3.0	22.	33.	42.	100.	2265
GERMANY.......................	8.0	21.	46.	25.	100.	789
FRANCE........................	8.0	39.	25.	28.	100.	427
ITALY.........................	34.	29.	37.	0.	100.	130
BELGIUM AND LUXEMBURG.........	5.1	16.	27.	52.	100.	272
THE NETHERLANDS...............	0.	21.	0.	79.	100.	425
SWEDEN........................	8.4	56.	0.	36.	100.	167
SWITZERLAND...................	0.	4.8	78.	17.	100.	393
JAPAN.........................	13.	37.	12.	38.	100.	481
CANADA........................	24.	32.	0.	44.	100.	197
OTHER NON-U.S.................	5.1	5.1	0.	90.	100.	99

CROSS-TABULATION 28.27.1: PERCENTAGE BREAKDOWN OF NUMBER (AS OF 1/1/71) OF
MANUFACTURING SUBSIDIARIES OF NON-U.S.-BASED PARENT SYSTEMS BY
NO. OF INDUSTRIES IN WHICH PARENT SYSTEM MANUFACTURED OUTSIDE NATIONAL BASE AS OF 1/1/71
FOR SUBSIDIARIES CLASSIFIED BY
NO. OF INDUSTRIES IN WHICH PARENT SYSTEM MANUFACTURED WITHIN NATIONAL BASE AS OF 1/1/71

NO. OF INDUSTRIES IN WHICH PARENT SYSTEM MANUF. WITHIN NATIONAL BASE AS OF 1/1/71	NO. OF INDUSTRIES IN WHICH PARENT SYSTEM MANUFACTURED OUTSIDE NATIONAL BASE AS OF 1/1/71					
	ONE TO THREE	FOUR TO NINE	TEN TO NINETEEN	TWENTY OR MORE	TOTAL PERCENT	TOTAL NUMBER
ONE TO THREE.............	27.	33.	24.	16.	100.	418
FOUR TO NINE.............	8.0	38.	24.	30.	100.	1719
TEN TO NINETEEN..........	3.6	21.	44.	31.	100.	2392
TWENTY OR MORE...........	1.4	4.8	11.	82.	100.	1116

CROSS-TABULATION 28.27.2: PERCENTAGE BREAKDOWN OF NUMBER (AS OF 1/1/68) OF
MANUFACTURING SUBSIDIARIES OF U.S.-BASED PARENT SYSTEMS BY
NO. OF INDUSTRIES IN WHICH PARENT SYSTEM MANUFACTURED OUTSIDE NATIONAL BASE AS OF 1/1/68
FOR SUBSIDIARIES CLASSIFIED BY
NO. OF INDUSTRIES IN WHICH PARENT SYSTEM MANUFACTURED WITHIN NATIONAL BASE AS OF 1/1/68

NO. OF INDUSTRIES IN WHICH PARENT SYSTEM MANUF. WITHIN NATIONAL BASE AS OF 1/1/68	NO. OF INDUSTRIES IN WHICH PARENT SYSTEM MANUFACTURED OUTSIDE NATIONAL BASE AS OF 1/1/68					
	ONE TO THREE	FOUR TO NINE	TEN TO NINETEEN	TWENTY OR MORE	TOTAL PERCENT	TOTAL NUMBER
ONE TO THREE............	45.	55.	0.	0.	100.	388
FOUR TO NINE............	15.	61.	17.	8.0	100.	1447
TEN TO NINETEEN.........	10.	71.	14.	4.8	100.	1460
TWENTY OR MORE..........	0.7	30.	52.	17.	100.	867

TABULATION 29.1: PERCENTAGE BREAKDOWN OF NUMBER OF SUBSIDIARIES BY
PARENT SYSTEM'S R&D EXPENDITURES AS A PERCENTAGE OF SALES IN YEAR PRIOR TO TERMINAL DATE
FOR VARIOUS CATEGORIES OF SUBSIDIARIES

CATEGORY OF SUBSIDIARY	PARENT SYSTEM'S R&D EXPENDITURES AS A PERCENTAGE OF SALES IN YEAR PRIOR TO TERMINAL DATE				
	LESS THAN 1%	1% - 4%	MORE THAN 4%	TOTAL PERCENT	TOTAL NUMBER
NON-U.S.-BASED SYSTEMS (AS OF 1/1/71):					
ALL SUBSIDIARIES..........	28.	42.	30.	100.	8838
MANUFACTURING SUBS........	23.	43.	34.	100.	3682
SALES SUBSIDIARIES........	30.	35.	35.	100.	2193
U.S.-BASED SYSTEMS (AS OF 1/1/68):					
ALL SUBSIDIARIES..........	35.	43.	23.	100.	3754
MANUFACTURING SUBS........	20.	55.	24.	100.	1540
SALES SUBSIDIARIES........	30.	36.	34.	100.	738
WORLD SUBSET OF SYSTEMS (AS OF 1/1/68):					
NON-U.S.-BASED SYSTEMS:					
ALL SUBSIDIARIES..........	22.	45.	33.	100.	4162
MANUFACTURING SUBS........	20.	46.	35.	100.	1802
SALES SUBSIDIARIES........	24.	38.	38.	100.	1233
U.S.-BASED SYSTEMS:					
ALL SUBSIDIARIES..........	40.	43.	17.	100.	3189
MANUFACTURING SUBS........	24.	59.	17.	100.	1239
SALES SUBSIDIARIES........	36.	37.	26.	100.	597

498

TABULATION 29.2: PERCENTAGE BREAKDOWN OF SALES OF SUBSIDIARIES IN 1970 BY
PARENT SYSTEM'S R&D EXPENDITURES AS A PERCENTAGE OF SALES IN 1970
FOR ALL SUBSIDIARIES, MANUFACTURING SUBSIDIARIES AND SALES SUBSIDIARIES
OF NON-U.S.-BASED SYSTEMS

CATEGORY OF SUBSIDIARY	PARENT SYSTEM'S R&D EXPENDITURES AS A PERCENTAGE OF SALES IN 1970				
	LESS THAN 1%	1% - 4%	MORE THAN 4%	TOTAL PERCENT	TOTAL ($ MIL)
ALL SUBSIDIARIES............	23.	45.	31.	100.	95626
MANUFACTURING SUBSIDIARIES...	19.	47.	34.	100.	60407
SALES SUBSIDIARIES..........	34.	36.	30.	100.	16117

CROSS-TABULATION 29. 1.1: PERCENTAGE BREAKDOWN OF NUMBER (AS OF 1/1/71) OF MANUFACTURING SUBSIDIARIES OF NON-U.S.-BASED PARENT SYSTEMS BY PARENT SYSTEM'S R&D EXPENDITURES AS A PERCENTAGE OF SALES IN 1970 FOR SUBSIDIARIES CLASSIFIED BY SUBSIDIARY'S COUNTRY

SUBSIDIARY'S COUNTRY	PARENT SYSTEM'S R&D EXPENDITURES AS A PERCENTAGE OF SALES IN 1970				TOTAL NUMBER
	LESS THAN 1%	1% - 4%	MORE THAN 4%	TOTAL PERCENT	
UNITED STATES.	20.	53.	27.	100.	283
CANADA.	34.	41.	25.	100.	110
MEXICO.	19.	42.	39.	100.	77
CENTRAL AMERICA AND CARIB.	28.	39.	33.	100.	57
VENEZUELA.	23.	46.	31.	100.	26
COLOMBIA.	25.	30.	45.	100.	20
PERU.	28.	24.	48.	100.	25
CHILE.	13.	50.	38.	100.	16
ARGENTINA.	23.	43.	34.	100.	86
BRAZIL.	25.	45.	30.	100.	143
OTHER SOUTH AMERICA.	21.	36.	43.	100.	14
GERMANY.	27.	45.	27.	100.	220
FRANCE.	13.	28.	59.	100.	323
ITALY.	22.	37.	41.	100.	150
BELGIUM AND LUXEMBURG.	31.	44.	25.	100.	95
THE NETHERLANDS.	32.	39.	29.	100.	77
UNITED KINGDOM.	20.	57.	23.	100.	213
IRELAND.	41.	37.	22.	100.	59
DENMARK.	12.	50.	38.	100.	26
NORWAY.	24.	24.	52.	100.	29
SWEDEN.	11.	41.	48.	100.	46
FINLAND.	27.	27.	45.	100.	11

TABLE CONTINUED ON NEXT PAGE

CROSS-TABULATION 29. 1.1: PERCENTAGE BREAKDOWN OF NUMBER (AS OF 1/1/71) OF
MANUFACTURING SUBSIDIARIES OF NON-U.S.-BASED PARENT SYSTEMS BY
PARENT SYSTEM'S R&D EXPENDITURES AS A PERCENTAGE OF SALES IN 1970
FOR SUBSIDIARIES CLASSIFIED BY
SUBSIDIARY'S COUNTRY
(CONTINUED)

SUBSIDIARY'S COUNTRY	PARENT SYSTEM'S R&D EXPENDITURES AS A PERCENTAGE OF SALES IN 1970				
	LESS THAN 1%	1% - 4%	MORE THAN 4%	TOTAL PERCENT	TOTAL NUMBER
SWITZERLAND............	24.	47.	29.	100.	38
AUSTRIA...............	15.	29.	55.	100.	65
PORTUGAL..............	25.	35.	40.	100.	40
SPAIN.................	24.	40.	36.	100.	149
GREECE................	16.	21.	63.	100.	19
TURKEY................	17.	17.	67.	100.	24
OTHER EUROPE + ISRAEL..	35.	35.	29.	100.	17
PAKISTAN..............	12.	35.	54.	100.	26
IRAN..................	15.	30.	55.	100.	20
OTHER MID EAST+EGYPT+LIBYA...	15.	20.	65.	100.	20
UNION OF SOUTH AFRICA.........	24.	52.	24.	100.	223
RHODESIA..............	58.	32.	11.	100.	19
ZAMBIA................	40.	60.	0.	100.	10
TANZANIA..............	44.	44.	11.	100.	9
KENYA.................	41.	36.	23.	100.	22
NIGERIA...............	29.	47.	24.	100.	17
OTHER (BRITISH) AFRICA.....	33.	50.	17.	100.	18
MOROCCO, ALGERIA + TUNISIA...	34.	41.	24.	100.	41
OTHER (FRENCH) AFRICA......	21.	56.	24.	100.	34
OTHER AFRICA..........	71.	29.	0.	100.	14
AUSTRALIA.............	25.	56.	19.	100.	257
NEW ZEALAND...........	29.	42.	29.	100.	65

TABLE CONTINUED ON NEXT PAGE

CROSS-TABULATION 29. 1.1: PERCENTAGE BREAKDOWN OF NUMBER (AS OF 1/1/71) OF MANUFACTURING SUBSIDIARIES OF NON-U.S.-BASED PARENT SYSTEMS BY PARENT SYSTEM'S R&D EXPENDITURES AS A PERCENTAGE OF SALES IN 1970 FOR SUBSIDIARIES CLASSIFIED BY SUBSIDIARY'S COUNTRY (CONTINUED)

SUBSIDIARY'S COUNTRY	PARENT SYSTEM'S R&D EXPENDITURES AS A PERCENTAGE OF SALES IN 1970				
	LESS THAN 1%	1% - 4%	MORE THAN 4%	TOTAL PERCENT	TOTAL NUMBER
JAPAN..........	8.2	45.	47.	100.	73
CHINA (TAIWAN)...........	10.	64.	26.	100.	50
HONG KONG.....	5.6	61.	33.	100.	18
THE PHILIPPINES...........	39.	28.	33.	100.	18
MALAYSIA..............	26.	38.	36.	100.	39
SINGAPORE............	26.	32.	41.	100.	34
INDONESIA.............	7.1	50.	43.	100.	14
THAILAND...........	27.	43.	30.	100.	44
INDIA...............	21.	36.	42.	100.	99
OTHER ASIA AND OCEANIA........	14.	51.	34.	100.	35

CROSS—TABULATION 29. 1.2: PERCENTAGE BREAKDOWN OF NUMBER (AS OF 1/1/68) OF MANUFACTURING SUBSIDIARIES OF U.S.-BASED PARENT SYSTEMS BY PARENT SYSTEM'S R&D EXPENDITURES AS A PERCENTAGE OF SALES IN 1967 FOR SUBSIDIARIES CLASSIFIED BY SUBSIDIARY'S COUNTRY

SUBSIDIARY'S COUNTRY	PARENT SYSTEM'S R&D EXPENDITURES AS A PERCENTAGE OF SALES IN 1967				
	LESS THAN 1%	1% - 4%	MORE THAN 4%	TOTAL PERCENT	TOTAL NUMBER
UNITED STATES	0.	0.	0.	100.	0
CANADA	19.	61.	20.	100.	166
MEXICO	15.	56.	29.	100.	102
CENTRAL AMERICA AND CARIB	32.	50.	18.	100.	50
VENEZUELA	22.	64.	13.	100.	45
COLOMBIA	27.	43.	30.	100.	37
PERU	31.	46.	23.	100.	13
CHILE	6.7	73.	20.	100.	15
ARGENTINA	10.	48.	43.	100.	40
BRAZIL	7.9	65.	27.	100.	63
OTHER SOUTH AMERICA	25.	50.	25.	100.	12
GERMANY	30.	47.	23.	100.	100
FRANCE	20.	53.	27.	100.	91
ITALY	22.	47.	32.	100.	73
BELGIUM AND LUXEMBURG	16.	63.	21.	100.	43
THE NETHERLANDS	20.	46.	34.	100.	35
UNITED KINGDOM	18.	51.	31.	100.	134
IRELAND	25.	75.	0.	100.	8
DENMARK	60.	40.	0.	100.	10
NORWAY	17.	67.	17.	100.	6
SWEDEN	0.	82.	18.	100.	11
FINLAND	0.	100.	0.	100.	2

TABLE CONTINUED ON NEXT PAGE

CROSS-TABULATION 29. 1.2: PERCENTAGE BREAKDOWN OF NUMBER (AS OF 1/1/68) OF MANUFACTURING SUBSIDIARIES OF U.S.-BASED PARENT SYSTEMS BY PARENT SYSTEM'S R&D EXPENDITURES AS A PERCENTAGE OF SALES IN 1967 FOR SUBSIDIARIES CLASSIFIED BY SUBSIDIARY'S COUNTRY (CONTINUED)

SUBSIDIARY'S COUNTRY	PARENT SYSTEM'S R&D EXPENDITURES AS A PERCENTAGE OF SALES IN 1967				
	LESS THAN 1%	1% - 4%	MORE THAN 4%	TOTAL PERCENT	TOTAL NUMBER
SWITZERLAND	33.	56.	11.	100.	9
AUSTRIA	33.	33.	33.	100.	9
PORTUGAL	0.	100.	0.	100.	4
SPAIN	24.	42.	33.	100.	45
GREECE	0.	80.	20.	100.	10
TURKEY	33.	67.	0.	100.	3
OTHER EUROPE + ISRAEL	14.	71.	14.	100.	7
PAKISTAN	0.	38.	63.	100.	8
IRAN	44.	33.	22.	100.	9
OTHER MID EAST+EGYPT+LIBYA	85.	7.7	7.7	100.	13
UNION OF SOUTH AFRICA	5.3	72.	23.	100.	57
RHODESIA	11.	89.	0.	100.	9
ZAMBIA	0.	100.	0.	100.	4
TANZANIA	0.	0.	0.	100.	0
KENYA	0.	100.	0.	100.	4
NIGERIA	0.	100.	0.	100.	7
OTHER (BRITISH) AFRICA	0.	100.	0.	100.	2
MOROCCO, ALGERIA + TUNISIA	17.	83.	0.	100.	6
OTHER (FRENCH) AFRICA	43.	57.	0.	100.	7
OTHER AFRICA	0.	0.	0.	100.	0
AUSTRALIA	29.	49.	22.	100.	93
NEW ZEALAND	23.	55.	23.	100.	22

TABLE CONTINUED ON NEXT PAGE

CROSS-TABULATION 29. 1.2: PERCENTAGE BREAKDOWN OF NUMBER (AS OF 1/1/68) OF MANUFACTURING SUBSIDIARIES OF U.S.-BASED PARENT SYSTEMS BY PARENT SYSTEM'S R&D EXPENDITURES AS A PERCENTAGE OF SALES IN 1967 FOR SUBSIDIARIES CLASSIFIED BY SUBSIDIARY'S COUNTRY (CONTINUED)

SUBSIDIARY'S COUNTRY	PARENT SYSTEM'S R&D EXPENDITURES AS A PERCENTAGE OF SALES IN 1967				
	LESS THAN 1%	1% - 4%	MORE THAN 4%	TOTAL PERCENT	TOTAL NUMBER
JAPAN......	21.	55.	25.	100.	77
CHINA (TAIWAN)......	33.	33.	33.	100.	6
HONG KONG......	0.	100.	0.	100.	2
THE PHILIPPINES......	19.	50.	31.	100.	16
MALAYSIA......	25.	75.	0.	100.	4
SINGAPORE......	17.	83.	0.	100.	6
INDONESIA......	0.	100.	0.	100.	1
THAILAND......	0.	86.	14.	100.	7
INDIA......	15.	41.	44.	100.	27
OTHER ASIA AND OCEANIA......	30.	70.	0.	100.	10

CROSS-TABULATION 29.21.1: PERCENTAGE BREAKDOWN OF NUMBER (AS OF 1/1/71) OF MANUFACTURING SUBSIDIARIES OF NON-U.S.-BASED PARENT SYSTEMS BY PARENT SYSTEM'S R&D EXPENDITURES AS A PERCENTAGE OF SALES IN 1970 FOR SUBSIDIARIES CLASSIFIED BY NATIONAL BASE OF SUBSIDIARY'S PARENT SYSTEM

NATIONAL BASE OF SUBSIDIARY'S PARENT SYSTEM	PARENT SYSTEM'S R&D EXPENDITURES AS A PERCENTAGE OF SALES IN 1970				
	LESS THAN 1%	1% - 4%	MORE THAN 4%	TOTAL PERCENT	TOTAL NUMBER
UNITED KINGDOM............	25.	49.	26.	100.	1069
GERMANY..................	12.	18.	70.	100.	661
FRANCE...................	40.	48.	12.	100.	318
ITALY....................	16.	68.	17.	100.	103
BELGIUM AND LUXEMBURG....	40.	60.	0.	100.	108
THE NETHERLANDS..........	1.6	98.	0.	100.	425
SWEDEN...................	60.	5.6	35.	100.	72
SWITZERLAND..............	40.	0.	60.	100.	393
JAPAN....................	25.	43.	32.	100.	292
CANADA...................	21.	78.	0.7	100.	145
OTHER NON-U.S............	7.3	0.	93.	100.	96